Authorized Self-Study Guide

Building Cisco Multilayer Switched Networks (BCMSN)

Richard Froom, CCIE No. 5102
Balaji Sivasubramanian
Erum Frahim, CCIE No. 7549

Cisco Press

Cisco Press
800 East 96th Street
Indianapolis, IN 46240 USA

Authorized Self-Study Guide
Building Cisco Multilayer Switched Networks (BCMSN)

Richard Froom, Balaji Sivasubramanian, Erum Frahim, Troy Houston

Copyright© 2007 Cisco Systems, Inc.

Published by:
Cisco Press
800 East 96th Street
Indianapolis, IN 46240 USA

Printed in the United States of America 1 2 3 4 5 6 7 8 9 0

First Printing: February 2007

ISBN: 1-58705-273-3

ISBN13: 9781587052736

Library of Congress Cataloging-in-Publication Data

Froom, Richard.

 Building Cisco multilayer switched networks (BCMSN) / Richard Froom, Balaji Sivasubramanian, Erum Frahi. -- 4th ed.

   p. cm.

 ISBN 1-58705-273-3 (hardback)

 1. Telecommunication--Switching systems--Examinations--Study guides. 2. Telecommunications engineers--Certification--Examinations--Study guides. I Froom, Richard II. Sivasubramanian, Balaji. III. Frahim, Erum. IV. Title.

TK5103.8.F76 2007

004.6'6--dc22

                        2006039558

Warning and Disclaimer

This book provides information about the CCNP Building Multilayer Switched Networks (BCMSN) course in preparation for taking the CCNP BCMSN exam 642-812. Every effort has been made to make this book as complete and as accurate as possible, but no warranty or fitness is implied.

The information is provided on an "as is" basis. The authors, Cisco Press, and Cisco Systems, Inc. shall have neither liability nor responsibility to any person or entity with respect to any loss or damages arising from the information contained in this book or from the use of the discs or programs that may accompany it.

The opinions expressed in this book belong to the author and are not necessarily those of Cisco Systems, Inc.

Trademark Acknowledgments

All terms mentioned in this book that are known to be trademarks or service marks have been appropriately capitalized. Cisco Press or Cisco Systems, Inc. cannot attest to the accuracy of this information. Use of a term in this book should not be regarded as affecting the validity of any trademark or service mark.

Corporate and Government Sales

Cisco Press offers excellent discounts on this book when ordered in quantity for bulk purchases or special sales.

For more information please contact: **U.S. Corporate and Government Sales 1-800-382-3419**
corpsales@pearsontechgroup.com

For sales outside the U.S. please contact: **International Sales international@pearsoned.com**

Feedback Information

At Cisco Press, our goal is to create in-depth technical books of the highest quality and value. Each book is crafted with care and precision, undergoing rigorous development that involves the unique expertise of members from the professional technical community.

Readers' feedback is a natural continuation of this process. If you have any comments regarding how we could improve the quality of this book, or otherwise alter it to better suit your needs, you can contact us through e-mail at feedback@ciscopress.com. Please make sure to include the book title and ISBN in your message.

We greatly appreciate your assistance.

Publisher	Paul Boger
Cisco Representative	Anthony Wolfenden
Cisco Press Program Manager	Jeff Brady
Executive Editor	Mary Beth Ray
Associate Publisher	David Dustimer
Production Manager	Patrick Kanouse
Senior Development Editor	Christopher Cleveland
Project Editor	Jennifer Gallant
Copy Editor	Bill McManus
Technical Editors	Don Johnston, John Tiso
Team Coordinator	Vanessa Evans
Book and Cover Designer	Louisa Adair
Composition	Mark Shirar
Indexer	Tim Wright
Proofreader	Karen Gill

CISCO

Americas Headquarters	Asia Pacific Headquarters	Europe Headquarters
Cisco Systems, Inc.	Cisco Systems, Inc.	Cisco Systems International BV
170 West Tasman Drive	168 Robinson Road	Haarlerbergpark
San Jose, CA 95134-1706	#28-01 Capital Tower	Haarlerbergweg 13-19
USA	Singapore 068912	1101 CH Amsterdam
www.cisco.com	www.cisco.com	The Netherlands
Tel: 408 526-4000	Tel: +65 6317 7777	www-europe.cisco.com
800 553-NETS (6387)	Fax: +65 6317 7799	Tel: +31 0 800 020 0791
Fax: 408 527-0883		Fax: +31 0 20 357 1100

Cisco has more than 200 offices worldwide. Addresses, phone numbers, and fax numbers are listed on the Cisco Website at **www.cisco.com/go/offices**.

About the Authors

Richard Froom, CCIE No. 5102, is an engineering manager for the Data Center Business Unit Customer Operations Group at Cisco Systems. Richard is currently testing Cisco storage solutions with customers and has been involved in customer testing, proof-of-concept testing, and post-sales support of Cisco storage solutions. He has been with Cisco for nine years, previously serving as a support engineer troubleshooting customers' networks and a technical leader working with Cisco Catalyst products. Richard, being involved with Catalyst product field trials, has been crucial in driving troubleshooting capabilities of Catalyst and MDS products and software. He has also contributed substantially to the Cisco.com LAN Technologies Technical Tips and has written white papers about 802.3 auto-negotiation and HSRP. Richard is also the coauthor of *Cisco Catalyst QoS: Quality of Service in Campus Networks* (ISBN 1-58705-120-6) from Cisco Press. He attended Clemson University and completed his bachelor of science degree in computer engineering.

Balaji Sivasubramanian, CCNP, is a product manager for the Internet Systems Business Unit (ISBU) at Cisco Systems. He is involved in defining product requirements for the next generation switching products for the Catalyst 6500 Switch Series. Previously, Balaji served as a team leader for the Cisco Systems Technical Assistance Center (TAC) LAN Switching team and as an escalation engineer for the Gigabit Switching Business Unit (GSBU). He has been with Cisco for more than seven years. He was a technical reviewer for the Cisco Press title, *Cisco Catalyst QoS: Quality of Service in Campus Networks* (ISBN 1-58705-120-6). In addition, Balaji has authored and reviewed many technical white papers on Cisco.com for the LAN Technologies subject area. He has been a presenter at Cisco Networkers and Technical Virtual Chalk Talk seminars for partners. Balaji holds a master of science degree in electronics and computer engineering from the University of Arizona and holds a bachelor of engineering degree in electrical and electronics engineering from Anna University, India.

Erum Frahim, CCIE No. 7549, is a team lead working for the Data Center, Business unit in SAN Test Lab at Cisco Systems. Erum is currently testing SAN solutions for various Cisco customers to aid them in deployment of the Cisco storage technologies. In addition, she is testing new features and products as well as handling crucial customer issues concerning Catalyst switches and Cisco MDS switches. She has been working for Cisco for the past six years and has been involved in early field trial testing of Catalyst products. In addition, Erum has contributed and authored articles on Cisco.com and in *Certification Magazine* on LAN and SAN technologies. Erum attended the Illinois Institute of Technology, Chicago, where she completed her master of science degree in electrical engineering, and she received her bachelor's degree from the N.E.D University of Engineering and Technology in Pakistan.

For questions regarding this book, you can contact Richard at richard-froom@nc.rr.com and Erum at e_frahim@yahoo.com.

About the Contributing Author

Troy Houston, CCNP, CCDP, and CCIE-written, independently provides contracted business and knowledge solutions to enterprise customers in the Mid-Atlantic area. The first half of his career was in the Aerospace industry where he gained extensive RF knowledge making him the WLAN SME today. Over the past ten years, Troy has planned, designed, implemented, operated, and troubleshot LANs, WANs, MANs, and WLANs. He attained his bachelor of science degree in management of information systems from Eastern University. Additionally, he is an inventor and holds a patent for one of his many ideas. Formerly in the military, Troy returned to the military on a reserve basis after 9/11. He provides the Air Force Reserves his skills and knowledge as a Computers–Communications Systems Specialist (3C0). He can be contacted at troy@houstonshome.com.

About the Technical Reviewers

Don Johnston has more than 20 years' technical, management, consulting, and training experience in networking. He is a certified Cisco Systems instructor and has developed well-received courses and labs. As a consultant, Don has successfully designed and installed LANs and WANs, provided trouble-shooting expertise, and managed technical staff for insurance brokerage, reinsurance, and marketing companies. An instrument-rated pilot, Don and his family live in the Chicago area.

John Tiso, **CCIE No. 5162**, **MCSE**, **CCDP**, holds a bachelor's of science degree from Adelphi University in New York. He currently serves as a customer support engineer in the Cisco Heartland TAC. Before joining the team at Cisco, John was the lead AVVID consultant and installer for a Cisco Gold Partner. John has written and edited for Cisco Press for many years. He has also published papers in several industry publications and coauthored a book for Cisco Learning Systems.

Dedications

I would like to dedicate this book to my wife, Elizabeth, and my son, Nathan. Thanks for giving me the time to complete this book.

—Richard Froom

I would like to dedicate this book to my siblings (Sridhar, Bhuvana, and Raji), who have been very supportive of me throughout my life. Thanks guys.

—Balaji Sivasubramanian

I would like to dedicate this book to my parents, Frahim and Perveen, who always guide me and support me in all the endeavors of my life. Especially my mother, Perveen, is my inspiration in my life and I am here because of her support and her prayers. Thank you, Mom. I also want to dedicate this book to my siblings, who are my best friends and who inspire me to achieve my goals in life. I would like to thank all my family members for their never-ending support and love that helps and encourages me to move forward.

—Erum Frahim

My dedication and service is, first and foremost, to God; additionally, my dedication and love to what is in my heart: my wife Cristina, my sons Grant and Cole, and my newborn daughter Paige. I cannot forget Walter and Stef Houston's loving parental support—thank you.

—Troy Houston

Acknowledgments

Richard Froom would like to thank his coauthors for such great work, especially Troy in his authoring of the wireless chapters. Furthermore, Richard would like to thank all the Cisco Press employees who helped make this book happen.

Balaji Sirasubramanian would like to thank coauthors Richard, Erum, and Troy for all their hard work toward this project. He would also like to thank his former manager Scott Lawrence, for allowing him to work on the second edition of this book project. In conclusion, Balaji would also like to personally thank all the technical reviewers and Chris Cleveland for their excellent review and assistance in this project.

Erum Frahim and Troy Houston would like to thank Rich Froom, Mary Beth Ray, Chris Cleveland, Don Johnston, and John Tiso for their dutiful efforts and reviews.

This Book Is Safari Enabled

The Safari® Enabled icon on the cover of your favorite technology book means the book is available through Safari Bookshelf. When you buy this book, you get free access to the online edition for 45 days.

Safari Bookshelf is an electronic reference library that lets you easily search thousands of technical books, find code samples, download chapters, and access technical information whenever and wherever you need it.

To gain 45-day Safari Enabled access to this book:

- Go to http://www.ciscopress.com/safarienabled
- Complete the brief registration form
- Enter the coupon code PZLM-XSTJ-LMRT-GAJZ-SIYD

If you have difficulty registering on Safari Bookshelf or accessing the online edition, please e-mail customer-service@safaribooksonline.com.

Contents at a Glance

Contents

Icons Used in This Book

 Router

 Bridge

 Hub

 DSU/CSU

 Catalyst Switch

 Modem

 ATM Switch

 ISDN/Frame Relay Switch

 Communication Server

 Gateway

 PC

 PC with Software

 Sun Workstation

 Macintosh

 Terminal

 Multilayer Switch

 Web Server

 File Server

 Laptop

 Printer

 Access Server

 Cisco Works Workstation

 IBM Mainframe

 Front End Processor

 Cluster Controller

——————— Line: Ethernet

Line: Serial

Line: Switched Serial

〜〜〜〜〜 Wireless Connection

Token Ring

FDDI

Network Cloud

 Access Point

 Lightweight Single Radio Access Point

 WLAN Controller

Command Syntax Conventions

The conventions used to present command syntax in this book are the same conventions used in the IOS Command Reference. The Command Reference describes these conventions as follows:

- **Boldface** indicates commands and keywords that are entered literally as shown. In actual configuration examples and output (not general command syntax), boldface indicates commands that are manually input by the user (such as a **show** command).

- *Italics* indicate arguments for which you supply actual values.

- Vertical bars (|) separate alternative, mutually exclusive elements.

- Square brackets [ ] indicate optional elements.

- Braces { } indicate a required choice.

- Braces within brackets [{ }] indicate a required choice within an optional element.

Foreword

Authorized Self-Study Guide Building Cisco Multilayer Switched Networks (BCMSN), Fourth Edition, is an excellent self-study resource for the CCNP BCMSN exam. Whether you are studying to become CCNP certified or are simply seeking to gain a better understanding of switching technology, implementation and operation, planning and design, and troubleshooting, you will benefit from the information presented in this book.

Cisco Press Self-Study Guide titles are designed to help educate, develop, and grow the community of Cisco networking professionals. As an early-stage exam preparation product, this book presents a detailed and comprehensive introduction to the technologies used to build scalable multilayer switched networks. Developed in conjunction with the Cisco certifications team, Cisco Press books are the only self-study books authorized by Cisco Systems.

Most networking professionals use a variety of learning methods to gain necessary skills. Cisco Press Self-Study Guide titles are a prime source of content for some individuals and can serve as an excellent supplement to other forms of learning. Training classes, whether delivered in a classroom or on the Internet, are a great way to quickly acquire new understanding. Hands-on practice is essential for anyone seeking to build, or hone, new skills. Authorized Cisco training classes, labs, and simulations are available exclusively from Cisco Learning Solutions Partners worldwide. Please visit http://www.cisco.com/go/training to learn more about Cisco Learning Solutions Partners.

I hope and expect that you'll find this guide to be an essential part of your exam preparation and a valuable addition to your personal library.

Don Field
Director, Certifications
Cisco Systems, Inc.
February, 2007

Introduction

Over the past several years, switching has evolved from simple Layer 3 switches to switches supporting Layer 4 through Layer 7 features such as, server load balancing, URL inspection, firewalls, VPNs, access-based control, and so on with large port densities. The multilayer switch has become an "all-in-one" component of the network infrastructure. As a result of this evolution, enterprise and service providers are deploying multilayer switches in place of multiple network components such as routers and network appliances. Switching is no longer a part of the network infrastructure; it is now *the* network infrastructure, with wireless as the latest evolution.

As enterprises, service providers, and even consumers deploy multilayer switching, the need for experienced and knowledgeable professionals to design, configure, and support the multilayer switched networks has grown significantly. CCNP and CCDP certifications offer the ability for network professionals to prove their competency.

CCNP and CCDP are more than résumé keywords. Individuals who complete the CCNP and CCDP certifications truly prove their experience, knowledge, and competency in networking technologies. A CCNP certification demonstrates an individual's ability to install, configure, and operate LAN, WAN, and dial access services for midsize to large networks deploying multiple protocols. A CCDP certification demonstrates an individual's ability to design high-performance, scalable, and highly available routed and switched networks involving LAN, WAN, wireless, and dial access services.

Both the CCNP and CCDP certification tracks require you to pass the Building Cisco Multilayer Switched Networks exam. For the most up-to-date information about Cisco certifications, visit the following website: http://www.cisco.com/en/US/learning/le3/ learning_career_certifications_and_learning_paths_home.html.

Goals and Purpose

The goal of this Self-Study Guide is to prepare and aid you in passing the Building Cisco Multilayer Switched Networks certification exam and assist you in taking the BCMSN course. To accomplish these tasks, this text includes in-depth theoretical explanations of BCMSN topics and provides illustrative design and configuration examples. The theoretical explanations of BCMSN topics include background information, standards references, and document listings from Cisco.com. Each chapter concludes with a lab exercise that assesses, in detail, your knowledge of the subject matter presented.

This book goes beyond just presenting the necessary information found on the certification exam and in the BCMSN course. This book attempts to present topics, theory, and examples in such a way that you truly understand the topics that are necessary to build multilayer switched networks in today's demanding networks. The examples and questions found in the chapters of this book make you contemplate and apply concepts found in each chapter. The goal is to have you understand the topics and then apply your understanding when you attempt the certification exam or take the BCMSN course.

This book includes several discussions, topics, examples, and extra credit chapters that are not covered on the BCMSN certification test. In addition, it has been our experience that network professionals are missing several key concepts that are necessary not only for certification tests but also for practical application. This book reviews and discusses these key concepts, beginning with Chapter 1, "Introduction to Building Cisco Multilayer Switched Networks."

Who Should Read This Book?

Besides network professionals preparing for the CCNP or CCDP certification exams, this book is an excellent resource for network professionals who want to learn about switching or to discover more about Catalyst switches. In addition, this book serves as a reference book, especially for Catalyst switches running Cisco IOS Software. Individuals at a variety of experience and knowledge levels are able to read this book. The book begins with the basics in Chapter 1 and continues in depth in subsequent chapters. At a minimum, readers of this text should have a basic understanding of networking. No previous certification is a requirement for reading this text, but a CCNA or equivalent level of knowledge is suggested for individuals to take full advantage of the topics covered. Furthermore, this book also covers switching topics found on the CCIE certification exam. The examples in this text are demonstrated on the Catalyst 3550 and 6500 families of switches. As a result, candidates who are preparing for the CCIE certification exam may find this text useful for preparing for the switching portions of the CCIE exam.

Methods

Each chapter ends with a summary and review questions to aid you in applying and assessing your understanding of the chapter contents. In addition, chapters that cover Catalyst configurations also include configuration exercises. Most of these exercises are small-scale exercises that can be performed on a single switch. The goal of using small-scale exercises is to enable network professionals to practice the configuration exercises with only a single switch.

How to Read This Book

Although this book is intended to be read cover to cover, it is designed to be flexible and allow you to easily move between chapters and sections of chapters to cover just specific material that you need more work with. For those who are reading this book for configuration, Chapter 3, "Initial Configuration and Troubleshooting of Cisco Multilayer Switches," is a prerequisite for any subsequent chapter. For those who are reading this book to learn about multilayer switching network design, Chapter 1 and Chapter 2, "The Roles of Switches in Designing Cisco Multilayer Switched Networks," are prerequisites for any later chapters.

How This Book Is Organized

This book is organized such that the fundamentals of multilayer switched network design are covered in the first two chapters. Thereafter, the book continues with a discussion of basic multilayer switch configuration in Chapter 3, followed by discussions of specific design features such as spanning tree, quality of service (QoS), and high availability. This book is organized as follows:

- **Chapter 1, "Introduction to Building Cisco Multilayer Switched Networks"**—This chapter opens with several key definitions and discussions pertaining to multilayer switched networks. In addition, the chapter presents the main model for designing multilayer switched networks—the Enterprise Composite Network Model. The chapter concludes with a brief review of each Catalyst switch.

- **Chapter 2, "The Roles of Switches in Designing Cisco Multilayer Switched Networks"**—This chapter applies the Enterprise Composite Network Model introduced in Chapter 1 and shows you how to build different network topologies based on this model, using specific Catalyst switches, features, and data-link technologies.

- **Chapter 3, "Initial Configuration and Troubleshooting of Cisco Multilayer Switches"**—This chapter illustrates the basic configuration parameters for any Catalyst switch, including configuring Secure Shell (SSH), the system host name, and management IP addresses.

- **Chapter 4, "Implementing and Configuring VLANs"**—This chapter covers virtual LANs (VLANs), including discussions on private VLANs, VTP, and 802.1Q trunking.

- **Chapter 5, "Understanding and Configuring the 802.1D, 802.1s, and 802.1w Spanning Tree Protocols"**—This chapter begins the discussion of spanning tree by covering the standard 802.1D STP specification and the more recent 802.1s and 802.1w STP specifications.

- **Chapter 6, "Adding Resiliency to Spanning Tree Using Advanced Features and Troubleshooting STP Issues"**—This chapter continues the discussion of spanning tree by covering the 802.1s and 802.1w STP specifications and advanced Cisco STP features such as UplinkFast and Root Guard.

- **Chapter 7, "Enhancing Network Stability, Functionality, Reliability, and Performance Using Advanced Features"**—This chapter discusses advanced features of Catalyst switches that aid in network stability, functionality, reliability, and performance. Included in this chapter are discussions of aggressive mode Unidirectional Link Detection (UDLD), the Cisco Discovery Protocol (CDP), and jumbo Ethernet frames.

- **Chapter 8, "Understanding and Configuring Inter-VLAN Routing"**—This chapter transitions into discussing Layer 3 switching by covering inter-VLAN routing. This chapter also includes a section on User Datagram Protocol (UDP) broadcast forwarding and Dynamic Host Configuration Protocol (DHCP) relaying.

- **Chapter 9, "Understanding and Configuring Multilayer Switching"**—This chapter builds on the Chapter 1 discussion of multilayer switching by covering the architecture of multilayer switching from a Catalyst switch perspective. Included in this chapter is a discussion of Cisco Express Forwarding (CEF)-based MLS.

- **Chapter 10, "Understanding and Implementing Quality of Service in Cisco Multilayer Switched Networks"**—This chapter covers quality of service on Catalyst switches for Layer 2 and Layer 3 switching.

- **Chapter 11, "Deploying Multicast in the Multilayer Switched Network"**—This chapter covers multicasting for both Layer 2 and Layer 3 features. Included in this chapter are discussions of Internet Group Management Protocol (IGMP) snooping, IGMP version 3, and IP multicast routing.

- **Chapter 12, "Designing Network Resiliency, Redundancy, and High Availability in Multilayer Switched Networks"**—This chapter covers high-availability component- and network-level options that are available on Catalyst switches. Included in this chapter are discussions of Virtual Router Redundancy Protocol (VRRP), Hot Standby Routing Protocol (HSRP), Cisco IOS Software Modularity, and Supervisor Engine redundancy.

- **Chapter 13, "Best Practices for Deploying Cisco IP Telephony Using Cisco Catalyst Switches"**—This chapter briefly covers the requirements for IP telephony in multilayer switched networks. Included in this chapter is a discussion of voice (auxiliary) VLANs.

- **Chapter 14, "Securing Your Multilayer Switched Network to Minimize Service Loss and Data Theft"**—This chapter covers a critical component of multilayer switched networks: security. This chapter primarily focuses on both control plane (management) security and data plane (traffic) security. Included in this chapter are topics on Layer 2 attacks, Dynamic Address Resolution Protocol Inspection (DAI), and AAA.

- **Chapter 15, "Introduction to the Catalyst Switching Architectures"**—This chapter builds on material in Chapters 1 and 9 and provides an overview of Catalyst switching architectures.

- **Chapter 16, "Designing, Building, and Connecting Cisco Multilayer Switched Networks Using Metro Solutions"**—This chapter covers connecting remote data centers over distance. This chapter includes discussions on coarse wavelength-division multiplexing (CWDM) and dense wavelength-division multiplexing (DWDM).

- **Chapter 17, "Performance and Connectivity Troubleshooting Tools for Multilayer Switches"**—This chapter covers management and performance monitoring techniques of Catalyst switches. Included in this chapter are discussions of the Enhanced Remote SPAN (ERSPAN) feature, the Embedded Event Manager (EEM), and the Network Analysis Module (NAM).

- **Chapter 18, "Introducing Wireless into the Campus Network"**—This chapter introduces wireless LANs (WLANs), including their components, topologies, usage, and configurations. This chapter includes a comparison of WLANs to wired LANs, a history of wireless, a discussion of RF fundamentals, and an overview of access point (AP) types—autonomous and lightweight.

- **Appendix A, "Answers to Review Questions"**—This appendix provides answers and explanations for the review questions that appear at the end of each chapter.

This chapter covers the following topics:

- Multilayer Switching Overview
- The Enterprise Composite Network Model for Building Cisco Multilayer Switched Networks
- Introduction to the Cisco Catalyst Switches

## CHAPTER 1

Introduction to Building Cisco Multilayer Switched Networks

Imagine a global network with multiple active data centers where one data center is able to handle all the functions of multiple data centers in the event of disaster. Consider that each data center network has a 100 percent uptime for normal operations that never interrupts user traffic, prevents worms and viruses, maintains stability and integrity during anomalous events, replicates data among different Data Centers, provides for immediate disaster recovery, routes inbound calls for employees through local Voice over IP (VoIP) networks, provides Virtual Private Network (VPN) access to remote-site users as if they were at the main site, migrates storage effortlessly, provides quality of service (QoS) adaptively, supports high-performance computing applications, and is self-maintaining, self-defending, self-upgrading, and self-repairing.

Although these types of data centers and campus networks might sound far-fetched, you can build these networks today by leveraging Cisco multilayer switched networks using the latest Cisco products and features. Convergence has many benefits, including reducing costs by consolidating procedures in network operation centers (NOC), consolidating platforms, reducing staff education curves, and so on. For example, consider training operation staff on multiple networks versus individual distinct networks.

This book focuses primarily on the Cisco Enterprise Campus Architecture of enterprise networks. However, a new focus in enterprise networks is developing—the data center. The data center has slightly different requirements than does the campus, but both use Cisco Catalyst switches and similar hierarchical designs. By definition in this book, the campus network includes the infrastructure for connecting the host devices, such as workstations. The campus network includes the server farm, but the server farm is now referred to as the data center. Unfortunately, as with network terms, the use of the terms *campus network* and *data center* is rather loose. This chapter intends to clarify each role.

By Cisco.com definition,

[the] Cisco Enterprise Campus Architecture empowers all enterprise users with advanced services, taking advantage of an intelligent, enterprise-wide network to increase revenue, productivity, and customer satisfaction while reducing the operational inefficiencies across the business.

The Enterprise Campus Architecture combines a core network infrastructure with an overlay of productivity-enhancing advanced technologies, including IP communications, mobility, and advanced security. This combination helps enterprises implement a resilient, highly available network that allows them to adapt more quickly to changing requirements, rapidly and securely enable new and emerging services, and streamline processes through optimized access to information and communications that increases employee effectiveness.

The server farm discussed in previous editions of this book has evolved into a more important component: the data center. By Cisco.com definition,

[the] Cisco Data Center Network Architecture provides a cohesive foundation for IT executives to better align data center resources with business priorities.

The Cisco Data Center Network Architecture allows IT organizations to achieve lower total cost of ownership (TCO), enhanced resilience, and greater agility by evolving data center infrastructures through consolidation, virtualization, and automation.

The data center encompasses many components including servers, server fabrics, applications, disk storage, storage-area networks (SAN), LANs, optical transports, and so on. As these technologies assemble into a single reference architecture, the phrases *convergence* and *data center* are becoming the new buzzwords.

In the previous edition, the motivation behind building multilayer switched networks was *productivity*. Although productivity is still a main reason for deploying Cisco converged switched networks, availability, security, and disaster-recovery techniques are the additional reasons. The new buzzword for building converged switched networks is *virtualization*.

In terms of productivity, Cisco multilayer switched networks are driving business productivity by building network architectures that are capable of boundless features, including voice, video, wireless data, and vast, reliable storage. These architectures embrace applications that support VoIP, wireless networking, remote access, and storage networking technologies. VoIP applications drive down the cost of ownership for telephony while effortlessly providing a multitude of telephony features to the end-user base on the intranet and on remote and wireless networks. Wireless technologies in the campus network are freeing individuals from their desks and increasing the productivity of mobile workers at the home and office for data and voice. Technologies such as VPNs are enabling telecommuters to be as productive as onsite workers. Therefore, the campus networks of yesterday are implementing design changes to quickly adopt these emerging applications to increase enterprise productivity. As a result, the traditional components of the Cisco multilayer switched networks are including specialized hardware for performance, high availability, and scalability to enable these applications. Multilayer switched networks are no longer networks of Layer 2 and Layer 3 switching, but rather are networks of Layer 2 through 7 switching with components for VoIP, wireless networking, storage networking, enhanced network management, and security.

In terms of availability, the requirements for these emerging applications such as voice, video, and data are 100 percent availability, high performance in terms of terabits per second (Tbps), and effortless scalability. Legacy data networks supported availability, performance, and scalability, but not to the degree needed by new applications for voice, video, and data. To provide for these applications and their needs, campus networks use a new design model, the Enterprise Composite Network Model, as a building block for enterprise networks. The model and its network components support features that are sophisticated, yet easily managed and sustained.

In terms of security, Cisco multilayer switched networks provide remote-site VPN solutions, firewall services, access control, and virus and worm mitigation and control. As companies continue to merge and add other companies, firewalls are no longer a requirement of just the Enterprise Edge. Firewalls are becoming more popular in local LANs where Catalyst switches support integrated firewall modules for the multigigabit speeds required for local LANs. Security features such as Secure Shell (SSH), 802.1x, access control lists (ACL), QoS, and private virtual LANs (VLAN) are necessary features that prevent unauthorized access. Companies cannot afford to allow free access to their private network and must account for every application and every user's security in the entire network. With Cisco switches and routers, following security best practices and designs is easy and well integrated.

In terms of disaster recovery, Cisco multilayer switched networks are the networks for which newer storage solutions opt to transport data for replication and migration. The end goal of data replication is to provide instantaneous data recovery in the event of disaster or anomalous occurrence. As Network Area Storage (NAS) and Fibre Channel over IP (FCIP) solutions become more popular, the performance, features, and availability found with Cisco multilayer switched networks become even more crucial.

This book covers the building blocks of Cisco multilayer switched networks from mostly a Catalyst switch and Cisco IOS perspective. Both the hardware components, such as Cisco Express Forwarding (CEF)-based multilayer switching (MLS), and software features, such as the Hot Standby Routing Protocol (HSRP) and the Spanning Tree Protocol (STP), are covered in this text for an understanding of building Cisco multilayer switched networks in today's highly demanding, highly available, secure, productive, and indestructible enterprise network environment.

This chapter provides a discussion of the basic elements of the Cisco multilayer switched network. The chapter begins with a synopsis of regulatory standards driving enterprise architectures, followed by a brief review of multilayer switching terminology, and then a discussion of the following elements of the network architecture:

- Service Oriented Network Architecture (SONA)
- The Enterprise Composite Network Model
- The Cisco Catalyst Switches

The section on Cisco Catalyst switches is a brief introduction to the capabilities of each platform and the role it can play within modern campus networks. Chapter 2, "The Roles of Switches in Designing Cisco Multilayer Switched Networks," provides a high-level overview of designing Cisco multilayer switched networks using these two elements: the Enterprise Composite Network Model and the Cisco Catalyst switches. Chapter 3, "Initial Configuration and Troubleshooting of Cisco Multilayer Switches," introduces basic configuration of Catalyst switches using both Cisco IOS and Cisco CatOS. The remaining chapters focus specifically on implementing software and hardware features to support high performance, scalability, and availability in Cisco multilayer switched networks based on the network designs that are discussed in Chapter 2.

Regulatory Standards Driving Enterprise Architectures

Many regulatory standards are driving enterprise architectures. Although most of these regulatory standards focus on data and information, they nonetheless drive network architectures. For example, to ensure that data is as safe as the Health Insurance Portability and Accountability Act (HIPAA) specifies, integrated security infrastructures are becoming paramount. Furthermore, the Sarbanes-Oxley Act, which specifies legal standards for maintaining the integrity of financial data, requires public companies to have multiple redundant data centers with synchronous copies of financial data.

Because the purpose of this book is to focus on enterprise architectures, you will not see detailed coverage of regulatory compliance. Nevertheless, these are important concepts for data centers, disaster recovery, and business continuance. You are encouraged to check out the following regulatory compliance standards:

- Sarbanes-Oxley (http://www.sarbanes-oxley.com)
- HIPAA (http://www.hippa.com)
- SEC 17a-4, "Records to Be Preserved by Certain Exchange Members, Brokers and Dealers" (http://www.sec.gov/rules/interp/34-47806.htm)

The next section on hardware- and software-switching terminology begins the technical discussion of building Cisco converged switched networks.

Hardware- and Software-Switching Terminology

This book refers to the terms *hardware-switching* and *software-switching* regularly throughout the text. The industry term *hardware-switching* refers to the act of processing packets at any layer, 2 through 7, via specialized hardware components referred to as *application-specific integrated circuits* (ASIC). ASICs, application-specific integrated circuits, are generally able to reach throughput at wire speed without performance degradation for advanced features such as QoS marking, ACL processing, or IP rewriting.

NOTE   Other terms used to describe *hardware-switching* are *in hardware*, *using ASICs*, and *hardware-based*. These terms are used interchangeably throughout the text. *MLS (multilayer switching)* is another term commonly used to describe hardware-switching. The term MLS can be confusing; for example, with the Catalyst 5500, the term *MLS* described a legacy hardware-switching method and feature. With today's terminology, MLS describes the capability to route and switch frames at line-rate (the speed of all ports sending traffic at the same time, full-duplex, at the maximum speed of the interface) with advanced features such as Network Address Translation (NAT), QoS, access-controls, and so on using ASICs. Chapter 9, "Understanding and Configuring Multilayer Switching," discusses the MLS terminology in more detail. For the next several chapters, MLS and hardware-switching simply represent switching and routing packets and frames in hardware at high speeds.

Switching and routing traffic via hardware-switching is considerably faster than the traditional software-switching of frames via a CPU. Many ASICs, especially ASICs for Layer 3 routing, use specialized memory referred to as *ternary content addressable memory* (TCAM) along with packet-matching algorithms to achieve high performance, whereas CPUs simply use higher processing rates to achieve greater degrees of performance. Generally, ASICs are able to achieve higher performance and availability than CPUs. In addition, ASICs scale easily in switching architecture, whereas CPUs do not. ASICs integrate not only on Supervisor Engines but also on individual line modules of Catalyst switches to hardware-switch packets in a distributed manner.

ASICs do have memory limitations. For example, the Catalyst 6500 family of switches is able to accommodate ACLs with a larger number of entries compared to the Catalyst 3500 family of switches due to the larger ASIC memory on the Catalyst 6500 family of switches. Generally, the size of the ASIC memory is relative to the cost and application of the switch. Furthermore, ASICs do not support all the features of the traditional Cisco IOS. For instance, the Catalyst 6500 family of switches with a Supervisor Engine 720 and an MSFC3 (Multilayer Switch Feature Card) must software-switch all packets requiring NAT without the use of specialized line modules. As products continue to evolve and memory becomes cheaper, ASICs gain additional memory and feature support.

NOTE   This section oversimplifies the view of hardware switching and software switching. As new technologies emerge, switching products are now using multiple hierarchical hardware- and software-switching components.

Multilayer Switching Overview

Traditionally, switches provided only Layer 2 functionality based on the MAC address. Current-generation switches, however, are capable of not only Layer 3 IP routing but also advanced features such as Layer 7 network access control (NAC), content-intelligence, load balancing, high availability, power distribution for IP phones, and a multitude of other features. In most campus networks, Layer 3 switches are replacing traditional routers. Furthermore, Layer 3 switches are migrating to the commercial and Internet service provider (ISP) markets because they are versatile and have high port density. This section of the chapter highlights the fundamentals of Layer 2 and Layer 3 switching. Later sections of this book discuss the Enterprise Composite Network Model for building multilayer switched networks and introduce the Cisco Catalyst switches.

Understanding Layers 2, 3, 4, and 7 Switching Terminology

Product marketing in the networking technology field uses many terms to describe product capabilities. In many situations, product marketing stretches the use of technology terms to distinguish products among multiple vendors. One such case is the terminology of Layers 2, 3, 4, and 7 switching. These terms are generally exaggerated in the networking technology field and need careful review.

The Layer 2, 3, 4, and 7 switching terminology correlates switching features to the OSI reference model. Figure 1-1 illustrates the OSI reference model and its relationship to protocols and network hardware.

Figure 1-1   *OSI Layer Relationship to Protocols and Networking Hardware*

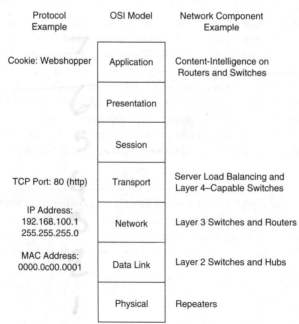

Protocol Example	OSI Model	Network Component Example
Cookie: Webshopper	Application	Content-Intelligence on Routers and Switches
	Presentation	
	Session	
TCP Port: 80 (http)	Transport	Server Load Balancing and Layer 4–Capable Switches
IP Address: 192.168.100.1 255.255.255.0	Network	Layer 3 Switches and Routers
MAC Address: 0000.0c00.0001	Data Link	Layer 2 Switches and Hubs
	Physical	Repeaters

Layer 2 Switching

Layer 2 switching strictly focuses on the data link layer, which means that Layer 2 switches are capable of switching packets only based on MAC addresses. Layer 2 switches increase network bandwidth and port density without much complexity. The term *Layer 2 switching* implies that frames forwarded by the switch are not modified in any way; however, Layer 2 switches such as the Catalyst 2960 are capable of QoS marking and network access control at Layer 4, whereas QoS does indeed modify the frame, and QoS and network access control do not affect the performance of the switch. An example of QoS marking at Layer 4 is marking the differentiated services code point (DSCP) bits in the IP header based on the TCP port number in the TCP header.

Legacy Layer 2 switches are limited in network scalability due to many factors. Consequently, all network devices on a legacy Layer 2 switch must reside on the same subnet and, as a result, exchange broadcast packets for address resolution purposes. Network devices that are grouped together to exchange broadcast packets constitute a *broadcast domain.* Layer 2 switches flood unknown unicast, multicast, and broadcast traffic throughout the entire broadcast domain. As a result, all network devices in the broadcast domain process all flooded traffic. As the size of the broadcast domain grows, its network devices become overwhelmed by the task of processing this unnecessary traffic. This caveat prevents network topologies from growing to more than a few legacy Layer 2 switches. Lack of QoS and security features further prevents the use of Layer 2 switches in campus networks and data centers.

However, all current and most legacy Cisco Catalyst switches support VLANs, which segment traffic into separate broadcast domains and, as a result, IP subnets. VLANs overcome several of the limitations of the basic Layer 2 networks, as discussed in the previous paragraph. This book discusses VLANs in Chapter 4, "Implementing and Configuring VLANs."

Figure 1-2 illustrates an example of a Layer 2 switch with workstations attached. Because the switch is only capable of MAC address forwarding, the workstations must reside on the same subnet to communicate. The "Layer 2 Switching in Depth" section discusses Layer 2 switching in more detail.

Figure 1-2   *Layer 2 Switching Example*

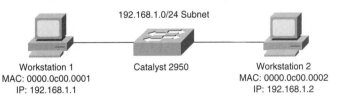

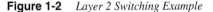

192.168.1.0/24 Subnet

Workstation 1
MAC: 0000.0c00.0001
IP: 192.168.1.1

Catalyst 2950

Workstation 2
MAC: 0000.0c00.0002
IP: 192.168.1.2

Layer 3 Switching

Layer 3 switches include Layer 3 routing capabilities. Many of the current-generation Catalyst Layer 3 switches are able to use routing protocols such as BGP, RIP, OSPF, and EIGRP to make optimal forwarding decisions. Catalyst Layer 3 switches are also capable of PIM multicasting and redundancy using the HSRP or the Virtual Router Redundancy Protocol (VRRP). These Layer 3 features are discussed in later chapters. Figure 1-3 illustrates a Layer 3 switch with several workstations attached. In this example, the Layer 3 switch routes packets between the two subnets.

Figure 1-3   *Layer 3 Switching Example*

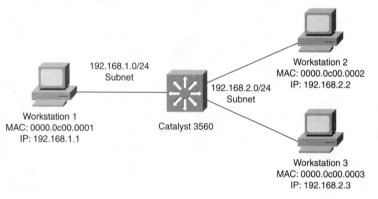

Layer 4 Switching

Layer 4 and 7 switching terminology is not as straightforward as Layers 2 and 3 switching terminology. Layer 4 switching implies switching based on protocol sessions. In other words, Layer 4 switching uses not only source and destination IP addresses in switching decisions, but also IP session information contained in the TCP and User Datagram Protocol (UDP) portions of the packet. The most common method of distinguishing traffic with Layer 4 switching is to use the TCP and UDP port numbers. Server load balancing, a Layer 4 to Layer 7 switching feature, can use TCP information such as TCP SYN, FIN, and RST to make forwarding decisions. (Refer to RFC 793 for explanations of TCP SYN, FIN, and RST.) As a result, Layer 4 switches are able to distinguish different types of IP traffic flows, such as differentiating the FTP, Network Time Protocol (NTP), HTTP, Secure HTTP (S-HTTP), and Secure Shell (SSH) traffic. Layer 4 switches generally use this differentiation for traffic filtering, QoS, and load balancing versus basic IP packet routing. All Cisco Layer 3 switches, such as the Catalyst 3560, 3750, 4500 (with Supervisor Engines II plus, III, IV, and V), 4900, and 6500 families of switches are capable of Layer 4 switching features, including load balancing, traffic filtering, and QoS based on IP TCP and UDP port numbering. Figure 1-4 illustrates a Layer 3 switch that is capable of Layer 4 QoS. In this example, the Layer 3 switch marks packets destined for a voice gateway with a DSCP value of 46 to differentiate service versus the management traffic from the management workstations.

Figure 1-4   *Layer 3 Switch Executing Layer 4 Feature*

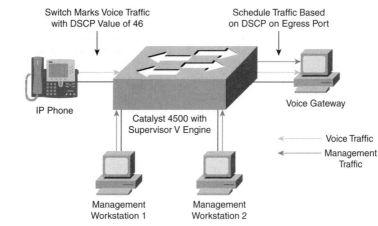

To achieve a high level of performance, Layer 4 switching requires hardware-forwarding capabilities with large memory capabilities. Later chapters of this book discuss the hardware-forwarding capabilities of several Catalyst platforms and their limitations.

Layer 7 Switching

Layer 7 switches operate at the application layer of the OSI reference model. Layer 7 switching capability implies content-intelligence. Content-intelligence with respect to web browsing implies features such as inspection of URLs, cookies, host headers, and so on. Content-intelligence with respect to VoIP may include distinguishing call destinations such as local or long distance for purposes of QoS. Content-intelligence is a powerful feature; however, switches use content-intelligence primarily for QoS and security rather than basic packet forwarding. At the time of publication, Cisco Catalyst Layer 3 switches are capable of Layer 7 switching on specific Catalyst switch models through the use of specialized hardware, software, or line modules.

Table 1-1 summarizes the layers of the OSI model with their respective protocol data units (PDU), which represent the data exchanged at each layer. The table also contains a column illustrating sample device types that are operating at the specified layer.

Table 1-1 *PDU and Sample Device Relationship to the OSI Model*

OSI Level	OSI Layer	PDU Type	Device Example	Address
1	Physical	Electrical signals	Repeater, transceiver	None
2	Data link	Frames	Switches	MAC address
3	Network	Packet	Router, multilayer switches	IP address
4	Transport	TCP or UDP data segments	Multilayer switch load balancing based on TCP port number	TCP or UDP port numbering
7	Application	Embedded application information in data payload	Multilayer switch using Network-Based Application Recognition (NBAR) to permit or deny traffic	Embedded information in data payload

Layer 2 Switching in Depth

Layer 2 switching is hardware-based bridging. In a Layer 2 switch, ASICs handle frame forwarding. Moreover, Layer 2 switches deliver the ability to increase bandwidth to the wiring closet without adding unnecessary complexity to the network. At Layer 2, no modification is required to the frame content when going between Layer 1 interfaces, such as Fast Ethernet to 10 Gigabit Ethernet.

In brief, the network design properties of current-generation Layer 2 switches include the following:

- Is designed for near wire-speed performance
- Is built using high-speed, specialized ASICs
- Has low latency
- Is scalable to several switches
- Supports Layer 3 functionality such as Internet Group Management Protocol (IGMP) snooping and QoS marking
- Offers limited scalability in large networks without Layer 3 boundaries

NOTE   Some Layer 2 switches are able to do packet rewriting for QoS marking. One such example is the Cisco Catalyst 2960's ability to mark ingress frames with a Layer 2 class of service (CoS) value or a Layer 3 DSCP value. This book explains QoS in more detail in later chapters.

At the time of publication, the only shipping Cisco Catalyst switches that fit into the pure Layer 2 switch category are the Catalyst 2940, 2950, 2955, 2960, 2970, and 4500 with Supervisor II+ families of switches. All other currently shipping switches are capable of Layer 3 routing.

Layer 3 Switching In-Depth

Layer 3 switching is hardware-based routing. Layer 3 switches overcome the inadequacies of Layer 2 scalability by providing routing domains. The packet forwarding in Layer 3 switches is handled by ASICs and other specialized circuitry. A Layer 3 switch performs everything on a packet that a traditional router does, including the following:

- Determines the forwarding path based on Layer 3 information

- Validates the integrity of the Layer 3 packet via the Layer 3 checksum

- Verifies and decrements packet TTL (Time-to-Live) expiration

- Rewrites the source and destination MAC address during IP rewrites

- Updates Layer 2 CRC during Layer 3 rewrite

- Processes and responds to any option information in the packet such as the Internet Connectivity Management Protocol (ICMP) record

- Updates forwarding statistics in the Management Information Base (MIB)

- Applies security controls and QoS if required

Layer 3 routing requires the ability of packet rewriting. Packet rewriting occurs on any routed boundary. Figure 1-5 illustrates the basic packet rewriting requirements of Layer 3 routing in an example in which two workstations are communicating using ICMP.

Figure 1-5   *Layer 3 Packet Rewriting Example*

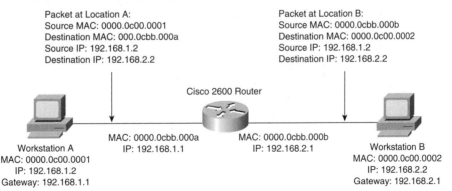

Address Resolution Protocol (ARP) plays an important role in Layer 3 packet rewriting. When Workstation A in Figure 1-5 sends five ICMP echo requests to Workstation B, the following events occur (assuming all the devices in this example have yet to communicate):

1 Workstation A sends an ARP request for its default gateway. Workstation A sends this ARP to obtain the MAC address of the default gateway. Without knowing the MAC address of the default gateway, Workstation A is unable to send any traffic outside of the local subnet. Note, in this example, that Workstation A's default gateway is the Cisco 2600 router with two Ethernet interfaces.

2 The default gateway, the Cisco 2600, responds to the ARP request with an ARP reply, sent to the unicast MAC address and IP address of Workstation A, indicating the default gateway's MAC address. The default gateway also adds an ARP entry for Workstation A in its ARP table upon receiving the ARP request.

3 Workstation A sends the first ICMP echo request to the destination IP address of Workstation B with a destination MAC address of the default gateway.

4 The router receives the ICMP echo request and determines the shortest path to the destination IP address.

5 Because the default gateway does not have an ARP entry for the destination IP address, Workstation B, the default gateway drops the first ICMP echo request from Workstation A. The default gateway drops packets in the absence of ARP entries to avoid storing packets that are destined for devices without ARP entries as defined by the original RFCs governing ARP.

6 The default gateway sends an ARP request to Workstation B to get Workstation B's MAC address.

7 Upon receiving the ARP request, Workstation B sends an ARP response with its MAC address.

8 By this time, Workstation A is sending a second ICMP echo request to the destination IP of Workstation B via its default gateway.

9 Upon receipt of the second ICMP echo request, the default gateway now has an ARP entry for Workstation B. The default gateway in turn rewrites the source MAC address to itself and the destination MAC to Workstation B's MAC address, and then forwards the frame to Workstation B.

10 Workstation B receives the ICMP echo request and sends an ICMP echo reply to the IP address of Workstation A with the destination MAC address of the default gateway.

Figure 1-5 illustrates the Layer 2 and Layer 3 rewriting at different places along the path between Workstation A and B. This figure and example illustrate the fundamental operation of Layer 3 routing and switching.

The primary difference between the packet-forwarding operation of a router and Layer 3 switching is the physical implementation. Layer 3 switches use different hardware components and have greater port density than traditional routers.

These concepts of Layer 2 switching, Layer 3 forwarding, and Layer 3 switching are applied in a single platform: the multilayer switch. Because it is designed to handle high-performance LAN traffic, a Layer 3 switch is locatable when there is a need for a router and a switch within the network, cost effectively replacing the traditional router.

Multilayer Switching

Multilayer switching combines Layer 2 switching and Layer 3 routing functionality. Generally, the networking field uses the terms *Layer 3 switch* and *multilayer switch* interchangeably to describe a switch that is capable of Layer 2 and Layer 3 switching. In specific terms, multilayer switches move campus traffic at wire speed while satisfying Layer 3 connectivity requirements. This combination not only solves throughput problems but also helps to remove the conditions under which Layer 3 bottlenecks form. Moreover, multilayer switches support many other Layer 2 and Layer 3 features besides routing and switching. For example, many multilayer switches support QoS marking at Layer 2 using the CoS field and QoS marking at Layer 3 using DSCP. Combining both Layer 2 and Layer 3 functionality and features allows for ease of deployment and simplified network topologies.

NOTE   The remainder of this text uses the term *multilayer switch* to represent a Layer 3 switch that is capable of Layers 2, 4, and 7 switching. The term *Layer 3 switching*, for the remainder of this text, represents the act of Layer 3 packet rewriting of frames by Layer 3–capable switches.

Enterprise Network Architectures

Now that you have an understanding of some basic switching concepts, this section provides a high-level overview of building Cisco multilayer switched networks by describing the Enterprise Composite Network Model, a hierarchy of functional areas, each with its own components. Figure 1-6 shows the Enterprise Composite Network Model at a high-level view. This section discusses each functional area and component in Figure 1-6. Furthermore, this section begins with an explanation of the Cisco Architecture for Voice, Video and Integrated Data (AVVID) framework upon which the campus design architecture is built.

Figure 1-6 *High-Level View of Enterprise Composite Network Model*

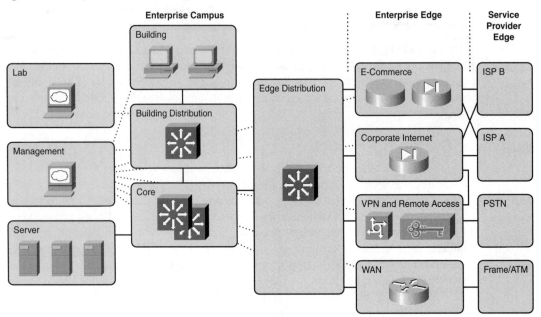

Specifically, this section covers the following topics:

- The Cisco Service-Oriented Network Architecture (SONA)
- The Cisco Intelligent Information Network (IIN)
- The Cisco AVVID framework
- The purpose of layer 3 networks
- The enterprise models
- The Enterprise Composite Network Model hierarchy
- The Enterprise Campus functional area
- The Enterprise Edge functional area
- The Service Provider Edge functional area
- The Cisco Enterprise Data Center

Cisco Service-Oriented Network Architecture

So far, the primary focus in this chapter has been on building a campus network for moving bits of data, voice, and video. As we all know, building campus networks is more than just moving bits. Many enterprises find themselves unlinked between network components and information assets. Furthermore, many enterprises have hundreds of "siloed" applications and databases that cannot communicate with each other. These disparate applications and databases are usually a result of specific requirements, delivery timelines, and distinct enterprise organizational structures. For example, information cannot be accessed easily by sales, customer service, or purchasing groups without creating different overlaying networks that join applications and information. Many enterprises have found that this unplanned expansion has left them with multiple systems and distributed resources that are uncoordinated and underused. These disparate systems are also difficult and costly to manage.

Consider your enterprise network. How many different database systems does your enterprise use? Do human resources, staff, shipping, sales, support, and marketing all use the same database or applications? How many diverse networks does your enterprise contain? Does your network have SAN islands or InfiniBand clusters?

The campus network still remains as the platform that can connect and enable all components of IT infrastructure transparently. Using Cisco SONA, enterprises can optimize applications, processes, and resources to deliver greater business benefits. By making the network more capable and intelligent, enterprises can improve the efficiency of everything the network touches while freeing funds for new strategic investments and innovation. Standardization increases asset efficiency by lowering operational costs to support the same number of assets. Virtualization optimizes use of assets such that extra physical resources can be logically segmented to be used across distributed departments. The widespread effect of the newly gained efficiencies across the network offers increased flexibility and scalability, thus creating a significant impact on growth, customer loyalty, and profitability—thereby improving the overall ability to compete.

The Cisco SONA framework outlines how enterprises can evolve to an Intelligent Information Network that accelerates applications, business processes, and resources and enables IT to have a greater impact on business. Cisco SONA leverages Cisco and Cisco partner solutions, services, and experience working with enterprises across industries to deliver proven, scalable business solutions. The Cisco SONA framework illustrates how to build integrated systems across a fully converged, intelligent network that significantly improves flexibility and increases efficiency. Enterprises can implement this comprehensive intelligence into the entire network, including the data center, branch offices, and campus environments. Figure 1-7 illustrates Cisco SONA.

Figure 1-7 *Cisco SONA Framework*

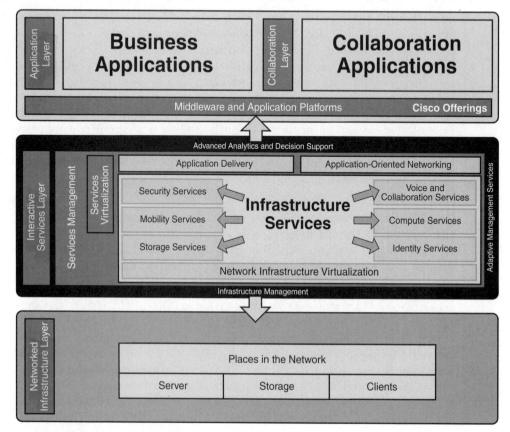

Three Layers of Cisco SONA

SONA is divided into the following three layers:

- **Network infrastructure layer**—The interconnected and converged network foundation

- **Interactive services layer**—The services structure that delivers efficient allocation of resources to applications and business processes

- **Application layer**—The business and collaborative applications that take advantage of the efficiencies of the interactive services and the network infrastructure

The network infrastructure layer is essentially the network itself. In terms of building converged switched networks, the network infrastructure includes the campus network and the data center. However, the network infrastructure layer includes all other networking components such as optical transports, firewalls, load-balancers, security appliances, and so on.

The interactive services layer includes the tools and network appliances that provide intelligent services and virtualization. For example, the VMWare product allows multiple operating systems to run on a single server and reuse wasted resources for applications. VMWare is an intelligent service. In terms of Cisco products, VFrame is an intelligent service because it has the capability to virtualize a cluster of servers to perform tasks as a single entity rather than as separate services. VFrame reduces cost and effectively uses resources in the network.

The application layer is the application itself that uses both the intelligent services and network infrastructure. Examples include SAP, Oracle, .NET, Microsoft Exchange, and so on.

In relation to building converged switched networks, this book focuses primarily on the network infrastructure layer. For more information on SONA, search for **SONA** on Cisco.com.

Cisco Intelligent Information Network

The IIN is a Cisco Systems 3- to 5-year vision for growing business value through increasing investment in the network.

The Cisco vision of the future IIN encompasses these features:

- **Integration of networked resources and information assets that have been largely unlinked**—The modern converged networks with integrated voice, video, and data require that IT departments more closely link the IT infrastructure with the network.

- **Intelligence across multiple products and infrastructure layers**—The intelligence built into each component of the network is extended network-wide and applies end to end.

- **Active participation of the network in the delivery of services and applications**—With added intelligence, the IIN makes it possible for the network to actively manage, monitor, and optimize service and application delivery across the entire IT environment.

With the listed features, the IIN offers much more than basic connectivity, bandwidth for users, and access to applications. The IIN offers end-to-end functionality and centralized, unified control that promotes true business transparency and agility.

The IIN technology vision offers an evolutionary approach that consists of three phases in which functionality can be added to the infrastructure as required:

- **Integrated transport**—Everything—data, voice, and video—consolidates onto an IP network for secure network convergence. By integrating data, voice, and video transport into a single, standards-based, modular network, organizations can simplify network management and generate enterprise-wide efficiencies. Network convergence also lays the foundation for a new class of IP-enabled applications delivered through Cisco IP Communications solutions.

- **Integrated services**—After the network infrastructure has been converged, IT resources can be pooled and shared or "virtualized" to flexibly address the changing needs of the organization. Integrated services help to unify common elements, such as storage and data center server capacity. By extending virtualization capabilities to encompass server, storage, and network elements, an organization can transparently use all its resources more efficiently. Business continuity is also enhanced because shared resources across the IIN provide services in the event of a local system failure.

- **Integrated applications**—With Application-Oriented Networking (AON) technology, Cisco has entered the third phase of building the IIN. This phase focuses on making the network "application-aware" so that it can optimize application performance and more efficiently deliver networked applications to users. In addition to capabilities such as content caching, load balancing, and application-level security, Cisco AON makes it possible for the network to simplify the application infrastructure by integrating intelligent application message handling, optimization, and security into the existing network.

The Cisco IIN vision and Cisco SONA yield today's Enterprise Composite Network Model. Before discussing the Enterprise Composite Network Model, the section that follows provides a quick review of the Cisco AVVID framework.

The Cisco AVVID Framework

The Cisco AVVID framework still exists, yet it has given way to Cisco SONA. Nevertheless, many enterprise design reference architectures still use the Cisco AVVID framework.

Cisco AVVID is an enterprise-wide, standards-based network architecture that provides a road map for combining business and technology strategies into a cohesive model. Figure 1-8 illustrates this model.

Figure 1-8 *Cisco AVVID Framework*

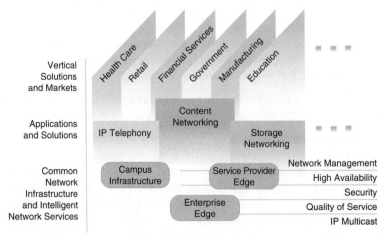

The goal of any network architecture is to provide a road map and a guide for ongoing network planning, design, and implementation. In addition, network architectures provide a coherent framework that unifies disparate solutions onto a single foundation.

To satisfy the network architecture goal, the Cisco AVVID framework establishes several components. The primary components include network infrastructure, intelligent network services, and network solutions. These components build solutions and applications such as storage, Internet service, and IP telephony.

In summary, the Cisco AVVID framework supports the following key components:

- Network infrastructure
- Intelligent network services
- Network solutions

The network infrastructure component includes the hardware and software used to send, receive, and manage packets that are transmitted between network devices throughout the enterprise. The network infrastructure includes the transmission media and devices that control transmission paths, such as private and public transport media. Examples of these devices include routers, LAN switches, WAN switches, call gateways, and private branch exchanges (PBX).

The intelligent network services allow end users to operate in a controlled, secure environment in which the network provides differentiated services. Intelligent network services essentially add intelligence to the network infrastructure beyond just moving a datagram between two network devices. Intelligent network services allow for application awareness and content-intelligence. Intelligent network services also include functions such as security, network management, quality of service, IP multicast, and high availability.

The network solutions include the hardware and software that use the network infrastructure and intelligent network services to their advantage. Network solutions allow enterprises to make business decisions about the business itself as well as about networks and the technologies and applications that run on them. Network-based applications enable an enterprise organization to interact more effectively with customers, suppliers, partners, and employees. Customer service, commerce, supplier, and other intranet applications run over the network infrastructure enabled by intelligent network services. The end result of these applications is increased profitability and productivity. Examples of network solutions that run over network infrastructures using the Cisco AVVID framework are IP telephony, multi-unit applications, content networking, and storage networking.

An example of an application that benefits from using the Cisco AVVID framework is IP telephony. Figure 1-9 illustrates a basic network topology using the Cisco AVVID framework. In this example, IP telephony itself is the network solution. The multilayer switches provide the network infrastructure, whereas QoS features of the multilayer switch provide the intelligent network service. In this specific example, the multilayer switches prioritize all IP telephony voice and signaling traffic over standard data traffic to ensure voice quality.

Figure 1-9 *Network Topology Example*

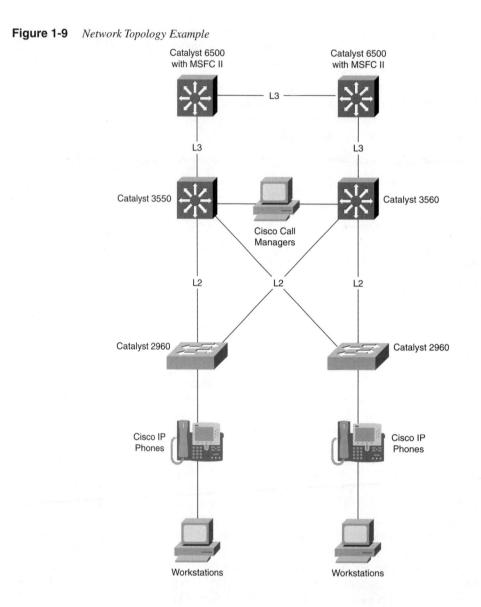

Purpose of Layer 3 Networks

The motivation behind building Layer 3 networks in the LAN is simple and straight-forward—Layer 3 networks add security, availability, performance, and features that are not available with Layer 2 networks. This book could discuss in detail how Layer 2 networks send broadcast frames to every port, broadcast unknown unicast packets to every port, and so on. However, the reasons for using Layer 3 networks today are security, availability, performance, and the ability to configure advanced features.

Security in Layer 3 networks is done via ACLs. Attempting to use Layer 2-based ACLs would be an impossible task in large networks. Access control via IP address or application (Layer 4 port number or Layer 7 application awareness) is far simpler than trying to apply access control by using MAC addresses that are unique for each host. Just imagine trying to apply security by using MAC address-based access control lists with over 1000 hosts, or even 10,000 hosts? Furthermore, Layer 3 redundancy is much faster, more stable, more consistent, and easier to configure than Layer 2 redundancy. For example, Layer 3 routing protocols converge significantly faster than the traditional STP. In addition, routing protocols are session-based, whereas STP is not.

Features are another important aspect of Layer 3 networks; server load balancing, NAT, and NetFlow (static analysis of IP flows) are not available at Layer 2. The list of reasons for deploying Layer 3 networks could go on almost indefinitely; however, most of the reasons are legacy now, and Layer 3 networks are the focus of any network designs today. The next section introduces the Enterprise Composite Network Model for building Cisco multilayer switched networks.

A common situation in which Layer 3 networks might not be the best choice is in data centers where a service module is needed in the distribution layer. In this case, due to bandwidth restrictions on the service module, Layer 2 topologies can be extended up to the distribution layer.

The Enterprise Models

Cisco provides the enterprise-wide systems architecture that helps companies to protect, optimize, and grow the infrastructure that supports business processes. The architecture provides integration of the entire network—campus, data center, WAN, branches, and teleworkers—offering staff secure access to the tools, processes, and services.

- **Cisco Enterprise Campus Architecture**—Combines a core infrastructure of intelligent switching and routing with tightly integrated productivity-enhancing technologies, including IP Communications, mobility, and advanced security. The architecture provides the enterprise with high availability through a resilient multilayer design, redundant hardware and software features, and automatic procedures for reconfiguring network paths when failures occur. Multicast provides optimized bandwidth consumption, and QoS prevents oversubscription to ensure that real-time traffic, such as voice and video, or critical data is not dropped or delayed. Integrated security protects against and mitigates the impact of worms, viruses, and other attacks on the network, even at the port level. Cisco enterprise-wide architecture extends support for standards, such as 802.1x and Extensible Authentication Protocol (EAP). The Cisco enterprise-wide architecture also provides the flexibility to add IP Security (IPsec) and Multiprotocol Label Switching VPNs (MPLS VPN), identity and access management, and VLANs to compartmentalize access. This helps improve performance and security and decreases costs.

- **Cisco Enterprise Data Center Architecture**—A cohesive, adaptive network architecture that supports the requirements for consolidation, business continuance, and security while enabling emerging service-oriented architectures, virtualization, and on-demand computing. IT staff can easily provide departmental staff, suppliers, or customers with secure access to applications and resources. This approach simplifies and streamlines management, significantly reducing overhead. Redundant data centers provide backup using synchronous and asynchronous data and application replication. The network and devices offer server and application load balancing to maximize performance. This solution allows enterprises to scale without major changes to the infrastructure.

- **Cisco Enterprise Branch Architecture**—Allows enterprises to extend head-office applications and services, such as security, IP Communications, and advanced application performance, to thousands of remote locations and users, or to a small group of branches. Cisco integrates security, switching, network analysis, caching, and converged voice and video services into a series of integrated services routers in the branch so that enterprises can deploy new services when they are ready without buying new equipment. This solution provides secure access to voice, mission-critical data, and video applications anywhere, anytime. Advanced network routing, VPNs, redundant WAN links, application content caching, and local IP telephony call processing provide a robust architecture with high levels of resilience for all the branch offices. An optimized network leverages the WAN and LAN to reduce traffic and save bandwidth and operational expenses. Enterprises can easily support branch offices with the ability to centrally configure, monitor, and manage devices located at remote sites, including tools, such as AutoQoS, that proactively resolve congestion and bandwidth issues before they affect network performance.

- **Cisco Enterprise Teleworker Architecture**—Allows enterprises to securely deliver voice and data services to remote small or home offices over a standard broadband access service, providing a business-resiliency solution for the enterprise and a flexible work environment for employees. Centralized management minimizes IT support costs, and robust integrated security mitigates the unique security challenges of this environment. Integrated security and identity-based networking services enable the enterprise to help extend campus security policies to the teleworker. Staff can securely log into the network over an "always-on" VPN and gain access to authorized applications and services from a single cost-effective platform. The productivity can further be enhanced by adding an IP phone, providing cost-effective access to a centralized IP Communications system with voice and unified messaging services.

- **Cisco Enterprise WAN Architecture**—Offers the convergence of voice, video, and data services over a single IP Communications network. This approach enables enterprises to cost-effectively span large geographic areas. QoS, granular service levels, and comprehensive encryption options help ensure the secure delivery of high-quality corporate voice, video, and data resources to all corporate sites, enabling staff to work productively and efficiently from any location. Security is provided with multiservice VPNs (IPsec and MPLS) over Layer 2 or Layer 3 WANs, hub-and-spoke, or full-mesh topologies.

This book focuses primarily on the Cisco Enterprise Campus Architecture, which uses the Enterprise Composite Network Model to divide and modularize the architecture into multiple functional areas. This division and modularity allows for flexibility in network design and facilitates ease of implementation and troubleshooting. The next section goes into detail regarding the Enterprise Composite Network Model.

Enterprise Composite Network Model

The Enterprise Composite Network Model provides a modular framework for designing networks. The modularity within this model allows for flexibility in network design and facilitates implementation and troubleshooting. This section describes the Enterprise Composite Network Model and, at a high-level overview, how the model addresses enterprise network requirements for performance, scalability, and availability.

Nearly a decade ago, Cisco introduced a hierarchical design model as a tool for network designers to approach network design from the physical, logical, and functional viewpoints. The hierarchical model divides networks into the access, distribution, and core layers. Figure 1-10 illustrates the network design hierarchical model.

Figure 1-10 *Network Design Hierarchical Model*

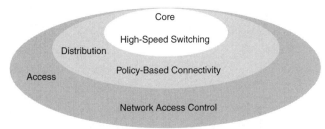

The access layer provides user access to network devices. In a network campus, the access layer generally incorporates Layer 2 switches that interconnect LAN devices such as workstations and servers. In the WAN environment, the access layer provides sites with access to the corporate network using a WAN technology such as broadband or Frame Relay.

The distribution layer aggregates the wiring closets and uses Layer 2 and Layer 3 switching to segment workgroups, implement security policies, restrict bandwidth, and isolate network problems. These measures prevent anomalous events in the distribution and access layers from affecting the core layer. Furthermore, routing and packet manipulation such as NAT and QoS marking commonly occur in the distribution layer. Redundancy in this scenario is carried out by HSRP or the Gateway Load Balancing Protocol (GLBP) and the use of routing protocols. Later chapters discuss these features in more detail.

The core layer describes a high-speed backbone, in which packets are switched as fast as possible. Because the core is critical for connectivity, it provides for high availability and adapts quickly to routing and topology changes.

Figure 1-11 illustrates a sample network topology that uses the hierarchical model. This sample network topology scales the distribution and access layers to two switches for simplicity. In an applied network topology, the distribution and access layers comprise numerous switches.

The hierarchical model was useful for designing basic enterprise networks. However, enterprise networks that employ multiple applications and services need additional modularity because the hierarchical model is difficult to scale logically. This need for additional modularity, or building blocks, led to the development of the Enterprise Composite Network Model.

Figure 1-11 *Hierarchical Sample Network Design*

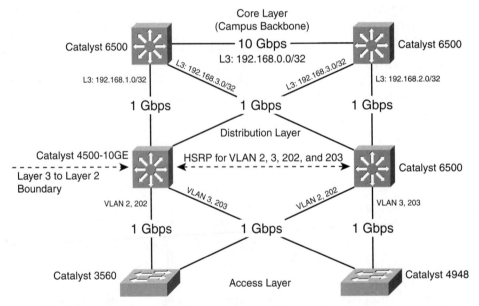

The Enterprise Composite Network Model introduces additional modularity into the network structure. The entire network is divided into functional areas that represent several distinct regions of the network. The functional areas of the Enterprise Composite Network Model still use the hierarchical model as the basic building block.

The Enterprise Composite Network Model includes the following four major functional areas:

- Enterprise Campus
- Enterprise Edge
- Service Provider Edge
- Data Center

The Enterprise Campus contains the modules that are required to build a hierarchical, highly robust campus network that offers performance, scalability, and high availability. This functional area contains the network elements that are required for independent operation within a single campus. This functional area does not offer remote connections or Internet access.

| NOTE | In the context of this chapter, a *campus* is defined as one or more buildings, with multiple virtual and physical networks, connected across a high-performance, multilevel switched backbone. |

The Enterprise Edge aggregates connectivity from the various elements at the edge of the enterprise network. The Enterprise Edge functional area filters traffic from the Edge modules and routes it into the Enterprise Campus functional area. The Enterprise Edge functional area contains all the network elements for efficient and secure communication between the Enterprise Campus and remote locations, remote users, home users, and the Internet.

The Service Provider Edge provides connectivity to services that are implemented by service providers. The Service Provider Edge functional area enables communications with other networks using different WAN technologies and ISPs.

The Data Center provides connectivity to server frames and services and consolidates the data processing and storage-related functions of the enterprise network.

Figures 1-12 and 1-13 illustrate, respectively, the Enterprise Composite Network Model and a sample implementation of the Enterprise Composite Network Model.

Figure 1-12 *Enterprise Composite Network Model*

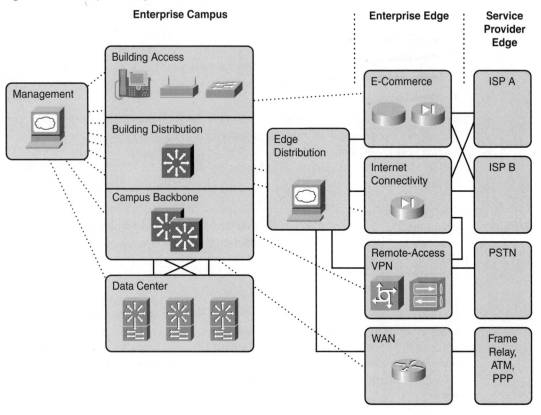

Figure 1-13 shows an enterprise network with the major components of the Enterprise Composite Network Model. The network is divided into the Enterprise Campus and Enterprise Edge functional areas, connected by the Campus Backbone submodule.

Figure 1-13 *Sample Implementation of the Composite Network Model*

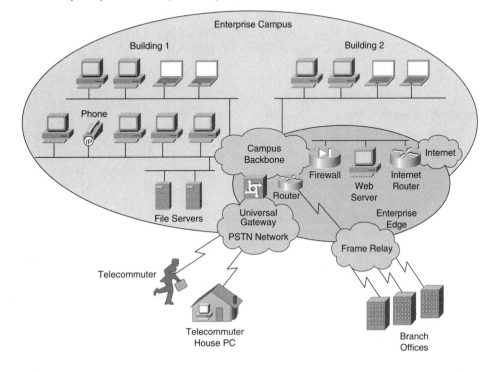

The functional areas of the Enterprise Composite Network Model orchestrate the following criteria for designing multilayer switched networks:

- Define a deterministic network with clearly defined boundaries between modules. The model has clear demarcation points such that the designer knows exact traffic patterns.

- Increase network scalability and ease the design task by making each module discrete.

- Provide scalability by allowing enterprises to add modules easily. As network complexity grows, designers are able to add new functional modules without disrupting other modules.

- Offer more network integrity in network design, allowing the designer to add services and solutions without changing the underlying network infrastructure or network design.

In brief, the Enterprise Composite Network Model divides the network into physical, logical, and functional areas. These functional areas establish their own hierarchical model of Building Access, Building Distribution, and Campus Backbone submodules. Usually, the Campus Backbone connects multiple functional areas that extend into each functional area as a set of interfaces.

Enterprise Campus

The Enterprise Campus defines a functional area of the Enterprise Composite Network Model, as described in the previous section. The Enterprise Campus functional area includes the following Enterprise Composite modules:

- Campus Infrastructure
- Network Management
- Edge Distribution

Each module has a specific function within the campus network. This section describes the modules that comprise an Enterprise Campus network and explains how the infrastructure meets the need for performance, scalability, and availability. Figure 1-14 illustrates the Enterprise Campus functional area.

Figure 1-14 *Enterprise Campus Functional Area*

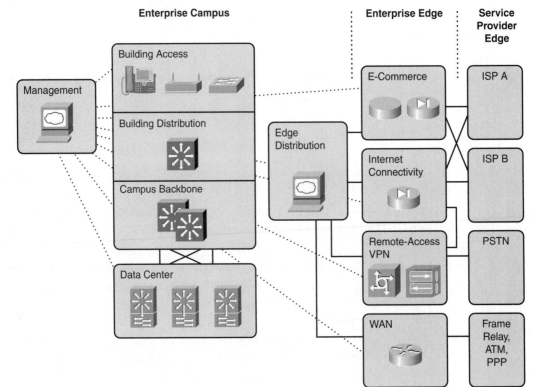

Enterprise Campus Infrastructure

The Campus Infrastructure module connects the other Enterprise Campus modules. This module connects multiple physical areas in a Campus Backbone submodule. The physical areas may be floors of a building, lab areas, buildings, or any other physical boundary. These physical areas connect to the Campus Backbone submodule through Building Access and Distribution submodules.

Generally, the Building Access and Building Distribution submodules are referred to as such because buildings are the usual boundaries. However, the access and distribution submodules may apply to any single physical or logical boundary, such as an intermediate distribution frame (IDF), floor, department, or area. The remainder of this text uses the terms *Building Access submodule* and *access layer submodule* interchangeably and uses the terms *Building Distribution submodule* and *distribution layer submodule* interchangeably as well.

Building Access, Building Distribution, and Campus Backbone Submodules

The Building Access submodule, also known as the access layer submodule, contains end-user workstations, IP phones, and the Layer 2 access switches that connect devices to the Building Distribution submodule. The Building Access submodule provides for network access and performs important services such as Layer 2 and Layer 3 broadcast and multicast suppression; access control, such as 802.1x, packet filtering, and protocol filtering; and QoS.

The Building Distribution submodule, also known as the distribution layer submodule, provides an aggregation of Building Access devices, often using Layer 3 switching. The Building Distribution submodule generally performs IP routing and implements features such as QoS and access control. This module intends to provide for fast failure recovery. Because each Building Distribution submodule switch maintains two equal-cost paths in the routing table to every destination network via the campus core, failover occurs immediately.

The Campus Backbone submodule, also known as the *core layer submodule*, provides redundant and fast-converging connectivity between Building Distribution submodules. The Campus Backbone submodule intends to route and switch traffic as fast as possible from one module to another. This module generally uses Layer 3 switches for high-throughput functions with added routing, QoS, and security features. In special circumstances, the Campus Backbone may use Layer 2 switches. Figure 1-15 depicts a sample Enterprise Campus infrastructure.

Network Management, Data Center, and Edge Distribution Submodules

In addition to the Campus Infrastructure module, which consists of the access layer, distribution layer, and core layer modules, the Enterprise Campus functional area includes the following modules:

- Network Management
- Data Center
- Edge Distribution

Figure 1-15 *Sample Enterprise Campus Infrastructure*

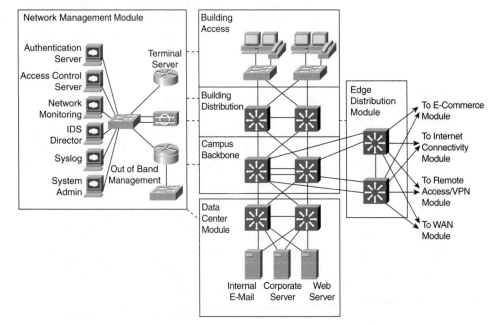

The Network Management module contains hosts and management workstations that receive system logging, perform authentication and network monitoring, and apply general configuration-management functions. This module is essential for capacity planning, monitoring, and network troubleshooting. For security and disaster-recovery purposes, the design recommends an out-of-band (a network on which no production traffic resides) connection to all network components. In the event of a network disaster, a redundant method of accessing the network equipment is crucial. Furthermore, the Network Management module provides configuration management for nearly all devices in the network using Cisco routers, specialized software, and dedicated network-management stations.

The Edge Distribution module aggregates the connectivity from the various elements at the Enterprise Edge functional area and routes the traffic into the Campus Backbone submodule. Its structure is similar to the Building Distribution submodule. Both modules use access control to filter traffic, although, the Edge Distribution module relies on the edge devices to perform additional security.

Figure 1-16 shows an example of an Enterprise Campus network divided into easily manageable building blocks, including the Campus Infrastructure, Network Management, Data Center, and Edge Distribution modules. Notice in the figure that the Enterprise Edge functional area is reachable only through the Edge Distribution module.

Figure 1-16 *Sample Implementation of an Enterprise Campus Network*

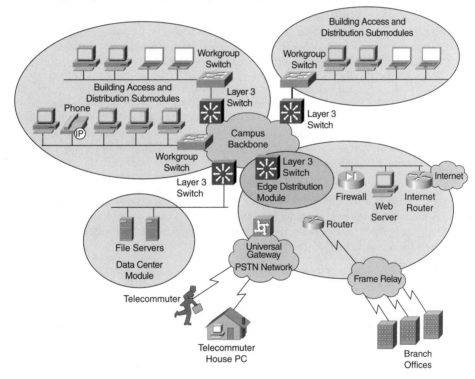

How Enterprise Campus Modules Meet the Needs of Enterprise Networks

The Enterprise Campus modules meet the needs of enterprise networks by providing security, performance, scalability, and availability. The last section of this chapter introduces the Cisco Catalyst switches that are used in the Enterprise Campus modules to meet the performance, scalability, and availability requirements of each module or submodule. This section briefly discusses how each network module provides performance, scalability, and availability in the enterprise. Later chapters of this book describe the exact features that are used to meet these requirements, such as 802.1D STP, EtherChannel, distributed Cisco Express Forwarding (dCEF), and VRRP.

Implementing security features at every submodule is crucial to a secure environment. Network-based security should be implemented as close as possible to the edge (access layer). Nevertheless, security control throughout the campus is required for a secure environment.

The Building Access submodule is critical to end-user performance. Generally, switches occupying the Building Access submodule are switches with high port density. The switches within this submodule generally achieve availability through path redundancy to the Building Distribution submodule. Because end-user workstations only connect via a single connection, switch redundancy is crucial, as in the Building Distribution or Campus Backbone.

The Building Distribution, Campus Backbone, and Data Center submodules require high-performance switching, scalability, and availability. Choosing the appropriate Cisco Catalyst switches with high-capacity switching fabrics, modularity for scaling port density, and high-availability features such as dual-processing engines and redundant switch fabrics is crucial for implementing these submodules.

The Enterprise Distribution submodule meets enterprise network needs by providing security, high performance, switch modularity, and redundancy. WAN deployments are available via many Catalyst switches that support WAN interface modules. Simply adding additional modules provides scalability, whereas using the switching fabric for WAN connectivity provides performance. The use of multiple interfaces and paths along with hardware redundancy provides WAN redundancy in the Enterprise Edge.

The Network Management submodule meets enterprise network needs by monitoring and administering the requirements for security, performance, scalability, and availability. This module is useful in determining whether capacity increases are necessary and is able to monitor network availability.

Table 1-2 summarizes how the Enterprise Campus modules meet the requirements for performance, scalability, availability and security in the enterprise.

Table 1-2 *How Enterprise Campus Modules Meet Enterprise Network Needs*

Module/Submodule	Performance	Scalability	Availability	Security
Building Access	Critical to desktop performance	Provides port density	Important to provide redundancy	Critical in providing a secure network
Building Distribution	Critical to campus performance	Provides switch modularity	Critical to provide redundancy	Critical in providing a secure network
Campus Backbone	Critical to overall network performance	Provides switch modularity	Critical to provide redundancy and fault tolerance	Critical in providing a secure network
Data Center	Critical to server and application performance	Provides switch modularity	Critical to provide redundancy and fault tolerance	Critical in providing a secure network
Enterprise Distribution	Critical to WAN and Internet performance	Provides switch modularity	Important to provide redundancy	Critical in providing a secure network

Enterprise Edge

The Enterprise Edge functional area aggregates the Internet portion of the enterprise network that is responsible for providing services outside the domain of the Enterprise Campus network. Each module connects individually to the Enterprise Distribution module to gain connectivity to the Enterprise Campus network. Figure 1-17 illustrates the Enterprise Edge functional area.

Figure 1-17 *Enterprise Edge Functional Area*

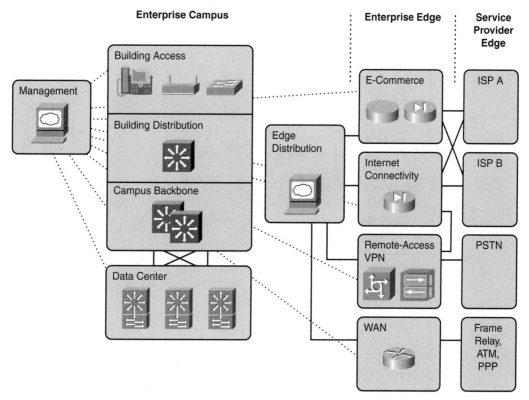

Four separate modules comprise the Enterprise Edge functional area. These modules are as follows:

- E-Commerce
- Internet Connectivity
- Remote Access and VPN
- WAN

Figure 1-18 illustrates the Enterprise Edge modules.

Figure 1-18 *Enterprise Edge Modules*

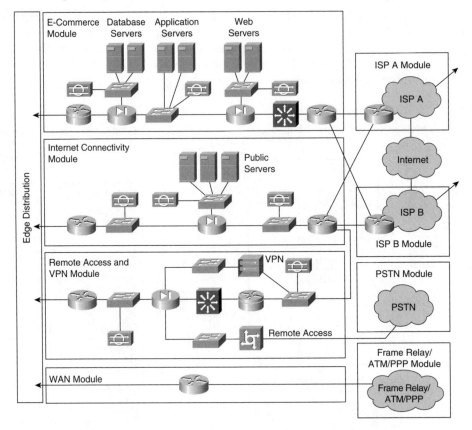

E-Commerce Module

The E-Commerce module enables enterprises to successfully deploy e-commerce applications and take advantage of the powerful competitive opportunities that are provided by the Internet. Online retail is an example of e-commerce. All e-commerce transactions pass through a series of intelligent services to provide performance, security, scalability, and availability within the overall e-commerce network design.

To build an e-commerce solution, enterprises deploy any of the following types of servers:

- **Web servers**—Provide the front end to the e-commerce site. Their primary role is to act as a customer interface for the e-commerce site.

- **Application servers**—Process data and make decisions about the processed data. An example is an application server configured to handle credit card transactions for an online store.

- **Database servers**—Contain all the information of an e-commerce site. Database servers, for example, may contain data about past records, inventory, or future events. In addition, database information may reside on Fibre Channel SANs because they are increasingly popular in enterprise networks.

- **Security servers**—Govern communication between the various levels of security in the system, often using firewalls, intrusion detection systems, encryption systems, and access-level control systems.

Any physical server may perform more than one role. For example, a single server may handle web- and application-server roles. Generally, enterprise networks deploy security servers as a separate entity.

Internet Connectivity Module

The Internet Connectivity module provides internal users with connectivity to Internet services. Internet users can access the information on publicly available servers. Additionally, this module accepts VPN traffic from remote users and remote sites and forwards it to the Remote Access and VPN module. Internet connectivity is crucial in all enterprise networks because it provides a means of communication outside the company.

The major components of the Internet Connectivity module are as follows:

- **E-mail servers**—Communicate between the Internet and intranet mail servers to exchange corporate e-mail with other companies.

- **DNS servers**—Act as an authoritative external DNS server for the enterprise and relay internal requests to the Internet. As a result, internal DNS servers replace the need for enterprise networks to connect to Internet DNS servers for domain name resolution. In addition, internal DNS servers may contain additional DNS entries for web services that are only available on the intranet.

- **Public web servers**—Provide public information about the organization and access to online services such as catalogs and online sales to the Internet.

- **Security systems**—Govern communication between the various levels of security in the network. Security systems include intrusion detection systems, firewalls, and access control systems such as TACACS+ and RADIUS. Security systems are generally appliances in corporate networks with specific functions; however, servers loaded with special software may act as a security system.

- **Edge routers**—Impart Layer 3 connectivity to the Internet. Generally, large enterprises deploy multiple Internet edge routers for redundancy. Internet edge routers always use security features such as basic packet filtering, NAT, and a few firewall capabilities. However, the security features deployed on Internet edge routers are not as secure and as sophisticated as security features implemented in the security systems component.

Remote Access and VPN Module

All enterprise networks deploy some methods of remote access. VPN is the most common method of remote access because of the availability of Internet access at home over broadband or DSL networks. Dial-in networks are also available for legacy remote-access methods. The components of the Remote Access and VPN module are as follows:

- **Dial-in access concentrators**—Terminate and authenticate dial-in connections. Dial-in access is a legacy technology, but it is still a useful method of remote access, especially for remote users who do not have access to a LAN or broadband network. Dial-in access also provides a backup to the other remote-access methods during disaster recovery. An example of a dial-in access concentrator is the Cisco AS5400.

- **VPN concentrators**—Terminate IP tunnels, forwarded by the Internet Connectivity module, from remote users or remote sites. An example of a VPN concentrator is the Cisco VPN 3000 concentrator. Examples of the VPN client are the Cisco VPN Client (software-based) and Cisco VPN 3002 Hardware Client. Note that Cisco routers may act as VPN clients or concentrators depending on software versions and hardware models.

- **Firewalls and intrusion detection systems (IDS)**—Firewalls provide network-level protection of resources and stateful filtering of traffic. IDSs detect and protect against unauthorized network traffic within the network.

- **Layer 2 switches**—Provide Layer 2 connectivity between the devices. Layer 3 switches may also be used in the Remote Access and VPN module but generally are used only as Layer 2 switches because Layer 3 routing is done by the Remote Access or VPN head-in (concentrator) device.

WAN Module

The WAN module routes traffic between the central sites, remote sites, or multiple campuses. The major difference between the WAN module and the Remote Access and VPN module is that with the Remote Access and VPN module, remote users and sites connect over a shared medium such as DSL or cable broadband to the enterprise network, whereas with the WAN module, remote users and sites connect to enterprise networks over point-to-point connections. Examples of these point-to-point connections include physical technologies such as leased lines, optical, cable, DSL, and wireless. Other methods of point-to-point connections include data-link protocols such as Frame Relay, ATM, and Point-to-Point Protocol (PPP). Note that cable and DSL are listed as point-to-point technologies as well. In special configurations, these technologies are able to achieve or emulate point-to-point connections. Moreover, ISDN and dial-up are alternative legacy remote-access options for remote users. Generally, dial-up access for remote users is a backup feature where broadband services are not available.

Figure 1-19 shows a sample Enterprise Edge module implementation.

Figure 1-19 *Sample Enterprise Edge Module Implementation*

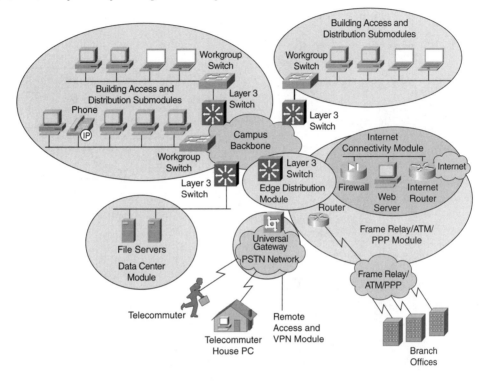

Service Provider Edge

The Service Provider Edge functional area defines modules for the physical connections to ISPs for Internet or intranet connectivity. The Service Provider Edge functional area defines the following three modules:

- ISP
- Public Switched Telephone Network (PSTN)
- Frame Relay, ATM, and PPP

Figure 1-20 illustrates the Service Provider Edge and its modules.

ISP Module

The ISP module enables enterprise connectivity to the Internet. This service is essential to enable Enterprise Edge services, such as the E-Commerce, Remote Access and VPN, and Internet Connectivity modules. To provide redundant connections to the Internet, enterprises connect to two or more ISPs. Physical connections between the ISP and the Enterprise Campus Backbone originate from any WAN technologies.

Figure 1-20 *Server Provider Edge*

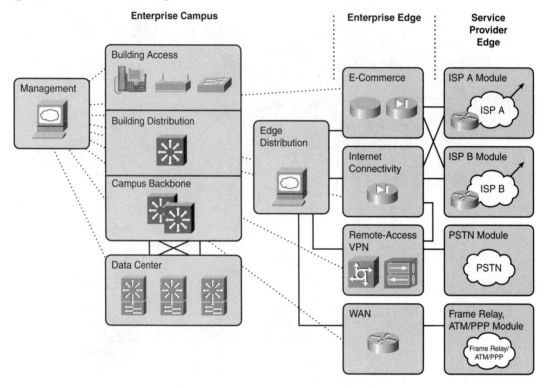

PSTN Module

The PSTN module represents the dial-up infrastructure used to access the enterprise network using ISDN, analog, and wireless (cellular) technologies. Enterprises can also use the PSTN module to back up existing WAN links. Connections are established on demand and are torn down when they are determined to be idle.

Frame Relay, ATM, and PPP Module

The Frame Relay, ATM, and PPP module includes all WAN technologies for permanent connectivity with remote locations. Frame Relay and ATM are common WAN technologies used today. PPP over any medium is another common WAN technology. PPP is used to connect networks across WAN mediums. Metro Ethernet, a MAN technology, is growing in popularity in the WAN as well. Nevertheless, many technologies can fit into the same model.

Figure 1-21 illustrates a sample implementation of the Service Provider Edge functional area.

Figure 1-21 *Sample Implementation of the Service Provider Edge*

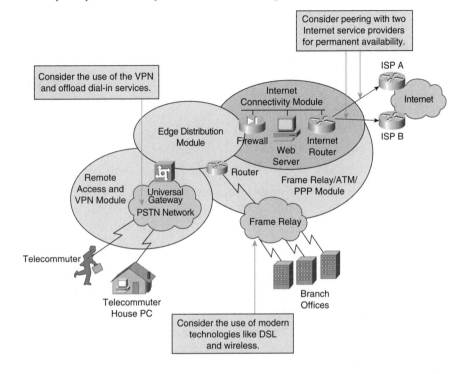

The Cisco Enterprise Data Center

Cisco Systems, Inc. has recently made a strong push to organize its products in the data center. From an executive point of view, a Cisco Data Center architecture enables IT executives to do the following:

- Consolidate and virtualize computing, storage, and network resources
- Deliver secure and optimized employee, partner, and customer access to information and applications
- Protect and rapidly recover IT resources and applications

At a high level, the Cisco Data Center uses the following network components:

- **Networked Infrastructure**—Gigabit/10 Gigabit, InfiniBand, storage switching and optical transport
- **Interactive Services**—Storage Fabric Services, computer services, security services, and application optimization services
- **Management**—Fabric manager (element and network management) and Cisco VFrame (server and service provisioning)

As with all current enterprise architectures, the Cisco Data Center is based on SONA, which is the enterprise implementation of the IIN technology vision. As discussed previously, Cisco SONA emphasizes the value of the interactive services provided in the networked infrastructure, such as application optimization, security, and server and storage fabric switching, to enhance business applications.

More specifically, the Cisco Data Center is grouped into the following four key areas:

- Server Fabrics
- Storage Areas Networks/Fabrics
- Data Center Interconnects
- Access Networks

The sections that follow discuss these key areas in more detail. As an example, Figure 1-22 illustrates a sample Cisco Data Center topology.

Server Fabrics

Server fabrics are used to interconnect servers for the purpose of high-performance cluster computers. To support high-performance clusters, the transport has to be not only high speed but over very low latency.

Applications that use server fabrics include financial modeling, fluid dynamics, and any type of data-mining application. Oracle-SAP and SAS are two popular applications that may benefit from server fabrics.

Currently, a leading data-link technology of interconnecting server fabrics is InfiniBand. InfiniBand is a new technology to financial enterprises but is not new to the scientific community. To achieve the high speed necessary for server fabrics (multiple 10 Gbps) and low latency, the servers using InfiniBand must deploy Remote Direct Memory Access (RDMA), compared with the latent and blocking server PCI bus architecture. An alternative to InfiniBand is, of course, Ethernet. However, Ethernet is not as well suited as InfiniBand for high-performance computing (HPC). As such, there are IEEE drafts discussing a revised Ethernet architecture that can offer RDMA, high performance, and lower latency than traditional Ethernet and low latency loss to InfiniBand. This revised Ethernet architecture has a proposed name of Data Center Ethernet (DCE). Search Google.com for more details on Data Center Ethernet.

The current Cisco products architected for server fabrics are the Cisco SFS 3000 Series Multifabric Server Switches, the Cisco SFS 7000 Series InfiniBand Server Fabric Switches, the Cisco InfiniBand Host Channel Adapters, and blade switches integrated into IBM and Dell blade servers.

Figure 1-22 *Sample Cisco Data Center Topology*

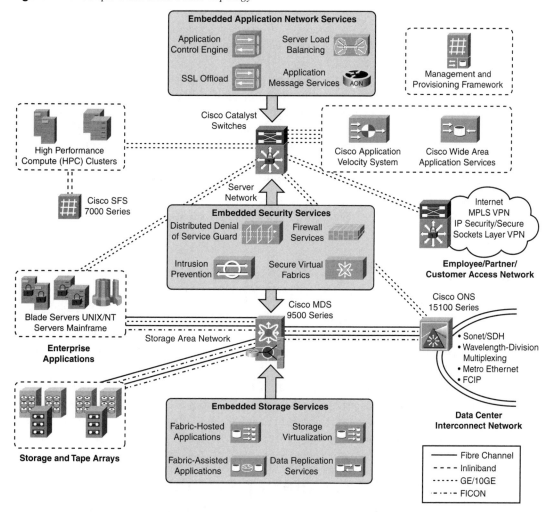

Storage Area Networks/Fabrics

SANs consolidate and virtualize storage resources such that the resources can be shared more effectively. Cisco SANs consolidate storage through the use of advanced features such as virtual SANs (VSAN), Fibre Channel over IP (FCIP), SCSI over IP (iSCSI), and Fibre Channel write acceleration. In addition, Cisco SANs enable large heterogeneous networks to support storage services such as virtualization, serverless backup, and continuous data protection, which in turn allow for enhanced business continuance data protection and data migration.

The current Cisco products that are enabling SANs are the Cisco MDS 9000, 9100, 9200, and 9500 director and fabric switches.

Data Center Interconnect

The data center interconnect connects the primary data center to a backup or secondary data center over optical or traditional WAN circuits. Data replication and business continuance best practices mandate the need for high-speed, low-latency connections between data center locations. An optical network's inherent features—low latency, high bandwidth, and high density—are ideal for interconnecting SANs, cluster nodes, and server farms between multiple data centers. When optical networks are not feasible, data center protocols including Fibre Channel can be transported over IP across traditional WANs.

The data center interconnect comprise multiple Cisco products, but primarily the Cisco ONS 15454 and ONS 15000 series and Cisco Catalyst 6500 switches are used in the designs.

Access Network

The access network secures access to employees, customers, or partners connected remotely over the intranet, Internet, or extranet. The majority of users are not located close to the data center, so robust, secure connectivity to the data center is mandatory. In terms of the Enterprise Composite Network Model, the access network is essentially the campus network.

The remainder of the book focuses primarily on the campus network and not the Data Center aspect of the enterprise. However, the concepts presented are the same ones applied on the front-end IP network of the Data Center design, which includes Catalyst switches in a hierarchical design.

Introducing the Cisco Catalyst Switches

The previous section introduced the building blocks of the Enterprise Composite Network Model. These building blocks include the components of the functional areas of the Enterprise Composite Network Model. This section introduces the Cisco Catalyst switches that are used in the modules and submodules of the Enterprise Composite Network Model. These switches may take on many different roles and are easily adaptable to access, distribution, and core layer roles. These switches are also applicable to any functional area because select models of Catalyst switches offer features such as security and WAN aggregation.

This section specifically covers the following current Cisco switching product lines:

- Catalyst 6500 family of switches
- Catalyst 4500 and 4900 families of switches

- Catalyst 3560 family of switches
- Catalyst 2960 family of switches

Many other Cisco Catalyst platforms exist and are still shipping; however, the Catalyst 6500, 4500, 4900, 3560, and 2960 families of switches are the most popular switches of today.

NOTE   The lists of performance, scalability, and availability features per family of switches are abbreviated. For a complete list, consult the Cisco product documentation for each Catalyst family of switches.

Catalyst 6500 Family of Switches

The Cisco Catalyst 6500 family of switches is the Cisco elite intelligent multilayer switching platform for delivering secure, converged services from the Building Access to the Campus Backbone of any functional area of the Enterprise Composite Network Model. In addition, the Catalyst 6500 is the leading platform for the core and distribution layers in Data Centers. The Cisco Catalyst 6500 platform uses a modular chassis. Line modules are available in a variety of models, including models with interfaces for 10/100/1000BASE-T Ethernet, Gigabit Ethernet, and 10 Gigabit Ethernet. Interfaces for DS0, OC-3, OC-12, OC-48, and WAN-capable line modules are also available.

The Catalyst 6500 family of switches supports the following features that meet the needs for performance in the enterprise:

- Up to 6510 Gigabit Ethernet ports
- Hundreds of millions of packets per second for Layers 2 through 4 switching of packets and frames, depending on the Supervisor Engine model and line card models
- Distributed CEF architecture
- Multiple performance options including 32-Gbps, 256-Gbps, and 720-Gbps bandwidth options with system throughput of 15 million packets per second (mpps), 30 mpps, 210 mpps, or up to 400 mpps
- 400 Mbps using dCEF720 hardware
- Hardware support for enterprise-class and service-provider-scale routing tables for high performance
- IPv6 support in hardware using Supervisor Engine 720
- Legacy protocol support (such as IPX and DECNET) for specific hardware models
- Cisco security solutions, including intrusion detection, firewall, VPN, and SSL at multigigabit speeds
- Gigabit Network Analysis Module for remote administration and network monitoring

- Available integrated Content Switching Module (CSM) for high-performance, feature-rich server and firewall load balancing
- Cisco Firewall Services Module (FWSM) offers unsurpassed firewall and virtualization services
- GRE support and Layer 2 bridging support in hardware at 400 mpps
- Hardware-assisted NAT support
- NBAR network management and control support at gigabit speeds

With regard to scalability, the Catalyst 6500 family of switches embraces the following characteristics:

- Forward-thinking architecture with investment protection
- Available in a 3-, 6-, 9-, and 13-slot modular chassis
- Up to 1152 10/100/1000BASE-T Ethernet ports per chassis using RJ-45 or RJ-21
- Multiple Gigabit and 10 Gigabit trunk ports per chassis
- Data and voice integration with 802.3af Power over Ethernet (PoE)
- MPLS support
- Support for up to 1,000,000 IPv4 routes and 500,000 IPv6 routes in hardware
- Support for up to 128,000 NetFlow entries
- Support for Layer 3 classification, aggregate rate limiting, and flow-based rate limiting
- Available dense T1/E1 and Foreign Exchange Station (FXS) VoIP gateway interfaces for PSTN access and traditional phone, fax, and PBX connections
- LAN, WAN, and MAN convergence
- Long product life cycle
- Application-Oriented Networking (AON)

In terms of availability, the Catalyst 6500 supports network high availability through features such as spanning tree and HSRP, and it supports component redundancy such as dual supervisor, dual route processors, and dual switch fabrics. The following list summarizes the major high-availability features of the Catalyst 6500 family of switches:

- Nonstop Forwarding and Stateful Switchover (NSF/SSO)
- Cisco IOS Software Modularity
- Designed for redundancy
- HSRP and VRRP
- 802.1D/802.1s/802.1w Spanning-Tree redundancy
- 802.3ad and EtherChannel link redundancy
- Highly available, stateful protocol redundancy

- Image versioning
- Cisco IOS Software redundancy
- Individual component redundancy
- Dual, redundant Supervisor Engines
- Redundant switching fabrics
- Redundant power supplies
- Intelligent network services redundancy
- Redundant clocking system
- Redundant fan system

In terms of security, the Catalyst 6500 family of switches offers the following features in addition to the features mentioned previously. (Later chapters explain these features in more detail.)

- Denial-of-service (DoS) attack mitigation
- Security Service Modules
- Man-in-the-middle attack mitigation
- Identity Based Networking Services (IBNS)
- Access list counters for monitoring traffic using specific details
- Port security
- IEEE 802.1x and 802.1x extensions for access-based security
- VLAN and router ACLs and Port ACLs for traffic filtering
- Security ACL entries
- Reflexive ACLs
- Unicast Reverse Path Forwarding (uRPF) check in hardware for multicast forwarding protection
- CPU rate limiters for DoS protection
- Private VLANs for host-to-host protection
- Support for large number interfaces with unique ACLs
- MAC ACLs on IP
- TCP intercept hardware acceleration

Catalyst 4500 and 4900 Families of Switches

The Catalyst 4500 and 4900 families of switches serve primarily as Building Access or Building Distribution switches in the Campus Infrastructure. The members of the 4900 family of switches are the Catalyst 4948 and Catalyst 4948-10GE. The Cisco Catalyst 4948-10GE switch offers 48 ports of wire-speed 10/100/1000BASE-T with 2 ports of wire-speed 10 Gigabit Ethernet (X2 optics). The Catalyst 4948-10GE switch is becoming extremely popular as an access-layer switch in the campus for host workstations and in the data center for server aggregation. In terms of performance, the 10GE model supports up to 102 mpps and 136 Gbps.

In reference to the Catalyst 4500 family of switches, the leading-edge supervisor is the Supervisor Engine V-10GE, which also supports up to 102 mpps and 136 Gbps in throughput performance.

In remote offices, these switches may function as the sole switch or as a Campus Backbone switch in a small network of only a few switches. In ISP networks, these switches are designed for business services aggregation and subscriber access in the metropolitan area because of the Cisco Long-Reach Ethernet capabilities of the platform.

In terms of performance, the Catalyst 4500 family of switches accommodates up to 64 Gbps or 48 mpps at Layer 2, 3, or 4 using the CEF-based hardware architecture of the Supervisor III or IV Engine. The Supervisor Engine V-10GE is capable of 136 Gbps and 102 mpps. The Supervisor II+ is only Layer 2 capable but is able to switch at 64 Gbps.

For the Catalyst 4500 family of switches, the following list indicates the scalabilities of the platform:

- 3-, 6-, 7-, and 10-slot modular chassis
- Integrates voice, video, and data
- Up to 336 10/100/1000BASE-T Gigabit Ethernet ports in a 10-slot chassis
- Integrated inline power for IP phones
- Multiple Gigabit Ethernet trunks
- WAN edge support through a specialized module
- 802.1Q-in-Q

In terms of high availability, the Catalyst 4500 supports the following features:

- Nonstop Forwarding with Stateful Switchover (NSF/SSO)
- HSRP and VRRP
- 802.1D/802.1s/802.1w spanning-tree redundancy
- 802.3ad and EtherChannel link redundancy
- Redundant Supervisor Engines for the Supervisor II+, IV, and V with 7-slot or 10-slot chassis
- Power supply redundancy

In terms of security, the Catalyst 4500 supports the following features:

- Network access control (NAC)
- Storm Control
- Per-Port QoS
- Standard and extended ACLs on all ports
- 802.1x user authentication (with VLAN assignment, voice VLAN, port security, and guest VLAN extensions)
- 802.1x accounting
- Trusted boundary
- Router ACLs (RACL) on all ports (no performance penalty)
- VLAN ACLs (VACL)
- Port ACLs (PACL)
- Private VLANs (PVLAN) on access and trunk ports
- DHCP snooping and Option 82 insertion
- Port security
- Sticky port security
- VLAN Management Policy Server (VMPS) client
- Unicast MAC filtering
- Unicast port flood blocking
- Dynamic ARP inspection
- IP source guard
- Community VLANs
- Voice VLAN sticky-port security

Catalyst 3560 Family of Switches

The Cisco Catalyst 3560 family of switches, generally deployed as Building Access switches, offers fixed port density with similar features to high-end switches but at a lower cost. The previous generation 3550 and 3750 switches can be grouped into the 3560 category, minus a few features.

Despite the lower cost associated with these switches, they support many switching features, including QoS, security, IP routing, and access control. These switches are available in fixed port configurations of 10/100BASE-T Fast Ethernet, 10/100/1000BASE-T Gigabit Ethernet, and Gigabit Ethernet over fiber interfaces. The Cisco Catalyst 3560 Series differs from the Catalyst 3550 in that it offers IEEE 802.3af and Cisco pre-standard PoE functionality in Fast Ethernet and Gigabit Ethernet configurations.

NOTE	For the remainder of this book, any mention of the Catalyst 3560 family of switches refers to the Catalyst 3550 and 3750 families of switches as well, unless otherwise stated.

In terms of performance, the 3560 supports up to 32 Gbps of traffic forwarding at Layer 2 or Layer 3 and supports jumbo frames up to 9018 bytes. Despite having fixed port densities, the Catalyst 3560 family supports the following scalabilities features:

- Baby Giants
- Up to 48 10/100 Fast Ethernet ports or 48 10/100/1000 Gigabit Ethernet Ports (3750G models)
- Integration for voice, video, and data
- Inline power for IP phones that adhere to the 802.3af standards
- Support for Cisco GigaStack or StackWise technology for switch stacking

In terms of availability, the Catalyst 3560 family of switches does not support component redundancy; however, the Catalyst 3560 family of switches does support the following availability features:

- HSRP and VRRP
- 1:N stateful redundancy for stack forwarding redundancy (Catalyst 3750 only)
- 802.1D/802.1s/802.1w spanning-tree redundancy
- 802.3ad and EtherChannel link redundancy
- Power supply redundancy through an external Redundant Power Supply (RPS)

In terms of security, the Catalyst 3560 switches offer the following security features:

- 802.1x.
- MAC address-based port security.
- Cisco security VLAN ACLs (VACLs) on all VLANs to prevent unauthorized data flows to be bridged within VLANs.
- Cisco standard and extended IP security Router ACLs (RACL) define security policies on routed interfaces for control plane and data plane traffic.
- Port-based ACLs (PACL) for Layer 2 interfaces allow security policies to be applied on individual switch ports.
- Time-based ACLs allow the implementation of security settings during specific periods of the day or days of the week.

- Private VLAN edge provides security and isolation between ports on a switch, ensuring that users cannot snoop on other users' traffic.

- User-selectable address-learning mode simplifies configuration and enhances security.

Catalyst 2960 Family of Switches

The Cisco Catalyst 2960 family of switches, also generally deployed as Building Access switches, offers fixed port density with similar features to high-end switches but at a lower cost. Despite the lower cost associated with these switches, they support many advanced switching features including integrated security, NAC, advanced QoS, and resiliency.

These switches are available as 24 or 48 10/100 or 10/100/1000BASE-T ports with dual-purpose uplinks for Gigabit Ethernet uplink flexibility, allowing use of either a copper or a fiber uplink—each dual-purpose uplink port has one 10/100/1000 Ethernet port and one Small Form-Factor Pluggable (SFP)-based Gigabit Ethernet port, with one port active at a time.

NOTE   The Catalyst 2950, 2955, and 2970 family of switches can be grouped into the same category as the Catalyst 2960 family of switches. The Catalyst 2960 family is the current-generation platform; the former switches (2950, 2955, and 2970) support a similar subset of features, QoS, NAC, security, and so on.

In terms of performance, the Catalyst 2960 family of switches offers the following features:

- Wire-speed Fast Ethernet and Gigabit Ethernet Layer 2 switching

- 32-Gbps switching fabric

- ACL and QoS Layer 2 and Layer 3 features at wire-speed Fast Ethernet and Gigabit Ethernet

- Jumbo Ethernet support of up to 9000-byte frames

With regard to the scalability of the platform, the Catalyst 2960 family of switches includes the following features:

- Up to 48 10/100 Fast Ethernet interfaces and 2 dual-purpose Gigabit Ethernet ports

- Support for 10/100/1000BASE-T Gigabit Ethernet, 100BASE-FX Fast Ethernet, and Gigabit Ethernet

- Configurable up to 8000 MAC addresses

- Integrated Cisco IOS Software features for bandwidth optimization

- Granular rate limiting

As for reliability, the Catalyst 29560 family supports the following availability features:

- Bandwidth aggregation up to 8 Gbps through Cisco Gigabit EthernetChannel technology
- 802.1D/802.1s/802.1w Spanning-Tree redundancy
- 802.3ad and EtherChannel link redundancy
- Power supply redundancy through an external RPS

In terms of security, the Catalyst 2960 family supports the following security features:

- 802.1x and a plethora of 802.1x advanced features
- MAC address notification
- Private VLAN edge
- Port Security
- Port-Based Access Control (based on MAC address, IP address, or TCP/UDP port)
- DHCP Interface Tracker and DHCP snooping
- TACACS+ and RADIUS authentication
- Port-based ACLs for Layer 2 interfaces, allowing application of security policies on individual switch ports
- SSHv2 and SNMPv3, providing network security by encrypting administrator traffic during remote-access and SNMP sessions

In terms of manageability, the Catalyst 2960 family supports the following manageability features:

- Cisco IOS CLI.
- Cisco Service Assurance Agent (SAA) support facilitates service-level management throughout the LAN.
- Switching Database Manager templates for security and QoS allow administrators to easily adjust memory allocation to the desired features based on deployment-specific requirements.
- Cisco Network Assistant is a no-charge, Windows-based application that simplifies the administration of networks of up to 250 users. It supports a wide range of Cisco Catalyst intelligent switches. With Cisco Network Assistant, users can manage Cisco Catalyst switches and launch the device managers of Cisco integrated services routers and Cisco Aironet WLAN access points.
- Express Setup simplifies initial configuration of a switch through a web browser, eliminating the need for terminal-emulation programs and CLI knowledge.
- CiscoWorks network-management software provides management capabilities on a per-port and per-switch basis, providing a common management interface for Cisco routers, switches, and hubs.

Study Tips

The following bullets review important BCMSN certification exam preparation points of this chapter. The bullets briefly highlight only the main points of this chapter related to the BCMSN exam and should be used only as supplemental study material. Consult the text of this chapter for additional information regarding these topics. Table 3-9 lists important commands to review for the BCMSN certification exam.

- Cisco SONA provides the framework for today's Internet business solutions. Moreover, Cisco SONA provides the baseline infrastructure that enables enterprises to design networks that scale to meet Internet business demands for performance, security, availability, and scalability. Cisco IIN is the future vision of the Cisco enterprise network.

- The functional areas of the Enterprise Composite Network Model represent specific modeling points of the Enterprise Campus network.

- Each functional area of the Enterprise Composite Networks is composed of its own Catalyst switches in a hierarchical model.

- The hierarchical model includes the Building Access submodule (access layer), Building Distribution submodule (distribution layer), and Campus Backbone submodule (core layer).

- Implementing the hierarchical model is unique for each enterprise, and the design is dependent on performance, scalability, availability, and security requirements.

- Layer 2 switching is defined as forwarding frames based on MAC address only. However, Layer 2 switches may support Layer 3 features such as QoS marking.

- Layer 3 switching involves forwarding frames based on IP addresses.

- The term *multilayer switching (MLS)* describes a switch designed to perform both Layer 2 and Layer 3 switching functions on a single platform.

- Layer 4 through 7 switching involves advanced IP features such as TCP/UDP access control lists and content intelligence.

- The Data Center has evolved as a separate entity that used to be logically referred to as the Server Farm. The Data Center includes not only the IP network but also the high-performance computing infrastructure and the back-end storage.

Summary

Cisco SONA is an enterprise-wide, standards-based network architecture that provides a road map for combining business and technology strategies into a cohesive model. The Enterprise Composite Network Model provides a modular framework for designing networks built on the premise of Cisco SONA. The modularity model allows flexibility in network design and facilitates implementation and troubleshooting.

The following list summarizes the key concepts of the Enterprise Composite Network Model:

- The Cisco Service-Oriented Network Architecture (SONA) is an architectural framework that guides your evolution to an Intelligent Information Network to accelerate applications, business processes, and profitability. This comprehensive framework provides guidelines to help you evolve your IT infrastructure and transform your business processes with network investments that increase business growth, agility, efficiency, and productivity.

- The Cisco Intelligent Information Network (IIN) is a strategy that addresses the evolving role of the network within your business and directly addresses your desire to align IT resources with business priorities. The resulting network delivers active participation, process optimization, service delivery, and application responsiveness, which results in better IT awareness.

- The Enterprise Composite Network Model comprises the Enterprise Campus, Enterprise Edge, and Service Provider Edge functional areas.

- The functional areas of the Enterprise Composite Network Model represent specific modeling points of the enterprise network.

- The Enterprise Campus functional area includes the Campus Infrastructure, Network Management, and Edge Distribution modules.

- The Enterprise Edge functional area includes the E-Commerce, Internet Connectivity, Remote Access and VPN, and WAN modules.

- Each module of the Enterprise Edge functional area connects to the Edge Distribution module, which connects the Enterprise Edge and the Campus Backbone.

- The Service Provider Edge includes the ISP, PSTN, and Frame Relay/ATM/PPP module.

- All modules of the Enterprise Composite Network Model are composed of their own access, distribution, and core layers.

The Enterprise Composite Network Model functional areas consist of Cisco Catalyst switches. Each Cisco Catalyst switch supports a varying degree of performance, scalability, and availability. Selecting the appropriate Cisco Catalyst switch depends on the needs for performance, scalability, availability, and other design principles, including cost.

Review Questions

For multiple-choice questions, there might be more than one correct answer.

1 True or False: If you are not deploying security features in your multilayer switched network, network security (and your job) is at risk.

2 True or False: Security is the single most important aspect of designing multilayer switched networks.

3 True or false: Hardware-switching of frames provides for additional scalability in switching platforms.

4 True or False: The Enterprise Composite Network Model creates modularity for the hierarchical network design model of access, distribution, and core layers.

5 True or False: In large enterprise networks, the Enterprise Data Center is its own functional area, combining the IP network, high-performance computer, and back-end storage-area networks.

6 Denote each switching feature as a Layer 2, 3, 4, or 7 switching feature and property.

   a Load balancing per IP destination across multiple Layer 2 switch interfaces

   b Applying QoS based on IP precedence for signaling frames from Cisco IP phones

   c Restricting specific IP broadcast traffic on a subnet using traffic rate policing

   d Applying access control using 802.1x authentication

   e Distributing TCP sessions to multiple servers behind a virtual IP address for the purpose of load balancing

   f Blocking third-party cookies for intranet hosts connecting to the Internet

   g Applying Network Address Translation for egress packets

   h Scheduling packets based on QoS CoS values

7 Which of the following is not a Layer 2 switching feature? You may need to consult later chapters for guidance in answering this question.

   a Forwarding based upon MAC address

   b Multicast and broadcast suppression

   c QoS marking of CoS on ingress frames

   d Segmenting a network into multiple broadcast domains using VLANs

   e Output scheduling packets based on DSCP values

8 Match each Enterprise Composite Network Model functional area to a description.

1. Enterprise Edge	a. Contains the modules required to build a hierarchical, highly robust campus network that offers performance, scalability, and availability
2. Enterprise Campus	b. Provides for secure communications between the Enterprise Campus network and remote or VPN networks
3. Service Provider Edge	c. Provides for connectivity to services implemented by service providers

9 Match each Enterprise Campus module to a description.

1. Edge Distribution module	a. Aggregates the connectivity from the various elements at the Enterprise Edge and routes the traffic to the campus core
2. Network Management module	b. Contains internal e-mail and corporate servers providing application, file, print, e-mail, and DNS services to internal users
3. Campus Infrastructure module	c. Interconnects Data Centers and high-performance computing clusters, and contains back-end SANs
4. Data Center	d. Useful in troubleshooting to gather information about the network

10 Match each Enterprise Edge module to a description.

1. E-Commerce	a. Routes traffic between remote sites and a central site
2. Internet Connectivity	b. Terminates VPN traffic from remote users and remote sites
3. Remote Access and VPN	c. Enables enterprises to successfully deploy e-commerce applications and take advantage of the powerful competitive opportunities provided by the Internet
4. WAN	d. Consists of e-mail servers to exchange intranet e-mail with Internet e-mail

11 Match each Service Provider Edge module with its description.

1. PSTN	a. Enables enterprise connectivity to the Internet
2. Frame Relay/ATM/ PPP	b. Includes all WAN technologies for permanent connectivity with remote locations
3. ISP	c. Represents the dial-up infrastructure used to access the enterprise network using ISDN and analog technologies

12 Which of the following switches support(s) IP routing?

a Catalyst 6500

b Catalyst 4500

c Catalyst 3750, 3550

d Catalyst 2960

13 Which of the following switches is well suited for metro Ethernet deployments because of its Long-Reach Ethernet functionality?

a Catalyst 6500

b Catalyst 4500

c Catalyst 3560

d Catalyst 2960

14 Which of the following switches support(s) highly available power via redundant power?

a Catalyst 6500

b Catalyst 4500

c Catalyst 3750, 3560

d Catalyst 2960

15 Which of the following switches use(s) a modular architecture?

a Catalyst 6500

b Catalyst 4500

c Catalyst 3750, 3560

d Catalyst 2960

16 Which of the following switches supports ATM interfaces natively?

    a Catalyst 6500

    b Catalyst 4500

    c Catalyst 3750, 3560

    d Catalyst 2960

17 Which of the following switches is well suited for any role in the Enterprise Composite Network Model regardless of network size?

    a Catalyst 6500

    b Catalyst 4500

    c Catalyst 3750, 3560

    d Catalyst 2960

18 What are the advantages of using modular switches rather than fixed port density switches?

    a Performance

    b Scalability

    c Availability

    d Low cost

19 Which of the following features applies modular switch benefits to fixed port density switches?

    a Spanning Tree

    b Stacking

    c EtherChannel

    d None of the above

20 In Figure 1-23, Workstation A is sending a frame to Workstation B. Assuming that all ARP tables are complete with correct entries, what is the destination MAC address of the frame destined for Workstation B at Location A?

21 In Figure 1-23, Workstation A is sending a frame to Workstation B. Assuming all ARP
tables are complete with correct entries, what is the source MAC address, destination
MAC address, and destination IP address of the frame destined for Workstation B at
Location B?

22 In Figure 1-23, Workstation A is sending a frame to Workstation B. Assuming all ARP
tables are complete with correct entries, what is the source MAC address, the
destination MAC address, and the source IP address of the frame destined for
Workstation B at Location C?

Figure 1-23 *Figure for Questions 20–22*

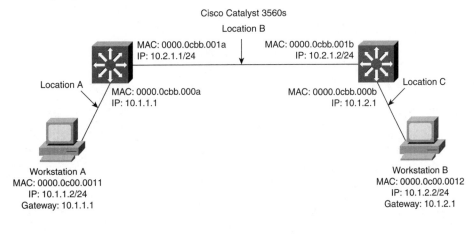

This chapter covers the following topics:

- Data Link Layer Technologies Used to Interconnect Multilayer Switches
- Designing Cisco Multilayer Switched Networks Using the Cisco Catalyst Switches and Current Data Link Technologies

## CHAPTER 2

The Roles of Switches in Designing Cisco Multilayer Switched Networks

Chapter 1, "Introduction to Building Cisco Multilayer Switched-Networks," discussed the design and the switching components of the multilayer switched network. The first section of this chapter continues the tour of building Cisco multilayer switched networks by discussing the data link technologies used to interconnect modules and submodules of the Enterprise Composite Network Model and Cisco Catalyst switches. The second section elaborates on designing Cisco multilayer switched networks using the Enterprise Composite Network Model, the Cisco Catalyst switches, and the data link technologies.

Data Link Technologies

Ethernet-based data link layer technologies that are available on Cisco Catalyst switches include Ethernet, Fast Ethernet, Long-Reach Ethernet (LRE), Gigabit Ethernet, and 10-Gigabit Ethernet. Moreover, for long distances, technologies that provide transparent delivery of Gigabit Ethernet and 10-Gigabit Ethernet are dense wavelength-division multiplexing (DWDM), Synchronous Optical Network (SONET), and coarse wavelength-division multiplexing (CWDM). These topics are covered in Chapter 17, "Performance and Connectivity Troubleshooting Tools for Multilayer Switches." The original 10-Mbps Ethernet is legacy and should no longer be considered an option for building enterprise networks. 100-Mbps Ethernet is slowly becoming extinct due to the low cost of 10/100/1000-Gbps Ethernet. This section discusses the various data link layer technologies for interconnecting switches and modules in the designing and building of multilayer switched networks.

10-Mbps Ethernet

Legacy Ethernet switching dynamically allocates dedicated 10-Mbps connections to each user on the network. Given advances in Fast Ethernet and Gigabit Ethernet technology and the lower costs associated with these technologies, 10-Mbps Ethernet is not typically used in Enterprise networks except for connection to legacy devices. However, 10-Mbps Ethernet used to be found on the ISP (WAN) interface of the DSL or cable modem for broadband networks in home offices. At the time of publication, most broadband consumer networks only provide up to 6 Mbps of bandwidth; therefore, 100-Mbps Fast Ethernet on the ISP interface of broadband modems is not necessary.

Increasing the speed of the link increases network performance at a very low cost. Whereas Ethernet supports 10 Mbps, Fast Ethernet supports 100 Mbps, Gigabit Ethernet supports up to 1000 Mbps, and 10-Gigabit Ethernet supports up to 10,000 Mbps. In addition, Fast Ethernet technologies generally, and Gigabit Ethernet technologies always, support full-duplex operation. *Full-duplex operation* is the ability to transmit and receive at the same time, effectively doubling the available bandwidth. Fast Ethernet and Gigabit Ethernet technologies both support auto-negotiation, which is useful in upgrading to higher-speed Ethernet while maintaining interoperability for legacy Ethernet speeds.

Moreover, the availability of powerful, affordable personal computers and workstations is driving the requirement for speed and availability in the campus network. In addition to existing applications, the new generation of multimedia, imaging, and database products easily overwhelms a network running at the traditional Ethernet speeds of 10 Mbps. For example, a high-definition TV broadcast in either 1920 × 1080I (interlaced) or 1280 × 720P (progressive) resolution requires between 11 Mbps and 18 Mbps of bandwidth. As a result, many enterprises are opting to design networks with Gigabit (Ethernet) to the desktop (GTTD).

Figure 2-1 illustrates a sample network design that uses different Ethernet technologies together in a single network design.

Figure 2-1   *Sample Network Topology Using Multiple Ethernet Technologies*

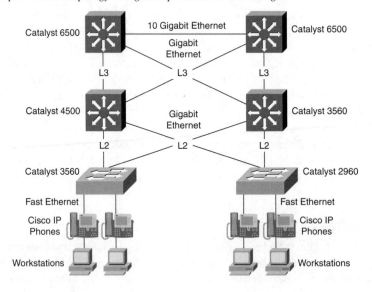

Regarding cable installations of Ethernet, most cable plant installers recommend following the 100-meter rule when installing unshielded twisted-pair (UTP) cable connections. The 100-meter rule is broken down into the following distance recommendations:

- Five meters from the switch to the patch panel
- Ninety meters from the patch panel to the office punch-down block (office faceplate)
- Five meters from the office punch-down block to the desktop connection

Short cables in a noisy wiring closet result in less induced noise on the wire compared to long cables and result in less crosstalk when used in large multiple-cable bundles. *Noise* in this context refers to interference caused by fans, power systems, motors, air-conditioning units, and so on. Nevertheless, short cables may restrict switch location in large wiring closets, so the 100-meter rule is occasionally overlooked.

The next section discusses the Fast Ethernet technology that is frequently used in wiring closets to provide device access to the network. However, Gigabit Ethernet technology deployment is rapidly evolving as a choice for device access. A discussion of Gigabit Ethernet follows the discussion of Fast Ethernet.

Fast Ethernet

From a deployment standpoint, Fast Ethernet in today's networks provides legacy PC and workstation network access at 100 Mbps. At 100 Mbps, data can move from 10 to 100 Mbps without protocol translation or changes to application and networking software. Fast Ethernet also maintains the 10BASE-T error control functions, frame format, and frame length. The most important aspect of Fast Ethernet is backward-compatibility. Fast Ethernet interfaces and the IEEE 802.3ab Gigabit Ethernet over copper interfaces optionally support auto-negotiation to 10 Mbps, and 100 Mbps in the case of Gigabit Ethernet. In this manner, new deployments that maintain backward capability ease installation while allowing for scaling to new, higher-speed Ethernet technologies. The "Fast Ethernet and Gigabit Ethernet Auto-Negotiation" section of this chapter discusses this topic in more detail. In addition, the IEEE 802.3-2002 standard now encompasses all Gigabit Ethernet specifications.

Fast Ethernet devices generally support full-duplex operation, which doubles the effective bandwidth to 200 Mbps. While Fast Ethernet defaults to half-duplex operation in the absence of auto-negotiation, Gigabit Ethernet defaults to full-duplex operation in the absence of auto-negotiation. With Gigabit Ethernet, the 802.3ab specification requires that all Gigabit Ethernet–capable devices support auto-negotiation. Current Cisco Catalyst switches support 10/100-Mbps auto-negotiation on all copper Fast Ethernet interfaces and full duplex on all fiber Fast Ethernet interfaces.

Specifications define Fast Ethernet to run over both UTP and fiber cable plants. Table 2-1 illustrates the wire category and maximum cable length for the Fast Ethernet standards.

Table 2-1 *Ethernet Wire Standards and Maximum Distances*

Standard	Wire Category	Maximum Cable Length in Switch Media
100BASE-TX	EIA/TIA Category 5 (UTP) Unshielded twisted-pair 2 pair	100 meters
100BASE-T4 (not supported on a Cisco device)	EIA/TIA Category 3, 4, 5 (UTP) Unshielded twisted-pair 4 pair	100 meters
100BASE-FX	MMF cable, with a 62.5-micron fiber-optic core and 125-micron outer cladding (62.5/125)	400 meters (half duplex) 2000 meters (full duplex)

Gigabit Ethernet

Gigabit Ethernet is the most effective choice for interconnecting and designing the Building Access submodule, Building Distribution submodule, Campus Backbone submodule, and the Data Center.

The current design recommendations call for Gigabit Ethernet to connect the access layer switches in the Building Access submodule to the distribution layer switches in the Building Distribution submodule with at least multiple Gigabit Ethernet links if not 10-Gbps Ethernet. Another guideline in designing the campus infrastructure is to use multiple Gigabit Ethernet interfaces for redundancy and load balancing where possible. Figure 2-1 in the previous section illustrates a sample topology using multiple Gigabit links to connect switches in the Building Access submodule to the distribution switches in the Building Distribution submodule.

In the Building Distribution and Campus Backbone submodules, the current design recommendations call for all Building Distribution and Campus Backbone submodules to interconnect with at least multiple Gigabit Ethernet links if not 10-Gbps Ethernet. For high-bandwidth networks, deploying multiple Gigabit Ethernet links between switches for load balancing and redundancy in the Campus Backbone and Building Distribution submodules is necessary. Two methods of combining multiple Gigabit Ethernet interfaces for load balancing are Cisco EtherChannel and 803.ad port channeling. Chapter 7, "Enhancing Network Stability, Functionality, Reliability, and Performance Using Advanced Features," discusses these port-channeling technologies in more detail. 1 0-Gigabit Ethernet has emerged as the leading choice for interconnecting switches in high-bandwidth enterprise campus networks and Data Centers.

Gigabit Ethernet is also well suited for connecting high-performance servers and even desktop workstations to the network. A high-performance UNIX, Windows application, or video server is easily capable of flooding three or four Fast Ethernet connections simultaneously. In addition, current-generation network interface cards (NIC) for servers are capable of TCP checksum calculations, IP checksum calculations, TCP/IP packet builds, and iSCSI (SCSI over IP) protocols in hardware, enabling 200-MBps throughput with very low CPU utilization. As servers and server NICs grow in power and throughput, along with the trend for centralizing servers within the campus network, Gigabit Ethernet has become a necessity within the Data Center.

Although 10-Gbps Ethernet is becoming available for servers, it is not yet widely deployed. Even high-end servers cannot fully achieve 10 Gbps of line rate network speed. In addition, x86 and SPARC architectures are really not capable of achieving such high sustained data rates of 10 Gbps. As such, future technologies will yield lower-latency protocols such as InfiniBand and newer server technologies such as virtualization and Remote Direct Memory Access (RDMA) that will allow data rates of 10 Gbps and beyond.

To achieve load balancing, a Gigabit Ethernet–capable switch is typically centrally located in the Data Center module. The design recommends that the servers in this module connect to switches via multiple autonomous NICs for load balancing and redundancy. Table 2-2 summarizes the Gigabit Ethernet deployment strategy for building Cisco multilayer switched networks. An alternate popular design is "top of rack," where a Catalyst 6503, 6504, or 4948G is used to aggregate server connections on a per-rack basis.

Table 2-2   *Gigabit Ethernet Deployment Strategy in the Enterprise Composite Network Model*

Module	Deployment Strategy
Building Access submodule	Gigabit Ethernet is becoming the de facto standard for workstations and end-user devices in today's networks; that said, almost all mid- to high-end workstations and laptops are beginning to ship with Gigabit Ethernet interfaces installed.
Building Distribution submodule	Gigabit Ethernet provides multiple high-speed connections between the Building Access and Building Distribution devices. It is recommended to use port-channel to aggregate multiple Gigabit Ethernet links in this submodule.
Campus Backbone submodule	Gigabit Ethernet and 10-Gigabit Ethernet provide high-speed connectivity to the Building Distribution submodule and to the Data Center module with multiple Gigabit Ethernet links. Gigabit Ethernet also provides high-speed interconnectivity between Campus Backbone submodule devices with multiple Gigabit Ethernet links. As with the Building Distribution submodule, use port-channel to aggregate multiple Gigabit Ethernet links.
Data Center Module	Gigabit Ethernet provides Gigabit Ethernet speeds to servers and network appliances. Most servers require Gigabit Ethernet because they are able to achieve throughput in hundreds of megabytes per second. New technologies such as ROMA are forthcoming.

Architecturally, Gigabit Ethernet upgrades the Ethernet physical layer, increasing data-transfer speeds tenfold over Fast Ethernet, to 1000 Mbps (1 Gbps). Gigabit Ethernet runs over copper or fiber.

Because Gigabit Ethernet makes significant use of the Ethernet specification and is optionally backward-compatible with Fast Ethernet on copper interfaces, customers are able to leverage existing knowledge and technology to install, manage, and maintain Gigabit Ethernet networks.

To increase speeds from 100-Mbps Fast Ethernet up to 1 Gbps, several changes were made to the physical interface. Gigabit Ethernet looks identical to Ethernet from the data link layer and upward of the OSI reference model. The IEEE 802.3 Ethernet and the American National Standards Institute (ANSI) X3T11 Fibre Channel were merged to create a specification for providing 1-Gbps throughput over fiber.

Table 2-3 defines the Gigabit Ethernet specifications and distance limitations per media type.

Table 2-3   *Distance Limitations for Gigabit Ethernet*

Standard	Wire Category	Maximum Cable Length in Switch Media
1000BASE-CX (not supported on any Cisco device)	Copper shielded twisted-pair	25 meters
1000BASE-T	Copper EIA/TIA, Category 5, unshielded twisted-pair (4 pair)	100 meters
1000BASE-SX	Multimode fiber cable using a 62.5- or 50-micron fiber-optic core with a 780-nanometer laser	260 meters with 62.5-micron fiber-optic core (multimode fiber) 550 meters with 50-micron fiber-optic core (multimode fiber)
1000BASE-LX	Single-mode fiber cable with 9 micron core and 1300-nanometer laser	3 km (Cisco supports up to 10 km)
1000BASE-ZX	Single-mode fiber cable with 9 micron core and 1550-nanometer laser	70 to 100 km depending on whether premium single-mode fiber or dispersion-shifted single-mode fiber

NOTE   1000BASE-LX and 1000BASE-ZX require minimum distances, and short distances may require attenuators to prevent burnout of the internal receivers. In the case of 1000BASE-ZX, 5-dB or 10-dB attenuators are necessary for fiber-optic cable spans of less than 15.5 miles (25 km).

In addition, Gigabit Ethernet defaults to full-duplex operation, for effective bandwidth of 2 Gbps, and all Gigabit technologies require auto-negotiation that includes methods for link integrity and duplex negotiation. As a result, Gigabit Ethernet auto-negotiation is superior in compatibility and resiliency to Fast Ethernet.

Fast Ethernet and Gigabit Ethernet Auto-Negotiation

Fast Ethernet and Gigabit Ethernet auto-negotiation is useful in scaling networks to newer Ethernet technologies while maintaining backward compatibility. Until recently, auto-negotiation was not resilient in its interoperability. At press time, the technologies covered in this section are almost considered legacy, because Gigabit Ethernet auto-negotiation has brought more stability to the feature. Furthermore, because of recent improvements in the capability of auto-negotiation and vendor testing, however, auto-negotiation is becoming a useful tool in upgrading networks, especially networks migrating to 10/100/1000 Gigabit Ethernet in the Building Access submodule.

One caveat with auto-negotiation is that manual configurations of 100 Mbps at full duplex do not interact properly with interfaces configured for auto-negotiation. This is a result of the IEEE 802.3u specification requiring interfaces to send auto-negotiation parameters for link partners only when those partners are configured for auto-negotiation. If one link partner is hard-coded to 100 Mbps, full duplex and the other link partner is configured for auto-negotiation, a duplex mismatch results because the auto-negotiating link partner did not receive auto-negotiation parameters from the other link partner; when such a situation occurs, the auto-negotiating link defaults to half duplex, as defined in the IEEE 802.3u specification. Duplex mismatches result in very poor performance and Layer 2 error frames.

Table 2-4 summarizes the valid auto-negotiation settings. Appendix A discusses these issues and auto-negotiation in more detail.

Table 2-4   *Valid Fast Ethernet Auto-Negotiation Configuration Table*

Configuration of NIC (Speed, Duplex)	Configuration of Switch (Speed, Duplex)	Resulting NIC (Speed, Duplex)	Resulting Switch (Speed, Duplex)	Comments
AUTO	AUTO	100 Mbps, full duplex	100 Mbps, full duplex	Assuming maximum capability of Catalyst switch and NIC is 100 full duplex
100 Mbps, full duplex	AUTO	100 Mbps, full duplex	100 Mbps, half duplex	Duplex mismatch
AUTO	100 Mbps, full duplex	100 Mbps, half duplex	100 Mbps, full duplex	Duplex mismatch
100 Mbps, full duplex	100 Mbps, full duplex	100 Mbps, full duplex	100 Mbps, full duplex	Correct manual configuration
100 Mbps, half duplex	AUTO	100 Mbps, half duplex	100 Mbps, half duplex	Link is established, but switch does not see auto-negotiation information from NIC and defaults to half duplex

continues

Table 2-4 *Valid Fast Ethernet Auto-Negotiation Configuration Table (Continued)*

Configuration of NIC (Speed, Duplex)	Configuration of Switch (Speed, Duplex)	Resulting NIC (Speed, Duplex)	Resulting Switch (Speed, Duplex)	Comments
10 Mbps, half duplex	AUTO	10 Mbps, half duplex	10 Mbps, half duplex	Link is established, but switch will not see FLP and will default to 10 Mbps, half duplex
10 Mbps, half duplex	100 Mbps, half duplex	No link	No link	Neither side will establish link due to speed mismatch
AUTO	10 Mbps, half duplex	10 Mbps, half duplex	10 Mbps, half duplex	Link is established, but NIC will not see FLP and will default to 10 Mbps, half duplex

NOTE Always manually configure speed and duplex settings for 10/100-Mbps Fast Ethernet and 10/100/1000-Mbps Gigabit Ethernet on both link partners for critical connections to servers or third-party equipment. Use auto-negotiation for interconnecting Cisco devices and user workstations.

Interfaces capable of 10/100/1000BASE-T operation use auto-negotiation to first recognize 100-Mbps capability and then exchange encoded information to determine 1000BASE-T operation.

10-Gigabit Ethernet

10-Gigabit Ethernet uses the IEEE 802.3 Ethernet MMAC protocol, the IEEE 802.3 Ethernet frame format, and the IEEE 802.3 frame size. 10-Gigabit Ethernet is full duplex, and it minimizes the user's learning curve from Gigabit Ethernet by maintaining the same management tools and architecture.

The 10-Gigabit Ethernet is becoming the de facto standard for new deployments by both service providers and enterprise networks. One primary use of 10-Gigabit Ethernet in the LAN is to aggregate multiple Gigabit Ethernet segments, such as those between buildings, to build a single, high-speed backbone. Technologies such as video and mass data storage require extremely high bandwidth. These applications are steadily growing into multiple Gigabit Ethernet speeds and eclipsing into the 10-Gigabit Ethernet range. Figure 2-2 illustrates a network using 10-Gigabit Ethernet in the Campus Backbone submodule.

Figure 2-2   *Campus Backbone Submodule Interconnected Using 10-Gigabit Ethernet*

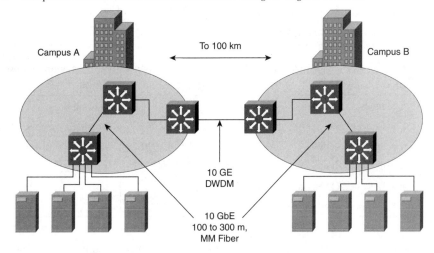

Currently, 10-Gigabit Ethernet is useful in implementing the following topologies:

- Server interconnections for clusters of servers operating at Gigabit Ethernet speeds
- Aggregation of multiple 1000BASE-X or 1000BASE-T segments into 10-Gigabit Ethernet uplinks and downlinks
- Switch-to-switch links for very high-speed connections between switches in the same data center, in an enterprise backbone, or in different buildings
- Interconnecting multiple multilayer switched networks
- High-speed server connections

10-Gigabit Ethernet physical layer interfaces, written as 10GBASE-*xyz*, tend to use the following general naming convention:

- **Prefix (10GBASE-)**—10-Gbps baseband communications
- **First suffix (*x*)**—Media type or wavelength, if media type is fiber
- **Second suffix (*y*)**—PHY encoding type
- **Optional third suffix (*z*)**—Number of wide wavelength-division multiplexing (WWDM) wavelengths or XAUI lanes

In the example in Table 2-5, a 10GBASE-LX4 optical module uses a 1310-nanometer (nm) laser, LAN PHY (8B/10B) encoding, and four WWDM wavelengths. A 10GBASE-SR optical module uses a serial 850-nm laser, LAN PHY (64B/66B) encoding, and one wavelength. The IEEE 802.3an task force is targeting to finalize the standard for 10-Gigabit Ethernet over twisted-pair copper cabling (10GBASE-T) by early 2007.

Table 2-5   *10GBASE Written Nomenclature*

Prefix	First Suffix = Media Type or Wavelength	Second Suffix = PHY Encoding Type	Third Suffix = Number of WWDM Wavelengths or XAUI Lanes
10GBASE-	Examples: C = Copper (twin axial) S = Short (850 nm) L = Long (1310 nm) E = Extended (1550 nm) Z = Ultra extended (1550 nm)	Examples: R = LAN PHY (64B/66B) X = LAN PHY (8B/10B) W = WAN PHY (64B/66B)	Examples: If omitted, value = 1 (serial) 4 = 4 WWDM wavelengths or XAUI lanes

Table 2-6 summarizes the operating ranges and media types supported for various 10-Gigabit Ethernet interfaces that would be used in enterprise deployments.

Table 2-6   *10-Gigabit Ethernet Typical Deployments and Distances*

10GE Physical Interface	Typical Deployment	Operating Range Over:			
		62.5-micron Multimode Fiber (FDDI Grade)	50-micron Multimode Fiber (MMF)	10-micron Single-Mode Fiber (SMF)	Twin-axial Copper
10GBASE-CX4	Data Center	N/A	N/A	N/A	15m
10GBASE-SR	Data Center	26–33m	66–300m	N/A	N/A
10GBASE-LX4	Campus or Data Center	300m	240–300m	N/A	N/A
10GBASE-LR	Campus or Metro	N/A	N/A	10 km	N/A
10GBASE-ER	Metro	N/A	N/A	40 km	N/A
10GBASE-ZR	Metro or Long-Haul	N/A	N/A	80 km	N/A
DWDM	Metro or Long-Haul	N/A	N/A	80 km-32 wavelengths over single-strand SMF	N/A

NOTE   More than 75 percent of existing fiber cabling plants from the campus distribution layer to the wiring closet is FDDI-grade (62.5 micron) MMF, and the distance requirements are typically greater than 100 meters (m). Thus, deploying 10-Gigabit Ethernet to wiring closets over existing FDDI-grade MMF will typically require the 10GBASE-LX4 optical module.

Gigabit Interface Converters

A Gigabit Interface Converter (GBIC) is an industry-standard modular optical interface transceiver for Gigabit Ethernet ports. The GBIC's primary role is to link the physical port with the fiber-optic cable. The use of modular GBICs allows for scalability by providing a method for each Gigabit Ethernet interface to use different media types. These media types include 1000BASE-T, 1000BASE-SX, 1000BASE-LX, and 1000BASE-ZX. GBICs are hot-swappable and are available in standard form for fiber with SC connectors and in Small Form-Factor Pluggable (SFP) form for fiber with LC connectors.

Cisco Long-Reach Ethernet

For buildings, infrastructures, neighborhoods, and campuses with existing Category 1, 2, or 3 wiring, LRE technology extends Ethernet at speeds from 5 to 15 Mbps (full duplex) and distances up to 5000 feet. The Cisco LRE technology delivers broadband service on the same lines as plain old telephone service (POTS), digital telephone, and ISDN traffic. In addition, Cisco LRE supports modes that are compatible with asymmetric digital subscriber line (ADSL), allowing service providers to provide LRE for buildings where broadband services already exist.

The Cisco LRE solution includes Cisco Catalyst LRE switches, the Cisco LRE customer premises equipment (CPE) device, and the Cisco LRE POTS splitter. Figure 2-3 illustrates a sample LRE topology. The topology in this example illustrates a service provider that is providing access to users throughout a neighborhood.

Figure 2-3   *Sample Long-Reach Ethernet Topology*

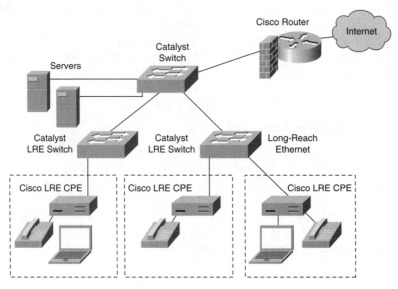

Metro Ethernet

You can extend Ethernet links between enterprise campuses through a service provider network using metro Ethernet solutions. As shown in Figure 2-4, two enterprise campuses use a metro Ethernet network, connected through multilayer switches, to connect to each other and to a backup data center.

Metro Ethernet is popular in enterprise networks where remote sites need high bandwidth that technologies such as Frame Relay, ISDN, POTS, and broadband are not able to provide. The main difference between metro Ethernet and LRE is speed. Metro Ethernet is meant to connect many high-bandwidth sites, whereas LRE is meant to connect many remote users or low-bandwidth remote sites. LRE has distance limitations of 5000 feet but is capable of using legacy wiring for connections. Metro Ethernet includes DWDM and Ethernet over SONET solutions.

Figure 2-4   *Sample Metro Ethernet Topology*

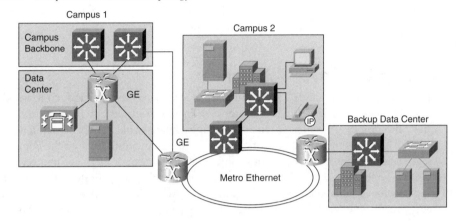

Designing Cisco Multilayer Switched Networks Using the Cisco Catalyst Switches and Data Link Technologies

Chapter 1 presented the Enterprise Composite Network Model of the enterprise network and the individual Cisco Catalyst switches that build the Enterprise Composite Network Model. The previous section illustrated the methods by which to interconnect the Cisco Catalyst switches in the Enterprise Composite Network Model. This section uses all these building blocks to illustrate sample network topologies using the Enterprise Composite Network Model, the Cisco Catalyst switches, and the data link technologies.

Reviewing the Campus Infrastructure Module of the Enterprise Composite Network Model

The Campus Infrastructure module includes the Building Access, Building Distribution, and Campus Backbone submodules, as discussed in Chapter 1. Layer 2 access switches in the Building Access submodule connect end-user workstations, IP phones, and devices to the Building Distribution submodule. Switches here, typically placed in a wiring closet, perform important services such as broadcast suppression, protocol filtering, network access, multicast services, access control, and QoS.

In the Building Distribution submodule, switches are almost always multilayer but could be Layer 2 switches depending on implementation needs. The switches provide aggregation of wiring closets, usually performing routing, QoS, and access control.

In the Campus Backbone submodule, Layer 3 switches provide redundant and fast-converging connectivity between Building Distribution submodules, and between the Data Center and Edge Distribution modules. Layer 3 switches in this module typically route and switch traffic as quickly as possible from one network module to another. In special circumstances, Layer 2 switches are used for port density. In this layer, the switches almost always perform routing, QoS, and security features.

Selecting Layer 2 or Layer 3 Switches

The development of Layer 2 switching in hardware several years ago led to network designs that emphasized Layer 2 switching. These designs are often characterized as "flat" because they are most often based on the campus-wide VLAN model in which a set of VLANs spans the entire network. This type of architecture favored the departmental segmentation approach where, for example, all marketing or engineering users needed to exist on their own broadcast domain to avoid crossing slow routers. Because these departments could exist anywhere within the network, VLANs had to span the entire network. Chapter 4, "Implementing and Configuring VLANs," discusses VLANs in more detail.

Layer 3 switches provide the same advantages as Layer 2 switches and add routing capability. Layer 3 switches perform IP routing in hardware for added performance and scalability. Adding Layer 3 switching in the Building Distribution and Campus Backbone submodules of the Campus Infrastructure module segments the campus into smaller, more manageable pieces. This approach also eliminates the need for campus-wide VLANs, allowing for the design and implementation of a far more scalable architecture. In brief, using Layer 3 switches in the Campus Backbone and Building Distribution submodules provides the following characteristics to the network design:

- Added scalability
- Increased performance
- Fast convergence
- High network availability
- Minimized broadcast domains
- Segmentation of IP subnets and network devices
- Access control at Layer 3, including IP access lists
- QoS classification, marking, policing, and scheduling using IP header information of frames
- Easier management
- Increased security
- Easier troubleshooting

Small Campus Network Design

A small campus network design is appropriate for a building-sized network with up to several hundred networked devices. Small campus networks optionally collapse the Campus Backbone and Building Distribution submodules into one layer. The Campus Backbone submodule provides aggregation for Building Access switches. Cost effectiveness in this model comes with a trade-off between scalability and investment protection. The lack of distinct Campus Backbone and Building Distribution submodules and limited port density in the Campus Backbone submodule restrict the scalability of this design.

The building design shown in Figure 2-5 comprises a single redundant building block. The two Layer 3 switches form a collapsed Campus Backbone submodule. The design uses Layer 2 switches in the wiring closets for desktop connectivity. Each Layer 2 switch has redundant Gigabit Ethernet uplinks to the backbone switches. The building design supports servers connected directly to Layer 2 switches or directly to the Layer 3 backbone switches, depending on performance and density requirements.

Figure 2-5   *Small Campus Network Design*

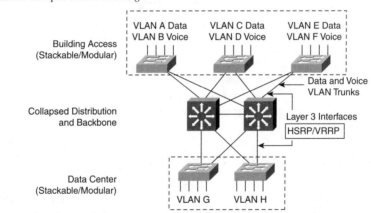

Figure 2-6 illustrates an example of a small enterprise switched network. In this example, the Catalyst 3550 family of switches frames the collapsed Distribution and Campus Backbone submodule. The Catalyst 2960 family of switches in Figure 2-6 comprises the Building Access submodule.

With this design, the network does not contain a single point of failure in the collapsed Distribution and Campus submodule because it provides switch and link redundancy. However, the Catalyst 3560 family of switches does not provide component redundancy and is composed of 32-Gbps switching fabrics, depending on model. (Consult the Cisco product documentation for more details.) For higher-bandwidth networks, consider using the Catalyst 4500 or 6500 family of switches.

In the access layer, the Catalyst 2960 family of switches provides Layer 2 redundancy via Spanning-Tree Protocol. The only downside to using the Catalyst 2960 family of switches is that these switches support only up to a 32-Gbps switching fabric, depending on the model, and up to 48 Gigabit ports. The Catalyst 2960 family of switches currently does not support inline power for Cisco IP phones. Nevertheless, both the Catalyst 2960 and 3560 families of switches support a wide range of QoS features adequate for VoIP deployments.

Figure 2-6 *Sample Small Enterprise Switched Network*

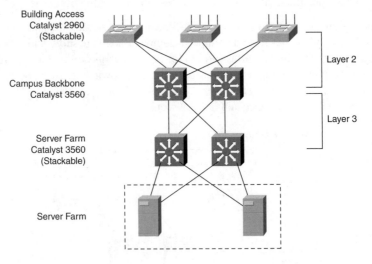

Medium-Sized Campus Network Design

Figure 2-7 shows a medium-sized campus network design with higher availability and higher capacity than the small campus network design. This design includes Layer 3 switches for a more flexible and scalable Campus Backbone submodule. The switches in the Campus Backbone submodule interconnect via routed, Layer 3, Gigabit Ethernet links or routed, Layer 3, Gigabit EtherChannel links.

Using the routed Gigabit Ethernet connections between the backbone switches offers the following advantages:

- Reduced router peering for additional stability and scalability
- Flexible and fast-converging topology with redundancy based on HSRP or VRRP instead of Spanning-Tree
- Multicast and broadcast control in the backbone
- Scalability to arbitrarily large network sizes

Figure 2-8 shows an example of a medium-sized multilayer switched network. In this example, the Campus Backbone submodule is composed of a Catalyst 6500 or Catalyst

4500, depending on performance, availability, and scalability requirements. The Catalyst 4500 is able to switch at 64 Gbps with a Supervisor Engine III or IV. With a Supervisor Engine V, the Catalyst 4500 switches up to 96 Gbps. Networks requiring more bandwidth need to use the Catalyst 6500 in the Campus Backbone or Building Distribution submodules as necessary. In this topology, the links between the Campus Backbone and Building Distribution submodules are Layer 3 routed interfaces. In the Building Distribution submodule of Figure 2-8, the Catalyst 4500 acts as a Building Distribution switch while the Catalyst 4500 or 3550 PWR switches provide user and IP phone ports. In this topology, each switch connects to two VLANs: one for voice and one for data. In this manner, HSRP or VRRP is the primary method of redundancy instead of the traditional Spanning-Tree. Later chapters of this book compare and contrast the redundancy methods of Spanning Tree, HSRP, and VRRP.

Figure 2-7 *Medium-Sized Campus Network Design*

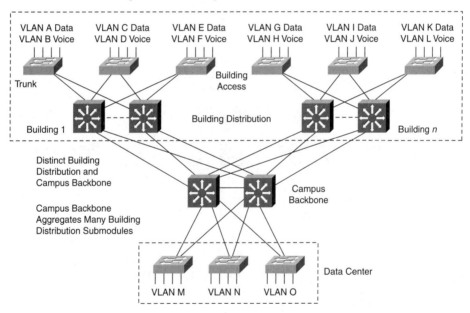

Large Campus Network Design

Figure 2-9 shows a multilayer campus design for a large network. One advantage of this multilayer campus design is scalability. An enterprise can easily add new buildings and Data Centers without changing the design. The redundancy of the building block is extended with redundancy in the backbone. If a separate backbone layer is configured, it should always consist of at least two separate switches. Ideally, these switches should be located in different buildings to maximize the redundancy benefits.

Figure 2-8 *Sample Medium Campus Network*

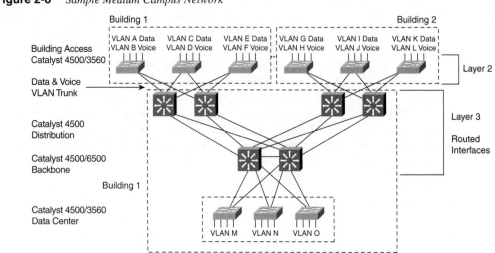

Figure 2-9 *Large Campus Network Design*

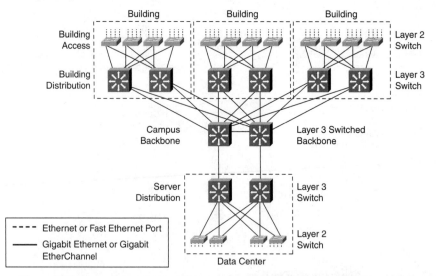

The multilayer campus design takes maximum advantage of many Layer 3 services, including segmentation, load balancing, and failure recovery. Broadcasts kept off the Campus Backbone submodule include Dynamic Host Configuration Protocol (DHCP) broadcasts. Cisco Layer 3 routers and switches are able to convert broadcasts such as DHCP to unicasts before packets leave the building block, to minimize broadcast flooding in the Campus Backbone submodule.

In the multilayer model, each Building Distribution submodule switch has two equal-cost paths into the backbone. This model provides fast failure recovery because each distribution switch maintains two equal-cost paths in the routing table to every destination network. All routes immediately switch to the remaining path after detection of a link failure; this switchover typically occurs in one second or less.

Using the Catalyst 6500 family of switches in all submodules is recommended for large campus network designs. By using the Catalyst 6500 family of switches in all submodules, the network design provides for greater availability, scalability, and performance over any other Catalyst family of switches.

Figure 2-10 shows a Layer 3 switched Campus Backbone submodule on a large scale. This Layer 3 switched backbone easily integrates and supports additional arbitrary topologies because a sophisticated routing protocol, such as Enhanced Interior Gateway Routing Protocol (EIGRP) or Open Shortest Path First (OSPF), is used extensively. Furthermore, the backbone consists of four Layer 3 switches with Gigabit Ethernet or Gigabit EtherChannel links. All links in the backbone are routed links; as a result, the Campus Backbone submodule switches do not use spanning-tree as a redundancy method. Figure 2-10 illustrates the actual scale by showing several gigabit links connected to the backbone switches. A full mesh of connectivity between backbone switches is possible depending on application, traffic patterns, and utilization but is not required by the design. In addition, the Data Center module in this design uses Layer 3 switches.

Figure 2-10 *Large Campus Network*

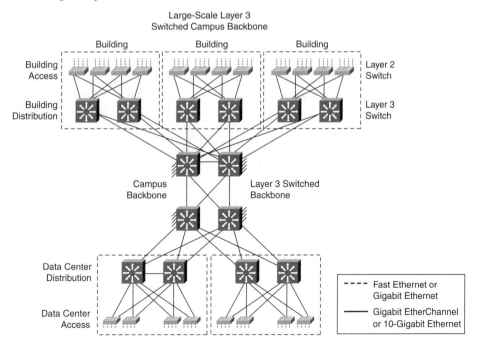

Figure 2-11 shows an example of a large enterprise switched network. In this example, the design is composed of the Catalyst 6500 family of switches in every submodule. The design optionally allows for the Catalyst 4500 family of switches in the Building Distribution and Building Access submodules for campus infrastructures that do not require the performance, scalability, and availability of the Catalyst 6500 platform.

Figure 2-11 *Sample Large Campus Network*

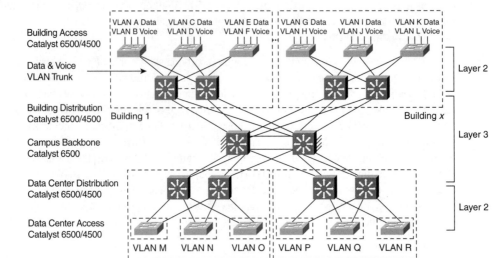

Data Center

Within the Data Center, switches provide connectivity between the Data Center and the Campus Backbone submodule in some designs, and possibly providing access between servers and storage-area networks (SAN). This section discusses the role of switches in the Data Center.

The Data Center contains internal e-mail and corporate servers that provide services such as applications, files, and print services, e-mail, and DNS to internal users. In financial data centers, servers in the Data Center mostly provide application services such as databases and data processing. Nevertheless, because access to these servers is vital to the servers connect to two different switches, enabling full redundancy and load sharing. The Data Center switches cross-connect with Campus Backbone submodule switches, enabling high reliability and availability of all interconnected switches. Figure 2-12 illustrates an example of a Cisco Data Center.

Depending on the type of the enterprise storage model, enterprise networks may use SANs to interconnect storage devices. Because of the recent growth of the iSCSI and FCIP protocols, SANs extension over IP is becoming a popular choice in enterprise networks for disaster-recovery designs. SANs use FCIP networks as FCIP to interconnect autonomous SANs over IP.

Figure 2-12 *Roles of Switches in the Data Center*

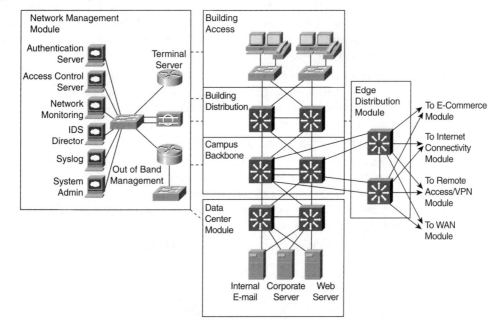

Figure 2-13 *Role of SANs in the Data Center*

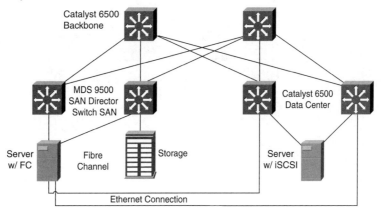

Data Center Infrastructure Architecture

The Data Center module logically divides the overall Data Center infrastructure into the following layers:

- **Data Center access layer**—Provides Layer 2 connectivity to directly connected servers. Layer 2 switching in the layer provides flexibility and speed. Layer 2 switches also allow deployment of legacy applications and systems that may inherently expect Layer 2–level connectivity.

- **Data Center distribution layer**—Consists of devices in multiple layers. This layer provides a transit between the Layer 2 and Layer 3 networks. The Data Center distribution layer leverages Layer 3 scalability characteristics while benefiting from the flexibility of Layer 2 services on egress ports to the access layer.

- **Campus Backbone layer**—Shared by the Campus Infrastructure, Enterprise Edge, and Data Center distribution devices. The Campus Backbone layer consists of high-end switches providing Layer 3 transport between the distribution and edge layers. The design allows for combining the distribution and core layers physically and logically into a collapsed backbone to provide connectivity with the edge layer and the Building Access submodule.

Figure 2-14 illustrates the Data Center infrastructure architecture.

Figure 2-14 *Data Center Infrastructure Architecture*

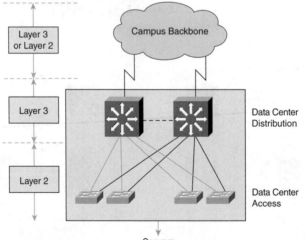

Figure 2-15 illustrates the Data Center distribution layer. The Data Center module architecture calls for the following best practices for designing the Data Center distribution layer:

- Deploy high- to mid-range multilayer switches, such as the Catalyst 6500 series, whenever possible.

- Implement redundant switching and links with no single points or paths of failure.

- Deploy caching systems where appropriate using Cisco Content Networking solutions.

- Implement server load balancing using Cisco Content Networking solutions or Cisco IOS.

- Implement server content routing using Cisco Content Networking solutions.

- In a large network, deploy multiple network devices; in a small network, deploy a single device with redundant logical elements.

- Layer 2 in the distribution layer is an option when using service modules for features such as VPN, firewalls, IP Contact Center (IPCC), and IDS.

   "Top-of-rack" design is becoming an option to consolidate server Gigabit Ethernet interfaces into several 10-Gbps Ethernet interfaces.

Figure 2-15 *Data Center Distribution Layer*

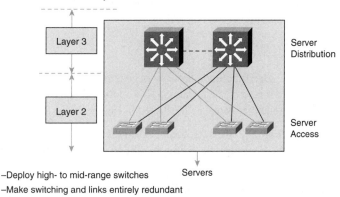

Figure 2-16 illustrates the Data Center access layer. The network model calls for the following best practices for designing the Data Center access layer:

- At minimum, deploy mid-range switches such as the Catalyst 6500, 4948G, or 4500 series. A popular choice is the Cisco Catalyst 4948G-10GE switch.

- Dual-home all servers with two separate NICs.

Figure 2-16 *Data Center Access Layer*

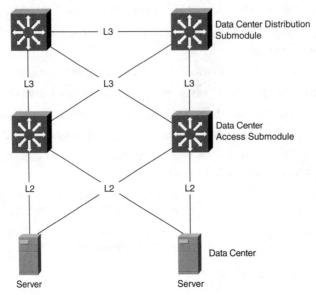

Enterprise Edge

In the Enterprise Edge functional area, switches provide functionality in the E-Commerce and Remote Access and VPN modules. This section discusses the roles of switches in the Enterprise Edge functional area, as illustrated in Figure 2-17.

As illustrated in Figure 2-17, switches perform the distribution function in the Edge Distribution module between the Enterprise Edge module and the Campus Backbone submodule.

In addition, switches play an important role in the various Enterprise Edge submodules. For example, in the E-Commerce module, all e-commerce transactions may pass through a series of intelligent services provided by the Catalyst switches. Intelligent services may include traffic filtering via firewall capabilities and load balancing. The switches themselves provide for the overall e-commerce network design by offering performance, scalability, and availability. Switches also play a role in the server and storage aspects of an e-commerce solution by providing interswitch connectivity and connections to SAN environments.

Figure 2-17 *Roles of Switches in the Enterprise Edge Functional Area*

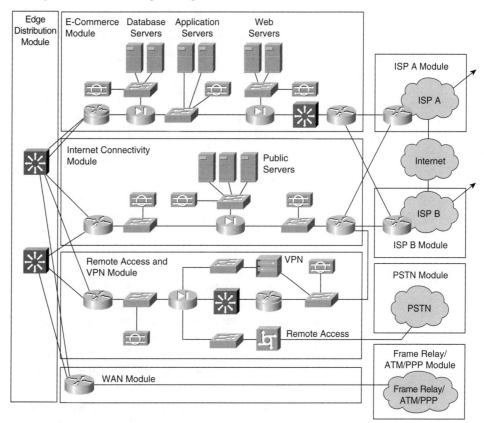

Another example of Catalyst switch involvement in the Enterprise Edge module, aside from switching traffic and providing individual switches, is remote access and VPN. With specialized hardware and specific software versions, the Catalyst switches can terminate VPN traffic from remote users and remote sites that are reachable through the Internet.

Case Study: Designing a Cisco Multilayer Switched Campus Network

Designing a Cisco multilayer switched network is a fairly detailed task. Designing a switched network requires forethought and research into traffic patterns, utilization, workstation use, end-user applications, and so on. To add a new building to a Campus Infrastructure of a switched network, you need information about the performance, scalability, and availability requirements of all the end devices to be connected to the network.

Consider, for example, having the following performance, scalability, and availability requirements for adding a new building to an enterprise campus:

- 2000 end users segmented in a single building with approximately 100 users per floor.
- Each user has a minimum available bandwidth requirement of 500 kbps to the Campus Backbone submodule.
- Application software typically bursts up to 20 MBps (160 Mbps).
- Support for a new IP/TV multicast application for end users.
- Support for nightly backups.
- High availability for IP telephony and data accessibility.
- Inline power for IP phones.

The Campus Backbone submodule is already in place, and four Gigabit Ethernet interfaces are available for use. The Data Center is located on a separate module adjoining the Campus Backbone submodule. Therefore, all you need to do is add a Building Distribution submodule and a Building Access submodule for the purpose of adding additional users.

In the Building Access submodule, each floor has 100 users. Five Catalyst 3560-24 PWR switches per floor suffice as the Building Access switches because this switch provides the needed switching fabric capacity, port density for minimum growth per floor, inline power, QoS, and redundant Gigabit Ethernet connections to the Campus Backbone submodule. Although the Catalyst 3560 family of switches is capable of Layer 3 switching, this design uses the Catalyst 3560 switches strictly as Layer 2 switches with Layer 4 QoS features for IP telephony. An alternate solution is to use the Catalyst 3750 family of switches in a stacking configuration per floor.

The use of five switches per floor results in a total of 100-Gigabit Ethernet connections to each Building Distribution switch. To accommodate this large number of Gigabit Ethernet connections per floor, a Catalyst 6500 with a Sup720 is preferable over the Catalyst 4500. Although the Catalyst 4500 is able to accommodate 100-Gigabit Ethernet connections, it cannot achieve line rate on all 100-Gigabit Ethernet interfaces simultaneously because of its limitation of 64 Gbps and line module restrictions. An alternative would be the Catalyst 49486-10GE.

To maintain a stable network in the event of an anomalous incident and to use a network design that does not rely on Spanning-Tree, the Building Distribution submodule provides Layer 3 connectivity and acts as a Layer 3 aggregation point to each Building Access submodule. HSRP carries out the redundancy for this topology.

For the connection to the Campus Backbone submodule, each Building Distribution Catalyst 6500 connects to the core via two links that load-share using EtherChannel. In this manner, each switch scales to 2 Gbps to the Campus Backbone submodule with each having link redundancy in the case of link failure.

Figure 2-18 illustrates this sample topology on a scale of two distribution layer switches and two access layer switches.

Figure 2-18 *Case Study Diagram*

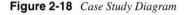

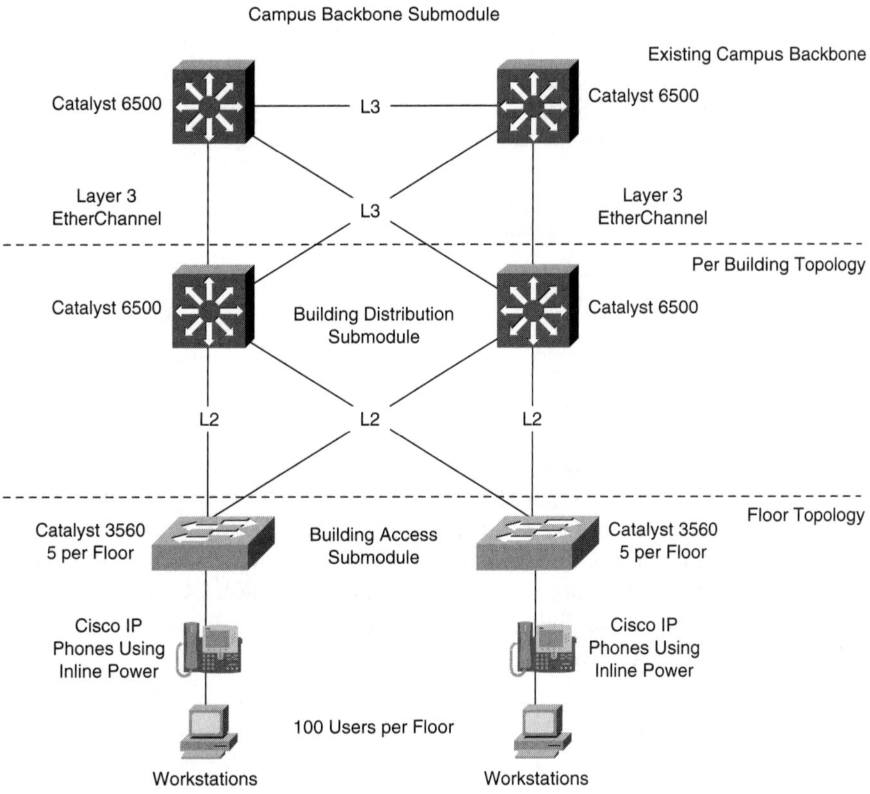

Campus Backbone Submodule

Existing Campus Backbone

Catalyst 6500 —— L3 —— Catalyst 6500

Layer 3 EtherChannel —— L3 —— Layer 3 EtherChannel

Per Building Topology

Catalyst 6500   Building Distribution Submodule   Catalyst 6500

L2   L2   L2

Floor Topology

Catalyst 3560 5 per Floor   Building Access Submodule   Catalyst 3560 5 per Floor

Cisco IP Phones Using Inline Power   Cisco IP Phones Using Inline Power

100 Users per Floor

Workstations   Workstations

Study Tips

The following bullets review important BCMSN certification exam preparation points of this chapter. The bullets only briefly highlight the main points of this chapter related to the BCMSN exam and should only be used as supplemental study material:

- Full-duplex Ethernet connections are able to transmit and receive at the same time. Full duplex is the default operation of Gigabit Ethernet and 10-Gigabit Ethernet.

- You should deploy Gigabit Ethernet even to the desktop in today's network. To aggregate bandwidth using multiple Gigabit Ethernet interfaces, use EtherChannel (port-channeling).

- Plan for, at minimum, Gigabit Ethernet connections to each server in the Date Center. However, design for oversubscription, because only the most powerful servers utilize the full bandwidth of 1 Gbps.

- The type of network design you should use depends on your design performance, scalability, security, and availability requirements.

- Always plan for adequate redundancy by designing redundant paths in your network.

- The main reasons for deploying Layer 3 switches instead of Layer 2 switches in the campus network are as follows:

  — Added scalability

  — Increased performance

  — Higher availability

  — Increased security

Summary

Data link technologies interconnect the building blocks of the Enterprise Composite Network Model. Selecting the speed of the data link technology is dependent on performance considerations and scalability factors. For designing and building networks, use a Gigabit Ethernet connection for all switch, module, server, and desktop interconnections at the data link layer. Strongly consider using 10-Gigabit Ethernet for high-performance servers and links connecting modules and switches, because 10-Gigabit Ethernet has clearly emerged as a legitimate option.

The role of Cisco Catalyst switches in the Enterprise Composite Network Model depends on design. Generally, fixed configuration switches such as the Catalyst 2960, 3560, 3750, and 4948G-10GE families of switches bode well as Building Access submodule switches. In medium- to large-scale network designs, the Catalyst 4500 and 6500 families of switches integrate well in the Building Distribution submodule, whereas the Catalyst 6500 family is the ultimate choice for the Campus Backbone submodule. Furthermore, the Catalyst 6500 fits into any submodule or module of the Enterprise Composite Network Model and remains the choice for most Campus Backbone submodule, Edge Distribution module, and Data Center switches.

Review Questions

For multiple-choice questions, there might be more than one correct answer.

1 True or False: Ethernet collisions can occur at full duplex. (Explain your answer.)

2 True or False: Using auto-negotiation with Gigabit Ethernet over copper is optional per the IEEE 802.3ab specification.

3 If auto-negotiation is configured on one link partner, and the other link partner is configured for speed and duplex manually, the end result will be which of the following? (Choose one.)

a Duplex mismatch

b Always a duplex mismatch

c Duplex mismatch if the manually configured link partner is set to 100 Mbps, full duplex

d No link

e Correct operation at 100 Mbps, full duplex

4 What are the primary differences between the packet-forwarding operation and design of a traditional Cisco IOS router such as a Cisco 3660 versus that of a Layer 3 switch such as Catalyst 6500? (Choose three.)

a The MIB update function

b The physical implementation

c The hardware design

d The port density

e The forwarding path determination

f The method of verifying Layer 3 header integrity

5 What are three likely applications for 10-Gigabit Ethernet?

a Providing remote access

b Interconnecting clusters of servers

c High-performance computing (HPC)

d Interconnecting access-layer switches

e Connecting hosts to access-layer switches

f Very high-speed switch-to-switch connections

g Connecting multiple campuses

6 Why are Data Center switches cross-connected with Campus Backbone submodule switches? (Choose the best answer.)

   a To enable routing

   b To reduce server load

   c To enable high availability

   d To provide high-speed access

7 Why is it necessary, for true redundancy, to dual-home servers by using two separate NICs instead of one? (Choose the best answer.)

   a To load-balance traffic into the network

   b To protect against failure of internal components of the NIC

   c To provide additional scalability

   d To increase performance

8 Servers in the Data Center may reach storage arrays, disks, and tapes via which methods? (Choose the two best answers.)

   a Using the iSCSI protocol via Ethernet-attached NICs

   b Via Fibre Channel Host Bus Adapters (NIC equivalent in Fibre Channel) connected directly to the SAN

   c Via web access over TCP/IP via Ethernet-attached NICs

9 What are two ways switches can be deployed in an E-Commerce module? (Choose two.)

   a Connectivity to the ISP

   b Connectivity to the PSTN

   c Connectivity to the WAN module

   d Server and storage connectivity

   e Switching between edge router and remainder of module

10 A small company occupies several floors of an office building. To date, the company employs 175 workers. The company uses a small-scale VoIP installation where availability is crucial. This company needs Layer 3 capability to isolate data and voice subnets. The company anticipates growing only 10 to 15 percent over the next several years. Of the following topologies, which one is best suited for this company?

a Small network design consisting of Catalyst 3560 with inline power in both the access layer and the collapsed Building Distribution and Campus Backbone submodules

b Medium-sized network design with separate access, distribution, and core layers using Catalyst 4500 and 6500s

c Small network design consisting exclusively of Catalyst 2960s in a single-layer network

d Small network design consisting of a single Catalyst 2960 and several low-cost hubs

11 A company of 10,000 employees occupies a campus network of several buildings. The company intends to increase the number of employees at a rate of 20 to 25 percent a year. In addition, the company is deploying IP telephony, remote access via VPN, and e-commerce. Of the following topologies listed, which one is best suited for this company?

a Small network design consisting of Catalyst 3560 with inline power in both the access layer and the collapsed Building Distribution and Campus Backbone submodules

b Large network design using Catalyst 6500 switches, end to end, for all modules of the enterprise

c Medium-sized network design using Catalyst 4500s as the Campus Backbone submodule to aggregate the Catalyst 3560s in the Building Access and Building Distribution submodules of the separate office buildings

d Small network design consisting exclusively of Catalyst 2960s in a single-layer network

12 A company of 1000 employees occupies several small office buildings in a small office center. This company edits high-definition videos for movie studios by using computers and vast amounts of storage. This company also uses IP telephony. Of the following topologies listed, which one is best suited for this company?

    a Large network design using Catalyst 6500 switches end to end

    b Medium-sized network design using Catalyst 4500s as the Campus Backbone submodule to aggregate the Catalyst 3560s in the Building Access and Building Distribution submodules of the separate office buildings

    c Medium-sized network design using Catalyst 4500s as the Campus Backbone submodule to aggregate the Catalyst 3560s in the Building Access and Building Distribution submodules of the separate office buildings and a small SAN network for redundant disk arrays

    d Small network design using only Catalyst 2960s in the collapsed Building Distribution and Campus Backbone submodules and in the access layer

13 When should Layer 3 routing in the distribution layer be implemented?

14 When should a network design integrate SANs?

This chapter covers the following topics:

- Comparing Cisco CatOS and Cisco IOS
- Handling Initial Configuration of Management Parameters for Cisco Catalyst Switches
- Managing Catalyst Switch Configurations
- Handling Cisco IOS File System and Software Images for Catalyst Switches
- Upgrading Software Versions on Catalyst Switches
- Implementing Basic Troubleshooting Practices

## CHAPTER 3

Initial Configuration and Troubleshooting of Cisco Multilayer Switches

Cisco Systems, Inc. ships most Catalyst switches today with Cisco IOS (Native Mode) Software. The only exceptions are by order request for the Catalyst 6500 with a Multilayer Switch Feature Card (MSFC) module with Cisco CatOS. All Catalyst 6500 families of switches with an MSFC, MSFC2, or MSFC3 are capable of running Cisco CatOS or Cisco IOS software. In terms of product life cycle, the only Catalyst switch that currently supports new features and hardware support in Cisco CatOS is the Catalyst 6500 family of switches. CatOS 8.x, at the time of publication, is deemed the last version of CatOS with maintenance releases for bug fixes lasting the next few years. New features will no longer be added to Cisco CatOS.

When building Cisco multilayer switched networks, it is important to understand the features that are available and the initial configuration of each operating system (OS). Foremost, before configuring any Catalyst switch for operation in a multilayer switched network, you need to understand the basic OS command-line interface (CLI) to upgrade to specific software versions for network consistency, hardware support, code updates, and new features. In addition, you must understand how to configure basic system parameters, such as IP addresses, and other basic management functions, such as DNS and system logging (syslog), and prevent unauthorized access to the switch and multilayer switched network. To prepare you for initial installations of Catalyst switches, this chapter discusses the following CLI configuration topics:

- Switch name
- Management IP configuration
- Telnet and SSH
- DNS
- System logging
- SNMP

In addition, this chapter covers the following specific topics to aid in the initial setup of Catalyst switches:

- Where to find documentation on how to migrate from Cisco CatOS to Cisco IOS on the Catalyst 6500 family of switches

- The usefulness of the **show** and **debug** commands in troubleshooting initial configurations
- Used of **debug** commands and their impact

This chapter concludes with a summary and a lab exercise. In terms of CCNP BCMSN exam preparation, focus on all sections except the section on SNMP. The SNMP section is outside the scope of the CCNP BCMSN exam, yet is important to both Enterprise Campus and Data Center deployments.

In addition, concentrate on Cisco IOS because the BCMSN exam focuses on Cisco IOS instead of Cisco CatOS.

Comparing Cisco CatOS and Cisco IOS

Cisco CatOS is the traditional Layer 2 operating system for Cisco Catalyst switches. Configuring Catalyst 6500 for Layer 3 features with Cisco CatOS requires a separate Layer 3 or router module running Cisco IOS software version. The term *hybrid mode* refers to the use of Cisco CatOS for configuring Layer 2 features and Cisco IOS for Layer 3 interfaces on the same platform.

Cisco IOS Software is capable of configuring both Layer 2 and Layer 3 features. Cisco IOS runs on any Cisco router or switch that can have interfaces that act as router ports (Layer 3) or as switched ports (Layer 2). Furthermore, Cisco IOS supports Layer 2–only switches such as the Catalyst 2950. Ports act as router or switch ports depending on the software configuration and hardware support of the respective interface. Cisco IOS running on Catalyst switches is also referred to as integrated IOS because Cisco IOS integrates the functions of multiple layers. Cisco IOS ships on all Catalyst families of switches, including the Catalyst 2940, 2950, 2970, 3550, 3560, 3750, 4500, and 6500 families. An alternative name for Cisco IOS running on the Cisco Catalyst 6500 family of switches is *Native IOS*. Likewise, another term for running Cisco IOS on any Catalyst switch is *Cisco IOS Native Mode*. This book uses the term *Cisco IOS* to describe Cisco IOS running on a Catalyst switch. Furthermore, Cisco IOS also supports Layer 2–only switches.

With the 6500 family of switches, support exists for either a hybrid-mode (running CatOS on the Supervisor Engine and Cisco IOS on the MSFC) or Cisco IOS when an MSFC module is present on the Supervisor Engine. When running Cisco CatOS on a Catalyst 6500 Supervisor Engine with an MSFC module, the MSFC itself runs a separate Cisco IOS image. The terms commonly used to describe a Catalyst 6500 running CatOS on the Supervisor Engine for Layer 2 functionality and Cisco IOS on the MSFC are *hybrid mode* and *Hybrid OS*. All other models of Catalyst switches support either Cisco CatOS or Cisco IOS but not specifically the hybrid-mode software. Currently, Cisco still supports the Cisco CatOS operating system on the Catalyst 4500 and 6500 families of switches. Table 3-1 illustrates which Catalyst switches run Cisco CatOS, Hybrid OS, and Native IOS. This book uses hybrid mode to represent a Catalyst 6500 running CatOS on the Supervisor Engine and Cisco IOS on the MSFC.

Feature parity does exist between hybrid-mode Cisco CatOS and Cisco IOS, although some differences exist between platform uses of Cisco IOS. The ultimate goal of Cisco IOS is complete feature and configuration parity with Cisco CatOS.

Table 3-1   *Cisco CatOS, Hybrid OS, and Cisco IOS Platform Matrix*

Platform	Cisco OS
Catalyst 6500 with MSFC or MSFC2	Either hybrid-mode (Hybrid OS) or Cisco IOS
Catalyst 6500 without an MSFC or MSFC2	Cisco CatOS
Catalyst 6500 with Supervisor Engine 720, PFC3, and MSFC3	Either hybrid-mode (Hybrid OS) or Cisco IOS
Catalyst 6500 with Supervisor Engine 32	Either hybrid-mode (Hybrid OS) or Cisco IOS
Catalyst 4000 or 4500 with Supervisor Engine II+, III, IV, or V; Catalyst 4948	Cisco IOS
Catalyst 4912G	Cisco CatOS (Layer 2–only platform)
Catalyst 4000 or 4500 with Supervisor Engine I or II	Cisco CatOS (Layer 2–only platform)
Catalyst 3550, 3560, or 3750	Cisco IOS
Catalyst 3500XL	Cisco IOS (Layer 2–only platform)
Catalyst 2940, 2950, 2955, 2960, or 2970	Cisco IOS (Layer 2–only platform)
Catalyst 2948G, 2980G, or 2948-GE-TX	Cisco CatOS (Layer 2–only platform)
2948G-L3 or 4908G-L3	Cisco IOS
Cisco Catalyst Express Switches	Cisco IOS

NOTE   This text focuses primarily on Cisco IOS. Most examples include Cisco CatOS for completeness and for those individuals using Cisco CatOS switches to prepare for the BCMSN switching exam. The BCMSN switching exam does not currently include coverage of Cisco CatOS commands.

Not surprisingly, differences do exist between the two types of operating systems. Table 3-2 illustrates the main system differences between Cisco CatOS and Cisco IOS.

Table 3-2   *Cisco CatOS and Cisco IOS System Differences*

Feature	Cisco CatOS	Cisco IOS
Configuration file	Two configuration files: one for the Supervisor Engine, or Network Management Processor (NMP), and one for the MSFC.	One configuration file. Use standard Cisco IOS commands such as **copy** to save the configuration.
Software image	Two images: one for the Supervisor Engine and one for the MSFC in the case of the Catalyst 6500.	One software image. An MSFC boot image is also required to allow the MSFC to load properly.
Default port mode	Every port is a Layer 2 switched port.	Every port is a Layer 3 interface (routed port) on the Cisco 6500 family of switches.

continues

Table 3-2   *Cisco CatOS and Cisco IOS System Differences (Continued)*

Feature	Cisco CatOS	Cisco IOS
Default port status	Every port is enabled.	Every port is in the shutdown state for the Catalyst 6500 family of switches. Some switches allow for an option to configure all interfaces up or down during the automated setup program.
Configuration commands format	The command keyword **set** precedes each configuration command.	Cisco IOS command structure with global and interface-level commands.
Configuration mode	No configuration mode (**set**, **clear**, and **show** commands).	The command **configure terminal** activates the VLAN configuration mode.
Removing/ changing the configuration	Via use of **clear**, **set**, or **enable/ disable** commands.	Same as Cisco IOS command structure; keyword **no** negates a command.

Initial Configuration of Management Parameters of Cisco Catalyst Switches

Before you deploy Cisco Catalyst switches, you must configure them to ease administration and troubleshooting. The basic configuration-management parameters are as follows:

- System name
- Management IP configuration
- Clock and Network Time Protocol (NTP) settings
- Telnet and Secure Shell (SSH)
- DNS
- System logging
- Simple Network Management Protocol (SNMP)

These configuration parameters are necessary for proper management and to simplify troubleshooting during initial installation. Your enterprise network may deploy other configuration parameters such as RMON. The preceding list of basic configuration-management parameters are those necessary to establish a switch in the network for in-band management and troubleshooting during initial installation.

System Name

Configuration of a meaningful system name is essential in managing Catalyst switches effectively. The default names of Switch, Router, and Console on multiple switches are not easily distinguishable from the CLI when multiple Telnet, SSH, or console sessions are open to multiple switches. Configuring meaningful and unique switch system names throughout the enterprise network is extremely useful, particularly system names that allude to location. For example, a system name of Sw4thFlRm2 abbreviates "Switch 4th Floor Room 2." Meaningful system names provide for quick examination of the precise switch currently being accessed. To configure the Catalyst switch system name on Cisco IOS–based switches, use the following command:

hostname *name-string*

name-string refers to the switch name. To configure the Catalyst switch system name on Cisco CatOS–based switches, use the following command:

set system name *name-string*

Examples 3-1 and 3-2 illustrate a user configuring the Catalyst switch system name on a Cisco IOS–based and Cisco CatOS–based switch, respectively.

Example 3-1   *Configuring Switch System Name on Cisco IOS–Based Switches*

```
Switch(config)#hostname Access-Floor1

Access-Floor1(config)#
```

Example 3-2   *Configuring Switch System Name on Cisco CatOS–Based Switches*

```
Console (enable) set system name Core-2

System name set.

Core-2> (enable)
```

Management IP Configuration

The management IP address allows for administrative access to the switch using Telnet, SSH, and HTTP. For Layer 2 switches and for Layer 3 switches acting solely as Layer 2 switches, use a single IP address for administrative access. This IP address occupies a specific VLAN. For example, Figure 3-1 illustrates a medium-sized network in which each access layer switch consists of two VLANs: one for voice and one for data. The switch management IP address resides in the data VLAN in this example. If VLAN A represents VLAN 101, then you should configure an interface VLAN 101 on your access layer switch with an IP address in VLAN 101.

Use the following command to configure an IP address on a Cisco IOS–based switch:

ip address *ip-address subnet-mask*

Example 3-3 illustrates configuration of an IP address on a VLAN interface on a Cisco IOS–based switch.

Figure 3-1 *Network Topology for Examples 3-3 and 3-4*

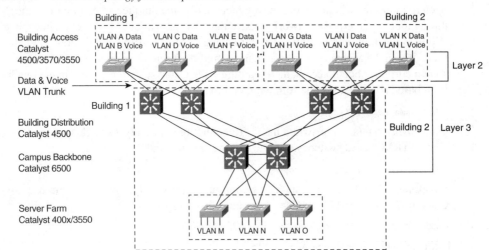

Example 3-3 *Configuring an IP Address and Subnet Mask on a VLAN Interface on a Cisco IOS–Based Switch*

```
Switch(config)#interface vlan 101

Switch(config-if)#ip address 10.1.101.10 255.255.255.0

Switch(config-if)#no shut
```

Because Layer 2 switches do not perform routing functions, Layer 2 switches require a default gateway IP address to reach subnets beyond the local subnet. Use the following command to configure an IP default gateway on a Cisco IOS–based switch:

```
ip default-gateway ip-address
```

Example 3-4 illustrates the configuration of an IP default gateway on a Cisco IOS–based switch.

Example 3-4 *Configuring an IP Default Gateway on a Cisco IOS–Based Switch*

```
Switch(config)#ip default-gateway 10.1.101.1
```

Cisco CatOS–based switches are Layer 2 switches. As a result, these switches use a specialized interface for management, known as the sc0 interface. The sc0 configuration parameters include IP address, subnet mask, and VLAN. Use the following command to configure the sc0 management interface on Layer 2–only Cisco CatOS–based switches:

```
set interface sc0 [vlan] [ip_address [netmask [broadcast]]]
```

Then use the following command to configure the default gateway for a Cisco CatOS–based switch:

```
set ip route default gateway [primary]
```

To view the current sc0 interface configuration, use the following command:

```
show interface
```

Example 3-5 illustrates the configuration of an IP address on the sc0 interface and default gateway configuration on a Cisco CatOS–based switch in VLAN 5. Note that the broadcast address is automatically configured unless otherwise specified.

Example 3-5 *Configuring an IP Address, Subnet Mask, VLAN Assignment, and Default Gateway on a Cisco CatOS–Based Switch*

```
Console (enable) set interface sc0 5 10.1.101.11 255.255.255.0

Interface sc0 vlan set, IP address and netmask set.

Console (enable) set ip route default 10.1.101.1

Route added.

Console (enable) show interface
sl0: flags=51<UP,POINTOPOINT,RUNNING>
        slip 0.0.0.0 dest 0.0.0.0
sc0: flags=63<UP,BROADCAST,RUNNING>
        vlan 5 inet 10.1.101.1 netmask 255.255.255.0 broadcast 10.1.101.255
```

The Building Distribution and Campus Backbone submodule switches in Figure 3-1 are Layer 3 switches; these switches are composed of multiple IP subnets on either VLANs or Layer 3 interfaces. Consequently, these switches have multiple IP addresses, which may act as a management IP address. As long as the management IP address is reachable from any network for in-band access, any IP address configured on the Layer 3 switches suffices as a management IP address. However, it is nonetheless recommended to separate out a specific subnet for management purposes. In addition, these switches do not require default gateways because they are performing routing functions and using routing protocols. Later chapters of this book discuss Layer 3 routing configuration in more detail.

Clock and NTP Settings

Clock settings to accurately display the time and date are essential in monitoring and troubleshooting Catalyst switches. Knowing exactly when events occur is crucial to maintaining control and stability of an enterprise network because system logging functionality uses timestamps. Furthermore, NTP is useful for synchronizing the system clocks for all network devices in the enterprise. Events for which time stamping is crucial include SNMP traps, SNMP inform messages, and system logging messages such as link state change, system reload, and so on. Use the following commands on Cisco IOS–based switches to configure the time and date along with the time zone; the **clock set** commands have two alternative formats:

```
clock set hh:mm:ss day month year
clock set hh:mm:ss month day year
clock timezone zone hours-offset [minutes-offset]
```

The **clock set** command is an executable command; the **clock timezone** command is a global configuration command. For the **clock timezone** configuration command, *zone* represents the time zone in abbreviations such as EST and PST, and *hours-offset* indicates the number of hours the current time zone is offset from UTC.

For Cisco CatOS–based switches, use the following commands to accomplish the same time and date configuration tasks:

```
set time [day_of_week] [mm/dd/yy] [hh:mm:ss]
set timezone [zone_name] [hours [minutes]]
```

Examples 3-6 and 3-7 illustrate configuration of the time, date, and time zone on Cisco IOS–based switches and Cisco CatOS–based switches, respectively.

Example 3-6 *Setting the Time, Date, and Time Zone on Cisco IOS–Based Switches*

```
Switch#clock set 12:30:00 May 1 2005
Switch#show clock
08:09:38.922 EST Mon Feb 7 2005
Switch#configure terminal

Enter configuration commands, one per line.  End with CNTL/Z.

Switch(config)#clock timezone EST -5
```

Example 3-7 *Setting the Time, Date, and Time Zone on Cisco CatOS–Based Switches*

```
Console> (enable) set time 05/01/2005 13:30:00

Sun May 1 2005, 12:30:00



Console> (enable) set timezone EST -5

Timezone set to 'EST', offset from UTC is -5 hours
```

Daylight savings time adjustments are configurable to automatically update the system clock if your location observes yearly time adjustments. Use the following commands to configure recurring or one-time time adjustments, respectively, on a per-time basis for Cisco IOS–based switches:

```
clock summer-time zone recurring [week day month hh:mm week day month hh:mm [offset]]
clock summer-time zone date date month year hh:mm date month year hh:mm [offset]
clock summer-time zone date month date year hh:mm month date year hh:mm [offset]
```

Use the following commands to configure recurring or one-time clock adjustments, respectively, for Cisco CatOS–based switches:

```
set summertime {enable | disable} [zone]
set summertime recurring [{week} {day} {month} {hh:mm} {week | day | month | hh:mm}
   [offset]]
set summertime date {month} {date} {year} {hh:mm} {month | date | year | hh:mm} [offset]
```

Examples 3-8 and 3-9 illustrate the configuration of the standard United States recurring daylight savings time on Cisco IOS–based switches and Cisco CatOS–based switches, respectively.

Example 3-8 *Configuring Recurring Time Adjustments on Cisco IOS–Based Switches*

```
Switch(config)#clock summer-time EST recurring second sunday March 2:00 first sunday
november 2:00 1
```

Example 3-9 *Configuring Recurring Time Adjustments on Cisco CatOS–Based Switches*

```
Switch> (enable) set summertime recurring second Sunday March 2:00 first Sunday
november 2:00 1f

Summertime is enabled and set to ''

  Start : Sun Mar 11 2007, 02:00:00

  End   : Sun Nov 4 2007, 02:00:00

  Offset: 1 hour

  Recurring: yes, starting at 02:00am of second Sunday of March and ending on 02:00am
of first Sunday of November.
```

The United States summertime parameters are the default and do not appear in the configuration. However, between 2007 and 2009, there is a shift to extend the period of daylight saving time in the United States as part of the Energy Policy Act of 2005. After 2009, a study will be presented to Congress to determine whether the extended period for daylight saving time is valuable and should continue.

Moreover, NTP is useful in synchronizing all the system clocks in the enterprise. Time synchronization is helpful in troubleshooting and network monitoring. To configure a Cisco IOS–based switch to synchronize its clock to an NTP server, use the following command:

  ntp server *ip-address*

For information about the switch itself acting as an NTP server and additional NTP configuration options such as authentication keys and preferences, consult the configuration guide for the respective Catalyst switch.

To configure a Cisco CatOS–based switch to synchronize its clock to an NTP server, use the following command:

  set ntp server *ip_address*

Examples 3-10 and 3-11 illustrate the configuration of NTP server associations on Cisco IOS–based switches and Cisco CatOS–based switches, respectively.

Example 3-10 *Configuring an NTP Association on a Cisco IOS–Based Switch*

```
Switch(config)#ntp server 10.192.1.1
```

Example 3-11 *Configuring an NTP Association on a Cisco CatOS–Based Switch*

```
Switch> (enable) set ntp server 10.192.1.1
```

Telnet and SSH

Both Cisco IOS–based and Cisco CatOS–based switches support administrative access via Telnet and SSH. Catalyst switches running Cisco IOS require a virtual terminal password configuration for command-line access, and both Cisco IOS and CatOS require an enable password for configuration access. Telnet passes passwords in clear-text. As a result, SSH, which does not transmit passwords in clear-text, is the preferable in-band connection method for CLI access to Catalyst switches. SSH requires the configuration of usernames and passwords and may optionally use RADIUS and TACACS+ methods of centralized security access. Cisco Secure supports both the TACACS+ and Radius Server features.

To configure a Cisco IOS–based switch's virtual terminal password and an enable password, use the following virtual terminal interface and global configuration commands, respectively:

```
password password
enable password [level level] {password | [encryption-type] encrypted-password}
```

For this command, **encryption-type** specifies the Cisco-proprietary algorithm used to encrypt the password. Currently, the only encryption type available is 7. If you specify *encryption-type*, the next argument you supply must be an encrypted password (a password already encrypted by a Cisco router). For simplicity, do not use the *encryption-type* option; simply enter a nonencrypted password in the command line when configuring the enable password.

To configure a Cisco CatOS–based switch's virtual terminal password and an enable password, use the following commands to generate prompt scripts for changing passwords:

```
set password
set enablepass
```

Examples 3-12 and 3-13 illustrate the configuration of Catalyst Cisco IOS–based switches and Cisco CatOS–based switches for enabling passwords and virtual terminal passwords, respectively.

NOTE The **line vty** command in Example 3-12 specifies virtual terminal lines 0 through 15 inclusively, the default number of virtual terminal lines for remote access.

In Example 3-13, if this is the first time you are configuring a password in Cisco CatOS, press **Enter** to enter a null password for the old password.

Example 3-12 *Configuring the Enable Password and Virtual Terminal Password on a Cisco IOS–Based Switch*

```
Switch(config)#enable password cisco

Switch(config)#line vty 0 15

Switch(config-line)#password cisco
```

Example 3-13 *Configuring the Enable Password and Virtual Terminal Password on a Cisco CatOS–Based Switch*

```
Console> (enable) set enablepass

Enter old password:

Enter new password: cisco
Retype new password: cisco

Password Changed


Console> (enable) set password

Enter old password:

Enter new password: cisco

Retype new password: cisco

Password Changed
```

As mentioned previously, SSH does not transmit passwords in clear-text and is the preferable method of in-band access. The SSH feature is available only on recent versions of Cisco IOS for the Catalyst switches. Table 3-3 lists the Cisco IOS versions for which the SSH feature is available.

Table 3-3 *Software Support for SSH on Catalyst IOS–Based Switches*

Platform	Cisco IOS Software Release
Catalyst 6500	12.1(11b)E and later
Catalyst 4000 and 4500	12.1(13)EW and later
Cat 3550 and 3750	12.1(11)EA1 and later
Cat 2950, 2955, and 2970	12.1(11)EA1 and later

To enable SSH on a Cisco IOS–based switch, use the following command to generate the necessary keys for SSH:

```
crypto key generate rsa
```

Other types of keys besides RSA are available in different versions of Cisco IOS. In addition to the **crypto key generate** command, enabling SSH requires the global configuration of **aaa new-model**. This command enables the use of local usernames and passwords for authentication, DNS name configuration, and virtual terminal configuration for inbound SSH sessions. Chapter 14 discusses additional security configurations and explains the **aaa new-model** command in more detail.

Example 3-14 illustrates the enabling of SSH as the only method of in-band access on a Cisco IOS–based switch.

Example 3-14 *Configuring a Switch for SSH for Exclusive In-Band Access on a Cisco IOS–Based Switch*

```
Switch(config)#ip domain-name cisco.com

Switch(config)#aaa new-model

Switch(config)#username cisco password cisco

Switch(config)#crypto key generate rsa modulus 2048

The name for the keys will be: Switch.cisco.com


% The key modulus size is 2048 bits

Generating RSA keys ...

[OK]



00:02:36: %SSH-5-ENABLED: SSH 1.5 has been enabled

Switch(config)#line vty 0 15

Switch(config-line)#transport input ssh
```

For additional configuration parameters and examples of configuring SSH on Cisco IOS routers and switches, refer to the following technical document on Cisco.com:

"Configuring Secure Shell on Routers and Switches Running Cisco IOS"

In regard to Cisco CatOS software, Table 3-4 illustrates the software support of the SSH feature on Cisco CatOS–based Catalyst switches.

Table 3-4   *Software Support for SSH on Cisco CatOS–Based Switches*

Platform	Cisco CatOS Version
Catalyst 6000	K9 images as of 6.1
Catalyst 4000	K9 images as of 6.1
Catalyst 2980G/2948G	K9 images as of 6.1

Example 3-15 illustrates the enabling of SSH as the only method of in-band access on a Cisco CatOS–based switch. Enabling an IP permit list without entries prevents access via the configured protocol.

Example 3-15 *Configuring a Catalyst Switch for Exclusive In-Band Access via SSH on a Cisco CatOS–Based Switch*

```
Switch (enable) set crypto key rsa 2048

Generating RSA keys.............. [OK]




Switch (enable) set ip permit enable telnet

TELNET permit list enabled.

WARNING!! IP permit list has no entries.
```

Although SSH is fairly secure, there are several inherent vulnerabilities that exist as a result of the protocol itself. Aside from protocol vulnerabilities, implementation and hardware or software defects on specific Cisco products might yield additional vulnerabilities. Keeping up-to-date on Cisco field notices, product vulnerabilities, and software versions minimizes security issues with SSH. The following list describes possible vulnerabilities with SSH, most of which have been addressed in the latest software versions of Cisco IOS and other vendor SSH server and client software:

- Buffer overflows or DoS attacks, for example, continuous unauthorized login attempts.

- Transmitting invalid fields. Incorrect packet lengths or invalid string lengths in the IP, TCP, or data fields of the packet to the router or switch can yield unexpected behavior such as a software crash or unauthorized access (DoS attack).

- Transmitting invalid padding and padding length of IP frame. This can yield unexpected behavior such as a software crash or unauthorized access (DoS attack).

- Attempting to transmit anomalous algorithms to network device.

- Software or hardware defect that can yield anomalous behavior.

- Weak usernames and passwords that are easily broken. Such passwords include the user's default username and simple passwords such as the user's birthday without the use of special characters.
- Key analysis by intercepting large number of frames.

NOTE   For Cisco products in your enterprise network, disable Telnet and enable SSH with RADIUS or TACACS+ authentication, authorization, and accounting for reasons of security.

DNS

Configuring DNS on Catalyst switches is useful for resolving domain names to IP addresses for management and troubleshooting purposes. To configure Cisco IOS–based switches for DNS, use the following commands:

```
ip name-server address [address2...address6]
ip domain-name domain
ip domain-lookup
```

The **ip name-server** *address* command configures up to eight domain servers to query for DNS resolution. The **ip domain-name** *domain* command specifies the domain on which the switch resides, and the **ip domain-lookup** command enables DNS resolution.

To configure Cisco CatOS–based switches for DNS, use the following commands:

```
set ip dns server ip-addr [primary]
set ip dns domain name
set ip dns {enable | disable}
```

The **set ip dns server** *ip-addr* command adds DNS servers to configured lists of servers. The Catalyst switch queries the primary DNS server before moving to other DNS servers in the list if there is no response to the DNS query. The **set ip dns enable** command enables the switch to perform DNS queries.

Examples 3-16 and 3-17 illustrate configuring Catalyst Cisco IOS–based switches and Cisco CatOS–based switches for DNS functionality, respectively.

Example 3-16 *Configuring DNS Lookup on a Cisco IOS–Based Switch*

```
Switch(config)# ip domain-name cisco.com

Switch(config)# ip name-server 10.4.1.209 10.4.1.210

Switch(config)# ip domain-lookup
```

Example 3-17 *Configuring DNS Lookup on a Cisco CatOS–Based Switch*

```
Console> (enable) set ip dns server 10.4.1.209

10.4.1.209 added to DNS server table as primary server.

Console> (enable) set ip dns server 10.4.1.210

10.4.1.210 added to DNS server table as backup server.

Console> (enable) set ip dns domain cisco.com

Default DNS domain name set to cisco.com

Console> (enable) set ip dns enable

DNS is enabled
```

System Logging

System logging is another useful tool to manage Catalyst switches. By default, Catalyst switches log critical information to a local buffer that is configurable in size. In addition, Catalyst switches support various logging levels, from emergency-level settings to debugging-level settings of various features and components, such as the Cisco Discovery Protocol (CDP) and the IEEE 802.1D Spanning Tree Protocol (STP). Generally, it is advisable to log all messages up to the critical status to a syslog server. Using a syslog server centralizes monitoring of multiple Catalyst switches in the enterprise.

For more information about syslog levels, facilities, and components, refer to the technical documentation for the respective Catalyst switch on Cisco.com. Recommended practice is to configure all Catalyst switches to log to syslog servers as part of their initial configuration.

To configure a Cisco IOS–based switch for system logging to a syslog server, use the following command:

> **logging** *ip-address*

To configure a Cisco CatOS–based switch for system logging to a syslog server, use the following commands:

> **set logging server** *ipaddress*
> **set logging server** {**enable** | **disable**}

Examples 3-18 and 3-19 illustrate the configuration of Catalyst Cisco IOS–based switches and Cisco CatOS–based switches for DNS functionality, respectively.

Example 3-18 *Configuring a Syslog Destination on a Cisco IOS–Based Switch*

```
Switch(config)# logging 10.1.1.118
```

Example 3-19 *Configuring a Syslog Destination on a Cisco CatOS–Based Switch*

```
Console> (enable) set logging server 10.1.1.118

10.1.1.118 added to system logging server table.
```

For information about different logging levels of Catalyst features and system capabilities, consult Cisco.com.

SNMP

Simple Network Management Protocol (SNMP) is a powerful and standards-based protocol by which to manage network devices. Example use of SNMP includes the following:

- Configuration and configuration file management
- Interface link up and down tracking
- Feature monitoring, such as HSRP tracking
- Interface statistics and performance measuring

In small networks, SNMP is mostly useful for monitoring; however, in large enterprise networks, SNMP is useful for configurations as well. Due to the large size of enterprise networks, centralized management and configuration is essential to successful deployments of multilayer switched networks.

All Cisco Catalyst switches support SNMP. A complete discussion of SNMP is outside the scope of the BCMSN; nevertheless, it is important to review the basic configuration needed to allow remote management of Cisco Catalyst switches through SNMP. Applications such as CiscoWorks, HP OpenView, and What's Up use SNMP to manage, track, monitor, and gather performance data from Cisco network devices.

There are three main versions of SNMP:

- Version 1 (RFC 1157)
- Version 2c (RFC 1901, 1905, 1906)
- Version 3 (RFCs 2273-2275)

Most enterprise networks currently use version 2c with a defined upgrade path to version 3. Version 3 is the only version that supports a high level of security using encryption. Table 3-5 shows the security levels available with SNMP.

Table 3-5 *SNMP Security Models and Levels*

Model	SNMP Level	Authentication	Encryption	Description
v1	noAuthNoPriv	Community String	No	Uses a plaintext community string for authentication.
v2c	noAuthNoPriv	Community String	No	Uses a plaintext community string for authentication.
v3	noAuthNoPriv	Username	No	Uses a username match for authentication.

Table 3-5   *SNMP Security Models and Levels (Continued)*

Model	SNMP Level	Authentication	Encryption	Description
v3	authNoPriv	MD5 or SHA	No	Provides authentication based on the HMAC-MD5 or HMAC-SHA algorithms.
v3	authPriv	MD5 or SHA	DES	Provides authentication based on the HMAC-MD5 or HMAC-SHA algorithms. Provides DES 56-bit encryption in addition to authentication based on the CBC-DES (DES-56) standard.

Recommended practice is to use SNMPv3 with secure authentication and command encryption; however, most enterprise networks have built their management applications around SNMPv2, and it might be some time before enterprise networks fully migrate to SNMPv3. Nevertheless, avoid using the read-only and read-write community strings as public and private, because those strings tend to be the standard default in enterprise networks. In review, SNMPv3 provides enhanced network security through the following features:

- Data can be collected securely from SNMP devices without fear of the data being tampered with or corrupted (message integrity).

- Encrypting confidential information. For example, SNMP set command packets that change a router's configuration can be encrypted to prevent the packet contents from being exposed on the network in plaintext.

- User authentication is optionally based on encryption algorithms (verifies valid source).

For more information on configuring SNMP with Cisco IOS on Catalyst switches, search the Cisco.com website for SNMP.

SNMP Configuration

To configure Cisco IOS with an SNMPv2 community string, use the following command:

```
snmp-server community string [view view-name] [ro | rw] [number]
```

In this command, **ro** represents read-only and **rw** represents read-write. *string* represents the community string. Most network devices are configured with strings public and private for the **ro** and **rw** community strings. In terms of security, recommended practice is that these strings be something other than the common public and private strings. Nevertheless, with SNMPv2, these strings are transmitted in clear-text. *number* represents an optional ACL for restricting access.

Example 3-20 illustrates configuring a Catalyst switch with a public and private community string.

Example 3-20 *Configuring SNMPv2 Community Strings*

```
Cat6500-MSFC(config)#snmp-server community public ro
Cat6500-MSFC(config)#snmp-server community private rw
```

To specify an identification name (ID) for either the local or remote SNMP engine on the router, use the following command in global configuration mode:

snmp-server engineID [**local** *engineid-string*] | [**remote** *ip-address* **udp-port** *port-number engineid-string*]

To configure the recipient of an SNMP trap operation, use the following command in global configuration mode:

snmp-server host *host* [**traps** | **informs**][**version** {**1** | **2c** | **3** [**auth** | **noauth** | **priv**]}] *community-string* [**udp-port** *port*] [*notification-type*]

Example 3-21 illustrates configuring the SNMP server engine ID and trap destination.

Example 3-21 *Configuring SNMP EngineID and a Trap Destination*

```
Cat6500-MSFC(config)#snmp-server EngineID local MSFC123
Cat6500-MSFC(config)#snmp-server host 10.1.1.12 traps version 2c public
```

To configure a new SNMP group or a table that maps SNMP users to SNMP views, use the following command in global configuration mode:

snmp-server group [*groupname* {**v1** | **v2c** | **v3** [**auth** | **noauth** | **priv**]}][**read** *readview*] [**write** *writeview*] [**notify** *notifyview*] [**access** *access-list*]

To configure a new user to an SNMP group, use the following command in global configuration mode:

snmp-server user username [*groupname* **remote** *ip-address* [**udp-port** *port*] {**v1** | **v2c** | **v3** [**encrypted**] [**auth** {**md5** | **sha**} *auth-password* [**priv des56** priv password]] [**access** *access-list*]

Note that the options for the **snmp-server user** command allow for encrypted username and passwords. In addition, the preceding commands require additional configurations and usually occupy AAA configurations. Refer to the SNMP configuration documentation at Cisco.com for more details. As previously noted, SNMP is outside the scope of the current BCMSN switching examination.

Managing Catalyst Switch Configurations

Cisco IOS software and Cisco CatOS software use the **copy** command to move configurations from one component or device to another, such as RAM, NVRAM, or a TFTP server. In addition to using AutoInstall, the setup utility, or the CLI to load or create a configuration, the **copy** command allows configurations to exist on servers elsewhere in the network.

The syntax of the **copy** command requires that the first argument indicate the source (from where the configuration is to be copied), followed by the destination (to where the configuration is to be copied), such as the **copy tftp flash** command when moving files on the Cisco IOS File System (IFS). For example, the **copy running-config tftp** command copies the running configuration in RAM to a TFTP server. The command prompts the user for the source filename, destination filename, and TFTP server address.

Furthermore, the **copy** command can copy the running configuration to NVRAM for nonvolatile storage. Startup-config is the term in Cisco IOS to refer to the configuration in NVRAM, and running-config represents the configuration currently running in RAM. To save a running-config to the startup-config, use the **copy running-config startup-config** command. This command performs the same operation as the **write memory** command. Similarly, using the command **copy startup-config running-config** copies the startup-config to the running-config. Analogous commands exist for copying files between a TFTP server and either NVRAM or RAM as indicated in the "Upgrading Software Versions on Catalyst Switches" section later in this chapter. The **erase startup-config** and **write erase** commands delete the saved startup-config in NVRAM. These commands are useful when resetting switches back to factory default.

Cisco CatOS–based switches immediately write configuration changes to NVRAM. There is no concept of running and startup configuration on Cisco CatOS–based switches.

Figure 3-2 illustrates the use of TFTP and Cisco IOS commands to move and store Cisco IOS configuration files in RAM and NVRAM. Example 3-22 illustrates a user saving a switch configuration to NVRAM followed by saving the configuration to a TFTP server on a Cisco IOS–based Catalyst switch.

Figure 3-2   *Representation of the Use of TFTP to Store Configuration Files in RAM and NVRAM*

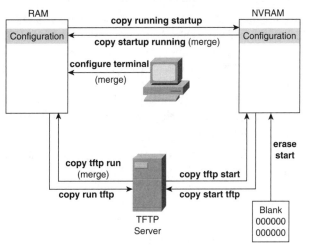

Example 3-22 *Managing Configuration Files on Catalyst Switches*

```
Switch#copy running-config startup-config

Destination filename [startup-config]?

Building configuration...
```

continues

Example 3-22 *Managing Configuration Files on Catalyst Switches*

```
[OK]

Switch#copy startup-config tftp

Address or name of remote host []? 10.18.118.100

Destination filename [Switch-confg]?

!!

3007 bytes copied in 1.028 secs (2925 bytes/sec)
```

NOTE   Do not alter the destination filename when saving the running-configuration to NVRAM. Doing so may result in the configuration being written to Flash memory instead of NVRAM. Configurations can also be managed by SNMP.

Understanding the Cisco IOS File System (IFS) and Software Images on Catalyst Switches

All currently shipping Catalyst switches, both with Cisco CatOS and Cisco IOS, use the Cisco IFS. The Cisco IFS uses physical, local flash file systems containing memory space to store OS images and configuration files. This memory space size is generally between 16 MB and 2 GB, depending on platform. The flash file system acts similarly to a UNIX file system where files may be added, deleted, renamed, and so on, depending on platform. All Cisco Catalyst switches include an internal Flash file system (referred to as *bootflash memory*), while several Cisco Catalyst switches include a PCMCIA or Flash Disk slot or slots for adding memory space.

In addition to the physical Flash file systems, the IFS supports using network file systems such as TFTP, remote copy protocol (rcp), and FTP. Furthermore, the IFS supports other endpoints for reading or writing data, including NVRAM, DRAM, ROM, and so on. Example 3-23 displays a user formatting a PCMCIA Flash card, copying an image to it, verifying the image on the Flash card, and then deleting the image.

Example 3-23 *Formatting and Copying Images on the IFS in Cisco CatOS*

```
Console> (enable) format slot0:

All sectors will be erased, proceed (y/n) [n]? y


Enter volume id (up to 31 characters):
```

Example 3-23 *Formatting and Copying Images on the IFS in Cisco CatOS (Continued)*

```
Formatting sector 1

Format device slot0 completed

Console> (enable) dir slot0:


No files on device


24772608 bytes available (0 bytes used)

Console> (enable) dir bootflash:

-#- -length- -----date/time------ name

  1  6238120 Nov 26 2002 14:10:11 cat6000-sup2k8.7-4-3.bin


25743320 bytes available (6238248 bytes used)

Console> (enable) copy bootflash:cat6000-sup2k8.7-4-3.bin slot0:


24772480 bytes available on device slot0, proceed (y/n) [n]? y

CCCCCCCCCCCCCCCCCCCCCCCCCCCCCCCCCCCCCCCCCCCCCCCCCCCCCCCCCCCCCCCCCCCCCCCCCCCCCCC
! Output omitted for brevity

File has been copied successfully.

Console> (enable) dir slot0::

-#- -length- -----date/time------ name

  1  6238120 Nov 26 2002 14:10:11 cat6000-sup2k8.7-4-3.bin
```

continues

Example 3-23 *Formatting and Copying Images on the IFS in Cisco CatOS (Continued)*

```
25743320 bytes available (6238248 bytes used)

Console> (enable) delete slot0:cat6000-sup2k8.7-4-3.bin
```

Cisco CatOS and Cisco IOS use network file systems to copy OS images and configurations to local file systems. Table 3-6 illustrates the file systems and their associated prefixes for use on Cisco CatOS–based and Cisco IOS–based (Native Mode) Catalyst switches.

Table 3-6   *The IFS Prefix Descriptions*

Prefix	Description
bootflash:	Bootflash memory.
disk0:	ATA Flash disk occupying the first (or only) PCMCIA or SanDisk slot.
disk1:	ATA Flash disk occupying the second (or only) PCMCIA or SanDisk slot.
flash:	Flash memory. This prefix is available on all platforms. For platforms that do not have a device named flash:, the prefix flash: is aliased to bootflash: or slot0:. Therefore, you can use the prefix flash: to refer to the main Flash memory storage area on all platforms.
flh:	Flash load helper log files.
ftp:	FTP network server.
nvram:	NVRAM.
rcp:	Rcp network server.
scp:	Secure copy protocol server.
sftp:	Secure FTP server.
slot0:	First PCMCIA Flash memory card.
slot1:	Second PCMCIA Flash memory card.
system:	Contains the system memory, including the running configuration.
tftp:	TFTP network server.

NOTE   As a standard practice, always use secure copy methods such as SFTP and SCP for copying images, because passwords and data that is passed through the network are encrypted.

Determining the IFS Size and Contents

To determine the size, available space, and contents of the Cisco IFS, use the following command in both Cisco CatOS and Cisco IOS:

```
show flash
```

Example 3-24 illustrates a user displaying information about the IFS on a Catalyst 2950 and 4500 running Cisco IOS and a Catalyst 6500 running Cisco CatOS, respectively. Note that the Catalyst 4500 does not support the **show flash** command on the current software version.

Example 3-24 *Displaying Information About the IFS on Cisco CatOS and Cisco IOS Switches*

```
! Catalyst 2950 Switch:

Switch#show flash


Directory of flash:/


    2  -rwx     2664051   Mar 01 1993 00:03:38  c2950-i6q4l2-mz.121-11.EA1.bin

    3  -rwx         616   Mar 06 1993 01:45:22  vlan.dat

    4  -rwx     2774747   Mar 03 1993 18:35:17  c2950-i6q4l2-mz.121-12c.EA1.bin

   22  -rwx         316   Mar 03 1993 20:11:35  env_vars

    7  drwx         896   Mar 03 1993 18:36:23  html

   19  -rwx         110   Mar 03 1993 18:37:12  info

   20  -rwx         110   Mar 03 1993 18:37:12  info.ver


7741440 bytes total (571392 bytes free)
```
```
! Catalyst 4500 Switch running Cisco IOS
Switch#show bootflash:

-#- ED ----type---- --crc--- -seek-- nlen -length- -----date/time------ name

1   .. config     76481B10 12B1018   15     56610 Jan 31 2000 22:08:56 Backup

2   .. image      40A9D879 2E07B90   28  8150708 Aug 18 2000 15:39:37 cat4000-is-
mz.121-12c.EW.bin


13599856 bytes available (47741840 bytes used)
```
```
! Catalyst 6500 Switch running Cisco CatOS:

Console> (enable) show flash
```

continues

Example 3-24 *Displaying Information About the IFS on Cisco CatOS and Cisco IOS Switches (Continued)*

```
-#- ED --type-- --crc--- -seek-- nlen -length- -----date/time------ name

 1 .. ffffffff f61a1629 673028  24 6238120 Nov 26 2002 14:10:11 cat6000-sup2k8.7-
4-3.bin


25743320 bytes available (6238248 bytes used)
```

Cisco IOS Image Naming

The name of the Cisco IOS or Cisco CatOS image indicates the appropriate platform and version. For the Cisco IOS images, the filename contains multiple parts specifying platform, software release number, features, and type. For example, the filename **c2950-i6q412-mz.121-11.EA1.bin** contains this information:

- **c2950**—Identifies the platform on which the image runs.

- **i6q412**—Identifies the special capabilities of the image file. A letter or series of letters identifies the features supported in that image. In the case of the 2950, two software versions exist: a standard version and an enhanced version with additional features.

- **mz**—Specifies where the image runs and whether the file is compressed. In this example, mz indicates that the image runs from RAM and is zip-compressed.

- **12.1(11)EA1**—Indicates the version number.

- **.bin**—Indicates the file extension. (In this example, .bin indicates that this is a binary executable file.)

The Cisco IOS software naming conventions, field meanings, image content, and other details are subject to change. For the most updated list of Cisco IOS software naming conventions, consult the following document on Cisco.com:

"White Paper: Cisco IOS(R) Reference Guide"

Naming Conventions Used by Hybrid and Cisco IOS Images on the Catalyst 6500 Family of Switches

Cisco IOS (hybrid mode) and Cisco CatOS use unique naming conventions to specify software versions. Because of the different models of Supervisor Engines available, unique naming conventions are necessary to ensure that a switch is using the correct image.

In the case of Cisco CatOS, software images for the Catalyst 6500 use the prefixes in Table 3-7 to indicate the applicable Supervisor Engine.

Table 3-7 *Cisco CatOS Image Name to Supervisor Engine Mapping*

Image Demarcation	Example	Supervisor Engine
cat6000-sup.<features>.<version>.bin	cat6000-supcv.6-4-4.bin	Supervisor Engine I
cat6000-sup2.<features>.<version>.bin	cat6000-sup2k8.7-6-1.bin	Supervisor Engine II
cat6000-sup720.<features>.<version>.bin	cat6000-sup720cvk8.8-1-2.bin	Supervisor 720

The **cv** prefix indicates CiscoView ADP flash image bundling, and the **k8** prefix indicates basic encryption support, whereas **k9** indicates SSH server support. The corresponding Cisco IOS image running on the MSFC for Catalyst 6500 Supervisors uses an image file with a **c6msfc** prefix.

In the case of Cisco IOS, software images for the Catalyst 6500 use the prefixes in Table 3-8 to indicate the applicable Supervisor Engine.

Table 3-8 *Cisco IOS Image Name to Supervisor Engine Mapping*

Image Demarcation	Example	Supervisor Engine
c6sup.<version>.bin	cat6000-sup.6-1-1.bin	Supervisor Engine I with MSFC
c6sup11.<version>	c6sup11-js-mz.121-19.E	Supervisor Engine I with MSFC (replaces c6sup for clarity)
c6sup12.<version>	c6sup12-jsv-mz.121-19.E	Supervisor Engine I with MSFC2
c6sup22.<version>	c6sup22-jo3sv-mz.121-19.E	Supervisor Engine II with MSFC2
s72033.<version>.bin	s72033-psv-mz.122-14.SX.bin	Supervisor Engine 720 with PFC3 and MSFC3

In summary, the following Cisco IOS prefixes indicate the use of the following hardware:

- **c6sup (original name for Integrated Cisco IOS image)**—For use with the Supervisor Engine I with an MSFC1
- **c6sup11**—For use with the Supervisor Engine I with an MSFC1
- **c6sup12**—For use with the Supervisor Engine I with an MSFC2
- **c6sup22**—For use with the Supervisor Engine II with an MSFC2
- **s72033**—For use with the Supervisor Engine 720 with an MSFC3 and PFC3

NOTE   All the previously mentioned images, with a complete list of other images, are available at the "LAN Switching Software" and the "Cisco IOS Software" sections of the Software Center on Cisco.com.

Upgrading Software Versions on Catalyst Switches

Upgrading software images on current-generation Catalyst switches is a straightforward process of loading a new image on the IFS and configuring the switch to load the new image on the next reload. When deleting the existing flash image, take extreme care not to reload the switch while copying a new image. If the switch loads without a proper image, a recovery mechanism such as Xmodem is required to load a bootable image.

The most common method of copying an image to a Catalyst switch is via TFTP using the following **copy** command for both Cisco IOS–based and Cisco CatOS–based Catalyst switches:

```
copy tftp flash
```

The **copy tftp flash** command asks the user for additional information when executed. This additional information includes the source filename, destination filename, and TFTP server IP address. After you confirm these entries, the procedure may prompt you to erase the Flash. Erasing Flash memory makes room for the new image. You should perform this task if there is not sufficient Flash memory for more than one Cisco IOS image. Generally, all current Cisco Catalyst switches contain enough memory in Flash for at least two software images.

Alternatively, you can back up the Catalyst switches' images and configuration to a TFTP server. To copy existing images in Flash to a TFTP server, use the following command:

```
copy flash tftp
```

In summary, the following steps are necessary to load a new image on a Catalyst switch:

Step 1   Copy the appropriate software image file to the appropriate TFTP directory on the workstation or server.

Step 2   Log in to the switch through the console port or via a Telnet or SSH session.

Step 3   Download the software image from the TFTP server using the **copy tftp flash** command. When prompted, enter the IP address or host name of the TFTP server and the name of the file to download. On those platforms that support the Flash file system, a prompt appears for the Flash device to which to copy the file and the destination filename.

The switch downloads the image file from the TFTP server to the respective file system after you finish entering the necessary prompts for the **copy tftp flash** command.

Step 4   After the image completes the download process, modify the BOOT environment variable on the switch using the **boot system flash** *device:filename* command for Cisco IOS–based switches or the **set boot system flash** *device:filename* **prepend** command for Cisco CatOS–based switches. The purpose of modifying the BOOT environment is to ensure that the switch boots the correct image on the next reload.

Step 5   For Cisco IOS–based switches, save the configuration using the **copy running-config startup-config** command to retain the boot variable configuration changes.

Step 6   Reset the switch using the **reload** command on a Cisco IOS–based switch or the **reset system** command for Cisco CatOS–based switches. Any open Telnet or SSH sessions disconnect during switch reload.

Step 7   When the switch reboots, enter the **show version** command to verify the version of software running on the switch.

NOTE   When you are using Telnet or SSH to access the switch during an upgrade procedure, the current Telnet or SSH session disconnects when power-cycling the switch to run the new software.

TFTP is not a secure protocol method to transfer images. Moreover, most TFTP server software does not support files larger than 16 MB or 24 MB, which are found with Cisco IOS 12.2 and 12.3 images for Catalyst switches. As a result, you should not attempt to copy images using TFTP over congested or low-speed interfaces. Opt for protocols such as SFTP, available on newer versions of Cisco CatOS and Cisco IOS, for more resilient file copies.

Example 3-25 illustrates a user backing up the existing Cisco IOS image to a TFTP server and copying a new image to the switch. In this example, the user configures the switch to load the correct software image by manipulating the boot parameters using the **boot system** command. The switch used in this example is a Catalyst 3550 switch running Cisco IOS software.

Example 3-25 *User Upgrading Cisco IOS Image*

```
Switch#copy flash tftp

Source filename [/c3550-i5q3l2-mz.121-12c.EA1/c3550-i5q3l2-mz.121-12c.EA1]? c3550-
i5q3l2-mz.121-12c.EA1.bin
```

continues

Example 3-25 *User Upgrading Cisco IOS Image (Continued)*

```
Address or name of remote host []? 10.1.118.100

Destination filename [c3550-i5q3l2-mz.121-12c.EA1.bin]? c3550-i5q3l2-mz.121-
12c.EA1.bin

!!!!!!!!!!!!!!!!!!!!!!!!!!!!!!!!!!!!!!!!!!!!!!!!!!!!!!!!!!!!!!!!!!!!!!!!!!!!!!!!!!!
! Output omitted for brevity
!!!!!!!!!!!!!!!!!!!!!!!!!!!!!!!!!!!!!!!!!!!!!!!!!!!!!!!!!!!!!!!!!!!!!!!!!!!!!!!

3823261 bytes copied in 11.640 secs (328459 bytes/sec)



Switch#copy tftp flash

Address or name of remote host [10.1.118.100]? 10.1.118.100

Source filename [c3550-i5q3l2-mz.121-13.EA1a.bin]? c3550-i5q3l2-mz.121-13.EA1a.bin

Destination filename [c3550-i5q3l2-mz.121-13.EA1a.bin]? c3550-i5q3l2-mz.121-
13.EA1a.bin

Accessing tftp://10.1.118.100/c3550-i5q3l2-mz.121-13.EA1a.bin...

Loading c3550-i5q3l2-mz.121-13.EA1a.bin from 10.1.118.100 (via FastEthernet0/1):
!!!!!!!!!!!!!!!!!!!!!!!!!!!!!!!!!!!!!!!!!!!!!!!!!!!!!!!!!!!!!!!!!!!!!!!!!!!!!!!!!!!
! Output omitted for brevity
!!!!!!!!!!!!!!!!!!!!!!!!!!!!!!!!!!!

[OK - 3993235 bytes]

3993235 bytes copied in 94.716 secs (42160 bytes/sec)



Switch#configure terminal

Enter configuration commands, one per line.  End with CNTL/Z.

Switch(config)#boot system flash:c3550-i5q3l2-mz.121-13.EA1a.bin

Switch(config)#end

Switch#copy run start

Destination filename [startup-config]?

Building configuration...
```

Example 3-25 *User Upgrading Cisco IOS Image (Continued)*

```
[OK]



Switch#reload

Proceed with reload? [confirm]



00:32:35: %SYS-5-RELOAD: Reload requestedBase ethernet MAC Address:
00:0b:5f:cf:6f:80

Xmodem file system is available.

The password-recovery mechanism is enabled.

Initializing Flash...

flashfs[0]: 34 files, 5 directories

flashfs[0]: 0 orphaned files, 0 orphaned directories

flashfs[0]: Total bytes: 15998976

flashfs[0]: Bytes used: 11586048

flashfs[0]: Bytes available: 4412928

flashfs[0]: flashfs fsck took 18 seconds.

...done Initializing Flash.

Boot Sector Filesystem (bs:) installed, fsid: 3

Loading "flash:c3550-i5q3l2-mz.121-13.EA1a.bin"...
##############################################################################
##############################################################################
##############################################################################
##############################################################################
##############################################################################
#################################################

#######
```

continues

Example 3-25 *User Upgrading Cisco IOS Image (Continued)*

```
File "flash:c3550-i5q3l2-mz.121-13.EA1a.bin" uncompressed and installed, entry
point: 0x3000

executing...

(text deleted)

00:00:36: %SYS-5-RESTART: System restarted --

Cisco Internetwork Operating System Software

IOS (tm) C3550 Software (C3550-I5Q3L2-M), Version 12.1(13)EA1a, RELEASE SOFTWARE
(fc1)

Copyright (c) 1986-2003 by cisco Systems, Inc.

Compiled Tue 25-Mar-03 23:42 by yenanh
```

NOTE   The Catalyst 3550 includes an archive and install software feature to ease installation of the software image and web interface files. See the software release notes for more details.

NOTE   The exclamation point (!) or pound sign (#) indicates the successful transfer of a UDP segment of the complete software image file.

For Cisco CatOS–based switches, follow the same procedure as upgrading Cisco IOS–based switches, except use the **set boot system flash** *device:filename* **prepend** command to manipulate the system image to boot.

Other modes of copying images to Flash exist, such as FTP, SFTP, and Xmodem. In general, only use the serial protocols such as Xmodem for disaster-recovery processes, such as when all the images have been accidentally removed from Flash. Example 3-26 illustrates the available transport methods on a Catalyst 3550 switch running Cisco IOS 12.1.13.EA1.

Example 3-26 *Available Image Transport Methods*

```
Switch#copy ?

  /erase        Erase destination file system.

  bs:           Copy from bs: file system
```

Example 3-26 *Available Image Transport Methods (Continued)*

```
flash:          Copy from flash: file system

ftp:            Copy from ftp: file system

null:           Copy from null: file system

nvram:          Copy from nvram: file system

rcp:            Copy from rcp: file system

running-config  Copy from current system configuration

startup-config  Copy from startup configuration

system:         Copy from system: file system

tftp:           Copy from tftp: file system

vb:             Copy from vb: file system

xmodem:         Copy from xmodem: file system

ymodem:         Copy from ymodem: file system

zflash:         Copy from zflash: file system
```

Overview of Converting Cisco CatOS to Cisco Native IOS

Most current Catalyst switches use the Cisco IOS operating system instead of the traditional Cisco CatOS Software. For the Catalyst 6500 family of switches with an MSFC that runs either Cisco Native IOS or Cisco CatOS, the option exists to convert switches currently running Cisco CatOS to Cisco IOS. The exact commands that are used to convert from Cisco CatOS to Cisco IOS depend on the Multilayer Feature Switch Card (MFSC) model and configuration specifics that are used on the switch. Check the reference documentation for the hardware in question for specific instructions on configuration migrations.

The following steps illustrate, at a high-level overview, the steps necessary to convert Cisco CatOS to Cisco IOS:

Step 1 Back up the configuration files by using the **copy** command.

Step 2 Obtain the appropriate Cisco IOS software image.

Step 3   Boot to ROMMON by setting the configuration register and rebooting. (ROMMON is a ROM-based program used by Catalyst switches for power-up and recovery from fatal exception errors. In addition, switches enter the ROMMON mode if there is no valid configuration file, if the NVRAM contents are corrupted, or by specific settings of the configuration-register.)

Step 4   Compare the current running configurations to the backup copy of the configuration from Step 1.

Step 5   Change the boot variables so that the switch will boot Cisco IOS the next time it restarts.

Step 6   Reload the original configuration from the backup copy from Step 1.

Step 7   Make any necessary manual configuration changes.

For specific instructions about how to convert the Catalyst 6500 family of switches from Cisco CatOS to Cisco IOS, refer to the following locations on the Cisco Technical Assistance Center (TAC) website. (These locations require you to be a registered Cisco.com user.)

> http://www.cisco.com/warp/customer/473/81.shtml
> http://www.cisco.com/warp/customer/473/80.shtml

In addition, Cisco.com provides useful tools to aid in converting from Cisco CatOS to Cisco IOS software and configurations on a Catalyst 6500 switch for registered Cisco.com users. Refer to the following documents, respectively, for information about the tools:

> http://www.cisco.com/cgi-bin/tablebuild.pl/cat6000-config-converter
> http://www.cisco.com/cgi-bin/Support/CatCfgConversion/catcfg_xlat.pl

Basic Troubleshooting Practices

Basic troubleshooting of Catalyst switches involves the use of **show** and **debug** commands. The **show** commands provide state information, and the **debug** commands provide real-time information about specific events. The use of **show** commands is always a first step in troubleshooting anomalies. In addition to **show** and **debug** commands, logging information with time stamps is useful in monitoring and debugging Catalyst switches. This section discusses these topics in the order listed in the following outline:

- **show** and **debug** commands
- Configurations and commands useful when troubleshooting
- The impact of **debug** commands and recommended use

show and debug Commands

Cisco IOS **show** and **debug** commands are important tools for troubleshooting network anomalies, connectivity problems, performance issues, and other anomalous behavior. The **show** commands provide a static collection of information about the status of a network device, neighboring switches and routers, and network performance. Use **show** commands when gathering facts for isolating problems in an enterprise network, including problems with interfaces, nodes, media, servers, clients, or applications. An example of using **show** commands for troubleshooting is using the **show interface** command to gather error statistics such as the number of Layer 2 cyclic redundancy check (CRC) frames received from a directly attached device.

The **debug** commands provide a flow of information about the traffic being seen (or not seen) on an interface, error messages generated by nodes on the network, protocol-specific diagnostic packets, and other useful state troubleshooting data. Use **debug** commands when you need to see process operations on the router or network to determine whether events or packets are working properly. One such example is debugging Cisco Express Forwarding (CEF) switching to verify behavior of packet flows.

Use **debug** commands only to isolate problems, not to monitor network or switch operation. Generally, it is advisable to use **debug** commands only under the supervisor of a TAC engineer because debugs may result in high CPU overhead. The following list summarizes important notes about the use of **debug** commands:

- Be aware that the **debug** commands may generate too much data that is of little use for a specific problem. You need to have knowledge of the protocol(s) being debugged to properly interpret the debug outputs.

- **debug** commands may generate high CPU overhead that may disrupt network device operation; therefore, only use debug commands when you are looking for specific types of traffic or solutions to problems and have narrowed problems to a likely subset of causes.

- When using the debug troubleshooting tools, be aware that output formats vary with each protocol. Some protocols generate a single line of output per packet, whereas others generate multiple lines of output per packet.

- Some **debug** commands generate large amounts of output; others generate only occasional output. Some generate lines of text, and others generate information in field format.

- **debug** commands can obtain information about network traffic and router or switch status. Use these commands with great care.

NOTE   For more details about the impact of a **debug** command, check Cisco.com or consult with a technical support representative.

Configurations and Commands Useful When Troubleshooting

Time stamping of debug and log messages is essential to proper debugging. Knowing time frames and exact instances when events occur is critical to troubleshooting performance issues. To configure Cisco IOS–based switches to time stamp debug and log messages, use the following Cisco IOS global configuration commands:

```
service timestamps debug {datetime | uptime} [{msec} {localtime} {show-timezone}]
service timestamps log {datetime | uptime} [{msec} {localtime} {show-timezone}]
```

Other parameters exist for configuring debug and logging time stamps; the commands listed with the **msec** and **localtime** options add millisecond time stamps using the switch's current time to all messages. These parameters are found to be the most useful when troubleshooting from the CLI. For Cisco CatOS–based switches, use the following command to enable and disable logging:

```
set logging timestamp [enable | disable]
```

On Cisco CatOS–based switches, time-stamp logging is a default configuration.

Noting CPU load before enabling debugging is necessary to prevent high CPU conditions. To determine the current CPU load before enabling debug commands, use the following Cisco IOS command:

```
show processes
```

This command reveals the current processes that are running and the total CPU utilization. It is not advisable to enable debugging when the CPU utilization is over 70 percent; doing so may further increase CPU utilization and cause anomalous behavior on the switch. Recall that current Catalyst switches use hardware switching for packet forwarding, and CPU utilization is not a direct correlation of packet performance.

Two other useful commands when enabling and disabling debugs are the **no debug all** and **undebug all** commands. These commands are useful for immediately disabling all debugs to prevent further CPU utilization.

The Impact of debug Commands and Recommended Use

Generally, if an abnormal situation results in the use of debugs, temporarily trading off switching and CPU efficiency for the opportunity to rapidly diagnose and correct the problem may be ideal. To effectively use debugging tools, determine the following information:

- The impact that the troubleshooting tool has on router or switch performance
- The most selective and focused use of the diagnostic tool
- How to minimize the impact of your troubleshooting on other processes that are competing for resources on the network device
- How to stop the troubleshooting tool when you are finished diagnosing so that the router or switch can resume its most efficient switching

Using debugs to troubleshoot a lab network that lacks end-user application traffic is different from troubleshooting in a production network. Without proper precautions, the impact of broadly focused **debug** commands could worsen the issue. With the proper, selective, and temporary use of these tools, though, debugs can obtain potentially useful information without needing a protocol analyzer or other third-party tool.

Some considerations for using **debug** commands are as follows:

- You are highly advised to use **debug** commands only during periods of lower network traffic and fewer users. Debugging during these periods reduces the effect these commands have on other users on the system.

- Gather the information from the **debug** commands in a timely manner and immediately disable the **debug** command (and any other related configuration settings, if any) to enable the router or switch to resume its normal behavior. Then, using the information collected during the **debug** window, continue problem solving and create a better-targeted action plan for additional **debug** commands if necessary.

All **debug** commands are entered in privileged EXEC mode, and most **debug** commands do not require parameters. Nevertheless, debug parameters are useful in isolating debug information to a specific interface or feature.

NOTE   Do not use the **debug all** command, because this debug can cause a system crash due to the overwhelming number of processes being debugged.

To list and see a brief description of all the debugging command options, enter the **debug ?** command in privileged EXEC mode.

By default, the network server sends the output from **debug** commands and system error messages to the console. Monitoring debugging output by using a virtual terminal connection is the preferable debugging method to the console port. However, in certain situations, virtual terminal access may be affected by the issue you are trying to debug. To redirect debugging output, use the **logging** command options within configuration mode. Possible destinations include the console, virtual terminals, internal buffer, and UNIX hosts running a syslog server. The syslog format is compatible with 4.3 Berkeley Standard Distribution (BSD) UNIX and its derivatives. Note that by default, virtual terminal sessions do not display debug or logging output; enter the **terminal monitor** EXEC command to enable display of logging and debug output to the current virtual terminal session.

For additional information about troubleshooting using protocol analyzers and other debugging and baselining tips, see Chapter 17, "Performance and Connectivity Troubleshooting Tools for Multilayer Switches."

Initial Configuration Troubleshooting Tips

This section discusses several basic and common initial configuration issues that arise when configuring a Catalyst switch for the first time. Specifically, the section covers the following issues:

- What to do when you are unable to connect to a Cisco Catalyst switch via the console port
- What to do when you are unable to establish IP connectivity to or from the switch using Telnet or SSH

What to Do When You Are Unable to Connect to the Switch via the Console Port

If you are unable to connect to the switch via the console port, perform the following troubleshooting steps. The order of the steps is not significant:

Step 1 Verify that you are using the correct type of cable: straight-through or rollover. (Refer to the hardware documentation for your switch Supervisor Engine to find out which cable to use.) Furthermore, several models of Catalyst switches have a front panel selectable toggle switch for selecting either console connectivity via straight-through or rollover cable. Select the opposite setting, and determine whether console connectivity is working.

Step 2 Make sure the terminal configuration matches the switch console port configuration. The Cisco default console port settings are 9600 baud, 8 data bits, no parity, 1 stop bit for any current Catalyst switch.

Step 3 Make sure the cable pinouts for the terminal serial port are correct for your Catalyst Supervisor Engine or fixed-port density Catalyst switch. (Refer to the hardware documentation for your switch Supervisor Engine.)

Step 4 Attempt to make console connectivity via more than one workstation or terminal server to rule out the possibility that the workstation or terminal server is contributing to the console connectivity problem.

Step 5 Check and verify whether the Catalyst switch is receiving sufficient power and airflow.

Step 6 Locate the front panel status LINK LEDs and note any light illumination. Check the product documentation for an explanation of these indicators because they may indicate a hardware fault or other state that is preventing console access.

Step 7 Occasionally, the console speed of a Cisco router, switch, or other network device might be set to 38400 bps for troubleshooting purposes. If all other attempts to connect to the console port have failed, attempt to establish a connection through the console port with a serial speed of 38400 bps.

What to Do When You Are Unable to Establish IP Connectivity to or from a Switch Using Telnet or SSH

If you are unable to establish connectivity to or from a switch using Telnet or SSH, perform the following troubleshooting steps. The order of these steps is significant:

Step 1 Make sure the LINK LED for the port connecting the switch to the network and the port connecting the respective workstation is green. In addition, verify that all switch ports connecting switches and workstations from the CLI are in the UP state using the **show interface** command with Cisco IOS and show port with Cisco CatOS.

Step 2 Check the cabling and ensure that the port connecting the switch to the network is properly cabled. Switch-to-switch connections typically use crossover cables.

Step 3 For SC-type or ST-type fiber connections, make sure the transmit (Tx) connectors on each link attach to the receive (Rx) connectors on the other end of the link.

Step 4 Using the **show interface** command, make sure the respective management interface (sc0, VLAN, or interface) states are in the UP state and properly configured.

Step 5 Make sure the IP address, subnet mask, and VLAN membership of the switch interface (sc0, me1, VLAN interface, or Layer 3 interface) are correct using the **show interface** command.

Step 6 Verify the default gateway configuration or IP routing configuration by using the **show ip route** command.

Step 7 Make sure the host configuration for the IP address, subnet mask, default gateway, speed, and duplex setting used by remote access software (Telnet, SSH or Java) to the switch is correct.

Step 8 If the host is in the same subnet as the switch interface, verify that the switch interface to which the host connects resides in the same VLAN. Use the **show interface** and **show configuration** commands to verify the VLAN settings.

Step 9 If the host resides in a different subnet than the management IP address, make sure the default gateway on the switch resides in the same subnet as the default gateway router. Use the **show ip route** command to verify the default gateway settings.

Step 10 Using the **show interface** command on Cisco IOS–based switches and the **show port** command on Cisco CatOS–based switches, make sure the speed and duplex settings on the host and the appropriate switch ports are correct.

Step 11 Using the **show mac address dynamic** command on Cisco IOS–based switches and the **show cam dynamic** command on Cisco CatOS–based switches, make sure the switch is learning the MAC address of the host.

Step 12 Attempt to establish IP connectivity on the same IP subnet in which the management IP address of the switch resides.

Step 13 Move the switch and the host to different switch interfaces and retry connecting to the switch over IP.

Study Tips

The following bullets review important BCMSN certification exam preparation points of this chapter. The bullets only briefly highlight the main points of this chapter related to the BCMSN exam and should be used only as supplemental study material. Consult the text of this chapter for additional information regarding these topics:

- Always use SSH instead of Telnet for remote access to Cisco devices because of the security risks involved with Telnet transmitting passwords in clear-text and other security issues.

- Although more secure than Telnet because of encryption, SSH still has vulnerabilities.

- Layer 2–only switches require a default-gateway configuration to reach non-local IP subnets.

- Always configure the following features for management and troubleshooting purposes on Cisco routers: privileged passwords, remote access passwords, IP management, timestamps, syslog, NTP, and SNMP.

- To copy a file to a Catalyst switch's bootflash, use the **copy tftp bootflash:** command.

- To copy a file to a Catalyst switch PCMCIA Flash card, use the **copy tftp slot0:** command.

- To copy a file to a Catalyst switch ATA disk (PCMCIA or SanDisk), use the **copy tftp disk0:** command.

- When troubleshooting, use **show** commands to get state information and **debug** commands to gather real-time information.

- Currently, all shipping Catalyst switches run exclusively Cisco IOS, with the exception of the Catalyst 6500 family of switches. The Catalyst 6500 family of switches still has the option of running either Cisco IOS or Cisco CatOS.
- Before loading Cisco IOS onto a Catalyst switch, always check for required features, versions, bug fixes, and memory requirements.

Table 3-9 lists important commands to review for the BCMSN certification exam.

Table 3-9   *Commands to Review*

Command	Description
configure terminal	Enters the global configuration mode
copy running-config bootflash:	Copies the running-configuraton to bootflash
copy running-config startup-config	Copies the running-configuration to the startup-configuration (i.e., saves the configuration to NVRAM)
copy running-config tftp:	Copies the running-configuration to a TFTP server
copy tftp bootflash:	Initiates a macro to copy a software image from a TFTP server to bootflash
copy tftp disk0:	Initiates a macro to copy a software image from a TFTP server to an ATA disk in disk0
copy tftp slot0:	Initiates a macro to copy a software image from a TFTP server to the PCMCIA card in slot0
delete *flash-device:filename*	Deletes an image on the device
format *flash-device:filename*	Formats a device for use on the current system; all data on device is deleted during format
(config-if)#**ip address** *ipaddr subnet-mask*	Configures the IP address and subnet mask of an interface
(config)#**ip default-gateway** *ip-address*	Configures a Layer 2-only switch or a Layer 3 switch with IP routing disabled for a default gateway
no debug all	Immediately disables all enabled debugs
show arp	Displays the ARP table contents
show hardware	Displays hardware information (similar to the **show version** command)
show interface	Displays all interfaces with statistics
show ip interface brief	Displays, in brief output, all interfaces on the system with an IP address and state
show ip route	Displays the IP routing table
show running-config	Displays the running-configuration
show version	Displays the software version, uptime and so on.

continues

Table 3-9 *Commands to Review (Continued)*

Command	Description
squeeze *flash-device:filename*	Removes deleted files on the device and recovers file system space
(config)#[**no**] **shutdown**	Administratively shuts down an interface
(config)#[**no**] **switchport**	Configures an interface as a Layer 2 interface
terminal monitor	Configures the virtual terminal to monitor system messages

Summary

All Cisco Catalyst families of switches are moving to supporting only Cisco IOS for new platforms and new feature support. The only Catalyst switch still using Cisco CatOS for new features and products is the Catalyst 6500 family of switches. As a result, consider upgrading and planning for Cisco IOS–based Catalyst switches as appropriate.

The initial configuration of a Catalyst switch involves basic management and IP configuration parameters that ease administration and troubleshooting. These management and IP configuration parameters include clock settings, NTP, DNS, and SSH configurations.

When performing basic troubleshooting, use **show** commands to gather state information and **debug** commands to gather real-time information. Note that the **debug** commands may affect the performance of the router, so you need special consideration when enabling these **debug** commands on production networks.

Configuration Exercise: Configuring a Cisco IOS–Based Catalyst Switch

Complete this configuration exercise to familiarize yourself with the initial configuration of a Cisco IOS–based Catalyst switch discussed in the chapter.

Required Resources

The resources and equipment required to complete this exercise are as follows:

- A Cisco IOS–based Catalyst switch such as a Catalyst 2950, 3550, 3560, 3750, 4500, or 6500
- A terminal server or workstation connected directly to the console port of the Catalyst switch
- Ethernet connection for IP connectivity

- Available IP address for assignment to the management IP address of the switch
- IP addresses of DNS and syslog servers
- Network connectivity via another switch or router
- TFTP server
- Workstation capable of Telnet and SSH

Exercise Objective

The purpose of this exercise is to demonstrate the initial configuration of a Cisco IOS–based Catalyst switch acting as a Layer 2 switch. At the end of this exercise, you will be able to execute the following initial configurations on Cisco IOS–based Catalyst switches:

- Connect to Catalyst switch via the console port
- Configure the switch for management access via IP
- Configure IP services such as DNS, Telnet, and SSH
- Upgrade the Cisco IOS to a different software version

The exercise exposes topics (such as VLANs) that are found in later chapters; however, the main purpose of this exercise is to demonstrate initial switch configuration.

Network Diagram

Figure 3-3 shows the network layout for this lab exercise.

Figure 3-3   *Network Diagram for Lab Exercise*

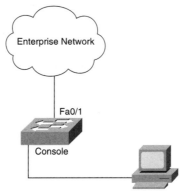

Command List

In this lab exercise, you will use the commands listed in Table 3-10. These commands are in alphabetical order so that you can easily locate the information you need. Refer to this table if you need configuration command assistance during the lab exercise. The table includes only the specific parameters used in the example and not all the available options for the command.

Table 3-10 *Command List for Lab Exercise*

Command	Description
archive download-sw /*overwrite source-url*	Automates software upgrade procedure on Catalyst 2950 and 3550 family of switches
boot system *filesystem:filename*	Configures the system boot image
clock set *hh:mm:ss month day year*	Configures the clock date and time
clock summer-time *zone* **recurring** [*week day month hh:mm week day month hh:mm* [**offset**]]	Configures recurring time adjustments, such as daylight saving time
clock timezone *zone hours-offset*	Configures the time zone in offset from UTC
configure terminal	Enters the configuration mode
copy running-config startup-config	Copies the running configuration to NVRAM
copy tftp flash	Executes a procedure to copy a file from a TFTP server to the IFS
dir flash:	Displays the contents of the IFS
enable	Enters the privilege mode
end	Configuration EXEC command to end the configuration mode
exit	Ends the current configuration mode leaf
hostname *hostname*	Configures switch with a descriptive name
interface FastEthernet ׀ **GigabitEthernet** *interface*	Enters an interface configuration mode
interface vlan *vlan-id*	Enters the VLAN configuration interface mode
ip address *ip-addr subnet-mask*	Configures an IP address and subnet mask
ip default-gateway *ip-addr*	Configures a default gateway for switches that do not perform Layer 3 routing
ip domain-lookup	Enables domain name lookup via DNS
ip domain-name *domain-name*	Configures the Internet domain suffix for the switch name

Table 3-10   *Command List for Lab Exercise (Continued)*

Command	Description
ip name-server *ip-addr*	Configures the domain name servers (DNS)
logging *ip-addr*	Configures the system that is logging the server destination IP address
ntp server *ip-addr*	Configures the NTP server IP address
no shutdown	Configures an interface in the Administrative UP state
ping *ip-addr*	Sends ICMP echoes to a specific destination
reload	Soft reboots the switch
show clock	Displays the current time and date
show ntp associations	Displays the NTP associations
show version	Displays the running software version, and so on.
switchport access vlan *vlan-id*	Configures an interface for a specific VLAN ID
transport input	Configures the virtual terminal for allowable protocols
vlan *vlan-id*	Adds or removes a VLAN ID in the VLAN database
write erase	Erases the startup-config

Task 1: Establish Console (Out-of-Band) Connectivity and Configure the Switch Name

Step 1   Connect the Catalyst switch to a terminal server or directly to a workstation's serial port for out-of-band connectivity.

Step 2   Verify the serial port configuration for out-of-band access.

Step 3   Using the terminal server or PC from Step 1, verify connectivity to the console port of the switch. If this is an initial install of a Catalyst switch, the prompt will indicate Switch> or a prompt asking to enter initial configuration dialog.

```
IOS (tm) C3550 Software (C3550-I5K2L2Q3-M), Version 12.1(13)EA1a,
RELEASE SOFTWARE (fc1)
Copyright (c) 1986-2003 by cisco Systems, Inc.
Compiled Tue 25-Mar-03 23:56 by yenanh
00:00:42: %LINK-3-UPDOWN: Interface FastEthernet0/1, changed state to up
00:00:43: %LINEPROTO-5-UPDOWN: Line protocol on Interface
FastEthernet0/1, changed state to up
00:01:14: %LINEPROTO-5-UPDOWN: Line protocol on Interface Vlan1,
changed state to up
Would you like to enter the initial configuration dialog? [yes/no]: n
```

```
Press RETURN to get started!


Switch>
```

Note	If previous configuration parameters exist on the Catalyst switch, issue the **erase start** command to restore the configuration back to the default. Next, after issuing the **write erase** command, issue the **reload** command and answer **no** to the prompt for saving the configuration to reload the switch with the default configuration. Some versions of Cisco IOS software store VLAN information in a vlan.dat file in bootflash. Simply delete this file to delete the VLAN configuration.

Step 4 Configure the system switch name using the global configuration command hostname *hostname*.

```
Switch>enable


Switch#configure terminal
Enter configuration commands, one per line.  End with CNTL/Z.
Switch(config)#hostname Fl1Rm226


Fl1Rm226(config)#
```

Task 2: Configure the Switch for IP Connectivity

Step 1 Using an available IP address, configure the switch with an IP address in the appropriate VLAN.

```
Fl1Rm226(config)#vlan 1
Fl1Rm226(config-vlan)#exit
Fl1Rm226(config)#interface vlan 1
Fl1Rm226(config-if)#ip address 10.1.118.103 255.255.255.0
Fl1Rm226(config-if)#no shutdown
Fl1Rm226(config-if)#exit
Fl1Rm226(config)#interface FastEthernet0/1
Fl1Rm226(config-if)#switchport access vlan 1
```

```
Fl1Rm226(config-if)#no shutdown
Fl1Rm226(config-if)#exit
```

Step 2   Configure the switch for the appropriate default gateway for the configured IP subnet.

```
Fl1Rm226(config)#ip default-gateway 10.1.118.1
Fl1Rm226(config)#exit
```

Step 3   Verify IP connectivity using the **ping** command.

```
Fl1Rm226#ping 10.1.118.1

Type escape sequence to abort.
Sending 5, 100-byte ICMP Echos to 10.1.118.1, timeout is 2 seconds:
!!!!!
Success rate is 100 percent (5/5), round-trip min/avg/max = 1/1/4 ms
Fl1Rm226#ping 10.1.116.1

Type escape sequence to abort.
Sending 5, 100-byte ICMP Echos to ping 10.1.116.1, timeout is 2 seconds:
!!!!!
Success rate is 100 percent (5/5), round-trip min/avg/max = 1/1/4 ms
```

Step 4   Configure the switch for DNS lookup.

```
Fl1Rm226(config)#ip name-server 10.1.1.200 10.1.1.201
Fl1Rm226(config)#ip domain-lookup
Fl1Rm226(config)#exit
```

Step 5   Verify DNS operation using the **ping** command.

```
Fl1Rm226#ping www.cisco.com
Translating "www.cisco.com"...domain server (10.1.1.200) [OK]

Type escape sequence to abort.
Sending 5, 100-byte ICMP Echos to 10.1.1.200, timeout is 2 seconds:
!!!!!
Success rate is 100 percent (5/5), round-trip min/avg/max = 60/60/64 ms
```

Task 3: Configure the Switch Usernames and Passwords for Privileged and In-Band Access

Step 1   Configure the enable password and virtual terminal password.

```
Fl1Rm226#configure terminal
Enter configuration commands, one per line.  End with CNTL/Z.
Fl1Rm226(config)#enable password cisco
Fl1Rm226(config)#line vty 0 4
Fl1Rm226(config-line)#password cisco
Fl1Rm226(config-line)#exit
```

Step 2   Configure local usernames and passwords for SSH sessions.

```
Fl1Rm226(config)#username cisco password cisco
```

Task 4: Configure the Switch for SSH and Disable Telnet Access

Step 1   Enable AAA authentication for SSH connectivity.

```
Fl1Rm226(config)#aaa new-model
```

Step 2   Configure the switch for SSH.

```
Fl1Rm226(config)#ip domain-name cisco.com


Fl1Rm226(config)#crypto key generate rsa
The name for the keys will be: Fl1Rm226.cisco.com
Choose the size of the key modulus in the range of 360 to 2048 for your
   General Purpose Keys. Choosing a key modulus greater than 512 may take
   a few minutes.

How many bits in the modulus [512]: 2048
Generating RSA keys ...
[OK]


00:56:19: %SSH-5-ENABLED: SSH 1.5 has been enabled
```

Step 3   Configure the switch for in-band connectivity via SSH only.

```
Fl1Rm226(config)#line vty 0 15
Fl1Rm226(config-line)#transport input ssh
Fl1Rm226(config-line)#exit
Fl1Rm226(config)#exit
```

Step 4   Verify that the switch is only accessible via SSH for in-band connectivity.

```
SUN_Workstation:43> ssh -l cisco 10.1.118.103
cisco@10.18.118.103's password: cisco

Fl1Rm226>exit
Connection to 172.18.118.103 closed.
SUN_Workstation:44> telnet 10.1.118.103
Trying 10.1.118.103...
telnet: Unable to connect to remote host: Connection refused
```

Task 5: Configure the Switch Time Settings, NTP Configuration, and System Logging Configuration

Step 1   Set the clock correctly, and configure NTP on the switch to update its time to an NTP server.

```
Fl1Rm226#clock set 11:22:00 november 6 2003
Fl1Rm226#show clock
11:22:02.051 UTC Fri Jun 6 2003

Fl1Rm226#configure terminal
Fl1Rm226(config)#clock timezone EST -5
Fl1Rm226(config)#clock summer-time EST recurring
Fl1Rm226(config)#ntp server 10.1.1.202
Fl1Rm226(config)#exit
Fl1Rm226#show ntp associations

address        ref clock    st  when  poll reach  delay  offset    disp
*~10.1.1.202   .GPS.         1   253   256   377    5.4    0.09     0.1
 * master (synced), # master (unsynced), + selected, - candidate,
   ~ configured
```

Step 2   Configure the switch to log all default messages to a syslog server.

```
Fl1Rm226(config)#logging 10.1.1.199
```

Task 6: Upgrade the Switch Cisco IOS Version to a Later Release

Step 1   Download the latest software version for the switch from Cisco.com.

Step 2   Following the upgrade instructions for the specific Catalyst switch used for this exercise, upgrade the switch to the latest software version.

Method 1:

```
Fl1Rm226#copy tftp flash
Address or name of remote host []? 10.1.1.21
Source filename []? c3550-i5k2l2q3-mz.121-13.EA1a.bin
Destination filename [c3550-i5k2l2q3-mz.121-13.EA1a.bin]?

Accessing tftp://10.1.1.21/c3550-i5k2l2q3-mz.121-13.EA1a.bin...
Loading c3550-i5k2l2q3-mz.121-13.EA1a.bin from 10.1.1.21 (via Vlan118): !!
(text deleted)
!!!!!!!!!!!!!!!!!!!!!!!!!!!
[OK - 4578754 bytes]

4578754 bytes copied in 116.884 secs (39173 bytes/sec)
Switch#dir flash:
```

```
Directory of flash:/

    3  -rwx      1955   Mar 05 1993 23:00:14   config.text
    4  -rwx         5   Mar 05 1993 23:00:14   private-config.text
    6  -rwx       856   Mar 03 1993 16:23:01   vlan.dat
   23  -rwx         0   Mar 04 1993 00:26:17   env_vars
    7  -rwx       346   Mar 04 1993 00:26:17   system_env_vars

Fl1Rm226#configure terminal
Enter configuration commands, one per line.  End with CNTL/Z.
Fl1Rm226(config)#boot system flash:c3550-i5k2l2q3-mz.121-13.EA1a.bin
Fl1Rm226(config)#no boot system flash:c3550-i5q3l2-mz.121-12c.EA1.bin
Fl1Rm226(config)#end

Fl1Rm226#copy running-config startup-config

Fl1Rm226#show boot
BOOT path-list:        flash:c3550-i5k2l2q3-mz.121-13.EA1a.bin
Config file:           flash:/config.text
Private Config file:   flash:/private-config.text
Enable Break:          no
Manual Boot:           no
HELPER path-list:
NVRAM/Config file
     buffer size:      393216
Fl1Rm226#reload
Proceed with reload? [confirm]

01:27:11: %SYS-5-RELOAD: Reload requested

(text deleted)

00:00:37: %SYS-5-RESTART: System restarted --
Cisco Internetwork Operating System Software
IOS (tm) C3550 Software (C3550-I5K2L2Q3-M), Version 12.1(13)EA1a,
RELEASE SOFTWARE (fc1)
Copyright (c) 1986-2003 by cisco Systems, Inc.
Compiled Tue 25-Mar-03 23:56 by yenanh

Fl1Rm226>en

Password: cisco
Fl1Rm226#show version
Cisco Internetwork Operating System Software
```

```
IOS (tm) C3550 Software (C3550-I5K2L2Q3-M), Version 12.1(13)EA1a,
RELEASE SOFTW
ARE (fc1)
Copyright (c) 1986-2003 by cisco Systems, Inc.
Compiled Tue 25-Mar-03 23:56 by yenanh
Image text-base: 0x00003000, data-base: 0x008BA914


ROM: Bootstrap program is C3550 boot loader

Fl1Rm226 uptime is 4 minutes
System returned to ROM by power-on
System restarted at 12:42:04 EST Sat Jun 21 2003
System image file is "flash:c3550-i5k2l2q3-mz.121-13.EA1a.bin"


(text deleted)
```

Method 2:

```
Fl1Rm226#archive download-sw /overwrite tftp://198.30.20.19/c3550-
i5q3l2- tar.121-13.EA1.tar

(text deleted)
Loading c3550-i5k2l2q3-tar.121-13.EA1a.tar from 172.18.118.184 (via
Vlan118): !
(text deleted)
!!!!!!!!!!!!!!!!!!!!!!!!!
extracting info (261 bytes)!
[OK - 6597120 bytes]


Image info:
    Version Suffix: i5k2l2q3-121-13.EA1a
    Image Name: c3550-i5k2l2q3-mz.121-13.EA1a.bin
    Version Directory: c3550-i5k2l2q3-mz.121-13.EA1a
    Ios Image Size: 4580864
    Total Image Size: 6596096
    Image Feature: LAYER_3|MIN_DRAM_MEG=64
    Image Family: C3550
Extracting files...
Loading c3550-i5k2l2q3-tar.121-13.EA1a.tar from 172.18.118.184 (via
Vlan118): !
c3550-i5k2l2q3-mz.121-13.EA1a/ (directory)
c3550-i5k2l2q3-mz.121-13.EA1a/html/ (directory)
extracting c3550-i5k2l2q3-mz.121-13.EA1a/html/homepage.htm (3992
bytes)!
(text deleted)

extracting c3550-i5k2l2q3-mz.121-13.EA1a/info (261 bytes)
```

```
extracting info (261 bytes)!
extracting info.ver (261 bytes)
[OK - 6597120 bytes]

New software image installed in flash:c3550-i5k2l2q3-mz.121-13.EA1a
Configuring system to use new image...done.

Fl1Rm226#reload

Proceed with reload? [confirm]

01:27:11: %SYS-5-RELOAD: Reload requested

(text deleted)

00:00:37: %SYS-5-RESTART: System restarted --
Cisco Internetwork Operating System Software
IOS (tm) C3550 Software (C3550-I5K2L2Q3-M), Version 12.1(13)EA1a,
RELEASE SOFTWARE (fc1)
Copyright (c) 1986-2003 by cisco Systems, Inc.
Compiled Tue 25-Mar-03 23:56 by yenanh

Fl1Rm226>en


Password: cisco
Fl1Rm226#show version
Cisco Internetwork Operating System Software
IOS (tm) C3550 Software (C3550-I5K2L2Q3-M), Version 12.1(13)EA1a,
RELEASE SOFTW
ARE (fc1)
Copyright (c) 1986-2003 by cisco Systems, Inc.
Compiled Tue 25-Mar-03 23:56 by yenanh
Image text-base: 0x00003000, data-base: 0x008BA914

ROM: Bootstrap program is C3550 boot loader

Fl1Rm226 uptime is 4 minutes
System returned to ROM by power-on
System restarted at 12:42:04 EST Sat Jun 21 2003
System image file is "flash:c3550-i5k2l2q3-mz.121-13.EA1a.bin"

(text deleted)
```

Review Questions

For multiple-choice questions, there might be more than one correct answer.

1 True or False: Telnet sends passwords in clear-text, making interception of these passwords easy. (Explain your answer.)

2 True or False: Layer 3 switches require a default gateway to reach remote networks. (Explain your answer.)

3 True or False: Although SSH supports encryption, it still has protocol vulnerabilities.

4 True or False: When configuring a switch for management access that is used for Layer 3 routing, a default gateway is required to reach non-local subnets.

5 True or False: TFTP is not a secure method of copying images to and from a Cisco router, switch, or other network device.

6 By default on the Catalyst 6500, all interfaces are Layer 3 routed ports in the administratively down state. Which of the following interface-level commands in Cisco IOS enables the interface?

  a **shutdown**

  b **no shutdown**

  c **up**

  d **link-up**

  e **switchport mode access**

  f **no switchport mode shutdown**

7 Which of the following commands display(s) information about an interface state as being up or down in Cisco IOS?

  a **show port**

  b **show mac**

  c **show interface status**

  d **show ip interface brief**

  e **show switchport**

  f **show hardware**

8 Which of the following file systems is (are) not supported on Catalyst switches?

  a PCMCIA flash card

  b Flash disk

  c FTP

  d TFTP

  e NFS

9 Which of the following Catalyst 6500 Supervisor Engines uses a Cisco IOS image with the s72033 prefix?

  a Supervisor Engine I with an MSFC

  b Supervisor Engine I with an MSFC2

  c Supervisor Engine II with an MSFC2

  d Supervisor Engine 720 with an MSFC3 and PFC3

10 Which of the following commands immediately disables all running debugs?

  a **undebug all**

  b **no all**

  c **no debug all**

  d **debug no all**

11 Which of the following are valid types of cables, depending on connection method, for making console connections to any Cisco Catalyst switch?

  a Crossover cable

  b Rollover cable

  c Straight-through cable

12 Should public and private strings not be used for SNMPv2 community strings?

13 What is the default console baud setting of Cisco Catalyst switches? Can this be changed? Is there another baud setting that is sometimes used?

14 Which command shows the hardware modules installed in a Cisco Catalyst switch?

15 Which command should be sent to the Cisco TAC when opening a case?

16 Which command is used to determine the existing contents and the remaining space available in the IFS?

17 Which command displays the current software version and the uptime of a switch?

18 Which command saves the current running configuration to NVRAM?

19 Which command copies a software image via FTP to disk0:?

20 Which command loads a configuration from TFTP to the running configuration?

This chapter covers the following topics:

- Implementing, Configuring, Verifying, and Troubleshooting VLANs, and the Benefits of VLANs in a Multilayer Switched Network

- Understanding and Configuring Private VLANs

- Implementing, Configuring, Verifying, and Troubleshooting VLAN Trunks in a Multilayer Switched Network

- Configuring, Verifying, and Troubleshooting the VLAN Trunking Protocol

## CHAPTER 4

Implementing and Configuring VLANs

Previous chapters have discussed the network architectures that are associated with Cisco multilayer switched networks and the basic configuration of multilayer switches. This and subsequent chapters discuss the features of multilayer switches in detail, along with each feature's implementation and benefits to the multilayer switched network.

VLANs, trunking, and the VLAN Trunking Protocol (VTP) are significant features of multilayer switched networks, and implementation of these features in multilayer switched networks improves overall network performance, scalability, security, and availability. Cisco Systems, Inc. provides VLAN-capable solutions across its entire suite of internetworking switches and mid-range to high-end routers. VLANs not only solve many of the immediate problems associated with administrative changes, but they also provide for improved scalability, interoperability, and increased dedicated throughput.

A VLAN trunk is a physical point-to-point link that is primarily used to carry frames for multiple VLANs. VLAN trunks are common in any multilayer switched network; therefore, network architects need to understand VLANs to be able to implement and troubleshoot them appropriately.

Furthermore, Cisco switches use VTP to distribute and synchronize information about VLANs that are configured throughout a switched network. VTP reduces the manual configuration that is needed on each switch in the network. In a large switched network, VTP allows enterprises to manage the VLAN implementation consistently.

This chapter discusses VLANs, trunking, VTP, and their inherent advantages within a Cisco multilayer switched network. In brief, this chapter covers the following topics:

* VLANs
* Private VLANs
* VLAN trunking
* VLAN Trunking Protocol

In terms of preparing for the CCNP BCMSN switching exam, focus on all the sections in this chapter except the section on VTP version 3. VTP version 3 is a new feature that is not widely deployed or covered on the CCNP BCMSN switching exam.

VLANs

A *VLAN* is a logical group of end devices with a common set of requirements independent of their physical location, as shown in Figure 4-1, where Sales, HR, and Engineering are three different VLANs spread on all three floors. End devices include end-user workstations, servers, routers, and the like.

Figure 4-1 *VLAN Overview*

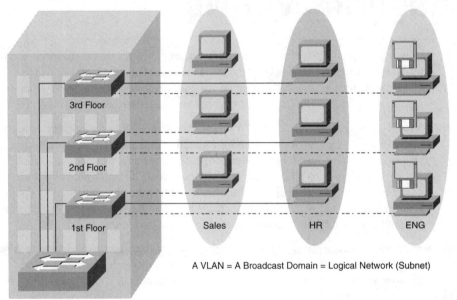

A VLAN = A Broadcast Domain = Logical Network (Subnet)

Larger, flat networks generally consist of many end devices where broadcasts and unknown unicast packets are flooded on all ports in the network, as shown in the top portion of Figure 4-2. One advantage of using VLANs is the ability to segment the Layer 2 broadcast domain. All devices in a VLAN are members of the same broadcast domain. If an end device transmits a Layer 2 broadcast, all other members of the VLAN receive the broadcast. Switches filter the broadcast from all the ports or devices that are not part of the same VLAN, as shown in the bottom portion of Figure 4-2.

Although switches do not propagate Layer 2 broadcasts between VLANs, VLANs are slightly different from a physical subnet. A physical subnet consists of devices on a physical cable segment. A logical subnet consists of devices that communicate with each other regardless of their physical location. As a result, VLANs are a type of logical subnet where interconnectivity of end devices is not directly limited by physical location. Instead, switch configurations limit interconnectivity of VLANs. Furthermore, VLANs may exist anywhere in the switch network. Because a VLAN is a single broadcast domain, a VLAN generally belongs to one IP subnet. To communicate between VLANs, packets need to pass through a router or Layer 3 device.

Figure 4-2   *Layer 2 New Broadcast Domain Boundary with VLANs*

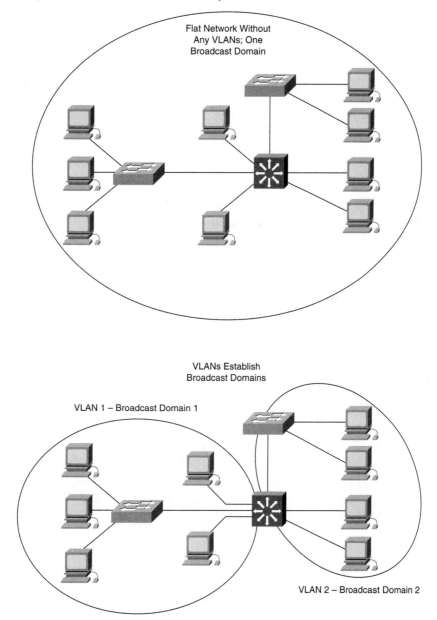

End-to-end VLANs are VLANs that span throughout the entire network. Local VLANs are VLANs that are local to a specific domain, such as Building Access submodule switches and their respective Building Distribution submodule. An end-to-end VLAN may span several wiring closets or even several buildings. End-to-end VLANs are usually associated with a workgroup, such as a department or project team. For redundancy, end-to-end VLANs need the Spanning Tree Protocol (STP), which is discussed in subsequent chapters. As a result of large spanning-tree topologies and simplified network management and troubleshooting with the use of local VLANs compared to end-to-end VLANs, designs using local VLANS, illustrated in Chapters 1 and 2, are becoming more popular.

Because VLANs are an important aspect of any multilayer switched network, all Cisco Catalyst switches support VLANs. A Catalyst switch implements VLANs by virtually limiting data forwarding to ports within the same VLAN. For example, when a broadcast frame arrives on a switch port, the switch retransmits the frame only to ports that belong to the same VLAN. The implication is that using VLANs on Catalyst switches improves scalability by limiting the transmission of unicast, multicast, and broadcast traffic.

Generally, a port carries traffic only for the single VLAN. For a VLAN to span across multiple switches, Catalyst switches use trunks. A trunk carries traffic for multiple VLANs by using Inter-Switch Link (ISL) encapsulation or IEEE 802.1Q. This chapter discusses trunking in more detail in the "VLAN Trunking" section.

This section continues the discussion of VLAN by explaining the following topics related to the implementation and configuration of VLANs:

- Implementing VLANs in multilayer switched networks
- Mapping VLANS to a hierarchical network
- Static and dynamic VLANS
- VLAN ranges
- Configuring VLANs
- Verifying the VLAN configurations
- Troubleshooting VLANs

Implementing VLANs in Multilayer Switched Networks

VLANs are helpful in improving the scalability of multilayer switched networks. The following subsections discuss the benefits and implementation of VLANs in multilayer switched networks.

Understanding the Role and Benefits of VLANs in the Multilayer Switched Network Design

Implementation of VLANs in multilayer switched networks provides scalability, improved performance, and higher availability. The following list details several benefits inherent to VLANs in multilayer switched networks:

- **Efficient bandwidth utilization**—VLANs solve the scalability problems found in large, flat networks by dividing the network into smaller broadcast domains or subnets. Furthermore, end devices require the use of routers to route packets across VLANs.

- **Security**—VLANs provide a basic level of security by allowing segregation of frames that contain sensitive or critical information from unauthorized users on separate VLANs. In addition, VLAN boundaries are marked by a Layer 3 interface where additional security measures, such as access lists, are applicable. In addition, several Catalyst switches support VLAN access lists for Layer 2 application.
- **Load balancing multiple paths**—Combined with routing, VLANs intelligently determine the best path to a destination and offer the ability to load-balance when multiple paths to a destination exist.
- **Isolation of failure domains**—One of the most important reasons to implement VLANs is to reduce the impact of network problems. In a flat network, a faulty device, a Layer 2 loop, or a broadcast-intensive application may potentially affect the entire network to the point of a total failure. One of the most effective measures against such network failures is to properly segment the network into VLANs with the use of a router. Using a router with VLANs effectively prevents these types of issues from being propagated from a VLAN to other segments or VLANs while maintaining the ability to route traffic between VLANs.

Benefits of End-to-End and Local VLANs in Campus Networks

An end-to-end VLAN spans the entire switched network, while a local VLAN is limited to a single switch or group of Building Access submodule and Building Distribution submodule switches.

A network that is deploying end-to-end VLANs has the following characteristics:

- End devices such as workstations are grouped into VLANs regardless of physical location.
- When the users and their workstations move around the campus, their VLAN membership typically remains the same.
- Each VLAN has a common set of security and resource requirements for all members across the campus.

Mapping VLANs to a Hierarchical Network

As enterprises move to centralize their network resources, end-to-end VLANs are becoming more difficult to maintain. As a result, enterprise networks are now creating "local" VLAN boundaries around physical boundaries, such as Building Access submodules, rather than around commonality boundaries, such as organizations or departments. In addition, enterprise networks deploy applications that access many resources outside the local VLAN. These types of applications include storage applications, stock tickers, databases, and intranet web services. Although this design of creating local VLANs results in user traffic crossing a Layer 3 router or multilayer switch to reach network resources, this design still allows the network to provide for a deterministic, secure, and consistent method of transporting data, voice, and video. Nevertheless, the use of local VLANs for user end devices maintains the performance and efficiency advantages of VLANs, including collision and broadcast domain segmentation.

Local VLANs, typically used in the Building Access submodule, are also easier to manage and conceptualize than VLANs spanning different areas of the network. A typical VLAN organization configures the minimum number of VLANs on a single access switch within a wiring closet, rather than having VLANs from multiple departments configured on the same switch. Figure 4-3 shows that every Building Access submodule switch belongs to two VLANs, one for voice and one for data, which terminate at the Building Distribution submodule switches.

Figure 4-3   *Local VLANs*

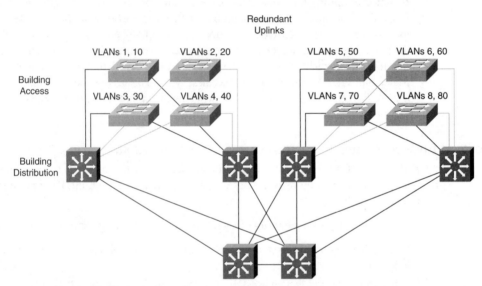

The goal of local VLANs is not to extend the VLANs beyond the Building Distribution submodule, as shown in Figure 4-3. Using the local VLAN structure to provide access into the network and to provide Layer 3 connectivity allows users to move from one VLAN to another without involving network administrators when using features such as DHCP. In addition, local VLANs provide users with the same level of performance regardless of their location, because Layer 3 devices also switch and route at wire rate due to hardware-switching.

Troubleshooting local VLANs that are contained within a single area is much easier than troubleshooting a VLAN and modules that span an entire functional area in the end-to-end design. In addition, because STP is configured for redundancy, the switch limits the STP to only the Building Access and Building Distribution submodules.

Static and Dynamic VLANs

Static VLANs constitute switch ports that are manually assigned to a particular VLAN, as shown in Figure 4-4. Dynamic VLANs, on the other hand, are VLANs that are assigned based on a source Media Access Control (MAC) address that has been entered into a VLAN Management Policy Server (VMPS).

Figure 4-4   *Static VLANs*

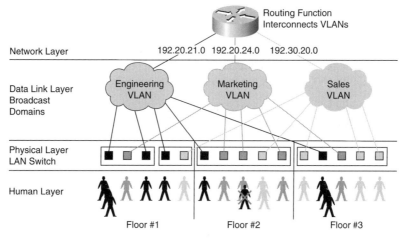

Static VLAN configurations on switches require a VLAN-management application or the use of the command line to assign a specific switch port to a particular VLAN. Although static VLANs require manual entry changes, they are secure, easy to configure, and straightforward to monitor. This type of VLAN assignment method works well in networks where adds, moves, and changes are rare. As shown in Figure 4-4, with the manual configuration of ports with the proper VLAN, if a person who belongs in the Engineering VLAN on Floor 2 tries to connect to the port configured for the Marketing VLAN, that person will not be able to communicate with the members of the Engineering VLAN (as indicated by the "X") until the Engineering VLAN uses Layer 3 routing.

Dynamic VLAN configuration is accomplished by using the VMPS. With dynamic VLANs, the switch assigns a VLAN to a host based on information in the MAC address-to-VLAN mapping on the VMPS. When a host moves from a port on one switch in the network to a port on another switch in the network, the switch assigns the new port to the proper VLAN for that host dynamically. The VMPS contains a database that maps the MAC addresses to VLAN assignments. When VMPS is enabled, the switch downloads a MAC address-to-VLAN mapping database from a Trivial File Transfer Protocol (TFTP) server and begins to service client requests. When a frame arrives on a dynamic port at the Catalyst access switch, the Catalyst switch queries the VMPS for the VLAN assignment based on the MAC address of the arriving frame. A dynamic port belongs to only one VLAN at a time. Multiple hosts may be active on a dynamic port only if they all belong to the same VLAN.

However, VMPS requires its own management overhead. Unless adds, moves, and changes create a significant management overhead, do not use VMPS to maintain end-station MAC addresses and custom filtering tables. Nonetheless, enterprises rarely deploy VMPS and opt for IEEE 802.1X as a security access feature instead. Chapter 14, "Securing Your Multilayer Switched Network to Minimize Service Loss and Data Theft," discusses 802.1X in more detail.

The Catalyst 4000, 5000, and 6500 families of switches running Cisco CatOS support VMPS functionality. In addition, an external server may act as a VMPS. Note, however, that several switches, such as the Cisco Catalyst 2900XL, Catalyst 2950/3550/3560, and Cisco Catalyst 4000 and 4500 families of switches running Cisco IOS, do not support the VMPS functionality, but they do support VMPS client functionality.

This chapter discusses static VLANs in more detail but does not discuss dynamic VLANs any further. To learn more about dynamic VLANs, consult the document "Configuring Dynamic Port VLAN Membership with VMPS" on Cisco.com:

> http://www.cisco.com/en/US/products/hw/switches/ps708/
> products_configuration_guide_chapter09186a00803f586e.html

VLAN Ranges

Cisco Catalyst switches support up to 4096 VLANs depending on platform and software version. Table 4-1 illustrates the VLAN division for Cisco Catalyst switches.

Table 4-1   *VLAN Ranges*

VLAN Ranges	Range	Usage	Propagated via VTP
0, 4095	Reserved	For system use only. You cannot see or use these VLANs.	
1	Normal	Cisco default. You can use this VLAN, but you cannot delete it.	Yes
2–1001	Normal	For Ethernet VLANs. You can create, use, and delete these VLANs.	Yes
1002–1005	Normal	Cisco defaults for FDDI and Token Ring. You cannot delete VLANs 1002–1005.	Yes
1006–1024	Reserved	For system use only. You cannot see or use these VLANS.	
1025–4094	Extended	For Ethernet VLANs only.	Not supported in VTP versions 1 and 2. The switch must be in VTP transparent mode to configure extended-range VLANS. Only supported in version 3.

Configuring VLANs

All Cisco Catalyst switches support VLANs. That said, each Cisco Catalyst switch supports a different number of VLANs, with high-end Cisco Catalyst switches supporting as many as 4096 VLANs. Table 4-2 notes the maximum number of VLANs supported by each model of Catalyst switch.

Table 4-2   *VLAN Support Matrix for Catalyst Switches*

Type of Switch	Maximum No. of VLANs	VLAN IDs Range
Catalyst 2940	4	1–1005
Catalyst 2950/2955	250	1–4094
Catalyst 2960	255	1–4094
Catalyst 2970/3550/3560/3750	1005	1–4094
Catalyst 2848G/2980G/4000/4500	4094	1–4094
Catalyst 6500	4094	1–4094

NOTE   The Catalyst 2950 and 2955 support as many as 64 VLANs with the Standard Software image, and up to 250 VLANs with the Enhanced Software image. Cisco Catalyst switches do not support VLANs 1002 through 1005; these are reserved for Token Ring and FDDI VLANs. Furthermore, the Catalyst 4500 and 6500 families of switches do not support VLANs 1006 through 1024. In addition, several families of switches support more VLANs than the number of Spanning Tree instances. For example, the Cisco Catalyst 2970 supports 1005 VLANs but only 128 Spanning Tree instances. For information on the number of supported Spanning Tree instances, refer to Cisco Product Technical Documentation.

As mentioned in previous chapters, Catalyst switches use either Cisco CatOS or Cisco IOS. This section covers the configuration of VLANs with respect to both Cisco CatOS and Cisco IOS, with emphasis on Cisco IOS.

Understanding the VLAN Configuration Modes in Cisco IOS

In Cisco IOS, two methods exist to create VLANs:

- **Global configuration mode**—A relatively new method to configure VLANs, this mode adds support for configuring extended VLANs not configurable by the VLAN database configuration mode.

- **VLAN database configuration mode**—Another method to configure VLANs, this mode supports only the configuration of VLANs in normal VLAN range (from 1 to 1005).

To create a new VLAN in global configuration mode, follow these steps:

Step 1   Enter global configuration mode.

```
Switch#configure terminal
```

Step 2 Create a new VLAN with a particular ID number.

```
Switch(config)#vlan vlan-id
```

Step 3 (Optional.) Name the VLAN.

```
Switch(config-vlan)#name vlan-name
```

Step 4 Exit global configuration mode.

```
Switch(config-vlan)#exit
```

Example 4-1 shows how to configure a VLAN in global configuration mode.

Example 4-1 *Creating a VLAN in Global Configuration Mode in Cisco IOS*

```
Switch#configure terminal
Switch(config)#vlan 5
Switch(config-vlan)#name Engineering
Switch(config-vlan)#exit
```

To configure VLANs in the VLAN database configuration mode, you use the **vlan database** privileged EXEC command.

NOTE The VLAN database command mode is different from other modes because it is session oriented. When you add, delete, or modify VLAN parameters, the switch does not apply the changes until you exit the session by entering the **apply** or **exit** command. Use the **abort** command to not apply the changes made to the VTP database.

To create a new VLAN in VLAN database configuration mode, follow these steps:

Step 1 Enter VLAN database configuration mode.

```
Switch#vlan database
```

Step 2 Create a new VLAN with a particular ID number.

```
Switch(vlan)#vlan vlan-id
```

Step 3 Name the VLAN.

```
Switch(vlan)#vlan vlan-id name vlan-name
```

Step 4 Exit VLAN database configuration mode.

```
Switch(vlan)#exit
```

Example 4-2 shows an example of creating a VLAN via the VLAN database configuration mode.

Example 4-2 *Creating a VLAN in VLAN Database Configuration Mode*

```
Switch#vlan database
Switch(vlan)#vlan 3
VLAN 3 added:
    Name: VLAN0003
Switch(vlan)#vlan 3 name Engineering
Switch(vlan)#exit
APPLY completed.
Exiting....
```

NOTE   Cisco recommends using global configuration mode to define VLANs. Future Cisco IOS releases for Catalyst switches may not support VLAN database configuration mode because it has been deemed an obsolete method of configuring VLANs.

To delete a VLAN in global configuration mode, follow these steps:

Step 1   Enter global configuration mode.

```
Switch#configure terminal
```

Step 2   Delete the VLAN by referencing its ID number.

```
Switch(config)#no vlan vlan-id
```

Step 3   Exit global configuration mode.

```
Switch(config)#end
```

NOTE   After a VLAN is deleted, the access ports that belong to that VLAN move into the inactive state until the ports are moved to another VLAN. As a security measure, ports in the inactive state do not forward traffic.

Example 4-3 shows deletion of a VLAN in global configuration mode.

Example 4-3 *Deleting a VLAN in Global Configuration Mode*

```
Switch#configure terminal
Switch(config)#no vlan 3
Switch(config)#end
```

To delete an existing VLAN in VLAN database configuration mode, follow these steps:

Step 1   Enter VLAN database configuration mode.

```
Switch#vlan database
```

Step 2   Delete the VLAN by referencing its ID number.

```
Switch(vlan)#no vlan vlan-id
```

Step 3   Exit VLAN database configuration mode.

```
Switch(vlan)#exit
```

To assign a switch port to a previously created VLAN, follow these steps:

Step 1   From global configuration mode, enter the configuration mode for the particular port you want to add to the VLAN.

```
Switch(config)#interface {FastEthernet | GigabitEthernet} slot/port
```

Step 2   Specify the port as an access port.

```
Switch(config-if)#switchport mode access
Switch(config-if)#switchport host
```

Note   The **switchport host** command effectively configures a port for a host device such as a workstation or server. This feature is a macro for enabling Spanning Tree PortFast and disabling EtherChanneling on a per-port basis. These features are discussed in Chapters 5–7.

Step 3   Remove or place the port in a particular VLAN.

```
Switch(config-if)#[no] switchport access vlan vlan-id
```

Example 4-4 illustrates configuration of an interface as an access port in VLAN 200.

Example 4-4   *Assigning an Access Port to a VLAN*

```
Switch#configure terminal
Enter configuration commands, one per line.  End with CNTL/Z.
Switch(config)#interface FastEthernet 5/6
Switch(config-if)#description PC A
Switch(config-if)#switchport
Switch(config-if)#switchport host
Switch(config-if)#switchport mode access
Switch(config-if)#switchport access vlan 200
Switch(configif)#no shutdown
Switch(config-if)#end
```

NOTE   Use the **switchport** command with no keywords to configure interfaces as Layer 2 interfaces on Layer 3 switches. After configuring the interface as a Layer 2 interface, use additional **switchport** commands with keywords to configure Layer 2 properties such as access VLANs or trunking.

Configuring VLANs in Cisco CatOS

To configure a VLAN in Cisco CatOS, use the following command:

```
set vlan vlan-id [vlan-name]
```

vlan-id represents the VLAN number. The *vlan-name* is an optional description for the VLAN.

NOTE   In Cisco CatOS, Cisco Catalyst switches require the configuration of a VTP name or a change of the VTP mode to transparent before new VLANs can be created. This chapter discusses VTP in the "VLAN Trunking Protocol" section.

Example 4-5 shows creation of a VLAN in Cisco CatOS.

Example 4-5   *Creating a VLAN in Cisco CatOS*

```
Console> (enable) set vtp domain cisco
VTP domain cisco modified
Console> (enable) set vlan 3
VTP advertisements transmitting temporarily stopped,
and will resume after the command finishes.
Vlan 3 configuration successful
```

To assign ports to a VLAN in Cisco CatOS, use the following command:

```
set vlan vlan-id [mod/port]
```

Example 4-6 shows assigning of ports to a VLAN in Cisco CatOS.

Example 4-6   *Assigning Ports to a VLAN in Cisco CatOS*

```
Console> (enable)  set vlan 3 2/1-4
VLAN 3 modified.
VLAN 1 modified.
VLAN  Mod/Ports
----  ----------------------
3     2/1-4
```

To delete VLANs in Cisco CatOS, use the **clear vlan** command, as shown in Example 4-7.

Example 4-7   *Deleting VLANs in Cisco CatOS*

```
Console> (enable) clear vlan 3
This command will deactivate all ports on vlan(s) 3
All ports on normal range vlan(s) 3
will be deactivated in the entire management domain.
Do you want to continue(y/n) [n]?y
VTP advertisements transmitting temporarily stopped,
and will resume after the command finishes.
Vlan 3 deleted
```

Verifying the VLAN Configuration

To verify the VLAN configuration of a Catalyst switch, use **show** commands. The **show vlan** command from privileged EXEC mode displays information about a particular VLAN. Table 4-3 documents the fields that are displayed by the **show vlan** command.

Table 4-3   **show vlan** *Field Descriptions*

Field	Description
VLAN	VLAN number
Name	Name, if configured, of the VLAN
Status	Status of the VLAN (active or suspended)
Ports	Ports that belong to the VLAN
Type	Media type of the VLAN
SAID	Security association ID value for the VLAN
MTU	Maximum transmission unit size for the VLAN
Parent	Parent VLAN, if one exists
RingNo	Ring number for the VLAN, if applicable
BrdgNo	Bridge number for the VLAN, if applicable
Stp	Spanning Tree Protocol type used on the VLAN
BrdgMode	Bridging mode for this VLAN
Trans1	Translation bridge 1
Trans2	Translation bridge 2
AREHops	Maximum number of hops for All-Routes Explorer frames
STEHops	Maximum number of hops for Spanning Tree Explorer frames

Example 4-8 displays information about a VLAN identified by number in Cisco IOS.

Example 4-8   *Displaying Information About a VLAN by Number in Cisco IOS*

```
Switch#show id vlan 3
VLAN Name                             Status    Ports
---- --------------------------------  --------- -------------------------------
3    VLAN0003                          active
VLAN Type  SAID       MTU   Parent RingNo BridgeNo Stp  BrdgMode Trans1 Trans2
---- ----- ---------- ----- ------ ------ -------- ---- -------- ------ ------
3    enet  100003     1500  -      -      -        -    -        0      0
------- -------- --------------------- --------------------------------------
```

Example 4-9 displays information about a VLAN identified by name in Cisco IOS.

Example 4-9 *Displaying Information About a VLAN by Name in Cisco IOS*

```
Switch#show vlan name VLAN0003
VLAN Name                             Status    Ports
---- -------------------------------- --------- --------------------
3    VLAN0003                         active

VLAN Type  SAID       MTU   Parent RingNo BridgeNo Stp  Trans1 Trans2
---- ----- ---------- ----- ------ ------ -------- ---- ------ ------
3    enet  100003     1500  -      -      -        -    0      0
```

To display the current configuration of a particular interface, use the **show running-config interface** *interface_type slot/port* command. To display detailed information about a specific switch port, use the **show interfaces** command. The command **show interface** *interface_type slot/port* with the **switchport** keyword displays not only a switch port's characteristics but also private VLAN and trunking information. The **show-mac address-table interface** *interface_type slot/port* command displays the MAC address table information for the specified interface in specific VLANs.

Example 4-10 displays the configuration of a particular interface.

Example 4-10 *Displaying Information About an Interface*

```
Switch#show running-config interface FastEthernet 5/6
Building configuration...
!
Current configuration :33 bytes
interface FastEthernet 5/6
 switchport access vlan 200
 switchport mode access
end
```

Example 4-11 displays detailed switch port information as the port VLAN and operation modes.

Example 4-11 *Displaying Detailed Switch Port Information*

```
BXB-6500-10:8A#show interfaces FastEthernet 4/1 switchport
Name: Fa4/1
Switchport: Enabled
Administrative Mode: static access
Operational Mode: static access
Administrative Trunking Encapsulation: negotiate
Operational Trunking Encapsulation: native
Negotiation of Trunking: Off
Access Mode VLAN: 2 (VLAN0002)
Trunking Native Mode VLAN: 1 (default)
Voice VLAN: none
Administrative private-vlan host-association: none
Administrative private-vlan mapping: none
Administrative private-vlan trunk native VLAN: none
```

continues

Example 4-11 *Displaying Detailed Switch Port Information (Continued)*

```
Administrative private-vlan trunk encapsulation: dot1q
Administrative private-vlan trunk normal VLANs: none
Administrative private-vlan trunk private VLANs: none
Operational private-vlan: none
Trunking VLANs Enabled: ALL
Pruning VLANs Enabled: 2-1001
Capture Mode Disabled
Capture VLANs Allowed: ALL

Voice VLAN: none (Inactive)
Appliance trust: none
```

Example 4-12 displays the MAC address table information for a specific interface in VLAN 1.

Example 4-12 *Displaying MAC Address Table Information*

```
Switch#show mac-address-table interface GigabitEthernet 0/1 vlan 1
          Mac Address Table
-------------------------------------------

Vlan    Mac Address      Type        Ports
----    -----------      ----        -----
   1    0008.2199.2bc1   DYNAMIC     Gi0/1
Total Mac Addresses for this criterion: 1
```

Troubleshooting VLANs

When troubleshooting problems related to VLANs, always review the following items:

- Physical connections
- Switch configuration
- VLAN configuration

Figure 4-5 shows, at a high level, VLAN problems that may occur on a switch.

Figure 4-5 *Troubleshooting VLAN Problems*

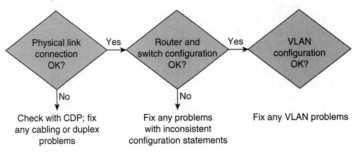

The following sections cover several common VLAN issues and the action plan to troubleshoot these issues.

Troubleshooting Slow Throughput

To troubleshoot slow-throughput issues within the same VLAN, perform the following steps:

- A point-to-point switch link consists of two ports where the problem may exist on either side of a link. Make sure the speed and duplex settings are consistent on both link partners.

- Using **show** commands, check to see what types of errors exist on the suspected interfaces. Combinations of frame check sequence (FCS) errors, alignment errors, and runts generally point to a duplex mismatch; auto-negotiation is the usual culprit, but it could also be a mismatched manual setting.

- Determine which Layer 2 path the packet is taking if there are redundant paths using spanning tree. For additional information on troubleshooting Spanning Tree Protocol (STP), consult Chapter 5, "Understanding and Configuring the 802.1D, 802.1s, and 802.1w Spanning Tree Protocols," and Chapter 6, "Adding Resiliency to Spanning Tree Using Advanced Features and Troubleshooting STP Issues."

If you see from the output of the **show interface** command that the number of collisions is increasing rapidly, the problem may be an oversubscribed half-duplex link, faulty hardware, a bad cable, or a duplex mismatch.

Troubleshooting Communication Issues

When one device cannot communicate with another device within a VLAN, troubleshoot the problem by doing the following:

- Ensure that the VLAN membership of the switch ports is correct by using the **show interface** command.

- Make sure the switch ports are up and connected. Try to reset the port by doing **shut** and **no shut** under the switch interface.

Private VLANs

Private VLANs (pVLAN) are VLANs that provide isolation between ports within the same VLAN. Cisco introduced pVLANs to provide security, to reduce the number of IP subnets, and to reduce the VLANs' utilization by isolating traffic between network devices residing in the same VLAN.

Service providers use pVLANs to deploy hosting services and network access where all devices reside in the same subnet but only communicate to a default gateway, backup servers, or another network. Service providers use pVLANs not only as a security feature but also as a method to minimize the use of IP address subnets.

In multilayer switching environments, enterprises generally use pVLANs to prevent network devices that are attached to interfaces or groups of interfaces from communicating between each other, but to allow communication to a default gateway such as a VLAN interface or router or to a particular group of devices. Although the network devices reside in different pVLANs, they use the same IP subnet. In this manner, network devices on the same VLAN can communicate only with the default gateway to reach networks beyond the default gateway or only to a particular group of devices if necessary.

Each pVLAN consists of two supporting VLANs:

- **A primary VLAN**—The Primary pVLAN is the high-level VLAN of the pVLAN. A primary VLAN can be composed of many secondary VLANs with the secondary VLANs belonging to the same subnet of the primary VLAN.

- **A secondary VLAN**—Every secondary VLAN is a child to a primary VLAN and is mapped to one primary VLAN. End devices are attached to secondary pVLANs. pVLANs define the use of promiscuous ports. All the devices in the pVLAN can communicate with the promiscuous ports. A promiscuous port is only part of one primary VLAN, but each promiscuous port can map to more than one secondary VLAN. Promiscuous ports are generally router ports, backup servers, or VLAN interfaces, as shown in Figure 4-6.

Figure 4-6   *pVLAN Port Structure*

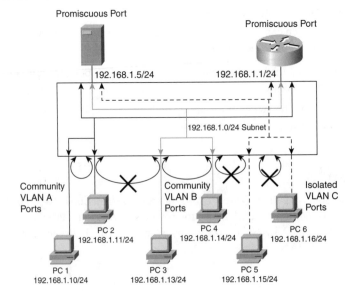

The following are the two types of secondary VLANs:

- **Community VLANs**—Ports that belong to the community VLAN are able to communicate with the other ports in the same community and promiscuous ports of the pVLAN. In Figure 4-6, PC 1 and PC 2, which belong to community VLAN A, can communicate with each other but (as indicated by the "X") not with PC 3 and PC 4, which belong to community VLAN B.

- **Isolated VLANs**—Ports that belong to an isolated VLAN can only communicate with promiscuous ports. Isolated ports cannot communicate with other ports in the same isolated VLAN, as reflected in Figure 4-6, where PC 5 and PC 6, although in the same isolated VLAN, cannot communicate with each other but can communicate with the promiscuous ports. Each pVLAN has only one isolated VLAN.

Figure 4-7 illustrates an example of implementing pVLANs in a service-provider environment. Here, a service provider has three customers under one primary VLAN. Customer A belongs to community VLAN 100, Customer B belongs to community VLAN 200, and Customer C belongs to isolated VLAN 300. Despite belonging to the same subnet, Customer A's, Customer B's, and Customer C's network devices cannot communicate with one another. All devices that reside in Customer A's community VLANs can communicate with one another even though the devices are spread across multiple switches. In addition, all devices that reside in Customer B's community VLANs can communicate with one another. However, devices in Customer C's isolated VLAN cannot communicate with one another.

Figure 4-7 *pVLAN Implementations*

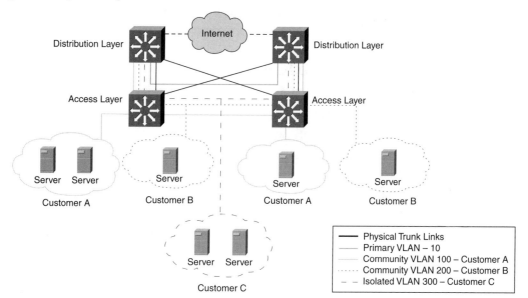

pVLANs can span multiple switches that support the pVLANs' trunking feature.

The Cisco Catalyst 6500 and 4500 families of switches support all the features of the pVLANs mentioned earlier in this chapter, except that a Cisco 4500 running IOS does not support community VLANs at this time. The low-end Catalyst switches, such as the Catalyst 2950, and the Catalyst 3550/3560 family of switches support only the isolated port feature of pVLANs. These switches refer to isolated ports as pVLAN edge (protected ports). The protected port is a feature that has only local significance to the switch, and there is no isolation between two protected ports located on different switches. A protected port cannot forward traffic (unicast, multicast, or broadcast) to any other port that is also a protected port in the same switch, hence providing isolation.

NOTE   There are some restrictions and limitations with the configuration of pVLANs. A few limitations and restrictions are as follows:

- pVLAN configuration requires VTP to be in transparent mode for VTP version 1 and 2.
- You cannot configure Layer 3 VLAN interfaces for secondary VLANs.
- Private VLANs are not supported on EtherChannels or span destination ports.

To view the complete list of restrictions and limitations, consult the following documents on the Cisco.com website.

For the Catalyst 4000 family of switches (Configuration Guide):

http://www.cisco.com/en/US/products/hw/switches/ps4324/
products_configuration_guide_chapter09186a008062cf2f.html

For the Catalyst 6500 family of switches:

http://www.cisco.com/univercd/cc/td/doc/product/lan/cat6000/122sx/swcg/pvlans.htm

---

Configuring PVLANs in Cisco IOS

To configure pVLANs in Cisco IOS, perform the following steps:

Step 1   Enter VLAN global configuration mode to configure the pVLANs.

```
Switch(config)# vlan pVLAN-id
```

Step 2   Configure the VLANs as a type of pVLAN.

```
Switch(config-vlan)# private-vlan {community | isolated | primary}
```

Step 3   Exit the configuration mode.

```
Switch(config-vlan)# exit
```

Step 4   Enter the VLAN global configuration mode to configure primary VLAN.

```
Switch(config)# vlan primary-vlan-id
```

Step 5   If it is a primary VLAN, make sure to associate the Layer 2 secondary VLAN to the primary VLAN.

```
Switch(config-vlan)#private-vlan association {secondary-vlan-list | add
secondary-vlan-list | remove secondary-vlan-list}
```

Step 6   Select the interface configuration mode for the primary VLAN.

```
Switch(config)#interface vlan  primary-vlan-id
```

Step 7   Map secondary VLANs to the Layer 3 VLAN interface of a primary
VLAN to allow Layer 3 switching of pVLAN ingress traffic.

```
Switch(config-if)#private-vlan mapping {secondary-vlan-list | add
secondary-vlan-list | remove secondary-vlan-list}
```

Step 8   Select the LAN port interface to configure as the pVLAN host or
promiscuous port.

```
Switch(config)#interface type slot/port
```

Step 9   Configure the LAN port for Layer 2 operation if the default behavior is
Layer 3 operation.

```
Switch(config-if)#switchport
```

Step 10   Configure the Layer 2 port as a pVLAN port either as host or
promiscuous port.

```
Switch(config-if)#switchport mode private-vlan {host | promiscuous}
```

Step 11   For access pVLAN ports, associate the community or isolated pVLAN
to the pVLAN.

```
Switch(config-if)#switchport private-vlan host-association primary-
vlan-id secondary-vlan-id
```

Step 12   For promiscuous ports, configure the interface by mapping the port to the
pVLAN.

```
Switch(config-if)#switchport private-vlan mapping primary-vlan-id
{secondary-vlan-list | add secondary-vlan-list | remove secondary-vlan-list}
```

Step 13   Exit the interface configuration mode.

```
Switch(config)#end
```

Example 4-13 represents the configuration of one community VLAN 200 and one isolated
VLAN 300 with a primary VLAN 100. Port 5/1 binds with community VLAN 200, and port
5/2 binds with isolated VLAN 300. The VLAN 100 interface permits routing of secondary
VLAN ingress traffic from VLANs 200 and 300.

Example 4-13 *Sample Configuration of pVLANs in Cisco IOS*

```
Switch# configure terminal
Switch(config)# vlan 100
Switch(config-vlan)# private-vlan primary
Switch(config)# vlan 200
Switch(config-vlan)# private-vlan community
Switch(config)# vlan 300
Switch(config-vlan)# private-vlan isolated
Switch(config)# vlan 100
```

continues

Example 4-13 *Sample Configuration of pVLANs in Cisco IOS (Continued)*

```
Switch(config-vlan)# private-vlan association 200,300
Switch(config-vlan)# exit
Switch(config)#interface vlan 100
Switch(config-if)#private-vlan mapping add 200,300
Switch(config-if)#exit
Switch(config)# interface FastEthernet 5/1
Switch(config-if)# switchport mode private-vlan host
Switch(config-if)# switchport private-vlan host-association 100 200
Switch(config)# interface FastEthernet 5/2
Switch(config-if)# switchport mode private-vlan host
Switch(config-if)# switchport private-vlan host-association 100 300
Switch(config-if)# end
```

Example 4-14 illustrates the commands used to verify the configuration of pVLANs in Cisco IOS.

Example 4-14 *Verifying pVLAN Configuration in Cisco IOS*

```
Switch# show vlan private-vlan
Primary Secondary Type Interfaces
------- --------- ---------------- ----------------------------------------
100 200 community
100 300 isolated

Switch# show interfaces FastEthernet 5/2 switchport
Name: Fa5/2
Switchport: Enabled
Administrative Mode: private-vlan host
Operational Mode: down
Administrative Trunking Encapsulation: negotiate
Negotiation of Trunking: On
Access Mode VLAN: 1 (default)
Trunking Native Mode VLAN: 1 (default)
Administrative private-vlan host-association: 100 (VLAN0200) 300 (VLAN0300)
Administrative private-vlan mapping: none
Operational private-vlan: none
Trunking VLANs Enabled: ALL
Pruning VLANs Enabled: 2-1001
Capture Mode Disabled
```

Configuring pVLANs in Cisco/CatOS

To configure pVLANs on the Catalyst 6000 and 4000 families of switches that are running Cisco CatOS, perform the following steps:

Step 1 Create a primary VLAN.

```
set vlan vlan-id pvlan-type primary
```

Step 2 Create secondary VLANs.

```
set vlan vlan-id pvlan-type {isolated | community}
```

Step 3   Map the primary VLAN to the secondary VLANs.

> **set pvlan** *primary-vlan-id* {*isolated-vlan-id* | *community-vlan-id*}

Step 4   Bind ports to the primary and secondary pVLANs.

> **set pvlan** *primary-vlan-id* {*isolated-vlan-id* | *community-vlan-id*} *mod/ports*

Step 5   Specify which ports will act as promiscuous ports.

> **set pvlan mapping** *primary-vlan-id* {*isolated-vlan-id* | *community-vlan-id*} *mod/ports*

Step 6   Verify the pVLAN configuration.

> **show pvlan** [*vlan-id*]
> **show pvlan mapping**

Example 4-15 represents the configuration of one community VLAN 200 and an isolated VLAN 300 associated with the primary VLAN 100. Port 5/1 binds to the community VLAN, port 5/2 binds to the isolated VLAN 300, and port 15/1 is the promiscuous port, which is a Catalyst 6500 Multilayer Switch Feature Card (MSFC) acting as a default gateway. As a result, devices that are connected on ports 5/1 and 5/2 cannot communicate with one another, but they are able to communicate with the promiscuous port, which is the MSFC port. Using the VLAN 100 interface on the MSFC, these ports can communicate with the rest of the network.

Example 4-15 *Sample Configuration of pVLANs*

```
Console> (enable) set vlan 100 pvlan-type primary
Vlan 100 configuration successful
Console> (enable) set vlan 300 pvlan-type isolated
Vlan 300 configuration successful
Console> (enable) set vlan 200 pvlan-type community
Vlan 200 configuration successful
Console> (enable) set pvlan 100 200 5/1
Successfully set the following ports to Private Vlan 100,200: 5/1
Console> (enable) set pvlan 100 300 5/2
Successfully set the following ports to Private Vlan 100,300:5/2
Console> (enable) set pvlan mapping 100,200 15/1
Successfully set mapping between 100 and 200 on 15/1
Console> (enable) set pvlan mapping 100 300 15/1
Successfully set mapping between 100 and 300 on 15/1
```

Example 4-16 illustrates several commands for verifying the configuration of pVLANs in Cisco CatOS.

Example 4-16 *Verifying pVLAN Configuration in Cisco CatOS*

```
Console> (enable) show pvlan
Primary Secondary Secondary-Type Ports
------- --------- -------------- -----------
100 300 isolated 5/2
100 200 community 5/1
Console> (enable) show pvlan mapping
Port Primary Secondary
----- -------- ----------
15/1 100 200,300
```

VLAN Trunking

Trunks carry the traffic for multiple VLANs across a single physical link. Trunking is used to extend Layer 2 operations across an entire network, such as end-to-end VLANs, as shown in Figure 4-8. The host in VLAN 2 can communicate with the host in VLAN 2 in the other switch over the single trunk link the same as a host in VLAN 1 can communicate with a host in another switch in VLAN 1.

Figure 4-8   *VLAN Trunking*

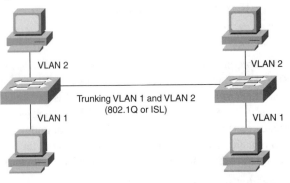

ISL and IEEE 802.1Q are two protocol-independent methods that Cisco Catalyst switches use to mark frames with a respective VLAN for transmission across the trunk interface. ISL is an encapsulation method for trunking, whereas 802.1Q trunking uses a tagging method. The 802.1Q frames place an additional 4-byte tag into the original packet. Catalyst switches add the tag before transmission on trunk lines and, as a result, compute a new FCS for each egress frame. At the receiving end, the link partners' trunking interface removes the tag and forwards the packet to the correct destination in the respective VLAN. ISL is a Cisco proprietary protocol, but Cisco licensed its use to many NIC vendors, including Intel and Compaq, for interoperability. Nevertheless, 802.1Q is the standard-based IEEE protocol that is commonly found in network devices regardless of manufacturer. The current generation of low-end Catalyst switches no longer supports ISL. As a result, when deploying multilayer switched networks, opt for trunking using 802.1Q instead of ISL.

The following sections discuss trunking implementation, configuration, and troubleshooting in a multilayer switched network in more detail, including coverage of the following topics:

- Implementing trunking in multilayer switched networks
- Trunking protocols
- Understanding DTP
- VLAN ranges and mappings
- Service provider–managed VLAN services
- Cisco trunking modes and methods
- Configuring ISL and 802.1Q Trunking in Cisco IOS

- Configuring VLAN trunking in Cisco CatOS
- Verifying trunking configurations
- Troubleshooting trunking

Implementing Trunking in Multilayer Switched Networks

Trunking is an important part of the multilayer switched network. The Campus Infrastructure module is hierarchical. The Building Distribution block is introduced to terminate local VLANs from many Building Access submodule switches using trunk links. Typically, several end-user nodes connect to single Building Access submodule switches with a selected number of access VLANs that provide basic connectivity to network resources, as shown in Figure 4-9.

Figure 4-9   *Trunk Implementations*

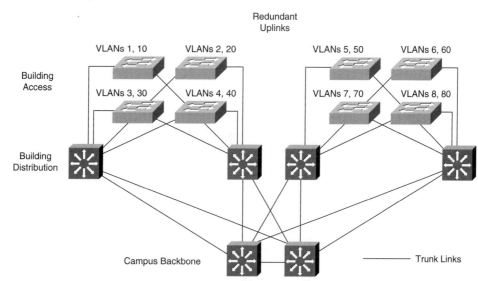

Cisco design guides recommend using redundant links for each Building Access submodule switch. Redundant links from the Building Distribution submodule switches to the Campus Backbone switches are recommended to provide multihomed redundancy.

Trunking Protocols

This subsection covers the following two trunking protocols in more detail:

- **Inter-Switch Link (ISL)**—A Cisco proprietary trunking encapsulation
- **IEEE 802.1Q**—An industry-standard trunking method

ISL

As mentioned in a previous section, ISL is a Cisco proprietary protocol for interconnecting Layer 2–capable devices that carry VLAN traffic, as illustrated in Figure 4-10. The dotted and shaded lines between the switches in Figure 4-10 show the trunk carrying traffic for three VLANs. Every PC belongs to a separate VLAN and can communicate with the other PCs connected to the remote switch in the same VLAN over the trunk link. Besides specific models of Cisco Catalyst switches, high-end routers and network appliances support ISL. This chapter highlights trunking on Catalyst switches exclusively. For configuration information regarding trunking on Cisco IOS routers or other network devices, refer to the Cisco Systems, Inc. technical documentation.

Figure 4-10 *ISL Implementations*

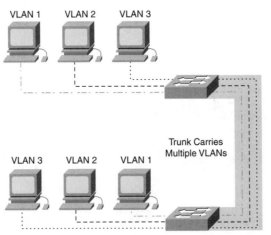

A non-ISL device that receives ISL-encapsulated Ethernet frames may consider those frames to be transmission errors if the size of the header plus the data frame exceeds the MTU size. Furthermore, devices that do not support ISL simply drop ISL frames on ingress because they cannot decode the ISL encapsulation. Figure 4-11 illustrates the ISL frame; note that the header encapsulation is 26 bytes plus an additional 4 bytes for a header cyclic redundancy check (CRC).

When you are examining the frame formats for Layer 2 frames, notice that the ISL Layer 2 header is placed before the other Layer 2 field information in the frame.

The ISL frame contains two FCS fields. The original transmitting device generates one FCS field, and the ISL trunk port generates the other FCS field. ISL encapsulates the frame without modifying its contents.

The ISL Ethernet frame header contains additional fields; consult Cisco.com for more details on these fields.

Figure 4-11 *ISL Frame*

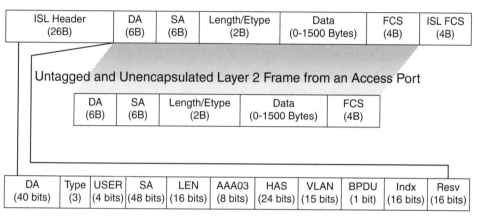

ISL Encapsulated Layer 2 Frame from an ISL Trunk Port

ISL Header (26B)	DA (6B)	SA (6B)	Length/Etype (2B)	Data (0-1500 Bytes)	FCS (4B)	ISL FCS (4B)

Untagged and Unencapsulated Layer 2 Frame from an Access Port

DA (6B)	SA (6B)	Length/Etype (2B)	Data (0-1500 Bytes)	FCS (4B)

DA (40 bits)	Type (3)	USER (4 bits)	SA (48 bits)	LEN (16 bits)	AAA03 (8 bits)	HAS (24 bits)	VLAN (15 bits)	BPDU (1 bit)	Indx (16 bits)	Resv (16 bits)

IEEE 802.1Q

All Catalyst switches support 802.1Q tagging for multiplexing traffic from multiple VLANs onto a single physical link, as shown in Figure 4-12.

Figure 4-12 *802.1Q Trunk Implementations*

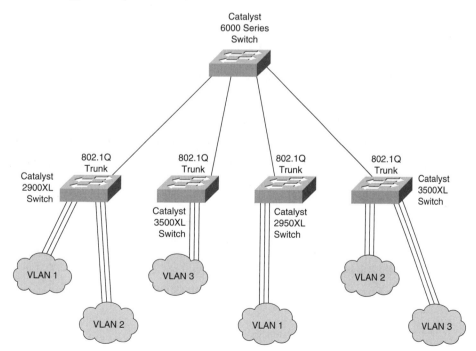

IEEE 802.1Q trunk links employ the tagging mechanism to carry frames for multiple VLANs, in which each frame is tagged to identify the VLAN to which the frame belongs. The IEEE 802.1Q/802.1p standard provides inherent architectural advantages over ISL:

- 802.1Q has smaller frame overhead than ISL. As a result, 802.1Q is more efficient than ISL, especially in the case of small frames. 802.1Q overhead is 4 bytes, whereas ISL is 30 bytes.

- 802.1Q is a widely supported industry-standard protocol.

- 802.1Q has the support for 802.1p fields for QoS.

Figure 4-13 describes the 802.1Q frame.

Figure 4-13 *802.1Q Frame*

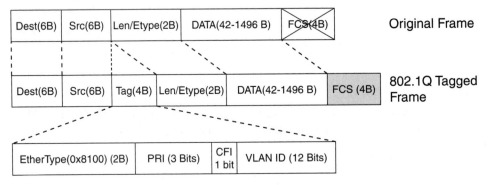

The 802.1Q Ethernet frame header contains the following fields:

- **Dest**—Destination MAC address (6 bytes)

- **Src**—Source MAC address (6 bytes)

- **Tag**—Inserted 802.1Q tag (4 bytes, detailed here)

  — **EtherType(TPID)**—Set to 0x8100 to specify that the 802.1Q tag follows.

  — **CFI**—Canonical Format Indicator is always set to 0 for Ethernet switches and to 1 for Token Ring-type networks.

  — **PRI**—3-bit 802.1p priority field.

  — **VLAN ID**—12-bit VLAN field. Of the 4096 possible VLAN IDs, the maximum number of possible VLAN configurations is 4094. A VLAN ID of 0 is used to indicate priority frames, and value 4095 (FFF) is reserved. CFI, PRI, and VLAN ID are represented as Tag Control information (TCI) fields.

- **Len/Etype**—2-byte field specifying length (802.3) or type (Ethernet II).

- **Data**—Data itself.

- **FCS**—Frame check sequence (4 bytes).

IEEE 802.1Q uses an internal tagging mechanism that modifies the original frame (as shown by the "X" over FCS in the original frame in Figure 4-13), recalculates the CRC value for the entire frame with the tag, inserts the new CRC value in a new FCS. ISL, in comparison, wraps the original frame and adds a second FCS that is built only on the header information but does not modify the original frame FCS.

IEEE 802.1p redefined the three most significant bits in the 802.1Q tag to allow for prioritization of the Layer 2 frame.

The 802.1Q tagged frame supports Layer 2 compatibility on any Layer 2 device. Layer 2 devices, except those with 802.1Q trunk ports, do not have the capability to discern the EtherType field or the tag. If a non-802.1Q-enabled device or an access port receives a frame, the device ignores the tagged portion of the frame and switches the packet at Layer 2 as if it were a standard Ethernet frame. This allows for the placement of Layer 2 intermediate devices, such as other switches or bridges, on the 802.1Q trunk link.

Baby giants are frames that are larger than the standard MTU of 1500 bytes but less than 2000 bytes. Because ISL and 802.1Q tagged frames increase the MTU beyond 1500 bytes, switches consider both frames as baby giants. ISL-encapsulated packets over Ethernet have an MTU of 1548 bytes, whereas 802.1Q has an MTU of 1522 bytes.

Understanding Native VLAN in 802.1Q Trunking

802.1Q trunks define a native VLAN for frames that are not tagged by default. Switches transmit any Layer 2 frames from a native VLAN on the trunk port untagged, as shown in Figure 4-14. The receiving switch forwards all untagged packets to its native VLAN. The native VLAN is the default VLAN configuration of the port. When the port is not trunking, the access VLAN configuration defines the native VLAN. In the case of Cisco switches, the default VLAN is VLAN 1 and is configurable.

Figure 4-14 *Native VLAN*

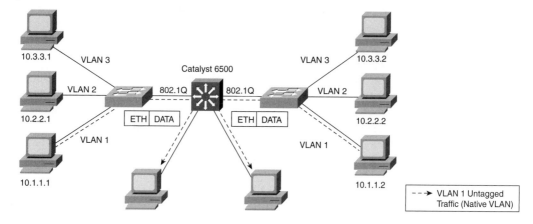

It is important that the 802.1Q trunk port between two devices has the same native VLAN configuration on both sides of the link. Misconfiguration of the native VLAN for 802.1Q trunk ports on the same trunk link might cause Layer 2 loops or black holes. With 802.1Q trunks, frames for the native VLAN are untagged, and if there is a native VLAN misconfiguration on peer switches, the untagged frames are received on the wrong VLAN on the peer switch. Furthermore, CDP issues a "VLAN mismatch" error message to any active consoles where native VLANs do not match. Note that there are some specific cases where CDP is either turned off or cannot be transmitted through an intermediate Layer 2 device in the same manner that 802.1Q frames are transmitted.

With an 802.1Q native VLAN, a switch forwards any Layer 2 frame that is received on a trunk port, whether tagged or not, to an intended VLAN. Compared to 802.1Q, ISL drops any unencapsulated frames that are received on a trunk port, and all frames that are transmitted from a trunk port are encapsulated, including the native VLAN.

Each physical port on the switch has a parameter called Port VLAN ID (PVID). Switches assign every 802.1Q port a PVID value based on its native VLAN ID. (The default is VLAN 1.) All switches assign all untagged frames to the VLAN that is specified in the PVID parameter. When a port receives a tagged frame, the tag is respected. If the frame is untagged, it is forwarded to the VLAN that is contained in the PVID. This allows the coexistence on the same Ethernet segment of VLAN-aware bridges or stations and VLAN-unaware bridges or stations.

Understanding DTP

All recent Cisco Catalyst switches, except for the Catalyst 2900XL and 3500XL, use a Cisco proprietary point-to-point protocol called Dynamic Trunking Protocol (DTP) on trunk ports to negotiate the trunking state. DTP negotiates the operational mode of directly connected switch ports to a trunk port and selects an appropriate trunking protocol. Negotiating trunking is a recommended practice in multilayer switched networks because it avoids network issues resulting from trunking misconfigurations.

VLAN Ranges and Mappings

ISL supports VLAN numbers in the range of 1 to 1005, whereas 802.1Q VLAN numbers are in the range of 1 to 4094. The default behavior of VLAN trunks is to permit all normal- and extended-range VLANs across the link if it is an 802.1Q interface and to permit normal VLANs in the case of an ISL interface. However, switches support configurations to restrict a single VLAN, range of VLANs, or group of VLANs across a trunk interface. Best practice is to limit the trunk to only the intended VLANs to reduce the possibility of loops and to improve bandwidth utilization by restricting unwanted VLAN data traffic from the link. Unnecessary VLANs can be limited by VTP pruning or manual removal of the VLANs from the trunk interfaces. This chapter discusses pruning later in the "VTP Pruning" section.

Cisco switches require VLAN mapping for the following reasons when traversing networks using both 802.1Q and ISL:

- In a network environment with devices that are connected to Cisco switches through 802.1Q trunks, 802.1Q VLANs in the range of 1 to 1000 are automatically mapped to the corresponding ISL VLAN; however, 802.1Q VLAN numbers greater than 1000 must be mapped to an ISL VLAN to be recognized and forwarded by Cisco network devices.

- In a network with non-Cisco devices that use reserved VLANs, VLANs must be mapped to nonreserved VLANs to work in Cisco networks.

The following restrictions apply when mapping 802.1Q VLANs to ISL VLANs:

- Limited to eight 802.1Q-to-ISL VLAN mappings on a switch.

- Limited to mapping 802.1Q VLANs to Ethernet-type ISL VLANs.

- It is important not to enter the native VLAN of any 802.1Q trunk in the mapping table to avoid overlapping numbers.

- Mapping an 802.1Q VLAN to an ISL VLAN blocks the traffic on the 802.1Q VLAN corresponding to the mapped ISL VLAN. For example, mapping 802.1Q VLAN 2000 to ISL VLAN 200 blocks the traffic on 802.1Q VLAN 200.

- VLAN mappings are local to each switch. Configure the same VLAN mappings on all appropriate switches in the network.

Service Provider–Managed VLAN Services

Another feature of 802.1Q is its capability to support tunneling features, such as 802.1Q-in-Q tunneling, which allows service providers to transport VLANs within VLANs, preserving individual customer's VLAN assignments without requiring them to be unique. Layer 2 protocol tunneling is a scaleable method for tunneling protocol data units (PDUs) through the service provider network, as shown in Figure 4-15. Chapter 16, "Designing, Building, and Connecting Cisco Multilayer Switched Networks Using Metro Solutions," discusses 802.1Q-in-Q tunneling in more detail.

Figure 4-15 *802.1Q-in-Q Tunneling*

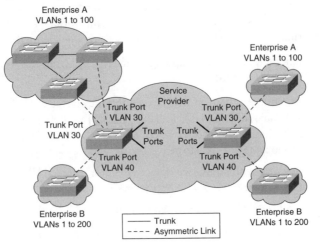

Cisco Trunking Modes and Methods

Table 4-4 describes the different trunking modes supported by Cisco switches.

Table 4-4 *Trunking Modes*

Mode in Cisco CatOS	Mode in Cisco IOS	Function
Off	Access	Puts the interface into permanent nontrunking mode and negotiates to convert the link into a nontrunk link. The interface becomes a nontrunk interface even if the neighboring interface does not agree to the change.
On	Trunk	Puts the interface into permanent trunking mode and negotiates to convert the link into a trunk link. The interface becomes a trunk interface even if the neighboring interface does not agree to the change.
Nonegotiate	Nonegotiate	Puts the interface into permanent trunking mode but prevents the interface from generating DTP frames. You must configure the neighboring interface manually as a trunk interface to establish a trunk link. Use this mode when connecting to a device that does not support DTP.
Desirable	Dynamic desirable	Makes the interface actively attempt to convert the link to a trunk link. The interface becomes a trunk interface if the neighboring interface is set to trunk, desirable, or auto mode. This is the default mode for all Ethernet interfaces in Cisco IOS.
Auto	Dynamic auto	Makes the interface willing to convert the link to a trunk link. The interface becomes a trunk interface if the neighboring interface is set to trunk or desirable mode. This is the default mode in Cisco CatOS.

Table 4-5 lists the Ethernet trunking modes that Cisco switches support.

Table 4-5   *Catalyst-Supported Ethernet Trunking Methods*

Trunking Method	Description
ISL	Encapsulates headers and trailers with a VLAN-ID.
802.1Q	Tags 4 additional bytes in the Ethernet header and marks these bytes with a VLAN-ID.

Table 4-6 lists which Catalyst switches support ISL and 802.1Q.

Table 4-6   *Cisco Catalyst Switches ISL and 802.1Q Support Matrix*

Family of Switch	ISL	802.1Q
Catalyst 2940	No	Yes
Catalyst 2948G/2980G	No	Yes
Catalyst 2950/2955/2960	No	Yes
Catalyst 2970/3550/3560/3750	Yes	Yes
Cisco CatOS–based Catalyst 4000/4500	No	Yes
Cisco IOS–based Catalyst 4000/4500	Yes	Yes
Catalyst 6500	Yes	Yes

NOTE   The Cisco Catalyst 4000 and 4500 switches run Cisco IOS or Cisco CatOS depending on the Supervisor Engine model. The Supervisor Engine I and II only support 802.1Q. Furthermore, specific oversubscribed line modules for the Catalyst 4000 and 4500 do not support ISL encapsulation on a per-port basis. Refer to the product documentation on Cisco.com for more details.

Configuring ISL and 802.1Q Trunking in Cisco IOS

To configure a switch port as an ISL trunking port in Cisco IOS, use the following commands:

Step 1   Enter the interface configuration mode.

```
Switch(config)#interface {FastEthernet | GigabitEthernet} slot/port
```

Step 2   Select the encapsulation type.

```
Switch(config-if)#switchport trunk encapsulation {isl | dot1q | negotiate}
```

Note   The **negotiate** option specifies that the port negotiates with the neighboring port to become an ISL (preferred) or 802.1Q trunk, depending on the configuration and capabilities of the neighboring port.

Step 3 Configure the interface as a Layer 2 trunk.

```
Switch(config-if)#switchport mode {dynamic {auto | desirable} | trunk}
```

Step 4 Specify the native VLAN.

```
Switch(config-if)#switchport trunk native vlan vlan-id
```

Step 5 Configure the allowable VLANs for this trunk.

```
Switch(config-if)#switchport trunk allowed vlan {add | except | all |
remove} vlan-id[,vlan-id[,vlan-id[,...]]]
```

NOTE With Cisco IOS Software Release 12.1(13)E and later, VLAN IDs may be in the range of 1 to 4094, except in the case of reserved VLANs. With Cisco IOS Release 12.1(11b)E or later, it is possible to remove VLAN 1 from a trunk port. Even after removing VLAN 1 from a trunk, the trunk interface continues to send and receive management traffic. For example, CDP, VTP, Port Aggregation Protocol (PAgP), and DTP all use VLAN 1, regardless of the existence of VLAN 1 on the port.

Example 4-17 shows configuration of a port for ISL trunking in Cisco IOS.

Example 4-17 *Configuring a Port for ISL Trunking in Cisco IOS*

```
Switch#configure terminal
Enter configuration commands, one per line. End with CNTL/Z.
Switch(config)#interface FastEthernet 5/8
Switch(config)#switchport
Switch(config-if)#switchport trunk encapsulation isl
Switch(config-if)#switchport mode trunk
Switch(config-if)#end
```

Example 4-18 shows configuration of interface Fast Ethernet 5/8 for 802.1Q trunking in the desirable mode and allowing only VLANs 1 through 100 on the trunk.

Example 4-18 *Configuring a Port for 802.1Q Trunking in Cisco IOS*

```
Switch#configure terminal
Enter configuration commands, one per line. End with CNTL/Z.
Switch(config)#interface FastEthernet 5/8
Switch(config-if)#switchport trunk encapsulation dot1q
Switch(config-if)#switchport mode dynamic desirable
Switch(config-if)#switchport trunk allowed vlan 1-100
Switch(config-if)#no shutdown
Switch(config-if)#end
```

Configuring VLAN Trunking in Cisco CatOS

To configure ISL trunks in Cisco CatOS, use the following commands in the privileged EXEC mode:

Step 1 The following command configures the trunking mode and method.

```
set trunk mod/port [on | desirable | auto | nonegotiate] [isl | dot1q]
```

Step 2   (Optional.) If not specified, all VLANs are allowed on the trunk. To specifically add VLANs on the trunk, use this command:

```
set trunk mod/port vlan-id1[,vlan-id[,vlan-id[,...]]]
```

Step 3   (Optional.) To remove VLANs from the trunk, use the following command:

```
clear trunk mod/port vlan IDs
```

clear also removes VLANs from the trunk. Another option to remove unnecessary VLANs is to use pruning with VTP, which this chapter discusses later in the "VTP Pruning" section.

Step 4   (Optional.) The following command tags all the VLANs including the native VLAN in 802.1Q. This is a global command.

```
set dot1q-all-tagged enable [all]
```

Step 5   (Optional.) To tag native VLANs only on specific ports, do the following:

```
set port dot1q-all-tagged mod/port enable | disable
```

Example 4-19 shows configuration of ISL trunking on Cisco CatOS to disallow VLANs 10 to 20 from the trunk.

Example 4-19 *Configuring a Port for ISL Trunking in CatOS*

```
Console> (enable) set trunk 1/2 desirable isl
Console> (enable) clear trunk 1/2 10-20
```

Example 4-20 shows configuration of 802.1Q trunking in Cisco CatOS.

Example 4-20 *Configuring a Port for 802.1Q Trunking in CatOS*

```
Console> (enable) set trunk 3/1 desirable dot1q
```

Verifying Trunking Configurations

To verify the trunk configuration in Cisco IOS, use the commands in Table 4-7.

Table 4-7   *Cisco IOS Commands to Verify Trunk Configuration*

Command	Notes
show running-config interface *type slot/port*	Displays the running configuration of the interface
show interfaces [*type slot/port*] **switchport**	Displays the switch port configuration of the interface
show interfaces [*type slot/port*] **trunk**	Displays the trunk configuration of the interface

Example 4-21 displays port configuration for trunking.

Example 4-21 *Displaying Port Information for Trunking*

```
Switch#show running-config interface FastEthernet 5/8
Building configuration...
Current configuration:
!
interface FastEthernet5/8
switchport mode dynamic desirable
switchport trunk encapsulation dot1q
end
```

Example 4-22 displays switchport information about interface FastEthernet 5/8, which is operating as an 802.1Q trunk.

Example 4-22 *Displaying Switchport Information for Trunking*

```
Switch#show interfaces FastEthernet 5/8 switchport
Name: Fa5/8
Switchport: Enabled
Administrative Mode: dynamic desirable
Operational Mode: trunk
Administrative Trunking Encapsulation: negotiate
Operational Trunking Encapsulation: dot1q
Negotiation of Trunking: Enabled
Access Mode VLAN: 1 (default)
Trunking Native Mode VLAN: 1 (default)
Trunking VLANs Enabled: ALL
Pruning VLANs Enabled: 2-1001
```

Example 4-23 displays trunk information for a particular port.

Example 4-23 *Displaying Trunk Information for a Particular Port*

```
Switch#show interfaces FastEthernet 5/8 trunk

Port        Mode       Encapsulation  Status       Native vlan
Fa5/8       desirable  n-802.1q       trunking     1

Port        Vlans allowed on trunk
Fa5/8  1-1005

Port        Vlans allowed and active in management domain
Fa5/8  1-6,10,20,50,100,152,200,300,303-305,349-351,400,500,521,524,570,801-8
02,850,917,999,1002-1005

Port        Vlans in spanning tree forwarding state and not pruned
Fa5/8  1-6,10,20,50,100,152,200,300,303-305,349-351,400,500,521,524,570,801-8
02,850,917,999,1002-1005
```

To verify the trunking configuration in Cisco CatOS, use the following command:

show trunk [*mod/port*]

Example 4-24 shows verification of the trunking configuration in Cisco CatOS in which port 3/1 is an ISL trunk and allows only VLANs 1, 5, and 10 through 20.

Example 4-24 *Verifying Trunking Configuration in Cisco CatOS*

```
Console> (enable) show trunk 3/1
Port      Mode         Encapsulation Status       Native vlan
--------  -----------  ------------- -----------  -----------
3/1       desirable    n-isl         trunking     1
Port      Vlans allowed on trunk
--------  ----------------------------------------------------------------
3/1       1,5,10-20
Port      Vlans allowed and active in management domain
--------  ----------------------------------------------------------------
3/1       1,5,10-20
Port      Vlans in spanning tree forwarding state and not pruned
--------  ----------------------------------------------------------------
3/1       1,5,10-20
```

Troubleshooting Trunking

To troubleshoot a problem with a trunk port, verify that the following configurations are correct:

- Interface modes
- Native VLAN
- Encapsulation types

A common problem with VLANs is where a device cannot establish a connection across a trunk link. Suggested solutions to the problem are as follows:

- Ensure that the Layer 2 interface mode configured on both ends of the link is valid. The trunk mode should be trunk or desirable for at least one side of the trunk. Use the **show interface** *interface* **trunk** command in Cisco IOS to verify the configuration.
- Ensure that the trunk encapsulation type configured on both ends of the link is valid and compatible.
- On IEEE 802.1Q trunks, make sure that the native VLAN is the same on both ends of the trunk.

VLAN Trunking Protocol

VTP is a protocol that is used to distribute and synchronize information about VLANs that are configured throughout a switched network. VTP minimizes misconfigurations and configuration inconsistencies that may result in various problems, such as duplicate VLAN names, incorrect VLAN-type specifications, and security violations. Switches transmit VTP messages only on 802.1Q or ISL trunks.

VTP is a Layer 2 messaging protocol that maintains VLAN configuration consistency by managing the additions, deletions, and name changes of VLANs within a VTP domain.

A VTP domain is one switch or several interconnected switches that share the same VTP environment. Catalyst switches support only a single VTP domain per switch.

By default, a Catalyst switch is in the "no-management-domain" state until it receives an advertisement for a VTP domain over a trunk link or until a VTP configuration is applied, as shown in Figure 4-16.

Figure 4-16 *VTP Protocol*

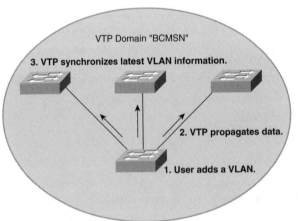

Configurations made to a single VTP server propagate across trunk links to all connected switches in the network in the following manner:

Step 1   An administrator adds a new VLAN definition.

Step 2   VTP propagates the VLAN information to all switches in the VTP domain.

Step 3   Each switch synchronizes its configuration to incorporate the new VLAN data.

VTP operates in one of the following modes: server mode, client mode, transparent mode, or off mode. Off mode currently is supported only in Cisco CatOS. The default VTP mode is server mode, but Catalyst switches do not propagate VTP information out trunk interfaces until a management domain name is specified or learned.

Table 4-8 describes the features of the VTP client, server, transparent, and off modes.

Table 4-8   *VTP Modes of Operation*

VTP Mode	Features
Client	Cannot create, change, or delete VLANs on command-line interface (CLI).
	Forwards advertisements to other switches.
	Synchronizes VLAN configuration with latest information received from other switches in the management domain.
	Does not save VLAN configuration in nonvolatile RAM (NVRAM).
Server	Creates, modifies, and deletes VLANs.
	Sends and forwards advertisements to other switches.
	Synchronizes VLAN configuration with latest information received from other switches in the management domain.
	Saves VLAN configuration in NVRAM.
Transparent	Creates, deletes, and modifies VLANs only on the local switch.
	Forwards VTP advertisements received from other switches in the same management domain.
	Does not synchronize its VLAN configuration with information received from other switches in the management domain.
	Saves VLAN configuration in NVRAM.
Off	Similar to transparent mode except this version drops advertisements on trunk interface.

NOTE   In VTP version 3, there is a concept of a primary server and a secondary server. This chapter discusses VTP version 3 later in the "VTP Version 3" section.

NOTE   VTP off mode is supported in Cisco CatOS only in version 7.1 and later.

Switches flood VTP advertisements throughout the management domain over trunk interfaces. The switch sends the messages every 5 minutes or whenever there is a change in VLAN configurations. Cisco switches transmit VTP advertisements over the management VLAN (VLAN 1 by default) using a Layer 2 multicast frame.

A device that receives VTP advertisements checks various parameters before incorporating the received VLAN information. First, the management domain name and password in the advertisement must match those configured in the local switch. Next, if the configuration revision number indicates that the message was created after the configuration currently in use, the switch incorporates the advertised VLAN information if the switch is a VTP server or client.

One of the most critical components of VTP is the configuration revision number. Each time a VTP server modifies its VLAN information, it increments the configuration revision number by 1. It then sends out a VTP advertisement with the new configuration revision number. If the configuration revision number that is being advertised is higher than the number stored on the other switches in the VTP domain, the rest of the switches in the domain overwrite their VLAN configurations with the new information being advertised, as shown in Figure 4-17.

Figure 4-17 *VTP Advertisements*

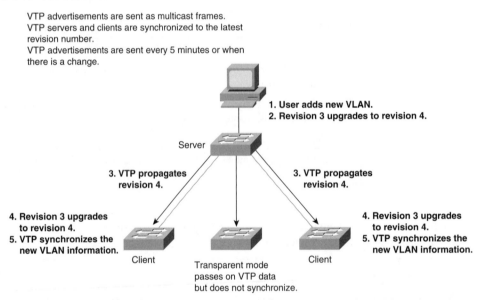

Because a VTP-transparent switch does not participate in VTP, that switch does not advertise its VLAN configuration or synchronize its VLAN database upon receipt of a VTP advertisement. Furthermore, a switch in VTP-transparent mode always has the configuration revision number of 0.

NOTE   The overwrite process means that if the VTP server deletes all VLANs and advertises with a higher revision number, the client devices in the VTP domain also delete their VLANs. Use this feature with caution.

The ensuing sections discuss the following properties of VTP:

- VTP pruning
- VTP versions
- VTP authentication
- Configuring VTP
- Verifying the VTP configuration
- Troubleshooting VTP

VTP Pruning

VTP pruning uses VLAN advertisements to determine when a trunk connection is flooding traffic needlessly. By default, a trunk connection carries traffic for all VLANs in the VTP management domain. Commonly, some switches in an enterprise network do not have local ports configured in each VLAN. In Figure 4-18, switches 1 and 4 support ports statically configured in the red VLAN.

Figure 4-18 *VTP Pruning*

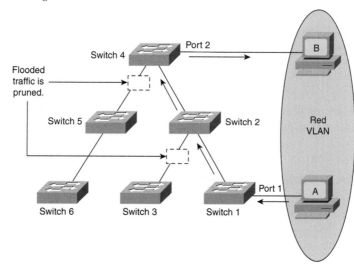

VTP pruning increases available bandwidth by restricting flooded traffic to those trunk links that the traffic must use to access the appropriate network devices. Figure 4-18 shows a switched network with VTP pruning enabled. The broadcast traffic from station A is not forwarded to switches 3, 5, and 6 because traffic for the red VLAN has been pruned on the links indicated on switches 2 and 4.

NOTE	Regardless of whether you use VTP pruning support, Catalyst switches run an instance of STP for each VLAN. An instance of STP exists for each VLAN even if there are no ports active in the VLAN or if VTP pruning removes the VLANs from an interface. As a result, VTP pruning prevents flooded traffic from propagating to switches that do not have members in specific VLANs. However, VTP pruning does not eliminate the switches' knowledge of pruned VLANs.

VTP Versions

Cisco Catalyst switches support three different versions of VTP: versions 1, 2, and 3. It is important to decide which version to use because they are not interoperable. In addition, Cisco recommends running only one VTP version for network stability. This chapter emphasizes VTP versions 1 and 2 because VTP version 3 is relatively new.

VTP Versions 1 and 2

VTP version 1 is supported in Cisco CatOS version 2.1 or later and in all versions of Cisco IOS. VTP version 2 is supported in Cisco CatOS version 3.1(1) or later and in all versions of Cisco IOS.

VTP version 2 supports these features that are not implemented in VTP version 1:

- **Token Ring support**—VTP version 2 supports Token Ring LAN switching and Token Ring VLANs.

- **Unrecognized Type-Length-Value (TLV) support**—A VTP version 2 server or client propagates configuration changes to its other trunks even for TLVs that it cannot parse. VTP version 2 servers and clients are still able to save unrecognized TLVs in NVRAM.

- **Version-independent transparent mode**—In VTP version 1, a VTP-transparent switch inspects VTP messages for the domain name and version and forwards a message only if the version and domain name match. Because only one domain is supported in the Supervisor Engine software, VTP version 2 forwards VTP messages in transparent mode—without checking the version.

- **Consistency checks**—VTP version 2 performs VLAN consistency checks (such as VLAN names and values) only when you enter new information through the CLI or via the Simple Network Management Protocol (SNMP). VTP version 2 does not perform checks when new information is obtained from a VTP message or when information is read from NVRAM. If the message digest algorithm 5 (MD5) on a received VTP message is correct, VTP version 2 accepts the information. Use VTP version 2 in a Token Ring environment, because VTP version 1 does not support Token Ring VLANs.

If all switches in a domain are capable of running VTP version 2, enable VTP version 2 on one switch. The VTP server propagates the version number to the other VTP version 2– capable switches in the VTP domain.

VTP Version 3

VTP version 3 is supported in Cisco CatOS software versions 8.1 and above and is not currently available for Cisco IOS. VTP version 3 differs from earlier VTP versions in that it does not directly handle VLANs. Instead, it is responsible for distributing a list of opaque databases over an administrative domain. The following items are enhancements in VTP version 3:

- Support for extended VLANs (1025 to 4094)
- Support for the creation and advertising of pVLANs
- Improved server authentication
- Enhancements to a mechanism for protection from the "wrong" database accidentally being inserted into a VTP domain
- Interaction with VTP versions 1 and 2
- Configurable on a per-port basis

VTP version 3 has the same features as VTP versions 1 and 2 except for the addition of the modes of primary and secondary server and the concept of database consistency.

The primary server is the sole server in the VTP domain that is used to modify VTP configuration. A VTP domain may operate without an active primary server because the secondary servers ensure persistence of the configuration over reloads. The primary server may initiate or change the VTP configuration. A VTP domain may operate without a primary server for the following reasons:

- If the switch reloads
- If a high-availability switchover occurs between the active and redundant Supervisor Engines
- If a forceful takeover from a secondary server occurs
- If a change in the VTP mode, version, or password configuration occurs

In server mode, the switch becomes a secondary server by default. The secondary server is the same as a VTP client in VTP version 2 in that a secondary VTP server cannot modify the configuration. The only exception is that the VTP server can save the VTP configuration in NVRAM. A secondary server can be changed to the primary server by using the **takeover** command from the switch; this switchover to the primary server is propagated to the entire domain. All other potential primary servers in the domain resign to secondary server mode to ensure that only one primary server exists in the VTP domain at any given time. This method avoids VLAN inconsistencies and provides a higher degree of stability.

A switch that is running VTP version 3 can modify reserved VLANs 1002 through 1005; however, these VLANs are set to their default in the scaled-down database for VTP version 2 peers. A switch that is running VTP version 3 does not accept a configuration from VTP version 1 or VTP version 2 neighbors. As a result, it is highly recommended that you change all the modes of the switches that are running versions 1 and 2 to VTP clients and reset their respective VTP revision versions.

VTP Authentication

VTP domains can be secured by using the VTP password feature. It is important to make sure that all the switches in the VTP domain have the same password and domain name; otherwise, a switch will not become a member of the VTP domain. Cisco switches use MD5 to encode passwords in 16-byte words. These passwords propagate inside VTP summary advertisements. In VTP, passwords are case-sensitive and can be 8 to 64 characters in length. The use of VTP authentication is a recommended practice.

Configuring VTP

When a network device is in VTP server mode, you can change the VLAN configuration on one switch and have the VLAN configuration propagate to all switches throughout the network. VLAN configuration changes include adding, removing, or changing the name of a VLAN. Default VTP configuration values depend on the switch model and software version. For example, the default values for the Catalyst 4500 and 6500 families of switches are as follows:

- **VTP domain name**—None
- **VTP mode**—Server
- **VTP pruning**—Disabled
- **VTP password**—None
- **VTP trap**—Disabled (SNMP traps communicating VTP status)

Cisco switches may learn or specify a VTP domain name. By default, the domain name is not set. To set a name and password for the VTP management domain, the name and password should be the same for all switches in the domain, and passwords are case-sensitive.

VTP pruning eligibility is one VLAN parameter that the VTP protocol advertises. Enabling or disabling VTP pruning with VTP versions 1 or 2 on a VTP server propagates the change throughout the management domain. However, in the case of VTP version 3, VTP pruning must be enabled manually on each switch.

Configuring VTP in Cisco IOS

To configure a VTP server in Cisco IOS in configuration mode for VTP versions 1 and 2, follow these steps from privileged EXEC mode:

Step 1 Enter global configuration mode.

```
Switch#configure terminal
```

Step 2 Configure the VTP mode as server.

```
Switch(config)#vtp server
```

Step 3 Configure the domain name.

```
Switch(config)#vtp domain domain_name
```

Step 4 (Optional.) Enable VTP version 2.

```
Switch(config)#vtp version 2
```

Step 5 (Optional.) Specify a VTP password.

```
Switch(config)#vtp password password_string
```

Step 6 (Optional.) Enable VTP pruning in the management domain.

```
Switch(config)#vtp pruning
```

Step 7 Exit global configuration mode.

```
Switch(config)#exit
```

NOTE Make sure the VTP password and VTP version are the same on all the switches that are part of the VTP domain.

NOTE Use these same steps to configure the VTP in the database mode except the VTP version. To change the VTP version under database mode, issue the **vtp v2-mode** command.

Example 4-25 shows configuration of a Catalyst switch as a VTP server in Cisco IOS in global configuration mode.

Example 4-25 *Configuring a Switch As a VTP Server in Cisco IOS*

```
Switch#configure terminal
Switch(config)#vtp mode server
Setting device to VTP SERVER mode.
Switch(config)#vtp domain Lab_Network
Setting VTP domain name to Lab_Network
Switch(config)#end
```

Configuring VTP in Cisco CatOS

To configure a VTP server in Cisco CatOS, follow these steps from the privileged EXEC mode:

Step 1   Define the VTP domain name on the switch.

> **set vtp domain** *name*

Step 2   Define the VTP mode.

> **set vtp mode client | off | server | transparent**

Step 3   (Optional.) Specify the password for the VTP domain.

> **set vtp passwd** *passwd*

Step 4   (Optional.) Specify the version of VTP. The default is 1.

> **set vtp version 1 | 2**

Step 5   (Optional.) Enable VTP pruning in the whole VTP domain.

> **set vtp pruning enable**

Step 6   (Optional.) Disable VTP pruning on the VLANs.

> **clear vtp pruneeligible** *vlan_range*

Step 7   (Optional.) Add VLANs to the VTP pruning list.

> **set vtp pruneeligible** *vlan_range*

Example 4-26 shows configuration of a VTP domain named Lab_Network in server mode in Cisco CatOS.

Example 4-26 *VTP Domain Configuration in Cisco CatOS*

```
Console> (enable) set vtp domain Lab_Network
VTP domain Lab_Network modified
Console> (enable) set vtp mode server
Changing VTP mode for all features
VTP domain Lab_Network modified
```

Example 4-27 shows configuration of VTP pruning for a VTP domain named BCMSN in Cisco CatOS. In addition, the example illustrates the removal of VLANs 100 through 500 from the pruning list in Cisco CatOS.

Example 4-27 *VTP Pruning in Cisco CatOS*

```
Console> (enable) set vtp pruning enable
Cannot modify pruning mode unless in VTP SERVER mode.
Console> (enable) set vtp mode server
Changing VTP mode for all features
VTP domain BCMSN modified
Console> (enable) set vtp pruning enable
This command will enable the pruning function in the entire management domain.
```

Example 4-27 *VTP Pruning in Cisco CatOS (Continued)*

```
All devices in the management domain should be pruning-capable before enabling.
Do you want to continue (y/n) [n]? y
VTP domain BCMSN modified
Console> (enable) clear vtp pruneeligible 100-500
Vlans 100-500 will not be pruned on this device.
VTP domain BCMSN modified.
```

Verifying the VTP Configuration

Use the **show vtp status** command to display information about the VTP configuration and current state in Cisco IOS. For Cisco CatOS, use the **show vtp domain** command to display similar information.

Example 4-28 shows how to verify the VTP configuration by using the **show vtp status** command. The output describes the VTP version, the number of VLANs supported locally, the VTP operating mode, the VTP domain name, and the VTP pruning mode.

Example 4-28 *Displaying VTP Status*

```
Switch#show vtp status

VTP Version                    : 2
Configuration Revision         : 247
Maximum VLANs supported locally : 1005
Number of existing VLANs       : 33
VTP Operating Mode             : Server
VTP Domain Name                : Lab_Network
VTP Pruning Mode               : Enabled
VTP V2 Mode                    : Disabled
VTP Traps Generation           : Disabled
MD5 digest                     : 0x45 0x52 0xB6 0xFD 0x63 0xC8 0x49 0x80
Configuration last modified by 0.0.0.0 at 8-12-99 15:04:4
```

Use the **show vtp counters** command to display statistics about VTP operation. Example 4-29 displays VTP statistics in Cisco IOS.

Example 4-29 *Displaying VTP Statistics in Cisco IOS*

```
Switch# show vtp counters

VTP statistics:
Summary advertisements received   : 7
Subset advertisements received    : 5
Request advertisements received   : 0
Summary advertisements transmitted : 997
Subset advertisements transmitted : 13
Request advertisements transmitted : 3
Number of config revision errors  : 0
Number of config digest errors    : 0
Number of V1 summary errors       : 0
```

continues

Example 4-29 *Displaying VTP Statistics in Cisco IOS (Continued)*

```
VTP pruning statistics:

Trunk           Join Transmitted Join Received    Summary advts received from
                                                  non-pruning-capable device
--------------- ---------------- ---------------- ------------------
Fa5/8                 43071           42766              5
```

Example 4-30 shows the output of the **show vtp domain** command in Cisco CatOS.

Example 4-30 *Verifying VTP Configuration in Cisco CatOS*

```
Console> (enable) show vtp domain
Version : running VTP1 (VTP3 capable)
Domain Name : Lab_Network Password : configured (hidden)
Notifications: disabled Updater ID: 172.20.52.19
Feature Mode Revision
-------------- -------------- ----------
VLAN Off 0
Pruning : disabled
VLANs prune eligible: 2-1000
```

Troubleshooting VTP

Problems with VTP configuration are usually a result of improperly configured trunk links, domain names, VTP modes, or passwords.

Perform the following steps to troubleshoot VTP issues in which VTP is not updating the configuration on other switches when VLAN configuration changes occur:

- Make sure the switches are connected through trunk links. VTP updates are exchanged only over trunk links. Check to make sure all switch-to-switch connections are using the same trunking protocol. In addition, verify that the operation of each link partner's operation speed and duplex is the same by using the **show interface** command in Cisco IOS.

- Make sure the VTP domain name, which is case-sensitive, is configured exactly the same way on the appropriate switches. Switches only exchange VTP updates between switches in the same VTP domain. Use the **show vtp status** command to verify these configurations.

- Check whether the switch is in VTP transparent mode. Only switches in VTP server or VTP client mode update their VLAN configuration based on VTP updates from other switches. Use the **show vtp status** command to verify the configured VTP modes.

- If you are using VTP passwords, make sure to use the same password and authentication on all switches in the VTP domain.

- Make a backup copy of VLAN.dat in Cisco IOS VLAN database configuration mode or the configuration in Cisco IOS by copying the configuration to a remote device such as a TFTP server before troubleshooting.

Case Study: Troubleshooting VLAN/Trunking Issues Across the Switches

If a particular host is not able to communicate with another host that is in the same VLAN but in a different switch, follow these steps:

Step 1   Make sure that a VLAN is created in the database by using the **show vlan** command.

Step 2   Check to determine if the hosts are members of the same VLAN by using the **show interface** command.

Step 3   Check to determine if the VLANs are active in the VLAN database by using the **show vlan membership** command. If this is not the problem, check to see if the VTP name and password, if configured, are correct or check to see that the VLAN is present in the VLAN database.

Step 4   Check to determine if the particular VLAN is active on the trunk interface. Even if active, if it is a dot1q trunk, check to see if the native VLAN is the same across both sides of the trunk interfaces by using the **show interface trunk** command.

Study Tips

The following bullets review important BCMSN exam preparation points of this chapter. The bullets only briefly highlight the important concepts. Table 4-9 lists and describes the functions of the important commands covered in this chapter. Consult the text of this chapter for additional information regarding these topics:

- A VLAN is a logical broadcast domain that facilitates a group of end devices with common requirements, irrespective of their physical locations. A VLAN generally encompasses a single IP subnet.

- In terms of configuring VLANs in Cisco IOS, make sure to define the VLAN before you assign the ports to the newly created VLAN.

- Always use the global configuration mode to configure VLANs in Cisco IOS.

- Recommended practice is to configure host ports to be static access ports using the **switchport mode access** command.

- Use the **switchport access vlan** *vlan* command to configure interfaces for a specific VLAN.

- Always use the **switchport host** command on the ports connected to a single host to disable EtherChanneling and to enable Spanning-Tree PortFast.

- Because 802.1Q is an industry-standard trunking protocol that has support for extended VLANs (VLAN IDs 1025 to 4094) and uses 802.1p fields for QoS, recommended practice is to always implement 802.1Q trunking instead of ISL trunking in multilayer switched networks.

- By default, the Native VLAN of an interface is 1.

- The Native VLAN of a trunk port is the configured VLAN ID as if the port were not trunking in Cisco CatOS.

- The Native VLAN is not tagged; therefore, the Native VLAN does not contain 802.1p fields for QoS. However, there is a configuration option in more recent Cisco IOS versions 12.1.13 or later to tag the Native VLAN on a trunk port (that is, tag all VLANs). With this option, the Native VLAN traffic is simply tagged with the associated VLAN ID, by default, VLAN 1. It is possible to remove VLAN 1 from a trunk; however, this only removes data traffic from VLAN 1. CDP, DTP, PAgP, and so on still transmit across VLAN 1.

- Dynamic Trunking Protocol (DTP) is a protocol that negotiates the operational mode of directly connected switch ports to a trunk port and chooses an appropriate trunking protocol.

- Always use the **switchport mode trunk** command to configure the trunk port in the on mode statically if the link partner (peer) does not support DTP or the desirable mode trunking configuration.

- VTP is also one of the important Layer 2 messaging protocols that is used to circulate and synchronize the VLAN database throughout the network within a VTP domain.

- VTP is configurable in server, client, and transparent modes within a particular domain. In server mode, the switch can add, delete, and update VLANs. In client mode, the switch cannot add or delete VLANs, but it can synchronize and forward VTP advertisements to other switches in a VTP domain. In transparent mode, the switch can add, delete, or modify VLANs only on a local switch, but it doesn't synchronize its VLAN database. Switches can forward VTP advertisement to other switches in a VTP domain, even when operating in the VTP transparent mode.

- The default VTP mode is the server mode.

- Use VTP pruning to stop flooding of unnecessary traffic on trunk ports.

- Configure switches in the VTP server or client mode to receive and synchronize the VLAN database using trunk links.

- Always add a new switch in either VTP transparent mode in the same domain name or in server mode with a different domain name first. Later, change the switch to the correct domain or change from VTP transparent mode to VTP server or client mode after all trunk links are up to properly synchronize the VLAN database.

- Private VLANs (pVLAN) are VLANs that provide Layer 2 isolation between end devices within the same VLAN. As such, private VLANs turn a single VLAN broadcast domain into multiple small broadcast domains to facilitate security and to reduce the number of IP subnets.

- Private VLANs consist of a primary and one or multiple secondary VLANs. Each secondary VLAN is associated with a primary VLAN.

- Isolated and community pVLANs are secondary pVLANs. Hosts that reside in isolated pVLANs can only converse with a promiscuous port (generally, a port with a connected router, whether it is logical, physical, or virtual), but they cannot communicate with hosts in the same isolated pVLAN. In community pVLANs, hosts that belong to the same community pVLAN can communicate with other ports in the same community VLAN and any promiscuous ports; however, the hosts in the community VLAN cannot communicate with hosts in the other community pVLANs or isolated pVLANs.

Table 4-9 *Commands to Review*

Command	Description
show vlan	Displays detailed information of all the VLANs configured on the switch.
show vlan brief	Displays brief information about the VLANs on the switch. This command describes the VLAN names, their status, and the ports assigned to the VLANs.
show vtp status	Provides information about VTP name, mode, version, and authentication.
show vlan *vlan-id*	Displays information about a particular VLAN by VLAN-ID.
show vlan summary	Displays a summary of active, suspended, and extended VLANs. This command is only available in Cisco CatOS.
show interfaces *type slot/port* **switchport**	Displays administrative and operational status of a switching interface, which includes VLAN information, pVLAN status, etc. *type* = **ethernet, fastethernet, gigabitethernet,** or **tengigabitethernet**
show interfaces *type slot/port* **trunk**	Displays the trunk information of an interface.
(config-if)#**description** *description*	Configures an interface with a description. This option is useful for quickly identifying interfaces.
(config-if)#**switchport host**	This command enables Spanning-Tree PortFast and turns off channeling on an interface. This command prevents timeouts on boot for host workstations and servers.
(config)#**interface** *type slot/port*	Configures an interface.

continues

Table 4-9 *Commands to Review (Continued)*

Command	Description
(config-if)#**switchport mode access**	Configures an interface with nontrunking single VLAN interface.
(config-if)#**switchport access vlan** *vlan_id*	Configures an interface to a VLAN-ID.
(config-if)#**switchport mode trunk**	Configures an interface for trunking unconditionally.
(config-if)#**switchport trunk encapsulation [dot1q | isl | negotiate]**	Configures the trunking protocol on a trunk interface.
(config-if)#**switchport trunk allowed vlan** *options*	Configures VLANs allowed to pass traffic on a trunk interface.
(config-if)#**switchport trunk native vlan** *vlan-id*	Configures the native VLAN on a trunk interface.

Summary

This chapter discussed VLANs in detail, including coverage of trunking and VTP.

In review, a VLAN is a logical grouping of switch ports that connects nodes of virtually any type, regardless of physical location. A VLAN is usually defined as end-to-end or local. An end-to-end VLAN spans the entire switched network, whereas a local VLAN is limited to the switches in the Building Access and Building Distribution submodules. VLANs usually are defined statically by manually assigning the switch ports to particular VLANs.

Furthermore, a trunk is a Layer 2 point-to-point link between networking devices that is capable of carrying the traffic of multiple VLANs. ISL and 802.1Q are the two trunking protocols to connect two switches. ISL is a Cisco proprietary protocol used for VLAN trunking. The 802.1Q protocol is an open-standard protocol also used for VLAN trunking. ISL supports VLAN numbers 1 to 1005, whereas 802.1Q supports VLAN numbers 1 to 4094.

VTP is used to distribute and synchronize information about VLANs configured throughout a switched network. VTP pruning helps to stop flooding of unnecessary traffic on trunk links. Review the study tips section for additional summarization of this chapter.

Configuration Exercise: Configuring VLAN, Trunking, and VTP in Multilayer Switched Networks

Complete this configuration exercise to familiarize yourself with the initial configuration of VLANs, VTP, and trunking on Cisco IOS–based Catalyst switches.

Required Resources

The only resources that are required for this exercise are access to Cisco IOS–based Catalyst switches via the console or in-band access such as SSH.

Exercise Objective

The purpose of this configuration exercise is to demonstrate the configuration of VLANs, trunking, and VTP in the multilayer switched environment. After completing this exercise, you will be able to perform the following types of configurations on Catalyst switches that are running Cisco IOS:

- Create a VTP management domain
- Configure trunking
- Configure VLANs
- Associate VLANs with ports on your switch
- Add a new switch to the existing network
- Verify the VTP and VLAN status
- Configure PVLANs

Network Diagram

Figure 4-19 shows the network layout for this exercise. In the multilayer switched network, the links between the Building Access submodule switch and the Building Distribution submodule switch (as well as the links between the distribution switches) are trunks, and all the switches belong to the same VTP domain. The access switches serve as VTP clients, while the distribution switches serve as VTP servers.

Figure 4-19 *Network Layout for Configuration Exercise*

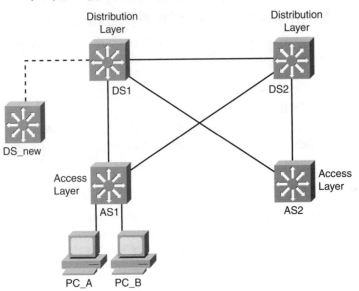

Command List

In this configuration exercise, you will use the commands listed in Table 4-10. The commands are in alphabetical order so that you can easily locate the information you need. Refer to this table if you need configuration-command assistance during the configuration exercise. The table includes only the specific parameters that are used in the example, not all the available options for the commands.

Table 4-10 *Command List for Configuration Exercise*

Command	Description
configure terminal	From privileged EXEC mode, enters global configuration mode
enable password *password*	Specifies a password used to authenticate a user to enter the privileged EXEC mode
exit	Exits the current mode
interface FastEthernet | **GigabitEthernet** *slot/port*	Enters the interface configuration mode for a Fast Ethernet or Gigabit Ethernet interface
interface range FastEthernet | **GigabitEthernet** *slot/ starting_port - ending_port*	Moves a range of interfaces into the interface configuration mode for applying the same configuration to the range of interfaces

Table 4-10 *Command List for Configuration Exercise (Continued)*

Command	Description
name *vlan-name*	Specifies a name for a VLAN in either the VLAN database or VLAN configuration mode
no interface vlan *vlan-id* **type**	Disables a VLAN interface
ping *ip-address*	Sends an ICMP echo to the designated IP address, using the default settings of size and response window time
private-vlan [primary I **isolated** I **community]**	Configures the VLAN as a pVLAN type
private-vlan association {*secondary_vlan_list* I **add** *secondary_vlan_list* I **remove** *secondary_vlan_list*}	Associates a secondary pVLAN to a primary pVLAN
private-vlan mapping {*secondary_vlan_list* I **add** *secondary_vlan_list* I **remove** *secondary_vlan_list*}	Maps the secondary pVLAN to the Layer 3 primary VLAN interface for routing
show interfaces [*type slot/port*] **switchport**	Displays the switchport configuration of the interface
show interfaces [*type slot/ port*]**trunk**	Displays the trunk configuration of the interface
show vlan	Displays VLAN information
show vlan private-vlan	Displays the pVLAN configuration
show vtp status	Verifies the VTP configuration
shutdown/no shutdown	Shuts down or enables an interface
switchport access vlan *vlan-id*	Specifies the default VLAN, which is used if the interface stops trunking
switchport mode access	Puts the interface into permanent nontrunking mode and negotiates to convert the link into a nontrunk link
switchport mode private-vlan {**host** I **promiscuous**}	Configures an interface as a pVLAN host port or a promiscuous port
switchport mode trunk	Puts the interface into permanent trunking mode and negotiates to convert the link into a trunk link
switchport nonegotiate	Turns off DTP negotiation
switchport private-vlan host-association *primary_vlan_ID* *secondary_vlan_ID*	Associates a Layer 2 interface with a pVLAN

continues

Table 4-10 *Command List for Configuration Exercise (Continued)*

Command	Description
switchport trunk allowed vlan [**remove**] *vlan-list*	Configures the list of VLANs allowed on the trunk
switchport trunk encapsulation dot1q	Specifies 802.1Q encapsulation on the trunk link
switchport trunk encapsulation isl	Specifies ISL encapsulation on the trunk link
telnet *ip-address*	Starts a terminal-emulation program that permits you to access network devices remotely over the network
vlan database	Enters VLAN configuration mode
vlan *vlan-id*	Creates a VLAN in either VLAN database or configuration mode
vtp domain *domain-name*	Sets the VTP domain name in either the VLAN database or configuration mode
vtp mode [**client** ⏐ **server** ⏐ **transparent**]	Sets the VTP mode

Task 1: Create a VTP Management Domain

Step 1 Enter privileged EXEC mode using the **enable** command, and then enter global configuration mode using the **configure terminal** command.

Step 2 From global configuration mode, configure the Building Access submodule switches, AS1 and AS2:

— Use the **vtp domain** *domain-name* command to configure the VTP domain name as "cisco."

— Use the **vtp mode** command to configure the switches as VTP clients.

— Use the **vtp password** command to configure a VTP domain password.

Also from global configuration mode, configure the Distribution layer switches, DS1 and DS2, with the same commands, except configure them as VTP servers.

```
as1(config)#vtp domain cisco
Changing VTP domain name from NULL to cisco
as1(config)#vtp password cisco
as1(config)#vtp mode client
Setting device to VTP CLIENT mode.
```

Step 3 Do the same configuration on the Building Distribution submodule switches DS1 and DS2, but configure them as server.

```
ds1(config)#vtp domain cisco
Changing VTP domain name from NULL to cisco
ds1(config)#vtp password cisco
```

Task 2: Configure Trunking

Step 1 Connect to your Building Access submodule switch AS1.

Step 2 Configure the interface on the Building Access submodule switches, AS1 and AS2, as 802.1Q trunk ports.

Note	If you need to configure the encapsulation type to dot-1Q on a switch that defaults to ISL, use the **switchport trunk encapsulation dot1q** command to configure the port as an 802.1Q trunk.
	The Catalyst 2950XL supports 802.1Q encapsulation only, and the Catalyst 3550XL/3560 supports both ISL and 802.1Q encapsulation.

```
as1(config)#interface GigabitEthernet 1/1
as1(config-if)#switchport
as1(config-if)#switchport trunk encapsulation dot1q
as1(config-if)#switchport mode trunk
```

Note	Use the **switchport** command to configure interfaces as Layer 2 interfaces in Cisco IOS. The Catalyst 6500 family of switches running Cisco IOS defaults to Layer 3 interfaces, whereas the Catalyst 2950, 3550, 3560, and 4500 default interface operation is Layer 2. Before applying trunking to interfaces on the Catalyst 6500 or to interfaces configured as Layer 3 interfaces, use the **switchport** command to force the interface into Layer 2 operation.

Step 3 Configure the Distribution switches DS1 and DS2 by repeating the preceding step.

```
ds1(config)#interface GigabitEthernet 1/1
ds1(config-if)#switchport
ds1(config-if)#switchport trunk encapsulation dot1q
ds1(config-if)#switchport mode trunk
ds1(config-if)#end
```

Task 3: Configure VLANs

Step 1   Configure VLANs 10, 20, and 30.

```
ds1#configure terminal
09:04:30: %SYS-5-CONFIG_I: Configured from console by console
Enter configuration commands, one per line.  End with CNTL/Z.
ds1(config)#vlan 10,20,30
ds1(config-vlan)#
```

Task 4: Assign VLANs with Ports on Your Switch

Step 1   Assign your PC port to its primary VLAN by using the **switchport access vlan** *vlan-id* command while in interface configuration mode.

```
as1(config)#interface FastEthernet 4/1
as1(config-if)#switchport
as1(config-if)#switchport mode access
as1(config-if)#switchport access vlan 10
as1(config-if)#exit
```

Step 2   Verify that your PC has connectivity with devices in the right VLAN by issuing a **ping** command.

Task 5: Add a New Switch to the Existing Network

To add the new switch, DS-new, to the existing network, as shown with the dotted lines in Figure 4-19, perform the steps that follow. Make sure the interfaces connecting to existing network are shut down before physically connecting the new switch.

Step 1   Change the VTP mode to transparent (or make it part of a temporary domain).

```
DS-new(config)#vtp mode transparent
Setting device to VTP TRANSPARENT mode.
```

Step 2   Configure the DS-new switch ports connected to the other switch as trunks ports with the static **on** setting and force 802.1Q encapsulation. Note that if the link partner is configured for dynamic trunking, the port may have already negotiated to a trunk.

```
DS-new(config)#interface gigabitEthernet 1/1
DS-new(config-if)#switchport
DS-new(config-if)#switchport trunk encapsulation dot1q
DS-new(config-if)#switchport mode trunk
DS-new(config-if)#no shutdown
```

Step 3   Configure the VTP mode to participate as client in the VTP domain.

```
DS-new(config)#vtp domain cisco
Changing VTP domain name from NULL to cisco
DS-new(config)#vtp mode client
Setting device to VTP CLIENT mode.
```

Task 6: Verify the VLAN and VTP Status

Use the **show running-config interface** *mod/port* commands to verify the interface config, **show vtp status** to verify the VTP configuration, and **show vlan** to verify the VLAN configuration:

```
as1#show running-config interface FastEthernet 4/1
Building configuration...
Current configuration : 141 bytes
!
interface FastEthernet4/1
 no ip address
 no logging event link-status
 switchport
 switchport access vlan 10
 switchport mode access
end

as1#show running-config interface GigabitEthernet 1/1
Current configuration : 154 bytes
!
interface GigabitEthernet1/1
 no ip address
 no logging event link-status
 switchport
 switchport trunk encapsulation dot1q
 switchport mode trunk
end
as1#show vtp status
VTP Version                     : 2
Configuration Revision          : 0
Maximum VLANs supported locally : 1005
Number of existing VLANs        : 6
VTP Operating Mode              : Client
VTP Domain Name                 : cisco
VTP Pruning Mode                : Disabled
VTP V2 Mode                     : Disabled
VTP Traps Generation            : Disabled
MD5 digest                      : 0x8C 0x59 0x58 0x5C 0xF6 0x03 0x51 0x9E
Configuration last modified by 0.0.0.0 at 0-0-00 00:00:00
as1#
as1#show vlan
VLAN Name                             Status    Ports
---- -------------------------------- --------- -------------------------------
1    default                          active    Gi1/1
10   VLAN0010                         active    Fa4/1
20   VLAN0020                         active
30   VLAN0030                         active
1002 fddi-default                     act/unsup
1003 token-ring-default               act/unsup
1004 fddinet-default                  act/unsup
1005 trnet-default                    act/unsup
```

```
VLAN Type  SAID        MTU    Parent RingNo BridgeNo Stp  BrdgMode Trans1 Trans2
---- ----- ----------  -----  ------ ------ -------- ---- -------- ------ ------
1    enet  100001      1500   -      -      -        -    -        0      0
10   enet  100010      1500   -      -      -        -    -        0      0
20   enet  100020      1500   -      -      -        -    -        0      0
30   enet  100030      1500   -      -      -        -    -        0      0
1002 fddi  101002      1500   -      -      -        -    -        0      0
1003 tr    101003      1500   -      -      -        -    -        0      0
1004 fdnet 101004      1500   -      -      -        ieee -        0      0
1005 trnet 101005      1500   -      -      -        ibm  -        0      0

Remote SPAN VLANs
------------------------------------------------------------------------------

Primary Secondary Type              Ports
------- --------- ----------------- --------------------------------------------
```

Task 7: Configure pVLANs

For this task, the first step is to configure the VTP mode to transparent because pVLANs are supported only in VTP transparent mode:

Step 1 Configure the VTP mode to transparent to configure pVLANs.

```
DS1(config-vlan)#vtp mode transparent
```

Step 2 Create a primary pVLAN 100, a community pVLAN 101, and an isolated pVLAN 102 on switches AS1 and DS1. In addition, associate the secondary pVLANs to the primary pVLAN.

```
DS1(config-vlan)#vlan 100
DS1(config-vlan)#private-vlan primary
DS1(config-vlan)#private-vlan association 101-102
DS1(config-vlan)#vlan 101
DS1(config-vlan)#private-vlan community
DS1(config-vlan)#vlan 102
DS1(config-vlan)#private-vlan isolated
```

Step 3 Configure an interface VLAN 100 for the primary pVLAN, and map the secondary pVLAN 101.

```
DS1(config)#interface vlan 100
DS1(config-if)#no shutdown
DS1(config-if)#private-vlan mapping 101,102
```

Step 4 Configure the Host's A interface as a member of pVLAN 101 and the Host's B interface as a member of pVLAN 102 on switch DS1.

```
DS1(config)#interface fastEthernet 2/3
DS1(config-if)#description Host_A
DS1(config-if)#switchport
DS1(config-if)#switchport mode private-vlan host
DS1(config-if)#switchport private-vlan host-association 100 101
DS1(config-if)#no shutdown
```

```
DS1(config-if)# interface fastEthernet 2/4
DS1(config-if)#description Host_B
DS1(config-if)#switchport
DS1(config-if)#switchport mode private-vlan host
DS1(config-if)#switchport private-vlan host-association 100 102
DS1(config-if)#no shutdown
```

Step 5   Verify the Private VLAN configuration, and make sure Host A is not able to send an ICMP ping to Host B.

```
DS1#show vlan private-vlan
Primary Secondary Type          Ports
------- --------- ---------     ------------------------------------------

100     101       community     Fa2/1, Fa2/3
100     102       isolated      Fa2/2, Fa2/4
```

Review Questions

For multiple-choice questions, there might be more than one correct answer.

1 True or False: It is important to have the same native VLAN on both switch link partners for ISL trunking.

2 True or False: The Cisco Catalyst 6500 supports up to 1024 VLANs in the most recent software releases.

3 True or False: When removing the native VLAN from a trunk port, CDP, Port Aggregation Protocol (PaGP), and DTP then use the lowest-numbered VLAN to send traffic.

4 True or False: Hosts that are members of different community VLANs are able to communicate to each other but not to members of isolated VLANs.

5 True or False: In VTP client mode, switches can add and delete VLANs.

6 True or False: Token Ring support is available in VTP version 1.

Questions 7 through 9 are based on the configuration in Example 4-31.

Example 4-31 *Configuration Example for Questions 7 through 9*

```
Catalyst6500-IOS#show run interface gigabitEthernet 3/9
Building configuration...

Current configuration : 137 bytes
!
interface GigabitEthernet3/9
 mtu 9216
 no ip address
 switchport
 switchport access vlan 5
 switchport trunk encapsulation dot1q
end
```

7 If the interface in Example 4-31 negotiates trunking, what would be the Native VLAN?

   a VLAN 1

   b VLAN 5

   c VLAN 9216

   d There would be no Native VLAN if the port negotiated trunking.

8 Under what condition can the interface in Example 4-31 negotiate ISL trunking?

   a If the port is a member of an EtherChannel.

   b If the link partner defaults to ISL trunking for negotiated ports.

   c If the link partner is configured for trunking in the on mode.

   d The interface cannot negotiate trunking because it is configured statically for 802.1Q trunking.

9 Which statements are true in regards to the configuration of the interface in Example 4-31?

   a The interface is a member of VLAN 5 and may negotiate to a trunk port.

   b The interface may negotiate to an ISL trunk with a Native VLAN of 5.

   c The interface may negotiate to an 802.1Q trunk and operate with a Native VLAN of 1.

   d The interface will not negotiate to a trunk port because it is configured in access VLAN 5.

   e If a host workstation is connected to the interface, it must be configured for trunking.

Questions 10 through 12 are based on the configuration in Example 4-32.

Example 4-32 *Configuration Example for Questions 10 Through 12*

```
svs-san-6509-2#show interfaces gigabitEthernet 3/9 switchport
Name: Gi3/9
Switchport: Enabled
Administrative Mode: dynamic auto
Operational Mode: down
Administrative Trunking Encapsulation: dot1q
Negotiation of Trunking: On
Access Mode VLAN: 1 (default)
Trunking Native Mode VLAN: 2 (VLAN0002)
Voice VLAN: none
```

Example 4-32 *Configuration Example for Questions 10 Through 12 (Continued)*

```
Administrative private-vlan host-association: none
Administrative private-vlan mapping: none
Operational private-vlan: none
Trunking VLANs Enabled: ALL
Pruning VLANs Enabled: 2-1001
Capture Mode Disabled
Capture VLANs Allowed: ALL
```

10 What is trunk Native VLAN based on configuration Example 4-32?

a   VLAN 1

b   VLAN 2

c   VLAN 5

d   There would be no Native VLAN if the port negotiated trunking.

11 Based on the configuration Example 4-32, what statement is true if the link partner (peer switch) is configured for the dynamic trunking mode?

a   The interface cannot negotiate to a trunk port because it is configured for dot1q encapsulation.

b   The interface cannot negotiate to a trunk port because the Native VLAN and access VLANs are mismatched.

c   The interface can negotiate to a trunk port if the peer is configured for the dynamic desirable trunking mode.

d   The interface can negotiate to a trunk port if access VLAN is the same on both sides.

12 What is the interface's access mode VLAN in configuration Example 4-32?

a   VLAN 1

b   VLAN 2

c   VLAN 5

d   VLAN 1001

13 How does implementing VLANs help improve the overall performance of the network?

   a By isolating problem employees

   b By constraining broadcast traffic

   c By grouping switch ports into logical communities

   d By forcing the Layer 3 routing process to occur between VLANs

14 What are two advantages of using local VLANs over end-to-end VLANs? (Choose two.)

   a Eases anagement

   b Eliminates the need for Layer 3 devices

   c Allows for a more deterministic network

   d Groups users by logical commonality

   e Keeps users and resources on the same VLAN

15 Which prompt indicates that you are in VLAN database configuration mode of Cisco IOS?

   a Switch#

   b Switch(vlan)#

   c Switch(config)#

   d Switch(config-vlan)#

16 Which switch port mode unconditionally sets the switch port to Access mode regardless of any other DTP configurations?

   a Access

   b Nonegotiate

   c Dynamic auto

   d Dynamic desirable

17 What information is contained in the FCS of an ISL-encapsulated frame?

   a CRC calculation

   b Header encapsulation

   c ASIC implementation

   d Protocol-independence

18 802.1Q uses an internal tagging mechanism, where a tag is inserted after the _____ field.

   a Type

   b SA

   c Data

   d CRC

19 Which command correctly configures a port with ISL encapsulation in Cisco IOS?

   a Switch(config-if)#**switchport mode trunk isl**

   b Switch(config-if)#**switchport mode encapsulation isl**

   c Switch(config-if)#**switchport trunk encapsulation isl**

   d Switch(config-if)#**switchport mode trunk encapsulation isl**

20 Which command correctly sets the native VLAN to VLAN 5?

   a **switchport native vlan 5**

   b **switchport trunk native 5**

   c **switchport native trunk vlan 5**

   d **switchport trunk native vlan 5**

21 If the Layer 2 interface mode on one link partner is set to dynamic auto, a trunk will be established if the link partner is configured for which two types of interface modes in Cisco IOS? (Choose two.)

   a Trunk

   b Access

   c Nonegotiate

   d Dynamic auto

   e Dynamic desirable

22 What is the default VTP mode for a Catalyst switch?

   a Client

   b Access

   c Server

   d Transparent

23 When is a consistency check performed with VTP version 2?

   a When information is read from NVRAM

   b When the digest on a received VTP message is correct

   c When new information is obtained from a VTP message

   d When you enter new information through the CLI or SNMP

24 Which command correctly sets the VTP version to version 1 in Cisco IOS global configuration mode?

   a **vtp v1-mode**

   b **vtp v2-mode**

   c **no vtp version**

   d **no vtp version 2**

25 Which of the following are valid VTP version 1 and 2 modes? (Check all that apply.)

   a   Primary server mode

   b   Server mode

   c   Client mode

   d   Transparent mode

26 After you complete the VTP configuration, which command should you use to verify your configuration?

   a   show vtp status

   b   show vtp counters

   c   show vtp statistics

   d   show vtp status counters

27 What command might correct a problem with incorrect VTP passwords?

   a   password vtp 0

   b   clear vtp password

   c   clear password vtp

   d   vtp password *password_string*

28 What is the purpose of pruning?

29 What are the advantages of pVLANs?

30 Suppose you have two workstations, A and B. If both workstations A and B are members of the same community pVLAN, can they communicate to each other? If they are members of different community pVLANs, can they communicate? If they are members of the same isolated pVLAN, can they communicate? Can they both communicate to the same promiscuous ports? Explain all your answers.

This chapter covers the following topics:

- The Basic Operation of the Spanning Tree Protocol (STP) and Its Use in a Multilayer Switched Network
- The 802.1D STP Standard, Including Concepts, States, Timers, and BPDU Format
- Configuration of Basic Parameters of Per VLAN Spanning Tree Plus (PVST+)
- The Difference Between 802.1D and Rapid Spanning Tree Protocol (RSTP)
- The Port States and Port Roles of Switches Running RSTP
- RSTP BPDU Format and Operation Details
- Multiple Spanning Tree (MST) and Its Advantages over PVST+
- Configuration of Basic Parameters of MST

Understanding and Configuring the 802.1D, 802.1s, and 802.1w Spanning Tree Protocols

High availability is of primary concern for enterprise networks that rely heavily on their multilayer switched network to conduct business. One method of ensuring high availability is to provide Layer 2 redundancy of devices, modules, and links throughout the network. Network redundancy at Layer 2, however, introduces the potential for bridging loops, where packets loop endlessly between devices, crippling the network. The Spanning Tree Protocol identifies and prevents such Layer 2 loops.

This chapter overviews the spanning-tree protocols. Chapter 6, "Adding Resiliency to Spanning Tree Using Advanced Features and Troubleshooting STP Issues," discusses Cisco-specific spanning-tree features and recommended troubleshooting practices for spanning tree.

Overview of the Spanning Tree Protocol

The basic STP functionality of a switch is identical to that of a transparent bridge. To understand STP, then, it is helpful to first look at the behavior of a switch as a transparent bridge without using spanning tree.

By definition, a transparent bridge

- Does not modify the frames that are forwarded.
- Learns addresses by "listening" on a port for the source MAC address of a device. The bridge then builds a MAC address table that indicates which MAC addresses are learned on specific ports; the switches use this table to forward frames based on the destination MAC address.
- Forwards packets with a destination multicast or broadcast MAC address out all ports except for the port that initially received the broadcast; this process is referred to as *flooding*. The exception to flooding multicast frames is with the use of multicast features such as IGMP snooping.
- Forwards a frame out all ports except for the port that initially received the frame, if the destination MAC address of that frame is unknown. Frames with unknown destination MAC addresses are referred to as *unknown unicast packets*.

Figure 5-1 illustrates the concept of transparent bridging using a switch. The switch treats each port as an individual segment; in Figure 5-1, both ports belong to the same Layer 2 broadcast domain. The switch in this scenario learns the MAC address of station A on port 1/1 and station B on port 1/2 upon receiving frames from those stations.

Figure 5-1   *Transparent Bridging*

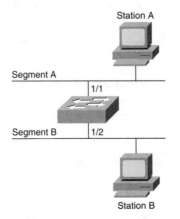

Transparent bridging by its very definition is transparent to the attached devices at Layer 2 and upper-layer protocols. This protocol transparency allows bridges to forward different packet types such as IP, IPX, and AppleTalk.

In a simple bridge environment without redundant links, transparent bridging works well. Transparent bridging of frames begins to have problems, however, as soon as bridged networks have redundant paths.

NOTE   In this chapter, the terms "bridges" and "switches" are used synonymously. Although bridges are obsolete devices, the term "bridging" is used by the IEEE 802.1 Standards Committee to refer to the Layer 2 relay process that is performed by switches. All Cisco LAN products are referred to as switches.

Identifying Bridging Loops

As Figure 5-2 illustrates, station A has two potential paths to station B by way of the switches. Consider a scenario in which station A sends to station B, but neither switch has learned station B's MAC address.

Station A transmits the frame to segment A. Both bridges on segment A receive the frame on their ports 1/1 and 2/1, respectively. The switches populate their respective address tables, indicating that station A resides on segment A, out ports 1/1 and 2/1, respectively.

Figure 5-2   *Bridging Loop*

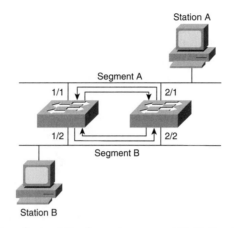

Both switches then forward the frame to segment B. Notice that not only does station B receive the frame twice, but both switches also receive the frame from the *other* switch. Because one of the basic characteristics of transparent bridging is to listen to the source MAC address to learn the correct port to use for that address, each switch relearns station A as residing on ports 1/2 and 2/2, respectively. The switches now incorrectly assume that all frames for station A need to be transmitted to segment B.

The switches forward the frame again to segment A, where the frame originated. The network is now seeing the beginning of a loop. Because neither switch is aware of the other, each switch continually forwards the frame on the other port. This loop continues forever. The loop manifests itself as the ability to get to station A and station B for brief periods of time. Other times, the switch believes that the destination is on the same segment as the receiving port and does not forward the frame.

Notice that if station A had originally sent a broadcast, the scenario would actually be much worse than a simple bridging loop. The two behaviors of always retransmitting a broadcast and never dropping the frame means that switches with more than two ports actually create broadcasts in an exponential fashion when a bridge loop occurs. This process of creating new broadcasts does not stop. Eventually, the bridging loop brings down the network as a result of this broadcast storm. Bridging loops stop when the physical loop no longer exists.

Preventing Bridging Loops

STP overcomes the problems of transparent bridging in redundant networks. The purpose of STP is to avoid and eliminate loops in the network by imposing a loop-free path. STP does this by determining where loops exist in the network and blocking redundant links. In this way, STP ensures that only one path to every destination exists. In the case of a link failure, the bridge transitions an interface in the blocking state to the forwarding state.

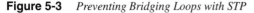STP executes an algorithm called the Spanning-Tree Algorithm (STA). To find the redundant links, the STA chooses a reference point in the network and locates the redundant paths to that reference point. The reference point is commonly known as the root of the spanning tree. If the STA finds a redundant path, it selects a single path back to the root and blocks any other redundancy paths. In the example shown in Figure 5-3, STP puts one of the switch ports in blocking mode, thus preventing the bridging loop in the scenario.

Figure 5-3   *Preventing Bridging Loops with STP*

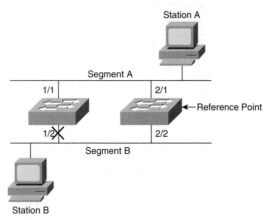

The blocked port continues to receive *bridge protocol data unit*s (*BPDU*), and the switch forwards through that port if a failure occurs on the current forwarding link. If multiple redundant paths exist, then more than one port goes into blocking mode, and the STP unblocks one of the previously blocked ports upon primary link failure.

Building Loop-Free Networks

A loop-free network is a network where Layer 2 traffic loops do not or cannot occur. The only downside of this design is that no Layer 2 redundancy exists. As such, you must use another form of redundancy, such as Layer 3 redundancy using the Hot Standby Routing Protocol (HSRP) and IP routing.

In Figure 5-4, port 1/2 on the switch is disabled, which effectively eliminates redundancy and hence the possibility of a loop.

Connecting servers and workstations with dual NICs is another form of redundancy that does not use STP. If the switch connected to the active NIC fails, the secondary NIC will start forwarding the packets through the alternate switch. This solution cannot detect non-switch or network-based failure scenarios in which the server NIC link does not go down, but traffic no longer flows down that link.

The most common way to design a Layer 2 loop-free network is to use Layer 3 links between the distribution switches so that HSRP or other Layer 3 default gateway redundancy protocols will be able to maintain connectivity for the end-users even if one of the links to the distribution switch fails. In Figure 5-5, when the link between switch C and A fails, switch B becomes the active HSRP router, and the access layer switch starts sending packets to switch B. Hence, connectivity is restored quicker due to the faster failover time of HSRP compared with Spanning Tree. See Chapter 12, "Implementing High Availability Options in Multilayer Switches," for more details regarding HSRP.

Figure 5-4 *Bridge Loop-Free Network*

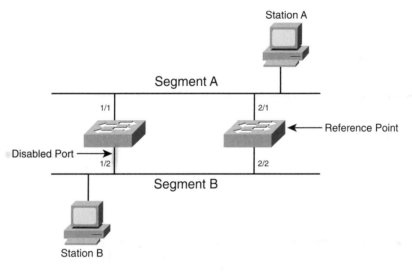

Figure 5-5 *Using Layer 3 Link to Form Loop-Free Network*

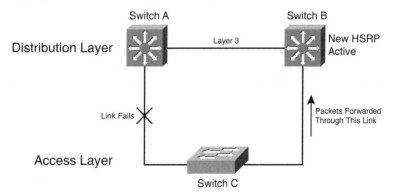

Despite the availability of these alternate designs, most of today's networks still use Layer 2 redundancy in some fashion and use STP to prevent bridging loops. Hence, your ability to understand the various STP standards and how to configure and troubleshoot the protocol is essential. Furthermore, networks that do not use STP for redundancy still have STP enabled to prevent Layer 2 loops on edge ports, effectively providing a security feature.

STP (IEEE 802.1D)

STP uses the concepts of root bridges, root ports, and designated ports to establish a loop-free path through the network. The following sections discuss the terms root bridge, root ports, and designated ports in more detail. This section discusses the operation of basic STP as defined in the STP-defining IEEE 802.1D standard.

Bridge Identifier

Spanning tree assigns each bridge or switch a unique identifier, called a *bridge ID*. A 2-byte priority value and the 6-byte MAC address make up the bridge ID, as shown in Figure 5-6.

Figure 5-6   *Bridge Identifier Format*

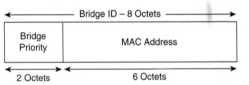

The default priority of Cisco Catalyst switches, in accordance with IEEE 802.1D, is 32,768 (1000 0000 0000 0000 in binary, or 0x8000 in hex), which is the midpoint value of possible values from 0 through 65,535. The bridge ID is always unique by virtue of the use of a unique MAC address.

NOTE   Cisco Catalyst switches use a MAC address from a pool of MAC addresses assigned either to the backplane or to the supervisor module, depending on the switch model. The **show module** *mod-no* command displays the pool of assigned MAC addresses.

Spanning-Tree Path Cost

Spanning-tree path cost is an accumulated total path cost based on the bandwidth of all the links in the path.

Table 5-1 shows several path costs specified in the IEEE 802.1D specification. Prior to 802.1D-1998, network managers with different media, such as FDDI, ATM-155, and ATM-622, had to manually scale the costs if they wanted to differentiate between the paths. Table 5-1 also shows the revised path cost of IEEE 802.1D-1998. The older specification calculated cost based on 1000-Mbps bandwidth, but the new specification adjusts the calculation by using a nonlinear scale to accommodate higher-speed interfaces.

Table 5-1   *Spanning-Tree Path Cost for Various Link Speeds*

Link Speed	Cost (Revised IEEE Spec)	Cost (Previous IEEE Spec)
10 Gbps	2	1
1 Gbps	4	1
100 Mbps	19	10
10 Mbps	100	100

Bridge Protocol Data Units

All switches in an extended LAN participating in STP gather information on other switches in the network through an exchange of control messages: BPDUs.

Switches that are running STP use BPDUs to relay LAN topology information to other switches; this information is refreshed at regular intervals—2 seconds by default on a switch that is running 802.1D. The IEEE 802.1D STP multicast destination address for BPDUs is 01-80-c2-00-00-00.

Switches that are running STP use BPDUs to do the following:

- Elect a root bridge
- Determine the location of redundant paths
- Block certain ports to prevent loops
- Notify the network of topology changes
- Monitor the state of the spanning tree

There are two types of BPDUs:

- **Configuration BPDU**—This type of BPDU is sent at periodic intervals (defined by the hello time interval, described later in the section) by the root bridge on all its ports; the BPDU includes the STP parameters. The STP parameters are critical for the stability of the STP. By generating the configuration BPDU only at the root bridge, the STP bridges are guaranteed to have no mismatch in the timers. In summary, the configuration BPDU is used to elect the root bridge and to keep the topology stable. If these BPDUs are not received from the root, topology change may occur.

- **Topology Change Notification (TCN) BPDU**—This type of BPDU is generated by the switch when it detects a topology change. More details about this BPDU are described in the section "STP Topology Changes" later in this chapter.

Table 5-2 shows the BPDU frame format and a brief description of the fields. More information about the fields and their use is provided in the following sections.

Table 5-2   *BPDU Frame Format*

Bytes	Field	Description
2	Protocol ID	This value is always 0.
1	Version	Version of STP (802.1D version is 0).
1	Message Type	BPDU type (configuration 00 and TCN BPDU 80).
1	Flags	Least Significant Bit (LSB) = TC flag; Most Significant Bit (MSB) = TCA flag. More details about a Topology Change (TC) are provided in the section "STP Topology Changes" later in this chapter.
8	Root ID	Bridge ID of the root bridge.
4	Cost of Path	STP cost for reaching the root bridge.
8	Bridge ID	BPDU sending bridge ID.
2	Port ID	BPDU sending bridge port ID.
2	Message Age	Seconds since root originated the BPDU. It is increased by 1 by each bridge (so it is essentially a hop count to the root bridge).
2	Maximum Time	The maximum time a bridge retains the root bridge ID before considering the root bridge as unavailable.
2	Hello Time	Time interval for subsequent BPDUs being sent from the root bridge.
2	Forward Delay	Time interval the bridge spends in each of the listening and learning STP states.

In normal STP operation, a bridge continuously receives configuration BPDUs from the root bridge on its root port, but it never sends out a configuration BPDU toward the root bridge. Note that the designated bridges or ports do send configuration BPDUs with root bridge information. Figure 5-7 shows a sample configuration BPDU frame layout.

When a bridge needs to signal a topology change, it starts sending the TCN BPDU. More details about how topology changes behavior are explained in the section titled "STP Topology Changes" later in this chapter.

Figure 5-7   *Configuration BPDU Frame Layout*

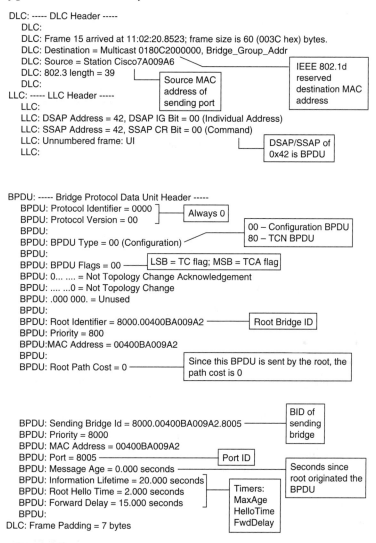

Spanning-Tree Port States and BPDU Timers

Propagation delays exist in switched networks due to the inherent latency of network devices. As a result, topology changes occur at different times and at different segments in a switched network. When a Layer 2 interface transitions directly from nonparticipation in the spanning-tree topology to the forwarding state, it potentially creates temporary data loops. To alleviate this problem, ports wait for new topology information to propagate through the switched LAN before starting to forward frames. Ports allow the frame lifetime to expire for frames that the bridges forwarded under the old topology.

Figure 5-8   *STP State Machine*

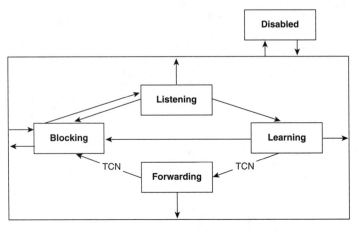

Each Layer 2 interface on a switch that uses spanning tree operates in one of the following five states, as shown in Figure 5-8:

- **Blocking**—In the blocking state, the Layer 2 interface does not participate in frame forwarding but listens to incoming BPDUs. The port does not learn MAC addresses of received frames.

- **Listening**—In the listening state, the switch resolves the root and selects the root port, the designated port, and the nondesignated ports. The port does not learn the unicast address of any received frames while in the listening state.

- **Learning**—In the learning state, the Layer 2 interface prepares to participate in frame forwarding. The port learns the MAC addresses of incoming frames in this state but does not forward the frames.

- **Forwarding**—In the forwarding state, the Layer 2 interface forwards frames. The port learns the source MAC address of received frames and forwards them appropriately based on the destination MAC address.

- **Disabled**—In the disabled state, the Layer 2 interface does not participate in spanning tree and does not forward frames.

The following three timers, carried in the BPDU frames, affect STP performance and state changes:

- **Hello time**—The *hello time* is the time between each BPDU that is sent on a port by the root bridge and forwarded by other designated bridges. This equals 2 seconds by default but is configurable between 1 and 10 seconds.

- **Forward delay**—The *forward delay* is the time spent in the listening and learning states. The forward delay by default is 15 seconds but is configurable between 4 and 30 seconds.

- **Max age**—The *max age timer* controls the maximum length of time a bridge port saves its configuration BPDU information. This is 20 seconds by default but is configurable between 6 and 40 seconds.

The spanning-tree topology of the network adheres to the timers of the root bridge. The root bridge passes the times in BPDUs to all switches in the Layer 2 topology.

When a bridge is powered on, the bridge assumes that it is the root bridge and transitions to the listening state. In general, two transitional states occur when a bridge recognizes a change in the network topology. During a topology change, a port temporarily implements the listening and learning states for the value of the forward delay timer. When a port is in the listening state, it can send and receive BPDUs to determine the active topology. When network topology is in transition, no user data passes.

During the listening state, the bridge processes the BPDU received by the bridge. Ports that remain as designated or root ports transition to the learning state after 15 seconds, the default forward delay. Ports that are not the designated or root ports transition back to the blocking state.

When a port is in the learning state, it can populate its MAC address table with MAC addresses heard on its ports, but it does not forward user data frames. The learning state also lasts 15 seconds, also the value of the forward delay timer, by default. At this point, the bridge is still not passing user data.

The learning state reduces the amount of flooding required when data forwarding begins. If a port is still a designated or root port at the end of the learning state, the port transitions to the forwarding state. Ports that are not the designated or root ports transition back to the blocking state. In the forwarding state, a port is capable of sending and receiving user data.

NOTE   Ports that are connected to hosts need not participate in the STP listening/learning process because forwarding on those links does not cause STP loops. To achieve the immediate forwarding on host ports, use Cisco's PortFast feature on those specific ports. For more information about the PortFast feature, see Chapter 6.

The normal time it takes for a port to transition from the blocking state to the forwarding state is 30 to 50 seconds. Although it is possible to tune the spanning-tree timers, the recommendation is to leave the spanning-tree timers at their default values.

STP Operation

STP initially converges on a logically loop-free network topology by performing these steps:

1 **Elects one root bridge**—The protocol uses a process to elect a root bridge. Only one bridge acts as the root bridge in a given network per VLAN. On the root bridge, all ports act as designated ports. Designated ports send and receive traffic as well as

configuration messages, or BPDUs. In the sample scenario in Figure 5-9, switch X wins the election as the root bridge because it has the lower priority parameter.

2 **Selects the root port on all nonroot bridges**—The protocol establishes one root port on each nonroot bridge. The root port is the lowest-cost path from the nonroot bridge to the root bridge. Root ports send and receive traffic. If a nonroot bridge has two or more equal-cost paths to the root, then the nonroot bridge selects the port that connects to the lowest bridge ID of the bridges that sent the BPDUs for the paths. If all the bridge IDs for the equal-cost paths are the same, then the nonroot bridge selects the port with the lowest port ID as the forwarding path. In the sample scenario in Figure 5-9, from switch Y, the lowest-cost path to the root bridge is through the 100BASE-TX Fast Ethernet link.

3 **Selects the designated port on each segment**—On each segment, STP establishes one designated port on the bridge that has the lowest path cost to the root bridge. In the sample scenario in Figure 5-9, the designated port for both segments is on the root bridge because the root bridge directly connects to both segments. The 10BASE-T Ethernet port on switch Y is a nondesignated port because there is only one designated port per segment. The switch primarily chooses a designated port as the least-cost path to the root bridge. In the event of a tie, the bridge ID acts as the tiebreaker.

Figure 5-9 *STP Operation*

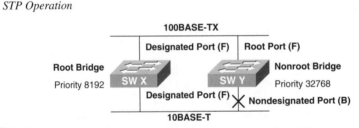

The following subsections review the STP operations in detail.

Root Bridge Election

The first step in creating the loop-free spanning tree is to elect a root bridge. The root bridge is the reference point that all switches use to determine whether there are loops in the network.

On bootup, the switch assumes that it is the root bridge and sets the bridge ID equal to the root ID. As previously discussed, two components make up the bridge ID:

- **Two-byte priority**—By default, each switch defaults to 0x8000 as the priority.

- **Six-byte MAC address**—This is the MAC address of the switch or bridge. The bridge ID is always unique by virtue of using a unique switch MAC address.

The bridge ID is created by concatenating the priority and MAC address values; this bridge ID is used to determine which switch becomes the root bridge. The lower the number, the more likely it is that this switch will become the root. By exchanging BPDUs, the switches determine which switch is the root bridge.

An example of the combination of the priority and bridge ID is as follows:

08.00.00.00.0c.12.34.56

The first 2 bytes in this example indicate the priority. The last 6 bytes signify the MAC address of the switch.

In the example shown in Figure 5-10, both switches are using the same default priority; as a result, the one with the lowest MAC address becomes the root bridge. In the example, switch X is the root bridge with a bridge ID of 0x08:00:00:0c00:11:11:11:11.

Figure 5-10 *Root Bridge Election*

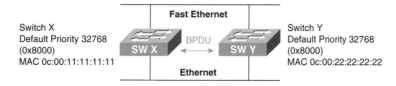

Planning Root Bridge Selection

Figure 5-11 illustrates the importance of locating the root bridge in the center of the network so that between any two hosts, the path cost is minimal. One of the considerations in Figure 5-11 is how traffic flows from hosts attached to switch F to hosts attached to switch C.

Figure 5-11 *Planning Root Bridge Selection*

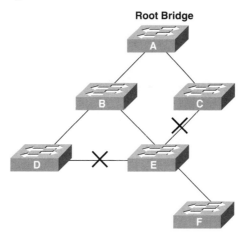

Traditional STP does not provide a means for the network administrator to securely enforce the topology of the switched Layer 2 network because bridge priority by itself does not guarantee that a bridge will be elected root. Consider the case of a new switch with a lower bridge ID connecting to switch F and how the STP topology changes.

NOTE   The Cisco root guard feature protects the Catalyst switch from accepting better BPDUs received on specifically configured ports. Enable root guard on the access-layer client ports and on the distribution switch ports leading to the access switches to protect against unauthorized root switches. The root guard feature is explained further in Chapter 6.

Although any switch is able to act as a root bridge in the network, it is better to place the root bridge manually in the Building Distribution submodule, assuming Layer 3 is configured on the Building Distribution submodule switch uplinks to the Campus Backbone submodule. This placement of the root bridge keeps the forwarding topology optimal.

Even if the administrator sets the root bridge priority to 0 to secure the root bridge position, there is still no guarantee of security of the root bridge position. For example, if a bridge with a priority of 0 and a lower bridge ID (due to a lower MAC address) is added to the network, it becomes the root bridge. Cisco's enhancement feature, root guard, may help to secure root switches in the network. More information about the root guard feature can be found in Chapter 6.

Selecting the root bridge and enforcing the topology is vital to complex Layer 2 networks to ensure that they are reliable, manageable, and secure.

Selecting and enforcing the Layer 2 network topology involves these steps:

Step 1   Configure the root and secondary root bridges.

Step 2   Set the port priorities.

Step 3   Set the port costs.

Step 4   Enable root guard on access-layer switches.

Selection of Root and Designated Port on Nonroot Bridges

When determining the loop-free topology, STP identifies the root bridge, root ports, and designated ports by evaluating BPDUs. Switches use the following five criteria in the decision-making process, in the following order:

1   Lowest root bridge ID

2   Lowest path cost to the root bridge

3   Lowest sender bridge ID

4   Lowest port priority

5   Lowest port ID

For example, when STP is trying to determine the root port of a switch, it may have two or more equal-cost paths to the root switch. As a result, STP looks at the bridge ID of the switches that sent the BPDUs for the paths, and if they are equal, STP looks at the priority of the ports; the port with the lowest port priority would be selected as the root port. If they are equal, STP uses the port identifiers and selects the port with the lowest port priority as the root port.

In the example shown in Figure 5-12, switch Y receives a BPDU from the root switch, from switch X, from a Fast Ethernet segment and from an Ethernet segment. The root path cost in both cases is 0. The local path cost on the Fast Ethernet port is 19, while the local path cost on the Ethernet port is 100. As a result, the port on the Fast Ethernet segment has the lowest path cost to the root bridge and is elected the root port for switch Y.

Figure 5-12 *STP Root Port Selection*

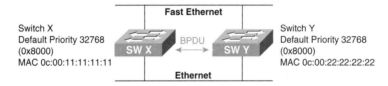

STP selects one designated port per segment to forward traffic. Other ports on the segment receive traffic but do not forward, to prevent loops. STP elects the port on the segment with the lowest path cost to the root bridge as the designated port. If multiple ports on the same bridge have the same cost, the port with the lowest port priority is chosen. If the port priority is the same, then the port with the lowest port ID becomes the designated port.

Because all ports on the root bridge have a root path cost of 0, STP designates all ports on the root bridge as designated ports. In the example shown in Figure 5-13, the root bridge ports act as the necessary designated ports in both the segments.

Figure 5-13 *STP Designated Port Selection*

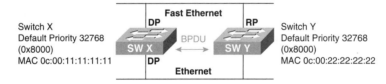

Understanding Primary and Backup Root Bridges

For each VLAN, the switch with the lowest bridge ID becomes the root bridge for that VLAN. The primary root bridge is the actual root bridge of a VLAN with the lowest bridge ID. Generally, you choose a centrally located or core switch in the network that has enough CPU power and switching capacity to forward traffic between various distribution-layer and access-layer switches to be the primary root bridge. The backup or secondary root bridges are selected in the event of a failure of the primary or current root bridge. The selection is done intentionally so that even in the event of primary root bridge failure, the new root bridge is still centrally located and has enough CPU power and switching capacity to take over the role of the primary switch. In a production network, it is essential that the backup root bridge have the same capacity as the primary. This ensures that there is no degradation of network performance in the case of primary root bridge failure.

Sample Scenario of STP Election Process

Consider the scenario depicted in Figure 5-14, in which three switches are using the same priority. As a result, the bridge with the lowest MAC address becomes the root bridge. In this case, switch ASW11 is the root bridge with a bridge ID of 00:00:0c:aa:aa:aa, and the other two switches are nonroot bridges. Root bridges designate all ports as designated ports.

Figure 5-14 *Root Bridge Selection*

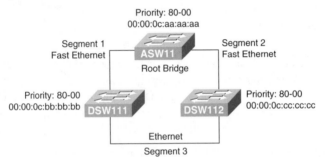

Figure 5-15 illustrates the same scenario as Figure 5-14, but it adds the process of selecting the root ports. DSW111 and DSW112 are nonroot bridges; therefore, each bridge elects a single root port. In both cases, the nonroot bridges receive a BPDU on segment 1 for DSW111 or segment 2 for DSW112 with a root path cost of 0 and a local path cost of 19, for a total cost of 19. Each nonroot bridge also receives a BPDU from the other on segment 3, with a root path cost of 19 and a local path cost of 100. As a result, each switch elects the port on segment 1 for DSW111 or segment 2 for DSW112 as the root port.

Figure 5-15 *Root Port Selection*

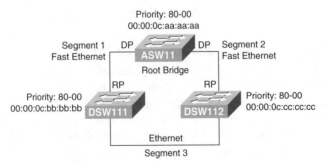

As the final step in the example, Figure 5-16 shows designated port selection. A port on either DSW111 or DSW112 ends up as the designated port for segment 3. Following the STP four-step decision process, bridges DSW111 and DSW112 examine the root bridge ID in the BPDUs. In this case, the root bridge IDs are the same. Therefore, as a second step, the bridges examine the root path cost. Again, the cost is the same for both ports. The third step is to check the sender bridge ID. Both bridges have the same priority, so the bridge with the lower of the two MAC addresses has the lowest bridge ID, DSW111. Therefore, the port on DSW111 becomes the designated port on segment 3, and the port on DSW112 becomes the nondesignated port, which consequently places the port into blocking state to prevent bridging loops.

Figure 5-16 *Designated Port Selection*

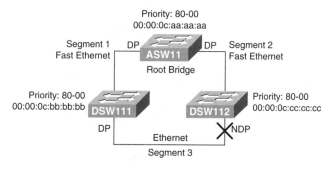

STP Topology Changes

When a bridge needs to signal a topology change, it starts sending the TCN BPDU. The switch sends a TCN when any of the following events occurs:

- Port in forwarding or listening state transitions to blocking (the case of a link failure)
- Port moves to forwarding state, and the bridge already has a designated port
- Nonroot bridge receives a TCN on its designated port (propagation TCN is sent)

The TCN is a simple BPDU. The TCN BPDU consists of three fields, which are the same as the first three fields of a configuration BPDU with the exception of the Type field. The Type field in a configuration BPDU is 0×00; the Type field in a TCN BPDU is 0×80. Refer to Figure 5-7 to see the BPDU format of the configuration and TCN BPDUs.

The designated bridge receives the TCN and acknowledges it by immediately sending back a normal configuration BPDU with the Topology Change Acknowledgement (TCA) bit set. The bridge that is notifying the topology change continues to send its TCN BPDU until the designated bridge has acknowledged it.

The designated bridge then generates another TCN for its own root port, and so on until the TCN BPDU reaches the root bridge.

Once the root bridge is aware there has been a topology change event in the network, it starts sending out its configuration BPDUs with the Topology Change (TC) bit set. Every bridge in the network relays these BPDUs with this bit set so that every bridge is aware of the topology-change situation, whereas each bridge reduces its MAC address table aging time to the value of the forward delay timer.

Figure 5-17 *Topology Change Notification from Source Bridge*

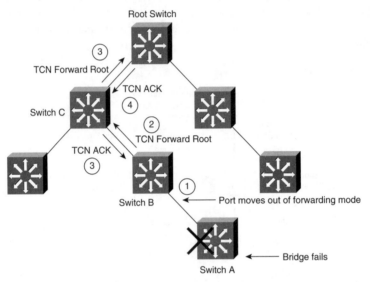

Figure 5-17 shows a sample topology change in a spanning-tree network. The steps occurring in this example follow:

1 Switch B notices that a change to a link has occurred when switch A fails.

2 Switch B sends a TC BPDU out the root port destined ultimately for the root switch. The switch continues to send the TC BPDU until the designated switch, switch C, responds with a TCA.

3 The designated switch, switch C, sends a TCA to the originating switch, switch B. The designated switch also sends a TC BPDU out the root port destined for either the designated switch or the root switch, this being the propagation TCN.

4 When the root switch receives the topology change message, it acknowledges the TC BPDU with a TCA to the sending bridge.

5 The root switch changes its configuration BPDU to indicate that a topology change is occurring. The root switch sets the topology change in the configuration BPDU for a period equal to the sum of the value of the forward delay timer and the value of the max age timer parameters.

6 A switch receiving the TC configuration BPDU message from the root switch uses the value of the forward delay timer to age out entries in the address table, as shown in

Figure 5-18. This allows the switch to age out MAC address entries faster than the normal 300-second default timer. This technique ensures MAC addresses of that station that are no longer available due to the topology change age out quickly. The switch continues this process until it no longer receives TC BPDU messages from the root switch.

Figure 5-18 *Root Switch Sets TC Flag Due to TCN*

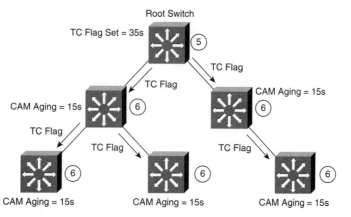

This process ensures that operation of the network has minimum impact on topology changes. In this example, if switch A has a redundant connection to the network, the backup link moves into the forwarding state, and the network quickly reconverges for the new topology.

NOTE   If there are continuous TCNs being generated due to flapping links because of faulty switch ports or faulty devices, the CAM table aging time remains at the value of the forward delay timer, which leads to fast aging of MAC addresses and unicast flooding in the network. Always identify and fix the cause of topology change to prevent performance problems from unicast flooding. Enabling spanning-tree PortFast on end workstations and server ports prevents the common reason for TCNs being generated in the network (edge port link up and down transitions).

Per VLAN Spanning Tree Plus

Per VLAN Spanning Tree Plus (PVST+) maintains a separate spanning-tree instance for each VLAN. By default, a single spanning tree runs on each configured VLAN, provided STP has not been manually disabled. Cisco switches allow STP enabling and disabling on a per-VLAN basis. For example, for the Catalyst 6500 family of switches, PVST+ runs on each VLAN on the switch, ensuring that each VLAN has a loop-free path through the network. The plus sign in PVST+ indicates that STP 802.1D has been enhanced by Cisco with proprietary features.

If configured, PVST+ provides for load balancing on a per-VLAN basis; PVST+ allows creation of different logical topologies using the VLANs on a switched network to ensure that all links can be used and that one link is not oversubscribed. For example, consider a typical Building Access submodule switch connected to two Building Distribution submodule switches, with one Building Distribution submodule switch STP root switch for one VLAN and the other Building Distribution submodule switch STP root switch for the second VLAN. The Building Access submodule switch in this scenario would use both the links, one for each VLAN, thus achieving load balancing.

Each instance of PVST+ on a VLAN has a single root bridge. This root bridge propagates the spanning-tree information associated with that VLAN to all other switches in the network. Providing different STP root switches per VLAN also creates a more robust network by allowing for the load balancing of root bridge responsibilities and link paths.

Figure 5-19 shows three switches configured with PVST+ and interconnected by VLAN trunks. One spanning-tree instance exists for the primary VLAN, with a second instance configured for the alternate VLAN. A single switch and even a single trunking port can serve different roles for each VLAN. In this example, on the access-layer switch, a port forwards for one VLAN while blocking for the other VLANs.

Figure 5-19 *Per VLAN Spanning Tree Plus*

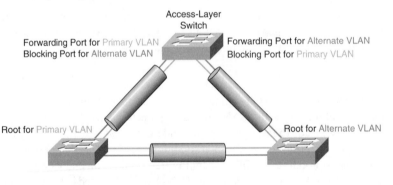

Access-Layer
Switch

Forwarding Port for Primary VLAN
Blocking Port for Alternate VLAN

Forwarding Port for Alternate VLAN
Blocking Port for Primary VLAN

Root for Primary VLAN

Root for Alternate VLAN

NOTE The desired STP configuration and resulting Layer 2 topology is not necessarily automatic. The network administrator needs to plan and configure it manually to ensure the traffic flow shown in Figure 5-19 and central location of the root switch.

Figure 5-20 shows how PVST+ is implemented for ten VLANs, with ports in different states for the different instances of spanning tree. In this case, each port is participating in all ten VLANs but is actively forwarding traffic for only half of them. With ten VLANs, each switch maintains ten spanning-tree instances.

Figure 5-20 *PVST+ Load Balancing Scenario*

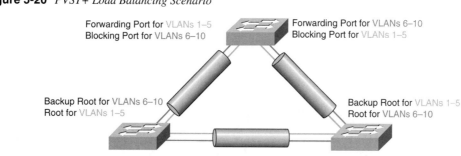

MAC Address Allocation and Reduction

The Catalyst switches typically have a pool of up to 1024 MAC addresses. This pool acts as the MAC addresses component of the bridge IDs for the VLAN spanning trees. The number of MAC addresses that are available depends on the switch model. Not all switches have 1024 MAC addresses. For example, the Catalyst 4500 Supervisor III and IV have a pool of only 64 MAC addresses.

A switch allocates MAC addresses sequentially, with the first MAC address in the range assigned to VLAN 1, the second MAC address in the range assigned to VLAN 2, and so on. The switch assigns the Supervisor Engine in-band (sc0) management interface the highest-order (last) MAC address in its range of allocated MAC addresses.

For example, if the MAC address range for a Supervisor Engine is 00-e0-1e-9b-2e-00 to 00-e0-1e-9b-31-ff, the VLAN 1 bridge ID is 00-e0-1e-9b-2e-00, the VLAN 2 bridge ID is 00-e0-1e-9b-2e-01, the VLAN 3 bridge ID is 00-e0-1e-9b-2e-02, and so forth. The in-band (sc0) interface MAC address is 00-e0-1e-9b-31-ff.

For switches that have fewer MAC addresses than the number of supported VLANs, the MAC address reduction feature is the solution. A Catalyst 6500, which supports up to 4094 VLANs, needs MAC address reduction to support 4094 STP instances.

Upon enabling MAC address reduction, the bridge ID that is stored in the spanning-tree BPDU contains an additional field called the *system ID extension*. The system ID extension with the bridge priority functions as the unique identifier for a VLAN or an MST instance (MSTI). The system ID extension is always the number of the VLAN or the MST instance; for example, the system ID extension for VLAN 100 is 100, and the system ID extension for MST instance 2 is 2. MST instances are discussed later in this chapter. Figure 5-21 depicts the bridge ID with MAC address reduction enabled.

Figure 5-21 *Bridge ID with MAC Address Reduction*

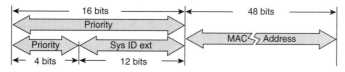

The bridge priority becomes a multiple of 4096 plus the VLAN ID if MAC address reduction is enabled. With MAC address reduction enabled, the switch can specify the switch priority only as a multiple of 4096. Hence, only the following values are possible: 0, 4096, 8192, 12288, 16384, 20480, 24576, 28672, 32768, 36864, 40960, 45056, 49152, 53248, 57344, and 61440.

STP and IEEE 802.1Q Trunks

IEEE 802.1Q VLAN trunks impose limitations on the spanning-tree features in a network. In a network of Cisco switches connected through 802.1Q trunks, the switches maintain one instance of spanning tree for each VLAN allowed on the trunks. However, non-Cisco 802.1Q switches maintain only one instance of spanning tree for all VLANs allowed on the trunks.

When you connect a Cisco switch to a non-Cisco device through an 802.1Q trunk, the Cisco switch combines the spanning-tree instance of the 802.1Q native VLAN of the trunk with the spanning-tree instance of the non-Cisco 802.1Q switch. However, Cisco switches separated by a cloud of non-Cisco 802.1Q switches maintain all per-VLAN spanning-tree information.

Cisco Catalyst switches treat the non-Cisco 802.1Q cloud separating them as a single trunk link between them and are able to share information across the non-Cisco cloud as follows:

1 Cisco Catalyst switches send the IEEE 802.1D BPDU on the Native VLAN to IEEE 802.1D MAC address 01-80-c2-00-00-00.

2 In addition, a Cisco Catalyst switch sends Cisco PVST+ BPDUs to Cisco-specific Shared STP (SSTP) MAC address 01-00-0c-cc-cc-cd. The switches send the BPDUs tagged with specific VLAN instances to the Cisco SSTP destination MAC address.

3 The non-Cisco device floods the BPDUs because the destination MAC address is an unknown multicast address on those devices.

Thus, Cisco switches can share information across a non-Cisco cloud.

Configuring the Basic Parameters of PVST+

The default mode for STP on Catalyst switches is PVST+, which runs an instance of STP per VLAN. Upon configuring a VLAN, Catalyst switches automatically enable STP with the default parameters. It is possible to disable STP on a per-VLAN basis as desired. Technically, bridging loops require physical topology redundancy or a Layer 2 loop to occur. Disabling STP in networks or VLANs without redundancy will not cause a loop; that said, it is highly recommended to have STP enabled to prevent intentional or unintentional loops that may create bridging loops.

Use the following global configuration command on Cisco IOS–based Cisco Catalyst switches to enable STP:

spanning-tree vlan *vlan-id*

Example 5-1 shows the enabling of STP on VLAN 100 on a Cisco IOS–based Catalyst switch.

Example 5-1   *Enabling STP on a Cisco IOS–Based Catalyst Switch*

```
Switch#configure terminal
Enter configuration commands, one per line.  End with CNTL/Z.
Switch(config)#spanning-tree vlan 100
Switch(config)#end
```

Configuring the Root Bridge

A Catalyst switch that is running PVST+ maintains an instance of spanning tree for each active VLAN configured on the switch. A bridge ID, consisting of the bridge priority and the bridge MAC address, is associated with each instance. For each VLAN, the switch with the lowest bridge ID becomes the root bridge for that VLAN. Whenever the bridge priority changes, the bridge ID also changes. This results in the recomputation of the root bridge for the VLAN.

To configure a switch to become the root bridge for a specified VLAN, lower its priority from the default value with the following command in Cisco IOS–based Catalyst switches:

spanning-tree vlan vlan-id **priority** value

Example 5-2 shows the setting of the priority of a Cisco IOS–based Catalyst switch to 4096.

Example 5-2   *Setting Bridge Priority*

```
Switch#configure terminal
Enter configuration commands, one per line.  End with CNTL/Z.
Switch(config)#spanning-tree vlan 100 priority 4096
Switch(config)#end
```

Assuming the other bridges in the VLAN 100 retain their default priority, a switch configured with a priority of 4096 becomes the root bridge. We suggest a root priority value of 4096 to designate the root bridge when configuring STP.

NOTE   The root switch for each instance of spanning tree should be on a switch in the Building Distribution submodule for network designs using Layer 3 in the distribution layer and Layer 2 in the Building Access submodule. In a network with a collapsed backbone and distribution layer, configure one of these backbones or distribution switches as the root switch. Do not configure a Building Access submodule as the spanning-tree primary root unless you are using Layer 3 routing in the Building Access submodule.

A secondary root is a switch that is likely to become the root bridge for specific VLANs if the primary root bridge fails. You specify a switch as the secondary root bridge by setting the priority to a value between the low value of the root bridge (4096) and the default value (32,768). Generally, the priority value 8192 is used. More than one switch can act as the backup root switch.

Catalyst switches also offer macro commands, which automatically detect the current root switch and lower the priority value of the respective switch so that it becomes the root. Use the following command to invoke the macro on Cisco IOS–based Catalyst switches:

```
spanning-tree vlan vlan-id root primary
```

To set the secondary root, which lowers the priority of the switch to a nondefault value but a higher value than the current root, use the following macro:

```
spanning-tree vlan vlan-id root secondary
```

If all the switches in a network are configured for the default priority value such that the current root bridge priority is using the default priority value of 32,768, setting the root bridge by using the root macro results in a priority of 8192 for the root switch. If the current root switch is not configured for the default value of 32,768, the macro selects one value below the current root to make the respective switch the root switch. For example, if the current root switch has a priority of 16384, using the root macro sets the priority of the current switch to 16383.

Manual configuration of priority results in a deterministic value for the root and secondary root bridge and is the recommended practice, as discussed earlier in this chapter.

Configuring Port Cost

STP considers port cost when selecting an interface to put into the forwarding state. Assign lower cost values to interfaces to make spanning tree select those first, and assign higher costs to interfaces that are less preferable for forwarding.

Interface media speed determines the default value for spanning tree port path cost. The possible cost range is 1 to 200,000,000. If all interfaces have the same cost value, STP puts the interface with the lowest interface priority in the forwarding state. If all the interfaces have the same priority, spanning tree puts the interface with the lower interface number in the forwarding state and blocks other interfaces.

STP uses the port cost value when the interface is an access port, and it uses VLAN port cost values when the interface is a trunk port.

To configure the STP port cost or VLAN port cost of an interface, use one of following interface-level commands on Cisco IOS–based Catalyst switches:

```
spanning-tree cost port-cost
spanning-tree vlan vlan-id cost port-cost
```

Example 5-3 shows the configuration of a nondefault port cost of 10 for interface FastEthernet 4/1, which is a better path cost than the default cost of 19 for FastEthernet interfaces. As a result of this configuration, spanning tree prefers interface FastEthernet 4/1 over other default cost ports for forwarding toward the root switch. Example 5-3 also shows the configuration of a nondefault port cost of 20 for trunking interface FastEthernet 4/2 for VLAN 10. A port cost of 20 is higher than the default port cost of 19; hence, STP gives less preference to this port as the forwarding path over any other Fast Ethernet interface with the default cost in this VLAN.

Example 5-3 *Configuring Nondefault Port Cost on Cisco IOS–Based Switches*

```
Switch#configure terminal
Enter configuration commands, one per line.  End with CNTL/Z.
Switch(config)#interface FastEthernet 4/1
Switch(config-if)#spanning-tree cost 10
Switch(config)#interface FastEthernet 4/2
Switch(config-if)#switchport trunk  encapsulation dot1q
Switch(config-if)#switchport mode trunk
Switch(config-if)#spanning-tree vlan 10 cost 20
Switch(config-if)#end
```

Verifying the STP Configuration

An exhaustive set of **show** commands exists in Cisco IOS and Cisco CatOS to display configuration and operational information about spanning tree.

On Cisco IOS–based Catalyst switches, use the following command to display the STP information for a specific VLAN:

```
show spanning-tree vlan vlan-id
```

Example 5-4 shows an example of displaying STP information on a Cisco IOS–based Catalyst switch, which acts as the root of the spanning tree for VLAN 1.

Example 5-4 *Displaying STP Information on Cisco IOS–Based Catalyst Switches*

```
Switch#show spanning-tree vlan 1

VLAN0001
  Spanning tree enabled protocol ieee
  Root ID    Priority    8193
             Address     0009.e845.6480
             This bridge is the root

             Hello Time   2 sec  Max Age 10 sec  Forward Delay  7 sec

  Bridge ID  Priority    8193    (priority 8192 sys-id-ext 1)
             Address     0009.e845.6480
             Hello Time   2 sec  Max Age 10 sec  Forward Delay  7 sec
             Aging Time 300

Interface        Role Sts Cost      Prio.Nbr Type
---------------- ---- --- --------- -------- --------------------------------
Fa3/24           Desg FWD 100        128.152  Shr

Fa3/42           Back BLK 19         128.170  P2p
```

The priority field in Example 5-4 is 8193 even though the configured priority value is 8192 due to the switch using the MAC address reduction feature. When using MAC address reduction, the priority fields include the VLAN ID information (8192 + 1 = 8193) as well. This feature was discussed previously in the section "MAC Address Allocation and Reduction."

The **show spanning-tree** command takes several arguments to display a variety of information about the STP configuration. Without arguments, the command displays general information about all STP configurations. The complete syntax is as follows:

```
show spanning-tree [bridge-group | active | backbonefast | {bridge [id]} | detail |
inconsistentports | {interface interface-type number} | root | summary [total] |
uplinkfast | {vlan vlan-id} | {port-channel number} | pathcost method]
```

Refer to the Cisco product software documentation for a complete explanation of each parameter. This section shows examples for common uses of the **show spanning-tree** command.

Example 5-5 illustrates how to display detailed information about STP for a specific VLAN. The information displayed includes the bridge ID, root bridge ID, BPDU parameters, last topology change information, and individual port details.

Example 5-5 *Displaying Detailed STP Information on Cisco IOS–Based Catalyst Switches*

```
Switch#show spanning-tree vlan 1 detail

 VLAN0001 is executing the ieee compatible Spanning Tree protocol
  Bridge Identifier has priority 8192, sysid 1, address 0009.e845.6480
  Configured hello time 2, max age 10, forward delay 7
  We are the root of the spanning tree
  Topology change flag not set, detected flag not set
  Number of topology changes 1 last change occurred 00:33:49 ago
          from FastEthernet3/24
  Times:  hold 1, topology change 17, notification 2
          hello 2, max age 10, forward delay 7
  Timers: hello 1, topology change 0, notification 0, aging 300
 Port 152 (FastEthernet3/24) of VLAN0001 is forwarding
   Port path cost 19, Port priority 128, Port Identifier 128.152.
   Designated root has priority 8193, address 0009.e845.6480
   Designated bridge has priority 8193, address 0009.e845.6480
   Designated port id is 128.152, designated path cost 0
   Timers: message age 0, forward delay 0, hold 0
   Number of transitions to forwarding state: 1
   Link type is shared by default
   BPDU: sent 2034, received 1
 ! Output omitted for brevity
 Port 170 (FastEthernet3/42) of VLAN0001 is blocking
   Port path cost 100, Port priority 128, Port Identifier 128.170.00
   Designated root has priority 8193, address 0009.e845.6480
   Designated bridge has priority 8193, address 0009.e845.6480
   Designated port id is 128.160, designated path cost 0
   Timers: message age 2, forward delay 0, hold 0
   Number of transitions to forwarding state: 0
   Link type is point-to-point by default
   BPDU: sent 2, received 1019
```

Example 5-6 shows how to display STP information on a trunk interface carrying VLANs (1 and 2) on a Cisco IOS–based Catalyst switch.

Example 5-6 *Displaying Detailed STP Information for a Trunk Interface on Cisco IOS–Based Catalyst Switches*

```
Switch#show spanning-tree interface FastEthernet 3/24 detail
 Port 152 (FastEthernet3/24) of VLAN0001 is forwarding
   Port path cost 100, Port priority 128, Port Identifier 128.152.
   Designated root has priority 8193, address 0009.e845.6480
   Designated bridge has priority 8193, address 0009.e845.6480
   Designated port id is 128.152, designated path cost 0
   Timers: message age 0, forward delay 0, hold 0
   Number of transitions to forwarding state: 1
   Link type is shared by default
   BPDU: sent 281, received 2

 Port 152 (FastEthernet3/24) of VLAN0002 is forwarding
   Port path cost 100, Port priority 128, Port Identifier 128.152.
   Designated root has priority 32770, address 0009.e845.6480
   Designated bridge has priority 32770, address 0009.e845.6480

   Designated port id is 128.152, designated path cost 0
   Timers: message age 0, forward delay 0, hold 0
   Number of transitions to forwarding state: 1
   Link type is shared by default
   BPDU: sent 142, received 2
! Output omitted for brevity
```

Example 5-7 illustrates how to display the spanning-tree bridge information on Cisco IOS–based Catalyst switches, which is useful in verifying the STP parameters for all VLANs.

Example 5-7 *Displaying Spanning-Tree Bridge Information on Cisco IOS–Based Catalyst Switches*

```
Switch#show spanning-tree bridge

                                          Hello  Max  Fwd
 Vlan                    Bridge ID         Time  Age  Dly  Protocol
 ---------------  --------------------------------  -----  ---  ---  --------
 VLAN0001            8193 (8192,1) 0009.e845.6480    2    10    7  ieee
 VLAN0002          32770 (32768,2) 0009.e845.6480    2    20   15  ieee
! Output omitted for brevity
```

Rapid Spanning Tree Protocol

Rapid Spanning Tree Protocol (IEEE 802.1w, also referred to as RSTP) significantly speeds the recalculation of the spanning tree when the network topology changes. RSTP defines the additional port roles of Alternate and Backup and defines port states as discarding, learning, or forwarding. This section describes the differences between STP (802.1D) and RSTP (802.1w).

The 802.1D STP standard was designed with the understanding that recovering connectivity after an outage within a minute or so gives adequate performance. With the advent of Layer 3 switching in LAN environments, bridging now competes with routed solutions, in which protocols such as Open Shortest Path First (OSPF) and Enhanced Interior Gateway Routing Protocol (EIGRP) can provide an alternate path in about 1 second.

Cisco enhanced the original 802.1D specification with features such as UplinkFast, BackboneFast, and PortFast to speed up the convergence time of a bridged network. The drawback is that these mechanisms are proprietary and need additional configuration.

The IEEE 802.1w standard (RSTP) is an evolution, rather than a revolution, of the 802.1D standard. The 802.1D terminology remains primarily the same, and most parameters are left unchanged, so users who are familiar with 802.1D can rapidly feel at home when configuring the new protocol. In most cases, RSTP performs better than the Cisco proprietary extensions, with negligible additional configuration. In addition, 802.1w is capable of reverting to 802.1D to interoperate with legacy bridges on a per-port basis. Reverting to 802.1D negates the benefits of 802.1w for that particular segment.

RSTP selects one switch as the root of an active spanning tree–connected topology and assigns port roles to individual ports on the switch, depending on whether the ports are part of the active topology.

RSTP provides rapid connectivity following the failure of a switch, switch port, or LAN. A new root port and the designated port of the connecting bridge transition to forwarding through an explicit handshake protocol between them. RSTP allows switch-port configuration so that the ports transition to forwarding directly when the switch reinitializes.

On Cisco Catalyst switches, a rapid version of PVST+, called RPVST+, is the per-VLAN version of the RSTP implementation. All of the current generation of Catalyst switches support RPVST+.

RSTP Port States

There are only three port states in RSTP, corresponding to the three possible operational statuses: discarding, learning, and forwarding. The RSTP 802.1w discarding state represents a merger of the 802.1D STP port states of disabled, blocking, and listening.

IEEE 802.1D STP mixes the state of a port, whether blocking or forwarding traffic, with the role it plays in the active topology. RSTP considers there to be no difference between a port in blocking state and a port in listening state; both discard frames, and neither learns MAC addresses. RSTP decouples the role of a port from the state of a port. Figure 5-22 provides a comparison of 802.1D port states with RSTP port states.

Figure 5-22 *Comparison of 802.1D Port States with RSTP Port States*

STP Port State	RSTP Port State	Port Included in Active Topology?	Port Learning MAC Addresses?
Disabled	Discarding	No	No
Blocking	Discarding	No	No
Listening	Discarding	No	No
Learning	Learning	No	Yes
Forwarding	Forwarding	Yes	Yes

RSTP Port Roles

RSTP uses the following definitions for port roles:

- **Root port**—The root port is the closest port to the root bridge in terms of path cost, identified with "R" in Figure 5-23. The STA elects a single root bridge for the whole bridged network, per-VLAN, or STP instance. The root bridge sends BPDUs that are better than the ones that any other bridge sends. The root bridge is the only bridge in the network that does not have a root port.

- **Designated port**—Bridges create a bridged domain by linking different network segments (Ethernet segments, for example). On a given segment, the requirement is to have only one path toward the root bridge; if there are two paths, a bridging loop occurs in the network. All bridges connected to a given segment listen to one another's BPDUs and agree that the bridge that is sending the best BPDU is the designated bridge for the segment. The corresponding port on that bridge is the designated port, identified with "D" in Figure 5-23.

- **Alternate port**—An alternate port is a port blocked from receiving root BPDUs from another bridge, as with the port on bridge A in Figure 5-23. The alternate port becomes the root port if the active root port fails.

- **Backup port**—A backup port is a port blocked from receiving root BPDUs from the designated port for a shared LAN segment from the same bridge on which the port is located, as with the port on bridge B in Figure 5-23. The backup port becomes the designated port if the existing designated port fails.

- **Disabled port**—A disabled port has no role within the operation of spanning tree.

Figure 5-23 depicts the various port roles in a sample topology of three bridges. RSTP calculates the final topology for the spanning tree by using the same criteria as 802.1D. There is no change in the way the different bridge and port priorities are used.

Figure 5-23 *RSTP Port Roles*

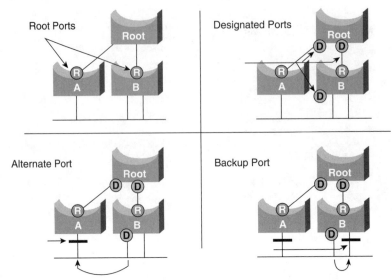

RSTP BPDU Format and BPDU Handling

RSTP introduces a few changes to the BPDU format. In 802.1D, only 2 bits in the Type field were used, namely TC and TC Acknowledgement. RSTP now uses all 6 remaining bits of the flag byte to do the following:

- Encode the role and state of the port originating the BPDU
- Handle the proposal and agreement mechanism

Another important change is that the RSTP BPDU is now of type 2, version 2. This property makes it easy for an 802.1w bridge to detect legacy bridges connected to it. Figure 5-24 shows the complete RSTP BPDU format.

Figure 5-24 *RSTP BPDU Format*

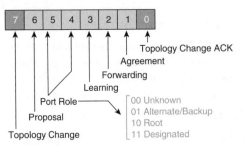

With 802.1D, a nonroot bridge generates a BPDU only when it receives one on its root port. With 802.1w, a bridge sends a BPDU with its current information every hello-time period, 2 seconds by default, even if it does not receive a BPDU from the root bridge.

If a given port receives no BPDUs for three consecutive hello times, the bridge immediately ages out protocol information. Immediate aging out of protocol information also happens if the max age timer expires. In RSTP, transmissions of BPDU act as keep-alive mechanisms between bridges; a bridge believes it has lost connectivity to its neighboring root or designated bridge if it misses three BPDUs in a row. This fast aging of the information allows quick failure detection. If a bridge fails to receive BPDUs from a neighbor, it is certain that the connection to that neighbor has been lost, as compared to 802.1D, where the problem potential exists anywhere on the path to the root or the root bridge itself. In RSTP mode, switches detect physical link failures much faster than in 802.1D.

The IEEE 802.1w committee also decided to incorporate a mechanism similar to the BackboneFast feature into RSTP.

In the scenario depicted in Figure 5-25, because bridge C still knows the root is alive and well, it immediately sends to bridge B a BPDU that contains information about the root bridge. As a result, bridge B stops sending its own BPDUs and accepts the port leading to C as its new root port.

Figure 5-25 *BackboneFast in RSTP*

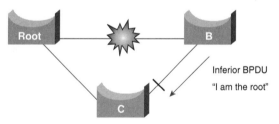

Rapid Transition to Forwarding

Rapid transition to forwarding is the most important feature introduced with IEEE 802.1w. Before the introduction of 802.1w, the Spanning-Tree Algorithm waited passively for the network to converge before transitioning a port to the forwarding state. The new RSTP actively confirms that a port transition to forwarding is safe without relying on a timer configuration. To achieve fast convergence on a port, the protocol relies upon two new variables:

- Edge port
- Link type

Ports that are directly connected to end stations are typically unable to create bridging loops in the network; therefore, they are allowed to transition directly to forwarding, skipping the listening and learning stages. Such ports are designated as edge ports through manual configuration. An edge port does not generate a topology change when its link transitions. If an edge port receives a BPDU, it immediately loses its edge port status and becomes a normal spanning-tree port.

RSTP-designated ports are only able to achieve rapid transition to forwarding on edge ports and point-to-point links. On today's switched networks, most switch-to-switch links are point-to-point; hence, this criterion is not an issue.

Switches automatically derive the link type from the duplex mode of a port. Figure 5-26 shows various RSTP link types in a typical network scenario. A port that is operating in full-duplex mode is point-to-point, while a port that is operating in half-duplex mode is assumed to be on a shared medium by default. Overriding of automatic link-type detection is possible with an explicit configuration.

Figure 5-26 *RSTP Link Types*

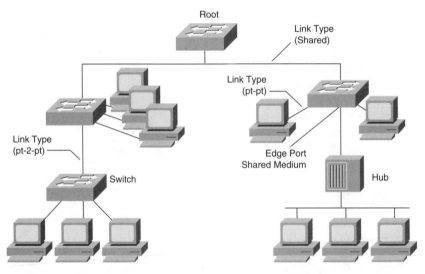

When the STA selects a port to become a designated port, 802.1D still waits two forward-delay periods (each delay is 15 seconds by default) before transitioning the port to the forwarding state.

In RSTP, the transition on point-to-point ports is rapid. Consider the scenario shown in Figure 5-27. Bridge A and bridge B connect through port a on bridge A and port b on bridge B. Bridge A is the root of the STP because of its superior BPDUs.

Figure 5-27 *Proposal and Agreement in RSTP*

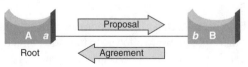

In this scenario, the following sequence of events occurs:

1 Ports a and b, the designated ports, start in discarding or learning state and send BPDUs with the proposal bit.

2 Port b receives the superior BPDU from bridge A and immediately knows that port b is the new root port.

3 Bridge B sends a BPDU back to bridge A with the agreement bit set in the BPDU.

4 Bridge A transitions to forwarding as soon as it receives the BPDU with the agreement bit set from bridge B.

The switched network has converged at the end of this proposal and agreement negotiation. The amount of time taken to converge with RSTP is the time it takes for the proposal and agreement BPDUs to reach both switches, which typically occurs in subsecond time.

Another form of immediate transition to the forwarding state included in RSTP is similar to the Cisco UplinkFast proprietary spanning-tree extension.

When a bridge loses its root port, it can put its best alternate port directly into forwarding mode. The selection of an alternate port as the new root port generates a topology change. The 802.1w topology change mechanism, discussed in the next section, clears the appropriate entries in the MAC address tables of the upstream bridges, removing the need for the dummy multicast generation process of UplinkFast.

RSTP Topology Change Mechanism

When an 802.1D bridge detects a topology change, it first notifies the root bridge by using a reliable mechanism. After the root bridge is aware of a change in the topology of the network, it sets the TC flag on the BPDUs that it sends out, which then gets relayed to all the bridges in the network through the normal mechanism. When a bridge receives a BPDU with the TC flag bit set, it reduces its bridging-table aging time to forward-delay seconds, ensuring a relatively quick flushing of stale information.

In RSTP, only non-edge ports that are moving to the forwarding state cause a topology change. Unlike with 802.1D, loss of connectivity does not generate a topology change. In other words, a port that is moving to blocking does not cause the respective bridge to generate a TC BPDU.

When an RSTP bridge detects a topology change, as depicted in Figure 5-28, it performs these actions:

1 The RSTP bridge starts the TC While timer with a value equal to twice the hello time for all its non-edge designated ports and its root port, if necessary. The TC While timer is the interval during which the RSTP bridge actively informs the rest of the bridges in the network of a topology change.

2 The RSTP bridge flushes the MAC addresses associated with all non-edge ports.

3 As long as the TC While timer is running on a port, the BPDUs sent out of that port have the TC bit set. While the timer is active, the bridge sends BPDUs even on the root port.

Figure 5-28 *Topology Change Mechanism in RSTP*

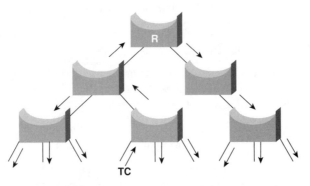

When a bridge receives a BPDU with the TC bit set from a neighbor, the bridge performs these actions:

1 The bridge clears the MAC addresses learned on all its ports, except the one that received the topology change.

2 The bridge starts the TC While timer and sends BPDUs with TC set on all its designated ports and root port; RSTP does not use the specific TCN BPDU anymore unless a legacy bridge needs to be notified.

In this way, the Topology Change Notification is flooded very quickly across the entire network. The topology change propagation is now a one-step process. In fact, the initiator of the topology change is flooding this information throughout the network, as opposed to with 802.1D, where only the root sends BPDUs with the TC bit set. This mechanism is much faster than the 802.1D equivalent. In RSTP implementation, there is no need to wait for the root bridge to be notified and then maintain the topology change state for the whole network for the value of the max age timer plus the value of the forward delay timer.

Compatibility with 802.1D

RSTP can operate with legacy STP protocols. However, it is important to note that 802.1w's inherent fast-convergence benefits are lost when interacting with legacy bridges.

Each port maintains a variable that defines the protocol to run on the corresponding segment. If the port consistently keeps receiving BPDUs that do not correspond to its current operating mode for two times the hello time, it switches to the other STP mode.

Multiple Spanning Tree

Multiple Spanning Tree (MST) extends the IEEE 802.1w RST algorithm to multiple spanning trees. The main purpose of MST is to reduce the total number of spanning-tree instances to match the physical topology of the network and thus reduce the CPU cycles of a switch. PVST+ runs STP instances for each VLAN and does not take into consideration the physical topology that may not require many different STP topologies. MST, on the other hand, uses a minimum number of STP instances to match the number of physical topologies present.

Figure 5-29 illustrates two links and 1000 VLANs. The 1000 VLANs map to two MST instances. Rather than maintaining 1000 spanning trees, each switch needs to maintain only two spanning trees, reducing the need for switch resources. This concept of two MST instances for the topology shown in Figure 5-29 extends to 4096 VLANs. MST converges faster than PVST+ and is backward compatible with 802.1D STP, 802.1w (RSTP), and the Cisco PVST+ architecture.

Figure 5-29 *VLAN Load Balancing*

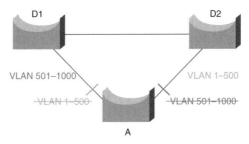

MST allows for the building of multiple spanning trees over trunks by grouping and associating VLANs to spanning-tree instances. Each instance may have a topology that is independent of other spanning-tree instances. This architecture provides multiple forwarding paths for data traffic and enables load balancing. A failure in one forwarding path does not affect other instances with different forwarding paths; hence, this architecture improves network fault tolerance.

In large networks, using different VLANs and a different spanning-tree topology enables better administration of the network and usage of the redundant paths that are available. An MST spanning-tree instance may exist only on bridges that have compatible VLAN instance assignments. Configuring a set of bridges with the same MST configuration information allows them to participate in a specific set of spanning-tree instances. The term *MST region* refers to the set of interconnected bridges that have the same MST configuration.

Figure 5-29 shows a common network design, featuring an access switch A, connected to two Building Distribution submodule switches D1 and D2. In this setup, there are 1000 VLANs, and the network administrator typically seeks to achieve load balancing on the access switch uplinks based on even or odd VLANs—or any other scheme deemed appropriate. In the following sections, we will compare PSVT+, 802.1Q, and MST solutions for the scenario in Figure 5-29, noting their relative advantages and disadvantages.

PVST+ Case

In a Cisco PVST+ environment, the switch achieves load balancing by tuning the spanning-tree parameters such that a specific number of VLANs are forwarding on each uplink trunk. Referring again to Figure 5-29, by electing bridge D1 to be the root for VLAN 501–1000 and bridge D2 to be the root for VLAN 1–500, the network topology achieves load balancing between the access and distribution layers. Switches maintain one spanning-tree instance for each VLAN, which means that 1000 instances are required for essentially only two different logical topologies. Maintaining 1000 instances consumes resources for all the switches in the network (in addition to the bandwidth used by each instance sending its own BPDUs).

In summary, PVST+ has the following characteristics:

- Provides the ability to optimize load balancing
- Maintains per-VLAN STP instance and hence results in more CPU utilization

802.1Q Case

The original IEEE 802.1Q standard defines much more than simple trunking. It defines a Common Spanning Tree (CST) instance, which is essentially one spanning-tree instance for the entire bridged network, regardless of the number of VLANs.

In a network running the CST instance, as depicted in Figure 5-30, the following is true:

- No load balancing is possible; one uplink needs to block for all VLANs.
- Switch CPU utilization is low; only one instance needs to be computed.

Figure 5-30 *Standard 802.1Q Case*

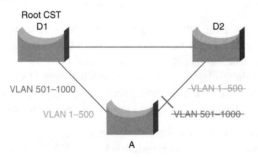

The Cisco implementation enhances 802.1Q to support PVST+. This feature behaves exactly as the PVST case. The Cisco per-VLAN BPDUs are tunneled by pure 802.1Q bridges.

MST Case

MST (IEEE 802.1s) combines the best aspects of PVST+ and 802.1Q, as shown in Figure 5-31. The idea is that most networks do not need more than a few topologies, and hence, mapping several VLANs reduces the number of spanning-tree instances. In the scenario described in Figure 5-31, only two different final logical topologies exist and therefore require only two spanning-tree instances. There is no need to run 1000 instances if, as shown in Figure 5-31, half of the 1000 VLANs map to a different spanning-tree instance.

In a network running MST, as depicted in Figure 5-31, the following is true:

- The desired load-balancing scheme is still possible because half the VLANs follow one separate instance.

- The switch utilization is low because it has to handle only two instances.

Figure 5-31 *MST Case*

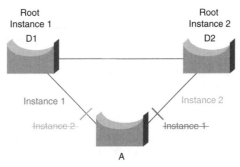

From a technical standpoint, MST is the best solution for the scenario presented in Figure 5-31. Because MST is a newer protocol, however, the following issues may arise:

- The protocol is more complex than the usual spanning tree and thus requires additional training of the operation staff.

- Interaction with legacy bridges is sometimes challenging.

MST Regions

The main enhancement introduced by MST is the ability to map several VLANs to a single spanning-tree instance. This raises the problem, however, of determining what VLAN is to be associated with what instance. More precisely, based on received BPDUs, devices need to identify these instances and the VLANs that are mapped to the instances.

In the case of the 802.1Q standard, all instances map to a unique and common instance and are therefore less complex. In the case of PVST+, each VLAN carries the BPDUs for its respective instance (one BPDU per VLAN).

Each switch that is running MST in the network has a single MST configuration that consists of three attributes:

- An alphanumeric configuration name (32 bytes)
- A configuration revision number (2 bytes)
- A 4096-element table that associates each of the potential 4096 VLANs supported on the chassis to a given instance

To be part of a common MST region, a group of switches must share the same configuration attributes. It is up to the network administrator to properly propagate the configuration throughout the region.

NOTE   If two switches differ on one or more configuration attributes, they are part of different regions.

To ensure a consistent VLANs-to-instance mapping, the protocol must be able to exactly identify the boundaries of the regions. For that purpose, the characteristics of the region are included in BPDUs. Switches do not propagate the exact VLANs-to-instance mapping in the BPDU, because the switches only need to know whether they are in the same region as a neighbor. Therefore, switches only send a digest of the VLANs-to-instance mapping table, along with the revision number and the name. Once a switch receives a BPDU, it extracts the message digest, a numerical value derived from the VLANs-to-instance mapping table through a mathematical function, and compares it with its own computed digest. If the digests differ, the port that is receiving the BPDU is at the boundary of a region.

In generic terms, a port is at the boundary of a region if the designated bridge on its segment is in a different region or if it receives legacy 802.1D BPDUs. In Figure 5-32, the port on B1 is at the boundary of region A, whereas the ports on B2 and B3 are internal to region B.

Figure 5-32   *Switches in Different MST Regions*

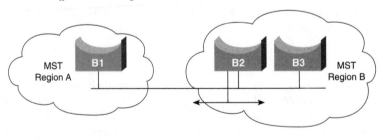

IST Instances

According to the IEEE 802.1s specification, an MST bridge must be able to handle at least one Internal Spanning Tree (IST) instance.

The IST instance enables interoperability between 802.1Q and 802.1s by extending the CST instance into the MST region.

The IST instance receives and sends BPDUs to the CST instance. The IST instance is capable of representing the entire MST region as a CST virtual bridge to the outside world.

Figure 5-33 shows two functionally equivalent diagrams. Notice the location of the different blocked ports. In a typical bridged network that is running 802.1D, the expectation is to see a blocked port between switches M and B. For the second loop, the expectation is to have a blocked port somewhere in the middle of the MST region; instead, the port on bridge D goes to blocking mode. To understand the reason for the location of blocked ports, consider the picture on the right as seen by the non-MST region running the CST. The MST region is seen as a single virtual bridge, which interacts with the non-MST region through the IST instance. The blocking port on switch B is an alternate port to the root and hence is blocked. Similarly, port D is blocked because it is another alternate port to the root bridge.

Figure 5-33 *IST Instance Interaction with the CST Instance*

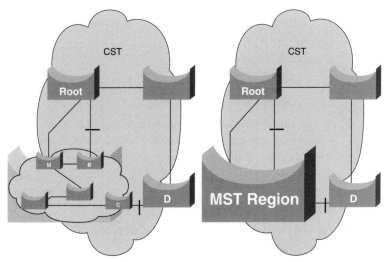

To summarize, a bridge that is running MST provides interoperability with CST bridges as follows:

- MST bridges run an IST instance, which augments the CST instance information with internal information about the MST region.

- The IST instances connect all the MST bridges in the region and appear as a subtree in the CST that includes the whole bridged domain. The MST region appears as a single bridge to adjacent CST bridges and MST regions.

The *Common and Internal Spanning Tree* (CIST) is the collection of the IST instances in each MST region, the CST instance that interconnects the MST regions, and the 802.1D bridges. The CIST is identical to an IST instance inside an MST region and identical to a CST instance outside an MST region. 802.1D STP and RSTP together elect a single bridge as the root of the CIST.

MST Instances

MST establishes and maintains additional spanning-tree instances within each MST region. These spanning-tree instances are termed MST instances (MSTI). The IST instance is numbered 0, and the MSTIs are numbered 1, 2, 3, and so on. Any MSTI is local to the MST region and is independent of MSTIs in other regions, even if the MST regions interconnect. MST interoperates with PVST+ as follows:

- MSTIs combine with the IST instance at the boundary of the MST region to become the CST. The MST region appears as a single bridge to adjacent single spanning-tree and MST regions.

- MST also generates PVST+ BPDUs for the non-CST VLANs.

- MST supports some of the PVST+ extensions, as follows:

  — UplinkFast and BackboneFast are not available in MSTP but are available as inherent features of RSTP.

  — PortFast is supported.

  — MST mode supports BPDU filtering and BPDU guard.

  — MST mode supports loop guard and root guard. MST preserves the VLAN 1 disabled functionality, but switches still transmit BPDUs in VLAN 1 when this feature is enabled.

  — An MST switch operates with MAC address reduction enabled. MAC address reduction, as discussed earlier in this chapter, enables extended-range VLAN identification.

  — For private VLANs, you must map a secondary VLAN to the same instance as the primary.

Configuring Basic Parameters of MST

Enabling MST is a multistep process that involves mapping ranges of VLANs to a single MSTI.

Because MST is applicable to multiple VLANs, it requires some additional configuration beyond that needed for PVST+ or RPVST+. After you have enabled MST with the command **spanning-tree mode mst**, you configure regions and instances with additional configuration commands:

Step 1   Enter the MST configuration submode to configure MST.

> `spanning-tree mst configuration`

Step 2   Configure the MST region name.

> `name` *name*

Step 3   Configure the MST configuration revision.

> `revision` *revision_number*

The revision number is any unsigned 16-bit integer. It is not incremented automatically when a new MST configuration is committed.

Step 4   Map the VLANs to MSTIs.

> `instance` *instance_number* `vlan` *vlan_range*

Use the **no** keyword to unmap all the VLANs that map to an MSTI when not specifying the **vlan** keyword. Use the **no** keyword to unmap a specified VLAN from an MSTI when specifying the **vlan** keyword.

Step 5   Save the configuration and exit the MST configuration submode.

> `end`

Example 5-8 illustrates a user changing the spanning-tree mode to MST and configuring the MST region by mapping the range of VLANs to instance 1.

Example 5-8   *Sample Output of Configuring MST and Mapping VLANs to Instances on Cisco IOS–Based Catalyst Switches*

```
Switch#configure terminal
Enter configuration commands, one per line.  End with CNTL/Z.
Switch(config)#spanning-tree mode mst
Switch(config)#spanning-tree mst configuration
Switch(config-mst)#show current
Current MST configuration
Name      []
Revision  0
Instance  Vlans mapped
--------  -----------------------------------------------------------
0         1-4094
------------------------------------------------------------------------
Switch(config-mst)#name cisco
Switch(config-mst)#revision 1
Switch(config-mst)#instance 1 vlan 1-10
Switch(config-mst)#show pending
Pending MST configuration
Name      [cisco]
Revision  1
```

continues

Example 5-8 *Sample Output of Configuring MST and Mapping VLANs to Instances on Cisco IOS–Based Catalyst Switches (Continued)*

```
Instance  Vlans mapped
--------  --------------------------------------------------------------
0         11-4094
1         1-10
Switch(config-mst)#end
```

The **show current** command in Example 5-8 displays the current MST configuration on the switch. The **show pending** command details the uncommitted MST configuration. Catalyst switches discard the pending configuration if the administrator aborts the configuration changes by using the **abort** command. In addition, Catalyst switches save the MST configuration when issuing the **end** command, as shown in Example 5-8.

Example 5-9 illustrates a user displaying the MST configuration on Cisco IOS–based Catalyst switches.

Example 5-9 *Displaying MST Configuration on Cisco IOS–Based Catalyst Switches*

```
Switch#show spanning-tree mst configuration
Name      [cisco]
Revision  1
Instance  Vlans mapped
--------  --------------------------------------------------------------
0         11-4094
1         1-10
          --------------------------------------------------------------
```

Example 5-10 illustrates a user displaying MST protocol information for MSTIs that are configured on the switch.

Example 5-10 *Displaying MST Protocol Information on Cisco IOS–Based Catalyst Switches*

```
Switch#show spanning-tree mst

###### MST00          vlans mapped:   5-4094
Bridge      address 0009.e845.6480  priority  32768 (32768 sysid 0)
Root        this switch for CST and IST
Configured  hello time 2, forward delay 15, max age 20, max hops 20


Interface        Role Sts Cost      Prio.Nbr Type
---------------- ---- --- --------- -------- --------------------------------
Fa3/24           Desg FWD 2000000   128.152  Shr
Fa3/32           Desg FWD 200000    128.160  P2p
Fa3/42           Back BLK 200000    128.170  P2p


###### MST01          vlans mapped:   1-2
Bridge      address 0009.e845.6480  priority  32769 (32768 sysid 1)
Root        this switch for MST01

Interface        Role Sts Cost      Prio.Nbr Type
```

Example 5-10 *Displaying MST Protocol Information on Cisco IOS–Based Catalyst Switches (Continued)*

```
---------------- ---- --- --------- -------- --------------------------------
Fa3/24          Desg FWD 2000000   128.152  Shr
Fa3/32          Desg FWD 200000    128.160  P2p
Fa3/42          Back BLK 200000    128.170  P2p

###### MST02        vlans mapped:  3-4
Bridge      address 0009.e845.6480  priority  32770 (32768 sysid 2)
Root        this switch for MST02

Interface       Role Sts Cost      Prio.Nbr Type
---------------- ---- --- --------- -------- --------------------------------
Fa3/24          Desg FWD 2000000   128.152  Shr
```

Example 5-11 illustrates a user displaying MST protocol information for a specific MSTI.

Example 5-11 *Displaying MST Protocol Instance Information*

```
Switch#show spanning-tree mst 1

###### MST01        vlans mapped:  1-2
Bridge      address 0009.e845.6480  priority  32769 (32768 sysid 1)
Root        this switch for MST01

Interface       Role Sts Cost      Prio.Nbr Type
---------------- ---- --- --------- -------- --------------------------------
Fa3/24          Desg FWD 2000000   128.152  Shr
Fa3/32          Desg FWD 200000    128.160  P2p
Fa3/42          Back BLK 200000    128.170  P2p
```

Example 5-12 illustrates a user displaying MST protocol information for a specific interface.

Example 5-12 *Displaying MST Protocol Information for a Specific Interface*

```
Switch# show spanning-tree mst interface FastEthernet 3/24

FastEthernet3/24 of MST00 is designated forwarding
Edge port: no           (default)       port guard : none      (default)
Link type: shared       (auto)          bpdu filter: disable   (default)
Boundary : internal                     bpdu guard : disable   (default)
Bpdus sent 81, received 81

Instance Role Sts Cost      Prio.Nbr Vlans mapped
-------- ---- --- --------- -------- --------------------------------
0        Desg FWD 2000000   128.152  5-4094
1        Desg FWD 2000000   128.152  1-2
2        Desg FWD 2000000   128.152  3-4
```

Example 5-13 illustrates a user displaying detailed information for a specific instance.

Example 5-13 *Displaying Detailed MSTI Information*

```
Switch#show spanning-tree mst 1 detail

###### MST01          vlans mapped:    1-2
Bridge      address 0009.e845.6480  priority  32769 (32768 sysid 1)
Root        this switch for MST01
FastEthernet3/24 of MST01 is designated forwarding
Port info            port id         128.152  priority    128  cost    2000000
Designated root      address 0009.e845.6480  priority  32769  cost          0
Designated bridge    address 0009.e845.6480  priority  32769  port id  128.152
Timers: message expires in 0 sec, forward delay 0, forward transitions 1
Bpdus (MRecords) sent755, received 0

FastEthernet3/32 of MST01 is designated forwarding
Port info            port id         128.160  priority    128  cost     200000
Designated root      address 0009.e845.6480  priority  32769  cost          0
Designated bridge    address 0009.e845.6480  priority  32769  port id  128.160
Timers: message expires in 0 sec, forward delay 0, forward transitions 1
Bpdus (MRecords) sent 769, received 1

FastEthernet3/42 of MST01 is backup blocking
Port info            port id         128.170  priority    128  cost     200000
Designated root      address 0009.e845.6480  priority  32769  cost          0
Designated bridge    address 0009.e845.6480  priority  32769  port id  128.160
Timers: message expires in 5 sec, forward delay 0, forward transitions 0
Bpdus (MRecords) sent 1, received 769
```

Study Tips

The following bullets review important BCMSN exam preparation points of this chapter. The bullets only briefly highlight the main points of this chapter related to the BCMSN exam. Consult the text of this chapter for additional information regarding these topics. Table 5-3 lists important commands to review for the BCMSN exam.

- MAC addresses of end stations are learned and stored in a MAC address table on Catalyst switches for directed forwarding.

- The five states of 802.1D Spanning Tree Protocol are

    — Listening

    — Learning

    — Forwarding

    — Blocking

    — Disabled

Of these states, only the Forwarding state actually allows forwarding of frames. All other states prevent frame forwarding.

- With 802.1D STP, the Bridge Identifier is made up of the Bridge Priority and MAC address of the switch, and the lowest identifier becomes the root of the spanning tree.

- With 802.1D STP, the Bridge Priority varies from 0 to 65535.

- With 802.1D STP, BPDUs carry three STP parameters—hello time, forward delay, and max age.

- RSTP (802.1w) has fast convergence due to a proposal and agreement mechanism instead of the timer-based mechanism of 802.1D.

- The three states of RSTP are

    — Disabled

    — Learning

    — Forwarding

- RSTP has five port roles:

    — Root port

    — Designated port

    — Backup port

    — Alternate port

    — Disabled port

    Of all these ports, only the root and designated port state allow forwarding of frames.

- In the traditional PVST mode, a spanning-tree instance is maintained for each VLAN.

- MST (802.1s) offers better performance (less CPU load and network traffic) by combining multiple VLANs into a single instance of spanning tree. MST also simplifies troubleshooting and allows for a large number of VLANs.

Table 5-3   *Important Commands*

Command	Description
show spanning-tree	Displays STP information for all VLANs configured on a switch
show spanning-tree active	Displays STP information regarding active interfaces for all VLANs
show spanning-tree interface *interface-id*	Displays STP information regarding the specified information
show spanning-tree statistics *mod/port vlan-id*	Displays STP statistical information for the specified port and specified VLAN on Catalyst switches running Cisco CatOS
show spanning-tree summary	Displays STP summary information for each VLAN configured on a switch

continues

Table 5-3 *Important Commands (Continued)*

Command	Description
show spanning-tree summary totals	Displays STP summary information for all VLANs configured on a switch
show spanning-tree detail	Displays detailed STP information for all VLANs configured on a switch
show spanning-tree vlan *vlan-id* **bridge**	Displays STP bridge information for a specified VLAN
show spanning-tree root	Displays the STP root information for all VLANs configured on a switch
show spanning-tree vlan *vlan-id*	Displays STP information for a specific VLAN
(config-if)#**spanning-tree cost** *port-cost*	Configures the interface spanning-tree cost value
(config)#**spanning-tree vlan** *vlan-id* **root primary**	Configures the switch as the root of the specified VLAN by automatically lowering its priority to a value lower than the current root
(config)#**spanning-tree vlan** *vlan-id* **priority** *value*	Configures the bridge priority for the specified VLAN

Summary

The Spanning Tree Protocol is a fundamental protocol to prevent Layer 2 loops and at the same time provide redundancy in the network. This chapter covered the basic operation and configuration of 802.1D, RSTP, and MST.

Chapter 6 reviews the configuration of 802.1D enhancements and advanced features available in Cisco Catalyst switches for STP. Chapter 6 also presents a methodology for troubleshooting STP problems.

Configuration Exercise: Configuring and Verifying Spanning-Tree Bridge Priorities and Spanning-Tree Port Cost

Complete this configuration exercise to practice using features discussed in this chapter.

Required Resources

The following resources and equipment are required to complete this exercise:

- Catalyst switches, as shown in Figure 5-34

- A terminal server connected to the console port of each laboratory device
- A PC connected to the terminal server to access the devices

Exercise Objective

The devices in the network should be preconnected and ready for use. In this exercise, you will configure and verify some of the features that were reviewed in this chapter.

After completing this exercise, you will be able to

- Configure and verify spanning tree root and backup bridges and STP bridge priorities.
- Configure and verify spanning-tree port cost.
- Identify STP topology changes.

The exercise assumes that the switches have been preconfigured with VLAN 1 and VLAN 2 and that the switches are already configured for VLAN trunking.

Network Diagram

Figure 5-34 shows the network layout for this exercise.

Figure 5-34 *Network Scenario*

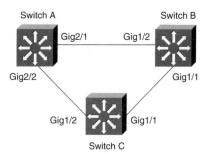

Command List

In this exercise, you will use the commands listed in Table 5-4. The commands are listed in alphabetical order so that you can easily locate the information you need. Refer to this table if you need configuration command assistance during the exercise.

Table 5-4   *Command List for Configuration Exercise*

Command	Description
configure terminal	From privileged EXEC mode, enters global configuration mode
end	Exits the configuration mode

continues

Table 5-4 *Command List for Configuration Exercise (Continued)*

Command	Description
exit	Exits the current mode
interface FastEthernet | GigabitEthernet *slot/ port*	Enters interface configuration mode for a Catalyst switch with a Fast Ethernet or Gigabit Ethernet interface installed
[no] shutdown	Enables or disables an interface.
show spanning-tree vlan *vlan-id*	Displays STP information for a VLAN
show spanning-tree vlan *vlan-id* **detail**	Displays detailed STP information for a VLAN
spanning-tree vlan *vlan-id* **cost** *cost*	Configures spanning tree port cost for a VLAN
spanning-tree vlan *vlan-id* **priority** *priority*	Configures a bridge priority for a VLAN

Task 1: Configure and Verify Spanning Tree Root and Backup Bridges and STP Priorities

Step 1   For VLAN 1, configure switch A to be the root switch and switch B to be the secondary root switch. For VLAN 2, configure switch B to be the root switch and switch A to be the secondary root switch. Use the **spanning-tree vlan** *vlan-id* **priority** *priority* command.

```
SwitchA#configure terminal
Enter configuration commands, one per line.  End with CNTL/Z.
SwitchA(config)#spanning-tree vlan 1 priority 4096
SwitchA(config)#spanning-tree vlan 2 priority 8192
SwitchA(config)#end
SwitchB#configure terminal
Enter configuration commands, one per line.  End with CNTL/Z.
SwitchB(config)#spanning-tree vlan 2 priority 4096
SwitchB(config)#spanning-tree vlan 1 priority 8192
SwitchB(config)#end
```

Step 2   Using the **show spanning-tree vlan** *vlan-id* command, verify that all three switches show the correct root bridge.

```
SwitchA#show spanning-tree vlan 1

VLAN0001
  Spanning tree enabled protocol ieee
  Root ID    Priority    4096
             Address     0030.7b4e.3401
```

```
                       This bridge is the root
                       Hello Time   2 sec  Max Age 20 sec  Forward Delay 15 sec

             Bridge ID  Priority    4096
                        Address     0030.7b4e.3401
                        Hello Time   2 sec  Max Age 20 sec  Forward Delay 15 sec
                        Aging Time 300

Interface          Role Sts Cost     Prio.Nbr Type
---------------- ---- --- --------- ---- --------------------------------
Gi2/1              Desg FWD 4        128.65   P2p
Gi2/2              Desg FWD 4        128.66   P2p
SwitchA#show spanning-tree vlan 2

VLAN0002
  Spanning tree enabled protocol ieee
  Root ID    Priority    4098
             Address     0009.e845.6480
             Cost        4
             Port        65 (GigabitEthernet2/1)
             Hello Time   2 sec  Max Age 20 sec  Forward Delay 15 sec

  Bridge ID  Priority    8192
             Address     0030.7b4e.3402
             Hello Time   2 sec  Max Age 20 sec  Forward Delay 15 sec
             Aging Time 300

Interface          Role Sts Cost     Prio.Nbr Type
---------------- ---- --- --------- ---- --------------------------------
Gi2/1              Root FWD 4        128.65   P2p
Gi2/2              Desg FWD 4        128.66   P2p

SwitchB#show spanning-tree vlan 1

VLAN0001
  Spanning tree enabled protocol ieee
  Root ID    Priority    4096
             Address     0030.7b4e.3401
             Cost        4
             Port        2 (GigabitEthernet1/2)
             Hello Time   2 sec  Max Age 20 sec  Forward Delay 15 sec

  Bridge ID  Priority    8193   (priority 8192 sys-id-ext 1)
```

```
                    Address      0009.e845.6480
                    Hello Time   2 sec  Max Age 20 sec  Forward Delay 15 sec
                    Aging Time 300


Interface          Role Sts Cost      Prio.Nbr Type
---------------- ---- --- --------- -------------------------------
Gi1/1              Desg FWD 4         128.1    P2p
Gi1/2              Root FWD 4         128.2    P2p
SwitchB#show spanning-tree vlan 2


VLAN0002
  Spanning tree enabled protocol ieee
  Root ID    Priority    4098
             Address     0009.e845.6480
             This bridge is the root
             Hello Time   2 sec  Max Age 20 sec  Forward Delay 15 sec


  Bridge ID  Priority    4098   (priority 4096 sys-id-ext 2)
             Address     0009.e845.6480
             Hello Time   2 sec  Max Age 20 sec  Forward Delay 15 sec
             Aging Time 15


Interface          Role Sts Cost      Prio.Nbr Type
---------------- ---- --- --------- -------------------------------
Gi1/1              Desg FWD 4         128.1    P2p
Gi1/2              Desg FWD 4         128.2    P2p
SwitchC#show spanning-tree vlan 1


VLAN0001
  Spanning tree enabled protocol ieee
  Root ID    Priority    4096
             Address     0030.7b4e.3401
             Cost        4
             Port        2 (GigabitEthernet1/2)
             Hello Time   2 sec  Max Age 20 sec  Forward Delay 15 sec


  Bridge ID  Priority    32769  (priority 32768 sys-id-ext 1)
             Address     000a.4172.df40
             Hello Time   2 sec  Max Age 20 sec  Forward Delay 15 sec
             Aging Time 300


Interface          Role Sts Cost      Prio.Nbr Type
---------------- ---- --- --------- -------------------------------
Gi1/1              Altn BLK 4         128.1    P2p
Gi1/2              Root FWD 4         128.2    P2p
```

```
SwitchC#show spanning-tree vlan 2

VLAN0002
  Spanning tree enabled protocol ieee
  Root ID    Priority    4098
             Address     0009.e845.6480
             Cost        4
             Port        1 (GigabitEthernet1/1)
             Hello Time   2 sec  Max Age 20 sec  Forward Delay 15 sec

  Bridge ID  Priority    32770  (priority 32768 sys-id-ext 2)
             Address     000a.4172.df40
             Hello Time   2 sec  Max Age 20 sec  Forward Delay 15 sec
             Aging Time 300

Interface         Role Sts Cost      Prio.Nbr Type
----------------- ---- --- --------- -------- --------------------------------
Gi1/1             Root FWD 4         128.1    P2p
Gi1/2             Altn BLK 4         128.2    P2p
```

Task 2: Configure and Verify Spanning Tree Port Cost

Step 1   Configure switch A to be the root switch and to be the root bridge for VLAN 2 as well. Use the **spanning-tree vlan** *vlan-id* **priority** *priority* command.

```
SwitchA#configure terminal
Enter configuration commands, one per line.  End with CNTL/Z.
SwitchA(config)#spanning-tree vlan 2 priority 4096
SwitchA(config)#end
SwitchB#configure terminal
Enter configuration commands, one per line.  End with CNTL/Z.
SwitchB(config)#spanning-tree vlan 2 priority 8192
SwitchB(config)#end
```

Step 2   Use the **show spanning-tree vlan** *vlan-id* command. On switch C, notice that for both VLAN 1 and VLAN 2, the same link is forwarding toward the root switch A.

```
SwitchC#show spanning-tree vlan 1

VLAN0001
  Spanning tree enabled protocol ieee
  Root ID    Priority    4096
             Address     0030.7b4e.3401
```

```
                      Cost        4
                      Port        2 (GigabitEthernet1/2)
                      Hello Time   2 sec  Max Age 20 sec  Forward Delay 15 sec

          Bridge ID  Priority    32769  (priority 32768 sys-id-ext 1)
                      Address     000a.4172.df40
                      Hello Time   2 sec  Max Age 20 sec  Forward Delay 15 sec
                      Aging Time 300


          Interface        Role Sts Cost      Prio.Nbr Type
          ---------------- ---- --- --------- -------- --------------------------------

          Gi1/1            Altn BLK 4          128.1    P2p
          Gi1/2            Root FWD 4          128.2    P2p


          SwitchC#show spanning-tree vlan 2


          VLAN0002
            Spanning tree enabled protocol ieee
            Root ID    Priority    4096
                       Address     0030.7b4e.3402
                       Cost        4
                       Port        2 (GigabitEthernet1/2)
                       Hello Time   2 sec  Max Age 20 sec  Forward Delay 15 sec
            Bridge ID  Priority    32770  (priority 32768 sys-id-ext 2)
                       Address     000a.4172.df40
                       Hello Time   2 sec  Max Age 20 sec  Forward Delay 15 sec
                       Aging Time 300


          Interface        Role Sts Cost      Prio.Nbr Type
          ---------------- ---- --- ------------- -------- -----------------------------

          Gi1/1            Altn BLK 4          128.1    P2p
          Gi1/2            Root FWD 4          128.2    P2p
```

Step 3 To achieve load balancing of the VLAN 1 and VLAN 2 traffic on switch C, change the spanning-tree port cost for VLAN 2 on Gigabit Ethernet 1/2 to 10. Use the **spanning-tree vlan** *vlan-id* **cost** *cost* command.

```
          SwitchC#configure terminal
          Enter configuration commands, one per line.  End with CNTL/Z.
          SwitchC(config-if)#interface gigabitEthernet 1/2
          SwitchC(config-if)#spanning-tree vlan 2 cost 10
          SwitchC(config-if)#end
```

Step 4 Verify that switch C load-balances between the two uplinks. Use the **show spanning-tree vlan** *vlan-id* command.

```
          SwitchC#show spanning-tree vlan 1
```

```
VLAN0001
  Spanning tree enabled protocol ieee
  Root ID    Priority    4096
             Address     0030.7b4e.3401
             Cost        4
             Port        2 (GigabitEthernet1/2)
             Hello Time   2 sec  Max Age 20 sec  Forward Delay 15 sec

  Bridge ID  Priority    32769  (priority 32768 sys-id-ext 1)
             Address     000a.4172.df40
             Hello Time   2 sec  Max Age 20 sec  Forward Delay 15 sec
             Aging Time 300


Interface        Role Sts Cost      Prio.Nbr Type
---------------- ---- --- --------- -------- --------------------------------
Gi1/1            Altn BLK 4         128.1    P2p
Gi1/2            Root FWD 4         128.2    P2p
```

SwitchC#**show spanning-tree vlan 2**

```
VLAN0002
  Spanning tree enabled protocol ieee
  Root ID    Priority    4096
             Address     0030.7b4e.3402
             Cost        8
             Port        1 (GigabitEthernet1/1)
             Hello Time   2 sec  Max Age 20 sec  Forward Delay 15 sec
  Bridge ID  Priority    32770  (priority 32768 sys-id-ext 2)
             Address     000a.4172.df40
             Hello Time   2 sec  Max Age 20 sec  Forward Delay 15 sec
             Aging Time 15


Interface        Role Sts Cost      Prio.Nbr Type
---------------- ---- --- --------- -------- --------------------------------
Gi1/1            Root FWD 4         128.1    P2p
Gi1/2            Altn BLK 10        128.2    P2p
```

Task 3: Identifying STP Topology Changes

Step 1   To simulate an STP topology change, bounce the link connecting switch A
and switch C. To bounce a link, use the **shutdown** and **no shutdown**
commands on switch C.

```
SwitchC#configure terminal
Enter configuration commands, one per line.  End with CNTL/Z.
```

```
SwitchC(config)#interface gigabitEthernet 1/2
SwitchC(config-if)#shutdown
SwitchC(config-if)#no shutdown
SwitchC(config-if)#end
SwitchC#
```

Step 2   Topology changes due to link failure or link bounce as simulated in the previous step need to be investigated. Use the **show spanning-tree vlan** *vlan-id* **detail** command on switch A to determine the source of the spanning-tree topology change.

```
SwitchA#show spanning-tree vlan 1 detail

VLAN0001 is executing the ieee compatible Spanning Tree protocol
 Bridge Identifier has priority 4096, address 000a.8adb.7600
 Configured hello time 2, max age 20, forward delay 15
 We are the root of the spanning tree
 Topology change flag not set, detected flag not set
 Number of topology changes 20 last change occurred 00:06:13 ago
        from GigabitEthernet2/2
 Times:   hold 1, topology change 35, notification 2
          hello 2, max age 20, forward delay 15
 Timers: hello 0, topology change 0, notification 0, aging 300

 Port 2 (GigabitEthernet2/2) of VLAN0001 is forwarding
  Port path cost 4, Port priority 128, Port Identifier 128.2.
  Designated root has priority 4096, address 000a.8adb.7600
  Designated bridge has priority 4096, address 000a.8adb.7600
  Designated port id is 128.2, designated path cost 0
  Timers: message age 0, forward delay 0, hold 0
  Number of transitions to forwarding state: 1
  Link type is point-to-point by default
  BPDU: sent 367, received 3
```

Review Questions

For multiple-choice questions, there might be more than one correct answer.

1   True or False: With redundant paths in the network, disabling STP will not cause a Layer 2 loop.

2   True or False: MST is always preferred if you have more than a single VLAN.

3   True or False: Secondary root bridges have a lower bridge priority than primary root bridges.

4 Which one of the following is the best bridge priority configuration for a spanning-tree root switch?

a 0

b 1

c 4096

d 8192

e 65536

5 Which command would display the spanning-tree root switch information for all VLANs configured on an IOS switch?

a **show spanning-tree-root**

b **show bridge root**

c **show root switch**

d **show spanning-tree root-switch**

e **show spanning-tree root**

6 What command is used to configure a distribution switch as the primary root of a spanning tree?

a **spanning-tree vlan** *vlan-id* **primary**

b **spanning-tree vlan** *vlan-id* **root primary**

c **spanning-tree root primary**

d **spanning-tree bridge root**

e None of the above

7 How many operational states does RSTP have?

a 1

b 2

    c 3

    d 4

    e None of the above

8 At what layer does STP operate in the OSI model?

    a Layer 1

    b Layer 2

    c Layer 3

    d Layer 4

9 What is a typical convergence time in network topology of just two directly connected RSTP-enabled switches?

    a 15 seconds

    b 50 seconds

    c 20 seconds

    d 2 seconds

    e <1 second

10 What is the default message interval for BPDUs in RSTP mode?

    a 1 second

    b 15 seconds

    c 20 seconds

    d 2 seconds

    e <1 second

11 Based on Figure 5-35, indicate which bridge is elected as root and why.

Figure 5-35 *Lab Topology*

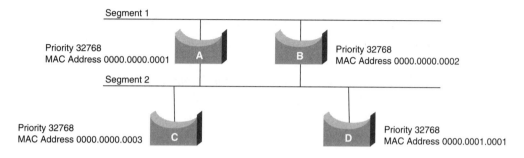

12 Based on Figure 5-35, indicate which port in segment 2 would be the designated port and why.

13 What are the criteria in a Layer 2 switched network for selecting a primary root bridge?

This chapter covers the following topics:

- Understanding and Configuring Cisco Enhancement Features to 802.1D STP

- Tuning and Adding Resiliency to STP Using the BPDU Guard, BPDU Filtering, and Root Guard Features

- Understanding How to Prevent Forwarding Loops in Multilayer Switched Networks

- Troubleshooting STP Problems

## CHAPTER 6

Adding Resiliency to Spanning Tree Using Advanced Features and Troubleshooting STP Issues

In Chapter 5, "Understanding and Configuring the 802.1D, 802.1s, and 802.1w Spanning Tree Protocols," you learned the theory behind how the Spanning Tree Protocol (STP) operates in preventing bridging loops and how it provides redundancy to a multilayer switched network. In addition, Chapter 5 covered some configuration commands and examples for configuring 802.1D STP. Although 802.1D is still the widely deployed STP in enterprise networks, it has many limitations, including slow convergence after a network topology change. In modern networks, because most of the connections between switches are point-to-point links, 802.1D STP takes too long to converge. The convergence usually takes tens of seconds—much too long by today's high-availability standards. As a result, Cisco introduced STP features such as PortFast, UplinkFast, and BackboneFast to achieve faster network convergence.

Moreover, 802.1D does not prevent unwanted devices from becoming the root bridge of the spanning tree, and no mechanism exists to selectively discard BPDUs from certain ports. Cisco introduced features such as Root Guard and BPDU Guard to solve the problem of unauthorized or inappropriate devices causing network topology changes.

In addition, network device failures can cause bridging loops or black holes in the network. The Cisco Unidirectional Link Detection (UDLD) and Loop Guard features prevent network device failures that are due to faulty hardware or software errors.

Problems such as link duplex mismatch, unidirectional link failure, frame corruption, resource errors, and misconfigurations may disrupt the spanning tree, which in turn disrupts network traffic. As a result, understanding how to troubleshoot spanning-tree problems is critical in maintaining high network availability. The following best practices for spanning tree prevent problems and aid in quick network recovery in the event of unforeseen anomalous events.

This chapter introduces the STP enhancements with sample configurations. This chapter also discusses how to tune STP for higher availability and resiliency. It concludes with a section on STP troubleshooting methodology.

Enhancements to 802.1D Spanning Tree Protocol

Cisco has developed several features to enhance the operation of STP, including the following:

- PortFast
- UplinkFast
- BackboneFast

Each one of these features speeds the convergence of the 802.1D spanning tree.

PortFast

Spanning Tree PortFast causes an interface configured as a Layer 2 access port to enter the forwarding state immediately, bypassing the listening and learning states. Enable PortFast on Layer 2 access ports connected to a single workstation or server to allow those devices to connect to the network immediately, rather than waiting for spanning tree to converge. In Figure 6-1, a server and workstation are attached to an access switch through ports that have the PortFast feature enabled.

Figure 6-1 *Sample PortFast Scenario*

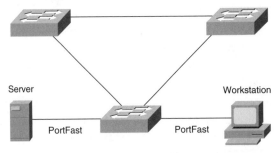

Figure 6-2 illustrates the modification in the STP state machine for interfaces configured for the PortFast feature. As illustrated in the figure, the STP state jumps directly from blocking to forwarding without going through the listening and learning state. In addition, PortFast suppresses topology change notifications.

NOTE   The purpose of PortFast is to minimize the time that access ports wait for STP to converge. The advantage of enabling PortFast is to prevent DHCP timeouts, Novell login problems, and AppleTalk address discovery problems on workstation bootup. Use this feature solely on access ports except in specific network designs. When enabling PortFast on a port connecting to another switch, there is a risk of creating a bridging loop.

Figure 6-2   *STP State Machine with PortFast*

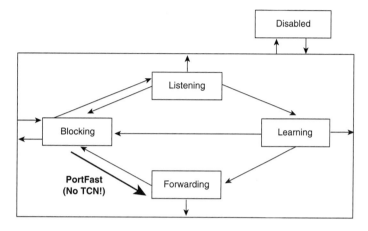

Configuring the PortFast Feature

On Cisco IOS–based Catalyst switches, use the following interface command to enable or disable the PortFast feature:

```
[no] spanning-tree portfast
```

Example 6-1 illustrates a user configuring the PortFast feature and verifying the configuration.

Example 6-1   *Configuration and Verification of PortFast on Cisco IOS–Based Catalyst Switches*

```
Switch#configure terminal
Enter configuration commands, one per line. End with CNTL/Z.
Switch(config)#interface FastEthernet 3/27
Switch(config-if)#spanning-tree portfast
%Warning: portfast should only be enabled on ports connected to a single
 host. Connecting hubs, concentrators, switches, bridges, etc... to this
 interface  when portfast is enabled, can cause temporary bridging loops.
 Use with CAUTION

%Portfast has been configured on FastEthernet3/27 but will only
 have effect when the interface is in a non-trunking mode.
Switch(config-if)#end
Switch#
Switch#show spanning-tree interface FastEthernet 3/27 portfast
VLAN0001          enabled
```

On switches in the Building Access submodule, enable PortFast globally so that there is no need to explicitly enable PortFast on each port individually. Remember to explicitly disable PortFast on uplink ports that connect to distribution layer switches.

Use the following command to enable PortFast globally in global configuration mode:

```
spanning-tree portfast default
```

NOTE   BPDU Guard puts the port in err-disable state if a PortFast-enabled port receives a BPDU. Err-disable port state, effectively the same as disable state, prevents any data ingress or egress from a port until the err-disabled configurable timeout period elapses or manual intervention occurs. A Catalyst switch uses the err-disable state to disable ports automatically in the case of other anomalous events or invalid configurations besides spanning tree. Enable the BPDU Guard feature on all ports configured for PortFast to prevent a network outage due to an accidental connection of a switching device on PortFast-enabled ports.

PortFast is a highly recommended configuration on end-user ports and server ports along with disabling negotiation of channeling and trunking. The end-result of these configurations is to allow immediate forwarding frames on link up. On Cisco IOS-based Catalyst switches, use the following command to place an interface into this desired configuration:

```
switchport mode host
```

Example 6-2 shows a user configuring an interface for connecting to a host.

Example 6-2   *Configuration of Host Interface on Cisco IOS–Based Catalyst Switch*

```
SwitchB#configure terminal
Enter configuration commands, one per line.  End with CNTL/Z.
SwitchB(config)#interface fastEthernet 3/9
SwitchB(config-if)#switchport host
switchport mode will be set to access
spanning-tree portfast will be enabled
channel group will be disabled
SwitchB(config-if)#end
SwitchB#
```

UplinkFast

UplinkFast provides fast convergence after a direct link failure if one or more redundant Layer 2 links exist. UplinkFast defines interfaces in an uplink group on a per-VLAN basis; only one interface is forwarding at any given time. Specifically, an uplink group consists of the root port (which is forwarding) and a set of blocked ports. Typically, only a single blocking interface exists, but there is no limit to the number of blocking or alternate links. The uplink group provides an alternate path in case the currently forwarding link fails.

Figure 6-3 shows an example of a topology with switch A deployed in the Building Access submodule with uplink connections to the root switch over link 2 and the backup root switch over link 3 (both of these switches are in the Building Distribution submodule.) Initially, the port on switch A connected to link 2 is in the forwarding state, and the port connected to link 3 is in the blocking state.

As shown in Figure 6-3, when switch A detects a link failure on the currently active link 2 on the root port (a direct link failure), UplinkFast unblocks the blocked port on switch A and transitions it to the forwarding state without going through the listening and learning states. This switchover occurs within 5 seconds.

NOTE UplinkFast is most useful in the Building Access submodule with at least one blocked port. This feature might not be useful for other types of applications.

Figure 6-3 *Network Scenario with UplinkFast Enabled*

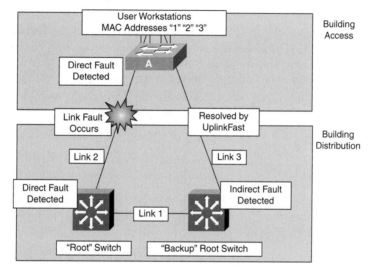

Configuration and Verification of UplinkFast

Use the following global configuration command to enable UplinkFast:

```
spanning-tree uplinkfast [max-update-rate max-update-rate]
```

The *max_update_rate* value represents the number of multicast packets transmitted per second; the default is 150 packets per second (pps). The purpose of the multicast packets is explained later in this section.

NOTE When you enable UplinkFast, it affects all VLANs on the switch. Catalyst switches do not support configuring UplinkFast on a per-VLAN basis.

Example 6-3 illustrates configuring UplinkFast on a Cisco IOS–based Catalyst switch.

Example 6-3 *Configuration of UplinkFast on Cisco IOS–Based Catalyst Switches*

```
Switch#configure terminal
Enter configuration commands, one per line. End with CNTL/Z.
Switch(config)#spanning-tree uplinkfast
Switch(config)#spanning-tree uplinkfast max-update-rate 400
Switch(config)#end
Switch#
```

UplinkFast increases the bridge priority to 49,152 and adds 3000 to the spanning-tree port cost of all interfaces on the switch, making it unlikely that the respective switch becomes a root switch. Catalyst switches do not support enabling UplinkFast for VLANs configured for a bridge priority. To enable UplinkFast on a VLAN with bridge priority configured, restore the bridge priority on the VLAN to the default value by entering the **no spanning-tree vlan** *vlan-id* **priority** command in global configuration mode.

To enhance the scalability of STP, UplinkFast also quenches the Topology Change Notification (TCN) messages that are normally transmitted toward the root bridge. Instead, the switch sends dummy multicast frames that proxy the MAC addresses of connected devices toward the root so that the upstream switch moves the MAC address table entries from the failed link to the new port immediately. This simple but effective mechanism updates the forwarding entries for the failed path without affecting other entries.

For more information on the operation of UplinkFast, refer to the following document on Cisco.com:

Document ID: 10575 Understanding and Configuring the Cisco UplinkFast Feature

UplinkFast is most useful in wiring-closet switches with a limited number of active VLANs. This feature might not be useful for other types of applications and should not be enabled on backbone or distribution layer switches.

Example 6-4 illustrates a user verifying the configuration of UplinkFast.

Example 6-4 *Displaying UplinkFast Information*

```
Switch#show spanning-tree uplinkfast
UplinkFast is enabled
Station update rate set to 400 packets/sec.
UplinkFast statistics
-----------------------
Number of transitions via uplinkFast (all VLANs)          :14
Number of proxy multicast addresses transmitted (all VLANs) :5308
Name                    Interface List
------------------- ------------------------------------
VLAN1                   Fa6/9(fwd), Gi5/7
VLAN2                   Gi5/7(fwd)
VLAN3                   Gi5/7(fwd)
```

BackboneFast

BackboneFast is a complementary feature to UplinkFast. Whereas UplinkFast quickly responds to failures on links directly connected to distribution switches, it does not help with indirect failures in the backbone core. BackboneFast reduces the default convergence time in situations where the root port is lost and the backup link leads through a different switch. The convergence is reduced to 30 seconds from the default 50 seconds in such scenarios. However, BackboneFast does not eliminate the forward delay time and does not support direct link failures.

NOTE	When configuring BackboneFast, enable it on every switch on the network. Some older Cisco Catalyst switch models may not support the BackboneFast feature.

When a switch receives a BPDU from a designated switch that identifies the root bridge and the designated bridge as the same switch, the switch considers the BPDU an *inferior BPDU*. When a switch receives an inferior BPDU, it indicates that a link to which the switch is not directly connected (an indirect link) has failed; that is, the designated switch has lost its connection to the root switch.

The designated switch transmits the BPDUs with the information that it is now the root switch and the designated switch. The receiving switch ignores the inferior BPDU for the time defined by the max age setting.

After receiving inferior BPDUs, the receiving switch tries to determine whether there is an alternate path to the root switch:

- If the port that received the inferior BPDUs is already in blocking mode, then the root port and other blocked ports on the switch become alternate paths to the root switch.

- If the switch receives inferior BPDUs on a root port (when another switch has been introduced to the topology), then all presently blocking ports become alternate paths to the root switch. In addition, if the switch receives inferior BPDUs on a root port and there are no other blocking ports on the switch, the receiving switch assumes that the link to the root switch is down. After the time interval defined by the max age setting expires, the switch starts the root switch election process by declaring itself as the root.

If the switch that receives the inferior BPDU has alternate paths to the root switch, it uses those alternate paths to send a root link query (RLQ) BPDU. The objective of the RLQ BPDU is to determine whether the current root switch is still alive. The RLQ BPDU propagates toward the root switch through the intermediate switches, and eventually the root switch responds. If the responding root switch is the same as the original root switch, the switch detecting the indirect link failure assumes that the root switch is still alive. The switch immediately skips to the listening state for the port receiving the inferior BPDU. This process enables faster convergence in the event of a backbone link failure.

Figure 6-4 shows an example of a topology with no link failures. Switch A, the root switch, connects directly to switch B over link L1 and to switch C over link L2. In this example, because switch B has a lower priority than switch A but a higher priority than switch C, switch B becomes the designated bridge for link 3. Consequently, the Layer 2 interface on switch C that connects directly to switch B is in the blocking state.

Next, assume that link L1 fails as shown in Figure 6-5. Switch A and switch B, the switches directly connected to this segment, instantly detect that the link is down. The blocking interface on switch C enters the forwarding state for the network to recover by itself. However, because link L1 does not directly connect to switch C, switch C does not start sending BPDUs on link L3 under the normal rules of STP until the time defined by the max age setting has expired.

Figure 6-4   *Network Topology with BackboneFast Enabled Before Link Failure*

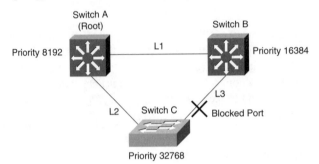

Figure 6-5   *Link Failure with BackboneFast Enabled*

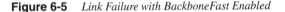
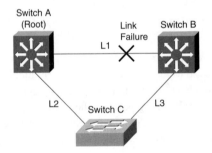

In an STP environment without BackboneFast, when link L1 fails, switch C cannot detect the failure because it does not directly connect to link L1. Because switch B directly connects to the root switch over link L1, switch B detects the failure and elects itself the root. Then, switch B begins sending configuration BPDUs to switch C, listing itself as the root.

The following steps detail actions taken by Catalyst switches with BackboneFast enabled, as shown in Figure 6-6:

1   When switch C receives the inferior BPDU from switch B, switch C infers that an indirect failure has occurred.

2   Switch C sends out an RLQ.

3   Switch A receives the RLQ. Because switch A is the root bridge, it replies with an RLQ response, listing itself as the root bridge.

4   When switch C receives the RLQ response on its existing root port, it knows that it still has a stable connection to the root switch. Because switch C originated the RLQ request, it does not need to forward the RLQ response to other switches.

5 BackboneFast enables the blocked port on switch C to move immediately to the listening state without waiting for the time defined by the port's max age setting to expire.

6 BackboneFast transitions the Layer 2 interface on switch C to the forwarding state, providing a path from switch B to switch A.

Figure 6-6   *Catalyst Switch with BackboneFast Enabled*

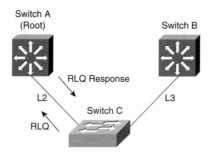

In this example, switch B can recover 20 seconds faster with BackboneFast enabled on the switches than without BackboneFast enabled. The total time for the switchover is approximately 30 seconds, twice the forward delay time (using the default forward delay time of 15 seconds).

Figure 6-7 shows a new switch introduced into a shared-medium topology. BackboneFast does not affect this situation because the inferior BPDUs did not come from the recognized designated bridge (switch B). The new switch begins sending inferior BPDUs that indicate the new bridge is the root switch. However, the other switches ignore these inferior BPDUs, and the new switch learns that switch B is the designated bridge to switch A (root switch). The new switch learns the path to the root bridge by using the normal STP processes.

Figure 6-7   *Adding New Switch with BackboneFast Enabled*

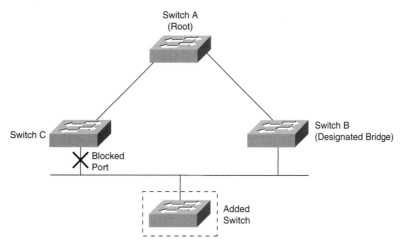

Configuration and Verification of BackboneFast

On Cisco IOS–based Catalyst switches, use the following global configuration command to enable or disable BackboneFast:

```
[no] spanning-tree backbonefast
```

For BackboneFast to function correctly, enable the feature on all switches in the network. Catalyst switches support BackboneFast for use with third-party switches.

Example 6-5 shows the configuration and verification of BackboneFast.

Example 6-5 *Configuring and Verifying BackboneFast on Cisco IOS–Based Catalyst Switches*

```
Switch#configure terminal
Enter configuration commands, one per line. End with CNTL/Z.
Switch(config)#spanning-tree backbonefast
Switch(config)#end
Switch#show spanning-tree backbonefast
BackboneFast is enabled

BackboneFast statistics
----------------------
Number of transition via backboneFast (all VLANs) : 0
Number of inferior BPDUs received (all VLANs)     : 0
Number of RLQ request PDUs received (all VLANs)   : 0
Number of RLQ response PDUs received (all VLANs)  : 0
Number of RLQ request PDUs sent (all VLANs)       : 0
Number of RLQ response PDUs sent (all VLANs)      : 0
```

Improving Spanning-Tree Resiliency

STP does not provide for checks and balances to ensure high availability in multilayer switched networks. As a result, Cisco introduced features such as the following to help fine-tune and increase resiliency of STP:

- **BPDU Guard**—Prevents accidental connection of switching devices to PortFast-enabled ports. Connecting switches to PortFast-enabled ports may cause Layer 2 loops or topology changes.

- **BPDU filtering**—Restricts the switch from sending unnecessary BPDUs out access ports.

- **Root Guard**—Prevents switches on access ports from becoming the root switch.

BPDU Guard

BPDU Guard puts an interface configured for STP PortFast in the err-disable state upon receipt of a BPDU. The BPDU Guard disables interfaces as a preventive step to avoid a potential bridging loop.

The STP BPDU Guard shuts down PortFast-configured interfaces that receive BPDUs, rather than putting them into the STP blocking state (the default behavior). In a valid configuration, PortFast-configured interfaces should not receive BPDUs. Reception of a BPDU by a PortFast-configured interface signals an invalid configuration, such as connection of an unauthorized device. BPDU Guard provides a secure response to invalid configurations, because the administrator must manually re-enable the err-disabled interface after fixing the invalid configuration. It is also possible to set up a time-out interval after which the switch automatically tries to re-enable the interface. However, if the invalid configuration still exists, the switch err-disables the interface again.

NOTE   STP applies the BPDU Guard feature globally to all PortFast-configured interfaces but can also be enabled/disabled per-interface basis.

To enable BPDU Guard or to disable BPDU Guard on a Cisco IOS–based Catalyst switch, use the following global configuration command:

    [no] `spanning-tree portfast bpduguard`

Example 6-6 illustrates a user configuring and verifying the spanning-tree PortFast BPDU Guard feature.

Example 6-6   *Configuring and Verifying BPDU Guard on Cisco IOS–Based Catalyst Switches*

```
Switch#configure terminal
Enter configuration commands, one per line. End with CNTL/Z.
Switch(config)# spanning-tree portfast bpduguard
Switch(config)# end
Switch#show spanning-tree summary totals

Root bridge for: none.
PortFast BPDU Guard is enabled
Etherchannel misconfiguration guard is enabled
UplinkFast is disabled
BackboneFast is disabled
Default pathcost method used is short

Name            Blocking Listening Learning Forwarding STP Active
------------------- -------- --------- -------- ---------- ---------
         34 VLANs 0        0         0        36         36
```

BPDU Filtering

BPDU filtering supports the ability to prevent Catalyst switches from sending BPDUs on PortFast-enabled interfaces. Ports configured for the PortFast feature typically connect to host devices. Hosts do not participate in STP and hence drop the received BPDUs. As a result, BPDU filtering prevents unnecessary BPDUs from being transmitted to host devices.

Catalyst switches support configuring BPDU filtering on a per-port or global basis. If explicitly configured on an interface, the switch does not send BPDUs and drops all BPDUs it receives.

If globally enabled, the switch changes the interface back to normal STP operation if the port receives BPDUs on the respective interface. For example, if a PortFast-enabled interface receives a BPDU, it immediately loses its PortFast status with BPDU filtering enabled. In this case, the switch disables PortFast BPDU filtering on the respective interface, and STP resumes sending BPDUs from the port toward the connected device.

CAUTION   Configuration of BPDU filtering on a port connected to another switch may result in a bridging loop; use caution when deploying BPDU filtering. BPDU filtering is not a recommended configuration.

Table 6-1 lists all the possible PortFast BPDU filtering combinations.

Table 6-1   *PortFast BPDU Filtering Port Configurations*

Per-Port Configuration	Global Configuration	PortFast State	PortFast BPDU Filtering State
Default	Enable	Enable	Enable
Default	Enable	Disable	Disable
Default	Disable	Not applicable	Disable
Disable	Not applicable	Not applicable	Disable
Enable	Not applicable	Not applicable	Enable

If you enable BPDU Guard on the same interface as BPDU filtering, BPDU Guard has no effect, because BPDU filtering takes precedence over BPDU Guard.

To enable PortFast BPDU filtering globally on the switch, use the following command on Cisco IOS–based Catalyst switches:

```
spanning-tree portfast bpdufilter default
```

To verify the configuration, use the following command on Cisco IOS–based Catalyst switches:

```
show spanning-tree summary totals
```

Root Guard

Root Guard is useful in avoiding Layer 2 loops during network anomalies. The Root Guard feature forces an interface to become a designated port, to prevent surrounding switches from becoming a root switch. In other words, Root Guard provides a way to enforce the root bridge placement in the network. Catalyst switches force Root Guard–enabled ports to be designated ports. If the bridge receives superior STP BPDUs on a Root Guard–enabled port, the port moves to a root-inconsistent STP state (effectively equal to a listening state), and the switch does not forward traffic out of that port. As a result, this feature effectively enforces the position of the root bridge.

Figure 6-8 shows a sample topology to illustrate the Root Guard feature. Switches A and B comprise the core of the network, and switch A is the root bridge for a VLAN. Switch C is an access layer switch. The link between switch B and switch C is blocking on the switch C side. Figure 6-8 shows the flow of STP BPDUs with arrows.

Figure 6-8   *Network Topology with Root Guard Disabled*

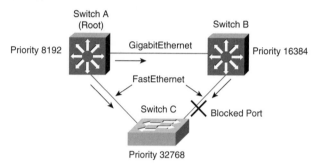

In Figure 6-9, when switch D is connected to switch C, it begins to participate in STP. If the priority of switch D is 0 or any value lower than that of the current root bridge, switch D becomes the root bridge for that VLAN based on normal STP guidelines. In this specific scenario, however, having switch D as the root causes the Gigabit Ethernet link that is connecting the two core switches to block, thus causing all the data in that particular VLAN to flow via a 100-Mbps link across the access layer. If there is more data flowing between the core switches in that VLAN than this link may accommodate, packet loss can occur, causing performance issues or network connectivity problems. An even worse scenario may occur if switch D is unstable and causes frequent reconvergence of the root bridge.

Figure 6-9   *New Switch Introduced with Root Guard Disabled*

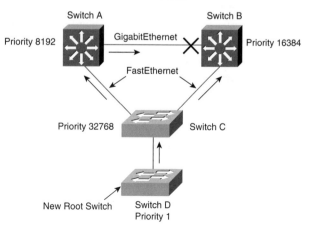

The Root Guard feature can protect against such issues. After the Root Guard feature is enabled on a port, the switch does not allow that port to become an STP root port. The port remains as an STP-designated port. In addition, if a better BPDU is received on the port, Root Guard disables (err-disables) the port rather than processing the BPDU. If an unauthorized device starts sending BPDUs with a better bridge ID, the normal STP process would elect the new switch as the root switch. By disabling the port, the network topology is protected.

The current design recommendation is to enable Root Guard on all access ports so that a root bridge is not established through these ports. In Figure 6-9, enable Root Guard on switches A, B, and C on the following ports:

- Switch A (Distribution/Core): Any access port
- Switch B (Distribution/Core): Any access port
- Switch C (Access): Any access port including the port connecting to switch D

In this configuration, switch C blocks the port connecting to switch D when it receives a better (superior) BPDU. The port transitions to a special STP state (root-inconsistent), which is effectively the same as the listening state. No traffic passes through the port in root-inconsistent state.

When switch D stops sending superior BPDUs, the port unblocks again and goes through regular STP transition of listening, learning, and eventually to the forwarding state. Recovery is automatic; no intervention is required.

In addition, Catalyst switches log the following message when a Root Guard–enabled port receives a superior BPDU:

```
%SPANTREE-2-ROOTGUARDBLOCK: Port 1/1 tried to become non-designated in VLAN 77.
    Moved to root-inconsistent state
```

To enable Root Guard on a Layer 2 access port to force it to become a designated port, or to disable Root Guard, use the following interface-level command on Cisco IOS–based Catalyst switches:

```
[no] spanning-tree guard root
```

Example 6-7 illustrates a user enabling the Root Guard feature on FastEthernet interface 5/8 and verifying the configuration.

Example 6-7 *Configuring and Verifying Root Guard on Cisco IOS–Based Catalyst Switches*

```
Switch#configure terminal
Enter configuration commands, one per line. End with CNTL/Z.
Switch(config)#interface FastEthernet 5/8
Switch(config-if)#spanning-tree guard root
Switch(config-if)#end
Switch#show running-config interface FastEthernet 5/8
Building configuration...
Current configuration: 67 bytes
!
interface FastEthernet5/8
switchport mode access
spanning-tree guard root
end
!
```

Example 6-8 shows how to determine whether any interfaces are in root-inconsistent state.

Example 6-8 *Displaying Root-Inconsistent Interfaces on Cisco IOS–Based Catalyst Switches*

```
Switch#show spanning-tree inconsistentports
Name                  Interface              Inconsistency
-------------------   --------------------   -----------------
VLAN0001              FastEthernet3/1        Port Type Inconsistent
VLAN0001              FastEthernet3/2        Port Type Inconsistent
VLAN1002              FastEthernet3/1        Port Type Inconsistent
VLAN1002              FastEthernet3/2        Port Type Inconsistent
Number of inconsistent ports (segments) in the system :4
```

Preventing Forwarding Loops and Black Holes

Prevention of forwarding loops and black holes in a network is a required aspect of network design. Cisco Catalyst switches support two important features to address such conditions:

- **Aggressive mode UDLD**—Aggressive mode UDLD detects and disables unidirectional links. UDLD is explained in detail in Chapter 7, "Enhancing Network Stability, Functionality, Reliability, and Performance Using Advanced Features."

- **Loop Guard**—The Loop Guard STP feature improves the stability of Layer 2 networks by preventing bridging loops. The following section discusses Loop Guard.

Loop Guard

Loop Guard provides additional protection against Layer 2 forwarding loops (STP loops). A bridging loop happens when an STP blocking port in a redundant topology erroneously transitions to the forwarding state. This usually occurs because one of the ports of a physically redundant topology (not necessarily the STP blocking port) has stopped receiving STP BPDUs. In STP, switches rely on continuous reception or transmission of BPDUs, depending on the port role. (A designated port transmits BPDUs, whereas a nondesignated port receives BPDUs.)

When one of the ports in a physically redundant topology stops receiving BPDUs, STP conceives the topology as loop-free. Eventually, the blocking port from the alternate or backup port transitions to a designated port and then moves to the STP forwarding state, creating a bridging loop.

With the Loop Guard feature, switches do an additional check before transitioning to the STP forwarding state. If switches stop receiving BPDUs on a nondesignated port with the Loop Guard feature enabled, the switch places the port into the STP loop-inconsistent blocking state instead of moving through the listening, learning, and forwarding states.

When the Loop Guard feature places a port into the loop-inconsistent blocking state, the switch logs the following message:

```
SPANTREE-2-LOOPGUARDBLOCK: No BPDUs were received on port 3/2 in vlan 3.
    Moved to loop-inconsistent state.
```

If a switch receives a BPDU on a port in the loop-inconsistent STP state, the port transitions through STP states according to the received BPDU. As a result, recovery is automatic, and no manual intervention is necessary. After the recovery, the switch logs the following message:

```
SPANTREE-2-LOOPGUARDUNBLOCK: port 3/2 restored in vlan 3.
```

To illustrate Loop Guard behavior, consider the example in Figure 6-10. Switch A is the root switch. Due to unidirectional link failure on the link between switch B and switch C, switch C is not receiving BPDUs from B.

Figure 6-10 *Unidirectional Link Without Loop Guard*

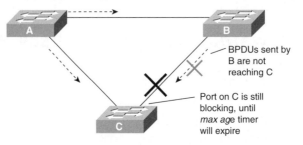

Without Loop Guard, the STP blocking port on switch C transitions to the STP listening state after the max age timer expires, and ultimately to the forwarding state after two times the forward delay time. When the port moves into the forwarding state, a bridging loop occurs, as shown in Figure 6-11.

Figure 6-11 *Bridging Loop Without Loop Guard*

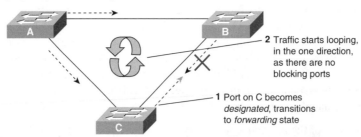

With the Loop Guard feature enabled, the blocking port on switch C transitions into the STP loop-inconsistent state when the max age timer expires, as shown in Figure 6-12. A port in the STP loop-inconsistent state does not pass data traffic; hence, a bridging loop does not occur. The loop-inconsistent state is effectively equal to the blocking state.

You configure the Loop Guard feature on a per-port basis, although the feature blocks inconsistent ports on a per-VLAN basis. For example, on a trunk port, if BPDUs are not received for only one particular VLAN, the switch blocks only that VLAN (that is, moves the port for that VLAN to the loop-inconsistent STP state). In the case of an EtherChannel interface, the channel status goes into the inconsistent state for all the ports belonging to the channel group for the particular VLAN not receiving BPDUs. (Recall that Catalyst switches consider EtherChannel as one logical port from the STP point of view.)

Figure 6-12 *Unidirectional Link with Loop Guard*

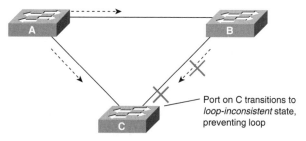

Figure 6-12 *Unidirectional Link with Loop Guard*

Port on C transitions to
loop-inconsistent state,
preventing loop

Enable the Loop Guard feature on all nondesignated ports, and not just for blocking ports. More precisely, Loop Guard should be enabled on root and alternate ports for all possible combinations of active topologies. Before enabling Loop Guard, however, consider all possible failover scenarios. Figure 6-13 shows a sample scenario and indicates the ports configured for Loop Guard.

Figure 6-13 *Loop Guard–Enabled Ports*

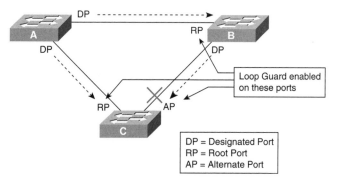

Loop Guard enabled
on these ports

DP = Designated Port
RP = Root Port
AP = Alternate Port

Loop Guard is disabled by default on Catalyst switches. Use the following interface-level configuration command to enable Loop Guard on Cisco IOS–based Catalyst switches:

```
spanning-tree guard loop
```

NOTE   Loop Guard and Root Guard cannot coexist on the same port. As a result, enabling Loop Guard disables any previous configuration of Root Guard on a per-port basis.

When you enable Loop Guard globally for application to all ports, the switch enables Loop Guard only on ports considered to be point-to-point links. Catalyst switches consider full-duplex ports as point-to-point links. It is still possible to configure, or override, the global configuration of Loop Guard on a per-port basis.

To enable Loop Guard globally on Cisco IOS–based Catalyst switches, use the following global configuration command:

```
spanning-tree loopguard default
```

To disable Loop Guard on any specific interface on Cisco IOS–based Catalyst switches, issue the following interface configuration command:

`no spanning-tree guard`

To verify the Loop Guard status on an interface, issue the following EXEC command on Cisco IOS–based Catalyst switches:

`show spanning-tree interface` interface-id `detail`

Example 6-9 illustrates a user verifying the status of Loop Guard on interface FastEthernet 3/42.

Example 6-9 *Verifying the Status of Loop Guard on an Interface on Cisco IOS–Based Catalyst Switches*

```
Switch#show spanning-tree interface FastEthernet 3/42 detail
 Port 170 (FastEthernet3/42) of VLAN0001 is blocking
    Port path cost 19, Port priority 128, Port Identifier 128.170.
    Designated root has priority 8193, address 0009.e845.6480
    Designated bridge has priority 8193, address 0009.e845.6480
    Designated port id is 128.160, designated path cost 0
    Timers: message age 1, forward delay 0, hold 0
    Number of transitions to forwarding state: 0
    Link type is point-to-point by default
    Loop guard is enabled on the port
    BPDU: sent 1, received 4501
```

Comparison Between Aggressive Mode UDLD and Loop Guard

Loop Guard and aggressive mode UDLD functionality overlap insofar as both protect against STP failures caused by unidirectional links. These two features are different, however, in their approach to the problem and in functionality. Table 6-2 compares and contrasts the Loop Guard and aggressive mode UDLD features.

Table 6-2 *Comparison Between Loop Guard and Aggressive Mode UDLD*

	Loop Guard	**Aggressive Mode UDLD**
Configuration	Per port	Per port
Action granularity	Per VLAN	Per port
Auto-recovery	Yes	Yes, with err-disable timeout feature
Protection against STP failures caused by unidirectional links	Yes, when enabled on all root ports and alternate ports in redundant topology	Yes, when enabled on all links in redundant topology
Protection against STP failures caused by problem in software resulting in designated switch not sending BPDUs	Yes	No
Protection against incorrect wiring	No	Yes

The most noticeable difference between aggressive mode UDLD and Loop Guard is in regard to STP. Aggressive mode UDLD cannot detect failures caused by problems in software in the designated switch not sending the BPDU. Problems resulting from software failures are less common than failures caused by unidirectional links that result from hardware failures. Nevertheless, aggressive mode UDLD is more robust in its ability to detect unidirectional links on EtherChannel. Loop Guard blocks all interfaces of the EtherChannel in such a failure by putting the EtherChannel into the loop-inconsistent state for a VLAN or for all VLANs, while aggressive mode UDLD disables the single port that is exhibiting problems. In addition, aggressive mode UDLD is not dependent on STP, so it supports Layer 3 links as well.

In addition, Loop Guard does not support shared links or interfaces that are unidirectional on switch Bootup. If a port is unidirectional on switch Bootup, the port never receives BPDUs and becomes a designated port. Loop Guard does not support this scenario, because the behavior is not distinguishable from normal STP operation. Aggressive mode UDLD does provide protection against such a failure scenario.

Enabling both aggressive mode UDLD and Loop Guard provides the highest level of protection against bridging loops and black holes in multilayer switched networks.

Troubleshooting STP

Bridging loops generally characterize STP problems. Troubleshooting STP involves identifying and preventing such loops.

The primary function of STP is to prevent loops created by redundant links in bridged networks. STP operates at Layer 2 of the OSI model. STP fails in specific cases, such as hardware or software anomalies. Troubleshooting these situations is typically very difficult, depending on the design of the network.

Potential STP Problems

The following subsections highlight common network conditions that lead to STP problems, listed as follows:

- Duplex mismatch
- Unidirectional link failure
- Frame corruption
- Resource errors
- PortFast configuration error
- Inappropriate STP diameter parameter tuning

Duplex Mismatch

Duplex mismatch on point-to-point links is a common configuration error. Duplex mismatch occurs specifically when one side of the link is manually configured as full duplex and the other side is using the default configuration for auto-negotiation. Such a configuration leads to duplex mismatch.

The worst-case scenario for a duplex mismatch is when a bridge that is sending BPDUs is configured for half duplex on a link while its peer is configured for full duplex. In Figure 6-14, the duplex mismatch on the link between switch A and switch B could potentially lead to a bridging loop. Because switch B is configured for full duplex, it starts forwarding frames even if switch A is already using the link. This is a problem for switch A, which detects a collision and runs the back-off algorithm before attempting another transmission of its frame. If there is enough traffic from switch B to switch A, every packet (including the BPDUs) sent by switch A is deferred or has a collision and is subsequently dropped. From an STP point of view, because switch B no longer receives BPDUs from switch A, it assumes the root bridge is no longer present. Consequently, switch B moves its port to switch C into the forwarding state, creating a Layer 2 loop.

Figure 6-14 *Duplex Mismatch*

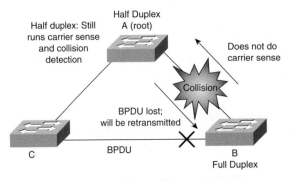

Unidirectional Link Failure

A unidirectional link is a frequent cause for a bridging loop. An undetected failure on a fiber link or a problem with a transceiver usually causes unidirectional links. With STP enabled to provide redundancy, any condition that results in a link maintaining a physical link connected status on both link partners but operating in a one-way communication state is detrimental to network stability because it could lead to bridging loops and routing black holes. Figure 6-15 shows such an example of a unidirectional link failure affecting STP.

Figure 6-15 *Unidirectional Link Failure*

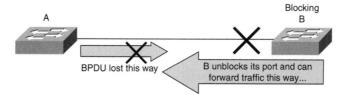

The link between switch A and switch B is unidirectional and drops traffic from switch A to switch B while transmitting traffic from switch B to switch A. Suppose, however, that the interface on switch B should be blocking. An interface blocks only if it receives BPDUs from a bridge that has a better priority. In this case, all the BPDUs coming from switch A are lost, and switch B eventually moves to the forwarding state, creating a loop. Note that in this case, if the failure exists at startup, STP does not converge correctly. In addition, rebooting of the bridges has absolutely no effect on this scenario.

To resolve this problem, Cisco introduced the UDLD and A-UDLD features on current-generation switches. These features can detect incorrect cabling or unidirectional links and automatically put the affected port in err-disable state. The recommended practice is to use A-UDLD on all point-to-point interfaces in any multilayer switched network. See Chapter 7 for more details about UDLD and A-UDLD.

Frame Corruption

Frame corruption is another cause for STP failure. If an interface is experiencing a high rate of physical errors, the result may be lost BPDUs, which may lead to an interface in the blocking state moving to the forwarding state. However, this case is rare, because STP default parameters are conservative. The blocking port needs to miss consecutive BPDUs for 50 seconds before transitioning to the forwarding state. In addition, any single BPDU that is successfully received by the switch breaks the loop. This case is more common for nondefault STP parameters and aggressive STP timer values. Frame corruption is generally a result of a duplex mismatch, bad cable, or incorrect cable length.

Resource Errors

Even on high-end switches that perform most of their switching functions in hardware with specialized application-specific integrated circuits (ASIC), STP is performed by the CPU (software-based). This means that if the CPU of the bridge is over utilized for any reason, it may lack the resources to send out BPDUs. STP is generally not a processor-intensive application and has priority over other processes; therefore, a resource problem is unlikely to arise. However, you need to exercise caution when multiple VLANs in PVST+ mode exist. Consult the product documentation for the recommended number of VLANs and STP instances on any specific Catalyst switch to avoid exhausting resources.

PortFast Configuration Error

As discussed in the section titled "PortFast" earlier in this chapter, the PortFast feature, when enabled on a port, bypasses the listening and learning states of STP, and the port transitions to the forwarding mode on linkup. The fast transition may lead to bridging loops if configured on incorrect ports.

In Figure 6-16, switch A has port p1 in the forwarding state and port p2 configured for PortFast. Device B is a hub. Port p2 goes to forwarding and creates a loop between p1 and p2 as soon as the second cable plugs into switch A. The loop ceases as soon as p1 or p2 receives a BPDU that transitions one of these two ports into blocking mode. The problem with this type of transient loop condition is that if the looping traffic is intensive, the bridge may have trouble successfully sending the BPDU that stops the loop. The BPDU Guard prevents this type of event from occurring.

Figure 6-16 *PortFast Configuration Error*

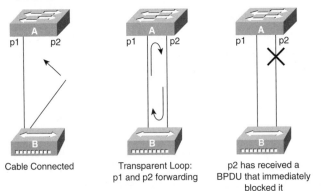

| Cable Connected | Transparent Loop: p1 and p2 forwarding | p2 has received a BPDU that immediately blocked it |

Inappropriate STP Diameter Parameter Tuning

A short timer value for the max age or the forward delay timers may lead to an unstable STP topology. The loss of BPDUs due to short timers may cause a momentary STP loop, and thus any tuning of the parameters should be done with caution. Another potential problem with short timer values relates to the diameter of the bridged network. The default max age timer for STP indicates a maximum network diameter of seven devices. As a result, two distinct bridges in the network should not be more than seven bridges away from one another. Part of this restriction comes from the age field carried by BPDUs: When a BPDU propagates from the root bridge toward the leaves of the tree, the age field gets incremented each time it goes though a bridge. Eventually, when the age field of a BPDU goes beyond max age, the bridge discards the BPDU. Typically, this discarding of the BPDU occurs only if the root is too far away from some bridges of the network. Hence, having a large STP diameter affects the convergence time.

Troubleshooting Methodology for STP Problems

Troubleshooting STP problems can be difficult if logical troubleshooting procedures are not deployed in advance. Occasionally, rebooting of the switches may resolve the problem temporarily, but without determining the underlying cause of the problem, the problem is likely to return.

The following steps provide a general overview of a methodology for troubleshooting STP:

Step 1 Know the network.

Step 2 Identify a bridging loop.

Step 3 Restore connectivity.

Step 4 Check the port status.

Step 5 Check for resource errors.

Step 6 Disable unneeded features.

The following subsections explain troubleshooting Layer 2 bridging loops in more detail.

Know the Network

Before you troubleshoot a bridging loop, you must understand the following basic characteristics of your network:

- The topology of the bridged network
- The location of the root bridge
- The location of the blocked ports and, therefore, the redundant links

Knowing the basic characteristics is essential in troubleshooting any Layer 2 issue. In addition, knowledge of the network helps to focus attention on the critical ports on key devices, because most of the STP troubleshooting steps simply involve using **show** commands to identify error conditions.

Identify a Bridging Loop

The best way to identify a bridging loop is to capture the traffic on a saturated link and to determine whether duplicate packets are propagating. If all users in a specific bridging domain have connectivity issues at the same time, a bridging loop is a possible cause. Check the port utilization on devices and look for abnormal values. In addition, you may see other protocols break down due to the bridging loops. For example, HSRP may complain of duplicate IP addresses if a loop causes it to see its own packets. Another common message during a loop is constant flapping of MAC addresses between interfaces. In a stable network, MAC addresses do not flap. In addition, be careful not to associate a bridging loop with a packet storm caused by another anomalous event such as an Internet worm or virus.

Restore Connectivity

Bridging loops have severe consequences on a bridged network. Administrators generally do not have time to look for the cause of a loop, however, preferring to restore connectivity as soon as possible and identify potential issues later. Restoring connectivity consists of the following two actions:

- **Breaking the loop**—A simple solution is to manually disable every port that is providing redundancy in the network. Identify the part of the network that is more affected and start disabling ports in that area. If possible, start by disabling ports that should be in the blocking state. Check to see whether network connectivity is restored while disabling one port at a time.

- **Logging events**—If it is not possible to identify the source of the problem or if the problem is transient, enable logging and increase the logging level of STP events on the switches experiencing the failure. At a minimum, enable logging on switches with blocked ports, because the transition of a blocked port to forwarding state creates the loop.

To log detailed events or to identify STP problems, use **debug** commands on Cisco IOS–based Catalyst switches. Debugging commands, if used with care, may help to identify the source of the problem.

Use the following command to enable STP debugging:

```
debug spanning-tree events
```

WARNING   As with all **debug** commands, be careful with **debug spanning-tree**, because it is extremely resource intensive.

Example 6-10 shows sample debug output for spanning-tree events.

Example 6-10 *Spanning-Tree Events Debug on Cisco IOS–Based Catalyst Switches*

```
Switch#debug spanning-tree events
Spanning Tree event debugging is on
Switch#
*Mar  5 21:23:14.994: STP: VLAN0013 sent Topology Change Notice on Gi0/3
*Mar  5 21:23:14.994: STP: VLAN0014 sent Topology Change Notice on Gi0/4
*Mar  5 21:23:14.994: STP: VLAN0051 sent Topology Change Notice on Po3
*Mar  5 21:23:14.994: STP: VLAN0052 sent Topology Change Notice on Po4
*Mar  5 21:23:15.982: %LINEPROTO-5-UPDOWN: Line protocol on Interface
GigabitEthernet0/1, changed state to down
*Mar  5 21:23:16.958: STP: VLAN0001 Topology Change rcvd on Po1
```

Use the following command from global configuration mode to capture debug information into the logging buffer of a Catalyst switch (see Chapter 3, "Initial Configuration and Troubleshooting of Cisco Multilayer Switches," for more details on system logging):

```
logging buffered
```

NOTE	When troubleshooting an IP subnet that spans multiple switches, it might be efficient to check the syslog server to collectively look at all the switches' logged messages. However, in the event of loss of network connectivity to the syslog server, not all messages may be available.

Check Port Status

Investigate the blocking ports first and then the other ports. The following are several guidelines for troubleshooting port status:

- **Blocked ports**—Check to make sure the switch reports receiving BPDUs periodically on root and blocked ports. Issue the following command on Cisco IOS–based Catalyst switches to display the number of BPDUs received on each interface:

  ```
  show spanning-tree vlan vlan-id detail
  ```

  Issue the command multiple times to determine whether the device is receiving BPDUs.

- **Duplex mismatch**—To look for a duplex mismatch, check on each side of a point-to-point link. Simply use the **show interface** command to check the speed and duplex status of the specified ports.

- **Port utilization**—An overloaded interface may fail to transmit vital BPDUs and is also an indication of a possible bridging loop. Use the **show interface** command to determine interface utilization using the load of the interface and packet input and output rates.

- **Frame corruption**—Look for increases in the input error fields of the **show interface** command.

Look for Resource Errors

High CPU utilization may lead to network instability for switches running STP. Use the **show processes cpu** command to check whether the CPU utilization is approaching 100 percent. Cisco Catalyst switches prioritize control packets such as BPDU over any lower-priority traffic; hence, the switch would be stable with higher CPU if it were just processing low-priority traffic.

Disable Unneeded Features

Disabling as many features as possible reduces troubleshooting complexity. EtherChannel, for example, is a feature that bundles several different links into a single logical port. It may be helpful to disable this feature while troubleshooting. In general, simplifying the network configuration reduces the troubleshooting effort. If configuration changes are made during the troubleshooting effort, note the changes. An alternate way is to save the configuration by maintaining a copy of the configuring in bootflash or on a TFTP server. After the root cause is found and fixed, the removed configurations can be easily reapplied.

Study Tips

The following bullets review important BCMSN exam preparation points of this chapter. The bullets only briefly highlight the main points of this chapter related to the BCMSN exam. Consult the text of this chapter for additional information regarding these topics. Table 6-3 lists important commands to review for the BCMSN exam:

- The STP PortFast feature enables host ports to transition to the forwarding state without the need to go through the listening and learning states. Therefore, this feature removes the STP delay, which enables a switch port to forward frames after link-up.

- The STP BPDU Guard feature prevents network interruptions in situations where devices connected to PortFast-enabled ports accidentally or maliciously loop back traffic including BPDU to the network.

- The BPDU filter feature prevents switches from sending BPDUs on host ports because hosts do not participate in STP and hence are unnecessary.

- The Root Guard feature prevents switches connected to undesirable ports, such as host or edge ports, from becoming a root switch, thus preventing network disruption.

- The Loop Guard feature prevents spanning-tree loops by preventing nondesignated ports from transitioning into the forwarding state when the port ceases to receive BPDUs. Aggressive mode UDLD provides additional loop prevention features and should be enabled on inter-switch links.

- STP UplinkFast provides fast convergence after a direct link failure if one or more redundant Layer 2 links exist.

- STP BackboneFast reduces the default convergence time in indirect link failure scenarios.

- STP problems can be caused by issues such as duplex mismatches on interfaces connecting switches, unidirectional link failures, frame corruption, incorrect PortFast configuration, resource errors, incorrect tuning of STP parameters, software defects, or hardware failures.

- Troubleshooting STP issues involves "knowing the network topology" ahead of time, knowing the backup and redundant connections, and being able to quickly remove redundancy.

Table 6-3   *Commands to Review*

Command	Description
`debug spanning-tree events`	Enables debugging for STP related events on a switch
`show processes cpu`	Displays the processor utilization information
`show spanning-tree backbonefast`	Displays the STP BackboneFast status and statistics
`show spanning-tree uplinkfast`	Displays the STP UplinkFast status and statistics
`(config-if)#spanning-tree guard loop`	Configures the Loop Guard on the specified interface
`(config-if)#spanning-tree guard root`	Configures the Root Guard feature on the specified interface
`(config-if)#spanning-tree portfast`	Configures the PortFast feature on the specified interface
`(config)#spanning-tree portfast bpdufilter default`	Configures the STP BPDU filter feature on all PortFast-enabled interfaces by default
`(config-if)#spanning-tree portfast bpduguard`	Configures the BPDU Guard feature on a PortFast-enabled interface

Summary

The Cisco STP enhancements provide robustness and resiliency to the protocol. These enhancements add availability to the multilayer switched network. These enhancements not only isolate bridging loops but also prevent bridging loops from occurring.

Configuration Exercise: Configuring BackboneFast, UplinkFast, Root Guard, and PortFast

Complete this exercise to practice configuring BackboneFast, UplinkFast, Root Guard, and PortFast features discussed in this chapter.

Required Resources

The following resources and equipment are required to complete this exercise:

- Catalyst switches, as shown in Figure 6-17
- Terminal server connected to the console port of each laboratory device
- PC connected to the terminal server to access the devices

Exercise Objective

The devices in the network should be connected and ready for use. In this configuration exercise, you will configure and verify some of the features reviewed in this chapter. After completing this exercise, you will be able to do the following:

- Configure and verify BackboneFast
- Configure and verify UplinkFast
- Configure and verify Root Guard
- Configure and verify PortFast

This exercise assumes that the switches are already configured as required in the configuration exercise found in Chapter 5.

Network Diagram

Figure 6-17 shows the network layout for this configuration exercise, which extends upon the topology in Figure 5-34 in Chapter 5. Tasks 1 and 2 only require switches A, B, and C. Task 3 requires the introduction of switch D.

Figure 6-17 *Lab Topology*

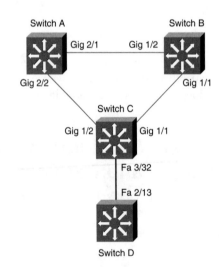

Command List

In this configuration exercise, you will use the commands listed in Table 6-4, which are listed in alphabetical order so that you can easily locate the information you need. Refer to this list if you need configuration command assistance during the configuration exercise.

Table 6-4   *Command List for Configuration Exercise*

Command	Description
configure terminal	From privileged EXEC mode, enters global configuration mode
end	Exits the configuration mode
exit	Exits the current mode
interface fastethernet | gigabitethernet *slot/ port*	Enters interface configuration mode for a Catalyst switch with a Fast Ethernet or Gigabit Ethernet interface installed
show running-config interface *interface-id*	Displays running configuration of the specific interface
show spanning-tree backbonefast	Displays STP BackboneFast status and statistics
show spanning-tree interface *interface-id* **portfast**	Displays STP PortFast status for the specified interface
show spanning-tree uplinkfast	Displays STP UplinkFast status and details
spanning-tree backbonefast	Configures STP BackboneFast on the switch
spanning-tree guard root	Configures STP Root Guard on an interface
spanning-tree uplinkfast	Configures STP UplinkFast on the switch

Task 1: Configure and Verify BackboneFast

Step 1   Configure BackboneFast on all three switches, A, B, C. Use the **spanning-tree backbonefast** command.

```
SwitchA#configure terminal
Enter configuration commands, one per line. End with CNTL/Z.
SwitchA(config)#spanning-tree backbonefast
SwitchA(config)#end

SwitchB#configure terminal
Enter configuration commands, one per line. End with CNTL/Z.
SwitchB(config)#spanning-tree backbonefast
SwitchB(config)#end

SwitchC#configure terminal
Enter configuration commands, one per line. End with CNTL/Z.
SwitchC(config)#spanning-tree backbonefast
SwitchC(config)#end
```

Step 2   Verify the BackboneFast configuration using the **show spanning-tree backbonefast** command.

```
SwitchA#show spanning-tree backbonefast
BackboneFast is enabled

BackboneFast statistics
-----------------------
Number of transition via backboneFast (all VLANs)    : 0
Number of inferior BPDUs received (all VLANs)        : 0
Number of RLQ request PDUs received (all VLANs)      : 0
Number of RLQ response PDUs received (all VLANs)     : 0
Number of RLQ request PDUs sent (all VLANs)          : 0
Number of RLQ response PDUs sent (all VLANs)         : 0
```

Switch B and switch C have similar output.

Task 2: Configure and Verify UplinkFast

Step 1   Configure UplinkFast on the access layer switch C. Use the **spanning-tree uplinkfast** command.

```
SwitchC#configure terminal
Enter configuration commands, one per line. End with CNTL/Z.
SwitchC(config)#spanning-tree uplinkfast
SwitchC(config)#end
```

Step 2   Verify the UplinkFast configuration using the **show spanning-tree uplinkfast** command.

```
SwitchC#show spanning-tree uplinkfast
UplinkFast is enabled

Station update rate set to 150 packets/sec.

UplinkFast statistics
-----------------------
Number of transitions via uplinkFast (all VLANs)            : 0
Number of proxy multicast addresses transmitted (all VLANs) : 0

Name                 Interface List
-------------------- ------------------------------------------
VLAN0001             Gi1/2(fwd), Gi1/1
VLAN0002             Gi1/1(fwd), Gi1/2
```

Task 3: Configure and Verify Root Guard

Step 1 As shown in Figure 6-17, a new switch, switch D, has been introduced into the topology. On Switch C, configure Root Guard on the interface connecting to switch D to prevent switch D from becoming the root switch. Use the **spanning-tree guard root** command.

```
SwitchC#configure terminal
Enter configuration commands, one per line. End with CNTL/Z.
SwitchC(config)#interface fastEthernet 3/32
SwitchC(config-if)#spanning-tree guard root
SwitchC(config-if)#end
SwitchC#
```

Step 2 Verify the Root Guard configuration using the **show running-config interface** *interface-id* command.

```
SwitchC#
SwitchC#show running-config interface fastEthernet 3/32
Building configuration...

Current configuration : 60 bytes
!
interface FastEthernet3/32
 spanning-tree guard root
end
```

Task 4: Configure and Verify PortFast

Step 1 Configure PortFast using the **spanning-tree portfast** command on switch C for the interface range FastEthernet 2/1–2/48, hypothetically where the workstations would be connected.

```
SwitchC#configure terminal
Enter configuration commands, one per line. End with CNTL/Z.
SwitchC(config)#interface range fastEthernet 2/1 - 2/48
SwitchC(config-if-range)#spanning-tree portfast
%Warning: portfast should only be enabled on ports connected to a single
 host. Connecting hubs, concentrators, switches, bridges, etc... to this
 interface  when portfast is enabled, can cause temporary bridging loops.
 Use with CAUTION

%Portfast will be configured in 48 interfaces due to the range command
 but will only have effect when the interfaces are in a non-trunking mode.
SwitchC(config-if-range)#end
SwitchC#
```

Step 2   Verify the PortFast configuration using the **show spanning-tree interface** *interface-id* **portfast** command.

```
SwitchC#show show spanning-tree interface fastEthernet 3/32 portfast
VLAN0001          enabled
```

Configuration Exercise: Identify and Resolve a Layer 2 Loop

Complete this exercise to practice how to identify and resolve a Layer 2 loop in a small network scenario and display some commands essential to troubleshooting a real network STP loop, as discussed in this chapter. For details on potential reasons for a bridging loop, refer to the "Troubleshooting STP" section of this chapter.

Required Resources

The following resources and equipment are required to complete this exercise:

- Catalyst switches, as shown in Figure 6-18
- A terminal server connected to the console port of each laboratory device
- A PC connected to the terminal server to access the devices

Figure 6-18 *Lab Exercise Topology*

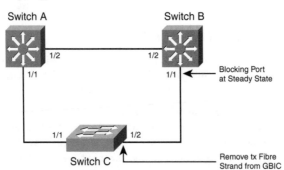

Exercise Objective

The devices in the network should be connected and ready for use. In this configuration exercise, you will locate and resolve a simulated failure leading to an STP loop. After completing this exercise, you will be able to do the following:

- Identify an STP loop
- Resolve an STP loop
- Be familiar with commands essential to troubleshooting an STP loop

Network Diagram

Figure 6-18 shows the network layout for this configuration exercise.

Command List

In this configuration exercise, you will use the commands listed in Table 6-5, which are listed in alphabetical order so that you can easily locate the information you need. Refer to this list if you need configuration command assistance during the configuration exercise.

Table 6-5   *Command List for Configuration Exercise*

Command	Description
configure terminal	From privileged EXEC mode, enters global configuration mode
end	Exits the configuration mode
exit	Exits the current mode
**interface fastethernet
gigabitethernet** *slot/ port*	Enters interface configuration mode for a Catalyst switch with a Fast Ethernet or Gigabit Ethernet interface installed
show catalyst6000 traffic-meter	Displays the backplane utilization on a Catalyst 6500 switch
show interface *interface-id* **counters errors**	Displays error counters for the specific interface
show logging	Displays the syslog messages on a switch
show processes cpu	Displays the processor utilization information
show spanning-tree vlan *vlan-id* **detail**	Displays detailed spanning tree instance information for the specific VLAN on a switch
show udld *interface-id*	Displays UDLD status and neighbor information for an interface
shutdown	Disables the interface

Task 1: Identifying the Layer 2 Loop

Step 1   Layer 2 loops caused by an STP issue generally also cause network connectivity issues for network users and are usually associated with certain symptoms. These symptoms include packet loss, HSRP duplicate IP address error messages, total loss of connectivity, MAC-address flapping error messages, and various other syslog error messages. As a result, the first step in troubleshooting a perceived Layer 2 loop or STP issue is to check the syslogs of all the core and Building Distribution switches in the network. Best practice is to maintain a syslog server in addition to the logging buffer on the Catalyst switch. (See Chapter 3 for more details.) To display logs on Cisco switches, use the **show logging** command. As a first step in this exercise, display the logs on switches A and C to verify the error messages.

```
SwitchA#show logging
Syslog logging: enabled (0 messages dropped, 0 messages rate-limited, 0
flushes, 0 overruns)
    Console logging: level debugging, 40 messages logged
    Monitor logging: level debugging, 0 messages logged
    Buffer logging: level debugging, 50 messages logged
    Exception Logging: size (8192 bytes)
    Count and timestamp logging messages: disabled
    Trap logging: level informational, 51 message lines logged


Log Buffer (4096 bytes):

00:24:50: %STANDBY-3-DUPADDR: Duplicate address 10.10.0.1 on Vlan10,
sourced by 0000.0c07.ac01
00:24:50: %STANDBY-3-DUPADDR: Duplicate address 10.10.0.1 on Vlan10,
sourced by 0000.0c07.ac01
<output truncated>
SwitchC#show logging
Syslog logging: enabled (0 messages dropped, 0 messages rate-limited, 0
flushes, 0 overruns)
    Console logging: level debugging, 23 messages logged
    Monitor logging: level debugging, 0 messages logged
    Buffer logging: level debugging, 23 messages logged
    Exception Logging: size (8192 bytes)
    Count and timestamp logging messages: disabled
    Trap logging: level informational, 24 message lines logged


Log Buffer (4096 bytes):
00:24:20: %C4K_EBM-4-HOSTFLAPPING: Host 00:00:65:00:00:02 is flapping
between port 1/2 and port 1/1
00:24:35: %C4K_EBM-4-HOSTFLAPPING: Host 00:00:65:00:00:02 is flapping
between port 1/2 and port 1/1
```

As indicated in the logging buffer, switch C is logging host flapping error messages. Also, switch A is reporting duplicate HSRP IP address messages, a common error associated with Layer 2 loops. These are a strong indication of a Layer 2 loop or STP issue. In addition, the flapping error message indicates that the flapping is occurring between ports 1/1 and 1/2, which indicates where the loop might be occurring. However, further investigation is needed, including investigating switches and devices connected off port 1/2.

Step 2   Another symptom of a Layer 2 loop or STP issue is high CPU utilization.
BPDUs, broadcasts, and multicast frames are generally "punted" to the
CPU (Layer 3 engine) for processing by the switch. Extreme abundance
of BPDUs, broadcasts, or multicast frames that occur during a Layer 2
loop condition results in high CPU utilization conditions. As such,
high CPU utilization conditions (over 75 percent) need investigation. To
display the CPU utilization on Catalyst switches in Cisco IOS, use
the **show processes cpu** command. In this step of the exercise, display
the processor utilization on switch C to verify a symptom of the Layer 2
loop.

```
SwitchC#show processes cpu
CPU utilization for five seconds: 75%/0%; one minute: 76%; five minutes:
76%
PID Runtime(ms) Invoked uSecs 5Sec   1Min  5Min  TTY   Process
  1          0       1 0     0.00%  0.00% 0.00%  0    Chunk Manager
  2         28  248759 0     0.00%0.00%0.00%0    Load  Meter
  3       5620  469937 11    0.00%  0.00% 0.00% 0      Exec
  4          0       1 0     0.00%  0.00% 0.00% 0      Deferred Events
  5     848512  168176 5045  0.00%  0.04% 0.05% 0 Check heaps
  6          0       2 0     0.00%  0.00% 0.00%  0 Pool Manager
  7          0       2 0     0.00%  0.00% 0.00%  0 Timers
  8          0       2 0     0.00%  0.00% 0.00%  0 Serial Backgroun
  9          4   20731 0     0.00%  0.00% 0.00%  0 IPC Dynamic Cach
 10          0       1 0     0.00%  0.00% 0.00%  0 IPC Zone Manager
 11        620 1243511 0     0.00%  0.00% 0.00%  0 IPC Periodic Tim
 12        320 1243511 0     0.00%  0.00% 0.00%  0 IPC Deferred Por
 13          0       1 0     0.00%  0.00% 0.00%  0 IPC Seat Manager
 14          0       1 0     0.00%  0.00% 0.00%  0 IFS Agent Manage
 15         12   20796 0     0.00%  0.00% 0.00%  0 ARP Input
 16          4      15 266   0.00%  0.00% 0.00%  0 Entity MIB API
 17          0       1 0     0.00%  0.00% 0.00%  0 SERIAL A'detect
 18        656 1243510 0     0.00%  0.00% 0.00%  0 Dynamic ARP Insp
 19        512  299181 1     0.00%  0.00% 0.00%  0 HC Counter Timer
 20          0       1 0     0.00%  0.00% 0.00%  0 Critical Bkgnd
 21        672  172885 3     0.00% 0.00%  0.00%  0 Net Backgroun
<output truncated>
```

Note	High CPU utilization is not always indicative of a Layer 2 or STP failure. There are numerous possibilities for high CPU utilization. Nevertheless, it is a common symptom of a Layer 2 loop.

Step 3   Another symptom of Layer 2 loops is that overall switch utilization (the
amount of traffic passing through the switch) is high due to excessive
traffic continuously looping through the switch. You can view the system

utilization LED lights present on the front panel of switches to note the utilization of the switch backplane. However, this requires physical access. During periods of high switch utilization, Telnet, SSH, and even console access might not be available. A simple ICMP ping to the switch management IP address might further indicate high switch utilization. On specific switches, such as the Catalyst 6500, the CLI might be available to check the backplane utilization. For example, on a Catalyst 6500 running Cisco IOS, the **show catalyst6000 traffic-meter** command indicates the backplane utilization. Use the **show system** command on all Cisco switches running CatOS. For this step, use the **show catalyst6000 traffic-meter** command on switch A, which is a Catalyst 6500 switch in this scenario, to view the backplane utilization.

```
SwitchA#show catalyst6000 traffic-meter
   traffic meter =   13%  Never cleared
             peak =   14%         reached at 12:08:57 CET Fri Sep 24 2004
```

Task 2: Divide and Conquer (Disconnect Redundancy)

Step 1   Disconnecting redundancy can immediately stop Layer 2 loops in a network if the culprit of the loop involves the redundant ports. To accomplish this task, you must "know your network." Selecting the erroneous forwarding port will quickly stop the loop. Breaking the redundant connection in this fashion can be done either by unplugging the physical port fiber or cable or by shutting down the interface. In this exercise, use the **shutdown** interface-level command to disconnect the steady-state blocking port (now forwarding) on switch B.

```
SwitchB#configure terminal
Enter configuration commands, one per line. End with CNTL/Z.
SwitchB(config)#interface gigabitEthernet 1/2
SwitchB(config-if)#shutdown
SwitchB(config-if)#end
```

Task 3: Find Root Cause of Layer 2 Loop (Investigate Network and Hardware)

Step 1   Check for faulty hardware as a possible root cause for the Layer 2 loop. Bad hardware includes a bad fiber cable, GBIC, port or module, or miswired or faulty patch panel. Useful commands to check for faulty hardware include **show interface**, **show hardware**, **show module**, and **show tech-support**.

Step 2 In this lab scenario, one of the fibers was purposefully left out of the GBIC with Gigabit auto-negotiation disabled to simulate a unidirectional link scenario. Reconnect the strand of fiber so that the link is no longer disconnected.

Task 4 (optional): Check Software Statistics

Step 1 The following list includes additional tasks for identifying root cause of a Layer 2 loops:

— **Investigate STP TCNs**—Investigating STP TCNs may lead to the chain of events that resulted in the Layer 2 loop. Furthermore, specific debugs and the syslog may yield additional clues. Use the Cisco IOS **show spanning-tree vlan** *vlan-id* **detail** command to display TCNs for a specific VLAN.

— **Check for port errors**—Checking for port errors might identify physical layer errors or hardware or software failures that lead to lost or corrupted BPDUs or "stuck" (unidirectional) ports. Use the Cisco IOS command **show interface** *interface-id* **counters errors** to quickly locate ports that received a large number of errors.

— **Check for UDLD state**—If aggressive mode UDLD is enabled, check the respective switch's syslog to verify if the switch-disabled ports are exhibiting a unidirectional condition. Use the **show udld** *interface-id* command to quickly view UDLD information on a per-port basis.

```
SwitchB# show spanning-tree vlan 10 detail

VLAN0010 is executing the ieee compatible Spanning Tree protocol
  Bridge Identifier has priority 32768, address 000a.8adb.7609
  Configured hello time 2, max age 20, forward delay 15
  Current root has priority 20490, address 000a.4172.df40
  Root port is 2 (GigabitEthernet1/2), cost of root path is 4
  Topology change flag not set, detected flag not set
  Number of topology changes 0 last change occurred 06:24:10 ago
  Times:  hold 1, topology change 35, notification 2
          hello 2, max age 20, forward delay 15
  Timers: hello 0, topology change 0, notification 0, aging 300

  Port 2 (GigabitEthernet1/2) of VLAN0010 is forwarding
    Port path cost 4, Port priority 128, Port Identifier 128.2.
    Designated root has priority 20490, address 000a.4172.df40
    Designated bridge has priority 20490, address 000a.4172.df40
```

```
       Designated port id is 128.2, designated path cost 0
       Timers: message age 2, forward delay 0, hold 0
       Number of transitions to forwarding state: 1
       Link type is point-to-point by default
       BPDU: sent 2, received 11505
SwitchB#show interfaces gigabitEthernet 1/2 counters errors

Port          CrcAlign-Err Dropped-Bad-Pkts Collisions    Symbol-Err
Gi1/2                 2533                0         0      80963727

Port          Undersize  Oversize  Fragments      Jabbers
Gi1/2             25308         2         52          310

Port          Single-Col Multi-Col   Late-Col    Excess-Col
Gi1/2                  0         0          0             0

Port          Deferred-Col False-Car  Carri-Sen Sequence-Err
Gi1/2                  0         0          0      68819058
SwitchB#


SwitchB#show udld gigabitEthernet 1/2

Interface Gi1/2
---
Port enable administrative configuration setting: Enabled / in
aggressive mode
Port enable operational state: Enabled / in aggressive mode
Current bidirectional state: Bidirectional
Current operational state: Advertisement - Single neighbor detected
Message interval: 7
Time out interval: 5

    Entry 1
    ---
    Expiration time: 44
    Device ID: 1
    Current neighbor state: Bidirectional
    Device name: FOX0627A001
    Port ID: Gi1/2
    Neighbor echo 1 device: FOX06310RW1
    Neighbor echo 1 port: Gi1/2

    Message interval: 15
    Time out interval: 5
    CDP Device name: SwitchC
```

Review Questions

For multiple-choice questions, there might be more than one correct answer.

1 True or False: Enabling PortFast is recommended on all ports to improve STP convergence.

2 True or False: Interfaces do not need both Loop Guard and A-UDLD.

3 True or False: Bridging loops can occur even when STP is disabled for a VLAN.

4 When BackboneFast is not enabled, how long does a switch take to change to the forwarding state upon detecting an indirect link failure?

    a   15 seconds

    b   20 seconds

    c   30 seconds

    d   50 seconds

    e   <1 second

5 What feature is used to detect and recover direct uplink failures on access layer switches connected redundantly to distribution layer switches?

    a   BackboneFast

    b   PortFast

    c   UplinkFast

    d   Root Guard

    e   LinkFast

6 Upon which one of the following features does the BPDU Guard depend?

    a   PortFast

    b   BPDU filtering

    c   UplinkFast

    d   Root Guard

7 What is a typical convergence time if a link fails on an UplinkFast-enabled switch?

   a 15 seconds

   b 50 seconds

   c 20 seconds

   d 2 seconds

   e <1 second

8 How does the Root Guard feature recover from the root-inconsistent state?

   a Automatically when the port stops receiving superior BPDUs

   b Automatically when the port stops receiving inferior BPDUs

   c Using an err-disable timeout mechanism

   d Manual shutdown/no shutdown of the port

   e Reload of the switch

9 BPDU filtering should only be enabled on ports connected to which of the following devices?

   a Hosts

   b Routers

   c Switches

   d Hubs

10 Select an activity that is not a recommended step in troubleshooting STP issues and Layer 2 loops.

   a Identifying the loop

   b Restoring connectivity

   c Rebooting the root switch or secondary root switch

   d Checking for bad hardware

   e Checking for port errors

11 Which command is used to collect debugging data regarding STP events on Catalyst switches?

   a   **logging spanning-tree events**

   b   **logging events spanning-tree**

   c   **debug stp events**

   d   **debug spantree events**

   e   None of the above

This chapter covers the following topics:

- EtherChannel
- Cisco Discovery Protocol (CDP)
- Protocol Filtering
- Broadcast and Multicast Suppression
- Multiple Default Gateways
- DHCP for Management IP Configuration
- MAC Address Notification
- Debounce Timer
- Baby Giants and Jumbo Frames
- Error-Disable
- IEEE 802.3 Flow Control
- Unidirectional Link Detection (UDLD) and Aggressive Mode UDLD

## CHAPTER 7

Enhancing Network Stability, Functionality, Reliability, and Performance Using Advanced Features

Previous chapters discussed the model for building Cisco multilayer switched networks and the building blocks of multilayer switched networks such as VLANs and the IEEE Spanning Tree Protocol. Cisco multilayer switches offer additional Layer 2 features to enhance the availability of networks, and to aid in troubleshooting. These services are not mandatory features of multilayer switched networks but using them is among the best practices in the industry.

Features such as the following prevent network outages due to network loops, unauthorized devices, or malfunctioning devices or software. In addition, these features can minimize network traffic packet loss:

- Unidirectional Link Detection
- Broadcast and multicast suppression
- Error-disable
- IEEE 802.3 flow control
- Protocol filtering
- Unicast flood blocking

In addition, the following features are services for adding functionality to the switches to support specific network devices or applications:

- Baby giants
- Jumbo frames
- Debounce timer

This chapter also reviews the EtherChannel feature, which provides link redundancy and increased bandwidth between devices. Finally, features such as DHCP-based management of IP configuration and CDP make management of Cisco devices easier.

These Layer 2 and Layer 3 features are value-adds to the multilayer switched network and help maintain the five 9s (99.999 percent) network uptime guarantee.

This chapter covers these multilayer switch features with a brief description of each feature's functionality and its support on various switches. Each section includes a sample configuration using Cisco CatOS– and Cisco IOS–based switches. This chapter also includes a case study on how the aggressive mode UDLD helps to prevent network outages. Upon completion of this chapter, you will understand how and where to use these Layer 2 and Layer 3 features to effectively administer the network with improved reliability and stability.

EtherChannel

Ethernet ports typically interconnect switches such that devices connected to one switch can pass frames to devices connected on another switch. Ethernet operates at 10 Mbps, 100 Mbps, 1000 Mbps, or 10 Gbps. With the increasing need for higher bandwidth, administrators look for alternate ways to increase the traffic bandwidth available between two devices. In most cases, opting for a higher-bandwidth port type, such as 10 Gigabit Ethernet, as a method of increasing bandwidth is not always feasible due to increased cost.

EtherChannel takes advantage of the existing ports by bundling ports to allow incremental additions to the available bandwidth. Cisco Catalyst switches allow as many as eight ports to be bundled together. In other words, with EtherChannel, Catalyst switches support the aggregation of single logical links for total bandwidth of up to 1600 Mbps (Fast Ethernet full duplex) or 16 Gbps (Gigabit Ethernet full duplex) for Fast Ethernet and Gigabit Ethernet interfaces, respectively. EtherChannel does not support channeling at 10 Mbps.

EtherChannel also provides redundancy in case of a link failure between the connecting devices by maintaining the connectivity through the other, non failing links. If the ports belong to the same module, then there is no significant loss in connectivity because only in-flight frames for the failing link are lost.

For more information on the system requirements of EtherChannel on various Catalyst switches, refer to the following document on Cisco.com:

> "System Requirements to Implement EtherChannel on Catalyst Switches," Document ID: 12025

Cisco IOS–based switches support Layer 2 EtherChannel as well as Layer 3 EtherChannel. Layer 3 EtherChannel bundles Layer 3 or routed interfaces. One of the primary advantages of link failure on Layer 3 EtherChannel is that routing protocols consider an EtherChannel as a single link; hence, no reconvergence of the routing protocols occurs during a link failure.

Figure 7-1 shows that EtherChannel is applicable to connections between switches, routers, and switches to routers.

Figure 7-1   *EtherChannel in Multilayer Switched Networks*

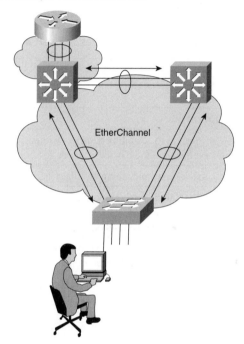

The Catalyst family of switches supports both the Cisco proprietary Port Aggregation Protocol (PAgP) and the industry standard 802.3ad-based protocol Link Aggregation Control Protocol (LACP). PAgP is a management function that checks the parameter consistency at either end of the link and assists the channel in adapting to link failure or addition. PAgP prevents STP loops or packet loss due to misconfigured channels and aids network reliability. LACP has similar functions.

Between Cisco Catalyst switches, EtherChannel typically uses either PAgP or LACP. However, EtherChannel supports an *on* mode that forces ports on both link partners to operate as an EtherChannel. Furthermore, channeling using PAgP is also possible between Cisco switches and other devices released by licensed vendors, such as network interface cards (NIC) from Intel. For interconnections between Cisco Catalyst switches and non-Cisco vendor switches or servers that support 802.3ad, use LACP to form an EtherChannel.

PAgP Modes

PAgP operates in different modes. The mode of operation determines whether a group of ports forms a channel. Table 7-1 lists and defines the various modes.

NOTE   The default channel protocol in Cisco switches is PAgP, and the default mode is auto.

Table 7-1   *PAgP Modes*

Mode	Description
On	Forces the ports to form an EtherChannel without the use of PAgP. EtherChannel on both link partners has to be in the on mode for an EtherChannel to operate correctly.
Off	Prevents the ports from forming an EtherChannel.
Auto	Places the port into a passive negotiating state and forms an EtherChannel if the port receives PAgP packets. However, in this mode, the port does not initiate the negotiation. This mode is the default.
Desirable	Places the port into a negotiating state to form an EtherChannel, using PAgP. This is the recommended mode between Catalyst switches for configuring an EtherChannel.

In addition, the auto and desirable PAgP modes of operation support the following options:

- **silent**—The default keyword used with auto or desirable mode to indicate that the switch does not expect PAgP frames from the partner device to prevent the switch from reporting the link to the STP as down. This mode is used to connect to non-PAgP-capable devices like traffic-generators.

- **non-silent**—Keyword used with auto or desirable mode to indicate that the switch expects PAgP frames from the partner device. This mode is used to detect unidirectional link problems because lack of PAgP frames from a partner indicates a loss of communication in one direction. The **non-silent** option is recommended between two PAgP-capable devices because it will report the link status to the STP as down upon unidirectional link detection.

Both the auto and desirable modes enable interfaces to negotiate with link partners' interfaces to determine whether they can form an EtherChannel, based on criteria such as interface speed and, for Layer 2 EtherChannel, trunking state and VLAN configuration.

NOTE   The Cisco recommendation for an EtherChannel mode is the desirable mode because it provides additional stability in the case of a misconfiguration or hardware or software failure.

Interfaces between two connected switches can form an EtherChannel when the interfaces are in different PAgP modes as long as the modes are compatible. On mode is only compatible with another interface in on mode; auto mode is only compatible with desirable mode; and desirable mode is compatible with either auto mode or desirable mode. Setting the port channel mode to on mode turns on EtherChannel manually, regardless of link-partner configuration.

LACP Modes

Table 7-2 lists and describes the various LACP operational modes.

Table 7-2   *LACP Modes*

Mode	Description
On	Forces the ports to form an EtherChannel without LACP. EtherChannel mode on both sides of the links has to be in on mode for a channel to operate.
Off	Prevents the ports from forming an EtherChannel.
Passive	Places the port into a passive negotiating state and forms an EtherChannel if the port receives LACP packets; however, in this mode, the port does not initiate the negotiation of an EtherChannel. This mode is the default.
Active	Places the port into an active LACP negotiating state where the port initiates to form an EtherChannel. Recommended mode between Catalyst switches.

Table 7-3 shows the parameters used in configuring LACP.

Table 7-3   *Parameters Used in Configuring LACP*

Parameter	Description
System priority	LACP requires that each link partner has a system priority. The switch determines the system priority automatically or through manual configuration. The switch uses the MAC address and the system priority to form the system ID used during negotiation with other systems.
Port priority	LACP requires that each port has a port priority. The switch determines the port priority automatically or through manual configuration. The port priority and the port number form the port ID. The switch uses the port priority to decide which ports to put in standby mode when a hardware limitation prevents all compatible ports from aggregating.
Administrative key	LACP requires each port involved in a channel to have a key value, which is determined automatically or administratively configured. The administrative key defines the ability of a port to aggregate with other ports. Port physical characteristics, such as data rate, duplex capability, and point-to-point or shared media, determine the ability of ports to form a channel. LACP also supports additional constraints set up by the configuration.

When enabled, LACP always tries to configure the maximum number of compatible ports in a channel, up to the maximum allowed by the hardware or eight ports. If LACP cannot aggregate all the ports that are compatible (for example, the remote system might have more restrictive hardware limitations), the switch places all the ports that cannot be actively included in the channel in a hot standby state. LACP uses these ports only if one of the channeled ports fails.

Cisco switches allow configuration of different channels with ports that have the same administrative key. For example, if eight ports are assigned the same administrative key, administrators may configure four ports in a channel using LACP active mode and the remaining four ports in a manually configured channel using on mode. An administrative key is meaningful only in the context of the switch that allocates it, and there is no global significance to administrative key values. The administrative key values range from 1 to 1024. It is possible to manually assign the administrative key or let the switch assign a key automatically. Example 7-1 shows a switch automatically assigning the administrative key.

Example 7-1 *Administrative Key Assignment for LACP EtherChannel*

```
Console> (enable) set port lacp-channel 6/4-8
Port(s) 6/4-8 are assigned to admin key 100.
```

Cisco IOS–based switches support an EtherChannel on Layer 2 or Layer 3 interfaces. Each EtherChannel has a corresponding numbered port-channel interface. A configuration applied to the port-channel interface affects all physical interfaces assigned to that interface. A configuration applied to the individual physical interface is applicable only to that interface.

EtherChannel Guidelines

The following list contains guidelines and best practices for configuring port channels:

- Cisco switches allow for a maximum of eight ports per EtherChannel. The ports do not have to be contiguous or on the same module. There may be restrictions on older-generation Catalyst switches; therefore, check the release notes for that specific product before implementing an EtherChannel.

- All ports in an EtherChannel must use the same protocol (PAgP or LACP).

- All ports in an EtherChannel must have the same speed and duplex mode. LACP requires that the ports operate only in full-duplex mode.

- A port cannot belong to more than one channel group at the same time.

- All ports in an EtherChannel must be configured to be in the same access VLAN configuration or be configured as VLAN trunks with the same allowable VLAN list and the same native VLAN.

- All ports in an EtherChannel require the same trunk mode to avoid unexpected results. (For instance, a trunk mode of dot1q is desirable.)

- All ports in an EtherChannel require the same VLAN cost configuration.

- An EtherChannel does not form if one of the ports is configured as a Switched Port Analyzer (SPAN) destination port.

- IP addresses should be configured on the port-channel interface for EtherChannels acting as Layer 3 interfaces instead of on the physical interface.

- An EtherChannel forms on compatible configured interfaces even with the interfaces configured for different STP port path costs.

EtherChannel Configuration Example

Figure 7-2 shows access layer Catalyst 3550s connecting to the distribution layer Catalyst 6500 switches. The administrator wants to configure a Layer 2 EtherChannel with VLAN trunking configured between pairs of access and distribution switches, as shown in Figure 7-2. Channeling provides increased bandwidth for the uplink from the access layer to the distribution layer and at the same time provides redundancy in case of link failure.

Figure 7-2   *EtherChannel Scenario in a Multilayer Switched Network*

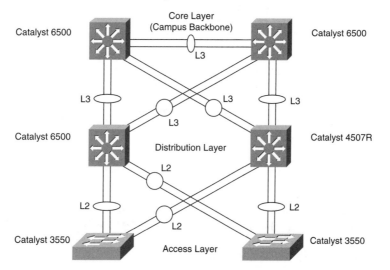

Examples 7-2 and 7-3 show the configuration and verification of one of the EtherChannels between the access layer Catalyst 3550 and distribution layer Cisco CatOS–based Catalyst 6500 switch, respectively.

Example 7-2   *Configuration and Verification of an EtherChannel on a Catalyst 3550 Switch*

```
3550(config)#interface GigabitEthernet 0/1
3550(config-if)#switchport
3550(config-if)#channel-group 1 mode desirable
Creating a port-channel interface Port-channel1
3550(config-if)#exit
3550(config)#interface GigabitEthernet 0/2
3550(config-if)#switchport
```

continues

Example 7-2 *Configuration and Verification of an EtherChannel on a Catalyst 3550 Switch (Continued)*

```
3550(config-if)#channel-group 1 mode desirable
3550(config-if)#interface port-channel 1
3550(config-if)#switchport mode trunk

3550#show etherchannel 1 summary
Flags:  D - down         P - in port-channel
        I - stand-alone  s - suspended
        R - Layer3       S - Layer2
        U - port-channel in use
Group Port-channel  Ports
-----+------------+----------------------------------------------------------
  1    Po1(SU)      Gi0/1(P)   Gi0/2(P)
```

Example 7-3 *Configuration and Verification of an EtherChannel on a Cisco CatOS–Based Catalyst 6500 Switch*

```
cat6000> (enable)set port channel 2/1-2 mode desirable
Port(s) 2/1-2 channel mode set to desirable.
Cat6000> (enable)set trunk 2/1 dot1q desirable
Port(s) 2/1-2 trunk mode set to desirable.
Port(s) 2/1-2 trunk type set to dot1q.

cat6000>show port channel 2/1
Port  Status      Channel Admin      Ch Mode Group Id
----- ----------  -------------------- ----- -----
 2/1  connected   desirable silent     174     815
 2/2  connected   desirable silent     174     815

----- ----------  -------------------- ----- -----
Port  Device-ID                        Port-ID                     Platform
----- ------------------------------   ------------------------    ----------------
 2/1  3550                             Gi0/1                       cisco WS-C3550-24
 2/2  3550                             Gi0/2                       cisco WS-C3550-24
----- ------------------------------   ------------------------    ----------------
```

For the topology shown in Figure 7-2, each access layer switch has redundant links connecting to the distribution layer and has backup links going to the backup distribution Catalyst 6500 switch. Backup links may stay in STP blocking mode until the primary link totally fails or the primary distribution switch fails. Such a configuration allows for high availability in case of link failure or switch failure. The current recommendation is to configure EtherChannel across multiple modules on the distribution switch to prevent a single module failure from causing a complete channel failure.

NOTE The **switchport** command in Cisco IOS configures an interface as a Layer 2 interface, and the **no switchport** command sets the interface as a Layer 3 or routed interface. Different model switches vary as to the default setting of interfaces as Layer 2 interfaces or a Layer 3 interfaces. Note that default settings do not appear in the configuration.

The connections between the distribution layers and the core layer are Layer 3 links. To provide link redundancy and increased bandwidth, the design uses Layer 3 port-channel configurations. Example 7-4 shows the configuration and verification of this Layer 3 EtherChannel connection between the Cisco IOS–based distribution layer Catalyst 4507R switch, whereas Example 7-5 shows the configuration and verification on the Cisco IOS–based core layer Catalyst 6500 switch.

Example 7-4 *Configuration and Verification of Layer 3 EtherChannel on a Cisco IOS–Based Catalyst 4500 Switch*

```
SwitchC-4500#configure terminal
Enter configuration commands, one per line.  End with CNTL/Z.
SwitchC-4500(config)#interface GigabitEthernet 1/1
SwitchC-4500(config-if)#no switchport
SwitchC-4500(config-if)#channel-group 1 mode desirable
Creating a port-channel interface Port-channel 1
2d14h: %EC-5-BUNDLE: Interface GigabitEthernet1/1 joined port-channel Port-channel1
SwitchC-4500(config-if)#interface GigabitEthernet 2/13
SwitchC-4500(config-if)#no switchport
SwitchC-4500(config-if)#channel-group 1 mode desirable
2d14h: %EC-5-BUNDLE: Interface GigabitEthernet2/13 joined port-channel Port-channel1
SwitchC-4500config)#interface port-channel 1
SwitchC-4500(config-if)#ip address 100.1.1.1 255.255.255.0
SwitchC-4500(config-if)#end
SwitchC-4500#
SwitchC-4500#show etherchannel 1 summary
Flags:  D - down        P - in port-channel
        I - stand-alone s - suspended
        R - Layer3      S - Layer2
        U - in use      f - failed to allocate aggregator
        u - unsuitable for bundling

Number of channel-groups in use: 1
Number of aggregators:           1

Group  Port-channel  Protocol    Ports
------+-------------+-----------+-------------------------------------------
1      Po1(RU)       PAgP        Gi1/1(P)   Gi2/13(P)
```

Example 7-5 *Configuration and Verification of Layer 3 Port-Channel on Cisco IOS–Based Catalyst 6500 Switch*

```
SwitchA-6500#configure terminal
Enter configuration commands, one per line.  End with CNTL/Z.
SwitchA-6500(config)#interface GigabitEthernet 2/1
SwitchA-6500(config-if)#no switchport
SwitchA-6500(config-if)#channel-group 1 mode desirable
Creating a port-channel interface Port-channel 1
2d14h: %EC-5-BUNDLE: Interface GigabitEthernet2/1 joined port-channel Port-channel1
SwitchA-6500(config-if)#interface GigabitEthernet 2/2
SwitchA-6500(config-if)#no switchport
SwitchA-6500(config-if)#channel-group 1 mode desirable
2d14h: %EC-5-BUNDLE: Interface GigabitEthernet2/2 joined port-channel Port-channel1
SwitchA-6500config)#interface port-channel 1
SwitchA-6500(config-if)#ip address 100.1.1.2 255.255.255.0
SwitchA-6500(config-if)#end
```

continues

Example 7-5 *Configuration and Verification of Layer 3 Port-Channel on Cisco IOS–Based*
Catalyst 6500 Switch (Continued)

```
SwitchA-6500#

SwitchA-6500#show etherchannel 1 summary
Flags:  D - down         P - in port-channel
        I - stand-alone s - suspended
        H - Hot-standby (LACP only)
        R - Layer3       S - Layer2
        U - in use       f - failed to allocate aggregator

Number of channel-groups in use: 1
Number of aggregators:           1

Group  Port-channel  Protocol    Ports
------+-------------+-----------+-------------------------------------------
1      Po1(RU)         PAgP      Gi2/1(P)   Gi2/2(P)
```

In Figure 7-2, because a Cisco CatOS–based distribution-layer Catalyst 6500 switch
connects to a Cisco IOS–based core-layer switch through a Layer 3 link, as per the design,
configuration of a Layer 2 EtherChannel is necessary. The ports are also in a dedicated
subnet and VLAN such that no local user traffic is present on that VLAN. As a result, the
EtherChannel carries only the routed traffic.

Example 7-6 shows the configuration and verification of a Layer 3 LACP EtherChannel
between two Cisco IOS–based Catalyst switches. In Example 7-6, the LACP system
priority, port priority, and administrative key are selected automatically by the switch.

Example 7-6 *Configuration and Verification of a Layer 3 LACP EtherChannel*

```
4506#configure terminal
Enter configuration commands, one per line.  End with CNTL/Z.
4506(config)#interface port-channel 2
4506(config-if)#no switchport
4506(config-if)#ip address 10.1.1.1 255.255.255.0
4506(config-if)#no shut
4506(config-if)#exit
4506(config)#interface gigabitEthernet 3/6
4506(config-if)#no switchport
4506(config-if)#channel-protocol lacp
4506(config-if)#channel-group 2 mode active
4506(config-if)#no shutdown
4506(config-if)#exit
4506(config)#interface gigabitEthernet 3/37
4506(config-if)#no switchport
4506(config-if)#channel-protocol lacp
4506(config-if)#channel-group 2 mode active
4506(config-if)#no shutdown
4506(config-if)#end
4506#
*Nov  5 09:12:50: %SYS-5-CONFIG_I: Configured from console by console
*Nov  5 09:13:51: %EC-5-BUNDLE: Interface Gi3/36 joined port-channel Po2
```

Example 7-6 *Configuration and Verification of a Layer 3 LACP EtherChannel (Continued)*

```
*Nov  5 09:14:08: %EC-5-BUNDLE: Interface Gi3/37 joined port-channel Po2
4506#show etherchannel 2 summary
Flags:  D - down         P - in port-channel
        I - stand-alone  s - suspended
        R - Layer3       S - Layer2
        U - in use       f - failed to allocate aggregator
        u - unsuitable for bundling
        w - waiting to be aggregated
        d - default port


Number of channel-groups in use: 1
Number of aggregators:           1

Group Port-channel  Protocol    Ports
------+-------------+-----------+-----------------------------------------------
2     Po2(RU)         LACP      Gi3/36(P)   Gi3/37(P)

4503#configure terminal
Enter configuration commands, one per line.  End with CNTL/Z.
4503(config)#interface port-channel 2
4503(config-if)#no switchport
4503(config-if)#ip address 10.1.1.2 255.255.255.0
4503(config-if)#no shutdown
4503(config-if)#exit
4503(config)#interface gigabitEthernet 3/39
4503(config-if)#no switchport
4503(config-if)#channel-protocol lacp
4503(config-if)#channel-group 2 mode active
4503(config-if)#no shutdown
4503(config-if)#exit
*Nov 12 00:06:01.103: %EC-5-BUNDLE: Interface Gi3/39 joined port-channel Po2
4503(config)#interface gigabitEthernet 3/40
4503(config-if)#no switchport
4503(config-if)#channel-protocol lacp
4503(config-if)#channel-group 2 mode active
4503(config-if)#no shutdown
4503(config-if)#end
4503#
*Nov 12 00:06:14.131: %SYS-5-CONFIG_I: Configured from console by console
*Nov 12 00:06:15.311: %EC-5-BUNDLE: Interface Gi3/40 joined port-channel Po2
4503#show etherchannel 2 summary
Flags:  D - down         P - in port-channel
        I - stand-alone  s - suspended
        R - Layer3       S - Layer2
        U - in use       f - failed to allocate aggregator
        u - unsuitable for bundling
        w - waiting to be aggregated
        d - default port


Number of channel-groups in use: 2
```

continues

Example 7-6 *Configuration and Verification of a Layer 3 LACP EtherChannel (Continued)*

```
Number of aggregators:        2

Group  Port-channel Protocol    Ports
------+------------+-----------+-----------------------------------------------
2      Po2(RU)         LACP     Gi3/39(P)   Gi3/40(P)
4503#show etherchannel 2 detail
Group state = L3
Ports: 2   Maxports = 8
Port-channels: 1 Max Port-channels = 1
Protocol:   LACP
                 Ports in the group:
                 -------------------
Port: Gi3/39
-----------


Port state    = Up Mstr In-Bndl
Channel group = 2             Mode = Active        Gcchange = -
Port-channel  = Po2           GC   = -             Pseudo port-channel = Po2
Port index    = 0             Load = 0x00          Protocol =   LACP

Flags:  S - Device is sending Slow LACPDUs   F - Device is sending fast LACPDUs.
        A - Device is in active mode.        P - Device is in passive mode.

Local information:
                           LACP port    Admin    Oper    Port     Port
Port       Flags   State   Priority     Key      Key     Number   State
Gi3/39     SA      bndl    32768        0x2      0x2     0x70     0x3D

Partner's information:

                        LACP port                Oper    Port    Port
Port       Flags   Priority Dev ID        Age    Key     Number  State
Gi3/39     SA      32768    000a.4172.df40 28s   0x2     0xBF    0x3D

Age of the port in the current state: 00d:01h:31m:17s


Port: Gi3/40
-----------


Port state    = Up Mstr In-Bndl
Channel group = 2             Mode = Active        Gcchange = -
Port-channel  = Po2           GC   = -             Pseudo port-channel = Po2
Port index    = 1             Load = 0x00          Protocol =   LACP

Flags:  S - Device is sending Slow LACPDUs   F - Device is sending fast LACPDUs.
        A - Device is in active mode.        P - Device is in passive mode.

Local information:
                           LACP port    Admin    Oper    Port     Port
Port       Flags   State   Priority     Key      Key     Number   State
Gi3/40     SA      bndl    32768        0x2      0x2     0x71     0x3D
```

Example 7-6 *Configuration and Verification of a Layer 3 LACP EtherChannel (Continued)*

```
Partner's information:

                    LACP port                        Oper    Port     Port
Port       Flags   Priority  Dev ID          Age     Key     Number   State
Gi3/40     SA      32768     000a.4172.df40   3s     0x2     0xC1     0x3D

Age of the port in the current state: 00d:01h:31m:04s

                Port-channels in the group:
                ---------------------------

Port-channel: Po2     (Primary Aggregator)


-----------

Age of the Port-channel  = 00d:01h:32m:11s
Logical slot/port    = 11/2          Number of ports = 2
Passive port list    = Gi3/39 Gi3/40
Port state           = Port-channel L3-Ag Ag-Inuse
Protocol             =   LACP

Ports in the Port-channel:

Index   Load   Port     EC state         No of bits
------+------+------+-----------------+-----------
  0     00     Gi3/39   Active              0
  1     00     Gi3/40   Active              0

Time since last port bundled:    00d:01h:31m:09s    Gi3/40
```

EtherChannel Load Balancing

EtherChannel supports load balancing of traffic across multiple interfaces. Without Ether-Channel, if two links are connected between switches, one of the links does not forward traffic due to STP, which views EtherChannel interfaces as one logical interface and therefore distributes traffic across all ports in the EtherChannel. By distributing the traffic across the EtherChannel, the amount of data loss is minimal in case of failure of the active link, and only in-flight traffic is lost. The traffic also immediately starts using the other links when any other link fails. EtherChannel load balancing selects a specific egress interface based on computation performed with a hash algorithm.

EtherChannel load balancing can use MAC addresses, IP addresses, or Layer 4 port numbers—source, destination, or both source and destination—as the determining factor for deciding to which egress port of the EtherChannel to transmit a frame. The parameters used in the hash algorithm vary depending on the user configuration to distribute the frames accordingly.

Use the option that provides the greatest flexibility in your configuration. For example, consider the scenario shown in Figure 7-3, where the destination MAC or IP address load-balancing algorithm is used. EtherChannel transmits frames only on a single link if the traffic on a channel is going to a single MAC or IP address. As shown in Figure 7-4, using the source MAC or IP address in determining the load-balancing scheme results in more efficient load balancing in this scenario. In addition, load balancing using Layer 4 TCP or User Datagram Protocol (UDP) ports results in more even distribution of traffic across both the links, as shown in Figure 7-5.

Figure 7-3 *Destination IP/MAC Address Load-Balancing Algorithm*

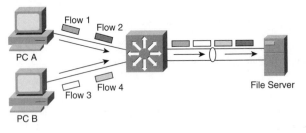

Figure 7-4 *Source-Destination IP/MAC Address Load-Balancing Algorithm*

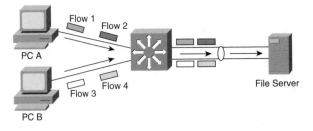

Figure 7-5 *Source-Destination Session Load-Balancing Algorithm*

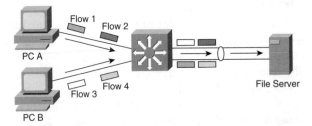

Load balancing operates at the switch level rather than per channel, applying globally for all channels on the switch. For the Cisco CatOS–based Catalyst 6500 family of switches, use the following command syntax:

```
set port channel all distribution {ip | mac | session} [source | destination | both]
```

For the Cisco IOS–based Catalyst 4500 or Catalyst 6500 family of switches, use the following command:

```
port-channel load-balance {src-mac | dst-mac | src-dst-mac | src-ip | dst-ip|
src-dst-ip | src-port | dst-port | src-dst-port}
```

For the Cisco IOS–based Catalyst 2950 family of switches, use the following command:

```
port-channel load-balance {dst-mac | src-mac}
```

Table 7-4 shows the varied support of the load-balancing algorithm Layer 2 (MAC address), Layer 3 (IP address), and Layer 4 (TCP/UDP ports) parameters.

Table 7-4   *Catalyst Switch Support of Load-Balancing Algorithm Parameters*

Catalyst Switch	Load-Balancing Algorithm Parameters
Catalyst 2950/Catalyst 2955/Catalyst 2940	L2
Catalyst 2970	L2/L3
Catalyst 3550/Catalyst 3560/Catalyst 3750	L2/L3
Catalyst 4500 family	L2/L3/L4
Catalyst 6500 family	L2/L3/L4

Also, the actual EtherChannel load-balancing algorithm varies depending on the family of switches. For more information, refer to the following technical document on Cisco.com:

"Understanding EtherChannel Load Balancing and Redundancy on Catalyst Switches," Document ID: 12023

Example 7-7 shows the configuration and verification of source-destination IP-based load balancing on a Cisco IOS–based Catalyst 6500 switch.

Example 7-7   *Configuration and Verification of EtherChannel Load-Balancing Algorithm*

```
6500(config)# port-channel load-balance src-dst-ip
6500(config)#end
6500# show etherchannel load-balance
Source XOR Destination IP address
```

To summarize, EtherChannel allows increasing bandwidth up to 16-Gbps (using Gigabit Ethernet interfaces) full duplex by bundling ports and provides redundancy in the case of link failure. EtherChannel is ubiquitous in typical networks of today.

CDP

CDP is a Layer 2 protocol enabled by default on Cisco devices and is an important protocol to identify connected device details. CDP is network protocol–independent and runs on all Cisco devices, including routers and Catalyst switches. The Link Layer Discovery Protocol (LLDP) is a vendor-neutral Layer 2 protocol equivalent to Cisco Discovery Protocol (CDP) that allows a network device to advertise its identity and capabilities on the local network.

The protocol has been formally ratified as IEEE standard 802.1AB in 2005, and support for LLDP is planned on the Catalyst switches in an upcoming Cisco IOS release.

CDP runs on all media that supports the Subnetwork Access Protocol (SNAP) frames type, including Ethernet, Frame Relay, and ATM physical media. CDP operates at Layer 2 in the OSI model and hence interacts with other Cisco devices regardless of network-layer protocols.

CDP works by sending periodic messages, called advertisement messages, on all CDP-enabled interfaces to the multicast MAC address 01-00-0c-cc-cc-cc. The devices learn information about the connected devices through these messages sent by neighboring devices.

The following list includes significant information related to switches carried by all CDP messages. Table 7-5 provides descriptions of all the fields carried by the CDP messages:

- Device ID
- Network addresses
- Port or interface sending the messages
- Capabilities of the sending device
- Hardware platform
- VTP management domain
- Native VLAN
- Duplex configuration
- Software version

CDP advertisement messages carry the information listed previously in embedded blocks called Type-Length-Value (TLV) fields.

Figure 7-6 shows the general format for a CDP version 2 packet. Table 7-5 describes the fields in the CDPv2 packet.

Figure 7-6   *CDP Version 2 Packet Format*

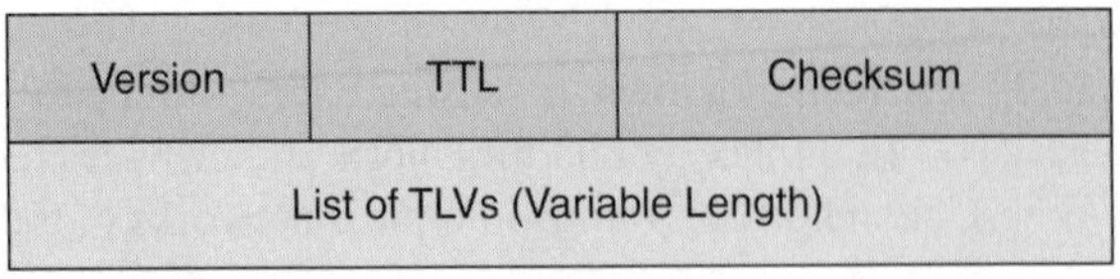

Version	TTL	Checksum
List of TLVs (Variable Length)		

Table 7-5   *CDP Version 2 Packet Fields Description*

Field	Length	Description
Version	8 bits	CDP version (0×02 for CDP v2)
Time-to-Live	8 bits	Length of time in seconds that a receiver should keep the information in this packet
Checksum	16 bits	Checksum of the CDP packet
List of TLVs	Variable length	List of TLVs

Figure 7-7 shows the TLV format, and Table 7-6 shows the descriptions of the fields.

Figure 7-7   *TLV Format*

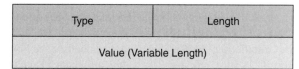

Table 7-6   *Description of Fields in TLV Format*

Field	Length	Description
Type	16 bits	Well-known values to define the type of TLV
Length	16 bits	Length of the TLV
Value	Variable	Data of the TLV

Table 7-7 shows the various TLV types and the description of the information carried in them.

Table 7-7   *CDPv2 TLV Types and Descriptions*

TLV Type	Description
Device-ID	Identifies the sending device
Address	Network layer address(es)—typically the address assigned on the interface sending the CDP packet
Port-ID	Identifies the interface from which the CDP packet is sent
Capabilities	The device's functional capability (for example, router or switch)
Version	Information about which software version the device is running
Platform	The hardware platform of the device
Native VLAN	802.1Q native VLAN (packets sent without 802.1Q tag on native VLAN)
Appliance VLAN-ID	Contains one or more tuples, each containing Appliance ID (for example, VoIP phone) and VLAN ID for that appliance
Trigger	Device receiving CDP packets with trigger TLV will respond on the interface of received packet instead of waiting to send packet at the periodic interval
Power Consumption	Maximum amount of inline power in milliwatts that the device connected on the interface expects to receive
sysName	System name (same as device's sysName MIB project)
sysObjectID	OBJECT-IDENTIFIER value of sending device's sysObjectID MIB object
Management-Address	Network layer addresses on which the device would accept SNMP messages

In addition to this information, the CDP advertisement contains the hold time, which indicates how long the receiving device should hold that CDP information before discarding it.

CDP Version 2 is the latest version of CDP, which provides additional TLVs. Some of the additional TLVs, which are typically used in Architecture for Voice, Video, and Integrated Data (AVVID) installations for Catalyst switches, include the Power Consumption, Extended Trust, COS for Untrusted Ports, and Appliance VLAN-ID TLVs.

For information about configuring the Catalyst switches in an AVVID environment, refer to the following publication:

"Cisco Catalyst QoS: Quality of Service in Campus Networks," Cisco Press, 2003

Cisco devices send and receive CDP by default. Example 7-8 shows a user displaying the neighboring Cisco devices on a Cisco IOS–based Catalyst switch using CDP.

Example 7-8 *Displaying CDP Information About Neighboring Cisco Devices*

```
4506#show cdp neighbor
Capability Codes: R - Router, T - Trans Bridge, B - Source Route Bridge
                  S - Switch, H - Host, I - IGMP, r - Repeater, P - Phone


Device ID        Local Intrfce    Holdtme    Capability  Platform  Port ID
TBA03501074(SwitcFa3/21           128         T S I      WS-C6506  3/36
SwitchC-4503     Fa3/27           150         R S I      WS-C4503  Fa3/14
4506#show cdp neighbor detail
-------------------------
Device ID: TBA03501074(SwitchA-6500)
Entry address(es):
  IP address: 10.18.2.137
Platform: WS-C6506,  Capabilities: Trans-Bridge Switch IGMP
Interface: FastEthernet3/21,  Port ID (outgoing port): 3/36
Holdtime : 170 sec

Version :
WS-C6506 Software, Version McpSW: 7.6(1) NmpSW: 7.6(1)
Copyright © 1995-2003 by Cisco Systems


advertisement version: 2
VTP Management Domain: '0'
Native VLAN: 1
Duplex: full


-------------------------
Device ID: SwitchC-4503
Entry address(es):
  IP address: 10.18.2.132
Platform: cisco WS-C4503,  Capabilities: Router Switch IGMP
Interface: FastEthernet3/27,  Port ID (outgoing port): FastEthernet3/14
Holdtime : 130 sec
```

Example 7-8 *Displaying CDP Information About Neighboring Cisco Devices (Continued)*

```
Version :
Cisco Internetwork Operating System Software
IOS (tm) Catalyst 4000 L3 Switch Software (cat4000-I5S-M), Version 12.1(19)EW, CISCO
ENHANCED PRODUCTION VERSION
Copyright © 1986-2003 by cisco Systems, Inc.
Compiled Tue 27-May-03 04:31 by prothero

advertisement version: 2
VTP Management Domain: 'cisco'
Native VLAN: 1
Duplex: full
```

CDP can be disabled globally or on a per-interface basis. On Cisco IOS–based Catalyst switches, use the following command to disable CDP globally:

no cdp run

Use the following interface-level command to disable CDP under individual interfaces on Cisco IOS–based switches:

no cdp enable

For Cisco CatOS–based Catalyst switches, use the following command to disable CDP globally:

set cdp disable

Use the following command to disable CDP for a specific port on Cisco CatOS–based switches:

set cdp disable *mod/port*

Voice VLAN and CDP

Figure 7-8 shows a typical VoIP implementation with a workstation connecting to an IP phone, which in turn connects to the Catalyst switch.

Figure 7-8 *IP Phone and Workstation Connecting to a Catalyst Switch*

Catalyst Switch   IP Phone   Workstation

In this configuration, the recommended configuration is to have two separate VLANs:

- One for the data traffic from the workstations
- Another for the voice traffic from the IP phones

Having two separate VLANs for voice and data traffic helps to apply QoS or other polices per VLAN and helps to differentiate between high-priority voice traffic and low-priority data traffic from the workstation.

To instruct the phone to tag (802.1Q tag) the voice traffic with voice VLAN (also known as auxiliary VLAN), the switch sends CDP packets with the appliance VLAN-ID TLV to the IP phone to mark the packets appropriately.

The following interface-level command is used on Cisco IOS–based Catalyst switches to specify the voice VLAN so that CDP can send it in its packet to the IP phone:

```
switchport voice vlan vlan-id
```

On Cisco CatOS–based Catalyst switches, use the following command to specify voice VLAN (auxiliary VLAN):

```
set port auxiliaryvlan mod/port vlan-id
```

In Figure 7-9, the native VLAN (untagged VLAN) for data traffic is 2 and the Voice VLAN is 111.

Figure 7-9   *Connecting IP Phone in Voice VLAN and Workstation in Data VLAN*

For more information on Voice VLANs, refer to Chapter 13, "Best Practices for Deploying Cisco IP Telephony using Cisco Catalyst Switches."

Security Issues

CDP provides useful information and helps in troubleshooting in most networks; however, CDP does cause security concerns because it sends information about the system on all the interfaces by default. The security concern is more evident when multiple organizations are interconnected. An example of such a connection is when the enterprise network connects to the service provider network. Best practice is to disable CDP on the interfaces connected to the service provider and the enterprise edge routers to avoid exchange of device information. In addition, disable CDP on a per-interface basis wherever you feel security can be compromised.

Multiple Default Gateways

The Multiple Default Gateway (MDG) feature is available exclusively to the Cisco CatOS–based Catalyst family of switches. The benefit of this feature is the redundancy associated with multiple default gateways to maintain management connectivity in case of a primary default gateway failure. In addition, the default gateway configured as the Hot Standby Routing Protocol (HSRP) virtual address offers redundancy in case of active router failure. The switches support as many as three default gateways, with one switch acting as the primary gateway and the other two as the backup gateways. Cisco IOS–based Catalyst switches support multiple default gateways via standard Cisco IOS Software IP routing commands. However, the MDG feature allows for additional failover monitoring that is not available on Layer 2–only Cisco IOS–based Catalyst switches.

When the MDG feature is enabled, the switch pings the configured default gateways every 10 seconds to verify that they are still available. If the primary gateway becomes unavailable, the switch automatically routes the packet to the backup gateway. This prevents the switch from becoming unreachable in case of primary gateway failure for any reason. This behavior is similar to the multiple-gateway feature available in Microsoft Windows XP and 2003.

Use the following command to enable or disable the MDG feature:

```
set feature mdg {enable| disable}
```

Example 7-9 shows a user configuring three default gateways and enabling the MDG feature on a Cisco CatOS–based Catalyst 6500 switch.

Example 7-9 *Configuration and Verification of the MDG Feature on Cisco CatOS–Based Switches*

```
6500> (enable) set ip route default 10.18.2.21
Route added.
6500> (enable) set ip route default 10.18.2.22
Route added.
6500> (enable) set ip route default 10.18.2.23
Route added.
6500> (enable) show ip route
Fragmentation    Redirect    Unreachable
-------------    --------    -----------
enabled          enabled     enabled

The primary gateway: 10.18.2.21
Destination        Gateway          RouteMask     Flags    Use        Interface
---------------    ---------------  ----------    -----    --------   ----------
default            10.18.2.23       0x0           G        0          sc0
default            10.18.2.22       0x0           G        0          sc0
default            10.18.2.21       0x0           UG       0          sc0
10.18.2.0          10.18.2.145      0xffffff00    U        13         sc0
default            default          0xff000000    UH       0          sl0
6500> (enable) set feature mdg enable
Multiple Default Gateway feature enabled.
```

In Example 7-9, the switch selects the first configured default gateway as the primary gateway. To configure the primary gateway explicitly, use the following command:

```
set ip route default ip-address-of-gateway primary
```

To summarize, the MDG feature is useful for adding redundancy for the default gateway for maintaining management connectivity for the Catalyst switch itself such that network connectivity from remote subnets is possible in the case of default gateway failure. To reiterate, this feature is available only on Cisco CatOS–based Catalyst switches.

MAC Address Notification

The MAC address notification feature can monitor new devices that connect to the network. In an "Ethernet To The Home (ETTH)" scenario, a typical access layer switch has each user port connecting to a different subscriber to provide network access. The MAC address notification feature helps control access and logs the network access of the subscribers. Furthermore, the MAC address notification feature is a useful troubleshooting tool in specific circumstances.

The MAC address notification feature works by sending Simple Network Management Protocol (SNMP) traps from the switch to a management system upon learning of one or more new MAC addresses on an access port. The information contained in the trap includes the specific port number of the user and the newly learned MAC addresses.

A DHCP server may be used for added flexibility. The DHCP server—upon receiving a request for a new IP address—verifies the MAC address with the switch and port information in its database to make sure the request is from a paying customer port. If this check verifies in the system, the DHCP server grants an IP address to the host, and the associated IP and MAC address information is stored in the database for tracking purposes.

This feature is currently available on the Cisco CatOS–based Catalyst 6500 family of switches and the Cisco IOS–based Catalyst 3750 family of switches.

Perform the following steps to enable the MAC address notification feature:

Step 1   Enable the MAC address notification feature globally.

```
set cam notification enable
```

Step 2   Enable MAC notification for additions or deletions per port, for tracking purposes.

```
set cam notification {added| deleted} enable {mod/port}
```

Step 3   Specify the MAC address notification interval.

```
set cam notification interval time
```

Step 4   Enable the switch to send MAC notification SNMP traps.

```
set snmp enable macnotification
```

Example 7-10 shows a user configuring the MAC address notification feature for MAC addresses learned on port 3/47 on a Cisco CatOS–based Catalyst 6500 switch.

Example 7-10 *Configuration of MAC Address Notification Feature*

```
6500> (enable) set cam notification enable
MAC address change detection globally enabled
Be sure to specify which ports are to detect MAC address changes
with the 'set cam notification [added | removed] enable <m/p> command.
SNMP traps will be sent if 'set snmp trap enable macnotification' has been set.
6500> (enable) set cam notification added enable 3/47
MAC address change notifications for added addresses are
enabled on port(s) 3/47.
6500> (enable) set cam notification interval 30
MAC address change notification interval set to 30 seconds
This interval will be applied when the process wakes up next time
6500> (enable) set snmp enable macnotification
SNMP enabled.
```

The MAC address notification feature is not currently widely available on Cisco IOS–based Catalyst switches. Currently, the Cisco Catalyst 3750-metro series of switches support this feature in Cisco IOS–based switches.

To summarize, the MAC address notification feature is useful in specific scenarios where the management station needs notification of MAC address changes. This feature is not used as commonly as some of the other features presented in this chapter, but it is nevertheless a valuable one.

Layer 3 Protocol Filtering

Layer 3 (L3) protocol filtering prevents forwarding of broadcast and unknown unicast flood traffic in a VLAN belonging to certain Layer 3 protocols based on configuration. For instance, a port configured for IP only does not forward IPX and AppleTalk broadcast traffic or IPX and AppleTalk unknown unicast traffic.

Catalyst switches classify protocols into the following groups:

- IP
- IPX
- AppleTalk, DECnet, and Banyan VINES (group mode)
- Other protocols

The default port protocol configuration is on for IP and auto for other protocol groups. The protocol-filtering configuration also allows explicit configuration of on mode for other protocol groups.

In auto mode, the switch port forwards broadcast and unknown unicast traffic other than the regular traffic of that protocol. For instance, if the port receives an IPX packet, the switch assumes that an IPX device connects to that port, and the switch forwards the broadcast and unknown unicast IPX traffic in addition to the traffic destined to the device using IPX. The switch stops forwarding IPX protocol packets out the respective port if it does not receive an IPX protocol packet within a 60-minute window. On a port configured for off mode for a particular protocol, the switch does not forward packets to or from that port for the specified protocol packets.

Example 7-11 shows the configuration of protocol filtering on ports 3/1 and 3/2. In this example, the administrator disallows IPX on ports 3/1 and 3/2.

Example 7-11 *Configuring and Verifying Protocol Filtering on Cisco CatOS–Based Catalyst Switches*

```
6500> (enable) set protocolfilter enable
Protocol filtering enabled on this switch.
6500> (enable) set port protocol 3/1-2 ipx off
IPX protocol disabled on ports 3/1-2.
6500> (enable) show port protocol 3/1-2
Port    Vlan      AuxVlan IP    IP    IPX    IPX  Group    Group
```
continues

Example 7-11 *Configuring and Verifying Protocol Filtering on Cisco CatOS–Based Catalyst Switches (Continued)*

```
                        Status   Hosts Status   Hosts Status   Hosts
-------- ---------- ------- -------- ----- -------- ----- -------- -----
  3/1    1          none    on       0     off      0     on       0
  3/2    1          none    on       0     off      0     on       0
6500> (enable)
```

Example 7-12 shows the configuration of protocol filtering on Cisco IOS–based Catalyst 6500 on the FastEthernet 5/8 interface. The administrator turns off IP and AppleTalk packet forwarding and turns on IPX packet forwarding for that interface.

Example 7-12 *Configuring and Verifying Protocol Filtering on Cisco IOS–Based Catalyst Switches*

```
6500#configure terminal
6500(config)#protocol-filtering
6500(config)#interface FastEthernet 5/8
6500(config-if)#switchport protocol appletalk off
6500(config-if)#switchport protocol ip off
6500(config-if)#switchport protocol ipx on
6500#show protocol-filtering interface FastEthernet 5/8
Interface IP Mode IPX Mode Group Mode Other Mode
-------------------------------------------------------------------
Fa5/8        OFF      ON       OFF        OFF
```

To summarize, protocol filtering is a useful feature in a multiprotocol environment where devices run certain protocols exclusively but may share the Layer 2 domains with other devices working with different protocols. Protocol-filtering features enable administrators to minimize the extent of traffic being flooded unnecessarily on all ports in a VLAN.

DHCP for Management IP Configuration

DHCP-based management IP configuration is a convenient feature to allow centralized configuration of IP addresses and switch configuration. The administrator configures the DHCP server with reserved leases that are bound to each switch interface by the MAC address.

The Cisco CatOS–based Catalyst family of switches uses a management interface, sc0, for the switch management. Refer to Chapter 3, "Initial Configuration and Troubleshooting of Cisco Multilayer Switches," for more information about sc0.

IP configuration through DHCP is possible only for the sc0 management interface. This eliminates the need for manual configuration that may lead to error. In the DHCP server, the supervisor's MAC address is manually bound to a predetermined IP address. This manual binding ensures that the IP address does not change each time the switch reboots.

To configure the switch to use DHCP for managing IP configuration with Cisco CatOS, use the **set interface sc0 0.0.0.0** command and reset the switch. When the module becomes available, the switch sends the DHCP request, as shown in Example 7-13. You can verify the assigned IP address using the **show interface** command.

Example 7-13 *Using DHCP for Management IP Configuration*

```
Sending RARP request with address 00:30:7b:4e:37:ff
Sending DHCP packet with address: 00:30:7b:4e:37:ff
Sending DHCP packet with address: 00:30:7b:4e:37:ff
10.18.2.21 added to DNS server table as primary server.
Default DNS domain name set to cisco.com
2003 May 23 17:28:41 %MGMT-5-DHCP_S:Assigned IP address 10.18.2.1 from DHCP Server
10.18.2.132
6500> (enable) show interface
sl0: flags=51<UP,POINTOPOINT,RUNNING>
        slip 0.0.0.0 dest 0.0.0.0
sc0: flags=63<UP,BROADCAST,RUNNING>
        vlan 1 inet 10.18.2.1 netmask 255.255.255.0 broadcast 10.18.2.255
sc1: flags=62<DOWN,BROADCAST,RUNNING>
        vlan 2 inet 0.0.0.0 netmask 0.0.0.0 broadcast 0.0.0.0
dhcp server: 10.18.2.132
```

To renew the IP configuration manually, use the following command:

```
set interface sc0 dhcp renew
```

To release the IP configuration manually, use the following command:

```
set interface sc0 dhcp release
```

On Cisco IOS–based switches, when you boot your switch, the switch automatically requests configuration information from a DHCP server only if a configuration file is not present on the switch.

DHCP-based IP configuration does not occur under these conditions:

- When the switch has a configuration file and the **service config** global configuration command is disabled.

- When the switch has a configuration file present in NVRAM and the **service config** global configuration command is enabled. In this case, the switch broadcasts TFTP requests for the configuration file.

NOTE   Without a configuration, the switch executes the setup program by default. Do not respond to any of the questions in the setup program until the switch receives the dynamically assigned IP address from the DHCP server and reads the switch configuration file.

For more information about DHCP-based auto-configuration, refer to the "Configuring the Switch for the First Time" section of the Catalyst 4500 software configuration guide at Cisco.com.

To summarize, DHCP for management of IP configuration is a convenient feature in a network scenario where manual configuration error is possible and a central assignment of IP addresses is preferred.

Debounce Timer Feature

Jitter tolerance, according to IEEE 802.3-2002, clause 25, shall not exceed 1.4 nanoseconds. However, there have been situations where NICs operating out of spec with respect to excessive jitter may cause repeated link flaps in the Catalyst family of switches. You can address this issue by troubleshooting the NIC and either updating the drivers or replacing the NIC.

However, Catalyst switches provide a workaround in such a scenario by increasing the jitter tolerance on the switch. The debounce timer feature is used to change the jitter tolerance timer such that the switch does not move the link into a down state for noncomplying NICs. It is highly recommended that you troubleshoot auto-negotiation before using this feature.

For more information about troubleshooting auto-negotiation issues with Ethernet ports, refer to the following technical document on Cisco.com:

"Configuring and Troubleshooting Ethernet 10/100/1000Mb Half/Full Duplex Auto-Negotiation," Document ID: 10561

In Cisco CatOS–based switches, use the following command:

```
set option debounce enable
```

Table 7-8 shows the port debounce timer with the debounce timer feature disabled and enabled on the Catalyst 6500 family of switches

Table 7-8   *Delay Time With and Without the Debounce Timer Feature*

Port Type	Delay Time with Debounce Timer Feature Disabled	Delay Time with Debounce Timer Feature Enabled
10BASE-FL	300 milliseconds	3100 milliseconds
10/100BASE-TX	300 milliseconds	3100 milliseconds
100BASE-FX	300 milliseconds	3100 milliseconds
10/100/1000BASE-TX	300 milliseconds	3100 milliseconds
1000BASE-TX	300 milliseconds	3100 milliseconds
1000BASE-FX	10 milliseconds	100 milliseconds
10-Gigabit Ethernet	1000 milliseconds	1000 milliseconds

CAUTION   Enabling the debounce timer feature causes delays in the detection of link up and down situations, which may cause loss of traffic. Only use this option as a temporary workaround.

Example 7-14 illustrates enabling the debounce timer feature on a Cisco CatOS–based Catalyst 6500 switch for port 3/15, which is connected to a user PC with a NIC operating incorrectly.

Example 7-14 *Enabling Debounce Timer Feature on Cisco CatOS–Based Catalyst Switches*

```
6500> (enable) set port debounce 3/15 enable
Debounce is enabled on port 3/15
Warning: Enabling port debounce causes Link Up/Down detections to be delayed.
It results in loss of data traffic during debouncing period, which might
affect the convergence/reconvergence of various Layer 2 and Layer 3 protocols.
Use with caution.
```

It is also possible to change the debounce timer from the default values upon enabling the debounce timer feature. This modifying option is available only for fiber-based Gigabit Ethernet ports.

On Cisco CatOS–based switches, use the following command syntax:

set port debounce {*mod/port*} **delay** {*time-in-milliseconds*}

Example 7-15 shows a user configuring the debounce timer feature on a fiber-based Gigabit Ethernet port 5/2 on a Catalyst 6500 switch.

Example 7-15 *Configuration and Verification of Debounce Timer Feature on Cisco CatOS–Based Catalyst 6500 Switches*

```
6500> (enable) set port debounce 5/2 delay 1500
Debounce time for port 5/2 set to 1500 ms.
Warning:Enabling port debounce causes Link Up/Down detections to be delayed.
It results in loss of data traffic during debouncing period, which might
affect the convergence/reconvergence of various Layer 2 and Layer 3 protocols.
Use with caution.
6500> (enable) show port debounce 5/3
Port   Debounce Debounce
       status   timer
-----  -------- ----------
 5/2   enabled    1500 ms
```

On Cisco IOS–based Catalyst switches, use the following interface command to enable the debounce timer feature:

link-debounce

On fiber-based Gigabit Ethernet interfaces, changing the debounce timer is supported using the following command:

link-debounce time *debounce-time*

Example 7-16 shows a network administrator configuring and verifying a debounce timer of 5000 milliseconds on GigabitEthernet 4/1 on a Cisco IOS–based Catalyst 6500 switch.

Example 7-16 *Configuration and Verification of Debounce Timer Feature on Cisco IOS–Based Catalyst Switch*

```
6500(config)#interface GigabitEthernet 4/1
6500(config-if)#link debounce time ?
  <100-5000>  Extended debounce time value
```

continues

Example 7-16 *Configuration and Verification of Debounce Timer Feature on Cisco IOS–Based Catalyst Switch (Continued)*

```
6500(config-if)#link debounce time 5000
Warning: Enabling debounce feature causes link down detection to be delayed

6500#show interfaces GigabitEthernet 4/1 debounce
Port    Debounce time   Value(ms)
Gi4/1   enable          5000
```

To summarize, the debounce timer feature is useful in a scenario where the switch needs to work with out-of-spec NIC workstations or servers. Enabling the debounce timer feature stabilizes the links to those devices and prevents unnecessary network device downtime. The recommended solution to this problem, though, is to replace the faulty NIC or upgrade the NIC driver instead of using the workaround.

Broadcast and Multicast Suppression

Broadcast packets have a unique characteristic in that every device in the broadcast domain processes them. If there is excessive broadcast traffic on a network segment, all devices are affected. Subsequently, if there is a broadcast storm, it ultimately leads to congestion and severe degradation of network performance. Unknown multicast addressed frames get flooded in the VLAN and affect the rest of the devices in the subnet. Hence, it is critical that the network protect against misbehaving faulty devices or malicious attacks caused by excessive multicast or broadcast traffic. Note that excessive broadcasts can also result from misconfiguration of applications or network devices.

The Catalyst family of switches offers the broadcast-suppression feature to alleviate excessive broadcasts. The action taken upon detection of broadcast suppression is to drop the excessive traffic or to disable the port receiving the excessive traffic.

This feature works by monitoring the traffic entering the port over a period of 1 second. If the broadcast traffic exceeds the configured threshold, the switches act on the configured violation action.

In the Catalyst 6500 family of switches, multicast and unicast suppression is configurable on Gigabit Ethernet ports. The feature is similar to broadcast suppression, described previously, except that multicast and unicast suppression controls excessive multicast or unicast traffic as well as broadcast traffic. This feature is extremely useful in controlling congestion and mitigating network loops.

On Cisco CatOS–based switches, use the following command to enable broadcast suppression:

```
set port broadcast mod/port threshold% [violation {drop-packets | err-disable}]
[multicast {enable | disable}][unicast {enable | disable}]
```

In the command syntax, *threshold%* is in terms of bandwidth of the port. For example, if you enable the broadcast suppression on a Fast Ethernet, a 10 percent threshold is 10 Mbps of traffic. Specifying a threshold of 100 percent does not suppress traffic. A 0 percent threshold means the switch suppresses all traffic. Choose the threshold percentage based on your network traffic pattern. Furthermore, make sure that you do not set the value too low such that the switch drops legitimate traffic. We recommend enabling broadcast and multicast suppression on user ports in the access layer to limit the amount of broadcast or multicast traffic that a specific host port can transmit into the network.

The violation action is to either drop the packets or err-disable the respective port. The action chosen depends on the network requirements. When a port goes into err-disabled state, the switch displays an error message and generates an SNMP trap message to notify the management station immediately of the excessive traffic.

Example 7-17 illustrates the configuration of broadcast suppression and multicast suppression on Gigabit Ethernet port 2/1 with a threshold set to 5 percent. In this configuration, if the combined broadcast and multicast traffic exceeds the threshold in a 1-second interval, the port transitions into the err-disabled state.

Example 7-17 *Configuration and Verification of Broadcast and Multicast Suppression*

```
6500> (enable) set port broadcast 2/1 5% violation err-disable multicast enable
Port 2/1 broadcast and multicast traffic limited to 5.00%.
On broadcast suppression port 2/1 is configured to move to err-disabled state.
6500> (enable) show port broadcast 2/1

Port    Broadcast-Limit Multicast Unicast Total-Drop          Action
-------- --------------- --------- ------- -------------------- -----------
 2/1            5.00 %    5.00 %       -                     0  err-disable
```

Table 7-9 shows support for broadcast, multicast, and unicast suppression features on various Catalyst families of switches.

Table 7-9 *Support of Broadcast, Multicast, and Unicast Suppression on the Catalyst Family of Switches*

Catalyst Switch	Broadcast Suppression	Multicast Suppression	Unicast Suppression
Catalyst 2950/Catalyst 2955/ Catalyst 2940/Catalyst 2970	Yes	Yes	Yes
Catalyst 3550/Catalyst 3560/ Catalyst 3750	Yes	Yes	Yes
Catalyst 4500 family	Yes	Yes	Yes
Catalyst 6500 family	Yes	Yes	Yes

Cisco IOS–based switches refer to broadcast suppression as storm control. With the storm-control feature, the only violation action is to drop packets for the Cisco IOS–based Catalyst 6500 family of switches. On the Cisco IOS–based Catalyst 4500 family of switches, violations include the shutdown action in addition to the option for dropping the packets. Use the following interface-level command syntax for enabling storm control:

```
storm-control {broadcast | multicast | unicast} level level
```

Example 7-18 shows a Cisco IOS–based Catalyst switch configuration of storm control. In this example, the user configures both the broadcast and multicast suppression threshold level to 5 percent.

Example 7-18 *Configuration of Broadcast and Multicast Suppression on Cisco IOS–Based Switches*

```
c6509a(config-if)#storm-control broadcast level 5
c6509a(config-if)#storm-control multicast level 5
```

To summarize, broadcast and multicast suppression aids in preventing unexpected attacks or misbehavior of network devices where an anomalous device sends a large number of broadcasts or multicasts. A large number of broadcasts per second may cause high CPU utilization on the network devices, which in turn may cause network outages. Configuring the suppression feature aids in preventing such outages and increases the stability of the network.

Baby Giants and Jumbo Frames

The standard Ethernet frame maximum transmission unit (MTU) is 1500 bytes. This does not include the Ethernet header (14 bytes) and cyclic redundancy check (CRC) trailer (4 bytes), which makes the total Ethernet frame size 1518 bytes. In this section, the MTU size or packet size refers only to the Ethernet payload. Ethernet frame size refers to the whole Ethernet frame, including the header and the trailer.

Baby giant frames are slightly larger than standard Ethernet frames and are designed to accommodate various encapsulations with an MTU of up to 1600 bytes. Some of the applications of baby giants include QinQ (802.1Q on top of 802.1Q tagged frame), Multiprotocol Label Switching (MPLS), Virtual Private Network (VPN), and Layer 2 Tunneling Protocol (L2TP). Figure 7-10 shows the frame formats of several applications that need frame size support greater than the standard MTU size of 1500 bytes.

NOTE The datagram size specified in the extended Cisco IOS PING utility refers to the Data field of the frame and does not include the Ethernet header and FCS fields.

A jumbo Ethernet frame is an Ethernet frame whose size is as large as 9236 bytes. The jumbo frame feature is used to increase Ethernet performance.

Figure 7-10 *Frame Formats*

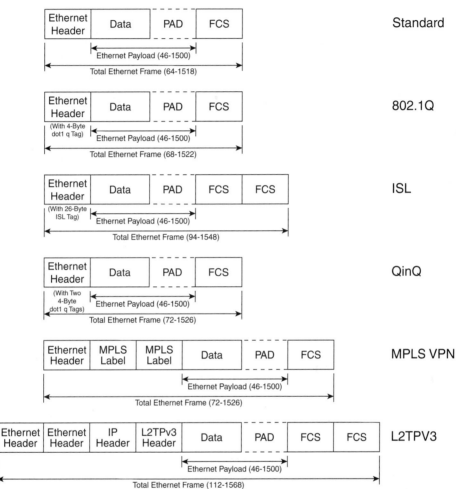

Theoretically, TCP throughput of a flow directly depends on the frame size of that flow. An example of an application that benefits from the jumbo frame feature is the NFS file transfer application. Servers require special NICs to send and receive jumbo frames. Nevertheless, jumbo frame support is becoming a standard feature of current-model NICs.

The Catalyst family of switches supports baby giants and the jumbo frame feature with many variations, but none of the Catalyst switches supports these features consistently on all of its modules. Also, if a frame gets forwarded from an interface that supports jumbo frames to an interface on the same switch in the same VLAN that does not support jumbo frames, the switch drops the frame because it can send only frames of the allowed size out of the egress interface. To avoid such a problem, make sure that all the interfaces that are communicating within a VLAN have jumbo frame support enabled.

If jumbo frames need to be routed between VLANs or subnets, the routing device needs to be configured to accept jumbo frames and to then fragment the frames if the egress interface does not support jumbo frames. Typically, the fragmentation and forwarding between VLANs is accomplished by software switching; it is not recommended to use software switching, however, because performance is decreased while the likelihood of higher CPU utilization is increased. As a result, the performance gain of using jumbo frames is lost.

The support of baby giant and jumbo frames varies across the Catalyst family of switches, as Table 7-10 briefly highlights.

Table 7-10 *Support of Baby Giants and Jumbo Frames on Catalyst Switches*

Catalyst Switch	Baby Giant Support	Jumbo Frame Support
Catalyst 2940	No	No
Catalyst 2950/Catalyst 2955	Yes (on some models)	No
Catalyst 2970	Yes	Yes
Catalyst 3550	Yes	No
Catalyst 3560/Catalyst 3750	Yes	Yes
Catalyst 4500 family	Yes	Yes
Catalyst 6500 family	Yes	Yes

For more information, see the following technical documents at Cisco.com:

"Configuring Jumbo/Giant Frame Support on Catalyst Switches," Document ID: 24048
"Understanding Baby Giant/Jumbo Frames Support on Catalyst 4000/4500 with Supervisor III/IV," Document ID: 29805

Example 7-19 shows the configuration and verification of jumbo frame support on port 2/1 on a Cisco CatOS–based Catalyst 6500 switch.

Example 7-19 *Configuration and Verification of Jumbo Frame Support on Cisco CatOS–Based Catalyst Switches*

```
Console> (enable) set port jumbo 2/1 enable
Jumbo frames enabled on port 2/1
Console> (enable) show port jumbo
Jumbo frames MTU size is 9216 bytes
Jumbo frames enabled on port(s) 2/1
```

On Cisco IOS–based switches, use the following global-level command to configure a baby giant:

```
system mtu size
```

This MTU size configuration is applicable to all interfaces in the system that have hardware support for it.

To enable jumbo frames, use the following interface-level command:

```
mtu size
```

NOTE	The interface-level configuration overrides the global system MTU configuration.

Example 7-20 shows the configuration and verification of baby giant support globally and jumbo frame support on interface Gigabit Ethernet 1/1, respectively, on a Cisco IOS–based Catalyst 4500 switch.

Example 7-20 *Configuration and Verification of Baby Giant and Jumbo Frame Support on Cisco IOS–Based Catalyst Switches*

```
4506(config)#system mtu 1552
Global Ethernet MTU is set to 1552 bytes.
Note: this is the Ethernet payload size, not the total
Ethernet frame size, which includes the Ethernet
header/trailer
4506(config)#interface gigabitEthernet 1/1
4506(config-if)#mtu ?
<1500-9198> MTU size in bytes

4506(config-if)#mtu 9198
4506(config-if)#end
4506#show system mtu
Global Ethernet MTU is 1552 bytes.
4506#show interfaces GigabitEthernet 1/1 mtu

Port    Name            MTU
Gi1/1                   9198
```

To summarize, baby giant and jumbo frame support provides support for frames greater than the standard Ethernet MTU size. Larger frame sizes are needed to support various encapsulations such as QinQ and to achieve higher TCP throughput. Also, make sure that there is no requirement for fragmentation (for example, switching jumbo frame packets to an interface that does not support jumbo frames), because fragmentation may lead to slower performance than using standard Ethernet frame sizes across the entire network.

Error-Disable Feature

The error-disable feature allows the switch to detect certain error conditions on interfaces and disable them before the error condition affects the entire switch or the rest of the network.

The error-disable feature can be activated for many error conditions, and it varies slightly per Catalyst switch and software version. For example, the Catalyst 4500 series switches can detect the following error conditions:

- UDLD
- BPDU guard detection
- Port-security violation
- EtherChannel misconfiguration
- VMPS client violation
- PAgP flapping
- DTP flapping
- Link flapping
- L2PT guard
- Invalid GBIC
- DHCP rate limit violation
- Unicast flood
- Storm control
- ARP inspection

When any one of the supported error conditions is detected, the switch can be configured to transition the interface into the err-disable state, which is an operational state similar to the link-down state.

There are two ways to recover from this error-disabled state of an interface:

- **Manual recovery**—Issue the **shutdown** command followed by the **no shutdown** interface level command to recover the error-disabled interface on Cisco IOS–based Catalyst switches. On Cisco CatOS–based switches, use the **set port disable** *mod/port* command followed by the **set port enable** *mod/port* command.

- **Automatic recovery**—The switch can be configured to automatically recover the error-disabled interface after a specified interval.

NOTE   If the error condition persists after the manual or automatic recovery, the interface goes into the error-disabled state again. Fixing the root cause of the problem prevents interfaces from error-disabling after the recovery.

To enable detection for the error-disable feature, use the following command on Cisco IOS–based Catalyst switches:

```
errdisable detect cause {all | arp-inspection | dhcp-rate-limit | dtp-flap |
    gbic-invalid | l2ptguard | link-flap | pagp-flap}
```

| NOTE | The error-disable feature is already integrated into features such as UDLD and Port-Security; hence, explicit enabling of those error condition causes is not required. |

To enable automatic recovery from error-disabled condition, use the following command on Cisco IOS–based Catalyst switches:

```
errdisable recovery cause {all | arp-inspection | bpduguard | channel-misconfig |
   dhcp-rate-limit | dtp-flap | gbic-invalid | l2ptguard | link-flap | pagp-flap |
   pesecure-violation | security-violation | storm-control | udld | unicastflood | vmps}
```

To enable automatic recovery on Cisco CatOS–based Catalyst switches, use the following command:

```
set errdisable-timeout {enable | disable} {bpdu-guard | channel-misconfig |
   duplex-mismatch | udld | other | all}
```

To specify the interval for attempting to recover from error-disabled state, use the following command on Cisco IOS–based Catalyst switches.

```
errdisable recovery interval interval
```

To specify the interval for recovery, use the following command on Cisco CatOS–based Catalyst switches:

```
set errdisable-timeout interval interval-in-seconds
```

Example 7-21 shows a user configuring the error-disable feature detection and recovery for all supported conditions. In addition, the user increases the recovery interval to 60 seconds from the default 30 seconds. Finally, the user verifies the configuration changes using the **show** commands.

Example 7-21 *Configuration and Verification of the Error-Disable Feature*

```
4500#configure terminal
Enter configuration commands, one per line.  End with CNTL/Z.
4500(config)#errdisable detect cause all
4500(config)#errdisable recovery cause all
4500(config)#errdisable recovery interval 60
4500(config)#end
4500#show errdisable detect
ErrDisable Reason    Detection status
----------------     ----------------
udld                 Enabled
bpduguard            Enabled
security-violatio    Enabled
channel-misconfig    Enabled
psecure-violation    Enabled
vmps                 Enabled
loopback             Enabled
unicast-flood        Enabled
pagp-flap            Enabled
dtp-flap             Enabled
link-flap            Enabled
l2ptguard            Enabled
gbic-invalid         Enabled
```

continues

Example 7-21 *Configuration and Verification of the Error-Disable Feature (Continued)*

```
dhcp-rate-limit        Enabled
unicast-flood          Enabled
storm-control          Enabled
ilpower                Enabled
arp-inspection         Enabled
4500#show errdisable recovery
ErrDisable Reason      Timer Status
----------------       -------------
udld                   Enabled
bpduguard              Enabled
security-violatio      Enabled
channel-misconfig      Enabled
vmps                   Enabled
pagp-flap              Enabled
dtp-flap               Enabled
link-flap              Enabled
l2ptguard              Enabled
psecure-violation      Enabled
gbic-invalid           Enabled
dhcp-rate-limit        Enabled
unicast-flood          Enabled
storm-control          Enabled
arp-inspection         Enabled
loopback               Enabled

Timer interval: 60 seconds

Interfaces that will be enabled at the next timeout:
```

Example 7-22 shows the error-disable feature in action where the BPDU guard feature error-disables an interface and the automatic recovery of error-disable feature recovers the interface after the specified interval. However, because the misconfiguration persists, the interface is immediately moved to the error-disabled state again. After the misconfiguration is corrected, the interface is recovered.

Example 7-22 *Error-Disable Feature in Action Sample Output*

```
4500#
*Oct 30 04:09:12.623: %SPANTREE-2-BLOCK_BPDUGUARD: Received BPDU on port
GigabitEthernet1/1 with BPDU Guard enabled. Disabling port.
4500#
*Oct 30 04:09:12.623: %PM-4-ERR_DISABLE: bpduguard error detected on Gi1/1, putting
Gi1/1 in err-disable state
4500#show interfaces gigabitEthernet 1/1 status

Port       Name           Status       Vlan    Duplex  Speed Type
Gi1/1                     err-disabled 10              full    1000 1000BaseSX
4500#show errdisable recovery
ErrDisable Reason      Timer Status
----------------       -------------
udld                   Enabled
```

Example 7-22 *Error-Disable Feature in Action Sample Output (Continued)*

```
bpduguard              Enabled
security-violatio      Enabled
channel-misconfig      Enabled
vmps                   Enabled
pagp-flap              Enabled
dtp-flap               Enabled
link-flap              Enabled
l2ptguard              Enabled
psecure-violation      Enabled
gbic-invalid           Enabled
dhcp-rate-limit        Enabled
unicast-flood          Enabled
storm-control          Enabled
arp-inspection         Enabled
loopback               Enabled


Timer interval: 60 seconds


Interfaces that will be enabled at the next timeout:


Interface     Errdisable reason     Time left(sec)
---------     -----------------     -------------
Gi1/1         bpduguard                  28


4500#
*Oct 30 04:10:04.299: %PM-4-ERR_RECOVER: Attempting to recover from bpduguard err-
disable state on Gi1/1
*Oct 30 04:10:08.643: %SPANTREE-2-BLOCK_BPDUGUARD: Received BPDU on port
GigabitEthernet1/1 with BPDU Guard enabled. Disabling port.
*Oct 30 04:10:08.643: %PM-4-ERR_DISABLE: bpduguard error detected on Gi1/1, putting
Gi1/1 in err-disable state
4500#configure terminal
Enter configuration commands, one per line.  End with CNTL/Z.
4500(config)#interface gigabitEthernet 1/1
4500(config-if)#spanning-tree bpduguard disable
4500(config-if)#end
4500#
4500#show interfaces gigabitEthernet 1/1 status


Port      Name              Status     Vlan    Duplex  Speed Type
Gi1/1                       err-disabled 10            full   1000 1000BaseSX
4500#
*Oct 30 04:11:02.011: %PM-4-ERR_RECOVER: Attempting to recover from bpduguard err-
disable state on Gi1/1
4500#show interfaces gig 1/1 status


Port      Name              Status     Vlan    Duplex  Speed Type
Gi1/1                       connected   10            full   1000 1000BaseSX
```

To summarize, the error-disable feature is an essential feature to prevent error conditions on one or more ports from affecting the entire switch or the rest of the network. This feature is a recommended best practice configuration.

IEEE 802.3 Flow Control

The IEEE 802.3 flow control feature is used to prevent the loss of traffic between two devices. This loss of traffic is due to buffer overflow on the receiving device. The amount of receiver buffer on the sending and receiving device might not be the same, even though either side is operating at the same speed. Also, the receiving device might not be able to empty receive buffers fast enough due to bottleneck issues within that device or from downstream switches. Similar issues happen between Catalyst switches and servers with Gigabit NICs. To prevent loss of traffic in these scenarios, the IEEE 802.3 flow control feature enables communication between the link partners about buffer full conditions of the receive buffer. When a link partner discovers that its peer is in a buffer full condition, it ceases transmitting traffic until its peer communicates that it is capable of accepting traffic again. This feature complements QoS and is useful in preventing buffer overflow and packet loss.

NOTE   IEEE 802.3 flow control is commonly called IEEE 802.3z to refer to the first version introduced for Gigabit Ethernet. Currently, flow control is supported for Fast Ethernet as well.

IEEE 802.3 uses specific frames called *pause frames* used to instruct its link partner to delay sending frames for a specified time. The specified time is not user configurable and is decided by the receiving switch port logic. Figure 7-11 shows a Catalyst switch using pause frames to instruct a file server to delay sending frames for a specified time due to congestion.

Figure 7-11 *Operation of IEEE 802.3 Flow Control*

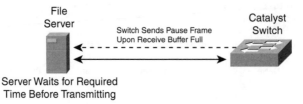

To configure IEEE 802.3 flow control, use the following interface command on Cisco IOS switches:

```
[no] flowcontrol [receive | send] {desired | off | on}
```

The **receive** keyword instructs the configured interface whether or not to process the received pause frames. The **send** keyword instructs the configured interface whether to send pause frames when congestion is experienced. The **desired** keyword is used if the link partner 802.3 flow control configuration is unknown.

Example 7-23 shows sample output of user configuration and verification of IEEE 802.3 flow control on a Cisco IOS–based Catalyst switch.

Example 7-23 *Configuration and Verification IEEE 802.3 Flow Control on a Cisco IOS–Based Catalyst Switch*

```
6500#configure terminal
Enter configuration commands, one per line.  End with CNTL/Z.
6500(config)#interface gigabitEthernet 1/1
6500(config-if)#flowcontrol receive on
6500(config-if)#flowcontrol send on
6500(config-if)#end
6500#show flowcontrol interface gigabitEthernet 1/1
Port      Send FlowControl  Receive FlowControl  RxPause TxPause
          admin    oper      admin    oper
--------  -------- --------  -------- --------    ------- -------
Gi1/1     on       on        on       on          0       0
```

Example 7-24 shows sample output of user configuration and verification of IEEE 802.3 flow control on a Cisco CatOS–based Catalyst switch.

Example 7-24 *Configuration and Verification of Flow Control on CatOS–Based Catalyst Switches*

```
Cat6500 (enable) set port flowcontrol 2/4 receive on
Port 2/4 flow control receive administration status set to on
(port will require far end to send flowcontrol)
Cat6500 (enable) set port flowcontrol 2/4 send on
Port 2/4 flow control send administration status set to on
(port will send flowcontrol to far end)
Cat6500 (enable) show port flowcontrol 2/4

Port  Send FlowControl  Receive FlowControl   RxPause     TxPause     Unsupported
      admin    oper      admin    oper                                opcodes
----- -------- --------  -------- --------    ----------- ----------- -----------
 2/4  on       disagree  on       on          0           0           0
```

To summarize, IEEE 802.3 flow control prevents packet loss in oversubscribed scenarios and is a recommended configuration for critical and high-end servers and workstations.

UDLD and Aggressive Mode UDLD

The UDLD protocol allows for detection of unidirectional link conditions on switch ports in situations where a link remains in the up state but the interface is not passing traffic. This situation typically arises in the case of faulty Gigabit Interface Converters (GBIC) or interfaces, software malfunction, hardware failure, or other anomalous behavior. UDLD aids in preventing catastrophic events that may occur during these types of failures.

UDLD is a Layer 2 protocol that works with Layer 1 mechanisms to determine the physical status of a link. At Layer 1, auto-negotiation takes care of the physical signaling and fault detection. UDLD performs tasks that auto-negotiation cannot, such as detecting the identities of neighbors and shutting down misconnected ports. When enabling both auto-negotiation and UDLD, Layer 1 and Layer 2 detections work together to prevent physical and logical unidirectional connections and the malfunctioning of other protocols.

With UDLD enabled, the switch periodically sends UDLD protocol packets to its neighbor and expects the packets to be echoed back before a predetermined timer expires. If the timer expires, the switch determines the link to be unidirectional and shuts down the port.

UDLD packets contain information about sending the port's device ID and port ID and the neighbor's device ID and port ID. Neighbor devices with UDLD enabled send the same hello message. The link is bidirectional if devices on both sides receive each other's UDLD packets.

Consider the network scenario shown in Figure 7-12 where the following is true:

- Switch A's tx strand is connected to switch B.
- Switch A's rx strand is connected to switch C.
- Switch B's tx strand is connected to switch C.

Figure 7-12 *UDLD Scenario Due to Miswiring*

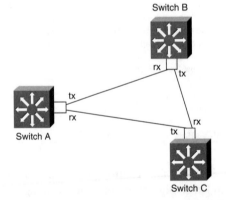

In Figure 7-12, the UDLD protocol on switch A detects that it is receiving UDLD advertisement from switch C, but switch C is advertising switch B as its neighbor. All switches in this topology detect the miswiring and potentially err-disable the ports. Note that when one link partner err-disables a port, the other link partner does not err-disable the port, because the link has already transitioned to the down state.

The default interval for UDLD message is 15 seconds, which is configurable for faster detection.

Aggressive mode UDLD is a variation of UDLD that provides additional benefits, as shown in Table 7-11. With aggressive mode UDLD enabled, when a port stops receiving UDLD packets, UDLD tries to re-establish the connection with the neighbor. After eight failed retries, the port state changes to the err-disable state, which effectively disables the port.

Table 7-11 *Differences in Behavior Between UDLD and Aggressive Mode UDLD*

Issue	UDLD State	Aggressive Mode UDLD State
Link is bidirectional; no issues.	Bidirectional.	Bidirectional.
Layer 1 remains up but with unidirectional link condition.	An error message is displayed and the port is put into the err-disable state.	An error message is displayed, and the port is put into the err-disable state.
One side of a link has a port stuck (both tx and rx).	Undetermined.	An error message is displayed, and the port is put into the err-disable state.
One side of a link remains up while the other side of the link has gone down.	Undetermined.	An error message is displayed, and the port is put into the err-disable state.

To re-enable the port after correcting the problem, use the following interface-level commands in Cisco IOS–based Catalyst switches:

```
shutdown
no shutdown
```

In Cisco CatOS–based Catalyst switches, use the following commands to recover an err-disabled port:

```
set port disable mod/port
set port enable mod/port
```

Spanning Tree Protocol prevents loops in the network by detecting loops and blocking the redundant ports. This loop detection is based on BPDUs received on switch ports. If a switch receives the same root BPDU from more than one port, it chooses the best port to the root bridge and blocks the other, redundant ports. Because receiving BPDUs is a critical part of the loop-prevention process, it is important to detect unidirectional links by another method to ensure that BPDUs are sent in the appropriate direction on all links at all times. Otherwise, a unidirectional link ultimately leads to spanning-tree loops or black holes for routed traffic. For instance, if a Layer 3 or routed interface is experiencing a unidirectional link condition but the interface, stays up, the switch continues to forward traffic to that interface but the packet never reaches the far-end device. In this situation, a routing black hole exists. The solution to preventing these issues is to use aggressive mode UDLD.

To illustrate this concept, consider the three switches shown in Figure 7-13. Switch A is the root bridge, and the link between switch B and switch C is in the blocking state because a physical loop is present in the network.

Now consider a situation where the link between switches B and C becomes unidirectional, as shown in Figure 7-14. Switch B can receive traffic from switch C, but switch C cannot receive traffic from switch B. On the segment between switches B and C, switch B is the designated bridge sending the root BPDUs, and switch C expects to receive the BPDUs.

Switch C waits until the max-age timer (20 seconds) expires before it takes action. When this timer expires, switch C moves through the listening and learning states of STP and then eventually to the STP forwarding state on the port toward switch B. At this moment, both switch B and switch C are forwarding to each other and, essentially, there is no blocking port in the network. This situation is a network loop where severe connectivity issues will exist.

Figure 7-13 *Steady State STP Behavior in the Topology*

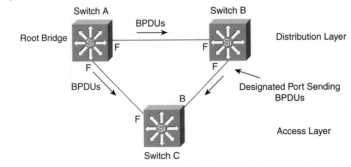

Figure 7-14 *Unidirectional Condition in the Topology*

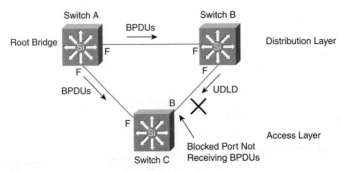

Aggressive mode UDLD running on switches B and C in this scenario would detect the condition and would be able to take corrective action before STP moves into the forwarding state.

UDLD works by exchanging UDLD protocol packets between connected switches. For UDLD to function correctly, it must be enabled on switches on both sides of the link. A UDLD-enabled switch sends UDLD protocol packets with its own device ID and port ID to the neighboring device. The UDLD is in determined status if the switch sees its own information in the packet sent by the neighbor. If the device does not see itself in the neighboring device's UDLD protocol packets, the link is determined as unidirectional.

Example 7-25 shows a user configuring and verifying aggressive mode UDLD on interface GigabitEthernet 5/1 on a Cisco IOS-based Catalyst switch.

Example 7-25 *Configuration and Verification of UDLD on Cisco IOS–Based Switches*

```
SwitchA#configure terminal
Enter configuration commands, one per line.  End with CNTL/Z.
SwitchA(config)#interface  gigabitEthernet 5/1
SwitchA(config-if)#udld port aggressive
SwitchA(config-if)#end
SwitchA#
SwitchA#show udld gigabitEthernet 5/1

Interface Gi5/1
---
Port enable administrative configuration setting: Enabled / in aggressive mode
Port enable operational state: Enabled / in aggressive mode
Current bidirectional state: Bidirectional
Current operational state: Advertisement - Single neighbor detected
Message interval: 15
Time out interval: 5

    Entry 1
    ---
    Expiration time: 38
    Device ID: 1
    Current neighbor state: Bidirectional
    Device name: FOX06310RW1
    Port ID: Gi1/1
    Neighbor echo 1 device: FOX0627A001
    Neighbor echo 1 port: Gi5/1

    Message interval: 15
    Time out interval: 5
    CDP Device name: SwitchB
```

Example 7-26 shows a user configuring and verifying aggressive mode UDLD on port 3/47 on a Cisco CatOS–based Catalyst switch.

Example 7-26 *Configuration and Verification of UDLD on Cisco CatOS–Based Switches*

```
6500> (enable) set udld enable
UDLD enabled globally
6500> (enable) set udld enable 3/47
UDLD enabled on port 3/47
6500> (enable) set udld aggressive-mode enable 3/47
Aggressive mode UDLD enabled on port 3/47.
6500> (enable) show udld port 3/47
UDLD            : enabled
Message Interval  : 15 seconds
Port      Admin Status  Aggressive Mode  Link State
--------  ------------  ---------------  ----------------
3/47      enabled       enabled          bidirectional
```

To summarize, UDLD and aggressive mode UDLD are critical features recommended on all ports to prevent various issues that may potentially cause network outages.

Case Study: Function of Aggressive Mode UDLD

This case study illustrates the advantages of aggressive mode UDLD using a Cisco CatOS–based Catalyst 6500 switch and Cisco IOS–based Catalyst 3550 switch interconnected by a fiber-based Gigabit Ethernet port, as shown in Figure 7-15.

Figure 7-15 *UDLD Scenario Between Cisco Catalyst Switches*

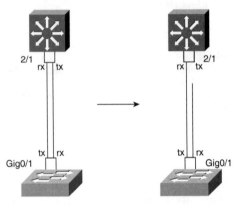

To simulate a UDLD link failure, the tx fiber strand was removed from the Catalyst 6500 port 2/1, leaving the rx fiber still receiving frames from the Catalyst 3550, as shown in Figure 7-15. To illustrate the behavior of UDLD in this example, auto-negotiation was disabled because auto-negotiation will detect the link-down status if the fiber strand fails. In a normal network scenario, auto-negotiation should remain enabled. If the link fails, auto-negotiation takes care of bringing the link down correctly. UDLD protects in cases where the link remains in the up state but behaves unidirectionally in the event of a hardware or software failure. To summarize, auto-negotiation is disabled in this case study, as shown in Example 7-27, to illustrate aggressive mode UDLD behavior compared to normal UDLD mode and is not a recommended practice.

Example 7-27 *Disabling Auto-Negotiation on a CatOS–Based Catalyst 6500 Switch*

```
6500> (enable) set port  negotiation 2/1 disable
Port 2/1 negotiation disabled.
6500> (enable) show port negotiation 2/1
Port   Link Negotiation Link Negotiation
       admin            oper
-----  ---------------- ----------------
 2/1   disabled         disabled
```

Examples 7-28 and 7-29 display the UDLD state with UDLD enabled on both sides and with aggressive mode UDLD disabled.

Example 7-28 *Checking the UDLD Status on Catalyst 6500 Switches*

```
6500> (enable) show udld port 2/1
UDLD           : enabled
Message Interval : 15 seconds
```

Example 7-28 *Checking the UDLD Status on Catalyst 6500 Switches (Continued)*

```
Port        Admin Status  Aggressive Mode  Link State
--------    ------------  ---------------  ----------------
 2/1        enabled       disabled         bidirectional
6500> (enable)
```

Example 7-29 *Checking the UDLD Status on Catalyst 3550 Switches*

```
3550#show udld GigabitEthernet 0/1

Interface Gi0/1
---
Port enable administrative configuration setting: Enabled
Port enable operational state: Enabled
Current bidirectional state: Bidirectional
Current operational state: Advertisement - Single neighbor detected
Message interval: 15
Time out interval: 5

   Entry 1
   ---
   Expiration time: 42
   Device ID: 1
   Current neighbor state: Bidirectional
   Device name: 00307b4e3400
   Port ID: 2/1
   Neighbor echo 1 device: CAT0606X0AL

   Neighbor echo 1 port: Gi0/1

   Message interval: 5
   CDP Device name: TBA03501074(6500)
```

Now the tx fiber strand of port 2/1 on the Catalyst 6500 is removed. The Catalyst 3550 shows the link-down status, whereas the Catalyst 6500 shows the port in connected status, as illustrated in Examples 7-30 and 7-31.

Example 7-30 *Checking the Interface Status of the Fiber Link on Cisco CatOS–Based Catalyst 6500 Switches*

```
6500> (enable) show port status 2/1
Port  Name                 Status     Vlan       Duplex Speed Type
----- -------------------- ---------- ---------- ------ ----- -----------
 2/1                       connected  1          full   1000  1000-LX/LH
```

Example 7-31 *Checking the Interface Status of the Fiber Link on a Catalyst 3550 Switch*

```
3550#show interfaces GigabitEthernet 0/1
GigabitEthernet0/1 is down, line protocol is down (notconnect)
  Hardware is Gigabit Ethernet, address is 0008.a391.0399 (bia 0008.a391.0399)
  MTU 1500 bytes, BW 1000000 Kbit, DLY 10 usec,
     reliability 255/255, txload 1/255, rxload 1/255
  Encapsulation ARPA, loopback not set
```

continues

Example 7-31 *Checking the Interface Status of the Fiber Link on a Catalyst 3550 Switch (Continued)*

```
     Keepalive set (10 sec)
     Auto-duplex, Auto-speed
     input flow-control is off, output flow-control is off
     ARP type: ARPA, ARP Timeout 04:00:00
     Last input 00:01:58, output 00:01:58, output hang never
     Last clearing of "show interface" counters never
     Input queue: 0/75/0/0 (size/max/drops/flushes); Total output drops: 0
     Queueing strategy: fifo
     Output queue :0/40 (size/max)
     5 minute input rate 0 bits/sec, 0 packets/sec
     5 minute output rate 0 bits/sec, 0 packets/sec
        2268443 packets input, 166039787 bytes, 0 no buffer
        Received 2149615 broadcasts, 0 runts, 0 giants, 0 throttles
        0 input errors, 0 CRC, 0 frame, 0 overrun, 0 ignored
        0 watchdog, 2149131 multicast, 0 pause input
        0 input packets with dribble condition detected
        618068374 packets output, 2539581729 bytes, 0 underruns
        0 output errors, 0 collisions, 28 interface resets
```

The Cisco Catalyst 6500 maintains the link because auto-negotiation is purposefully disabled. The UDLD state changes to undetermined on the Catalyst 6500, as shown in Example 7-32. Catalyst 3550 displays the current operational status as link down, as shown in Example 7-33.

Example 7-32 *Verification of UDLD Configuration on Cisco CatOS–Based Catalyst 6500 Switches*

```
6500> (enable) show udld port 2/1
UDLD             : enabled
Message Interval : 15 seconds
Port      Admin Status  Aggressive Mode  Link State
--------  ------------  ---------------  ---------------
 2/1      enabled       disabled         undetermined
6500> (enable)
6500> (enable) show spantree 2/1
Port                     Vlan Port-State   Cost      Prio Portfast Channel_id
-----------------------  ---- ----------   --------- ---- -------- ----------
 2/1                     1    forwarding              4   32 disabled 0
6500> (enable)
```

Example 7-33 *Verification of UDLD Configuration on Catalyst 3550 Switches*

```
3550#show udld GigabitEthernet 0/1

Interface Gi0/1
---
Port enable administrative configuration setting: Enabled
Port enable operational state: Enabled
Current bidirectional state: Bidirectional
Current operational state: Link down
Message interval: 15
Time out interval: 5
No neighbor cache information stored
Switch#
```

The UDLD scenario described in this section would lead to a routing black hole because the Catalyst 3550 interface is not up and operational but the Catalyst 6500 switch is still transmitting. To prevent this type of failure, use aggressive mode UDLD. In Examples 7-34 and 7-35, aggressive mode UDLD was enabled on both the switches after connectivity was restored.

Example 7-34 *Configuration and Verification of Aggressive Mode UDLD on Cisco CatOS–Based Catalyst 6500 Switches*

```
6500> (enable) set udld aggressive-mode enable 2/1
Aggressive mode UDLD enabled on port 2/1.
Warning: Aggressive Mode for UniDirectional Link Detectionb
should be enabled only on ports not connected to hubs,
media converters or similar devices.

6500> (enable) show udld port 2/1
UDLD             : enabled
Message Interval : 15 seconds
Port      Admin Status  Aggressive Mode  Link State
--------  ------------  ---------------  ----------------
 2/1      enabled       enabled          bidirectional
```

Example 7-35 *Configuration and Verification of Aggressive Mode UDLD on Catalyst 3550 Switches*

```
3550(config)#interface GigabitEthernet 0/1
3550(config-if)#udld port aggressive

3550#show udld GigabitEthernet 0/1

Interface Gi0/1
- - -
Port enable administrative configuration setting: Enabled / in aggressive mode
Port enable operational state: Enabled / in aggressive mode
Current bidirectional state: Bidirectional
Current operational state: Advertisement - Single neighbor detected
Message interval: 15
Time out interval: 5

   Entry 1
   - - -
   Expiration time: 40
   Device ID: 1
   Current neighbor state: Bidirectional
   Device name: 00307b4e3400
   Port ID: 2/1
   Neighbor echo 1 device: CAT0606X0AL
   Neighbor echo 1 port: Gi0/1

   Message interval: 5
   CDP Device name: TBA03501074(6500)
Switch#
```

If the tx strand of fiber is now removed from port 2/1, the 6500 switch detects the UDLD condition and err-disables the port, as shown in Example 7-36.

Example 7-36 *Aggressive Mode UDLD Err-Disables the Port*

```
2003 Jun 07 15:13:58 %UDLD-3-AGGRDISABLE:Neighbor(s) of port 2/1 disappeared on
bidirectional link. Port disabled
2003 Jun 07 15:13:58 %ETHC-5-PORTFROMSTP:Port 2/1 left bridge port 2/1
6500> (enable) show port status 2/1
Port  Name                  Status      Vlan     Duplex Speed Type
----- --------------------  ----------  -------- ------ ----- -----------
 2/1                        err-disable 1                full  1000 1000-LX/LH
```

This behavior demonstrates that aggressive mode UDLD is the preferable configuration over UDLD because it prevents black holes in the network by actively err-disabling interfaces instead of just informing the system of a unidirectional link. In addition, UDLD sends SNMP traps to the network management station, which are configurable as trigger alarms. These alarms can be set to notify the network administrator immediately upon a UDLD condition. The biggest advantage to aggressive mode UDLD is that it prevents spanning-tree loops, as described in the previous section.

Study Tips

The following bullets review important BCMSN exam preparation points of this chapter. The bullets only briefly highlight the main points of this chapter related to the BCMSN exam. Consult the text of this chapter for additional information regarding these topics. Table 7-12 lists important commands to review for the BCMSN exam:

- Two variations of the EtherChannel protocol exist—PagP and LACP.

- Catalyst switches support up to eight ports in an EtherChannel.

- CDP is a useful Cisco proprietary protocol to collect value information about neighboring devices in a network; however, CDP is considered a security risk on public interfaces.

- MAC address notification is used in service provider environments to track MAC addresses and control user access.

- The debounce timer feature enables Catalyst switches to work with noncompliant NICs by providing administrators the ability to configure higher jitter tolerance.

- Using the baby giant and jumbo frame features can increase TCP throughput performance between servers and allow various encapsulated packets to travel through the switch.

- DHCP for management IP configuration of Catalyst switches eases IP address assignment and avoids manual configuration.

- UDLD and aggressive mode UDLD prevent network outages due to hardware, software, or physical-layer fault resulting in unidirectional links.

- IEEE 802.3 flow control helps to prevent packet loss when a downstream switch receive buffer is full. Pause frames are sent to the upstream switch to indicate the congestion condition.

- The Layer 3 protocol filtering feature filters certain Layer 3 protocol packets from entering the network.

- The broadcast and multicast suppression feature prevents an unauthorized or malfunctioning device from flooding and disrupting the network.

- The error-disable feature prevents many erroneous conditions that generally disrupt the multilayer switch network. The error-disable features prevent these conditions by error-disabling (shutting down) the interface in question. In addition, error-disable is a major function of other features such as BPDU guard, UDLD, and so on.

Table 7-12   *Commands to Review*

Command	Description
`(config)#errdisable detect cause [all │arp-inspection │ dhcp-rate-limit │ dtp-flap │ gbic-invalid │ l2ptguard │ link-flap │ pagp-flap]`	Configures error-disable feature detection causes
`(config-if)#channel-group group-number mode {active │ auto │ desirable │ on │ passive}`	Configures the interface to be part of a EtherChannel group in the specified mode of operation
`(config-if)#udld port aggressive`	Configures aggressive mode UDLD on the interface regardless of global default
`errdisable recovery cause {all │ arp-inspection │ bpduguard │ channel-misconfig │ dhcp-rate-limit │ dtp-flap │ gbic-invalid │ l2ptguard │ link-flap │ pagp-flap │ pesecure-violation │ security-violation │ storm-control │ udld │ unicastflood │ vmps}`	Configures error-disable feature recovery causes
`show cdp neighbor`	Displays information about neighboring devices discovered via CDP
`show cdp neighbor detail`	Displays detailed information about neighboring devices discovered via CDP
`show etherchannel summary`	Displays a one-line summary for each EtherChannel group
`show interface`	Displays status and statistics regarding all the interfaces present in the system
`show interfaces interface-id switchport`	Displays information related to switchport configuration of the specified interface
`show interfaces interface-id trunk`	Displays information related to trunk configuration for the specified interface
`show interfaces port-channel {port-channel-interface-number}`	Displays the status and statistics information regarding the specified EtherChannel interface
`show ip interface brief`	Displays the status of IP protocol information of all interfaces present in the system

continues

Table 7-12 *Commands to Review (Continued)*

Command	Description
`show ip protocols`	Displays information regarding IP configured routing protocol process parameters and statistics
`show ip route`	Displays the IP routing table
`show running-config`	Displays the running configuration of the system
`show udld` *interface-id*	Displays the UDLD status information for the specified interface
`show version`	Displays the software and hardware version running on the system

Summary

Layer 2 and Layer 3 advanced features discussed in this chapter are essential to enhance network performance and to prevent unexpected network outages.

The features described in this chapter are not required in every network scenario. The administrator needs to understand and apply the features on appropriate switches to achieve maximum benefit.

Configuration Exercise

Complete this configuration exercise to practice features discussed in this chapter.

Required Resources

The following resources and equipment are required to complete this exercise:

- Catalyst switches, as shown in Figure 7-16
- Terminal server connected to the console port of each laboratory device
- PC connected to the terminal server to access the devices

Exercise Objective

The devices in the network should be connected and ready for use. In this exercise, you configure and verify some of the features reviewed in this chapter.

After completing this exercise, you will be able to

- Configure and verify PAgP EtherChannel
- Configure and verify LACP EtherChannel
- Configure and verify CDP

- Configure and verify UDLD and aggressive mode UDLD
- Configure and verify jumbo frames
- Configure and verify error-disable

Network Diagram

Figure 7-16 shows the network layout for this configuration exercise.

Figure 7-16 *Network Diagram for Configuration Exercise*

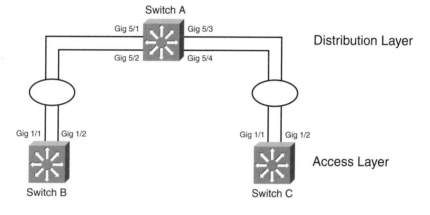

Command List

In this configuration exercise, you use the commands listed in Table 7-13. The commands are listed in alphabetical order so that you can easily locate the information you need. Refer to this table if you need configuration command assistance during the exercise.

Table 7-13 *Command List for Configuration Exercise*

Command	Description
`cdp enable`	Enables CDP protocol on a per-interface basis. To disable CDP on a per-interface basis, use the **no cdp enable** command.
`cdp run`	Enables CDP protocol globally on the router or switch.
`channel-group port-channel-number mode desirable`	Assigns and configures an interface to a PAgP EtherChannel.
`channel-protocol lacp`	Specifies the EtherChannel protocol as LACP.
`channel-group group-number mode active`	Assigns and configures an interface to an LACP EtherChannel.

continues

Table 7-13 *Command List for Configuration Exercise (Continued)*

Command	Description
`configure terminal`	From privileged EXEC mode, enters global configuration mode.
`end`	Exits configuration mode.
`errdisable detect cause all`	Enables error-disable detection for all supported error conditions.
`errdisable recovery cause all`	Enables error-disable recovery for all supported error conditions.
`exit`	Exits the current mode.
`interface FastEthernet | GigabitEthernet` *slot/port*	Enters interface configuration mode for a Catalyst switch with a Fast Ethernet or Gigabit Ethernet interface installed.
`mtu` *size*	Configures MTU size up to jumbo frame sizes (9k) on an interface of a Catalyst 4500 switch.
`show cdp`	Displays the CDP protocol status and parameters on the device.
`show cdp neighbors`	Displays a list of all the neighboring devices discovered through the CDP protocol.
`show errdisable detect`	Displays the status of the error-disable detection causes configured on the switch.
`show errdisable recovery`	Displays the status of the error-disable recovery causes configured on the switch as well as any interfaces about to be recovered from an error condition.
`show etherchannel summary`	Displays EtherChannel information for a channel with a one-line summary per channel group.
`show interfaces mtu module` *module-number*	Displays the configured MTU value of interfaces belonging to a specified module.
`show running-config module` *module-number*	Displays running configuration of the specific module.
`udld port aggressive`	Enables aggressive mode UDLD on an interface in Cisco IOS.

Task 1: Configure and Verify EtherChannel

Step 1   For EtherChannel to work properly, make sure the ports on Switch A, B, and C are configured similarly. To do so, use the **show running-config interface** *interface-id* or **show running-config module** *module-number* command on the Cisco IOS–based switches.

```
SwitchA#show running-config module 5
Building configuration...
```

```
Current configuration : 191 bytes
!
interface GigabitEthernet5/1
!
interface GigabitEthernet5/2
!
interface GigabitEthernet5/3
!
interface GigabitEthernet5/4
!
interface GigabitEthernet5/5
!
interface GigabitEthernet5/6
end
```

```
SwitchB#show running-config module 1
Building configuration...

Current configuration : 67 bytes
!
interface GigabitEthernet1/1
!
interface GigabitEthernet1/2
end
```

```
SwitchC#show running-config module 1
Building configuration...

Current configuration : 67 bytes
!
interface GigabitEthernet1/1
!
interface GigabitEthernet1/2
end
```

Step 2   Configure a Layer 2 EtherChannel between Switch A and B using the
PAgP protocol. To do so, use the interface-level **channel-group** *group-id*
command on Cisco IOS–based switches.

```
SwitchA#configure terminal
Enter configuration commands, one per line.  End with CNTL/Z.
SwitchA(config)#interface gigabitEthernet 5/1
SwitchA(config-if)#channel-group 10 mode desirable
Creating a port-channel interface Port-channel 10

SwitchA(config-if)#interface gigabitEthernet 5/2
SwitchA(config-if)#channel-group 10 mode desirable
SwitchA(config-if)#end
SwitchA#
```

```
*Nov  7 13:14:28: %SYS-5-CONFIG_I: Configured from console by console
*Nov  7 13:14:55: %EC-5-BUNDLE: Interface GigabitEthernet5/1 joined
port-channel Port-channel10
*Nov  7 13:14:59: %EC-5-BUNDLE: Interface GigabitEthernet5/2 joined
port-channel Port-channel10
```

```
SwitchB#configure terminal
Enter configuration commands, one per line.  End with CNTL/Z.
SwitchB(config)#interface gigabitEthernet 1/1
SwitchB(config-if)#channel-group 10 mode desirable
Creating a port-channel interface Port-channel 10

SwitchB(config-if)#interface gigabitEthernet 1/2
SwitchB(config-if)#channel-group 10 mode desirable
SwitchB(config-if)#end
6w2d: %EC-5-BUNDLE: Interface GigabitEthernet1/1 joined port-channel
Port-channel10
SwitchB#
6w2d: %SYS-5-CONFIG_I: Configured from console by console
6w2d: %EC-5-BUNDLE: Interface GigabitEthernet1/2 joined port-channel
Port-channel10
```

Step 3 Verify the PAgP EtherChannel operational status using the **show etherchannel summary** command on Cisco IOS–based switches.

```
SwitchA#show etherchannel summary
Flags:  D - down        P - in port-channel
        I - stand-alone s - suspended
        R - Layer3      S - Layer2
        U - in use      f - failed to allocate aggregator
        u - unsuitable for bundling
        w - waiting to be aggregated
        d - default port


Number of channel-groups in use: 1
Number of aggregators:           1

Group  Port-channel  Protocol    Ports
------+------------+-----------+----------------------------------------
10     Po10(SU)        PAgP      Gi5/1(P)    Gi5/2(P)
```

```
SwitchB#show etherchannel summary
Flags:  D - down        P - in port-channel
        I - stand-alone s - suspended
        R - Layer3      S - Layer2
        U - in use      f - failed to allocate aggregator
        u - unsuitable for bundling
```

```
            w - waiting to be aggregated
            d - default port


Number of channel-groups in use: 1
Number of aggregators:            1

Group  Port-channel  Protocol    Ports
------+-------------+-----------+---------------------------------
10     Po10(SU)       PAgP        Gi1/1(P)    Gi1/2(P)
```

Task 2: Configure and Verify LACP EtherChannel

Step 1   Configure a Layer 2 LACP EtherChannel between switch A and switch C. Use the **channel-protocol lacp** command to change the EtherChannel protocol, and use the **channel-group** *group-number* **mode active** command on Cisco IOS–based Catalyst switches to configure the EtherChannel.

```
SwitchA#configure terminal
Enter configuration commands, one per line.  End with CNTL/Z.
SwitchA(config)#interface gigabitEthernet 5/3
SwitchA(config-if)#channel-protocol lacp
SwitchA(config-if)#channel-group 20 mode active
Creating a port-channel interface Port-channel 20

SwitchA(config-if)#interface gigabitEthernet 5/4
SwitchA(config-if)#channel-protocol lacp
SwitchA(config-if)#channel-group 20 mode active
SwitchA(config-if)#end
SwitchA#
*Nov  7 13:23:04: %SYS-5-CONFIG_I: Configured from console by console
*Nov  7 13:23:06: %EC-5-L3DONTBNDL2: Gi5/3 suspended: LACP currently not
enabled on the remote port.
*Nov  7 13:23:12: %EC-5-L3DONTBNDL2: Gi5/4 suspended: LACP currently not
enabled on the remote port.
*Nov  7 13:23:35: %EC-5-BUNDLE: Interface Gi5/3 joined port-channel Po20
*Nov  7 13:23:36: %EC-5-L3DONTBNDL2: Gi5/4 suspended: LACP currently not
enabled on the remote port.
*Nov  7 13:23:38: %EC-5-BUNDLE: Interface Gi5/4 joined port-channel Po20
SwitchC#configure terminal
Enter configuration commands, one per line.  End with CNTL/Z.
SwitchC(config)#interface GigabitEthernet 1/1
SwitchC(config-if)#channel-protocol lacp
SwitchA(config-if)#channel-group 20 mode active
Creating a port-channel interface Port-channel 20
```

```
SwitchC(config-if)#interface GigabitEthernet 1/2
SwitchC(config-if)#channel-protocol lacp
SwitchA(config-if)#channel-group 20 mode active
SwitchC(config-if)#end
*Nov 14 04:15:44.746: %EC-5-BUNDLE: Interface Gi1/1 joined port-channel
Po20
SwitchC#
*Nov 14 04:15:46.474: %SYS-5-CONFIG_I: Configured from console by console
*Nov 14 04:15:47.646: %EC-5-BUNDLE: Interface Gi1/2 joined port-channel
Po20
```

Step 2 Verify the LACP EtherChannel operational status using the **show etherchannel summary** command on Cisco IOS–based Catalyst switches.

```
SwitchA#show etherchannel summary
Flags:  D - down        P - in port-channel
        I - stand-alone s - suspended
        R - Layer3      S - Layer2
        U - in use      f - failed to allocate aggregator
        u - unsuitable for bundling
        w - waiting to be aggregated
        d - default port


Number of channel-groups in use: 2
Number of aggregators:           2

Group  Port-channel  Protocol    Ports
------+-------------+-----------+-----------------------------------
10     Po10(SU)       PAgP        Gi5/1(P)    Gi5/2(P)
20     Po20(SU)       LACP        Gi5/3(P)    Gi5/4(P)
```

```
SwitchC#show etherchannel summary
Flags:  D - down        P - in port-channel
        I - stand-alone s - suspended
        R - Layer3      S - Layer2
        U - in use      f - failed to allocate aggregator
        u - unsuitable for bundling
        w - waiting to be aggregated
        d - default port


Number of channel-groups in use: 1
Number of aggregators:           1

Group  Port-channel  Protocol    Ports
------+-------------+-----------+-----------------------------------
20     Po20(SU)       LACP        Gi1/1(P)    Gi1/2(P)
```

Task 3: Configure and Verify CDP

Step 1   CDP is enabled by default on the Cisco Catalyst switches and routers on all interfaces. If for some reason CDP was disabled, you can turn it back on using the **cdp run** global command and **cdp enable** interface-level command. Enable CDP on the switch A GigabitEthernet 5/1 interface.

```
SwitchA#configure terminal
Enter configuration commands, one per line.  End with CNTL/Z.
SwitchA(config)#cdp run
SwitchA(config)#interface gigabitEthernet 5/1
SwitchA(config-if)#cdp enable
SwitchA(config-if)#end
SwitchA#
```

Step 2   Verify the CDP operation status and neighbors on all three switches.

```
SwitchA#show cdp
Global CDP information:
        Sending CDP packets every 60 seconds
        Sending a holdtime value of 180 seconds
        Sending CDPv2 advertisements is enabled
SwitchA#show cdp neighbors
Capability Codes: R - Router, T - Trans Bridge, B - Source Route Bridge
                  S - Switch, H - Host, I - IGMP, r - Repeater, P - Phone

Device ID      Local Intrfce    Holdtme    Capability  Platform  Port ID
SwitchB        Gig 5/2          178          R S I     WS-C4006  Gig 1/2
SwitchB        Gig 5/1          178          R S I     WS-C4006  Gig 1/1
SwitchC        Gig 5/4          153          R S I     WS-C4503  Gig 1/2
SwitchC        Gig 5/3          150          R S I     WS-C4503  Gig 1/1
SwitchB#show cdp
Global CDP information:
        Sending CDP packets every 60 seconds
        Sending a holdtime value of 180 seconds
        Sending CDPv2 advertisements is enabled
SwitchB#show cdp neighbors
Capability Codes: R - Router, T - Trans Bridge, B - Source Route Bridge
                  S - Switch, H - Host, I - IGMP, r - Repeater, P - Phone

Device ID      Local Intrfce    Holdtme    Capability  Platform  Port ID
SwitchA        Gig 1/2          160          R S I     WS-C4506  Gig 5/2
SwitchA        Gig 1/1          160          R S I     WS-C4506  Gig 5/1
SwitchC#show cdp
Global CDP information:
        Sending CDP packets every 60 seconds
        Sending a holdtime value of 180 seconds
        Sending CDPv2 advertisements is enabled
```

```
SwitchC#show cdp neighbors
Capability Codes: R - Router, T - Trans Bridge, B - Source Route Bridge
                  S - Switch, H - Host, I - IGMP, r - Repeater, P - Phone

Device ID      Local Intrfce     Holdtme    Capability  Platform   Port ID
SwitchA        Gig 1/2           144        R S I       WS-C4506   Gig 5/4
SwitchA        Gig 1/1           144        R S I       WS-C4506   Gig 5/3
```

Task 4: Configure and Verify Aggressive Mode UDLD

Step 1   On the interconnecting ports between switches, configure aggressive mode UDLD. To do so, use the interface-level **udld port aggressive** command on Cisco IOS–based switches.

```
SwitchA#configure terminal
Enter configuration commands, one per line.  End with CNTL/Z.
SwitchA(config)#interface  gigabitEthernet 5/1
SwitchA(config-if)#udld port aggressive
SwitchA(config-if)#interface  gigabitEthernet 5/2
SwitchA(config-if)#udld port aggressive
SwitchA(config-if)#interface  gigabitEthernet 5/3
SwitchA(config-if)#udld port aggressive
SwitchA(config-if)#interface  gigabitEthernet 5/4
SwitchA(config-if)#udld port aggressive
SwitchA(config-if)#end
SwitchA#
```

```
SwitchB#configure terminal
Enter configuration commands, one per line.  End with CNTL/Z.
SwitchB(config)#interface gigabitethernet 1/1
SwitchB(config-if)#udld port aggressive
SwitchB(config-if)#interface gigabitethernet 1/2
SwitchB(config-if)#udld port aggressive
SwitchB(config-if)#end
SwitchB#
```

```
SwitchC#configure terminal
Enter configuration commands, one per line.  End with CNTL/Z.
SwitchC(config)#interface gigabitethernet 1/1
SwitchC(config-if)#udld port aggressive
SwitchC(config)#interface gigabitethernet 1/2
SwitchC(config-if)#udld port aggressive
SwitchC(config-if)#end
SwitchC#
```

Step 2   Verify the UDLD status using the **show udld** *interface-id* command on
Cisco IOS–based switches.

```
SwitchA#show udld gigabitEthernet 5/1

Interface Gi5/1
---
Port enable administrative configuration setting: Enabled / in
aggressive mode
Port enable operational state: Enabled / in aggressive mode
Current bidirectional state: Bidirectional
Current operational state: Advertisement - Single neighbor detected
Message interval: 15
Time out interval: 5

     Entry 1
     ---
     Expiration time: 38
     Device ID: 1
     Current neighbor state: Bidirectional
     Device name: FOX06310RW1
     Port ID: Gi1/1
     Neighbor echo 1 device: FOX0627A001
     Neighbor echo 1 port: Gi5/1

     Message interval: 15
     Time out interval: 5
     CDP Device name: SwitchB

SwitchA#show udld gigabitEthernet 5/3

Interface Gi5/3
---
Port enable administrative configuration setting: Enabled / in
aggressive mode
Port enable operational state: Enabled / in aggressive mode
Current bidirectional state: Bidirectional
Current operational state: Advertisement - Single neighbor detected
Message interval: 15
Time out interval: 5

     Entry 1
     ---
     Expiration time: 34
     Device ID: 1
     Current neighbor state: Bidirectional
     Device name: FOX06210AXY
```

```
        Port ID: Gi1/1
        Neighbor echo 1 device: FOX0627A001
        Neighbor echo 1 port: Gi5/3

        Message interval: 15
        Time out interval: 5
CDP Device name: SwitchC
```

```
SwitchB#show udld gigabitEthernet 1/1

Interface Gi1/1
---
Port enable administrative configuration setting: Enabled / in
aggressive mode
Port enable operational state: Enabled / in aggressive mode
Current bidirectional state: Bidirectional
Current operational state: Advertisement - Single neighbor detected
Message interval: 15
Time out interval: 5

    Entry 1
    ---
    Expiration time: 36
    Device ID: 1
    Current neighbor state: Bidirectional
    Device name: FOX0627A001
    Port ID: Gi5/1
    Neighbor echo 1 device: FOX06310RW1
    Neighbor echo 1 port: Gi1/1

    Message interval: 15
    Time out interval: 5
    CDP Device name: SwitchA
```

```
SwitchC#show udld gigabitEthernet 1/1

Interface Gi1/1
---
Port enable administrative configuration setting: Enabled / in
aggressive mode
Port enable operational state: Enabled / in aggressive mode
Current bidirectional state: Bidirectional
Current operational state: Advertisement - Single neighbor detected
Message interval: 15
Time out interval: 5

    Entry 1
    ---
```

```
                    Expiration time: 42
                    Device ID: 1
                    Current neighbor state: Bidirectional
                    Device name: FOX0627A001
                    Port ID: Gi5/3
                    Neighbor echo 1 device: FOX06210AXY
                    Neighbor echo 1 port: Gi1/1

                    Message interval: 15
                    Time out interval: 5
            CDP Device name: SwitchA
```

Task 5: Configure and Verify Jumbo Frame

Step 1   Enable jumbo frames on all interconnecting interfaces on switch A, switch B, and switch C. Use the **mtu 9198** interface level command on a Cisco IOS–based Catalyst 4500 switch. Because you are changing the MTU for interfaces in an EtherChannel, apply the command on the logical port-channel interface.

```
SwitchA#configure terminal
Enter configuration commands, one per line.  End with CNTL/Z.
SwitchA(config)#interface port-channel 10
SwitchA(config-if)#mtu 9198
*Nov  7 14:57:34: %EC-5-UNBUNDLE: Interface GigabitEthernet5/2 left the
port-channel Port-channel10
*Nov  7 14:57:34: %EC-5-CANNOT_BUNDLE2: Gi5/2 is not compatible with
Gi5/1 and will be suspended (MTU of Gi5/2 is 9198, Gi5/1 is 1500)
*Nov  7 14:57:34: %EC-5-UNBUNDLE: Interface GigabitEthernet5/1 left the
port-channel Port-channel10
*Nov  7 14:57:34: %EC-5-COMPATIBLE: Gi5/2 is compatible with port-
channel members
*Nov  7 14:57:36: %EC-5-BUNDLE: Interface GigabitEthernet5/2 joined
port-channel Port-channel10
*Nov  7 14:57:36: %EC-5-BUNDLE: Interface GigabitEthernet5/1 joined
port-channel Port-channel10
SwitchA(config-if)#interface port-channel 20
SwitchA(config-if)#mtu 9198
*Nov  7 14:57:43: %EC-5-CANNOT_BUNDLE2: Gi5/4 is not compatible with
Gi5/3 and will be suspended (MTU of Gi5/4 is 9198, Gi5/3 is 1500)
*Nov  7 14:57:43: %EC-5-UNBUNDLE: Interface Gi5/4 left the port-channel
Po20
*Nov  7 14:57:43: %EC-5-COMPATIBLE: Gi5/4 is compatible with port-
channel members
*Nov  7 14:57:45: %EC-5-BUNDLE: Interface Gi5/4 joined port-channel Po20
SwitchA(config-if)#end
SwitchA#
```

```
SwitchB#configure terminal
Enter configuration commands, one per line.  End with CNTL/Z.
SwitchB(config)#interface port-channel 10
SwitchB(config-if)#mtu 9198
SwitchB(config-if)#end
SwitchB#
6w2d: %EC-5-UNBUNDLE: Interface GigabitEthernet1/2 left the port-
channel Port-channel10
6w2d: %EC-5-CANNOT_BUNDLE2: Gi1/2 is not compatible with Gi1/1 and will
be suspended (MTU of Gi1/2 is 9198, Gi1/1 is 1500)
6w2d: %EC-5-UNBUNDLE: Interface GigabitEthernet1/1 left the port-
channel Port-channel10
6w2d: %EC-5-COMPATIBLE: Gi1/2 is compatible with port-channel members
6w2d: %SYS-5-CONFIG_I: Configured from console by console
SwitchB#
6w2d: %EC-5-BUNDLE: Interface GigabitEthernet1/2 joined port-channel
Port-channel10
6w2d: %EC-5-BUNDLE: Interface GigabitEthernet1/1 joined port-channel
Port-channel10
```

```
SwitchC#configure terminal
Enter configuration commands, one per line.  End with CNTL/Z.
SwitchC(config)#interface port-channel 20
SwitchC(config-if)#mtu 9198
SwitchC(config-if)#end
SwitchC#
*Nov 14 05:52:19.025: %EC-5-CANNOT_BUNDLE2: Gi1/2 is not compatible with
Gi1/1 and will be suspended (MTU of Gi1/2 is 9198, Gi1/1 is 1500)
*Nov 14 05:52:19.025: %EC-5-UNBUNDLE: Interface Gi1/2 left the port-
channel Po20
*Nov 14 05:52:19.033: %EC-5-COMPATIBLE: Gi1/2 is compatible with port-
channel members
*Nov 14 05:52:19.649: %SYS-5-CONFIG_I: Configured from console by
console
*Nov 14 05:52:20.841: %EC-5-BUNDLE: Interface Gi1/2 joined port-channel
Po20
```

Step 2 Verify the jumbo frame configuration using the **show interface mtu** *interface-id* command or the **show interface mtu module** *module-number* command on Cisco IOS–based Catalyst switches.

```
SwitchA#show interfaces mtu module 5
```

Port	Name	MTU
Gi5/1		9198
Gi5/2		9198
Gi5/3		9198
Gi5/4		9198
Gi5/5		1500
Gi5/6		1500

```
SwitchA#
SwitchB#show interfaces mtu module 1

Port     Name                 MTU
Gi1/1                         9198
Gi1/2                         9198
SwitchB#
SwitchC#show interfaces mtu module 1

Port     Name                 MTU
Gi1/1                         9198
Gi1/2                         9198
SwitchC#
```

Task 6: Configure and Verify Error-Disable

Step 1   Enable error-disable detection and recovery for all causes on all three switches in this exercise. Use the **errdisable detect cause all** global level command for enabling detecton for all supported causes on Cisco IOS–based switches. Use the **errdisable recovery cause all** global command for enabling error-disable for all supported causes on Cisco IOS–based Catalyst switches.

```
SwitchA#configure terminal
Enter configuration commands, one per line.  End with CNTL/Z.
SwitchA(config)#errdisable detect cause all
SwitchA(config)#errdisable recovery cause all
SwitchA(config)#end
SwitchA#
SwitchB#configure terminal
Enter configuration commands, one per line.  End with CNTL/Z.
SwitchB(config)#errdisable detect cause all
SwitchB(config)#errdisable recovery cause all
SwitchB(config)#end
SwitchB#
SwitchC#configure terminal
Enter configuration commands, one per line.  End with CNTL/Z.
SwitchC(config)#errdisable detect cause all
SwitchC(config)#errdisable recovery cause all
SwitchC(config)#end
SwitchC#
```

Step 2   Verify the error-disable configuration on Switch A. Use the **show errdisable detect** command to display the status of error-disable detection for the various causes on Cisco IOS–based Catalyst switches. Furthermore, use the **show errdisable recovery** command to display the status of error-disable recovery for the various causes as well as any interfaces that are error-disabled and are about to be recovered.

```
SwitchA#show errdisable detect
ErrDisable Reason    Detection status
----------------     ----------------
udld                 Enabled
bpduguard            Enabled
security-violatio    Enabled
channel-misconfig    Enabled
psecure-violation    Enabled
vmps                 Enabled
loopback             Enabled
unicast-flood        Enabled
pagp-flap            Enabled
dtp-flap             Enabled
link-flap            Enabled
l2ptguard            Enabled
gbic-invalid         Enabled
dhcp-rate-limit      Enabled
unicast-flood        Enabled
storm-control        Enabled
ilpower              Enabled
arp-inspection       Enabled
```

```
SwitchC#show errdisable recovery
ErrDisable Reason    Timer Status
----------------     -------------
udld                 Enabled
bpduguard            Enabled
security-violatio    Enabled
channel-misconfig    Enabled
vmps                 Enabled
pagp-flap            Enabled
dtp-flap             Enabled
link-flap            Enabled
l2ptguard            Enabled
psecure-violation    Enabled
gbic-invalid         Enabled
dhcp-rate-limit      Enabled
unicast-flood        Enabled
storm-control        Enabled
arp-inspection       Enabled
loopback             Enabled

Timer interval: 300 seconds

Interfaces that will be enabled at the next timeout:
```

Review Questions

For multiple-choice questions, there might be more than one correct answer.

1 True or False: Aggressive mode UDLD is similar to normal UDLD except that it has a lower time interval between UDLD messages.

2 True or False: LACP-based EtherChannel can be applied only between Cisco switches.

3 Select the IEEE standard channeling protocol (803.2ad) from the following list:

    a PAgP

    b STP

    c LACP

    d 803.2

    e None of the above

4 On what layer does the UDLD operate in the OSI model?

    a 1

    b 2

    c 3

    d 4

5 What is the maximum default size of Ethernet frames, in bytes, including the Ethernet header and CRC (FCS)?

    a 1500 bytes

    b 1502 bytes

    c 1600 bytes

    d 1518 bytes

    e 9216 bytes

6 What is the maximum size, in bytes, of Ethernet 802.1Q tagged frames?

   a 1500 bytes

   b 1522 bytes

   c 1600 bytes

   d 1518 bytes

   e 9216 bytes

7 What is the size, in bytes, of Layer 2 CRC of an Ethernet frame?

   a 1500 bytes

   b 26 bytes

   c 18 bytes

   d 14 bytes

   e 4 bytes

8 What is the default message interval for UDLD?

   a 3 seconds

   b 20 seconds

   c 60 seconds

   d 15 seconds

   e 300 seconds

9 Select the channel mode that does not belong to LACP.

   a on

   b off

   c active

   d desirable

   e passive

10 Explain the difference between UDLD and aggressive mode UDLD.

11 Which of the following is the default recovery time for an err-disabled interface?

a   300 seconds

b   15 seconds

c   30 seconds

d   2 seconds

e   0 seconds

12 Which of the following error conditions is not supported by the error-disable feature?

a   PAgP flap

b   DTP flap

c   Link flap

d   Route flap

e   UDLD

13 Which of the following protocols prevents packet loss during network congestion on the receiving device?

a   IEEE 802.3af

b   IEEE 802.3

c   IEEE 802.3e

d   IEEE 802.3

e   IEEE 802.3ae

14 Explain why CDP may be a security risk when running on public interfaces.

This chapter covers the following topics:

- Understanding and Configuring Inter-VLAN Routing
- Understanding and Configuring a Router on a Stick
- Verifying Inter-VLAN Routing Configurations
- Understanding and Configuring IP Broadcast Forwarding Across VLANs

## CHAPTER 8

Understanding and Configuring Inter-VLAN Routing

Previous chapters emphasized Layer 2 features and their integration in the multilayer switched network. This and the following chapters discuss, in detail, the importance of Layer 3 routing and its advantages and integration in the multilayer switched network.

Network topologies generally associate VLANs with individual networks or subnetworks. VLANs, as discussed in Chapter 4, "Implementing and Configuring VLANs," limit the broadcast domain and add security. However, network devices in different VLANs cannot communicate with each other without a Layer 3 switch or a router to forward traffic between the VLANs, because inter-VLAN communication demands that the VLANs be in different IP subnets. Cisco provides several solutions to enable inter-VLAN routing. Many Catalyst switches have integrated Layer 3 routing capabilities using hardware switching to achieve line-rate performance. In addition, several families of switches use Layer 3 modules to provide inter-VLAN routing.

This chapter discusses inter-VLAN routing and its inherent advantages to the multilayer switched network. In brief, this chapter covers the following topics:

- IP address hierarchy in a multilayer switched network
- Inter-VLAN routing
- Cisco solutions for inter-VLAN routing
- IP broadcast forwarding to implement solutions such as DHCP relay agent

IP Address Hierarchy in a Multilayer Switched Network

Understanding how to appropriately apply an IP addressing hierarchy to a multilayer switched network is an important concept. If you are reading this book as preparation for the CCNP or CCDP BCMSN switching exam, however, you should understand the basic principle of applying an IP addressing hierarchy. If you need a refresher on IP addressing, consult the following documents at Cisco.com:

- "IP Addressing and Subnetting for New Users" http://www.cisco.com/en/US/tech/tk365/technologies_tech_note09186a00800a67f5.shtml, Document ID: 13788
- "IP Addressing Services" http://www.cisco.com/en/US/tech/tk648/tk361/tsd_technology_support_protocol_home.html

- "Configuring IP Address [in Cisco IOS]" http://www.cisco.com/en/US/customer/ products/ps6350/products_configuration_guide_book09186a008042f219.html (requires Cisco.com username and password)

Two important points to keep in mind when applying an IP addressing hierarchy to the multilayer switched network are as follows:

- For local or end-to-end VLANs, use subnets and supernets depending on the number of hosts that are planned to reside in the respective VLAN. The recommended practice is to have between 100 and 250 hosts per VLAN. Make sure you always plan for future growth in each respective VLAN.

- Use subnets with a 30-bit mask to conserve address space when designing an IP address hierarchy for Layer 3 point-to-point interfaces.

Introduction to Inter-VLAN Routing

Recall from Chapter 4 that a *VLAN* is a logical group of ports, usually belonging to a single IP subnet to control the size of the broadcast domain. Because VLANs isolate traffic to a defined broadcast domain and subnet, network devices in different VLANs cannot communicate with each other natively. In Figure 8-1, VLANs 10, 20, and 30 cannot communicate with each other without the use of a Layer 3 device.

Figure 8-1 *VLAN Isolation*

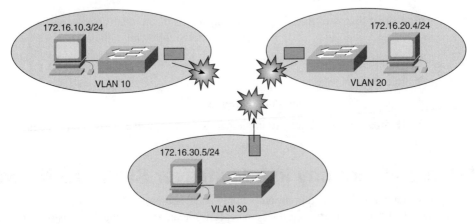

The devices in each VLAN can communicate to the network devices in another VLAN only through a Layer 3 routing device, referred to as an inter-VLAN router (see Figure 8-2).

Cisco recommends the implementation of Layer 3 routing and switching in the Building Distribution submodule or the Building Access submodule of the multilayer switched network to terminate local VLANs. This helps to isolate network problems and to prevent them from affecting the Campus Backbone submodule. In addition, packet manipulation and control of the traffic across VLANs is simplified by routing in the distribution layer instead of the core layer.

Figure 8-2 *Inter-VLAN Routing*

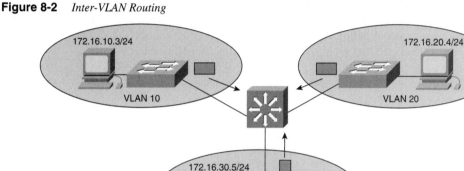

The following devices are capable of providing inter-VLAN routing:

- Any Layer 3 multilayer Catalyst switch
- Any external router with an interface that supports trunking (router on a stick)
- Any external router or group of routers with a separate interface in each VLAN

NOTE   Adding an external router with an individual interface in each VLAN is a nonscalable solution, especially when there are between 20 and 50 VLANs in the network. In addition, adding an external router for inter-VLAN routing on trunk interfaces does not scale beyond 50 VLANs. This chapter discusses only using Layer 3 switches and external routers with trunk interfaces (router on a stick) to route VLANs. Furthermore, Cisco IOS routers support trunking in specific Cisco IOS Software feature sets, such as the IP Plus Feature set. Refer to the documentation on Cisco.com for software requirements before deploying inter-VLAN routing on Cisco IOS routers.

Router on a stick is simple to implement because routers are usually available in every network, but most enterprise networks use multilayer switches to achieve high packet-processing rates using hardware switching. Recall from Chapter 1, "Introduction to Building Cisco Multilayer Switched Networks," that hardware switching yields line-rate performance, scalability, and high availability. In addition, Layer 3 switches usually have packet-switching throughputs in the millions of packets per second (pps), whereas traditional general-purpose routers provide packet switching in the range of 100,000 pps to just over 1 million pps.

Connecting VLANs with Multilayer Catalyst Switches

Many Cisco Catalyst switches support inter-VLAN routing either using integrated Layer 3 modules or with daughter cards. Table 8-1 lists the current models of Cisco Catalyst switches and identifies their inter-VLAN routing capabilities and solutions.

Table 8-1   *Cisco Catalyst Switches with Inter-VLAN Routing Support*

Type of Switch	Inter-VLAN Routing Capability	Inter-VLAN Routing Solutions
Catalyst 2940/2950/2955/ 2960/2970	No	
Catalyst 3550/3750/3760	Yes	Integrated
Catalyst 4000/4500/4948	Yes	Catalyst 4000 running Cisco CatOS with Supervisor I, II, using the Layer 3 module, WS-X4232-L3 Catalyst 4000 with a Supervisor II+, III, IV, or V running Cisco IOS using integrated routing
Catalyst 6500	Yes	Catalyst 6500 with an MSFC, MSFC II, or MSFC III daughter card running Cisco CatOS on the supervisors and Cisco IOS on the MSFC Catalyst 6500 with MSFC, MSFC II, or MSFC III running Cisco Native IOS Catalyst 6500 using a legacy MSM module

Multilayer switches allow for the configuration of interfaces as Layer 2 or Layer 3 interfaces to provide all solutions in one switch. This book discusses Layer 2 interfaces in detail in Chapter 4. The following list is a summary of Layer 2 interfaces and their functionality:

- **Access port**—Carries traffic for a single VLAN
- **Trunk port**—Carries traffic for multiple VLANs using Inter-Switch Link (ISL) encapsulation or 802.1Q tagging

In Cisco IOS, the **switchport** command configures an interface as a Layer 2 interface. The **no switchport** command configures an interface as a Layer 3 interface. Note that different models of Catalyst switches use different default settings for interfaces. For example, all members of the Catalyst 3550 and 4500 families of switches use Layer 2 interfaces by default, whereas members of the Catalyst 6500 family of switches running Cisco IOS use Layer 3 interfaces by default. Recall that default interface configurations do not appear in the running or startup configuration. As a result, depending on which Catalyst family of switches is being used, the **switchport** or **no switchport** command may or may not be present in the running-config or startup-config files. In Cisco CatOS, all interfaces are Layer 2 interfaces.

The Catalyst multilayer switches support three different types of Layer 3 interfaces:

* **Routed port**—A pure Layer 3 interface similar to a routed port on a Cisco IOS router.
* **Switch virtual interface (SVI)**—A virtual VLAN interface for inter-VLAN routing. In other words, SVIs are the virtual routed VLAN interfaces.
* **Bridge virtual interface (BVI)**—A Layer 3 virtual bridging interface.

With the advent of high-performance switches such as the Catalyst 6500 and Catalyst 4500, almost every function, from spanning tree to routing, is done through hardware switching using features such as MLS and Cisco Express Forwarding (CEF)-based MLS, both of which are discussed in detail in later chapters.

All Layer 3 Cisco Catalyst switches support routing protocols, but several models of Catalyst switches require enhanced software for specific routing protocol features. Table 8-2 illustrates the types of Catalyst switches that support routing and the types of routing protocols they support.

Table 8-2   *Routing Protocol Support for Cisco Catalyst Layer 3 Switches*

Model of Layer 3 Catalyst Switch	Routing Protocols	Notes
Catalyst 3550/ 3560/3750/3760	RIP, OSPF, IGRP, EIGRP, BGP, etc.	If the switch is running a Standard Multilayer Software Image (SMI), only default routing, static routing, and RIP are supported. All other routing protocols require the Enhanced Standard Multilayer Software Image (EMI).
Catalyst 4000/ 4500/4948	RIP, OSPF, IGRP, EIGRP, BGP, etc.	With Cisco IOS, the Catalyst 4000/4500 with a Supervisor III, IV, and V require a special license to run BGP, EIGRP, OSPF, and IGRP. Catalyst 4000/4500 with a Supervisor II+ supports only static routes and RIP versions 1 and 2. With the WS-X4232-L3 routing module, BGP is not supported.
Catalyst 6500	RIP, OSPF, IGRP, EIGRP, BGP, etc.	BGP, Exterior Gateway Protocol (EGP) and IS-IS, etc., require the InterDomain Routing Feature License.

Routed Ports

A *routed port* is a physical port that acts similarly to a port on a traditional router with Layer 3 addresses configured. Unlike an access port, a routed port is not associated with a particular VLAN. A routed port behaves like a regular router interface, except that it does not support subinterfaces as with Cisco IOS routers.

Routed ports are used for point-to-point links; connecting WAN routers and security devices are examples of the use of routed ports. In the multilayer switched network, routed ports are mostly configured between the switches in the Campus Backbone submodules and between switches in the Campus Backbone and Building Distribution submodules if Layer 3 routing is applied in the distribution layer. Figure 8-3 illustrates an example of routed ports for point-to-point links in a multilayer switched network.

Figure 8-3   *Routed Ports in a Multilayer Switched Network*

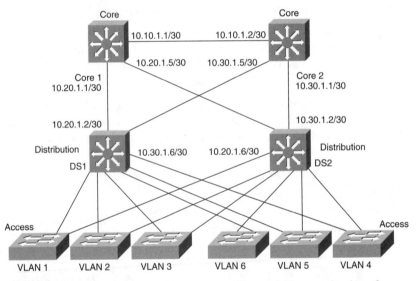

To configure routed ports, make sure to configure the respective interface as a Layer 3 interface using the **no switchport** interface command, if the default configurations of the interfaces are Layer 2 interfaces as with the Catalyst 3550 family of switches. In addition, assign an IP address and other Layer 3 parameters as necessary. After assigning the IP address, make certain that IP routing is globally enabled and that applicable routing protocols are configured. Note that routed ports are available only in Cisco IOS.

NOTE	Entering the **no switchport** interface configuration command shuts down the interface and then re-enables it, which might generate messages on the device to which the interface is connected. When you use this command to put the interface into Layer 3 mode, you delete any Layer 2 characteristics configured on the interface.

Example 8-1 illustrates the configuration of routed ports for a Catalyst 6500 switch running Cisco IOS. In this example, if the port is a Layer 2 port, the switch returns an error message upon attempted configuration.

Example 8-1   *Configuration of Routed Ports in Cisco IOS*

```
Core(config)#interface GigabitEthernet 1/1
Core(Coreonfig-if)#no switchport
Core(config-if)#ip address 10.10.1.1 255.255.255.252
Core(config-if)#exit
Core(config)#interface GigabitEthernet 1/2
Core(config-if)#ip address 10.20.1.254 255.255.255.252
% IP addresses may not be configured on L2 links.
Core(config-if)#no switchport
Core(config-if)#ip address 10.20.1.254 255.255.255.252
Core(config-if)#end
```

Switch Virtual Interfaces

Switch virtual interfaces (SVI) are Layer 3 interfaces that are configured on multilayer Catalyst switches that are used for inter-VLAN routing. An SVI is a VLAN interface that is associated with only one (that is, a unique) VLAN-ID to enable routing capability on that VLAN, as shown in Figure 8-4. In Figure 8-4, to configure communication between VLANs, such as VLAN 10 and VLAN 20, you must configure each SVI with an IP address and subnet mask in the chosen address range for that subnet. The IP address associated with the VLAN interface is the default gateway of the workstation. In this case, the switch routes frames from host A to host B directly on the switch via hardware switching without requiring an external router. An SVI is mostly implemented to interconnect the VLANs on the Building Distribution submodules or the Building Access submodules in the multilayer switched network.

Figure 8-4   *Routing Between VLANs Using a Multilayer Switch*

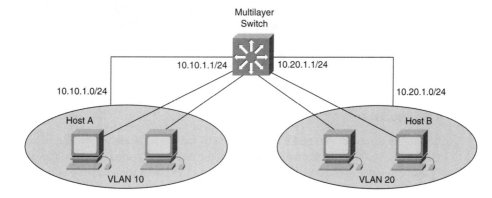

To configure an SVI for inter-VLAN routing on a Catalyst switch, such as the Catalyst 6000 Series, perform these steps:

Step 1   (Optional.) Enable IP routing on the router.

```
Switch(config)#ip routing
```

Step 2   (Optional.) Specify an IP routing protocol or use static routes.

```
Switch(config)#router ip_routing_protocol options
```

Step 3   Specify an SVI by using a VLAN interface command.

```
Switch(config)#interface vlan vlan-id
```

Step 4   Assign an IP address to the VLAN.

```
Switch(config-if)#ip address ip_address subnetmask
```

Step 5   Enable the interface.

```
Switch(config-if)#no shutdown
```

Example 8-2 shows the configuration of IP routing on a Catalyst 6500 by creating VLAN interfaces and assigning IP addresses and subnet masks to the interfaces.

Example 8-2   *Inter-VLAN Routing Using SVIs*

```
Switch#configure terminal
Enter configuration commands, one per line.  End with CNTL/Z.
Switch(config)#ip routing
Switch(config)#router rip
Switch(config-router)#network 10.0.0.0
Switch(config)#interface vlan 10
Switch(config-if)#ip address 10.10.1.1 255.0.0.0
Switch(config-if)#no shutdown
Switch(config-if)#interface vlan 20
Switch(config-if)#ip address 10.20.1.1 255.255.255.0
Switch(config-if)#no shutdown
```

NOTE   Make sure that VLANs are present in the VLAN database before creating SVI (VLAN) interfaces. Interfaces do not forward traffic for a VLAN until the VLAN is present in the VLAN database.

After applying the configuration shown in Example 8-2, hosts in VLAN 100 can communicate with hosts in VLAN 200 if each host is configured with a default gateway of the respective VLAN interface.

The number of routed ports and SVIs supported by the Layer 3 Catalyst switches is not limited by software; however, the relationship between the number of routed ports and the number of Layer 3 interfaces and other features might affect CPU utilization because of hardware limitations. One such example is NAT, because several models of Catalyst switches do not support NAT in hardware. Most Catalyst families of switches have different limitations with regard to the number of SVIs supported. In addition, the number of VLANs and SVIs supported per Catalyst family is not always the same. For example, a switch may support 256 VLAN, but only 64 SVIs (routed VLAN interfaces). Refer to Chapter 4 for details about the number of VLANs supported per Catalyst switch, and always refer to product release notes for the latest details about the number of VLANs and SVIs supported per Catalyst family of switch.

Bridge Virtual Interfaces

A bridge virtual interface (BVI) is a Layer 3 virtual interface that acts like a normal SVI to route packets across bridged or routed domains. Bridging Layer 2 packets across Layer 3 interfaces is a legacy method of moving frames in a network. To configure a BVI to route, use the integrated routing and bridging (IRB) feature, which makes it possible to route a given protocol between routed interfaces and bridge groups within the same device. Specifically, routable traffic is routed to other routed interfaces and bridge groups, while local or unroutable traffic is bridged among the bridged interfaces in the same bridge group. As a result, bridging creates a single instance of spanning tree in multiple VLANs or routed subnets. This type of configuration complicates spanning tree and the behavior of other protocols, which in turn makes troubleshooting difficult.

In today's network, however, bridging across routed domains is highly discouraged. A BVI is useful for migrating bridged networks to routed networks, while hosts on the bridged networks can reach hosts on the routed network during the migration phase.

Only Cisco IOS routers support BVIs. The exceptions to this rule are the Catalyst 2948G-L3 and 4908G-L3 switches and the WS-X4232 Layer 3 module for the Catalyst 4000 switches. These switches use BVIs in place of SVIs for configuration. However, these switches are the only models to use BVIs instead of SVIs. In addition, Cisco intends to have all future models of Catalyst switches use the SVI method of configuring inter-VLAN routing. Again, except for the Catalyst 2948G-L3 and 4908G-L3 switches and the WS-X4232 Layer 3 module, BVIs are not supported on multilayer switches, and the use of BVIs on Cisco IOS routers is discouraged.

Moreover, several Catalyst multilayer switches support fallback bridging methods of forwarding traffic between VLANs. Fallback bridging forwards traffic not routed by the switch, such as SNA, and connects multiple VLANs into one bridge domain by bridging between two or more SVIs or routed ports. As a result, bridging the spanning tree in multiple VLANs creates a single instance of spanning tree for all VLANs. When configuring fallback bridging, you assign SVIs or routed ports to bridge groups, with each SVI or routed port assigned to only one bridge group. All interfaces in the same group belong to the same bridge domain. Cisco does not recommend this practice, however. Instead, it recommends using fallback bridging exclusively for migration because of the hardware-switching limitations of fallback bridging, confusing spanning-tree topologies, and other factors that make troubleshooting difficult.

Router on a Stick (External Router)

An alternative method of implementing inter-VLAN routing is to use an external router, referred to as *router on a stick*. The router on a stick feature requires the use of trunking using either ISL or 802.1Q between the external router and the Catalyst switch. Most of the newer switches only support 802.1Q because it is an open standard. A single trunk can carry traffic for multiple VLANs.

When implementing the 802.1Q trunk, it is important to make sure that the native VLAN is assigned to the same VLAN on each link partner. Refer to Chapter 4 for additional details on configuring trunking on Catalyst switches.

In Figure 8-5, the host on VLAN 10 needs to establish IP TCP sessions with the host on VLAN 20. To perform inter-VLAN routing functions, the router must know how to reach all interconnecting VLANs. As a result, the router must have a separate logical connection for each VLAN using ISL or 802.1Q trunking on a single physical connection. The router then performs the inter-VLAN function in the following way:

1   Each host sends traffic for other subnets to its default gateway, which is a router configured for routing between VLAN 10 and VLAN 20 through a switch.

2   The switch accepts the packets from each VLAN and forwards them to the router with encapsulation or tag for the proper VLAN.

3   The router accepts the packets from each VLAN because the route processor is configured to route traffic between VLANs 10 and 20.

4   The router determines the egress interface and VLAN based on the destination Layer 3 network address.

5   The router rewrites the Layer 2 source and destination MAC address and Layer 2 CRC and then tags or encapsulates the packet to identify the appropriate VLAN.

6   The router places the packet in the output queue of the appropriate egress interface for transmission to the switch; the switch then forwards the packet to the appropriate egress host port.

NOTE   When a host sends traffic to other subnets in a router on a stick configuration, it sends the traffic to the default gateway, which is the IP address of the subinterface configured on the external router (router on a stick). This behavior is the same as the use of SVIs configured on an internal router or Layer 3 switch.

Figure 8-5   *Router on a Stick Solution*

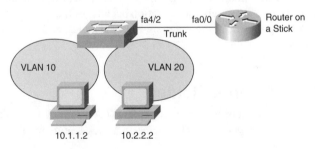

To configure inter-VLAN routing using router on a stick, perform the following steps:

Step 1   Enable trunking on the switch port connecting to the router. (Refer to Chapter 4 for details on configuring trunking on multilayer switches.)

Step 2   Enable the router interface by issuing the **no shutdown** interface command on the router.

```
router(config)#interface {FastEthernet | GigabitEthernet} slot/port
router(config-if)#no shutdown
```

Step 3   On the router, create the subinterfaces for each VLAN that requires inter-VLAN routing.

```
router(config)#interface {FastEthernet | GigabitEthernet}
slot/port.subinterface
```

Step 4   On the router, configure the trunking encapsulation and IP address on the subinterfaces corresponding to the VLANs.

```
router(config-subif)#encapsulation [dot1Q | isl] vlan-id {native}
router(config-subif)#ip address ip_address subnet_mask
```

NOTE   The **encapsulation dot1Q 1 native** command was introduced in Cisco IOS version 12.1(3)T. The **native** keyword indicates the native VLAN. Recall from Chapter 4 that Cisco switches and routers do not tag the native VLAN. The alternative method of configuring the native VLAN is to configure the Layer 3 properties, such as the IP address, on the main interface rather than on the subinterface.

NOTE   The subinterface number of the slot/port number configuration is arbitrary and does not have to match the encapsulation configuration. However, to make configuration easily readable, configure the subinterface ID number as the VLAN ID number.

Example 8-3 shows an example of configuring inter-VLAN routing on an external router and a Catalyst switch running Cisco IOS. Configuration of a router is followed by the switch configuration to configure an interface as a trunk port.

Example 8-3   *Inter-VLAN Routing Using External Router*

```
Router(config)#interface FastEthernet0/0
Router(config-if)#no shutdown
Router(config)#interface FastEthernet 0/0.1
Router(config-subif) description VLAN 1
Router(config-subif)#encapsulation dot1Q 1 native
Router(config-subif)#ip address 10.1.1.1 255.255.255.0
```

continues

Example 8-3 *Inter-VLAN Routing Using External Router (Continued)*

```
Router(config-subif)#exit
Router(config)#interface FastEthernet 0/0.2
Router(config-subif)# description VLAN 2
Router(config-subif)#encapsulation dot1Q 2
Router(config-subif)#ip address 10.2.2.1 255.255.255.0
Router(config-subif)#exit
Router(config)#end
#####Cisco IOS switch Trunking Configuration Connected to Interface FastEthernet0/0
switch(config)#interface FastEthernet 4/2
switch(config-if)#switchport trunk encapsulation dot1q
switch(config-if)#switchport mode trunk
switch(config-if)#end
```

Verifying the Inter-VLAN Routing Configuration

To verify the inter-VLAN routing configuration, use the **ping** command and the **show** commands. The following are the most useful commands for verifying inter-VLAN routing configurations:

- **ping**
- **show running-config**
- **show ip route**
- **show ip protocol**

After the router is properly configured and is connected to the network, it can communicate with other nodes on the network. To test IP connectivity to hosts, use the **ping** command.

To display and verify the current (running) configuration, IP routing information, and IP protocol information, use **show** commands. Example 8-4 displays the inter-VLAN configuration using the **show running-config** command.

Example 8-4 *Displaying Inter-VLAN Configuration*

```
Switch#show running-config
 (text deleted)
!
interface VLAN1
 ip address 10.100.1.1 255.255.255.0

!
interface VLAN11
 ip address 10.100.11.1 255.255.255.0
!
[text deleted]
```

In Example 8-5, the **show ip route** command shows the available IP routes in the router or multilayer switch.

Example 8-5 show ip route *Command*

```
Switch#show ip route
Codes: C -connected,S -static,I -IGRP,R -RIP,M -mobile,B -BGP
D -EIGRP,EX_-EIGRP external,O -OSPF,IA -OSPF inter area
N1 -OSPF NSSA external type 1,N2 -OSPF NSSA external type 2
E1 -OSPF external type 1, E2 -OSPF external type 2, E -EGP
I -IS-IS,L1 -IS-IS level-1,L2 -IS-IS level-2,ia -IS-IS inter area
* -candidate default,U -pre-user static route,o -ODR
P -periodic downloaded static route
Gateway of last resort is not set
10.100.0.0/24 is subnetted, 5 subnets
C  10.100.11.0 is directly connected, Vlan11
C  10.100.12.0 is directly connected, Vlan12
C  10.100.13.0 is directly connected, Vlan13
C  10.100.14.0 is directly connected, Vlan14
C  10.100.1.0 is directly connected, Vlan1
```

The **show ip protocol** command shows information about the routing protocols that are enabled on the switch or router, as shown in Example 8-6.

Example 8-6 show ip protocol *Command*

```
Switch#show ip protocol
Routing Protocol is "eigrp 1"
  Outgoing update filter list for all interfaces is not set
  Incoming update filter list for all interfaces is not set
  Default networks flagged in outgoing updates
  Default networks accepted from incoming updates
  EIGRP metric weight K1=1, K2=0, K3=1, K4=0, K5=0
  EIGRP maximum hopcount 100
  EIGRP maximum metric variance 1
  Redistributing: eigrp 1
  Automatic network summarization is in effect
  Maximum path: 4
  Routing for Networks:
    10.0.0.0
  Passive Interface(s):
   Vlan1
   Vlan11
   Vlan12
   Vlan13
   Vlan14
  Routing Information Sources:
   Gateway         Distance      Last Update
    10.100.117.202        90      20:25:10
    10.100.113.201        90      20:25:10
   Gateway         Distance      Last Update
    10.100.115.202        90      20:25:12
 10.100.111.201        90        20:25:12
  Distance: internal 90 external 170
```

IP Broadcast Forwarding

IP broadcast forwarding is necessary when using VLANs to centrally locate DHCP or other servers where clients rely on broadcasts to locate or communicate with the services running on the server. For example, DHCP requests are IP subnet broadcasts to the 255.255.255.255 address. Routers do not route these packets by default. However, Cisco routers and Layer 3 switches can be configured to forward these DHCP and other UDP broadcast packets to a unicast or directed broadcast address. The broadcast-forwarding features support more than DHCP and can forward any UDP broadcast. Another example of using IP broadcast forwarding is to forward NetBIOS over IP broadcasts for Microsoft Windows clients that are not using WINS servers.

The following list summarizes the solutions that Cisco IOS IP broadcast forwarding features provide:

- DHCP relay agent
- UDP broadcast forwarding

DHCP Relay Agent

DHCP is a client-server application, in which the DHCP client, usually a desktop computer, contacts a DHCP server for configuration parameters using a broadcast request. Today's enterprise networks consist of multiple VLANs, where inter-VLAN routing routes between the subnetworks. Because Layer 3 devices do not pass broadcasts by default, each subnet requires a DHCP server unless the routers are configured to forward the DHCP broadcast using the DHCP relay agent feature, as shown in Figure 8-6.

Figure 8-6 *DHCP Relay Agent*

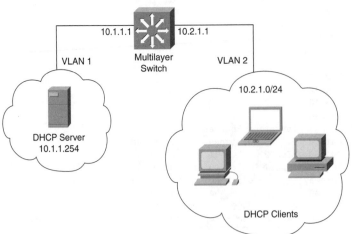

To enable the DHCP relay agent feature, configure the **ip helper-address** command with the DHCP server IP address on the client VLAN interfaces on Cisco Catalyst multilayer switches or on router interfaces in the router on a stick scenario. For multiple DHCP servers, use multiple commands. The **ip helper-address** command not only forwards DHCP UDP packets but also forwards TFTP, DNS, Time, NetBIOS, name server, and BOOTP packets by default.

Example 8-7 illustrates the configuration of the DHCP relay agent feature using the **ip helper-address** command, as shown in Figure 8-6. In this example, 10.1.1.254 is the DHCP server that resides in VLAN 1 and hosts the DHCP clients that reside on VLAN 2 in the 10.1.2.0/24 network.

Example 8-7 *Sample Configuration of DHCP Relay Agent*

```
6500(config)#interface vlan 1
 6500(configif)#description DHCP Server VLAN
6500(config-if)#ip address 10.1.1.1 255.255.255.0
6500(config-if)#no ip directed-broadcast
6500(config-if)#no shutdown
6500(config-if)#interface vlan 2
6500(config-ig)#description DHCP clients
6500(config-if)#ip address 10.2.1.1 255.255.255.0
6500(config-if)#no shutdown
6500(config-if)#no ip directed-broadcast
6500(config-if)#ip helper-address 10.1.1.254
6500(config-if)#exit
```

NOTE   When applying the **ip helper-address** command, make sure the **ip directed-broadcast** is not configured on any outbound interface that the UDP broadcast packets need to traverse. The **no ip directed-broadcast** command configures the router or switch to prevent the translation of a directed broadcast to a physical broadcast. This is a default behavior since Cisco IOS Release 12.0, implemented as a security measure. For more information, consult the following document:

http://www.cisco.com/warp/public/707/21.html Document ID: 13608

UDP Broadcast Forwarding

To specify additional UDP broadcasts for forwarding by the router when configuring the **ip helper-address** interface command, use the following command:

```
ip forward protocol udp udp_ports
```

You can also use this command to configure the router not to forward UDP broadcasts for specific ports. Table 8-3 shows the default UDP ports forwarded by the configuration of the **ip helper-address** command.

Table 8-3 *Default UDP Ports Forwarded by* **ip helper-address**

UDP Application	UDP Port Number
BOOTP/DHCP	Client: 68, Server: 67
DNS	53
Nameserver	42
NetBIOS	Name service: 137, Datagram service: 138
TFTP	69
Time	37

Example 8-8 illustrates the configuration to disallow the forwarding UDP broadcasts for the NetBIOS name service, a default behavior when configuring the **ip helper-address** command. This example also shows the configuration of forwarding UDP packets for mobile-ip and the other default UDP forwarded ports.

Example 8-8 **ip forward-protocol udp** *Command*

```
Router(config)#interface vlan 2
Router(config-if)#ip address 10.2.1.1 255.255.255.0
Router(config-if)#ip helper-address 10.1.1.254
Router(config-if)#no shutdown
Router(config-if)#exit
Router(config)#no ip forward-protocol udp netbios-ns
Router(config)#ip forward-protocol udp mobile-ip
```

Study Tips

The following bullets review important BCMSN exam preparation points of this chapter. The bullets only briefly highlight the important concepts. Consult the text of this chapter for additional information regarding these topics. Table 8-4, which follows this list, provides a summary of the key commands covered in this chapter:

- Inter-VLAN routing is required to route traffic between VLANs. Without inter-VLAN routing, VLANs are simple LAN islands.

- The three available solutions for inter-VLAN routing are Layer 3 switching, router on a stick, and external router without trunking. Most enterprise and service provider networks use Layer 3 switching.

- Layer 3 switching, compared to other inter-VLAN routing solutions, provides the highest packet-forwarding rate with the most features.

- In multilayer switched networks, SVIs are best suited for Distribution or Access submodules.

- Routed interfaces are mainly used for connecting Distribution submodules and Campus Backbone submodules. Routed interfaces commonly use IP address with 30-bit subnet masks.

- IP routing is a global configuration option on all Layer 3 switches.

- Make sure to create VLANs in the VLAN database before creating SVI (VLAN) interfaces. Interfaces do not forward traffic for a VLAN until the VLAN is present in the VLAN database.

- The recommended practice is *not* to bridge across VLANs unless necessary because doing so can create Layer 2 loops, make troubleshooting and topology rendering difficult, and might cause latency issues because packet flow does not follow the hardware-switching path on most Catalyst switches.

- Most Cisco Catalyst Layer 3 switches support all routing protocols; however, they might require special software licenses for specific routing protocols such as BGP.

- To forward DHCP requests to a DHCP server on different VLANs or subnets, configure the DHCP relay agent on first-hop Layer 3 interfaces by using the **ip helper address** command on the VLAN interfaces.

Table 8-4   *Commands to Review*

Command	Description
interface vlan *vlan-id*	Configures an SVI for a specific VLAN for Layer 3 routing.
interface {fastethernet | gigabitethernet} *slot/port.subinterface*	Creates a subinterface corresponding to a specific VLAN on an Ethernet interface of a Cisco IOS router. This command is not used on Layer 3 switches.
encapsulation [dot1Q | isl] *vlan-id* {**native**}	Configures trunking on Ethernet subinterfaces of a router. The **native** keyword specifies that the subinterface operates on the native VLAN.
show ip route	Displays the current routing table of a Cisco router or switch.
show ip protocol	Displays information about the routing protocols currently enabled on a Cisco router or switch.
ping	Tests connectivity between two or more IP-enabled devices.
ip helper-address *dhcp-ip-address*	Configures the DHCP relay agent's destination IP address for forwarding DHCP broadcast request across Layer 3 boundaries. This feature might be used for more than just DHCP broadcasts. In addition, the destination IP address can be unicast, multicast, or broadcast.
ip forward-protocol udp *udp-ports*	Configures additional UDP ports, besides the default ports, on a router or switch for forwarding UDP broadcast across a Layer 3 boundary.

Summary

This chapter discussed in detail Layer 3 routing and its implementation, including coverage of inter-VLAN routing and router on a stick. This chapter can be summarized as follows:

- Inter-VLAN routing provides communication between the devices in different VLANs. Recall that a VLAN is a single broadcast domain, and the devices within a VLAN are not able to communicate beyond VLAN boundaries unless through a Layer 3 device. Multilayer switches support two types of Layer 3 interfaces: routed ports and SVIs (VLAN interfaces).

- Routed ports are point-to-point connections such as those that interconnect the Building Distribution submodules and the Campus Backbone submodules when using Layer 3 in the distribution layer.

- SVIs are VLAN interfaces that route traffic between VLANs, and VLANs group ports together. In multilayer switched networks with Layer 3 in the distribution layer and Layer 2 in the access layer, SVIs are used to route traffic from VLANs on the access-layer switches.

- Using router on a stick is an alternative and legacy method of implementing inter-VLAN routing for low-throughput and latency-tolerant applications.

Configuration Exercise: Configuring Inter-VLAN Routing on Cisco IOS–Based Catalyst Switches

Complete this configuration exercise to familiarize yourself with the initial configuration of inter-VLAN routing on Cisco IOS–based Catalyst switches.

Required Resources

The only resource necessary for this lab exercise is access to a Cisco IOS–based Catalyst switch via the console or in-band access such as SSH. A host workstation for testing the configuration of inter-VLAN routing is optional.

Exercise Objective

The purpose of this exercise is to demonstrate the configuration of inter-VLAN routing in the multilayer switched environment. After completing this exercise, you will be able to perform the following types of configurations on Catalyst switches running Cisco IOS:

- Configure inter-VLAN routing in the distribution submodule switches using SVIs.
- Configure simple routing using EIGRP.

- Configure inter-VLAN routing on the external router using router on a stick.
- Configure SVI interfaces for DHCP forwarding.

Network Diagram

Figure 8-7 shows the network layout for this configuration exercise.

Figure 8-7   *Network Layout for Configuration Exercise*

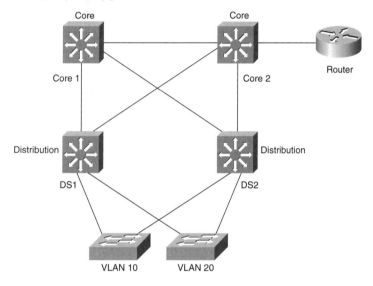

Command List

In this configuration exercise, you use the commands listed in Table 8-5. These commands are in alphabetical order so that you can easily locate the information you need. Refer to this list if you need configuration command assistance during the exercise. The table includes only the specific parameters used in the example and not all the available options for the command.

Table 8-5   *Command List for Configuration Exercise*

Command	Description
configure terminal	Enters global configuration mode.
enable password *password*	Sets the password used to move into privileged EXEC mode.

continues

Command	Description

Table 8-5 *Command List for Configuration Exercise (Continued)*

**encapsulation dot1q	isl** *vlan-id*	Enables trunking and identifies the VLAN for a subinterface on a Cisco IOS router. This command is not used on Layer 3 Catalyst switches.
exit	Exits the current mode.
**interface fastEthernet	gigabitEthernet** *slot/port*	Enters the interface configuration mode for a Catalyst switch with a Fast Ethernet or Gigabit Ethernet interface installed. *slot* refers to the module number, and *port* refers to the front-panel port number.
**interface fastEthernet	gigabitEthernet** *slot/port.number*	Creates a subinterface on an interface of a router. Used for configuring a router on a stick.
interface vlan *vlan-id*	Creates the VLAN interface for inter-VLAN routing.
ip address *address subnetmask*	Specifies the IP address for an interface.
ip helper-address *dhcp-server-address*	Forwards DHCP requests packets across the routed network.
network *network_address*	Enables routing on the networks.
no interface vlan *vlan-id*	Removes the VLAN interface.
no ip directed-broadcast	Configures the router or switch to prevent the translation of a directed broadcast to a physical broadcast. By default, routers are configured with the **no ip directed-broadcast** configuration.
no switchport	Configures an interface as a Layer 3 routed port; an interface is required to be a Layer 3 routed port to accept an IP address.
ping *ip-address*	Sends an ICMP echo to the designated IP address using the default size and response window time settings.
router eigrp *process-id*	Initiates EIGRP on the Layer 3 switches and routers with a specific process ID. Also enters the EIGRP configuration submode for configuring additional EIGRP parameters. The *process-id* is globally significant and should match all EIGRP routers in the AS.
show interfaces [*type slot/port*] **switchport**	Displays the switchport configuration of the interface.
show interfaces trunk	Displays the trunk configuration of the interface.
[no] shutdown	Administratively shuts down or enables an interface.
switchport access vlan *vlan-id*	Specifies the default (native) VLAN, which is used if the interface is not trunking.
switchport mode trunk	Puts the interface into permanent trunking mode and negotiates to convert the link into a trunk link.
Command	**Description**

Table 8-5   *Command List for Configuration Exercise (Continued)*

switchport trunk allowed vlan remove *vlan-list*	Configures the list of VLANs allowed on the trunk.
switchport trunk encapsulation dot1q	Specifies 802.1Q encapsulation explicitly on a trunk link.
switchport trunk encapsulation isl	Specifies ISL encapsulation explicitly on a trunk link.
telnet *ip-address*	Starts a terminal-emulation program from a PC, router, or switch that permits you to access network devices remotely over the network.
vlan database	Enters VLAN configuration mode.
vlan *vlan-id*	Creates a VLAN in the VLAN database and enters the VLAN configuration mode.

Task 1: Configure Inter-VLAN Routing Using SVIs on a Building Distribution Switch

Step 1   Connect to Building Distribution switches DS1 and DS2. Enter privileged EXEC mode using the **enable** command, and then enter global configuration mode using the **configure terminal** command.

Step 2   From global configuration mode, create VLAN virtual interfaces for VLAN 10 and VLAN 20 on each of the Building Distribution switches to enable inter-VLAN routing. The following is the configuration of Building Distribution switch DS1. Use the same steps for DS2, but with the appropriate IP addresses.

```
ds1(config)#ip routing
ds1(config)#interface vlan 10
ds1(config-if)#ip address 10.10.1.1 255.255.255.0
ds1(config-if)#no shutdown
ds1(config-if)#interface vlan 20
ds1(config-if)#ip address 10.20.1.1 255.255.255.0
ds1(config-if)#no shutdown
ds1(config-if)#end
```

Task 2: Configure Simple Routing Using EIGRP

Step 1   Configure EIGRP as the routing protocol on all the Building Distribution and Building Core switches. Consult Cisco.com for additional information regarding routing protocols:

```
DS1(config)#router eigrp 1
DS1(config-router)#network 10.0.0.0
```

Step 2 Verify that the switches are learning routes in the routing table using EIGRP by using the **show ip route** command:

```
DS1#show ip route
3w0d: %SYS-5-CONFIG_I: Configured from console by consoleoute
Codes: C - connected, S - static, I - IGRP, R - RIP, M - mobile, B - BGP
       D - EIGRP, EX - EIGRP external, O - OSPF, IA - OSPF inter area
       N1 - OSPF NSSA external type 1, N2 - OSPF NSSA external type 2
       E1 - OSPF external type 1, E2 - OSPF external type 2, E - EGP
       i - IS-IS, L1 - IS-IS level-1, L2 - IS-IS level-2, ia - IS-IS inter
       * - candidate default, U - per-user static route, o - ODR
       P - periodic downloaded static route

Gateway of last resort is not set
        10.0.0.0/8 is variably subnetted, 2 subnets, 2 masks
    C       10.10.1.0/24 is directly connected, VLAN10
    C       10.20.1.0/24 is directly connected, VLAN20
    D       10.1.2.0/24 [90/2169856] via 10.1.1.1, 00:00:47,
GigabitEthernet1/2
```

Task 3: Configure Inter-VLAN Routing Using a Router on a Stick

Step 1 Configure trunking on the Layer 2 Cisco IOS switch.

```
Core2(config)#interface FastEthernet 4/6
Core2(config-if)#switchport trunk encapsulation dot1q
Core2(config-if)#switchport mode trunk
```

Step 2 Configure inter-VLAN routing on the external 2600 router.

```
Router(config)#interface FastEthernet 0/1
Router(config-if)#no shutdown
Router(config)#int FastEthernet 0/1.1
Router(config-subif)#encapsulation dot1Q 1 native
Router(config-subif)#ip address 10.1.1.1 255.255.255.0
Router(config-subif)#no shutdown
Router(config-subif)#interface FastEthernet 0/1.2
Router(config-subif)#encapsulation dot1Q 2
Router(config-subif)#ip address 10.2.1.1 255.255.255.0
Router(config-subif)#no shutdown
Router(config-subif)#end
```

Task 4: Configure SVI Interfaces for DHCP Forwarding

Step 1 Configure the Building Distribution switches for DHCP forwarding because hosts that reside on the Access Layer switches used DHCP to get their IP addresses, default gateway, and so on.

```
ds1(config)#interface vlan 10
ds1(config-if)#no ip directed-broadcast
ds1(config-if)#ip helper-address 10.2.1.254
ds1(config-if)#interface vlan 20
ds1(config-if)#no ip directed-broadcast
ds1(config-if)# ip helper-address 10.2.1.254
```

Review Questions

For multiple-choice questions, there might be more than one correct answer.

1 True or False: A SVI is a physical Layer 3 interface, whereas a routed port is a virtual Layer 3 interface.

2 True or False: Multilayer switches generally outperform routers of multiple Ethernet interfaces.

3 True or False: A router can forward DHCP requests across VLAN or IP subnet boundaries by using the DHCP relay agent feature.

Questions 4 and 5 are based on the configuration in Example 8-9.

Example 8-9 *Configuration for Questions 4 and 5*

```
6500-5#show run interface vlan 10
Building configuration...

Current configuration : 60 bytes
!
interface Vlan10
 ip address 10.1.1.1 255.255.255.0
 no ip proxy-arp
end
6500-5#show run int vlan 20
Building configuration...

Current configuration : 60 bytes
!
interface Vlan20
 ip address 10.2.1.1 255.255.255.0
 no ip proxy-arp
end

6500-5#
```

4 Based on Example 8-9, can the hosts that reside in VLAN 20 communicate with hosts on VLAN 10 if their default gateway is set to 10.2.1.1?

    a Yes, if the hosts on VLAN 10 have their default gateway set to 10.1.1.1.

    b No, the default gateway of the hosts that reside in VLAN 20 should be set to 10.1.1.1.

    c Yes, but there is no need to define default gateways.

    d No, because the routing protocol or static routes are not defined.

5 Based on Example 8-9, if the hosts that reside on VLAN 10 have their default gateway defined as 10.1.1.1 and can ICMP ping 10.2.1.1 but not a host that resides in VLAN 20, what could be a possible reason?

    a Hosts on VLAN 10 are not configured with the correct default gateway.

    b Hosts on VLAN 20 are not configured with the correct default gateway.

    c The routing protocol or static routes are not defined on the Layer 3 switch.

    d VLAN 20 is not defined in the switch database.

6 What command is used on Cisco IOS switches to change the interface from a Layer 3 interface to a Layer 2 interface?

    a **switchport mode access**

    b **ip routing**

    c **switchport**

    d **switchport mode trunk**

7 Which Cisco IOS command enables IP routing on a Catalyst switch?

    a **ip routing**

    b **interface** *vlan-id*

    c **ip address** *n.n.n.n mask*

    d **router** *ip_routing_protocol*

8 What are the disadvantages of using BVIs on Cisco IOS routers?

9 What is the function of a DHCP relay agent?

10 Which of the following UDP protocols are forwarded in addition to DHCP when a Layer 3 interface is configured with the **ip helper-address** command? (Select all that apply.)

a   Mobile IP

b   DNS

c   Time

d   FTP

This chapter covers the following topics:

- Multilayer Switching Architecture on Catalyst Switches
- MLS Memory Table Architecture
- CEF-Based MLS Configuration, Verification, and Troubleshooting

## CHAPTER 9

Understanding and Configuring Multilayer Switching

The purpose of this chapter is to provide you with details, architecture, and methods of multilayer switching on Catalyst switches. An understanding of multilayer switching is necessary for network designers, administrators, and operators for deployment and troubleshooting purposes.

The term *multilayer switching* refers to the ability of a Catalyst switch to support switching and routing of packets in hardware, with optional support for Layers 4 through 7 switching in hardware as well. As mentioned in Chapter 1, "Introduction to Building Cisco Multilayer Switched Networks," switching and routing in hardware (hardware switching) yields high throughput at or near line rate even with all ports sending traffic simultaneously.

With multilayer switches, the prime area of focus is often raw performance. Multilayer switches tend to have packet-switching throughputs in the millions of packets per second (pps), while traditional general-purpose routers have evolved from the 100,000 pps range to just over a million pps. Cisco Catalyst switches achieve this high rate of performance by using hardware switching.

For Catalyst switches to perform hardware switching, a route processor (Layer 3 engine) must download software-based routing, switching, access lists, QoS, and other information to the hardware for packet processing. To accomplish multilayer switching (packet processing in hardware), Cisco Catalyst switches use either the traditional multilayer switching (traditional MLS) or the Cisco Express Forwarding (CEF)-based MLS architecture. Traditional MLS is a legacy feature, whereas all leading-edge Catalyst switches support CEF-based multilayer switching (CEF-based MLS). Table 9-1 illustrates Catalyst switch support of traditional MLS and CEF-based MLS.

In terms of CCNP BCMSN exam preparation, you should focus on the following:

- The path of a packet with CEF-based MLS
- Understanding the differences between centralized and distributed switching
- CEF troubleshooting commands

The section dealing with traditional MLS is outside the scope of the current CCNP BCMSN exam.

Table 9-1 *Layer 3 Catalyst Switch Support of Traditional MLS and CEF-Based MLS*

Catalyst Switch Family	MLS Mode of Operation
Catalyst 3550, 3560, and 3750	CEF-based MLS
Catalyst 4000 or 4500 running Cisco IOS and using Supervisor Engine II+, III, IV, or V	CEF-based MLS
Catalyst 5000 or 5500 with RSM or RSFC and NFFC or NFFC II	Traditional MLS
Catalyst 6500 with Supervisor Engine I with MSFC	Traditional MLS
Catalyst 6500 with Supervisor Engine II, Supervisor 32, or Supervisor 720 with MSFC	CEF-based MLS

Understanding Traditional MLS

MLS enables specialized application-specific integrated circuits (ASIC) to perform Layer 2 rewrite operations of routed packets. Layer 2 rewrites include rewriting the source and destination MAC addresses and writing a recalculated cyclic redundancy check (CRC). Because the source and destination MAC addresses change during Layer 3 rewrites, the switch must recalculate the CRC for these new MAC addresses.

For Catalyst switches that support traditional MLS, the switch learns Layer 2 rewrite information from an MLS router via an MLS protocol. Another name for traditional MLS is NetFlow-based switching. With traditional MLS, the Layer 3 engine (route processor) and switching ASICs work together to build Layer 3 entries on the switch. Each of these Layer 3 entries is populated in one of the following ways:

- Source IP address exclusively (S)
- Source and destination IP address (S/D)
- Full Flow Information with Layer 4 protocol information (FFI)

With traditional MLS, the switch forwards the first packet in any flow to the Layer 3 engine for processing using software switching. After the routing of the first packet in the flow, the Layer 3 engine programs the hardware-switching components for routing for subsequent packets. Figure 9-1 illustrates these fundamentals of traditional MLS.

In Figure 9-1, when workstation A sends a packet to workstation B, workstation A sends the packet to its default gateway. In this figure, the default gateway is the RSM. The switch (MLS-SE) recognizes this packet as an MLS candidate packet because the destination MAC address matches the MAC address of the MLS router (MLS-RP). As a result, the switch creates a candidate entry for this flow. Next, the router accepts the packets from workstation A, rewrites the Layer 2 destination MAC address and CRC, and forwards the packet to workstation B. The switch refers to the routed packet from the RSM as the enabler packet. The switch, upon seeing both the candidate and enabler packets, creates an MLS entry in hardware such that the switch rewrites and forwards all future packets matching this flow. The MLS switched packet arrow in Figure 9-1 indicates this flow. This behavior is very different from CEF-based MLS.

Figure 9-1   *Fundamentals of Traditional MLS*

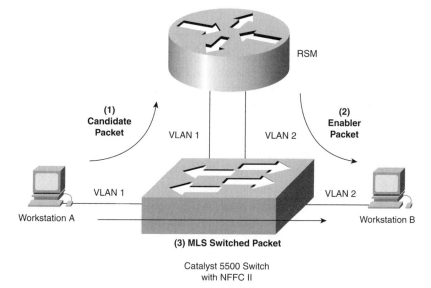

RSM

(1)
Candidate
Packet

VLAN 1   VLAN 2

(2)
Enabler
Packet

VLAN 1   VLAN 2

Workstation A   Workstation B

(3) MLS Switched Packet

Catalyst 5500 Switch
with NFFC II

On the Catalyst 5000 family of switches, MLS requires specialized supervisors and line modules and a router. In addition, MLS on Catalyst 5000 requires manual configuration. On the Catalyst 6500 family of switches with a Supervisor I Engine with an MSFC, all the line modules support MLS. In addition, this hardware combination uses MLS by default, and configuration of MLS is not required. For more details on and examples of the MLS architecture, consult the following technical documents at Cisco.com.

"Configuring and Troubleshooting IP MLS on Catalyst 6000 Switches with an MSFC," Document ID: 10566

"Troubleshooting IP Multilayer Switching," Document ID: 10554

Traditional MLS is a legacy feature; all leading-edge and future Catalyst switches support CEF-based MLS. The next section and the remainder of this chapter discuss CEF-based MLS and its architecture.

Understanding CEF-Based MLS

The leading-edge Catalyst switches, as listed in Table 9-1, use the CEF-based MLS forwarding model to download the control plane information such as the access lists to the data plane on the supervisor, port, or line card for hardware switching of packets. In the context of this chapter, the *control plane* represents the Layer 3 engine (route processor), and the *data plane* represents the hardware components such as ASICs used by the switch for hardware switching.

CEF is a topology-based forwarding model in which all routing information is pre-populated into a forwarding information base (FIB) and Layer 2 rewrite information is dynamically updated in an adjacency table. As a result of the pre-population of routing information, Catalyst switches can quickly look up routing information such as IP adjacencies and next-hop IP and MAC addresses.

The two main components of CEF are as follows:

- **Forwarding information base (FIB)**—CEF uses an FIB to make IP destination prefix-based switching decisions. The FIB is conceptually similar to a routing table or information base. It maintains a mirror image of the forwarding information contained in the IP routing table. When routing or topology changes occur in the network, the IP routing table is updated, and those changes are reflected in the FIB. The FIB maintains next-hop address information based on the information in the IP routing table. In the context of CEF-based MLS, both the Layer 3 engine and the hardware-switching components maintain an FIB.

- **Adjacency tables**—Network nodes in the network are said to be adjacent if they can reach each other with a single hop across a link layer. In addition to the FIB, CEF uses adjacency tables to store Layer 2 addressing information. The adjacency table maintains Layer 2 addresses for all FIB entries. As with the FIB, in the context of CEF-based MLS, both the Layer 3 engine and the hardware-switching components maintain an adjacency table.

Figure 9-2 depicts CEF-based MLS logically, applied to the Catalyst 6500 family of switches.

Figure 9-2 *Logical Depiction of CEF-Based MLS on the Catalyst 6500 Family of Switches*

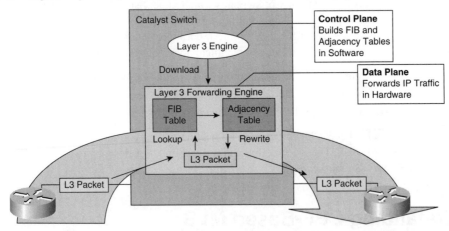

CEF-based MLS separates the control plane hardware from the data plane hardware switching. Nevertheless, the control plane is responsible for building the FIB table and adjacency tables in software and then downloading this information to the data plane.

On the Catalyst 6500 family of switches, the control plane hardware is easily distinguishable from the data plane hardware, especially in the case of hybrid software. The Catalyst 6500 MSFC daughter card is responsible for the control plane operations, whereas the Supervisor and PFC module are responsible for the data plane operations. The Catalyst 3550, 3560, 3750, and 4500 families of switches do not have distinguishable control plane and data plane modules or daughter cards.

Catalyst switches do not support routing of all types of frames in hardware. For example, the following list details common frame types that are not supported by hardware switching:

- Packets with IP header options
- Packets sourced from or destined to tunnel interfaces
- Packets using Ethernet encapsulation types other than ARPA
- Packets that require fragmentation

Upcoming models of Catalyst switches may support these frame types in hardware. In addition, each Catalyst switch family has its own distinct list of frames not supported by hardware switching.

Centralized and Distributed Switching

CEF-based Catalyst switches support one of two methods of hardware switching at Layer 3:

- **Centralized switching**—Centralized switching carries out forwarding decisions on a specialized ASIC that is *central* to all interfaces of a Layer 3 switch. With centralized switching, routing, ACL, QoS, and forwarding decisions are made on the Supervisor Engine in a modular chassis or by Layer 3 engines in fixed port density Layer 3 switches. As a result, all frames to be routed or switched must pass through the centralized engine via a fabric or bus. Furthermore, with centralized switching, the hardware-switching performance of the Catalyst switch is based on the central forwarding engine and the fabric or bus architecture. Figure 9-3 illustrates centralized switching, logically. Note in Figure 9-3 how frames must pass through the centralized switching engine.

Figure 9-3 *Logical Representation of Centralized Switching*

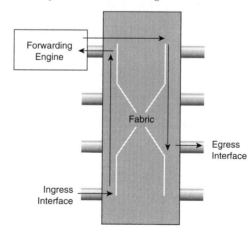

Examples of Catalyst switches that are engineered for centralized switching are the Catalyst 4500 family of switches and the Catalyst 6500 family of switches without the use of Distributed Forwarding Cards (DFC).

- **Distributed switching**—With distributed switching, interfaces or line modules on Layer 3 switches handle forwarding decisions independently. With distributed switching, a centralized switching engine synchronizes Layer 3 forwarding, routing, and rewrite tables to local tables on distributed switching–capable modules. As a result, individual line cards or ports make forwarding decisions without the aid of the centralized switching engine; frames pass between ports directly across the fabric. In other words, switches using distributed switching place additional copies of the CEF FIB and adjacency table on line modules or interfaces for routing and switching of frames. System performance with distributed switching is equal to the aggregate of all forwarding engines. Distributed forwarding enables Catalyst switches to achieve rates of over 100 million pps. The Catalyst 6500 supports distributed switching through the use of the Switch Fabric module or with a Supervisor 720 that has an integrated fabric and DFC line modules. The Catalyst 6500 maintains use of a centralized distributing switching engine even when using distributed switching–capable line modules for backward-compatibility. Figure 9-4 illustrates distributed switching logically.

Figure 9-4   *Logical Representation of Distributed Switching*

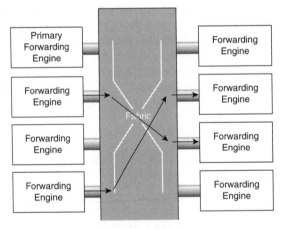

NOTE   Traditional MLS supports centralized switching only.

Address Resolution Protocol Throttling

An important feature of CEF-based Catalyst switches is Address Resolution Protocol (ARP) throttling; this feature requires explanation before CEF-based MLS is explored further. Make note that the ARP table builds the CEF adjacency table. This concept is explored in more detail throughout this chapter; however, it is important to consider when reading this section.

When a router is directly connected to a segment shared by multiple hosts such as Ethernet interfaces, the router maintains an additional prefix for the subnet. This subnet prefix points to a glean adjacency. When a router receives packets that need to be forwarded to a specific host, the adjacency database is gleaned for the specific prefix. If the prefix does not exist, the subnet prefix is consulted, and the glean adjacency indicates that any addresses within this range should be forwarded to the Layer 3 engine ARP processing.

One example where glean adjacencies are used is where a Catalyst switch receives a packet for which no rewrite information exists. In order to obtain rewrite information, the Layer 3 engine sends ARP requests to obtain the rewrite information. Catalyst switches using CEF-based MLS forward only the first several packets to the Layer 3 engine for new destinations without rewrite information. The switch installs a throttling adjacency such that the switch drops subsequent packets to the specific destination address in hardware until an ARP response is received. The switch removes the throttling adjacency when an ARP reply is received from the Layer 3 engine (and a complete rewrite adjacency is installed for the host). The switch removes the throttling adjacency if no ARP reply is seen within 2 seconds (to allow more packets through to the Layer 3 engine to reinitiate ARP). This relieves the Layer 3 engine from excessive ARP processing (or ARP-based denial-of-service [DoS] attacks).

Figure 9-5 shows an example of ARP throttling; an explanation of its stepwise behavior follows. Figure 9-5 depicts the Layer 3 forwarding engine and hardware switching forwarding engine as two separate hardware components for illustrative purposes.

Figure 9-5 *ARP Throttling Example*

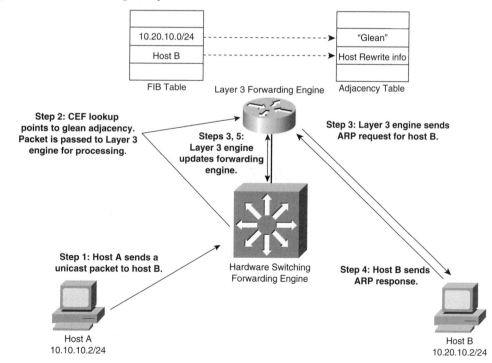

ARP throttling consists of the following steps:

Step 1 Host A sends a packet to host B.

Step 2 The switch forwards the packet to the Layer 3 engine based on the "glean" entry in the FIB.

Step 3 The Layer 3 engine sends an ARP request for host B and installs the drop adjacency for host B in hardware.

Step 4 Host B responds to the ARP request.

Step 5 The Layer 3 engine installs adjacency for host B and removes the drop adjacency.

Figure 9-9, later in this chapter, builds on Figure 9-5 to show CEF-based MLS in a larger context.

Switching Table Architectures

Multilayer switches build routing (CEF FIB and adjacency), bridging, QoS, and ACL tables for centralized or distributed switching in hardware using high-speed memory tables. Switches perform lookups in these tables for result information, such as to determine whether a packet with a specific destination IP address is supposed to be dropped according to an ACL. These tables support high-performance lookups and search algorithms such that multilayer switches maintain line-rate performance.

Multilayer switches deploy these memory tables using specialized memory architectures, referred to as content addressable memory (CAM) and ternary content addressable memory (TCAM). CAM tables provide only two results: 0 (true) or 1 (false). CAM is most useful for building tables that search on exact matches such as MAC address tables. TCAM provides three results: 0, 1, and "don't care." TCAM is most useful for building tables for searching on longest matches such as IP routing tables organized by IP prefixes.

In addition, Catalyst switch architecture supports the ability to perform multiple lookups into multiple distinct CAM and TCAM regions in parallel. As a result of this ability to perform multiple lookups simultaneously, Catalyst switches do not suffer any performance degradation by enabling additional hardware-switching features such as QoS and IP ACL processing.

CAM

Catalyst switches use CAM tables to house, for example, Layer 2 switching tables. Switches match results in CAM tables in binary (0 or 1 operations). With CAM tables, switches must find exact matches or use a default behavior. For example, in the case of Layer 2 switching tables, the switch must find an exact match to a destination MAC address or flood the packet out all ports in the VLAN.

The information that a switch uses to perform a lookup in a CAM table is called a *key*. For example, a Layer 2 lookup would use a destination MAC address and a VLAN ID as a key. Figure 9-6 depicts the use of keys in determining results using CAM.

Figure 9-6   *Content Addressable Memory*

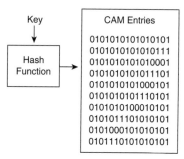

The following steps detail the process of determining a result based on a key:

Step 1   The switch feeds the key into a hashing algorithm for searching the CAM for a matching key.

Step 2   The hashing algorithm returns a pointer into the CAM table for the matched entry.

Step 3   The switch accesses the pointer and finds the result without searching the entire table sequentially.

In the case of Layer 2 tables, CAM tables contain information such as destination VLAN, destination MAC address, and destination ports.

Switches do not always search for an exact match in memory tables. For example, a switch that is looking up an IP route destination subnet with a 24-bit mask is concerned only with the first 24 bits of an IP address (i.e., the prefix). In this case, the switch is not looking for an exact match in CAM but rather a match on the first 24 bits of the IP address.

TCAM

TCAM is a specialized CAM designed for rapid table lookups. For example, the Catalyst 2950, 3550, 3560, 3750, 4500, and 6500 families of switches use TCAM to handle ACL lookups at line rate. As a result of using TCAM, applying ACLs does not affect the performance of the switch.

TCAM populates a limited number of entries, which varies per platform, with pattern values and mask values, each with an associated result. These are known as value, mask, and result (VMR) entries, respectively. The term *VMR* simply refers to the format of entries in TCAM.

The "value" in VMR refers to the pattern that is to be matched; examples include IP addresses, protocol ports, DSCP values, and so on. The "mask" refers to the mask bits associated with the pattern and determines the prefix. The "result" refers to the result or action that occurs in the case where a lookup returns a hit for the pattern and mask. This result might be a "permit" or "deny" in the case of a TCAM for ACLs. Another example of a result is a pointer to an entry in the hardware adjacency table that contains the next-hop MAC rewrite information in the case of a TCAM used for IP routing.

The TCAM structure is broken into a series of patterns and masks. Masks are shared among a specific number of patterns by using wildcard-specific content fields. To perform a lookup in a TCAM table, the switch checks all entries in parallel. The performance is independent of the number of entries. This allows a switch to use the longest match lookup when needed, and it provides fixed latency to unused fields.

Figure 9-7 illustrates a sample logical depiction of TCAM used for access lists in hardware. This figure represents the access list shown in Example 9-1.

Figure 9-7 *Sample TCAM Illustration*

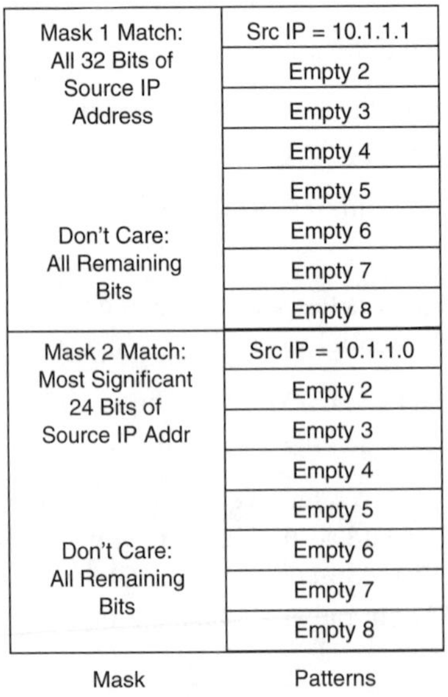

Mask	Patterns
Mask 1 Match: All 32 Bits of Source IP Address	Src IP = 10.1.1.1
	Empty 2
	Empty 3
	Empty 4
	Empty 5
Don't Care: All Remaining Bits	Empty 6
	Empty 7
	Empty 8
Mask 2 Match: Most Significant 24 Bits of Source IP Addr	Src IP = 10.1.1.0
	Empty 2
	Empty 3
	Empty 4
	Empty 5
Don't Care: All Remaining Bits	Empty 6
	Empty 7
	Empty 8

Example 9-1 *Sample ACL for Figure 9-7*

```
access-list 101 permit ip host 10.1.1.1 any

access-list 101 deny ip 10.1.1.0 0.0.0.255 any log
```

Moreover, TCAM defines three different match options that correlate to specific match regions. These match regions are as follows:

- **Exact-match region**—Consists of Layer 3 entries for regions such as IP adjacencies. IP adjacencies are the next-hop information (MAC address) for an IP address. Other examples of exact-match regions are Layer 2 switching tables and UDP flooding tables.

- **Longest-match region**—Consists of multiple "buckets" or groups of Layer 3 address entries organized in decreasing order by mask length. All entries within a bucket share the same mask value and key size. The buckets change their size dynamically by borrowing address entries from neighboring buckets. Although the size of the whole protocol region is fixed, several platforms support configuration of the region size. For most platforms, the reconfigured size of the protocol region is effective only after the next system reboot.

- **First-match region**—Consists of regions that stop lookups after the first match of the entry. An example of when a first-match region is used is for ACL entries.

Table 9-2 illustrates the common protocol regions, lookup type, and key size found on Catalyst switches. The size of the regions and the ability to configure the region varies on each Catalyst switch family.

Table 9-2   *Common TCAM Protocol Regions*

Region Name	Cisco IOS Region Name	Lookup Type	Key Size	Sample Result
IP adjacency	ip-adjacency	Exact-match	32 bits	MAC address rewrite info
IP prefix	ip-prefix	Longest-match	32 bits	Next-hop routing information
IP multicast	ip-mcast	Longest-match	64 bits	Next-hop routing information
Layer 2 switching	l2-switching	Exact-match	64 bits	Destination interface and VLAN
UDP flooding	udp-flooding	Exact-match	64 bits	Next-hop routing or MAC address rewrite info
Access lists	access-list	First-match	128 bits	Permit, deny, or wildcard

CEF-Based MLS Operation and Use of TCAM

The following list details the characteristics of CEF-based MLS operation and its use of the TCAM:

- Longest-match lookups in the FIB table are done for the Layer 3 destination address prefixes.

- CEF uses the IP routing table on the Layer 3 forwarding engine to build the FIB. Arrangement of the FIB is for maximum lookup throughput.

- CEF builds the adjacency table from the ARP table. The adjacency table contains Layer 2 rewrite (MAC) information for the next hop.

- FIB entries in the TCAM table are populated from the most specific to the least specific entry.

- Adjacency (rewrite) information and statistics are maintained by specialized components.

- CEF maintains one-to-one CEF-to-adjacency mappings for accurate statistics tracking.

- When the FIB table in TCAM is full, a wildcard entry redirects unmatched entries to the software switching Layer 3 forwarding engine.

- When the adjacency table in TCAM is full, an entry in the FIB table points to the Layer 3 forwarding engine to redirect the adjacency lookup.

- FIB and adjacency tables are dynamically updated when an ARP entry for a destination next hop changes, ages out, or is removed; the routing table changes; or next-hop rewrite information changes.

Sample CEF-Based MLS Operation

Figure 9-8 provides an example of CEF-based MLS operation.

Figure 9-8   *Sample of CEF-Based MLS Operation*

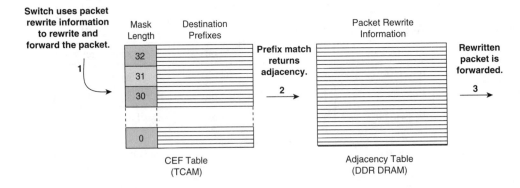

1. Layer 3 packets initiate TCAM lookup.
2. The longest match returns adjacency with rewrite information.
3. The packet is rewritten per adjacency information and forwarded.

Before a multilayer switch can route frames in the hardware, it sets up the necessary routing information in the hardware. After the switch has set up the necessary routing information in the hardware, frame routing in the hardware can start. The following steps illustrate an example of frame routing via hardware switching based on Figure 9-8. Figure 9-9 illustrates the steps. These steps assume the switch does not initially have rewrite information for the destination:

Step 1   Host A sends a packet to host B. The switch recognizes the frame as a Layer 3 packet because the destination MAC (0000.000c.0001) matches the Layer 3 engine MAC.

Step 2   The switch performs a CEF lookup based on the destination IP address (10.20.10.2) in the hardware. The packet hits the CEF FIB entry for the connected (VLAN 20) network and is redirected to the Layer 3 engine using a "glean" adjacency. The hardware-switching CEF table cannot forward this packet because it does not have rewrite information.

Figure 9-9   *Stepwise Example of CEF-Based MLS Operation*

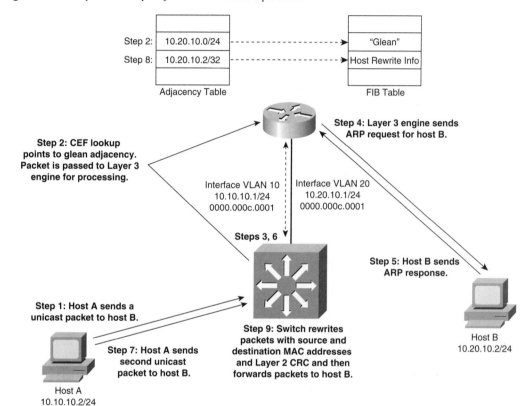

Step 3   The Layer 3 engine installs an ARP throttling adjacency in the switch for host B's IP address, because an ARP entry does not exist for host B since host A and B have not previously communicated.

Step 4   The Layer 3 engine sends an ARP request for host B on VLAN 20.

Step 5   Host B sends an ARP response to the Layer 3 engine.

Step 6   The Layer 3 engine installs the resolved adjacency in its local adjacency table and the hardware-switching components install the adjacency as well (removing the ARP throttling adjacency).

Step 7   The switch receives another packet for host B (10.20.10.2).

Step 8   The switch performs a Layer 3 lookup and finds a CEF entry for host B. The entry points to the adjacency with rewrite information for host B.

Step 9   The switch rewrites packets per the adjacency information (source and destination MAC address) and forwards the packet to host B on VLAN 20.

NOTE	The ARP throttling adjacency drops the first packet in any communication between hosts A and B due to ARP processing when no ARP entries exist for hosts A and B.

CEF-Based MLS Load Sharing

CEF-based MLS does support load sharing (equal-cost or nonequal-cost). However, CEF-based MLS does not support all the load-sharing features found in software-based CEF. With the current version of software on a Catalyst 6500 switch, a single FIB entry may have up to six adjacencies for load sharing per destination.

To achieve evenly distributed load balancing across multiple interfaces, CEF-based MLS selects a particular adjacency based on the hash (mathematical equivalent) of the following packet characteristics:

- Source IP address
- Destination IP address
- Source and destination IP Layer 4 ports

The load-sharing method and hashing algorithms vary slightly per Catalyst switch family. Consult the product documentation for specifics about load-sharing support on each Catalyst switch.

CEF-Based MLS Configuration, Verification, and Troubleshooting

In terms of designing multilayer switched networks, different modes of multilayer switching meet the requirements for different performance and scalability aspects. In terms of troubleshooting, understanding the basic operation of multilayer switches is paramount; multilayer switching requires a hierarchical approach to troubleshooting because several switching components determine the packet flow, not a single processing engine. CEF-based MLS configuration, verification, and troubleshooting vary slightly per Catalyst switch family but do have some commonalities.

CEF-Based MLS Configuration

Cisco Catalyst switches that use the CEF-based MLS architecture use CEF by default. Consequently, Catalyst switches perform hardware Layer 3 switching by default as well. For Catalyst switches that support CEF-based MLS, CEF-based MLS and per-destination load balancing with CEF-based MLS are enabled by default. As a result, no configuration is required for CEF-based MLS.

You should not disable CEF on Catalyst switches for any reason except under the supervision of a Cisco TAC engineer for the specific purpose of troubleshooting. Disabling

CEF on Cisco Catalyst switches yields low switching performance and may result in undesirable behavior.

CEF-Based MLS Verification and Troubleshooting

To display information about the Catalyst 6500 family of switches running Cisco IOS, use the **show interface** command, as shown in Example 9-2.

Example 9-2   *Displaying Layer 3 Switching Statistics on the Cisco IOS–Based Catalyst 6500 Family of Switches*

```
Router#show interface port-channel 9

Port-channel9 is up, line protocol is up (connected)

  Hardware is EtherChannel, address is 00d0.039b.e80a (bia 00d0.039b.e800)

  Description: POINT-TO-POINT TO CORE-4

! Output omitted for brevity

  Output queue: 0/40 (size/max)

  5 minute input rate 0 bits/sec, 0 packets/sec

  5 minute output rate 0 bits/sec, 0 packets/sec

  L2 Switched: ucast: 205744 pkt, 34282823 bytes - mcast: 216245 pkt, 66357101 bytes

  L3 in Switched: ucast: 367825 pkt, 361204150 bytes - mcast: 0 pkt, 0 bytes mcast

  L3 out Switched: ucast: 248325 pkt, 243855150 bytes

     682964 packets input, 431530341 bytes, 0 no buffer

     Received 311465 broadcasts (50899 IP multicast)

     0 runts, 0 giants, 0 throttles

     0 input errors, 0 CRC, 0 frame, 0 overrun, 0 ignored

     0 watchdog, 0 multicast, 0 pause input

     0 input packets with dribble condition detected

     554167 packets output, 309721969 bytes, 0 underruns

     0 output errors, 0 collisions, 8 interface resets

     0 babbles, 0 late collision, 0 deferred

     0 lost carrier, 0 no carrier, 0 PAUSE output

     0 output buffer failures, 0 output buffers swapped out
```

In Example 9-2, the lines beginning L2 Switched, L3 in Switched, and L3 out Switched indicate the Layer 3 hardware-switching statistics. Catalyst switches do not instantaneously update hardware-switching statistics for CLI **show** commands. For example, on the Catalyst 4500 family of switches running Cisco IOS, interface statistics may take up to 30 seconds to be updated in **show** commands. Furthermore, each Catalyst family of switches has its own troubleshooting methodology and commands for viewing hardware switching statistics. Consult Cisco.com for more details.

Viewing the Layer 3 Engine CEF Table

The Layer 3 Engine CEF table determines the hardware-switching CEF table. As such, when troubleshooting any CEF issues, the first step is to view the software CEF table. To view the CEF FIB table as per the Layer 3 switching engine in software, use the following commands:

```
show ip cef
show ip cef detail
```

Both commands display the FIB table per the Layer 3 switching engine. These commands do not display the FIB table according to the hardware-switching components such as TCAM, but instead display a "shadow" copy in software of the hardware-switching table. The "receive" entry in the Next Hop column indicates that the destinations for that specific prefix are passed to a normal Cisco IOS routing engine for processing. Examples 9-3 and 9-4 illustrate the use of these commands, respectively, on a Catalyst 3550 switch.

Example 9-3 *Sample Use of the* **show ip cef** *Command*

```
Router#show ip cef

Prefix              Next Hop           Interface

0.0.0.0/32          receive

10.5.1.1/32         10.20.248.2        Port-channel1

10.5.1.140/30       10.20.248.202      GigabitEthernet3/16

                    10.20.248.2        Port-channel1

224.0.0.0/4         0.0.0.0

224.0.0.0/24        receive

255.255.255.255/32  receive
```

Example 9-4 *Sample Use of the* **show ip cef detail** *Command*

```
Switch#show ip cef detail

IP Distributed CEF with switching (Table Version 8548), flags=0x0

  4156 routes, 0 reresolve, 0 unresolved (0 old, 0 new), peak 1000

  4156 leaves, 56 nodes, 680744 bytes, 6513 inserts, 2357 invalidations

  1023 load sharing elements, 343728 bytes, 1023 references

  universal per-destination load sharing algorithm, id 0C2C7438

  3(0) CEF resets, 3099 revisions of existing leaves

  Resolution Timer: Exponential (currently 1s, peak 2s)

  2048 in-place/0 aborted modifications

  refcounts:  11471 leaf, 6319 node


  Table epoch: 0 (4156 entries at this epoch)


Adjacency Table has 8 adjacencies

0.0.0.0/32, version 0, epoch 0, receive

10.5.1.1/32, version 52, epoch 0, cached adjacency 10.20.248.2

0 packets, 0 bytes

  via 10.20.248.2, Port-channel1, 0 dependencies

    next hop 10.20.248.2, Port-channel1

    valid cached adjacency

! Output omitted for brevity

  via 10.20.248.2, Port-channel1, 0 dependencies

    traffic share 1

    next hop 10.20.248.2, Port-channel1

    valid adjacency

  0 packets, 0 bytes switched through the prefix
```

continues

Example 9-4   *Sample Use of the* **show ip cef detail** *Command (Continued)*

```
224.0.0.0/4, version 30, epoch 0

0 packets, 0 bytes, Precedence routine (0)

  via 0.0.0.0, 0 dependencies

    next hop 0.0.0.0

    valid punt adjacency

224.0.0.0/24, version 2, epoch 0, receive

255.255.255.255/32, version 1, epoch 0, receive
```

Viewing the Layer 3 Engine Adjacency Table

CEF populates the adjacency tables when MAC addresses are learned via the ARP process. As a result, the adjacency table includes the MAC address rewrite information and destination interface for the adjacent node. All IP routing entries in the CEF table correspond to a next-hop address (adjacency).

When a switch hardware-switches an ingress packet with the destination MAC address as itself, it looks up the destination IP address in the CEF table. The first match in the CEF table points to an adjacency entry that contains the MAC rewrite information and destination interface. The switch rewrites the packet accordingly and sends it out the destination interface.

A single CEF entry may point to multiple adjacency entries when multiple paths to a destination exist. In addition, when a router is connected directly to several hosts, the FIB table on the router maintains a prefix for the subnet rather than for the individual host prefixes. The subnet prefix points to a glean adjacency. When packets need to be forwarded to a specific host, the adjacency database is gleaned for the specific prefix.

Certain IP prefixes or addresses require exception processing. Switches require exception processing of packets in cases where hardware switching does not support routing of the frame or in cases where the Layer 3 engine requires processing of the packet. Examples of packets that require exception processing include interfaces configured for NAT and received packets with IP options. Recall from Chapters 1 and 2 that support for hardware switching of frames varies on a per-switch basis.

The following types of adjacencies exist for special processing:

- **Punt adjacency**—Used for packets that require special handling by the Layer 3 engine or for features that are not yet supported by hardware switching.

- **Drop or discard adjacency**—Used to drop ingress packets.

- **Null adjacency**—Used to drop packets destined for a Null0 interface. The use of a Null0 interface is for access filtering of specific source IP packets.

To display adjacency table information, use the **show adjacency** command. The optional **detail** keyword displays detailed adjacency information, including Layer 2 information. Adjacency statistics are updated approximately every 60 seconds. Examples 9-5 and 9-6 illustrate sample output from the **show adjacency** and **show adjacency detail** commands, respectively.

Example 9-5 *Sample Use of the* **show adjacency** *Command*

```
Router#show adjacency

Protocol Interface            Address

IP       GigabitEthernet3/16  10.20.248.202(11120)

IP       FastEthernet9/48     10.192.15.254(7)

IP       FastEthernet9/1      100.1.1.1(2005)

IP       EOBC0/0              127.0.0.12(3)

IP       FastEthernet9/48     10.192.15.100(5)

IP       Port-channel1        10.20.248.2(11162)
```

Example 9-6 *Sample Use of the* **show adjacency detail** *Command*

```
Router#show adjacency detail

Protocol Interface            Address

IP       GigabitEthernet3/16  10.20.248.202(11120)

                              0 packets, 0 bytes

                              00D00178780A

                              00D00624440A0800

                              ARP         00:05:40

                              Epoch: 0

IP       FastEthernet9/48     10.192.15.254(7)

                              0 packets, 0 bytes

                              00D0BCF107C8

                              00D00624440A0800

                              ARP         00:39:20

                              Epoch: 0
```

continues

Example 9-6 *Sample Use of the* **show adjacency detail** *Command (Continued)*

```
IP      FastEthernet9/1          100.1.1.1(2005)

                                 0 packets, 0 bytes

                                 0007ECC57000

                                 00D00624440A0800

                                 ARP         03:19:20

                                 Epoch: 0
IP      EOBC0/0                  127.0.0.12(3)

                                 0 packets, 0 bytes

                                 000021000000

                                 0000210000000800
```

Debugging CEF on the Layer 3 Engine

To debug CEF on the Layer 3 engine, use the **debug ip cef** EXEC command. These debug commands display information about the CEF from the perspective of the Layer 3 engine. The interprocess communication (IPC) debugs provide information on CEF data to and from centralized and distributed switching engines. The syntax for these **debug ip cef** commands is as follows:

```
debug ip cef {drops [access-list] | receive [access-list] | events [access-list] |
    prefix-ipc [access-list] | table [access-list]} debug ip cef {ipc | interface-ipc}
```

The optional constraints for the **debug ip cef** command are as follows. Use the options to debug specific CEF operations on the Layer 3 engine:

- **drops**—Records dropped packets.
- **receive**—Records packets that are not switched using information from the FIB table but are received and sent to the next switching layer.
- **events**—Records general CEF events.
- **prefix-ipc**—Records updates related to IP prefix information, including the following:
  - — Debugging of IP routing updates in a line card
  - — Reloading of a line card with a new table
  - — Adding a route update from the route processor to a DFC-enabled line card where the CEF table is already full
  - — Control messages related to FIB table prefixes

- **table**—Produces a table showing events related to the FIB table. Possible types of events include the following:
    - Routing updates that populate the FIB table
    - Flushing of the FIB table
    - Adding or removing of entries to or from the FIB table
    - Table reloading process
- **ipc**—Records information related to interprocess communications in CEF. Possible types of events include the following:
    - Transmission status of IPC messages
    - Status of buffer space for IPC messages
    - IPC messages received out of sequence
    - Status of resequenced messages
    - Throttle requests sent from a line card to the route processor
- **interface-ipc**—Records IPC updates related to interfaces. Possible reporting includes an interface coming up or going down, and so on.

Specify an access list with the **debug** option to control collections of debugging information to specific IP address(es):

```
Switch#configure terminal
Switch(config)#access-list 99 permit host 192.168.1.100
Switch(config)#end
Switch#debug ip cef drops 99
```

CEF troubleshooting using the **debug ip cef** command should be coordinated with a Cisco TAC engineer because the **debug** output is not easily decoded.

CEF-Based MLS Troubleshooting Methodology

Previous subsections discussed several CEF troubleshooting techniques on the Layer 3 engine. Recall that the Layer 3 engine does not actually contain the hardware FIB and adjacency table. Rather, these tables are located in specialized hardware components in Supervisor Engines and line cards. The following highlights a stepwise approach to troubleshooting a unicast route on a CEF-based Catalyst switch. The troubleshooting steps are not inclusive but do review the hierarchical approach to troubleshooting CEF-based MLS:

Step 1   Verify that the IP routing information on the Layer 3 engine is correct. Use the **show ip route** or **show ip route** *destination-network* command to verify that the destination network routing entry exists and is associated with a valid next-hop address. If the route does not exist or the next-hop address is incorrect, troubleshooting of routing protocol, next hop interfaces, or route configuration is required.

Step 2 Verify that the next-hop address has a valid next-hop MAC address by using the **show ip arp** *IP-address* command. If the entry is incomplete, troubleshooting of the ARP process is required.

Step 3 Verify that the IP route entry in the FIB on the Layer 3 engine contains the same next-hop address as in Step 1 by using the **show ip cef** *destination-network* command.

Step 4 Verify that the CEF adjacency table contains the same rewrite information as the ARP table from Step 2 by using the **show adjacency detail** | **begin** *next_hop_IP_address* command.

Step 5 When all other troubleshooting steps have been exhausted and the CEF-based MLS switch is still experiencing unicast routing issues, verify the population of the FIB and adjacency table in TCAM under the supervision of a TAC engineer.

This chapter contains an example of CEF-based MLS troubleshooting in the configuration exercise at the end of this chapter. For more information on troubleshooting CEF on Catalyst switches, refer to the following documents on Cisco.com:

- "How-To Troubleshoot Unicast IP Routing CEF on Catalyst 6000s with a Supervisor 2 in Hybrid Mode," Document ID: 20626

- "Troubleshooting Cisco Express Forwarding Routing Loops," Document ID: 26083

- "Troubleshooting Incomplete Adjacencies with CEF," Document ID: 17812

- "Troubleshooting Prefix Inconsistencies with Cisco Express Forwarding," Document ID: 14540

Study Tips

The following bullets review important BCMSN exam preparation points of this chapter. The bullets only briefly highlight the main points of this chapter related to the BCMSN exam. Consult the text of this chapter for additional information regarding these topics. Table 9-3 lists important commands to review for the BCMSN exam:

- In describing CEF-based MLS in a few sentences, CEF-based MLS is the Layer 3 forwarding mechanism deployed currently on all shipping Catalyst switches. CEF-based MLS consists of two logical devices: a control plane and a data plane. In CEF, the control plane is generally referred to as the software-switching engine or Layer 3 forwarding engine. In addition, the data plane carries several common names, including the hardware-switching component, "in hardware," hardware forwarding engine, and ASICs.

- The control plane is responsible for building the IP routing table and ARP table. The IP routing table and ARP table ultimately build the IP CEF and CEF adjacency table. The CEF table contains prefixes of subnets, hosts, and so on, which are used to quickly search for an adjacency index. The index into the adjacency table provides the next-hop address, interface, and Layer 3 rewrite information.

- The control plane downloads its CEF and adjacency table to the data plane (hardware forwarding engine). The hardware forwarding engine consists of hardware components including TCAM that enable high-speed switching and routing of frames. All changes, updates, additions, and so on to the CEF and adjacency table are controlled by the Layer 3 forwarding engine.

- With the Catalyst 6500 family of switches, the control plane and data plane are easily distinguishable (MSFC and PFC, respectively). However, the other Catalyst switches do not have separate components from an end-user standpoint, yet these switches still have a distinct control plane and data plane.

- *Layer 3 switching* (or multilayer switching) is the term used to describe the ability of a Cisco Catalyst switch to perform Layer 3 routing in hardware (hardware-switching) using high-speed hardware components.

- Layer 3 switching is beneficial in the campus network because it provides versatility, high-availability, large port density, and high performance.

- Current shipping Layer 3 switches use CEF to populate IP routing tables and Layer 2 rewrite information in hardware.

- The terms *CEF-based MLS* or just plain *CEF* are used to describe the routing architecture of Catalyst switches.

- No specific configuration is needed for CEF-based MLS because it is enabled by default.

- ARP throttling is a feature that prevents ARP-based DoS attacks on Catalyst switches. The feature works by installing a throttling adjacency in the hardware CEF table such that hardware-switching drops subsequent identical ARP requests for a specific time until the respective ARP response is received.

- With CEF, when a router is connected directly to several hosts, the FIB table on the router maintains a prefix for the subnet rather than for the individual host prefixes. The subnet prefix points to a glean adjacency. When packets need to be forwarded to a specific host, the adjacency database is gleaned for the specific prefix.

- With CEF, punt adjacencies in TCAM on Catalyst switch hardware are used to send packets to the Layer 3 engine (for example, MSFC) that require special handling or that are used for special situations where the hardware does not yet support the packet flow in question (for example, NAT).

- Catalyst switches support two methods for CEF-based MLS: centralized switching and distributing switching.

- Centralized switching describes hardware-switching using a centralized hardware-switching engine found on the Supervisor Engine of a Cisco Catalyst switch. With centralized switching, data to be routed or switched must pass through the switching fabric of the Catalyst switch to the centralized hardware-switching engine for processing. After the forwarding decision has been made and the packet rewritten with new Layer 2 information, the centralized switching engine forwards the packet to the correct destination port and VLAN.

- The Catalyst 4500 family of switches is based on centralized switching.

- Distributed switching describes the hardware-switching method used by Catalyst switches that utilize hardware-switching engines on individual line cards and port groups. With distributed switching, individual line cards determine the routing destination and rewrite information for a packet. Therefore, with distributed switching line cards, a Catalyst switch is able to route a packet between source and destination without sending the packet to the Supervisor Engine for processing. In addition, the packet might never leave the line card if the source and destination of the line card are on the same switch.

- Review the "Sample CEF-Based MLS Operation" section and Figure 9-8, which illustrates the path of a packet during CEF-based MLS operation.

- Review the "CEF-Based MLS Troubleshooting Methodology" section of this chapter for details on how to approach CEF-based MLS troubleshooting.

Table 9-3   *Commands to Review*

Command	Description
debug ip cef	Enables debugging with IP CEF. Recommended practice is to use this **debug** option with optional parameters including ACLs to limit output. In addition, use this **debug** command in production only in coordination with a Cisco TAC engineer.
show adjacency detail	Displays the IP CEF Layer 2 rewrite information and statistical information from the perspective of the Layer 3 engine.
show arp	Displays the ARP table contents. This command is the first step in troubleshooting adjacency issues.
show ip cef	Displays the IP CEF information from the Layer 3 engine perspective. Displays the prefix, the next hop, and the next-hop interface (outgoing interface).
show ip route	Displays the IP routing table. This command is the first step in troubleshooting IP routing or IP CEF issues.

Summary

Outside the scope of the BCMSN course, the following notes along with the study tips in the previous section summarize the chapter:

- CEF-based MLS is a forwarding model implemented on the latest generation of Cisco multilayer switches. CEF-based MLS is topology based; the control plane and data plane are separate. The control plane downloads the routing table information to the data plane for hardware switching. CEF-based MLS scales to large networks and is not limited on the number of traffic flows.

- CEF-based MLS uses either centralized switching or distributed switching. Distributed switching provides higher performance than centralized switching.

- Switches use TCAM and other hardware-switching components not only for IP CEF but also for applying QoS and access lists to packets routed and switched using hardware switching.

- Cisco multilayer switches that support CEF-based MLS use CEF-based MLS by default.

- CEF-based MLS supports statistics via show commands with specific limitation.

Configuration Exercise: Troubleshooting CEF-Based MLS

Complete this configuration exercise to familiarize yourself with the basic troubleshooting steps of CEF-based MLS.

Required Resources

The resources and equipment required to complete this exercise are as follows:

- A Cisco IOS–based, Layer 3 CEF-based MLS Catalyst switch such as a Catalyst 3550, 3560, 3750, 4500, or 6500 with Supervisor II or 720 with an MSFC in a Layer 3 Building Distribution submodule or Layer 3 routing topology

- A terminal server or workstation connected directly to the console port of the Catalyst switch

Exercise Objective

The purpose of this exercise is to demonstrate the first steps in troubleshooting CEF-based MLS on a Cisco IOS–based Catalyst switch. Troubleshooting CEF-based MLS is generally a last step in troubleshooting connectivity problems. Generally, connectivity problems are the result of a physical layer issue or configuration issue. Troubleshoot CEF-based MLS after all other troubleshooting steps have been exhausted.

Network Diagram

Figure 9-10 shows the network layout for this configuration exercise. The configuration exercise uses a Catalyst 3560 switch from the Building Distribution submodule to illustrate commands. This switch learns IP routing entries from the Campus Backbone switches.

Figure 9-10 *Network Diagram for Configuration Exercise*

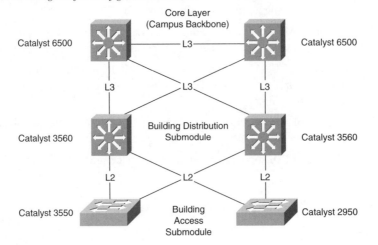

Command List

In this configuration exercise, you use the commands listed in Table 9-4. These commands are in alphabetical order so that you can easily locate the information you need. Refer to this list if you need configuration command assistance during the exercise. The table includes only the specific parameters used in the example and not all the available options for the command.

Table 9-4 *Command List for Configuration Exercise*

Command	Description
ping *ip_address*	Sends ICMP echo requests to a specific IP address
show adjacency detail	Displays the CEF adjacency table and rewrite information
show ip arp *ip-address*	Displays the ARP table for a specific IP address
show ip cef *destination-network* **detail**	Displays the IP CEF FIB table for a specific destination network
show ip route *destination-subnet*	Displays the Cisco IOS IP routing table

Task 1: Establish Console (Out-of-Band) Connectivity or Telnet or SSH Connectivity to the Switch

This task is self-explanatory.

Task 2: Determine the IP Routing Entry or Subnet That Is Experiencing Connectivity Problems or a CEF-Based MLS Issue

For this configuration exercise, use the destination subnet, 10.20.30.0/24, as an example.

Task 3: Verify the Cisco IOS IP Routing Table and ARP Entries for the Route

Step 1   Verify that a route exists to the destination network in the IP routing table.

```
Switch#show ip route 10.20.30.0 255.255.255.0
Routing entry for 10.20.30.0/24
  Known via "ospf 3738", distance 110, metric 2, type intra area
  Last update from 10.20.248.6 on Port-channel2, 05:59:50 ago
  Routing Descriptor Blocks:
  * 10.20.248.34, from 10.20.255.14, 05:59:50 ago, via Port-channel4
      Route metric is 2, traffic share count is 1
    10.20.248.6, from 10.20.255.13, 05:59:50 ago, via Port-channel2
      Route metric is 2, traffic share count is 1
```

Step 2   Verify the ARP entries for the next-hop addresses for the destination subnet obtained in Step 1.

```
Switch#show ip arp 10.20.248.34
Protocol  Address          Age (min)  Hardware Addr   Type    Interface
Internet  10.20.248.34            1   00d0.03e5.840a  ARPA    Port-channel4


Switch#show ip arp 10.20.248.6
Protocol  Address          Age (min)  Hardware Addr   Type    Interface
Internet  10.20.248.6             1   00d0.03eb.b40a  ARPA    Port-channel2
```

Step 3   Using the **ping** command, send ICMP echoes to the next-hop address to verify connectivity.

```
Switch#ping 10.20.248.34


Type escape sequence to abort.
Sending 5, 100-byte ICMP Echos to 10.20.248.34, timeout is 2 seconds:
!!!!!
Success rate is 100 percent (5/5), round-trip min/avg/max = 1/1/1 ms

Switch#ping 10.20.248.6


Type escape sequence to abort.
Sending 5, 100-byte ICMP Echos to 10.20.248.6, timeout is 2 seconds:
!!!!!
Success rate is 100 percent (5/5), round-trip min/avg/max = 1/1/1 ms
```

Task 4: Verify the IP CEF FIB and Adjacency Entries for the Route

Step 1   Verify the IP CEF FIB entry for the destination subnet in question.

```
Switch#show ip cef 10.20.30.0 detail
10.20.30.0/24, version 122, epoch 0, per-destination sharing
```

```
0 packets, 0 bytes
  via 10.20.248.34, Port-channel4, 0 dependencies
    traffic share 1
    next hop 10.20.248.34, Port-channel4
    valid adjacency
  via 10.20.248.6, Port-channel2, 0 dependencies
    traffic share 1
    next hop 10.20.248.6, Port-channel2
    valid adjacency
  0 packets, 0 bytes switched through the prefix
```

Step 2 Verify the CEF adjacency entry for the next-hop address obtained from Step 1, and compare the results to Step 2 in Task 3.

```
Switch#show adjacency detail | begin 10.20.248.34
IP          Port-channel4              10.20.248.34(170)
                                       0 packets, 0 bytes
                                       00D003E5840A
                                       00D00624440A0800
                                       ARP         00:05:42
                                       Epoch: 0


Switch#show adjacency detail | begin 10.20.248.6
IP          Port-channel2              10.20.248.6(166)
                                       0 packets, 0 bytes
                                       00D003EBB40A
                                       00D00624440A0800
                                       ARP         00:04:53
                                       Epoch: 0
```

Task 5: Debug the CEF FIB and Adjacency Table's Downloads to the Centralized Switching and Distributed Switching Engines, and Verify the TCAM Contents for FIB and Adjacency Tables

This task should be performed only under the supervision of a Cisco TAC engineer.

Review Questions

Note that more than one correct answer might be valid for multiple-choice questions.

1 True or False: CEF-based MLS Catalyst switches use the Layer 3 engine to route the first packet and build flows based in hardware for subsequent packets.

2 True or False: The performance of a Catalyst switch using distributed switching is the aggregate of all forwarding engines.

3 In CEF-based multilayer switching, which type of adjacency entry is used for features that require special handling or for features that are not yet supported in conjunction with CEF hardware-switching paths?

    a   Glean adjacency

    b   Punt adjacency

    c   Drop adjacency

    d   Default adjacency

4 Which statement describes a TCAM mask associated with the entry **access-list 101 deny ip 10.1.0.0 0.0.255.255?**

    a   All 32 bits of source address

    b   Most significant 8 bits of source address

    c   Most significant 16 bits of source address

    d   Most significant 24 bits of source address

5 When troubleshooting CEF-based MLS for issues such as being unable to reach a certain IP destination, what two tables need to be verified as a first step in troubleshooting?

    a   The IP routing table and the IP route-cache table

    b   The IP routing table and the CEF adjacency table

    c   The IP CEF FIB table and the adjacency table in TCAM

    d   The IP routing table and the ARP table

6 Which of the following statements is true with regard to CEF-based MLS?

    a   CEF-based MLS Catalyst switches use the IP CEF FIB and adjacency tables to build FIB and adjacency tables in TCAM for hardware switching.

    b   CEF-based MLS Catalyst switches use the IP routing and IP ARP tables to build FIB and adjacency tables in TCAM for software switching.

    c   CEF-based MLS Catalyst switches use the IP CEF FIB and adjacency tables to build MLS flows on-demand in TCAM for hardware switching.

7 Describe the steps a multilayer switched packet takes when using CEF-based MLS.

This chapter covers the following topics:

- Identifying Network Requirements and the Need for Quality of Service (QoS)
- Understanding Why QoS Is Needed in Networks That Have Ample Bandwidth
- Describing the IntServ and DiffServ QoS Architectures
- Understanding the QoS Components: Classification, Marking, Traffic Conditioning, Congestion Management, and Congestion Avoidance
- Applying QoS in Each Submodule of the Enterprise Composite Network Model

Understanding and Implementing Quality of Service in Cisco Multilayer Switched Networks

Cisco Catalyst switches provide a wide range of QoS features that address the needs of voice, video, and data applications sharing a single infrastructure. Cisco Catalyst QoS technology lets you implement complex networks that predictably manage services to a variety of networked applications and traffic types.

Using the QoS features and services in Cisco IOS and Cisco CatOS Software, you can design and implement networks that conform to either the Internet Engineering Task Force (IETF) integrated services (IntServ) model or the differentiated services (DiffServ) model. Cisco switches provide for differentiated services using QoS features such as classification and marking, traffic conditioning, congestion avoidance, and congestion management.

Table 10-1 indicates the predominant Catalyst switches at the time of publication. Each Catalyst switch supports each QoS component with specific restrictions and caveats. For brevity, this chapter focuses strictly on QoS using Cisco IOS. In addition, the examples, caveats, and restrictions discussed in this chapter involve the Catalyst 3550, 3560, and 6500 families of switches. Refer to the product-configuration guides or release notes on other Catalyst switches for the latest information regarding QoS-supported features and configurations. For information regarding Catalyst QoS using Cisco CatOS, refer to the configuration guides for those specific Catalyst switches on Cisco.com.

Table 10-1 *Leading Catalyst Switches Applicable to This Chapter*

Cisco IOS–Based Catalyst Switches
Catalyst 2940, 2950, 2955, 2960, and 2970
Catalyst 3550, 3560, and 3750
Catalyst 4000 or 4500 with Supervisor Engine II+, III, IV, V, VI, or VII
Catalyst 6500 with Supervisor Engine I with MSFC or MSFC2
Catalyst 6500 with Supervisor Engine II with MSFC2
Catalyst 6500 with Supervisor Engine 720 with MSFC3

Cisco IOS on routers and switches support many QoS capabilities, including the following:

- **Control over resources**—You have control over which network resources (bandwidth, equipment, wide-area facilities, and so on) are being used. For example, critical traffic such as voice, video, and data may consume a link with each type of traffic competing for link bandwidth. QoS helps to control the use of the resources (for example, dropping low-priority packets), thereby preventing low-priority traffic from monopolizing link bandwidth and affecting high-priority traffic such as voice traffic.

- **More efficient use of network resources**—By using network analysis management and accounting tools, you can determine how traffic is handled and which traffic experiences latency, jitter, and packet loss. If traffic is not handled optimally, you can use QoS features to adjust the switch behavior for specific traffic flows.

- **Tailored services**—The control and visibility provided by QoS enables Internet service providers to offer carefully tailored grades of service differentiation to their customers. For example, a service provider can offer different SLAs for a customer website that receives 3000–4000 hits per day, compared to another customer site that receives only 200–300 hits per day.

- **Coexistence of mission-critical applications**—QoS technologies make certain that mission-critical applications that are most important to a business receive the most efficient use of the network. Time-sensitive multimedia and voice applications require bandwidth and minimized delays, while other applications on a link receive fair service without interfering with mission-critical traffic.

This chapter discusses the preceding features with respect to Catalyst switches. Furthermore, it discusses QoS components and features that are available on Catalyst switches from the perspective of the Catalyst 6500, Catalyst 3560, and Catalyst 3550 families of switches. Later sections discuss recommendations for deploying the QoS components in different submodules of the Enterprise Composite Network Model.

In terms of BCMSN preparation, this chapter delves deeper into the QoS technology than what is tested on the BCMSN switching examination and what is covered in the course. However, the extra content only further explains QoS and provides you with a well-rounded understanding that aids in learning QoS and preparing for QoS questions on the BCMSN switching exam. You should focus on the main components of QoS in this chapter:

- Classification
- Trusting
- Policing
- Congestion management

Go through the study tips, the summary, and the lab exercise if you are seeking to quickly study the main points of QoS.

The Need for QoS

As introduced in the preceding section, even with adequate bandwidth available throughout a multilayer switched network, several network design properties may affect performance. The following network design properties may result in congestion even with networks of unlimited bandwidth; Figure 10-1 illustrates these network design properties.

Figure 10-1  *The Need for QoS*

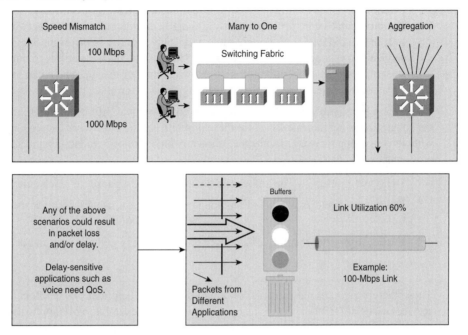

- **Ethernet speed mismatch**—Network congestion may occur when different-speed network devices are communicating. For example, a Gigabit Ethernet–attached server sending traffic to a 100-Mbps Ethernet–attached server may result in congestion at the egress interface of the 100-Mbps Ethernet–attached server due to buffer limitations of the switch.

- **Many-to-one switching fabrics**—Network congestion may occur when aggregating many-to-one switches. For example, when aggregating multiple access layer switches into a distribution layer switch, the sum of the switching fabric bandwidth of all access layer switches generally exceeds the switch fabric capability of the distribution layer switch.

- **Aggregation**—Network congestion may occur when multiple Ethernet-attached devices are communicating over Ethernet through a single connection or to a single network device or server.

- **Anomalous behavior**—Network congestion may occur because of anomalous behavior or events. Faulty hardware or software on any network device may cause a broadcast storm or other type of network storm yielding congestion on multiple interfaces. In this context, faulty software includes computer worms and viruses, which may cause packet storms that congest enterprises and even service provider networks. QoS can mitigate and control the behavior of the network during these types of anomalous events well enough that VoIP phone calls continue unaffected—even during an anomalous packet storm caused by an Internet worm—until the anomaly is resolved.

- **Security**—As implied in the previous bullet, QoS is a security feature. Applying policies and QoS trusting and scheduling limits the effect of unwarranted traffic or malicious attacks. For example, trusting and scheduling important data network traffic over unmarked data traffic might yield additional stability in the event of a denial-of-service (DoS) attack. Through policing, QoS limits an attacker's ability to impose or steal information. Although QoS cannot prevent theft of information, it can limit this behavior by explicitly discarding or limiting associated traffic.

Congestion greatly affects the network availability and stability problem areas, but congestion is not the sole factor for these problem areas. All networks, including those without congestion, may experience the following three network availability and stability problems:

- **Delay (or latency)**—The amount of time it takes for a packet to reach a destination.

- **Delay variation (or jitter)**—The change in interpacket latency within a stream over time.

- **Packet loss**—The measure of lost packets between any given source and destination.

NOTE   These factors are extremely crucial in deploying AVVID applications. Each network service places different expectations on the network. For example, VoIP applications require low latency and steady jitter factors, whereas storage protocols such as FCIP and iSCSI require very low packet loss but are less sensitive to jitter.

Latency, jitter, and packet loss may occur even in multilayer switched networks with adequate bandwidth. As a result, each multilayer switched network design needs to include QoS. A well-designed QoS architecture aids in preventing packet loss while minimizing latency and jitter. The following sections discuss these factors in more detail, as well as other benefits of QoS such as security and mitigating the effects of viruses and worms by using traffic conditioning.

Latency

End-to-end delay, or latency, between any given sender and receiver comprises two types of delay:

- **Fixed-network delay**—Includes encoding and decoding time and the latency required for the electrical and optical signals to travel the media en route to the receiver. Generally, applying QoS does not affect fixed-network delay because fixed-network delay is a property of the medium. Upgrading to higher-speed media such as 10-Gigabit Ethernet and newer network hardware with lower encoding and decoding delays, depending on application, may result in lower fixed-network delay.

- **Variable-network delay**—Refers to the network conditions, such as congestion, that affect the overall latency of a packet in transit from source to destination. Applying QoS does affect the variable-network delay.

In brief, the following list details the types of delay that induce end-to-end latency. (Note that the first four types of delay are fixed delay.)

- **Packetization delay**—Amount of time it takes to segment, sample, and encode signals, process data, and turn the data into packets.

- **Serialization delay**—Amount of time it takes to place the bits of a packet, encapsulated in a frame, onto the physical media.

- **Propagation delay**—Amount of time it takes to transmit the bits of a frame across the physical wire.

- **Processing delay**—Amount of time it takes for a network device to take the frame from an input interface, place it into a receive queue, and place it into the output queue of the output interface.

- **Queuing delay**—Amount of time a packet resides in the output queue of an interface.

Of all the delay types listed, queuing is the delay over which you have the most control with QoS features in Cisco IOS. The other types of delay are not directly affected by QoS configurations. Propagation delay is subject to the medium used for transport and hardware components. Indirectly, QoS has an overall effect on propagation delay as QoS might limit traffic on the wire, but QoS features do not directly lower propagation delay of individual frames. QoS might also reduce processing delay by limiting the amount data requiring processing. Nevertheless, QoS does not lower the processing delay of individual frames. For this reason, this chapter focuses mostly on queuing delay.

Jitter

Jitter is critical to network operation in maintaining consistent data rates. All end stations and Cisco network devices use jitter buffers to smooth out changes in arrival times of data packets that contain data, voice, and video. However, jitter buffers are only able to compensate for small changes in latency of arriving packets. If the arrival time of subsequent packets increases beyond a specific threshold, a *jitter buffer underrun* occurs. During jitter buffer exhaustion, there are no packets in the buffer to process for a specific stream. For example, if a jitter buffer underrun occurs while you are using an audio application to listen to an Internet radio station, the audio application stops playing music until additional packets arrive into the jitter buffer.

In contrast, when too many packets arrive too quickly, the jitter buffers may fill and be unable to handle further traffic. This condition is called a *buffer overrun*. In this condition, for example, an audio application will skip parts of the audio file. This is a result of the audio player always having packets to play but missing several packets of the audio stream. With regards to VoIP phone calls, jitter buffer underruns and buffer overruns are usually intolerable, making the calling experience difficult.

Packet Loss

Packet loss is a serious issue in multilayer switched networks. Packet loss generally occurs on multilayer switches when there is a physical layer issue such as an Ethernet duplex mismatch or an interface output queue full condition. A common scenario for packet loss is when an output queue is full of packets to be transmitted where there is no additional memory space for additional ingress packets; this condition is commonly referred to as an *output queue full condition*. In this condition, the network device that is queuing the packets has no choice but to drop the packet. For example, an output queue full condition can occur where a sender attached to an interface of a higher speed is sending to a receiver attached to an interface of a lower speed. Eventually, the output queue buffers become full, resulting in dropped packets. A specific example of this behavior is where a server attached to a Catalyst switch at Gigabit Ethernet is transmitting to a client workstation attached at 100-Mbps Fast Ethernet. In this situation, when the server sends data at a sustained rate higher than 100 Mbps, the output queue for the workstation fills and eventually the switch drops egress frames. Several QoS options are available to apply deterministic behavior to the packet drops.

QoS-Enabled Solutions

In brief, QoS addresses latency, jitter, and packet-drop issues by supporting the following components and features on Cisco network devices:

- Classifying and marking traffic such that network devices can differentiate traffic flows

- Traffic conditioning (policing) to tailor traffic flows to specific traffic behavior and throughput

- Marking traffic rates above specific thresholds as lower priority (policing)

- Dropping packets when rates reach specific thresholds (congestion avoidance)

- Scheduling packets such that higher-priority packets transmit from output queues before lower-priority packets (congestion management)

- Managing output queues such that lower-priority packets awaiting transmit do not monopolize buffer space (congestion management)

Applying QoS components and features to an enterprise or service provider network provides for deterministic traffic behavior. In other words, QoS-enabled infrastructures allow you to do the following:

- Predict response times for end-to-end packet flows, I/O operations, data operations, transactions, and so on

- Correctly manage and determine abilities of jitter-sensitive applications such as audio and video applications

- Streamline delay-sensitive applications such as VoIP

- Control packet loss during times of inevitable congestion
- Configure traffic priorities across the entire network
- Support applications or network requirements that entail dedicated bandwidth
- Monitor and avoid network congestion
- Limit anomalous behavior and maintain network stability in the event of a malicious attack

This chapter discusses in later sections how to apply QoS features to achieve deterministic traffic behavior on Catalyst switches. The next section discusses the two QoS service models that are the building blocks of any QoS implementation. These models are outside the scope of the BCMSN switching course and BCMSN switching examination; however, they provide some thoughtful insight into QoS behavior.

QoS Service Models

The two QoS architectures used in IP networks when designing a QoS solution are the IntServ and DiffServ models. The QoS service models differ by two characteristics: how the models enable applications to send data, and how networks attempt to deliver the respective data with a specified level of service.

A third method of service is best-effort service, which is essentially the default behavior of the network device without QoS. In summary, the following list restates these three basic levels of service for QoS:

- **Best-effort service**—The standard form of connectivity without guarantees. This type of service, in reference to Catalyst switches, uses first-in, first-out (FIFO) queues, which simply transmit packets as they arrive in a queue with no preferential treatment.

- **Integrated services**—IntServ, also known as *hard QoS*, is an absolute reservation of services. In other words, the IntServ model implies that traffic flows are reserved explicitly by all intermediate systems and resources.

- **Differentiated services**—DiffServ, also known as soft QoS, is class-based, where some classes of traffic receive preferential handling over other traffic classes. Differentiated services use statistical preferences, not a hard guarantee like integrated services. In other words, DiffServ categorizes traffic and then sorts it into queues of various efficiencies.

Choosing the type of service to use in a multilayer switched network depends on the following factors:

- Application support
- Technology upgrade speed and path
- Cost

The following two subsections discuss the IntServ and DiffServ architectures in more detail.

Integrated Services Architecture

The IntServ model, defined in RFC 1633, guarantees a predictable behavior of the network for applications. IntServ provides multiple services that accommodate multiple QoS requirements. IntServ is implemented through the use of the Resource Reservation Protocol (RSVP), enabled at both the endpoints and the network devices between. The RSVP-enabled application requests a specific kind of service from the RSVP-enabled network before it sends data. Explicit signaling via RSVP makes the request, and the application informs the network of its traffic profile and requests a particular kind of service that can encompass its bandwidth and delay requirements. The application is expected to send data only after it gets a confirmation from the network. The network also expects the application to send data that lies within its described traffic profile.

The RSVP-enabled network performs admission control based on information from the requesting host application and available network resources. It either admits or rejects the application's request for bandwidth. The network commits to meeting the QoS requirements of the application as long as the specific traffic flow for which the request was made remains within the profile specifications. Each flow of traffic must go through the admission control process.

Using Common Open Policy Service (COPS) centralizes admission control at a Policy Decision Point (PDP). COPS provides the following benefits when used with RSVP:

- Centralized management of services
- Centralized admission control and authorization of RSVP flows
- Increased scalability of RSVP-based QoS solutions

Together, RSVP and IntServ offer the following benefits:

- Explicit resource admission control (end-to-end)
- Per-request policy admission control (authorization object, policy object)
- Signaling of dynamic port numbers

The drawbacks to using RSVP and IntServ are that they are not scalable and they require continuous signaling from network devices.

Differentiated Services

The DiffServ model provides multiple levels of service that satisfy differing QoS requirements. However, unlike with the IntServ model, an application that uses DiffServ does not explicitly signal the network devices before sending data. DiffServ is a QoS implementation technique that is tailored for modern networks and their solutions. DiffServ reassigns bits in the type of service (ToS) field of an IP packet header. DiffServ uses differentiated services code points (DSCP) as the QoS priority descriptor value and supports 64 levels of classification. RFC 2474 defines the use of the ToS byte for DSCP. Catalyst switch configurations support IP Precedence and DSCP values.

Figure 10-2 illustrates the bits used in packets for classification. Network devices use either Layer 2 class of service (CoS) bits of a frame or Layer 3 IP Precedence or DSCP bits of a packet for classification. All Catalyst switches listed in Table 10-1 support QoS by Layer 3 classification as well as Layer 2 classification. At Layer 2, 3 bits are available in 802.1Q frames and Inter-Switch Link (ISL) frames for classification for up to eight distinct values (levels of service): 0 through 7. These Layer 2 classification bits are referred to as the CoS values. At Layer 3, QoS uses the 6 most significant ToS bits in the IP header for a DSCP field definition. This DSCP field definition allows for up to 64 distinct values (levels of service)—0 through 63—of classification on IP frames. The last two bits represent the Early Congestion Notification (ECN) bits. IP Precedence is only the 3 most significant bits of the ToS field. As a result, IP Precedence maps to DSCP by using IP Precedence as the 3 high-order bits and padding the lower-order bits with 0.

Figure 10-2 *DiffServ Packet Classification*

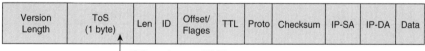

A practical example of the interoperation between DSCP and IP Precedence is with Cisco IP Phones. Cisco IP Phones mark voice traffic at Layer 3 with a DSCP value of 46 and, consequently, an IP Precedence of 5. Because the first 3 bits of DSCP value 46 in binary is 101 (5), the IP Precedence is 5. As a result, a network device that is only aware of IP Precedence understands the packet priority similarly to a network device that is able to interpret DSCP. Moreover, Cisco IP Phones mark frames at Layer 2 with a CoS value of 5.

Figure 10-3 illustrates the ToS byte. P2, P1, and P0 make up IP Precedence. T3, T2, T1, and T0 are the ToS bits. When viewing the ToS byte as DSCP, DS5 through DS0 are the DSCP bits. Table 10-2 illustrates the IP Precedence value to precedence designation mapping. For more information about bits in the IP header that determine classification, refer to RFCs 791, 795, and 1349.

Figure 10-3 *DiffServ Field*

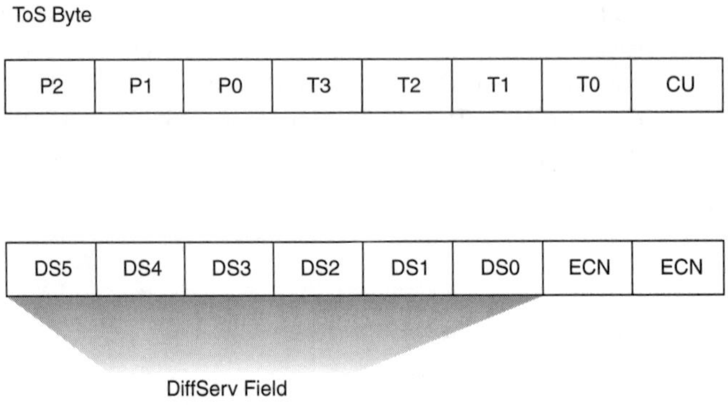

ToS Byte

P2	P1	P0	T3	T2	T1	T0	CU

DS5	DS4	DS3	DS2	DS1	DS0	ECN	ECN

DiffServ Field

Table 10-2 *IP Precedence Bit Mappings*

Bits (IP Precedence Value)	IP Precedence
111 (7)	Network control
110 (6)	Internetwork control
101 (5)	CRITIC/ECP
100 (4)	Flash override
011 (3)	Flash
010 (2)	Immediate
001 (1)	Priority
000 (0)	Routine

Using DSCP values for classification of packets is the leading method for classification in all enterprise and service provider multilayer switched networks.

For a differentiated service, the network tries to deliver a particular kind of service based on the QoS descriptor specified in each IP packet header on a per-hop basis, rather than per-traffic flow as in IntServ. You can use the DiffServ model for the same mission-critical applications as IntServ and to provide end-to-end QoS. Network devices forward each according to priorities designated within the packet on a per-device, per-hop basis. Typically, this DiffServ model is the preferable model within the multilayer switched network because of its scalability.

IntServ must maintain state information for every flow in the network. DiffServ overcomes this limitation by assigning different queuing policies, traffic policing, and drop parameters based on classification of packets to differentiate (prefer) traffic flows. In addition, DiffServ uses per-class polices instead of per-flow polices as with IntServ, such that flows can be aggregated into a small number of classes. This makes QoS administration and configuration easier than maintaining policies on a per-flow basis. Another advantage in using DiffServ is the ability to support complex traffic classification and conditioning performed at the network edge. As a result, the recommendation is to apply DiffServ QoS features in every submodule of the Enterprise Composite Network Model.

Assured Forwarding and Expedited Forwarding

RFC 2474 introduced DSCP and 64 possible markings on a single packet. IETF decided to standardize the meanings for several codepoint values into per-hop behaviors (PHB). Two main PHBs exist:

- Assured Forwarding (RFC 2597)
- Expedited Forwarding (RFC 2598)

Assured Forwarding

Assured Forwarding (AF) defines classes by using DSCP values. AF is important in understanding how to relate DSCP AF terminology to DSCP values. Example 10-1 illustrates an abbreviated list of configuration options for DSCP in Cisco IOS. The policy map configuration shown in this example is explained later in this chapter.

Example 10-1 *DSCP Configuration in Cisco IOS*

```
Switch(config-pmap-c)#set ip dscp ?
  <0-63>   Differentiated services codepoint value
  af11     Match packets with AF11 dscp (001010)
  af12     Match packets with AF12 dscp (001100)
! Output omitted for brevity
  af33     Match packets with AF33 dscp (011110)
  af41     Match packets with AF41 dscp (100010)
  af42     Match packets with AF42 dscp (100100)
  af43     Match packets with AF43 dscp (100110)
  cs1      Match packets with CS1(precedence 1) dscp (001000)
! Output omitted for brevity
  cs7      Match packets with CS7(precedence 7) dscp (111000)
  default  Match packets with default dscp (000000)
  ef       Match packets with EF dscp (101110)
```

AF has four AF classes, AF1x through AF4x, where the AF4 class is considered to have more importance than the AF1 class. Within each class, there are three drop probabilities. Depending on the policy of a given network, you can configure packets for a PHB based on required throughput, delay, jitter, loss, or according to priority of access to network services.

AF PHB defines a method by which traffic classes are given different forwarding assurances. A practical example of dividing a network into classes is as follows:

- Gold: 50 percent of the available bandwidth
- Silver: 30 percent of the available bandwidth
- Bronze: 20 percent of the available bandwidth

Table 10-3 illustrates the DSCP coding to specify the AF class with the drop probability. Bits 0, 1, and 2 define the class; bits 3 and 4 specify the drop probability; bit 5 is always 0.

Table 10-3 *Sample DSCP Coding to Specify AF Class*

	Class 1	Class 2	Class 3	Class 4
Low Drop	001010	010010	011010	100010
	AF11	AF21	AF31	AF41
	DSCP 10	DSCP 18	DSCP 26	DSCP 34
Medium Drop	001100	010100	011100	100100
	AF12	AF22	AF32	AF42
	DSCP 12	DSCP 20	DSCP 28	DSCP 36
High Drop	001110	010110	011110	100110
	AF13	AF23	AF33	AF43
	DSCP 14	DSCP 22	DSCP 30	DSCP 38

Expedited Forwarding

Expedited Forwarding defines the Expedited Forwarding (EF) PHB. Network devices use EF PHB to build a low-loss, low-latency, low-jitter, assured-bandwidth, end-to-end service through DiffServ domains. EF service appears to the endpoints as a point-to-point connection. An example is to apply EF PHBs to VoIP traffic. The remaining sections of this chapter explain the application of DSCP and DiffServ on Catalyst switches.

Catalyst QoS Fundamentals

Figure 10-4 illustrates the queuing components of a QoS-enabled Cisco IOS–based Catalyst switch. The figure illustrates the classification that occurs on ingress packets. After the switch classifies a packet, it determines whether to place the packet into a queue or drop the packet. Queuing mechanisms drop packets only if the corresponding queue is full without the use of congestion avoidance.

Figure 10-4 *Queuing Components of Cisco Catalyst Switches*

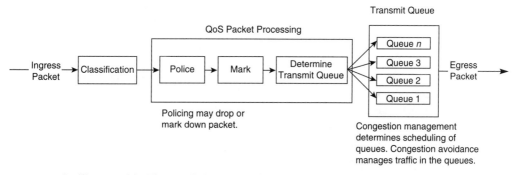

As illustrated in Figure 10-4, the queuing mechanism on Cisco IOS–based Catalyst switches has the following main components:

- Classification

- Marking

- Traffic conditioning: policing and shaping

- Congestion management

- Congestion avoidance

On the current Catalyst family of switches listed in Table 10-1, classification defines an internal DSCP value. The internal DSCP value is the classification value the Catalyst switches use in determining the egress marking, output scheduling, policing, congestion management, and congestion avoidance behavior of frames as the frames traverse and exit the switch. Marking and policing may alter this internal DSCP. Figure 10-5 illustrates how Catalyst switches use internal DSCP for QoS.

Figure 10-5 *Logical Depiction of Internal DSCP*

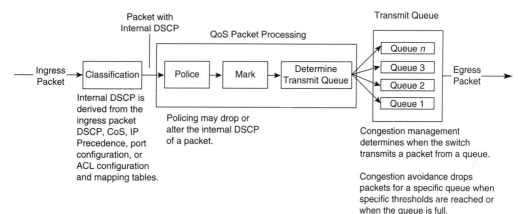

Figure 10-5 is an abbreviated logical depiction of QoS packet handling in Catalyst switches because it does not illustrate mapping tables and other QoS features. Nonetheless, the figure illustrates the basic QoS packet handling of Catalyst switches.

Example 10-2 introduces QoS on a Catalyst switch. In this simple example, the intended purpose of QoS is to provide a higher degree of service to VoIP traffic between Cisco IP Phones. The Catalyst switch used in this example is a Catalyst 3560 running Cisco IOS. To accomplish this configuration of applying differentiated service to VoIP traffic, the switch must classify voice frames with a DSCP value sufficient for applying high priority to the VoIP frames. By default, Cisco IP Phones mark voice frames with a DSCP value of 46; as a result, trusting is a valid option applying high priority.

A valid and simple method of classification for this example is to trust the DSCP value of ingress frames based on whether a Cisco IP Phone is attached to a Catalyst switch interface. The **mls qos trust device cisco-phone** interface configuration command accomplishes this configuration. Furthermore, the Cisco Catalyst 3560 family of switches uses four output queues. The default queue for frames with a DSCP value of 46 is queue 3. The Cisco Catalyst family of switches supports a priority queue option specifically for frames in queue 4. Therefore, the switch needs to map the respective CoS value of 5 (mapped from internal DSCP of 46) to queue 4 for priority queuing of the voice frames. The Catalyst 3550 interface command **priority-queue out** enables strict-priority queues on an interface such that the switch transmits frames out of queue 4 before servicing any other queue.

Example 10-2 illustrates the resulting configuration. Although this is a simplistic example of classification and output scheduling, it provides a brief overview of how to apply QoS. The **wrr-queue cos-map** commands in Example 10-2 are explained later in this section.

Example 10-2 *Basic Catalyst Switch QoS Configuration Applying Classification and Congestion Management*

```
! Output omitted for brevity
!
mls qos
!
!
! Output omitted for brevity
!
interface FastEthernet0/2
 switchport mode access
 mls qos trust device cisco-phone
 wrr-queue cos-map 1 0 1
 wrr-queue cos-map 2 2 3
 wrr-queue cos-map 3 4 6 7
 wrr-queue cos-map 4 5
 priority-queue out
 spanning-tree portfast
 !
 !
interface FastEthernet0/3
 switchport mode access
```

Example 10-2 *Basic Catalyst Switch QoS Configuration Applying Classification and Congestion Management (Continued)*

```
 mls qos trust device cisco-phone
 wrr-queue cos-map 1 0 1
 wrr-queue cos-map 2 2 3
 wrr-queue cos-map 3 4 6 7
 wrr-queue cos-map 4 5
 priority-queue out
 spanning-tree portfast
!
! Output omitted for brevity
!
```

Following subsections discuss each QoS component on Catalyst switches for high-speed Ethernet interfaces. In addition, the remainder of this chapter focuses on the Catalyst switches listed in Table 10-1 running Cisco IOS. The only Cisco CatOS switch to support a wide range of QoS features is the Catalyst 6500 with an MSFC.

For a complete understanding and an overview of configuring QoS with Cisco switches running CatOS, refer to Cisco.com. In addition, the following sections on QoS components cover Cisco IOS QoS in general. Not all of the switches listed in Table 10-1 support all of the features discussed in this chapter.

Classification

Classification distinguishes a frame or packet with a specific priority or predetermined criteria. In the case of Catalyst switches, classification determines the internal DSCP value on frames. Catalyst switches use this internal DSCP value for QoS packet handling, including policing and scheduling as frames traverse the switch.

The first task of any QoS policy is to identify traffic that requires classification. With QoS enabled and no other QoS configurations, all Cisco routers and switches treat traffic with a default classification. With respect to DSCP values, the default classification for ingress frames is a DSCP value of 0. The Catalyst switches listed in Table 10-1 use an internal DSCP of 0, by default, for all ingress frames regardless of the ingress DSCP value of DSCP of a frame. The terminology used to describe an interface configured for treating all ingress frames with a DSCP of 0 is untrusted. The following subsection discusses trusted and untrusted interfaces in more detail. Figure 10-6 simplistically illustrates classification and marking.

On Cisco Catalyst switches, the following methods of packet classification are available:

- Per-interface trust modes
- Per-interface manual classification using specific DSCP, IP Precedence, or CoS values
- Per-packet based on access lists
- Network-Based Application Recognition (NBAR)

Figure 10-6 *Representation of Classification and Marking*

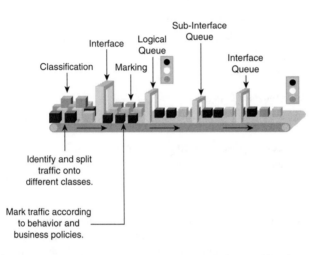

In multilayer switched networks, always apply QoS classification as close to the edge as possible. This application allows for end-to-end QoS with ease of management. The following sections discuss these methods of classification. The first section, "Trust Boundaries and Configurations," covers classification based on interface trust modes, interface manual classification, and packet-based access control lists. Classification using NBAR is then covered in the "NBAR" section.

Trust Boundaries and Configurations

Trust configurations on Catalyst switches allow trusting for ingress classification. For example, when a switch configured for *trusting DSCP* receives a packet with a DSCP value of 46, the switch accepts the ingress DSCP of the frame and uses the DSCP value of 46 for internal DSCP. Despite the ingress classification configuration, the switch may alter the DSCP and CoS values of egress frames by policing and egress marking.

The Catalyst switches support trusting via DSCP, IP Precedence, or CoS values on ingress frames. When trusting CoS or IP Precedence, Catalyst switches map an ingress packet's CoS or IP Precedence to an internal DSCP value. Tables 10-4 and 10-5 illustrate the default mapping tables for CoS-to-DSCP and IP Precedence-to-DSCP, respectively. These mapping tables are configurable.

Table 10-4 *Default CoS-to-DSCP Mapping Table*

CoS	0	1	2	3	4	5	6	7
DSCP	0	8	16	24	32	40	48	56

Table 10-5   *Default IP Precedence-to-DSCP Mapping Table*

IP Precedence	0	1	2	3	4	5	6	7
DSCP	0	8	16	24	32	40	48	56

Figure 10-7 illustrates the Catalyst QoS trust concept using port trusting. When the Catalyst switch trusts CoS on ingress packets on a port basis, the switch maps the ingress value to the respective DSCP value in Table 10-4. When the ingress interface QoS configuration is untrusted, the switch uses 0 for the internal DSCP value for all ingress packets. Recall that switches use the internal DSCP values for policing, egress polices, congestion management, congestion avoidance, and the respective CoS and DSCP values of egress frames.

Figure 10-7   *Catalyst QoS Trust Concept*

To configure a Cisco IOS–based Catalyst switch for trusting using DSCP, CoS, or IP Precedence, use the following interface command:

```
mls qos trust [dscp | cos | ip-precedence]
```

Example 10-3 illustrates a sample configuration of trusting DSCP in Cisco IOS.

Example 10-3 *Sample Interface Configuration for Trusting DSCP*

```
! Output omitted for brevity
!
mls qos
!
! Output omitted for brevity
!
interface FastEthernet0/16
 switchport mode dynamic desirable
 mls qos trust dscp
!
! Output omitted for brevity
!
```

Because an internal DSCP value defines how the switches handle a packet internally, the CoS-to-DSCP and IP Precedence-to-DSCP mapping tables are configurable. To configure CoS-to-DSCP mapping, use the following command:

```
mls qos map cos-dscp values
```

Here, *values* represents eight DSCP values, separated by spaces, corresponding to the CoS values 0 through 7; valid DSCP values are from 0 to 63. Example 10-4 illustrates an example of configuring CoS-to-DSCP mapping. In this example, the mapping table maps the CoS value of 0 to 0, 1 to 8, 2 to 16, 3 to 26, 4 to 34, 5 to 46, 6 to 48, and 7 to 56.

Example 10-4 *Sample CoS-to-DSCP Mapping Table Configuration*

```
! Output omitted for brevity
!
mls qos
!
(text deleted)
mls qos map cos-dscp 0 8 16 26 34 46 48 56
! Output omitted for brevity
!
```

To configure IP Precedence-to-DSCP mapping, use the following command:

```
mls qos map ip-prec-dscp dscp-values
```

Here, *dscp-values* represents DSCP values corresponding to IP Precedence values 0 through 7; valid values for *dscp-values* are from 0 to 63.

Furthermore, it is possible to map ingress DSCP values to different internal DSCP values using DSCP mutation or a policy map. Consult the configuration guide on Cisco.com for more details on configuring DSCP mutation.

Another method of trusting ingress frames is to trust DSCP or CoS based on whether the switch learns of a Cisco IP Phone attached to an interface through the Cisco Discovery Protocol (CDP). To configure this behavior of trusting ingress frames based on the switch learning that a Cisco IP Phone is attached, use the **mls qos trust device cisco-phone** interface configuration command in conjunction with the **mls qos trust dscp** or **mls qos trust cos** command.

Example 10-2 in the section "Catalyst QoS Fundamentals," earlier in this chapter, illustrates a sample configuration of trusting based on whether a Cisco IP Phone is attached to an interface.

The **mls qos trust dscp** and **mls qos trust cos** configuration options configure the switch to trust all ingress traffic, regardless. To trust only particular traffic on ingress, use traffic classes. Traffic classes apply ACLs to specific QoS functions, such as classification, marking, and policing. To configure a traffic class on a Cisco IOS–based Catalyst switch, perform the following steps:

Step 1 Create a class map with a user-defined class-name. Optionally, specify the class map with the **match-all** or **match-any** option.

```
Switch(config)#class-map [match-any | match-all] class-name
```

Step 2 Configure the class-map clause. Class-map clauses include matching against ACLs, the input interface, specific IP values, and so on. Note: CLI may show unsupported match clauses.

```
Switch(config-cmap)#match ?
  access-group        Access group
  any                 Any packets
  class-map           Class map
  destination-address Destination address
  input-interface     Select an input interface to match
  ip                  IP specific values
  mpls                Multi Protocol Label Switching specific values
  not                 Negate this match result
  protocol            Protocol
  source-address      Source address
  vlan                VLANs to match
Switch(config-cmap)#match access-group acl_number
```

Class maps only define traffic profiles. Policy maps apply class maps to QoS functions. To define a policy map and tie a class map to a policy map, perform the following steps:

Step 1   Create a policy map with a user-defined name.

```
Switch(config)#policy-map policy-name
```

Step 2   Apply the class-map clause.

```
Switch(config-pmap)#class class-map
```

Step 3   Configure policy map QoS actions.

```
Switch(config-pmap-c)#?
QoS policy-map class configuration commands:
  bandwidth  Bandwidth
  exit       Exit from QoS class action configuration mode
  no         Negate or set default values of a command
  trust      Set trust value for the class
  <cr>
  police     Police
  set        Set QoS values

Switch(config-pmap-c)#bandwidth ?
  <8-2000000>  Kilo Bits per second
  percent      % of Available Bandwidth

Switch(config-pmap-c)#trust ?
  cos           Trust COS in classified packets
  dscp          Trust DSCP in classified packets
  ip-precedence Trust IP precedence in classified packets[0801]
  <cr>

Switch(config-pmap-c)#set ?
  cos   Set IEEE 802.1Q/ISL class of service/user priority
  ip    Set IP specific values
  mpls  Set MPLS specific values
```

Step 4 Apply policy maps to interfaces on an ingress or egress basis. Not all Catalyst switches, including the Catalyst 6500 with a Supervisor I or II Engine, support egress policing.

```
Switch(config)#interface {vlan vlan-id | {FastEthernet | GigabitEthernet}
slot/interface | port-channel number}
Switch(config-if)#service-policy {input | output} policy-name
```

Step 5 Configure the ingress trust state of the applicable interface. The trust state preserves ingress DSCP, CoS, or IP Precedence values for application to the policy map.

```
Switch(config)#interface {vlan vlan-id | {FastEthernet | GigabitEthernet}
slot/interface | port-channel number}
Switch(config-if)#mls qos trust [dscp | cos | ip-precedence]
```

Step 6 Enable QoS globally, if not previously configured.

```
Switch(config)#mls qos
```

NOTE Always enable QoS globally using the **mls qos** or **qos** global command to enable a Catalyst switch to enact QoS configurations.

NOTE This example used a Cisco Catalyst 3560 for demonstration. Different Catalyst switches support additional or fewer options for policy maps and class maps depending on platform and software version. Check the product configuration guides on Cisco.com for exact product support of policy map and class map options.

NOTE The Catalyst 4000 and 4500 families of switches running Cisco IOS do not prefix QoS configuration commands with the keyword **mls**. For example, to configure an interface to trust DSCP on the Catalyst 4000 and 4500 families of switches running Cisco IOS, the command is **qos trust dscp** instead of **mls qos trust dscp**.

Example 10-5 illustrates a sample configuration for a policy map and class map configuration. In this example, the switch trusts DSCP of all ingress TCP traffic destined to the 10.1.1.0/24 subnet received on interface FastEthernet0/1. The switch maps all other ingress traffic with the interface default DSCP of 0 for internal DSCP.

Example 10-5 *Sample Configuration of Policy Map and Class Map for Trusting*

```
! Output omitted for brevity
!
mls qos
!
```

Example 10-5 *Sample Configuration of Policy Map and Class Map for Trusting (Continued)*

```
class-map match-all Voice-subnet
  match access-group 100
!
!
policy-map Ingress-Policy
  class Voice-subnet
    trust dscp
!
(text deleted)
!
interface FastEthernet0/1
 switchport mode access
 mls qos trust dscp
 service-policy input Ingress-Policy
!
(text deleted)
!
access-list 100 permit tcp any 10.1.1.0 0.0.0.255
```

NBAR

Network-Based Application Recognition adds intelligent network classification to switches and routers. ACL-based classification uses Layer 3 and Layer 4 properties of packets, such as IP address and TCP or UDP ports, to classify packets. NBAR can classify frames based on Layer 7 information, such as application type, URL, and other protocols that use dynamic TCP and UDP assignments. For example, NBAR supports these types of classification features:

- Classification of applications that dynamically assign TCP and UDP ports
- Classification of HTTP traffic by URL, host, or Multipurpose Internet Mail Extensions (MIME) type
- Classification of Citrix Independent Computer Architecture (ICA) traffic by application name
- Classification of applications using subport information

Example 10-6 illustrates several protocols that are available for NBAR classification on a Catalyst 6500 running Cisco IOS 12.2(17a)SX1 with a Supervisor Engine 720. Always refer to the product documentation for the latest supported NBAR protocol list.

Example 10-6 *Several Available NBAR Protocols on Catalyst 6500 with Sup720/MSFC3 Running Cisco IOS Version 12.2(18)SXD2B*

```
Switch(config-cmap)#match protocol ?
  arp             IP ARP
! Output omitted for brevity
  cdp             Cisco Discovery Protocol
(text deleted)
  eigrp           Enhanced Interior Gateway Routing Protocol
  exchange        MS-RPC for Exchange
                                                        continues
```

Example 10-6 *Several Available NBAR Protocols on Catalyst 6500 with Sup720/MSFC3 Running Cisco IOS Version 12.2(18)SXD2B (Continued)*

```
! Output omitted for brevity
  http              World Wide Web traffic
! Output omitted for brevity
  nfs               Network File System
  nntp              Network News Transfer Protocol
! Output omitted for brevity
  secure-ftp     FTP over TLS/SSL
  secure-http    Secured HTTP
  secure-irc     Internet Relay Chat over TLS/SSL
! Output omitted for brevity
  sqlserver      MS SQL Server
  ssh            Secured Shell
! Output omitted for brevity
```

For a complete and current list of protocols and applications that NBAR recognizes on a per-platform basis, consult Cisco.com.

NBAR configuration uses policy maps and class maps as with Cisco IOS–based classification. As such, use the following steps to configure NBAR-based classification:

Step 1   Specify the user-defined name of the class map.

```
Switch#configure terminal
Switch(config)#class-map [match-all | match-any] class-name
```

Step 2   Specify a protocol supported by NBAR as a matching criterion.

```
Switch(config-cmap)#match protocol protocol-name
```

Step 3   Create a traffic policy by associating the traffic class with one or more QoS features in a policy map.

```
Switch(config)#policy-map policy-name
```

Step 4   Specify the name of a predefined class.

```
Switch(config-pmap)#class class-name
```

Step 5   Enter QoS-supported parameters in the policy map class configuration mode. These parameters include marking the DSCP value, traffic policing, and so on and vary on a Catalyst switch basis.

```
Switch(config-pmap-c)#?
QoS policy-map class configuration commands:
    bandwidth      Bandwidth
    exit           Exit from QoS class action configuration mode
    no             Negate or set default values of a command
    police         Police
    <cr>
    fair-queue     Flow-based Fair Queueing
    priority       Low Latency Queueing
    queue-limit    Queue Max Threshold for Tail Drop
```

```
          random-detect  Weighted Random Early Detect (Precedence based)
          set            Set QoS values
          shape          Traffic Shaping
          trust          Set trust value for the class
        Switch(config-pmap-c)#exit
        Switch(config-pmap)#exit
```

Step 6   Attach the traffic policy to the interface for ingress or egress application.

```
        Switch(config)#interface {vlan vlan-id | {FastEthernet |
        GigabitEthernet} slot/interface | port-channel number}
        Switch(config-if)#service-policy [input | output] policy-name
```

Marking

Marking in reference to QoS on Catalyst switches refers to changing the DSCP, CoS, or IP Precedence bits on ingress frames. Marking is configurable on a per-interface basis or via a policy map. Marking alters the DSCP value of packets, which in turn affects the internal DSCP. For instance, an example of marking would be to configure a policy map to mark all frames from a video server on a per-interface basis to a DSCP value of 40, resulting in an internal DSCP value of 40 as well. Marking also might be a result of a policer. An example of marking using a policer is a Catalyst switch marking DSCP to a lower value for frames above a specified rate.

Figures 10-8 and 10-9 review the associated CoS and DSCP bits in frame headers for Layer 2 and Layer 3 marking, respectively. In deploying or designing new networks, use Layer 3 whenever possible. Note: The CoS field is only applicable to 802.1Q tagged frames.

Figure 10-8 *Layer 2 CoS Field of a 802.1Q Frame*

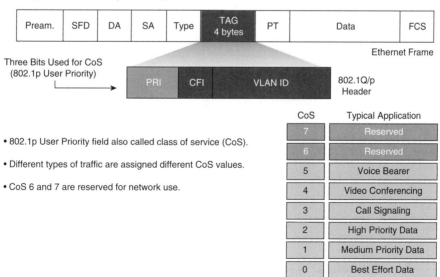

Figure 10-9 *Layer 3 IP ToS Byte*

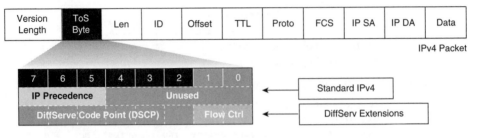

- IPv4
  - Three most significant bits of ToS byte are called IP Precedence.
  - Other bits are unused.
- DiffServ
  - Six most significant bits of ToS byte are called DiffServ Code Point (DSCP).
  - DSCP is backward-compatible with IP Precedence.
  - Remaining two bits are used for flow control.

To configure DSCP and CoS marking on the ingress queue of a Cisco IOS–based Catalyst switch, use the following commands, respectively:

```
mls qos dscp dscp-value
mls qos cos cos-value
```

Here, *dscp-value* represents a DSCP value from 0 to 63, whereas *cos-value* represents a CoS value between 0 and 7. These commands effectively yield classification as the switches use the new DSCP or CoS values for determining the internal DSCP value, which consequently overrides the existing DSCP or CoS value on the ingress frame. Example 10-7 illustrates marking CoS on ingress frames on a per-interface basis on a Cisco IOS–based Catalyst switch.

Example 10-7 *Marking CoS on Ingress Frames*

```
! Output omitted for brevity
!
mls qos
!
! Output omitted for brevity
!
interface FastEthernet0/20
 switchport mode dynamic desirable
 mls qos cos 5
!
! Output omitted for brevity
!
```

To configure marking as part of the policy map for classification based on ACLs, use any of the following policy-map action commands, depending on application:

```
set ip dscp ip-dscp-value
set ip precedence ip-precedence-value
set cos cos-value
```

Example 10-8 illustrates an example of a policy map with a class-map clause of marking frames with an IP DSCP value of 45.

Example 10-8 *Sample Configuration of Policy Map and Class Map for Marking*

```
(text deleted)
!
mls qos
!
class-map match-all Voice-subnet
  match access-group 100
!
!
policy-map Ingress-Policy
  class Voice-subnet
    set ip dscp 45
!
(text deleted)
!

interface FastEthernet0/1
 switchport mode access
 service-policy input Ingress-Policy
!
(text deleted)
!
access-list 100 permit tcp any 10.1.1.0 0.0.0.255
!
```

Traffic Conditioning: Policing and Shaping

Cisco routers that run Cisco IOS support two traffic-shaping methods: generic traffic shaping (GTS) and Frame Relay traffic shaping (FRTS). Cisco routers that run Cisco IOS support policing using the committed access rate (CAR) tool. Cisco Catalyst switches that run Cisco IOS support policing and shaping via slightly different methods and configurations compared to Cisco IOS on Cisco routers. The following sections discuss policing and shaping on Catalyst switches in more detail.

Shaping

Both shaping and policing mechanisms control the rate at which traffic flows through a switch. Both mechanisms use classification to differentiate traffic. Nevertheless, there is a fundamental and significant difference between shaping and policing.

Shaping meters traffic rates and delays (buffers) excessive traffic so that the traffic rates stay within a desired rate limit. As a result, shaping smoothes excessive bursts to produce a steady flow of data. Reducing bursts decreases congestion in downstream routers and switches and, consequently, reduces the number of frames dropped by downstream routers and switches. Because shaping delays traffic, it is not useful for delay-sensitive traffic flows such as voice, video, or storage, but it is useful for typical, bursty TCP flows. Figure 10-10 illustrates an example of traffic shaping applied to TCP data traffic.

Figure 10-10 *Traffic-Shaping Example*

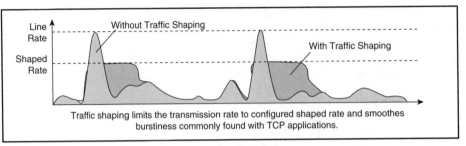

Traffic shaping limits the transmission rate to configured shaped rate and smoothes burstiness commonly found with TCP applications.

For more information on which Catalyst switches support shaping and configuration guidelines in regards to shaping, consult the Cisco.com website. In the multilayer switched networks, policing is more commonly used and is widely supported across the Catalyst platforms when compared to shaping.

Policing

In contrast to shaping, policing takes a specific action for out-of-profile traffic above a specified rate. Policing does not delay or buffer traffic. The action for traffic that exceeds a specified rate is usually *drop*; however, other actions are permissible, such as trusting and marking.

Policing on Catalyst switches follows the leaky token bucket algorithm, which allows for bursts of traffic compared to rate limiting. The leaky token bucket algorithm is as effective at handling TCP as it is at handling bursts of TCP flows. Figure 10-11 illustrates the leaky token bucket algorithm.

Figure 10-11 *Leaky Token Bucket*

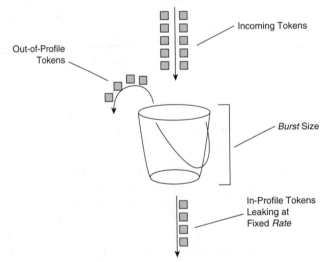

When switches apply policing to incoming traffic, they place a number of tokens proportional to the incoming traffic packet sizes into a token bucket in which the number of tokens equals the size of the packet. At a regular interval, the switch removes a defined number of tokens, determined by the configured rate, from the bucket. If the bucket is full and cannot accommodate an ingress packet, the switch determines that the packet is out of profile. The switch subsequently drops or marks out-of-profile packets according to the configured policing action.

It is important to note that the leaky bucket does not actually buffer packets, although the diagram in Figure 10-11 alludes to this point. The traffic is not actually flowing through the bucket; Catalyst switches simply use the bucket to determine out-of-profile packets. Furthermore, each Catalyst switch's hardware implementation of policing is different; therefore, only use the leaky token bucket explanation as a guide to understanding the difference between policing and shaping and how policing limits traffic.

A complete discussion of the leaky token bucket algorithm is outside the scope of this book. Consult the following document on Cisco.com for more information about the leaky token bucket algorithm:

"Understanding QoS Policing and Marking on the Catalyst 3550"

Policing is configured using several parameters. Policing configurations apply the following parameters. (Not all parameters are configurable on all Catalyst switches.)

- **Rate**—The effective policing rate in terms of bits per second (bps). Each Catalyst switch supports different rates and different rate increments.

- **Burst**—The number of packets that switches allow in the bucket before determining that the packet is out of profile. Various Catalyst switches support various burst ranges with various increments.

- **Conforming action**—Depending on the Catalyst switch model, optional supported conforming actions include drop, transmit, and mark.

- **Exceed action**—Depending on the Catalyst switch model, optional supported exceed actions for out-of-profile packets are drop, transmit, and mark.

- **Violate action**—Applies to Catalyst switches that support two-rate policers, where there is a second bucket in the leaky token bucket algorithm. The violate action adds a third measurement for out-of-profile traffic. Applicable violate actions are drop, transmit, and mark. RFC 2698 discusses three-color marking, the basis for the addition of violate action on Cisco Catalyst switches.

There are many white papers, books, and tech notes on how to correctly configure the burst size to handle TCP traffic effectively. One leading recommended formula for configuring burst is as follows:

$$\text{<burst\_size>} = 2 * \text{<RTT>} * \text{rate}$$

RTT is the round trip time for a TCP session. RTT can be determined from sophisticated methods such as traffic analysis tools or simple tools such as ping. Rate is throughput end-to-end. For more information on configuring recommended burst sizes, refer to Cisco.com.

In addition, there are three types of policing on Catalyst switches:

- **Individual policers**—An individual policer is a per-interface policer where the switch applies specified policing parameters on a per-interface basis. Applying a policer that limits traffic to 75 Mbps on each interface is an example of an individual policer.

- **Aggregate policers**—Aggregate policers are policers that apply policing parameters on a group of interfaces. For example, an aggregate policer that is defined to limit traffic to 75 Mbps to a group of interfaces limits the total traffic for all interfaces to 75 Mbps. As a result, the group of interfaces can achieve only 75 Mbps among all members with an aggregate policer, whereas an individual policer applies policing parameters on a per-interface basis.

- **Microflow policing**—Microflow policing is per-flow policing where a switch applies policing parameters to each class within a policy map.

NOTE   Several models of Catalyst switches support application of policing not only on a per-interface basis but also on a per-VLAN basis. Check the product configuration guide for support applications of policing on a per-VLAN basis.

Configuring individual or microflow policers on Catalyst switches is accomplished via policy maps. To specify an individual policer or microflow policer as a class map action clause, use the following command:

```
police [flow] bits-per-second normal-burst-bytes [extended-burst-bytes]
    [pir peak-rate-bps] [{conform-action action} {drop [exceed-action action]} |
    {set-dscp-transmit [new-dscp]} | {set-prec-transmit [new-precedence]} |
    {transmit [{exceed-action action} | {violate-action action}]]
```

Not all families of Catalyst switches and software versions support all the options listed in the preceding **police** command; always check the configuration guides on Cisco.com for supported actions.

To define an aggregate policer, use the following global command:

```
mls qos aggregate-policer policer_name bits_per_second normal_burst_bytes
    [maximum_burst_bytes] [pir peak_rate_bps] [[[conform-action {drop |
    set-dscp-transmit dscp_value | set-prec-transmit ip_precedence_value |
    transmit}] exceed-action {drop | policed-dscp | transmit}]
    violate-action {drop | policed-dscp | transmit}]
```

As with the policy map configuration, not all families of Catalyst switches support the entire options list with the **mls qos aggregate-policer** command. To tie an aggregate policer to a class map action clause in a policy map, use the following command:

```
police aggregate aggregate_policer_name
```

Example 10-9 illustrates a sample configuration of an individual policer on a Catalyst 3550 switch. This individual policer limits traffic ingress on interface FastEthernet0/3. The policer limits the traffic that matches the class map MATCH-UDP, which in turn matches access-list 101. Access-list 101 permits traffic on UDP 10000. As a result of this configuration on FastEthernet0/3, all traffic on UDP port 10000 is policed to 1,536,000 bps by dropping traffic exceeding the rate.

Example 10-9 *Sample Configuration of Policing*

```
!
mls qos
!
class-map match-all MATCH-UDP
  match access-group 101
!
!
policy-map LIMIT-UDP
  class MATCH-UDP
    police 1536000 20000 exceed-action drop
!
! Output omitted for brevity
!
interface FastEthernet0/3
 switchport mode dynamic desirable
 service-policy input LIMIT-UDP
!
(text deleted)
!
```

The following sections discuss congestion management and congestion avoidance. Congestion management is the key feature of QoS because it applies scheduling to egress queues.

Congestion Management

Catalyst switches use multiple egress queues for application of the congestion-management and congestion-avoidance QoS features. Both congestion management and congestion avoidance are a per-queue feature. For example, congestion-avoidance threshold configurations are per queue, and each queue may have its own configuration for congestion management and avoidance. In addition, each Catalyst switch has a unique hardware implementation for egress queues. For example, the Catalyst 3550 family of switches has four egress queues, whereas the Catalyst 6500 family of switches uses either one or two egress queues depending on line module.

Cisco IOS uses specific nomenclature for referencing egress queues. For a queue system XpYqZt, the following applies:

- X indicates the number of priority queues.
- Y indicates the number of queues other than the priority queues.
- Z indicates the configurable tail-drop or WRED thresholds per queue.

For example, the Catalyst 4000 and 4500 families of switches use either a 1p3q1t or 4q1t queuing system, depending on configuration. For the 1p3q1t queuing system, the switch uses a total of four egress queues, one of which is a priority queue, all of which support a single congestion-avoidance threshold.

Moreover, classification and marking have little meaning without congestion management. Switches use congestion-management configurations to schedule packets appropriately from output queues once congestion occurs. Catalyst switches support a variety of scheduling and queuing algorithms. Each queuing algorithm solves a specific type of network traffic condition.

Catalyst switches transmit frames on egress with a DSCP value mapped directly from the internal DSCP value. The CoS value of egress also maps directly from the internal DSCP value where the DSCP-to-CoS value for egress frames is configurable. Table 10-6 illustrates the default DSCP-to-CoS mapping table.

Table 10-6   *DSCP-to-CoS Mapping Table*

DSCP Value	0–7	8–15	16–23	24–31	32–39	40–47	48–55	56–63
CoS Value	0	1	2	3	4	5	6	7

To configure the DSCP-to-CoS mapping table, use the following command:

```
mls qos map dscp-cos dscp-values to cos_value
```

Congestion management comprises several queuing mechanisms, including the following:

- FIFO queuing
- Weighted round robin (WRR) queuing
- Priority queuing
- Custom queuing
- Shaped round robin (SRR)

The following subsections discuss these queuing mechanisms in more detail.

FIFO Queuing

The default method of queuing frames is FIFO queuing, in which the switch places all egress frames into the same queue, regardless of classification. Essentially, FIFO queuing does not use classification, and all packets are treated as if they belong to the same class. The switch schedules packets from the queue for transmission in the order in which they are received. This behavior is the default behavior of a Cisco IOS–based Catalyst switch without QoS enabled. Figure 10-12 illustrates the behavior of FIFO queuing.

Because FIFO queuing is the default configuration of Catalyst switches, it does not require configuration commands.

Figure 10-12 *FIFO Queuing*

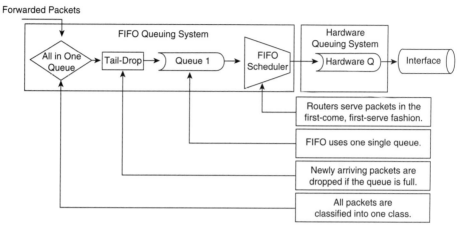

Forwarded Packets

FIFO Queuing System

All in One Queue

Tail-Drop

Queue 1

FIFO Scheduler

Hardware Queuing System

Hardware Q

Interface

Routers serve packets in the first-come, first-serve fashion.

FIFO uses one single queue.

Newly arriving packets are dropped if the queue is full.

All packets are classified into one class.

Weighted Round Robin Queuing

Scheduling packets from egress queues using WRR is a popular and simple method of differentiating service among traffic classes. With WRR, the switch uses a configured weight value for each egress queue. This weight value determines the implied bandwidth of each queue. The higher the weight value, the higher the priority that the switch applies to the egress queue. For example, consider the case of a Catalyst 3550 switch configured for QoS and WRR. The Catalyst 3550 uses four egress queues. If queues 1 through 4 are configured with weights 50, 10, 25, and 15, respectively, queue 1 can utilize 50 percent of the bandwidth when there is congestion. Queues 2 through 4 can utilize 10, 25, and 15 percent of the bandwidth, respectively, when congestion exists. Figure 10-13 illustrates WRR behavior with eight egress queues. Figure 10-13 also illustrates tail-drop and WRED properties, which are explained in later sections.

Figure 10-13 *Weighted Round Robin*

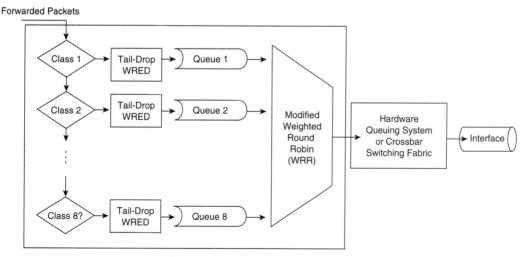

Forwarded Packets

Class 1 → Tail-Drop WRED → Queue 1

Class 2 → Tail-Drop WRED → Queue 2

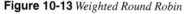

Class 8? → Tail-Drop WRED → Queue 8

Modified Weighted Round Robin (WRR)

Hardware Queuing System or Crossbar Switching Fabric

Interface

Although the queues utilize a percentage of bandwidth, the switch does not actually assign specific bandwidth to each queue when using WRR. The switch uses WRR to schedule packets from egress queues only under congestion. Another noteworthy aspect of WRR is that it does not starve lower-priority queues, because the switch services all queues during a finite time period.

To configure WRR on the Catalyst 6500 family of switches running Cisco IOS, perform the following steps:

Step 1 Enable QoS globally, if not previously configured.

```
Switch(config)#mls qos
```

Step 2 Select an interface to configure.

```
Switch(config)#interface {ethernet | fastethernet | gigabitethernet |
    tengigabitethernet} slot/port
```

Step 3 Assign egress CoS values to queues and queue thresholds. The switches use the CoS mapping for congestion avoidance thresholds, which are discussed in the next section.

```
Switch(config-if)#wrr-queue cos-map queue-id threshold-id cos-1...cos-n
```

You must assign the CoS-to-queue threshold for all queue types. The queues are always numbered starting with the lowest-priority queue possible, and ending with the strict-priority queue, if one is available. A generic example follows using variable number queues, termed n:

— Queue 1 will be the low-priority WRR queue.

— Queue 2 will be the high-priority WRR queue.

— Queue n will be the strict-priority queue.

The strict-priority queue is configured by using the **priority-queue** command, and the **wrr-queue cos-map** command configures the CoS to egress queue mapping. Repeat Step 3 for each queue, or keep the default CoS assignments.

Step 4 Configure the WRR weights for the WRR queues.

```
Switch(config-if)#wrr-queue bandwidth weight for Q1 weight for Q2 weight
    for Qn
```

Weight for Q1 relates to queue 1, which should be the low-priority WRR queue. Keep this weight at a level lower than the weight for Q2. The weight can take any value between 1 and 255. Assign the ratio by using the following formulas:

— To queue 1: [weight 1 / sum(weights)]

— To queue 2: [weight 2 / sum(weights)]

— To queue n: [weight n / sum(weights)]

You must define the weight for all types of queues. These weight types do not need to be the same.

Step 5 Define the transmit queue ratio. The weights are configurable percentages between 1 and 100.

```
Router(config-if)# wrr-queue queue-limit  low-priority-queue-weight
 [medium-priorityqueue-weights(s)]  high-priority-queue-weights
```

The transmit queue ratio determines the way that the buffers are split among the different queues. If you have multiple queues with a priority queue, the configuration requires the same weight on the high-priority WRR queues and for the strict-priority queue. These levels cannot be different on the Catalyst 6500 family of switches for hardware reasons. Generally, high-priority queues do not require a large amount of memory for queuing because traffic destined for high-priority queues is delay sensitive and often low volume. As a result, large queue sizes for high- and strict-priority queues are not necessary. The recommendation is to use memory space for the low-priority queues that generally contain data traffic that is not delay sensitive to buffering. The next section discusses strict-priority queuing with WRR.

NOTE   The Catalyst 2950 family of switches applies WRR configuration on a global basis and not on a per-interface basis, as do the Catalyst 6500 and 3550 families of switches. The preceding steps are applicable to the Catalyst 2950 except on a per-switch basis.

NOTE   The Catalyst 2970 and 3750 families of switches use a specialized WRR feature referred to as shaped round robin (SRR) for congestion management. Refer to the Catalyst 2750 and 3750 QoS configuration guides detailing SSR for more details.

NOTE   The Catalyst 4000 and 4500 families of switches running Cisco IOS do not use WRR, specifically, for congestion management. These switches use sharing and shaping instead. Sharing is different from WRR; it differentiates services by guaranteeing bandwidth per queue. These switches do support strict-priority queuing on queue 3.

Example 10-10 illustrates a sample congestion-management configuration on a Catalyst 6500 switch running Cisco IOS. In this configuration, egress CoS values 0 through 2 map to queue 1 threshold 1, CoS value 3 maps to queue 2 threshold 2, CoS value 4 maps to queue 2 threshold 1, and CoS value 6 maps to queue 2 threshold 2. The egress CoS values of 5 and 7 map to the priority queue, which is referenced as queue 1 and threshold 1.

Example 10-10 *Sample Configuration for Congestion Management for a Catalyst 6500 Switch Running Cisco IOS*

```
!
interface GigabitEthernet1/1
 no ip address
 wrr-queue bandwidth 50 75
 wrr-queue queue-limit 100 50
 wrr-queue cos-map 1 1 0 2
 wrr-queue cos-map 2 2 3
 wrr-queue cos-map 2 1 4
 wrr-queue cos-map 2 2 6
 priority-queue cos-map 1 1 5 7
 switchport
!
```

Shaped Round Robin (SRR)

The Catalyst 2970, 3560, and 3750 use the shaped round robin (SRR) feature for egress queuing. SRR supports the following two congestion management configurations:

- Shaped mode
- Shared mode

In shaped mode, egress queues are shaped to an exact percentage of interface bandwidth, similar to Cisco IOS rate limiting. As such, traffic from an egress queue cannot exceed a specified rate regardless of traffic in other queues. Shaping provides a more even flow of traffic over time and reduces the peaks and valleys of bursty traffic. Shaped mode is commonly used with delay-sensitive traffic and UDP/IP traffic flows.

In shared mode, egress queues also receive a percentage of bandwidth; however, the egress queues are not limited to that bandwidth. If other queues have no traffic to send, a single queue can consume the whole bandwidth. In other words, queues are able to use bandwidth from other queues if their queues do not have data to transmit. Furthermore, in shared mode, a percentage of bandwidth per queue is guaranteed when congestion exists. This concept is similar to Class-based Weighted Fair Queuing (CBWFQ) commonly found on Cisco IOS routers.

Because four egress queues exist on the Catalyst 3750, a hybrid configuration of shaped and shared bandwidth is possible. To configure SRR for shaping, use the following command:

```
srr-queue bandwidth shape weight1 weight2 weight3 weight4
```

For *weight1 weight2 weight3 weight4*, enter the weights to allocate the percentage of bandwidth that each egress queue is shaped. The inverse ratio (1/*weight*) controls the shaping bandwidth for this queue. If you configure a weight of 0, the corresponding queue operates in shared mode, and the weight specified with the **srr-queue bandwidth shape** command is ignored; instead, the weights specified with the **srr-queue bandwidth share** interface configuration command are used. When configuring queues in the same queue-set for both shaping and sharing, make sure that you configure the lowest number queue for shaping.

To explicitly configure the egress queue bandwidth share on an interface, use the following command:

srr-queue bandwidth share *weight1 weight2 weight3 weight4*

By default, all four weights are 25. For *weight1 weight2 weight3 weight4*, enter the weights to control the ratio of the frequency in which the SRR scheduler sends packets. The range is 1 to 255, similar to WRR configurations. The configuration of the expedite queue on the Catalyst 2960, 3560, and 3750 families of switches remains the same as the Catalyst 3560 as discussed in an earlier section. Example 10-11 demonstrates SRR queuing where queue 1 is shaped to 20 percent of the bandwidth while the rest of the queues are shared at the respective bandwidth percentages.

Example 10-11 *SRR Sample Configuration*

```
Switch#show run interface gigabitEthernet 1/0/1
Building configuration...

Current configuration : 132 bytes
!
interface GigabitEthernet1/0/1
 no ip address
 srr-queue bandwidth shape  20  0  0  0
 srr-queue bandwidth share 20 30 25 25
end
```

Priority Queuing

One method of prioritizing and scheduling frames from egress queues is to use priority queuing. Earlier sections noted that enabling QoS globally on Cisco IOS–based Catalyst switches enables the use of egress queues. When applying strict priority to one of these queues, the switch schedules frames from that queue as long as there are frames in that queue, before servicing any other queue. Catalyst switches ignore WRR scheduling weights for queues configured as priority queues; most Catalyst switches support the designation of a single egress queue as a priority queue.

Priority queuing is useful for voice applications where voice traffic occupies the priority queue. However, this type of scheduling may result in queue starvation in the nonpriority queue. The remaining nonpriority queues are subject to the WRR configurations.

Catalyst switches, in terms of configuration, refer to priority queuing as expedite queuing or strict-priority queuing, depending on the model. To configure the strict-priority queue on Catalyst 6500 switches running Cisco IOS, use the **priority-queue cos-map** command and assign the appropriate CoS values to the priority queue. Because voice traffic usually carries a DSCP value of 46, which maps to a CoS value of 5, the ideal configuration for priority queuing is to map the CoS value of 5 to the strict-priority queue.

On the Catalyst 3550 family of switches, use the **priority-queue out** command to enable strict-priority queuing on queue 4. For the Catalyst 4000 and 4500 families of switches, use the **priority high** command on the **tx-queue 3** interface to enable strict-priority queuing on queue 3. Note that not all line modules for the Catalyst support egress priority queuing. The Catalyst 3750 uses ingress priority along with SRR instead of egress priority scheduling for priority queuing–type configurations. See the configuration guides for these switches for more details regarding strict-priority queuing configurations. Example 10-10 also illustrates the priority-queuing configuration for an interface of Catalyst 6500 running Cisco IOS using the **priority-queue cos-map** command.

Custom Queuing

Another method of queuing available on Catalyst switches strictly for WAN interfaces is custom queuing. Custom queuing (CQ) reserves a percentage of available bandwidth for an interface for each selected traffic type. If a particular type of traffic is not using the reserved bandwidth, other queues and types of traffic may use the remaining bandwidth.

CQ is statically configured and does not provide for automatic adaptation for changing network conditions. In addition, CQ is not popular on high-speed WAN interfaces; refer to the configuration guides for CQ support on LAN interfaces and configuration details. See the configuration guide for each Catalyst switch for supported CQ configurations.

Other Congestion-Management Features and Components

This section highlights the most significant features of congestion management on Cisco IOS–based Catalyst switches, specifically focusing on the Catalyst 6500 family of switches. Each Catalyst switch is unique in configuration and supported congestion-management features; refer to the configuration guides and product documentation for more details.

In brief, the following additional congestion-management features are available on various Catalyst switches:

- Internal DSCP to egress queue mapping
- Sharing
- Transmit queue size per Catalyst switch and interface type

Congestion Avoidance

Congestion-avoidance techniques monitor network traffic loads in an effort to anticipate and avoid congestion at common network bottleneck points. Switches and routers achieve congestion avoidance through packet dropping using complex algorithms (versus the simple tail-drop algorithm). Campus networks more commonly use congestion-avoidance techniques on WAN interfaces (versus Ethernet interfaces) because of the limited bandwidth of WAN interfaces. However, for Ethernet interfaces of considerable congestion, congestion avoidance is very useful.

Tail Drop

When an interface of a router or switch cannot transmit a packet immediately because of congestion, the router or switch queues the packet. The router or switch eventually transmits the packet from the queue. If the arrival rate of packets for transmission on an interface exceeds the router's or switch's ability to buffer the traffic, the router or switch simply drops the packets. This behavior is called *tail drop* because all packets for transmission attempting to enter an egress queue are dropped until there is space in the queue for another packet. Tail drop is the default behavior on Cisco Catalyst switch interfaces.

Tail drop treats all traffic equally regardless of internal DSCP in the case of a Catalyst switch. For environments with a large number of TCP flows or flows where selective packet drops are detrimental, tail drop is not the best approach to dropping frames. Moreover, tail drop has these shortcomings with respect to TCP flows:

- The dropping of frames usually affects ongoing TCP sessions. Arbitrary dropping of frames with a TCP session results in concurrent TCP sessions simultaneously backing off and restarting, yielding a "saw-tooth" effect. As a result, inefficient link utilization occurs at the congestion point (TCP global synchronization).

- Aggressive TCP flows may seize all space in output queues over normal TCP flow as a result of tail drop.

- Excessive queuing of packets in the output queues at the point of congestion results in delay and jitter as packets await transmission.

- No differentiated drop mechanism exists; premium traffic is dropped in the same manner as best-effort traffic.

- Even in the event of a single TCP stream across an interface, the presence of other non-TCP traffic may congest the interface. In this scenario, the feedback to the TCP protocol is poor; as a result, TCP cannot adapt properly to the congested network.

Recall that TCP increases the window size slowly (TCP slow start) and linearly until a lost acknowledgment signals lost frames along the data path. It then decreases the window size logarithmically. If there are many flows that start slowly, each flow will increase the window size until congestion occurs, and then all will fall back at the same time. As the flows become synchronized, the link is used less efficiently.

Because routers and switches handle multiple concurrent TCP sessions, and because TCP flows are generally bursty, when egress traffic exceeds the buffer limit for egress queues, it vastly exceeds the buffer limit for the egress queues. In addition, the burstiness of TCP is of short duration and generally does not result in periods of prolonged congestion. Recall that tail-drop algorithms drop all traffic that exceeds the buffer limit by default. As a result of multiple TCP flows vastly exceeding the buffer limit, multiple TCP sessions simultaneously go into TCP slow start. Consequently, all TCP traffic slows down and then slow-starts again. This behavior creates a condition known as *global synchronization*, which occurs as waves of congestion crest only to be followed by troughs during which link utilization is not fully utilized.

One method of handling global synchronization is to apply weighted fair queuing (WFQ). WFQ uses an elaborate scheme for dropping traffic, because it can control aggressive TCP flows via its Congestion Discard Threshold (CDT)–based packet dropping algorithm. However, WFQ does not scale to the backbone speeds used in multilayer switched networks; instead, Catalyst switches use weighted random early detection (WRED) for congestion avoidance. The next subsection discusses this feature.

Tail drop is a congestion-avoidance mechanism when applied with classification to multiple thresholds. An example of congestion avoidance is configuring a Catalyst switch to tail-drop packets with DSCP values between 0 and 5 at a 50 percent queue full threshold compared to tail-dropping packets with DSCP values between 6 and 10 at a 100 percent queue full threshold. In this configuration, the switch drops packets with DSCP values between 0 and 5 at a lower threshold to avoid congestion on packets with DSCP values between 6 and 10.

Weighted Random Early Detection

WRED is a congestion-avoidance mechanism that is useful for backbone speeds. WRED attempts to avoid congestion by randomly dropping packets with a certain classification when output buffers reach a specific threshold. WRED is essentially a combination of two QoS features: random early detection (RED) and WRR.

Figure 10-14 illustrates the behavior of TCP with and without RED. As illustrated in the diagram, RED smoothes TCP sessions because it randomly drops packets, which ultimately reduces TCP windows. Without RED, TCP flows go through slow start simultaneously. The end result of RED is better link utilization.

Figure 10-14 *Link Utilization Optimizations with Congestion Avoidance*

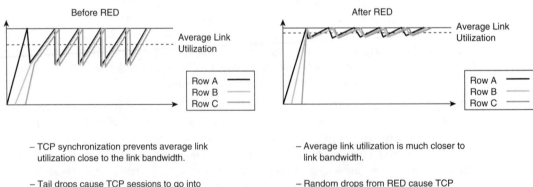

RED randomly drops packets at configured threshold values (percentage full) of output buffers. As more packets fill the output queues, the switch randomly drops frames in an attempt to avoid congestion without the "saw-tooth" TCP problem. RED only works when the output queue is not full; when the output queue is full, the switch tail-drops any additional packets that attempt to occupy the output queue. However, the probability of dropping a packet rises linearly as the output queue begins to fill above the RED threshold.

RED works very well for TCP flows but not for other types of traffic, such as UDP flows and voice traffic. WRED is similar to RED except that WRED takes into account classification of frames. For example, for a single output queue, a switch configuration may consist of a WRED threshold of 50 percent for all best-effort traffic for DSCP values up to 20, and 80 percent for all traffic with a DSCP value between 20 and 31. In this example, the switch drops existing packets in the output queue with a DSCP of 0 to 20 when the queue's threshold reaches 50 percent. If the queue continues to fill to the 80 percent threshold, the switch then begins to drop existing packets with DSCP values above 20. If the output queue is full even with WRED configured, the switch tail-drops any additional packets that attempt to occupy the output queue. The end result of the WRED configuration is that the switch is less likely to drop packets with higher priorities (higher DSCP value). Figure 10-15 illustrates the WRED algorithm pictorially.

Figure 10-15 *Weighted Random Early Detection*

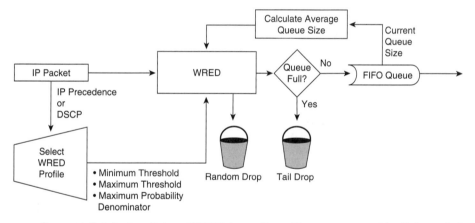

On most Catalyst switches, WRED is configurable per queue, with all the switches in Table 10-1 using four queues except the Catalyst 6500, for which the number of output queues varies per line card. Nevertheless, it is possible to use WRR and WRED together. A best-practice recommendation is to designate a strict-priority queue for high-priority traffic and use WRED for the remaining queues designated for data traffic.

For switches that support tail-drop and WRED configurations, the configurations vary depending on the number of output queues and whether the line modules support minimum configurable thresholds. Minimum thresholds specify the queue depth at which not to drop traffic. To configure tail-drop thresholds on the Catalyst 6500 family of switches running Cisco IOS for 1q4t or 2q2t interfaces, use the following command:

```
wrr-queue threshold queue-id thr1% thr2%
```

Here, *queue-id* specifies the respective queue number, and *thr1%* and *thr2%* specify the output queue full percentage at which to start dropping traffic and the maximum queue full percentage at which to apply tail-drop, respectively. Always set *thr2%* to 100 percent for tail-drop configurations. To configure WRED on the Catalyst 6500 family of switches running Cisco IOS for 1p2q2t, 1p3q1t, 1p2q1t, and 1p1q8t, use the following commands:

```
wrr-queue random-detect min-threshold queue-id thr1% [thr2% [thr3% thr4% thr5% thr6%
    thr7% thr8%]]
wrr-queue random-detect max-threshold queue-id thr1% [thr2% [thr3% thr4% thr5% thr6%
    thr7% thr8%]]
```

The **min-threshold** command specifies the low-WRED output queue percentage value for which the switch does not drop frames. The **max-threshold** command specifies the high-WRED queue percentage value for which to drop all frames in the queue. Example 10-12 illustrates an example of WRED on the Catalyst 6500 family of switches. In this example, the switch only applies WRED when queue 1 reaches 50 percent full for threshold 1 and 70 percent full for threshold 2. When the queue is 75 percent full in threshold 1, the switch drops all frames.

Example 10-12 *Sample WRED Configuration on Catalyst 6500 Switch Running Cisco IOS*

```
!
interface GigabitEthernet1/1
 no ip address
 wrr-queue bandwidth 50 75
 wrr-queue queue-limit 100 50
 wrr-queue random-detect min-threshold 1 50 70
 wrr-queue random-detect max-threshold 1 75 100
 wrr-queue cos-map 1 1 0 2
 wrr-queue cos-map 1 2 3
 wrr-queue cos-map 2 1 4
 wrr-queue cos-map 2 2 6
 priority-queue cos-map 1 1 5 7
 rcv-queue cos-map 1 1 0
 switchport
!
```

To configure all other interface output queue types on the Catalyst 6500 family of switches and all other Catalyst switches, refer to the product configuration guides for the respective Catalyst switch on Cisco.com.

Catalyst switches support WRED on ingress receive queues as well. Consult the configuration guides on Cisco.com for additional details on configuring WRED for ingress receive queues.

QoS in the Multilayer Switched Network

The QoS implementation for a campus network differs at the Campus Backbone, Building Access, and Building Distribution submodules. Because applying QoS classification at the edge is ideal, Layer 2 edge (Building Access) switches generally perform the following QoS functions:

- Classification on a per-packet basis
- Marking

- Congestion management
- Congestion avoidance

In general, backbone Layer 3 devices perform the following QoS functions, because backbone devices receive packets after classification and marking:

- Congestion management
- Congestion avoidance

For Edge submodules that connect Campus Backbones across MANs or WANs, deploy the following QoS features:

- Classification on a per-packet basis
- Policing or shaping
- Fragmentation
- Compression
- Congestion management
- Congestion avoidance

Figure 10-16 depicts the recommended QoS feature deployments.

Figure 10-16 *Recommended QoS Features in the Enterprise Composite Network Model*

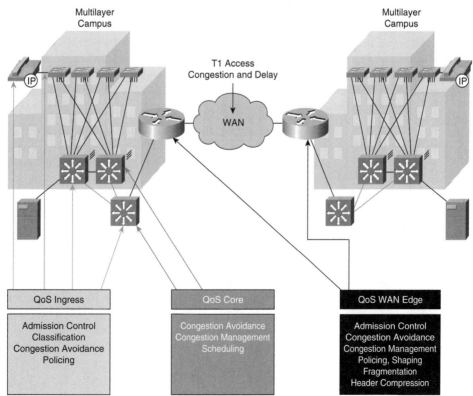

Networks with special applications of QoS may not exactly follow these guidelines, but these guidelines are a starting point for any QoS network policy.

QoS in the Building Access Submodule

The Building Access submodule is typically where the trust boundary is formed. In this submodule, the Catalyst switches set or trust the DSCP value of ingress packets for use through the entire network. Catalyst switches may set or trust the DSCP value of ingress packets by comparing ingress packets against an ACL or policer. When using ACLs, the Catalyst classifies or marks only packets that match specific criteria, such as TCP port number or IP addresses. In addition, using policers to set or trust DSCP values on ingress packets allows the Catalyst switches to determine the trust behavior by the traffic rate. Traffic that exceeds a specified rate and receives a lower DSCP value than traffic that complies with the specified rate is an example of the use of a policer to mark down DSCP values. These features are useful in differentiating traffic flows instead of differentiating traffic by ingress port.

Furthermore, policing is optional in the Building Access submodule. Catalyst switches in the Building Access submodule layer configured for policing apply traffic conditioning and may optionally classify or mark packets before reaching the Campus Backbone or Building Distribution submodule.

Congestion management is a requirement of the Building Access submodule for all interfaces. Classification only determines the internal DSCP of a packet as it traverses the Catalyst switch. Congestion management on the Catalyst switch acts on the internal DSCP values of packets to schedule and apply congestion avoidance accordingly. Congestion avoidance is another useful feature used in the access layer in preventing low-priority traffic from starving higher-priority traffic out of queues.

Not all the Cisco Catalyst switches support all QoS features. In addition, low-end Catalyst switches support the features with significant restrictions, such as restrictions on ACL size and types of ACLs for classification. Consult the product release notes and documentation before deciding which Catalyst switches to use in the QoS design.

QoS in the Building Distribution Submodule

Classification and marking other than trusting in the Building Distribution submodule is necessary only if the Building Access layer does not classify packets or if the Catalyst switches used in the Building Access submodule do not support adequate features necessary to apply QoS effectively. When applying QoS in the Building Distribution submodule, simply use the same principles used when applying QoS in the Building Access submodule. In this layer, configure all inter-switch links for trusting. In this manner, the Building Distribution submodule switches trust the classification from all other switches.

Policing is optional in the Building Distribution submodule as with any submodule. Policing is useful in constraining traffic flows and marking frames above specific rates. Policing is primarily useful for data flows and voice or video flows because voice and video usually maintain a steady rate of traffic.

Congestion management is necessary on all inter-switch links and any hosts or servers that may connect to the Building Distribution submodule. Congestion management applies proper scheduling of frames for differential service. Congestion avoidance is optional in any submodule but is not a requirement.

QoS in the Campus Backbone

The Campus Backbone QoS application is similar to the Building Distribution submodule; use classification and marking in situations where other submodules have not classified or marked traffic. Ideally, there should not be a need to classify or mark traffic in the Campus Backbone submodule. As with other submodules, policing is optional. However, congestion management is a requirement to differentiate traffic flows through the core of the network. Congestion avoidance is optional but recommended to handle congestion effectively.

Auto QoS

Cisco AutoQoS enables customers to deploy QoS features for converged IP telephony and data networks much more quickly and efficiently. Cisco AutoQoS generates traffic classes and policy map CLI templates. Cisco AutoQoS simplifies and automates the Modular QoS CLI (MQC) definition of traffic classes and the creation and configuration of traffic policies. Therefore, when Cisco AutoQoS is configured at the interface, the traffic receives the required QoS treatment automatically. In-depth knowledge of the underlying technologies, service policies, link efficiency mechanisms, and Cisco QoS best practice recommendations for voice requirements is not required to configure Cisco AutoQoS.

Cisco AutoQoS can be extremely beneficial for these scenarios:

- Small to medium-sized businesses that must deploy IP telephony quickly but lack the experience and staffing to plan and deploy IP QoS services
- Large customer enterprises that need to deploy Cisco Systems telephony solutions on a large scale, while reducing the costs, complexity, and time frame for deployment, and ensuring that the appropriate QoS for voice applications is being set in a consistent fashion
- International enterprises or service providers requiring QoS for VoIP where little expertise exists in different regions of the world and where provisioning QoS remotely and across different time zones is difficult

- Service providers requiring a template-driven approach to delivering managed services and QoS for voice traffic to large numbers of customer premises devices

Moreover, Cisco AutoQoS simplifies and shortens the QoS deployment cycle. Cisco AutoQoS helps in all five major aspects of successful QoS deployments:

- **Application classification**—Cisco AutoQoS leverages intelligent classification on routers using Cisco NBAR to provide deep and stateful packet inspection. Cisco AutoQoS uses CDP for voice packets to ensure that the device attached to the LAN is really an IP Phone.

- **Policy generation**—Cisco AutoQoS evaluates the network environment and generates an initial policy. The first release of Cisco AutoQoS provides the necessary Cisco AutoQoS VoIP feature to automate QoS settings for VoIP deployments. This feature automatically generates interface configurations, policy maps, class maps, and ACLs. Cisco AutoQoS VoIP automatically employs Cisco NBAR to classify voice traffic and mark the traffic with the appropriate DSCP value. Cisco AutoQoS VoIP can be instructed to rely on, or trust, the DSCP markings previously applied to the packets.

- **Configuration**—With one command, Cisco AutoQoS configures the port to prioritize voice traffic without affecting other network traffic, while still offering the flexibility to adjust QoS settings for unique network requirements. Not only will Cisco AutoQoS automatically detect Cisco IP Phones and enable QoS settings, it will disable the QoS settings to prevent malicious activity when a Cisco IP Phone is relocated or moved.

- **Monitoring and reporting**—Cisco AutoQoS provides visibility into the CoSs deployed via system logging and Simple Network Management Protocol (SNMP) traps, with notification of abnormal events (that is, VoIP packet drops).

- **Consistency**—When deploying QoS configurations using Cisco AutoQoS, the configurations that are generated are consistent among router and switch platforms. This level of consistency ensures seamless QoS operation and interoperability within the network.

There are two interface configuration options for enabling QoS on Catalyst switches running Cisco IOS:

- **VoIP Trust**—Configures the ingress classification on the interface to trust the CoS and DSCP bits received in the packet.

- **VoIP Cisco-phone**—Trusts ingress CoS and DSCP only if a phone is detected connected to the interface with CDP.

Furthermore, both options configure strict priority (expedited queuing) on the egress interface for voice traffic and WRR for scheduling of the voice and data traffic, where appropriate. For further details on AutoQoS, refer to the configuration guide for the respective Catalyst switch.

Study Tips

The following bullets review important BCMSN certification exam preparation points of this chapter. The bullets only briefly highlight the main points of this chapter related to the BCMSN exam and should be used only as supplemental study material. Consult the text of this chapter for additional information regarding these topics. Furthermore, review Chapter 13, "Best Practices for Deploying Cisco IP Telephony Using Cisco Catalyst Switches," in regards to voice VLANs, an important feature that supplements QoS. Table 10-7 lists important commands to review for the BCMSN certification exam:

- QoS, in respect to Catalyst switches, is composed of the following configuration components:

    — Classification

    — Marking

    — Traffic conditioning

    — Congestion management and avoidance

- Classification associates a priority value to a frame based on properties such as ingress port, and IP packet properties such as TCP port, embedded URL, application properties, or MAC address.

- *Marking* consists of statically marking the DSCP, CoS, or IP Precedence value of a frame (hence, classifying the frame) based on ingress port, IP packet properties, rate of traffic, and so on.

- Traffic conditioning includes both shaping and policing. The purpose of this feature is to limit traffic rates and drop or mark packets exceeding the traffic rate.

- Congestion management includes scheduling packets from egress queues in such a way as to provide higher priority to specific frames based on DSCP, CoS, or IP Precedence values (classified frames).

- Congestion avoidance includes queue management as to manage congestion effectively.

- To configure a Catalyst switch to trust DSCP on an interface, use the **mls qos trust dscp** Cisco IOS command.

- To configure a Catalyst switch to trust CoS on an interface, use the **mls qos trust cos** Cisco IOS command.

- To configure a Catalyst switch to override the CoS value of ingress frames on an interface, use the **mls qos cos** *value* command.

- Congestion management configurations vary based on Catalyst switch; however, the typical configuration is to map high-priority traffic to a priority queue and schedule other queues appropriately.

- For a single deployment of QoS where QoS technologies remain abstract, use the Cisco AutoQoS feature.

Table 10-7 *Commands to Review*

Command	Description
(config) #**mls qos**	Enables QoS globally on a Catalyst 2950, 2960, 2960, 3550, 3560, 3750, or 6500 switch
(config) #**policy-map** *policy-map-name*	Enters the policy-map submode for configuration of a policy map
(config-cmap) #**match access-group** *access-list-number*	Defines matching traffic for a class map
(config-cmap) #**set ip dscp** *dscp-value*	Configures the class action as rewriting DSCP to specified value
(config-if) #**mls qos cos** *value*	Manually sets ingress CoS values to the specified *value*
(config-if) #**mls qos trust cos**	Trusts CoS values of incoming frames
(config-if) #**mls qos trust device cisco-phone**	Trusts either DSCP or CoS based on whether a Cisco IP Phone is learned via CDP on the respective port
(config-if) #**mls qos trust dscp**	Trusts DSCP values of ingress frames
(config-if) #**service-policy** [**input** | **output**] *policy-map-name*	Applies a policy to an interface, ingress or egress
#**show mls qos**	Displays whether QoS is enabled globally
(config-if) #**wrr-queue bandwidth** *weight1 weight2 weight3 weight4*	Configures WRR bandwidths
(config-if) #**wrr-queue cos-map**	Configures CoS-to-egress queue mapping, globally or on a per-interface basis

Summary

QoS is an integral part of any multilayer switched network deployment. With QoS, you can build a network of predictable behavior for latency, jitter, and packet loss. In addition, QoS mitigates anomalous network behavior and provides for differentiation of traffic flows. The following list summarizes QoS:

- Classification associates a priority value to a frame.

- Catalyst switches support classification on a per-interface or per-packet basis using ACLs.

- Marking changes the DSCP value of a packet or CoS value of a frame on ingress or egress.

- Catalyst switches use policing or shaping to condition traffic rates.
- Catalyst switches support congestion management through the use of WRR, sharing, and shaping scheduling mechanisms.
- Congestion avoidance uses WRED on Catalyst switches to improve link utilization under congestion with TCP flows.

In brief, adhere to the following guidelines and recommendations for deploying QoS in a multilayer switched network:

- Before configuring Catalyst switches for QoS, develop a QoS plan that clearly outlines the necessary traffic classification.
- Opt to classify traffic based on DSCP values instead of CoS values.
- Apply classification as close to the edge as possible, preferably in the Building Access submodule.
- Trust interfaces that interconnect switches where classification configuration already exists.
- Use policing to effectively condition traffic data rates.
- Apply congestion management to all interfaces, and use priority queuing on interfaces that transmit VoIP traffic.
- Use congestion avoidance on interfaces where heavy congestion exists with TCP flows.

For additional information on QoS, refer to the following resource:

- "Cisco IOS Quality of Service," at http://www.cisco.com/warp/public/732/Tech/qos/

Configuration Exercise: Configuring QoS on Cisco IOS–Based Catalyst Switches

Complete this configuration exercise to familiarize yourself with basic QoS configuration on Cisco IOS–based Catalyst switches as discussed in this chapter.

Required Resources

The resources and equipment required to complete this exercise are as follows. (The last two items are optional.)

- Catalyst 3550.
- Terminal server or workstation connected directly to the console port of the Catalyst 3550 or out-of-band access to the Catalyst 3550.
- Cisco IP Phones infrastructure supporting voice calls. (This resource verifies the configuration and is not mandatory.)
- Traffic generator. (This resource verifies the configuration and is not mandatory.)

Exercise Objective

The purpose of this exercise is to configure a Cisco IOS–based Catalyst switch for the following QoS features:

- Classification
- Marking
- Policing
- Congestion management
- Congestion avoidance

The exercise exposes topics such as VLANs and spanning tree found in others chapters of this book. Nevertheless, the main purpose of this exercise is to demonstrate a QoS configuration. In this configuration exercise, your goal is to configure a Catalyst 3550 for the following QoS features:

- Trust ingress DSCP values for interfaces FastEthernet0/1 through 0/10 when a Cisco IP Phone is attached.
- Reclassify frames on interface FastEthernet0/11 for a CoS value of 4.
- Mark ingress TCP Port 30000 frames on interface FastEthernet0/12 with a DSCP value of 16.
- Apply strict-priority queuing for VoIP traffic.
- Configure high-priority queues to have a 2-to-1 (2:1) priority over low-priority queues.

Network Diagram

Figure 10-17 shows the network layout for this configuration exercise.

Figure 10-17 *Network Diagram for Lab Exercise*

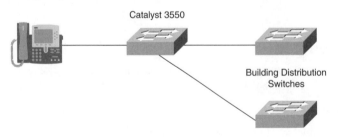

Command List

In this configuration exercise, you will use the commands listed in Table 10-8, which are in alphabetical order so that you can easily locate the information you need. Refer to this list if you need configuration command assistance during the configuration exercise. The table includes only the specific parameters used in the example and not all the available options for the command.

Table 10-8   *Command List for Configuration Exercise*

Command	Description
access-list *access-list-number*	Access list configuration command
class-map	Enters the class-map configuration submode
configure terminal	Enters the configuration mode
copy running-config startup-config	Copies the running configuration to NVRAM
enable	Enters privileged mode
end	Ends the configuration mode
exit	Exits a configuration mode to its antecedent mode
hostname *hostname*	Configures switch with a descriptive name
interface FastEthernet | GigabitEthernet *interface*	Enters an interface configuration mode
interface range FastEthernet | GigabitEthernet *interfaces*	Configures multiple interfaces simultaneously
interface vlan *vlan-id*	Enters the VLAN configuration interface mode
match access-group *access-list-number*	Configures class-map matching clauses
mls qos	Globally enables QoS
mls qos trust device cisco-phone	Trusts when a Cisco Phone is learned via CDP on the respective interface; works in conjunction with the **mls qos trust dscp** and **mls qos trust cos** commands
mls qos trust dscp	Trusts DSCP values for ingress frames
no shutdown	Configures an interface in the Administrative UP state
policy-map *policy_map_name*	Enters the policy-map configuration submode

continues

Table 10-8 *Command List for Configuration Exercise (Continued)*

Command	Description
priority-queue out	Configures queue 4 on the Catalyst 3550 family of switches as a priority queue
**service-policy input	output** *policy-map-name*	Maps a policy map to an interface for ingress or egress traffic
set ip dscp *dscp_value*	Marks DSCP
**show mls qos interface FastEthernet	GigabitEthernet** *interface*	Displays the trusting configuration of an interface
spanning-tree portfast	Configures an interface for the spanning-tree PortFast feature
switchport	Configures an interface for Layer 2 operation
switchport access vlan *vlan-id*	Configures an interface for a specific VLAN-ID
vlan *vlan-id*	Adds or removes a VLAN-ID in the VLAN database
wrr-queue bandwidth *weight1 weight2 weight3 weight4*	Enters the ratio that determines the frequency in which the WRR scheduler dequeues packets; separate each value with a space (the range is 1 to 65536)
wrr-queue cos-map *queue-id cos1 ... cos8*	Configures CoS value to egress queue mapping

Task 1: Globally Enable QoS

Step 1 Connect the Catalyst switch to a terminal server or directly to the workstation's serial port for in-band connectivity.

Step 2 Globally enable QoS features on the switch.

```
Switch#configure terminal
Switch(config)#mls qos
```

Step 3 Verify that QoS is globally enabled.

```
Switch(config)#do show mls qos
QoS is enabled
```

NOTE The Cisco IOS **do** command is a recent addition to Cisco IOS to allow execution of privileged mode commands within configuration mode. This command saves the time and annoyance of exiting out and re-entering configuration mode. The **do** command is found only in the most recent Cisco IOS version, so it may not be supported in your version. If not, exit configuration mode and type the command (minus the keyword **do**) in privileged mode.

NOTE	Recall that for the Catalyst 4000 and 4500 families of switches running Cisco IOS, **qos** commands are not prefixed with the keyword **mls**.

Task 2: Configure the Switch to Trust DSCP on Interfaces FastEthernet0/1 Through 0/10 if a Cisco IP Phone Is Attached

Step 1 Enter the **range** command to configure multiple interfaces simultaneously.

```
Switch(config)#interface range FastEthernet 0/1 -10
```

Step 2 Specify an access VLAN for IP Phones. (Voice VLANs are not used in this exercise.)

```
Switch(config-if-range)#switchport access vlan 500
```

Step 3 Configure the switch to trust DSCP for incoming frames only if Cisco IP Phones are attached to the interface.

```
Switch(config-if-range)#mls qos trust dscp
Switch(config-if-range)#mls qos trust device cisco-phone
```

Step 4 Configure the interfaces for Spanning-Tree PortFast.

```
Switch(config-if-range)#spanning-tree portfast
%Warning: portfast should only be enabled on ports connected to a single
   host. Connecting hubs, concentrators, switches, bridges, etc... to this
   interface when portfast is enabled, can cause temporary bridging loops.
   Use with CAUTION
%Portfast will be configured in 10 interfaces due to the range command
   but will only have effect when the interfaces are in a non-trunking mode.
```

Step 5 Enable the interfaces.

```
Switch(config-if-range)#no shutdown
```

Step 6 Verify the QoS configuration.

```
Switch#show mls qos interface FastEthernet 0/1
FastEthernet0/1
trust state: not trusted
trust mode: trust dscp
COS override: dis
default COS: 0
DSCP Mutation Map: Default DSCP Mutation Map
trust device: cisco-phone
```

Task 3: Configure the Switch to Classify All Incoming Frames on Interface FastEthernet 0/11 with a CoS Value of 4 for Untagged Frames

Step 1   Enter the interface configuration mode for FastEthernet0/11.

```
Switch(config)#interface FastEthernet 0/11
```

Step 2   Configure the interface to classify all ingress frames with a CoS value of 4.

```
Switch(config-if)#mls qos cos 4
```

Step 3   Verify the QoS configuration.

```
Switch#(config-if)#do show mls qos interface FastEthernet 0/11
FastEthernet0/11
trust state: not trusted
trust mode: not trusted
COS override: dis
default COS: 4
DSCP Mutation Map: Default DSCP Mutation Map
trust device: none
```

Task 4: Configure a Policy Map, a Class Map, and the Interface Such That All Ingress TCP Port 30000 Packets on FastEthernet0/11 Have Their DSCP Set to 16

Step 1   Configure an access list to match packets on TCP port 30000.

```
Switch(config)#access-list 100 permit tcp any any eq 30000
```

Step 2   Configure a traffic profile using a class map.

```
Switch(config)#class-map TCP-PORT-30k
Switch(config-cmap)#match access-group 100
Switch(config-cmap)#exit
```

Step 3   Configure a policy map to apply the class map in Step 2 to the class action of setting the DSCP to 16.

```
Switch(config)#policy-map BCMSN
Switch(config-pmap)#class TCP-PORT-30k
Switch(config-pmap-c)#set ip dscp 16
Switch(config-pmap-c)#exit
Switch(config-pmap)#exit
```

Step 4   Apply the policy-map ingress on interface FastEthernet0/11.

```
Switch(config)#interface FastEthernet 0/11
Switch(config-if)#service-policy input BCMSN
Switch(config-if)#exit
```

Step 5   Verify the policy-map configuration.

```
Switch#show policy-map interface FastEthernet 0/11

FastEthernet0/11

 service-policy input: BCMSN

   class-map: TCP-PORT-30k (match-all)
     0 packets, 0 bytes
     5 minute offered rate 0 bps, drop rate 0 bps
     match: access-group 100

   class-map: class-default (match-any)
     0 packets, 0 bytes
     5 minute offered rate 0 bps, drop rate 0 bps
     match: any
       0 packets, 0 bytes
       5 minute rate 0 bps
```

Task 5: Configure All Egress Queues Such That CoS Values 4, 6, and 7 Use Queue 3 and a CoS Value 5 Uses Queue 4

Step 1   Enter the **range** command to configure multiple interfaces simultaneously.

```
Switch(config)#interface range FastEthernet 0/1 -24
```

Step 2   Configure interfaces for appropriate CoS mapping.

```
Switch(config-if)#wrr-queue cos-map 4 5
Switch(config-if)#wrr-queue cos-map 3 4 6 7
Switch(config-if)#exit
```

Task 6: Configure Queue 4 as a Strict-Priority Queue

Step 1   Enter the **range** command to configure multiple interfaces simultaneously.

```
Switch(config)#interface range FastEthernet 0/1 -24
```

Step 2   Configure queue 4 as a strict-priority queue.

```
Switch(config-if)#priority-queue out
```

Task 7: Configure WRR Weights Such That Queue 3 Receives Twice as Much Service as Any Other Single Queue

Step 1 Enter the **range** command to configure multiple interfaces simultaneously.

```
Switch(config)#interface range FastEthernet 0/1 -24
```

Step 2 Configure queue 3 with twice the service level as that of any other queue.

```
Switch(config-if)#wrr-queue bandwidth 20 20 40 20
```

Step 3 Verify the WRR configuration.

```
Switch#show mls qos interface FastEthernet 0/1 queueing
FastEthernet0/1
Egress expedite queue: ena
wrr bandwidth weights:
qid-weights
 1 - 20
 2 - 20
 3 - 40
 4 - 20     when expedite queue is disabled
Cos-queue map:
cos-qid
 0 - 1
 1 - 1
 2 - 2
 3 - 2
 4 - 3
 5 - 4
 6 - 3
 7 - 3
```

Task 8: Verify All Configurations by Viewing Interface Statistics

```
Switch#show mls qos interface FastEthernet 0/1 statistics
FastEthernet0/1
Ingress
  dscp: incoming   no_change  classified policed    dropped (in bytes)
Others: 97663325   87828650   9834675    0          0
Egress
  dscp: incoming   no_change  classified policed    dropped (in bytes)
Others: 30540345     n/a        n/a      0          0
```

Review Questions

For multiple-choice questions, there might be more than one correct answer.

1 True or False: You should always apply QoS classification in the access layer and as close to the network device as possible.

2 True or False: Congestion management includes the RED, WRED, and tail-drop QoS features.

3 Which command overrides CoS values on ingress frames to 1?

   a   **mls qos dscp 1**

   b   **mls qos trust cos**

   c   **mls cos 1**

   d   **mls qos cos 1**

4 What is the purpose of trust boundaries?

   a   To determine the classification of a packet at a specific location in the network.

   b   To determine where in the network packets are dropped.

   c   To determine where in the network to reclassify packets.

   d   It is an administrative configuration in which Layer 2 or Layer 3 priority designations of frames or packets are either accepted or not.

5 Consider a network design in which a video server needs a higher class of service for video data compared to other regular data traffic. The server does not support 802.1q tagging or setting bits in the IP field for priority. Furthermore, the server transmits other management traffic besides the video. Which of the following QoS components and methods would correctly prioritize traffic from the video server?

   a   Port-based classification in which the configuration would set all ingress frames from the server to a DSCP value of 36.

   b   Port-based classification using a policy map that uses a class map with an ACL that distinctively marks frames for video traffic with a DSCP value of 36.

   c   Using a policer to mark all frames from the server above a certain rate with a DSCP value of 36.

   d   Using an input ACL to classify all frames from the server with a DSCP value of 36.

6 Which QoS model requires end-to-end configuration?

   a LFI

   b IntServ

   c DiffServ

   d Traffic conditioning

7 In designing a multilayer switched network, you are required to condition traffic on a Catalyst switch such that TCP flows do not achieve more than 10 Mbps out of a 100-Mbps interface. Which of the following methods of traffic conditioning achieves link utilization closest to 10 Mbps?

   a Shaping

   b Policing

8 Which of the following methods of traffic conditioning would you use to limit VoIP traffic?

   a Shaping

   b Policing

9 Figure 10-18 illustrates an IP Phone attached to a Catalyst 3550 switch. Consider a situation in which the IP Phone is sending voice packets to another IP Phone with a DSCP value of 46 and a CoS value of 5. If the Catalyst 3550 switch is configured to trust DSCP and is using the default mapping tables, what is the internal DSCP of the frame as it traverses the switch?

   a 5

   b 46

   c 40

   d 0

Figure 10-18 *QoS Topology for Questions 8–10*

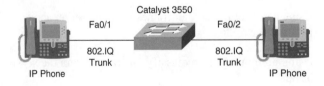

10 With regard to Figure 10-18, consider a situation in which the IP Phone is sending voice packets to another IP Phone with a DSCP value of 46 and a CoS value of 5. If the Catalyst 3550 switch is configured to trust CoS and the switch is using the default mapping tables, what is the internal DSCP of the frame as it traverses the switch?

a 5

b 46

c 40

d 0

11 With regard to Figure 10-18, consider a situation in which the IP Phone is sending voice packets to another IP Phone with a DSCP value of 46 and a CoS value of 5. If the Catalyst 3550 switch is configured to untrusted and the switch is using the default mapping tables, what is the internal DSCP of the frame as it traverses the switch?

a 5

b 46

c 40

d 0

Example 10-13 is for use in questions 12 and 13.

Example 10-13 *Sample Policing Configuration*

```
! Output omitted for brevity
!
class-map match-any LIMIT-TCP_File_Sharing
  match access-group 100
  match access-group 101
!
!
policy-map LIMIT_File_Sharing
  class LIMIT-TCP_File_Sharing
    police 1536000 20000 exceed-action drop
!
!
! Output omitted for brevity
!
```

12 With regard to Example 10-13, which configuration command is the class action of the policy map?

a **class LIMIT-TCP_File_Sharing**

b **police 1536000 20000 exceed-action drop**

c **match access-group 101**

13 With regard to Example 10-13, which action is taken for packets that conform to the policing rate?

a Transmit

b Drop

c Mark-down

This chapter covers the following topics:

- Introduction to Multicast and Its Functionality in the Multilayer Switched Network
- The Functionality of Important Multicast Layer 3 Protocols—For Example, PIM and IGMP
- Cisco Hardware-Switching Methods for Multicast
- Constraining Multicasts at Layer 2 Using CGMP or IGMP Snooping
- IP Multicast in Multilayer Switched Networks
- Configuring and Monitoring IP Multicast Routing in Multilayer Switched Networks

## CHAPTER 11

Deploying Multicast in the Multilayer Switched Network

Most campus networks today support intranet applications that operate between one sender and one receiver, referred to as *unicast*. In the emerging campus network, there is a demand for Internet, intranet, and multimedia applications where one sender transmits to a group of receivers simultaneously. Examples of these applications include the following:

- Transmitting a corporate message to all employees
- Broadcasting video and audio, including interactive video for distance learning
- Transmitting data from a centralized data warehouse to multiple departments
- Communicating stock quotes to brokers
- Computing collaboratively

Using IP multicast to distribute this information reduces the overall network load and bandwidth consumption. This is a result of IP multicast's simultaneous transmission of an IP data frame to a host group that is defined by a single multicast IP address, or flow.

This chapter discusses IP multicast routing and its inherent advantages, functionality, and configuration in the multilayer switched network. This chapter is unlike other chapters, as commands for configuring multicast on multilayer switches are covered after discussing the fundamentals of multicast. This chapter starts with an introduction to multicast and then discusses the fundamentals of the IP multicast. This chapter also discusses the important Layer 3 and Layer 2 multicast protocols and the design recommendation for deploying multicast in multilayer switched networks.

Introduction to Multicast

Multimedia applications offer the integration of sound, graphics, animation, text, and video. As the ways of conducting business have become more complex, these types of applications have become increasingly popular in the enterprise networks. However, applying several multimedia applications onto a multilayer switched network and sending the multimedia streams over a campus data network is a complicated process due to bandwidth consumption on the network.

Multimedia traffic uses one of the following methods of transmission, each of which has a different effect on network bandwidth:

- **Unicast**—With a unicast design, an application sends one copy of each packet to every client's unicast address. As a result, unicast transmission has significant scaling restrictions. If the group is large, the same information must be carried multiple times, even on shared links.

- **Broadcast**—In a broadcast design, an application sends only one copy of each packet using a broadcast address. Broadcasting a packet to all devices is inefficient, except in the case where only a small subset of the network actually needs to see the packet. Broadcast multimedia is dispersed throughout the network similarly to normal broadcast traffic, in that every host device must process the broadcast multimedia data frame. However, unlike standard broadcast frames, which are generally small, multimedia broadcasts may reach data rates as high as 13 Mbps or more. Even if an end station is not using multimedia applications, the device still processes the broadcast traffic. This requirement may use most, if not all, of the allocated bandwidth for each device. For this reason, Cisco highly discourages broadcast implementation for applications delivering data, voice, or video to multiple receivers.

- **Multicast**—The most efficient solution to transmit multimedia applications is multicast, which falls between unicast and broadcast. In multicast transmission, a multimedia server sends one copy of each packet to a special address that represents multiple clients. Unlike the unicast environment, a multicast server sends out a single data stream to multiple clients. Unlike the broadcast environment, the client device decides whether or not to listen to the multicast address. Multicasting saves bandwidth and controls network traffic by forcing the network to forward packets only when necessary. By eliminating traffic redundancy, multicasting reduces network bandwidth consumption and host processing. Furthermore, Catalyst switches can process IP multicast packets and deliver those packets only to receivers that request receipt of those packets at both Layer 2 and Layer 3.

IP multicast is the transmission of an IP data frame to a host group that is defined by a single IP address called a *multicast IP address*. A host can join or leave the multicast IP group dynamically regardless of the location or number of members. An important characteristic of the multicast is its capability to limit delivery variation in delivery time (jitter) of IP multicast frames along the complete server-to-client path.

In Figure 11-1, the video server transmits a single video stream for each multicast group. A *multicast*, or *host*, group is defined as a set of host devices listening to a specific multicast address. Cisco routers and switches replicate the video stream as required to the host groups that are in the path. This technique allows an arbitrary number of clients to subscribe to the multicast address and receive the stream. One host can be a part of one or more multicast groups for multiple applications. In addition, routers can transmit multiple data streams for different applications for a single group address.

In the multicast scenario shown in Figure 11-1, only 1.5 Mbps of server-to-network bandwidth is utilized, leaving the remaining bandwidth free for other uses.

Figure 11-1 *Multicast Traffic*

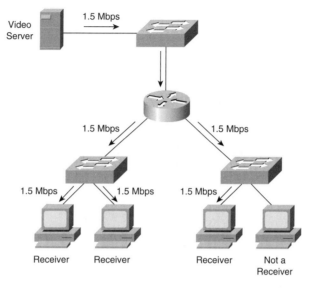

NOTE	In a unicast scenario, the server sequences through transmission of multiple copies of the data, so variability in delivery time is large, especially for large transmissions or large distribution lists.

IP multicast relies on the concept of a virtual group address called the *multicast IP address*. In IP unicast routing, a packet is routed from a source address to a destination address, traversing the IP network on a hop-by-hop basis. In IP multicast, the packet's destination address is not assigned to a single destination. Instead, receivers join a group; when they do, packets addressed to that group begin flowing to them. All members of the group receive the packet; a host must be a member of the group to receive the packet. Multicast sources do not need to be members of that group. In Figure 11-2, packets sent by group member 3 (represented by the solid arrows) are received by group members 1 and 2 but not by the nonmember of the group. The nonmember host can also send packets (represented by the dotted arrows) to the multicast group that are received by all three group members because all the new hosts are members of the multicast group. Group members 1 and 2 do not send multicast packets; they are just the receivers.

IP multicast traffic uses UDP as the transport layer protocol. Unlike TCP, UDP adds no reliability, flow control, or error-recovery functions to IP. Because of the simplicity of UDP, data packet headers contain fewer bytes and consume less network overhead than TCP. Reliability in multicast is therefore managed at the receiving client and by QoS in the network. Routers and switches can deliver multicast traffic using quality of service (QoS) capabilities just as they can do with unicast IP traffic.

Figure 11-2 *Multicast Group Membership*

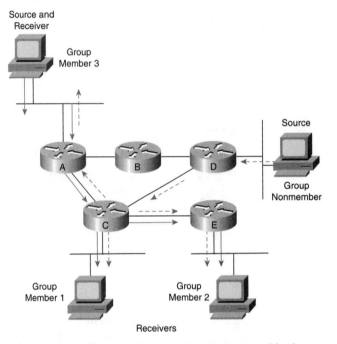

Because the location of hosts in the group is widely spread in the network, the multicast router sends the packets to respective multiple interfaces to reach all the hosts. This makes the multicast forwarding more complex. To avoid duplication, several multicast routing protocols use reverse path forwarding (RPF), discussed in the section "Reverse Path Forwarding," later in this chapter.

This chapter discusses the following fundamentals of IP multicast in more detail:

- Multicast IP address structure
- Multicast MAC address structure
- Reverse path forwarding
- Multicast forwarding tree

Multicast IP Address Structure

The range of IP addresses is divided into classes based on the high-order bits of a 32-bit IP address. IP multicast uses the Class D addresses, which range from 224.0.0.0 to 239.255.255.255. These addresses consist of binary 1110 as the most significant bits (MSB) in the first octet, followed by a 28-bit group address, as shown in Figure 11-3. Unlike with Class A, B, and C IP addresses, the last 28 bits of a Class D address are unstructured.

Figure 11-3 *Multicast IP Address Structure*

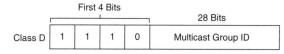

These remaining 28 bits of the IP address identify the multicast group ID, which is a single address that is typically written as decimal numbers in the range 224.0.0.0 to 239.255.255.255. The Internet Assigned Numbers Authority (IANA) controls the assignment of IP multicast addresses. The Class D address range is used only for the group address or destination address of IP multicast traffic. The source address for multicast datagrams is always the unicast source address.

IP multicast addresses specify a set of IP hosts that have joined a group and are interested in receiving multicast traffic designated for that particular group. Table 11-1 outlines the IPv4 multicast address conventions.

Table 11-1 *Multicast IP Address Ranges*

Description	Range
Reserved link local addresses	224.0.0.0 to 224.0.0.255
Globally scoped addresses	224.0.1.0 to 238.255.255.255
Source-specific multicast addresses	232.0.0.0 to 232.255.255.255
GLOP addresses	233.0.0.0 to 233.255.255.255
Limited-scope addresses	239.0.0.0 to 239.255.255.255

Applications allocate multicast addresses dynamically or statically. Dynamic multicast addressing provides applications with a group address on demand. Because dynamic multicast addresses have a specific lifetime, applications must request this type of address only for as long as the address is needed.

Statically allocated multicast addresses are reserved for specific protocols that require well-known addresses, such as Open Shortest Path First (OSPF). IANA assigns these well-known addresses, which are called *permanent host groups* and are similar in concept to the well-known TCP and UDP port numbers.

The following sections discuss the details of the multicast addresses listed in Table 11-1.

Reserved Link Local Addresses

IANA has reserved addresses in the range 224.0.0.0 to 224.0.0.255 (link local destination addresses) to be used by network protocols on a local network segment. Routers do not forward packets in this address range, because these packets are typically sent with a Time-to-Live (TTL) value of 1. Network protocols use these addresses for automatic router discovery and to communicate important routing information. For example, OSPF uses the IP addresses 224.0.0.5 and 224.0.0.6 to exchange link-state information.

Address 224.0.0.1 identifies the all-hosts group. Every multicast-capable host must join this group when initializing its IP stack. If you send an ICMP echo request to this address, all multicast-capable hosts on the network answer the request with an ICMP echo reply.

Address 224.0.0.2 identifies the all-routers group. Multicast routers join this group on all multicast-enabled interfaces.

Globally Scoped Addresses

Addresses in the range 224.0.1.0 to 238.255.255.255 are called *globally scoped addresses*. Companies use these addresses to multicast data between organizations and across the Internet. Multicast applications reserve some of these addresses for use through IANA. For example, IANA reserves the IP address 224.0.1.1 for the Network Time Protocol (NTP).

Source-Specific Multicast Addresses

Addresses in the 232.0.0.0 to 232.255.255.255 range are reserved for Source-Specific Multicast (SSM), an extension of the Protocol Independent Multicast (PIM) protocol that allows for an efficient data-delivery mechanism in one-to-many communications. In SSM, forwarding decisions are based on both group and source addresses, which is referred to as (S,G). The special notation of (S,G), pronounced "S comma G," uses S as the IP address of the source and G as the multicast group address. This unique (S,G) is known within SSM as a channel. SSM also removes address allocation problems because the source address makes each channel unique. SSM requires that the host be aware of the source as well as the group it desires data from and a method to signal this (S,G) requirement to the router.

GLOP Addresses

RFC 2770, "GLOP Addressing in 233/8," proposes that the 233.0.0.0 to 233.255.255.255 address range be reserved for statically defined addresses by organizations that already have an autonomous system number reserved. This practice is called *GLOP addressing*. The autonomous system number of the domain is embedded into the second and third octets of the 233.0.0.0 to 233.255.255.255 address range. For example, the autonomous system 62010 is written in hexadecimal format as F23A. Separating the two octets F2 and 3A results in 242 and 58 in decimal format, respectively. These values result in a subnet of 233.242.58.0/24 that is globally reserved for autonomous system 62010 to use.

Limited-Scope Addresses

Addresses in the 239.0.0.0 to 239.255.255.255 range are called *limited-scope addresses* or *administratively scoped addresses*. These addresses are described in RFC 2365, "Administratively Scoped IP Multicast," to be constrained to a local group or organization.

Companies, universities, or other organizations use limited-scope addresses to have local multicast applications where edge routers to the Internet do not forward the multicast frames outside their intranet domain. Edge routers typically deploy configurations with access lists to prevent multicast traffic in this address range from flowing outside of an autonomous system or any user-defined domain into the intranet. Within an autonomous system or domain, the limited-scope address range can be further subdivided so that local multicast boundaries can be defined. This subdivision is called *address scoping* and allows for address reuse between these smaller domains.

Multicast MAC Address Structure

Similar to the manner in which an IP address maps to a unique MAP address, an IP multicast address also maps to a unique multicast MAC address. The multicast MAC address is derived from the IP multicast address.

Multicast MAC addresses start with the 25-bit prefix 0x01-00-5E (which in binary is 00000001.00000000.01011110.0xxxxxxx.xxxxxxxx.xxxxxxxx) with the 25th bit set to 0. Because all the IP multicast addresses have the first 4 bits set to 1110, the remaining 28 least significant bits (LSB) of multicast IP addresses must map into the 23 LSBs of the MAC address. As a result, the MAC address loses 5 bits of uniqueness in the IP-to-MAC address mapping process. The 5 bits that are not used are the 5 MSBs of the 28 remaining LSBs after 4-bit, 1110, MSBs. This method for mapping multicast IP addresses to MAC addresses results in a 32:1 mapping, whereas each multicast MAC address represents a possible 32 distinct IP multicast addresses. Figure 11-4 shows an example of the multicast IP-to-MAC address mapping.

Figure 11-4 *Sample Multicast IP-to-MAC Mapping*

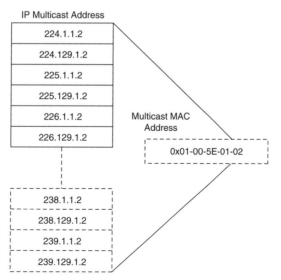

A host that joins one multicast group programs its network interface card to listen to the IP-mapped MAC address. If the same MAC address maps to a second MAC multicast address already in use, the host CPU processes both sets of IP multicast frames. Furthermore, because switches forward frames based on the multicast MAC address if configured for Layer 2 multicast snooping, they forward frames to all the members corresponding to other IP multicast addresses of the same MAC address mapping, even if the frames belong to a different IP multicast group. For example, multicast IP addresses 238.1.1.2 and 238.129.1.2 both map to the same multicast MAC address 01:00:5E:01:01:02. As a result, a host that registered to group 238.1.1.2 also receives the traffic from 238:129:1.2 because the same MAC multicast address is used by both IP multicast flows. It is recommended to avoid overlapping when implementing multicast applications in the multilayer switched network by tuning the destination IP multicast addresses at the application level.

Reverse Path Forwarding

Multicast-capable routers and multilayer switches create distribution trees that control the path that IP multicast traffic takes through the network to achieve loop-free forwarding. Reverse Path Forwarding (RPF) is the mechanism that performs an incoming interface check to determine whether to forward or drop an incoming multicast frame. RPF is a key concept in multicast forwarding. This RPF check helps to guarantee that the distribution tree for multicast is loop-free. In addition, RPF enables routers to correctly forward multicast traffic down the distribution tree.

In unicast routing, traffic is routed through the network along the path from the single source to the single destination host. A router that is forwarding unicast packets does not consider the source address, by default; the router considers only the destination address and how to forward the traffic toward the destination with the exception of specialized CEF features. Upon receipt of unicast packets, the router scans through its routing table for the destination address and then forwards a single copy of the unicast packet out the correct interface to the destination.

In multicast forwarding, the source is sending traffic to an arbitrary group of hosts that is represented by a single multicast group address. When a multicast router receives a multicast packet, it determines which direction is the upstream direction (toward the source) and which one is the downstream direction (toward the receivers). A router forwards a multicast packet only if the packet is received on the correct upstream interface determined by the RPF process.

For traffic flowing down a source tree, the RPF check procedure works as follows:

- The router looks up the source address in the unicast routing table to determine whether it arrived on the interface that is on the reverse path back to the source.

- If the packet has arrived on the interface leading back to the source, the RPF check is successful, and the router replicates and forwards the packet to the outgoing interfaces.

- If the RPF check in the previous step fails, the router drops the packet and records the drop as an *RPF failed drop.*

The top portion of Figure 11-5 illustrates an example where the RPF check fails. The router in the figure receives a multicast packet from source 151.10.3.21 on interface S0. A check of the unicast route table shows that this router uses interface S1 as the egress interface for forwarding unicast data to 151.10.3.21. Because the packet instead arrived on interface S0, the packet fails the RPF check, and the router drops the packet. In the bottom portion of Figure 11-5, the RPF check succeeds. With this example, the multicast packet arrives on interface S1. The router checks the unicast routing table and finds that interface S1 is the correct ingress interface. The RPF check passes, and the router forwards the packet.

Figure 11-5 *Reverse Path Forwarding*

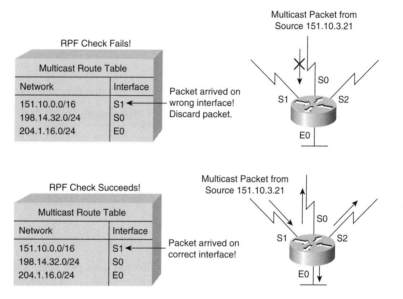

In multilayer switched networks where multiple routers connect to the same LAN segment, only one PIM-designated router forwards the multicast traffic from the source to the receivers on the outgoing interfaces, as shown in Figure 11-6. Router A, the PIM-designated router (PIM DR), forwards data to VLAN 1 and VLAN 2. Router B receives the forwarded multicast traffic on VLAN 1 and VLAN 2, and it drops this traffic because the multicast traffic fails the RPF check. Traffic that fails the RPF check is called *non-RPF traffic.* Specific models of Catalyst switches process non-RPF traffic in hardware. Another way of performing non-RPF packet drops in hardware is to use access lists on the interfaces. Performing excess RPF checks in software may yield high CPU.

Table 11-2 describes the switches that drop or rate-limit non-RPF traffic in hardware.

Figure 11-6 *Non-RPF Multicast Traffic*

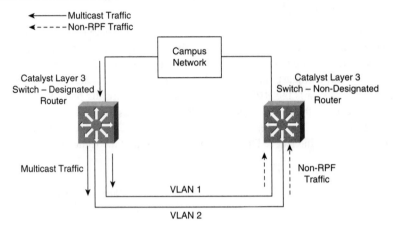

Table 11-2 *Support for Non-RPF Traffic in Hardware*

Type of Switch	Support Non-RPF Traffic in Hardware	Comments
Catalyst 3550/3560/ 3750	Yes	
Catalyst 4500	Yes	Only for Supervisor II+, III, IV, V, and VI
Catalyst 6500	Yes	Only with Supervisor 720 and Supervisor 2

Multicast Forwarding Tree

Multicast-capable routers create multicast distribution trees that control the path that IP multicast traffic takes through the network to deliver traffic to all receivers.

The following are the two types of distribution trees:

- Source trees
- Shared trees

Source Trees

The simplest form of a multicast distribution tree is a source tree with its root at the source and its branches forming a tree through the network to the receivers. Because this tree uses the shortest path through the network, it is also referred to as a *shortest path tree* (SPT).

Figure 11-7 shows an example of an SPT for group 224.1.1.1 rooted at the source, host A, and connecting two receivers, hosts B and C.

Using the (S,G) notation, the SPT for the example shown in Figure 11-7 is (192.168.1.1, 224.1.1.1).

The (S,G) notation implies that a separate SPT exists for each source sending to each group. For example, if host B is also sending traffic to group 224.1.1.1 and hosts A and C are receivers, a separate (S,G) SPT would exist with a notation of (192.168.2.2, 224.1.1.1).

Figure 11-7 *IP Multicast Source Distribution Tree*

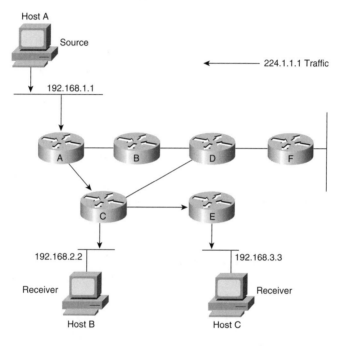

Shared Trees

Unlike source trees, which have their root at the source, shared trees use a single common root placed at some chosen point in the network. This shared root is called a *rendezvous point* (RP). Figure 11-8 shows a shared unidirectional tree for the group 224.1.1.1 with the root located at router D. Source traffic is sent toward the RP on a shared tree. The traffic is then forwarded down the shared tree from the RP to reach all the receivers unless the receiver is located between the source and the RP, in which case the multicast traffic is serviced directly.

In Figure 11-8, multicast traffic from the sources, hosts A and D, travels to the root (router D) and then down the shared tree to the two receivers, hosts B and C. Because all sources in the multicast group use a common shared tree, a wildcard notation written as (*,G), pronounced "star comma G," represents the tree. In this case, * means all sources, and G represents the multicast group. Therefore, the shared tree shown in the figure is written as (*, 224.1.1.1).

Figure 11-8   *IP Multicast Shared Tree Distribution*

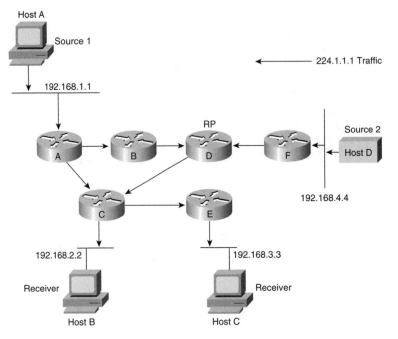

Comparing Source Trees and Shared Trees

Both source trees and shared trees are loop free. Routing devices replicate the multicast packets only where the tree branches.

Members of multicast groups join or leave at any time; as a result, the distribution trees update dynamically. When all the active receivers on a particular branch stop requesting traffic for a particular multicast group, the routers prune that branch from the tree and stop forwarding traffic down it. If one receiver on that branch becomes active and requests the multicast traffic, the router dynamically modifies the distribution tree and starts forwarding traffic again.

Source trees have the advantage of creating the optimal path between the source and the receivers. This advantage guarantees the minimum amount of network latency for forwarding multicast traffic. However, this optimization requires additional overhead because the routers maintain path information for each source. In a network that has thousands of sources and thousands of groups, this overhead quickly becomes a resource issue on routers or multilayer switches. Memory consumption and troubleshooting complexity from the size of the multicast routing table are factors that network designers need to take into consideration when designing multicast networks.

Shared trees have the advantage of requiring the minimum amount of state information in each router. This advantage lowers the overall memory requirements and complexity for a network that only allows shared trees. The disadvantage of shared trees is that, under certain circumstances, the paths between the source and receivers might not be the optimal paths, which may introduce additional latency in packet delivery. As a result, shared trees may overuse some links and leave others unused, whereas source-based trees (where sources are distributed) usually distribute traffic across a set of links. For example, in Figure 11-8, the shortest path between host A (source 1) and host B (a receiver) is between Router A and Router C. Because Router D is the root for a shared tree, the traffic traverses Routers A, B, D, and then C. Network designers need to carefully consider the placement of the RP when implementing a shared tree–only environment.

IP Multicast Protocols

Similar to IP unicast, IP multicast uses its own routing, management, and Layer 2 protocols. The following are two important multicast protocols:

- Protocol Independent Multicast (PIM)
- Internet Group Management Protocol (IGMP)

PIM

A multicast routing protocol is responsible for the construction of multicast delivery trees and enabling multicast packet forwarding. Different IP multicast routing protocols use different techniques to construct multicast trees and to forward packets. The PIM routing protocol leverages whichever unicast routing protocols are used to populate the unicast routing table to make multicast forwarding decisions.

Furthermore, routers use the PIM neighbor discovery mechanism to establish PIM neighbors using hello messages to the ALL-PIM-Routers (224.0.0.13) multicast address for building and maintaining PIM multicast distribution trees. In addition, routers use PIM hello messages to elect the designated router (DR) for a multicast LAN network.

PIM encompasses two distinct versions: PIM version 1 and PIM version 2. This chapter compares the two in the section "Comparison and Compatibility of PIM Version 1 and Version 2," later in this chapter.

PIM has the following four modes of operation, which are discussed in the following sections:

- PIM dense mode
- PIM sparse mode
- PIM sparse-dense mode
- PIM bidirectional

Sparse-dense mode is most common in large enterprise networks.

PIM Dense Mode

PIM dense mode (PIM-DM) multicast routing protocols rely on periodic flooding of the network with multicast traffic to set up and maintain the distribution tree. PIM relies on its neighbor information to form the distribution tree. PIM-DM uses a source distribution tree to forward multicast traffic, which is built by respective routers as soon as any multicast source begins transmitting. Figure 11-9 illustrates an example of PIM-DM.

Figure 11-9 *PIM Dense Mode*

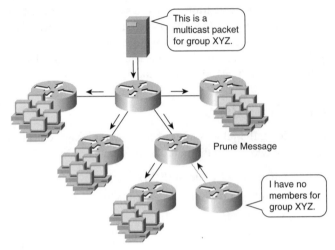

PIM-DM assumes that the multicast group members are densely distributed throughout the network and that bandwidth is plentiful, meaning that almost all hosts on the network belong to the group. When a router configured for PIM-DM receives a multicast packet, the router performs the RPF check to validate the correct interface for the source and then forwards the packet to all the interfaces configured for multicasting until pruning and truncating occurs. All downstream routers receive the multicast packet until the multicast traffic times out. PIM-DM sends a pruning message upstream only under the following conditions:

- Traffic arrives on a non-RPF, point-to-point interface; this is the next-hop router interface that does not have a best route toward the multicast source.

- A leaf router without receivers sends a prune message as shown in Figure 11-9, where the router, which does not have members or receivers, sends the prune message to the upstream router.

- A non-leaf router receives a prune message from all of its neighbors.

In summary, PIM-DM works best when numerous members belong to each multimedia group. PIM floods the multimedia packet to all routers in the network and then prunes routers that do not service members of that particular multicast group.

PIM-DM is most useful in the following cases:

- Senders and receivers are in close proximity to one another.

- There are few senders and many receivers.

- The volume of multicast traffic is high.

- The stream of multicast traffic is constant.

Nevertheless, PIM-DM is not the method of choice for enterprise and service provider customers because of its scalability and flooding properties.

PIM Sparse Mode

The second approach to multicast routing, PIM sparse mode (PIM-SM), is based on the assumptions that the multicast group members are sparsely distributed throughout the network and that bandwidth is limited.

It is important to note that PIM-SM does not imply that the group has few members, just that they are widely dispersed. In this case, flooding would unnecessarily waste network bandwidth and could cause serious performance problems. Therefore, PIM-SM multicast routing protocols rely on more selective techniques to set up and maintain multicast trees.

PIM-SM protocols begin with an empty distribution tree and add branches only as the result of explicit requests to join the distribution.

With PIM-SM, each data stream goes to a relatively small number of segments in the campus network. Instead of flooding the network to determine the status of multicast members, PIM-SM defines an RP. When a sender wants to send data, it first does so to the RP. When a receiver wants to receive data, it registers with the RP, as shown in Figure 11-10. When the data stream begins to flow from sender to RP to receiver, the routers in the path automatically optimize the path to remove unnecessary hops. PIM-SM assumes that no hosts want the multicast traffic unless they specifically ask for it. In PIM-SM, the shared tree mode can be switched to a source tree after a certain threshold to have the best route to the source. All Cisco IOS routers and switches, by default, have the SPT threshold set to 0, such that the last-hop router switches to SPT mode as soon as the host starts receiving the multicast, to take advantage of the best route for the multicast traffic.

PIM-SM is optimized for environments where there are many multipoint data streams. Deploying PIM-SM with IP multicast is most useful when

- There are few receivers in a group.
- The type of traffic is intermittent.

Figure 11-10 *Multicast PIM Sparse Mode*

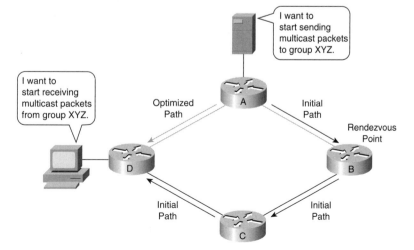

PIM Sparse-Dense Mode

PIM can simultaneously support dense mode operation for some multicast groups and sparse mode operation for others. Cisco has implemented an alternative to choosing just dense mode or just sparse mode on a router interface, however. This was necessitated by a change in the paradigm for forwarding multicast traffic via PIM that became apparent during its development. It turned out that it was more efficient to choose sparse or dense mode on a per-group basis rather than a per-router interface basis. Sparse-dense mode facilitates this ability.

PIM sparse-dense mode allows individual groups to use either sparse or dense mode depending on whether RP information is available for that group. If the router learns RP information for a particular group, sparse mode is used; otherwise, dense mode is used.

PIM Bidirectional

Bidirectional PIM (bidir-PIM) is an extension of the existing PIM-SM feature and shares many SPT operations. Bidir-PIM is suited for multicast with larger numbers of sources.

Bidir-PIM can unconditionally forward source traffic toward the RP upstream on the shared tree without registering for sources as in PIM-SM. This allows traffic to be passed up the shared tree toward the RP. To avoid multicast packet loops, bidir-PIM introduces a mechanism called *designated forwarder (DF)* election, which establishes a loop-free SPT rooted at the RP. The DF is responsible for forwarding multicast packets received on that network upstream to the RP. One DF exists for every RP of bidirectional groups.

A router creates only (*,G) entries for bidirectional groups. The outgoing interface list of multicast traffic (olist) of a (*,G) entry includes all the interfaces for which the router has been elected as DF and that have received either an IGMP or PIM join message. If a packet is received from the RPF interface toward the RP, the packet is forwarded downstream according to the olist of the (*,G) entry. Otherwise, once the router that is DF for the receiving interface forwards the packet toward the RP, all other routers must discard the packet. These modifications are necessary and sufficient to allow forwarding of traffic in all routers based solely on the (*, G) multicast routing entries. This feature eliminates any source-specific state and allows scaling capability to an arbitrary number of sources.

Automating Distribution of RP

PIM-SM and PIM sparse-dense modes use various methods, discussed in this section, to automate the distribution of the RP. This mechanism has the following benefits:

- It eliminates the need to manually configure RP information in every router and switch in the network.

- It is easy to use multiple RPs within a network to serve different group ranges.

- It allows load-splitting among different RPs and allows the arrangement of RPs according to the location of group participants.

- It avoids inconsistency; manual RP configurations may cause connectivity problems if not configured properly.

PIM uses the following mechanisms to automate the distribution of the RP:

- Auto-RP
- Bootstrap router (BSR)

Auto-RP

Auto-RP automates the distribution of group-to-RP mappings in a PIM network. Group-to-RP mappings define which multicast groups use which RP for sparse mode or sparse-dense mode.

All routers and Layer 3 devices in the PIM network learn about the active group-to-RP mapping from the RP mapping agent by automatically joining the Cisco-RP-discovery (224.0.1.40) multicast group. The *RP mapping agent* is the router that sends the authoritative discovery packets that notify other routers which group-to-RP mapping to use, as shown in Figure 11-11. The RP mapping agent sends this information every 60 seconds. Such a role is necessary in the event of conflicts (such as overlapping group-to-RP ranges).

Mapping agents also use IP multicast to discover which routers in the network are possible candidate RPs by joining the Cisco-RP-announce (224.0.1.39) group to receive candidate RP announcements. Candidate RPs send RP-announce multicast messages for the particular groups every 60 seconds. The RP mapping agent uses the information contained in the announcement to create entries in group-to-RP cache. RP mapping agents create only one entry per group. If more than one RP candidate announces the same range, then the RP mapping agent uses the IP address of the RP to break the tie.

Figure 11-11 *Auto-RP Mechanism*

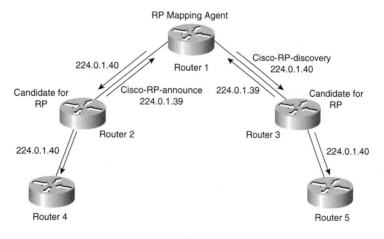

It is recommended that an RP mapping agent be configured on the router with the best connectivity and stability. All routers within the TTL number of hops from the RP mapping router receive the Auto-RP discovery messages.

Sparse mode environments require a default RP to join the Auto-RP discovery group, but sparse-dense mode environments do not need a default RP for Auto-RP. It is recommended to use RP for the global groups. There is no need to reconfigure the group address range that the RP serves. RPs that are discovered dynamically through Auto-RP take precedence over statically configured RPs. Typically, campus networks use a second RP for the local groups.

Bootstrap Router

A *bootstrap router* (BSR) is a router or Layer 3 device that is responsible for distributing RP. Using a BSR is another way to distribute group-to-RP mapping information in the PIM multicast network. However, BSR works only with PIM version 2. A BSR uses hop-to-hop flooding of special BSR messages instead of multicast to distribute the group-to-RP mapping.

BSR uses an election mechanism to select the BSR router from a set of candidate routers and multilayer switches in the domain. The BSR election uses the BSR priority of the device contained in the BSR messages that flow hop-by-hop through the network. Each BSR device examines the message and forwards it out all interfaces only if the message has either a higher BSR priority than the router's own BSR priority or has the same BSR priority but with a higher BSR IP address.

The elected BSR sends BSR messages with a TTL of 1 with its IP address to enable candidate BSRs to learn automatically about the elected BSR. Neighboring PIM version 2 routers or multilayer switches receive the BSR message and multicast the message out all other interfaces (except the one on which it was received) with a TTL of 1 to distribute the BSR messages hop-by-hop, as shown in Figure 11-12.

Candidate RPs send candidate RP advertisements showing the group range for which each is responsible to the BSR, which stores this information in its local candidate RP cache. The BSR includes this information in its bootstrap messages and disseminates it to all PIM routers using 224.0.0.13 with a TTL of 1 in the domain hop-by-hop. Based on this information, all routers can map multicast groups to specific RPs. As long as a router is receiving the bootstrap message, it has a current RP map. Routers and multilayer switches select the same RP for a given group because they all use a common RP hashing algorithm.

Figure 11-12 *BSR Mechanism*

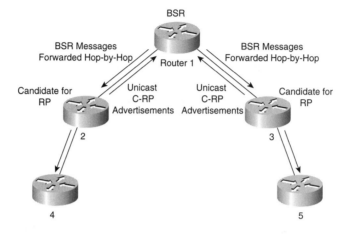

Comparison and Compatibility of PIM Version 1 and Version 2

PIM version 2 is a standards-based multicast protocol in the Internet Engineering Task Force (IETF). Cisco highly recommends using PIM version 2 in the entire multilayer switched network. The Cisco PIM version 2 implementation allows interoperability and transition between version 1 and version 2, although there are a few caveats. For example, if a PIM version 2 router detects a PIM version 1 router, the version 2 router downgrades itself to version 1 until all version 1 routers have been shut down or upgraded.

PIM version 2 uses the BSR to discover and announce RP-to-group mapping information for each group prefix to all the routers in a PIM domain. This is the same function accomplished by Auto-RP. However, the BSR feature is part of the PIM version 2 specifications because bootstrap messages are sent on a hop-by-hop basis, and a PIM version 1 router prevents these messages from reaching all routers in a network. Therefore, if a network has a PIM version 1 router with Cisco routers, it is best to use Auto-RP rather than the bootstrap mechanism. Nevertheless, Auto-RP is a standalone protocol, separate from PIM version 1, and is Cisco proprietary. The BSR mechanism interoperates with Auto-RP on Cisco routers.

A PIM version 2 BSR that is also an Auto-RP mapping agent automatically advertises the RP elected by Auto-RP. That is, Auto-RP prevails in its imposition of a single RP on every router in the group.

In summary, PIM version 2 includes the following improvements over PIM version 1:

- A single, active RP exists per multicast group, with multiple backup RPs. This single RP compares to multiple active RPs for the same group in PIM version 1.

- A BSR provides a fault-tolerant, automated RP discovery and distribution mechanism. Thus, routers dynamically learn the group-to-RP mappings.

- Sparse mode and dense mode are properties of a group, as opposed to an interface. Cisco strongly recommends sparse-dense mode configurations.

- PIM join and prune messages have more flexible encodings for multiple address families.

- A more flexible hello packet format replaces the query packet to encode current and future capability options.

- Register messages to an RP indicate whether they were sent by a border router or a designated router.

- PIM no longer uses the IGMP protocol for transport; PIM version 2 uses standalone packets.

IGMP

Hosts use IGMP to dynamically register themselves in a multicast group on a particular LAN. Hosts identify group memberships by sending IGMP messages to their local designated multicast router. Routers and multilayer switches, configured for IGMP, listen to IGMP messages and periodically send out queries to discover which groups are active or inactive on a particular subnet or VLAN.

The following list indicates the current versions of IGMP:

- IGMP version 1 (IGMPv1) RFC 1112
- IGMP version 2 (IGMPv2) RFC 2236
- IGMP version 3 (IGMPv3) RFC 3376
- IGMP version 3 lite (IGMPv3 lite)

IGMPv1

According to the IGMPv1 specification, one multicast router per LAN must periodically transmit host membership query messages to determine which host groups have members on the router's directly attached LAN networks. IGMP query messages are addressed to the all-host group (224.0.0.1) and have an IP TTL equal to 1. A TTL of 1 ensures that the corresponding router does not forward the query messages to any other multicast router.

When the end station receives an IGMP query message, the end station responds with a host membership report for each group to which the end station belongs. IGMP messages are specified in the IP datagram with a protocol value of 2.

Table 11-3 describes the fields of the IGMP message, which are shown in Figure 11-13.

Table 11-3   *IGMP Field Description*

Field	Definition
Version	1
Type	There are two types of IGMP messages of concern to hosts: 1 = host membership query 2 = host membership report
Unused	Unused field, zeroed when sent, ignored when received.
Checksum	Used to validate the integrity of the packet.
Group Address	In a host membership query message, the Group Address field is set to 0 when sent, ignored when received. In a host membership report message, the Group Address field holds the IP host group address of the group being reported.

Figure 11-13 *IGMPv1 Packet Format*

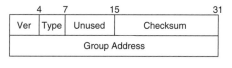

- Version = 1
- Type:
  − 1 = Host membership query
  − 2 = Host membership report
- Group Address:
  − Multicast group address

IGMPv2

Version 2 of IGMP made several enhancements to the previous version, including the definition of a group-specific query. The group-specific query message allows a router to transmit a specific query to one particular group. IGMPv2 also defines a leave group message for the hosts, which results in lower leave latency.

There are four types of IGMP messages of concern to the host-router interaction:

- Membership query

- Version 2 membership report

- Leave report

- Version 1 membership report

IGMPv2 uses the IGMPv1 membership report for backward-compatibility with IGMPv1. Newer versions of IGMP or multicast routing protocols use new message types. Any other or unrecognized message types are ignored.

Table 11-4 describes the IGMPv2 message fields, which are shown in Figure 11-14.

Table 11-4   *IGMPv2 Field Description*

Field	Value
Type	0x11 = membership query 0x12 = version 1 membership report 0x16 = version 2 membership report 0x17 = leave report
Maximum Response Time	10 seconds = default value. Meaningful only in a membership query. Specifies the maximum allowed time before sending a responding report in units of 1/10 second. 0 = All other messages.
Checksum	Calculated the same as for the ICMP checksum.
Group Address	0.0.0.0 in a general query. Group address queried in a group-specific query. Multicast group address in a report.

Figure 11-14 *IGMPv2 Packet Format*

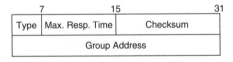

- Multiple Message Types
- Maximum Response Time
  - Maximum time before sending a responding report in 1/10 s (default = 10 s)
- Group Address:
  - Multicast group address (0.0.0.0 for general queries)

IGMPv3

IGMPv3 is the next step in the evolution of IGMP. IGMPv3 adds support for source filtering that enables a multicast receiver to signal to a router the groups from which it wants to receive multicast traffic and from which sources to expect traffic. This membership information enables Cisco IOS Software to forward traffic from only those sources from which receivers requested the traffic.

In IGMPv3, the following types of IGMP messages exist:

- Version 3 membership query
- Version 3 membership report

Table 11-5 describes the fields in the IGMPv3 query message, and Figure 11-15 shows the packet format.

Table 11-5   *IGMPv3 Query Message Field Description*

Field	Definition
Type = 0x11	IGMP query.
Max Resp. Code	Maximum response code (in seconds). Specifies the maximum time allowed before sending a responding report.
Group Address	Multicast group address. This address is 0.0.0.0 for general queries.
S	S flag. Indicates that processing by routers is being suppressed.
QRV	Querier Robustness Value. Affects timers and the number of retries.
QQIC	Querier's Query Interval Code (in seconds). Specifies the query interval used by the querier.
Number of Sources (N)	Number of sources present in the query. This number is nonzero for a group-and-source query.
Source Address [1...N]	Address of the sources.

Figure 11-15 *IGMPv3 Query Packet Format*

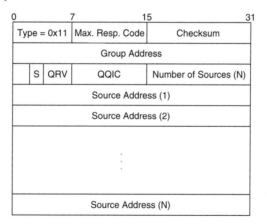

Table 11-6 describes the fields in the IGMPv3 report message, and Figure 11-16 shows the IGMPv3 report packet format with detailed group record format.

Table 11-6 *IGMPv3 Report Packet Field Description*

Field	Definition
Type=0x22	IGMPv3 report message
# of Group Records (M)	Number of group records present in the report.
Group Record (1...M)	Block of fields containing information regarding the sender's membership with a single multicast group on the interface from which the report was sent.
Record Type	The group record type (e.g., MODE_IS_INCLUDE, MODE_IS_EXCLUDE).
# of Sources (N)	Number of sources present in the record.
Source Address (1...N)	Address of the sources.

Figure 11-16 *IGMPv3 Report Packet Format with Detailed Group Record Internal Format*

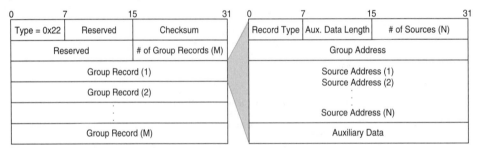

IGMPv3 supports applications that explicitly signal sources from which they want to receive traffic. With IGMPv3, receivers signal membership to a multicast host group in one of the following two modes:

- **INCLUDE mode**—In this mode, the receiver announces membership to a host group and provides a list of source addresses (the INCLUDE list) from which it wants to receive traffic.

- **EXCLUDE mode**—In this mode, the receiver announces membership to a multicast group and provides a list of source addresses (the EXCLUDE list) from which it does not want to receive traffic. The host will receive traffic only from sources whose IP addresses are not listed in the EXCLUDE list. To receive traffic from all sources, which is the behavior of IGMPv2, a host uses EXCLUDE mode membership with an empty EXCLUDE list.

IGMPv3 Lite

IGMPv3 lite is a Cisco-developed transitional solution for application developers to immediately start programming applications for SSM. Specifically, IGMPv3 lite allows application developers to write and run SSM applications on hosts that do not yet support IGMPv3 in their operating system kernel.

Applications require the Host Side IGMP Library (HSIL) for IGMPv3 lite. This software library provides applications with a subset of the IGMPv3 API that is required to write SSM applications. HSIL was developed for Cisco by Talarian.

One part of the HSIL is a client library linked to the SSM application. It provides the SSM subset of the IGMPv3 API to the SSM application. If possible, the library checks whether the operating system kernel supports IGMPv3. If it does, then the API calls simply are passed through to the kernel. If the kernel does not support IGMPv3, then the library uses the IGMPv3 lite mechanism.

When using the IGMPv3 lite mechanism, the library tells the operating system kernel to join to the whole multicast group, because joining to the whole group is the only method for the application to receive traffic for that multicast group for IGMPv1 or IGMPv2. In addition, the library signals the (S,G) channel subscriptions to an IGMPv3 lite server process. A server process is needed because multiple SSM applications may be on the same host. This server process then sends IGMPv3 lite-specific (S,G) channel subscriptions to the last-hop Cisco IOS router or multilayer switch.

This Cisco IOS router or multilayer switch then sees both the IGMPv1 or IGMPv2 group membership report from the operating system kernel and the (S,G) channel subscription from the HSIL daemon. If the router sees both of these messages, it interprets them as an SSM (S,G) channel subscription and joins the channel through PIM-SM. Refer to the documentation accompanying the HSIL software for more information on how to use IGMPv3 lite with your application.

Cisco supports IGMPv3 lite only through the API provided by the HSIL. By default, IGMPv3 lite is disabled on Cisco routers and switches. When IGMPv3 lite is configured through the **ip igmp v3lite** command on an interface, it becomes active only for IP multicast addresses in the SSM range.

Multicast Hardware-Based Switching Methods

All Layer 3 Cisco Catalyst switches accomplish high-performance multicast forwarding using the following hardware-based multicast switching and routing methods:

- Multicast multilayer switching (MMLS)
- CEF-based MMLS
- Multicast forwarding information base (MFIB) subsystem

Table 11-7 shows types of switches and their supported hardware-switching methods.

Table 11-7 *Catalyst Switches and Hardware-Switching Methods*

Type of Switches	Hardware-Switching Method	Comments
Catalyst 3550/3560/ 3750/3760	CEF-based MMLS	
Catalyst 4500/4948	MFIB or CEF-based MMLS	Supervisor III, IV, and V use the MFIB with CEF
Catalyst 6500	MMLS or CEF-based MMLS	Supervisor I with PFC I uses MMLS Supervisor I with PFC2 uses MMLS Supervisor II with PFC2 uses CEF-based MMLS Supervisor 720/32 with PFC3 uses CEF-based MMLS

MMLS

Multicast multilayer switching is the original hardware-based switching method that creates the multicast flow entries in hardware using multilayer switching, as discussed in Chapter 9, "Understanding and Configuring Multilayer Switching." Switches forward the packets in the hardware if the entry is present in the MLS cache; otherwise, the switch forwards the frames to the Layer 3 switching engine for processing and then updates the MLS cache. For each cache entry, the hardware ASIC maintains a list of outgoing interfaces for the destination IP multicast group and uses this list to replicate the packets on the outgoing interfaces.

CEF-Based MMLS

CEF-based MMLS is a forwarding model based on unicast CEF-based MLS, which uses the forwarding information base (FIB) and the adjacency table on the Supervisor or daughter card ASICs. Switches populate the (S,G) or (*,G) flows in the hardware FIB table with the suitable masks, such as (S/32, G/32) and (*/0, G/32), and with the RPF interface and the adjacency pointer information (adjacency table). Generally, multicast entries use a 32-bit mask with the indication of source and multicast group in the form of (*,G).

The adjacency table contains the rewrite information and a pointer to the replication entries. The Layer 3 CEF-switching cache contains flow information for all active multicast flows. If the multicast packets are identified as belonging to an existing flow, they can be hardware-switched based on the cache entry for that flow. For each cache entry, the adjacency table maintains a list of outgoing interfaces for the IP multicast group. From this list, the switch determines onto which VLANs traffic from a given multicast flow should be replicated. If a flow matches a FIB entry, the switch does an RPF check for the incoming interface or VLAN. A mismatch results in an RPF failure.

Switches can rate-limit RPF failures to avoid excessive RPF processing and high CPU. For example, host A (10.173.1.100) sends a multicast to the group 224.14.200.1. If there are members on this group that reside in other VLANs than the source VLAN, the switch checks the multicast entry for the particular source and group in the adjacency table to find the outgoing VLAN lists to replicate the packets.

MFIB

The multicast forwarding information base (MFIB) subsystem is the hardware multicast forwarding system that extracts the multicast routes that PIM and IGMP create and changes them into a protocol-independent format for hardware switching. Each entry in the MFIB table consists of an (S,G) or (*,G) route, an input RPF VLAN, and a list of Layer 3 output interfaces. The MFIB subsystem, together with platform-dependent management software, forwards this multicast routing information into the hardware FIB and hardware multicast expansion table (MET) for packet replication. At the time of publication, MFIB is only supported on the Catalyst 4500 family of switches running IOS.

Layer 2 Multicast Protocols

Similar to Layer 3 hardware switching properties of switches, switches also have Layer 2 features to control multicast traffic. The default behavior for a Layer 2 interface on a switch is to forward all multicast traffic to every Layer 2 interface that belongs to the destination VLAN on the switch. This behavior reduces the efficiency of multilayer switching at Layer 2, whose purpose is to limit traffic to the interfaces that need to receive the data.

For example, suppose a video client wants to watch a 1.5-Mbps IP multicast–based video feed sent from a corporate video server. The video client sends an IGMP join message to the video server. The next-hop designated router for the client logs the IGMP join message. The router transmits the IP multicast traffic downstream to the video client. The switch detects the incoming traffic and examines the destination MAC address to determine where the traffic should be forwarded. Because the destination MAC address is a multicast address and there are no entries in the switching table for where the traffic should be forwarded, the 1.5-Mbps video feed is simply sent to all Layer 2 ports in the VLAN.

Layer 2 switches have some degree of multicast awareness to avoid flooding multicasts to all switch ports. Switches provide an architecture that allows multicast traffic to be forwarded to a large number of attached group members without unduly loading the switch fabric. This function allows the switch to provide support for the growing number of new multicast applications without affecting other traffic. The following are the two methods to control multicast at Layer 2 on multilayer switches:

- IGMP snooping
- Cisco Group Management Protocol (CGMP)

Table 11-8 shows types of Cisco Catalyst switches and their supported multicast switching method.

Table 11-8 *Supported Layer 2 Multicast Protocol on Catalyst Switches*

Type of Switch	Layer 2 Multicast Method	Comments
Catalyst 2940/2950/2955/ 2970/2960	IGMP snooping	
Catalyst 3550/3650/3750/3760	IGMP snooping	
Catalyst 4000/4500/4948	CGMP or IGMP snooping	Catalyst 4000 using Cisco CatOS with Supervisor I or II supports CGMP. Catalyst 4000 with a Supervisor II+, III, IV, or V with integrated Layer 3 engine running Cisco IOS supports IGMP snooping. Catalyst 4948 supports IGMP snooping.
Catalyst 6500	IGMP snooping	

IGMP Snooping

IGMP snooping is an IP multicast constraining mechanism that examines Layer 2 and Layer 3 IP multicast information to maintain a Layer 2 multicast forwarding table. This constrains multicast traffic at Layer 2 by configuring Layer 2 LAN ports dynamically to forward multicast traffic only to those ports that want to receive it.

IGMP snooping operates on multilayer switches, even switches that do not support Layer 3 routing. IGMP snooping requires the LAN switch to examine, or "snoop," the IGMP join and leave messages sent between hosts and the first-hop designated multicast router.

NOTE   Without specialized ASICs for IGMP snooping to operate with hardware switching, CGMP is the preferable choice for low-end switches.

When the host joins multicast groups either by sending an unsolicited IGMP join message or by sending an IGMP join message in response to a general query from a multicast router, the switch sees an IGMP host report packet from a host for joining a particular multicast group. The switch snoops the IGMP packets and adds the host's interface from which the IGMP report packet originated to the associated multicast Layer 2 forwarding table entry. IGMP snooping forwards only the first host join message per multicast group to the multicast routers and suppresses the rest of the joining messages for that multicast group unlike CGMP. The switch receives the multicast traffic from the multicast router for that group specified in the join message and forwards that multicast traffic to the interfaces where join messages were received.

When hosts desire to leave a multicast group, either they ignore the periodic general IGMP queries sent by the multicast router (a process known as *silent leave*) or they send a group-specific IGMPv2 leave message. When the switch receives a group-specific IGMPv2 leave message from a host, the switch responds with a MAC-based group-specific query to determine whether any other devices connected on that VLAN are interested in receiving multicast traffic for the specific multicast group. If the switch does not receive an IGMP join message in response to the general query, the switch removes the table entry of the host. If the last leave message was from the only host in the group and the switch does not receive an IGMP join message in response to the general query, it removes the group entry and relays the IGMP leave message to the multicast router. The first-hop designated router then removes the group from that interface and stops forwarding multicast traffic on the interface for the group specified in the leave message.

NOTE   Multilayer switches that support Layer 3 routing perform both the Layer 2 and Layer 3 operations as a single device because both the router and switch act as a single platform.

IGMP snooping supports the "fast-leave processing" feature, which allows IGMP snooping to remove a Layer 2 interface from the multicast forwarding table without first responding with IGMP group-specific queries to the host port. Upon receiving a group-specific IGMP version 2 or 3 leave message, the switch immediately removes the interface from the Layer 2 forwarding table entry for that multicast group, unless a multicast router is detected on the respective interface. Fast-leave processing improves bandwidth management for all hosts in a VLAN on a multilayer switched network.

The IGMP protocol transmits messages as IP multicast packets; as a result, switches cannot distinguish IGMP packets from normal IP multicast data at Layer 2. Therefore, a switch running IGMP snooping must examine every multicast data packet to determine whether it contains pertinent IGMP control information. If IGMP snooping is implemented on a low-end switch with a slow CPU, this could have a severe performance impact when data is transmitted at high rates. The solution to this problem is to implement IGMP snooping with special ASICs that can perform IGMP snooping in hardware.

Cisco Group Management Protocol

CGMP is a Cisco-developed protocol that allows Catalyst switches to learn about the existence of multicast clients from Cisco routers and Layer 3 switches.

CGMP is based on a client/server model. The router is considered a CGMP server, with the switch taking on the client role. The basis of CGMP is that the IP multicast router sees all IGMP packets and, therefore, can inform the switch when specific hosts join or leave multicast groups. The switch then uses this information to construct a forwarding MAC-address table.

When the router sees an IGMP control packet, the router creates a CGMP packet. This CGMP packet contains the request type (either join or leave), the multicast group address, and the actual MAC address of the client. The packet is sent to a well-known address (0x0100.0cdd.dddd) to which all switches listen. Each switch then interprets the packet and creates the proper entries in a forwarding table.

Figure 11-17 illustrates a client that desires to join a multicast group by sending an IGMP join. When the next-hop designated router receives the IGMP join message, however, the router records the source MAC address of the IGMP message and issues a CGMP join message back downstream to the Catalyst switch. The Catalyst switch uses the CGMP message to dynamically build an entry in the switching table that maps the multicast traffic to the switch port of the client. In this example, the server delivers the 1.5-Mbps video feed only to switch ports defined in the multicast switching table. As a result, the switch does not propagate the multicast traffic to hosts that did not join the multicast group.

Figure 11-17 *CGMP Operation*

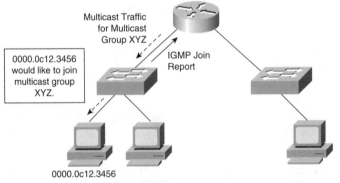

CGMP is a legacy multicast switching protocol. All current-generation (and future) Catalyst switches support IGMP snooping. IGMP snooping has several advantages over CGMP, such as the ability to operate without a first-hop router, and it is less CPU-intensive because it is implemented with special ASICs that can perform IGMP snooping in hardware.

IP Multicast in the Multilayer Switched Network

Multicast is a significant feature of multilayer switched networks. The following are design considerations for deploying multicast in the multilayer switched network:

- **Preferred PIM mode**—Most campus networks run sparse-dense mode because of its ability to work in both dense and sparse modes. The decision to use the sparse mode is based on whether the RP information is available for that group. Sparse-dense mode not only allows Auto-RP to work without preconfiguring the RP, but it also provides the mechanism to control which groups work under sparse mode and which groups work under dense mode.

- **Preferred Layer 2 Multicast Protocol**—By default, most Cisco Catalyst switches have special ASICs to support IGMP snooping in hardware. As a result, the recommendation is to use IGMP snooping on all switches in the multicast switched network. IGMP snooping is simple to implement and works seamlessly with IP multicast.

- **Preferred RP placement**—All Cisco devices that support IP multicast routing use an SPT threshold set to 0; therefore, all last-hop routers in PIM-SM networks immediately switch to SPT and bypass RP for any new sources. Even though the RP does not replicate or forward multicast traffic due to the Cisco SPT-threshold behaviors, the RP must maintain all (*,G) and (S,G) multicast routing entries. Large multicast routing tables consume additional CPU cycles and memory resources. As a result, it is considered best practice to place RPs in the Campus Backbone submodule.

Configuring Multicast

To configure IP multicast on Catalyst switches running Cisco IOS, perform the following steps:

Step 1 Enable multicast routing on Layer 3 globally.

```
Switch(config)#ip multicast-routing
```

NOTE The command syntax used to configure multicast is slightly different for each Cisco family of switches. For specific multicast configuration details of each Cisco family of switches, refer to the product configuration guides and command references on Cisco.com. In addition, refer to the *Multicast Quick-Start Configuration Guide* (Document ID: 9356) at the following URL for more information about configuring multicast on Cisco multilayer switches:

http://www.cisco.com/en/US/tech/tk828/technologies_tech_note 09186a0080094821.shtml

Step 2 Enable PIM on the interface that requires multicast.

```
Switch(config-if)#ip pim [dense-mode | sparse-mode | sparse-dense-mode]
```

Step 3 (Optional.) Configure RP if you are running PIM sparse mode or PIM sparse-dense mode. The Cisco IOS software can be configured so that packets for a single multicast group can use one or more RPs. It is important to configure the RP address on all routers (including the RP router). To configure the address of the RP, enter the following command in global configuration mode:

```
Switch(config)#ip pim rp-address ip-address [access-list-number]
   [override]
```

Step 4   (Optional.) To designate a router as the candidate RP for all multicast groups or for a particular multicast group by using an access list, enter the following command in global configuration mode:

```
Switch(config)#ip pim send-rp-announce interface-type interface-number
   scope ttl [group-list access-list-number] [interval seconds]
```

The TTL value defines the multicast boundaries by limiting the number of hops that the RP announcements can take.

Step 5   (Optional.) To assign the role of RP mapping agent on the router configured in Step 4 for Auto-RP, enter the following command in global configuration mode:

```
Switch(config)#ip pim send-rp-discovery scope ttl
```

Step 6   (Optional.) All systems using Cisco IOS Release 11.3(2)T or later start in PIM version 2 mode by default. In case you need to re-enable PIM version 2 or specify PIM version 1 for some reason, use the following command:

```
Switch(config-if)#ip pim version [1 | 2]
```

Step 7   (Optional.) Configure a BSR border router for the PIM domain so that bootstrap messages do not cross this border in either direction. This ensures that different BSRs will be elected on the two sides of the PIM border. Configure this command on an interface such that no PIM version 2 BSR messages will be sent or received through the interface.

```
Switch(config-if)#ip pim bsr-border
```

Step 8   (Optional.) To configure an interface as a BSR candidate, issue the following command:

```
Switch(config)#ip pim bsr-candidate interface-type hash-mask-length
   [priority]
```

hash-mask-length is a 32-bit mask for the group address before the hash function is called. All groups with the same seed hash correspond to the same RP.

priority is configured as a number from 0 to 255. The BSR with the largest priority is preferred. If the priority values are the same, the device with the highest IP address is selected as the BSR. The default is 0.

Step 9   (Optional.) To configure an interface as an RP candidate for BSR router for particular multicast groups, issue the following command:

```
Switch(config)#ip pim rp-candidate interface-type interface-number ttl
    group-list access-list
```

Example 11-1 shows a sample configuration of PIM sparse mode in Cisco IOS with an RP address of 10.20.1.254.

Example 11-1 *Configuration of PIM Sparse Mode in Cisco IOS*

```
Router#conf t
Router(config)#ip multicast-routing
Router(config)#interface vlan 1
Router(config-if)#ip pim sparse-mode
Router(config-if)#interface vlan 3
Router(config-if)#ip pim sparse-mode
Router(config-if)#exit
Router(config)#ip pim rp-address 10.20.1.254
```

Example 11-2 shows a sample configuration of PIM sparse-dense mode in Cisco IOS with a candidate BSR.

Example 11-2 *Multicast Configuration of Sparse-Dense Mode with BSR*

```
Router(config)#ip multicast-routing
Router(config)#interface vlan 1
Router(config-if)#ip pim sparse-dense-mode
Router(config-if)#exit
Router(config)#ip pim bsr-candidate vlan 1 30 200
```

Example 11-3 shows a sample Cisco IOS configuration of the Auto-RP that is advertising the IP address of VLAN 1 as the RP.

Example 11-3 *IP Multicast Configuration of Sparse-Dense Mode with Auto-RP*

```
Router(config)#ip multicast-routing
Router(config)#interface vlan 1
Router(config-if)#ip pim sparse-dense-mode
Router(config-if)#exit
Router(config)#ip pim send-rp-announce vlan 1 scope  15 group-list 1
Router(config)#access-list 1 permit 225.25.25.0.0.0.0.255
Router(config)#exit
```

In addition to the preceding commands, every Cisco Catalyst switch supports additional multicast tuning features such as rate limiting and altering the protocol timers. Refer to the product documentation for more information.

To configure IGMP snooping on a Cisco IOS switch, perform the following steps:

Step 1   Enable IGMP snooping globally. (By default, it is enabled globally.)

```
Switch(config)#ip igmp snooping
```

Step 2   (Optional.) Switches add multicast router ports to the forwarding table for every Layer 2 multicast entry. The switch learns of such ports through snooping IGMP queries, flowing PIM and DVMRP packets, or interpreting CGMP packets from other routers. Configure the IGMP snooping method. The default is PIM.

```
Switch(config)#ip igmp snooping vlan vlan-id mrouter learn [cgmp |
    pim-dvmrp]
```

Step 3   (Optional.) If needed, configure the router port statically. By default, IGMP snooping automatically detects the router ports.

```
Switch(config)#ip igmp snooping vlan vlan-id mrouter interface
    interface-num
```

Step 4   (Optional.) Configure IGMP fast leave if required.

```
Switch(config)#ip igmp snooping vlan vlan-id fast-leave
```

Note   To configure IGMP snooping fast leave on Cisco Catalyst 2940/2950/2955/2970, Catalyst 3550/3650/3750, and Catalyst 4500, use the following command:

```
Switch(config)#ip igmp snooping vlan vlan_id immediate-leave
```

Step 5   (Optional.) By default, all hosts register and add the MAC address and port to the forwarding table automatically. If required, configure a host statically on an interface. Generally, static configurations are necessary when troubleshooting or working around IGMP problems.

```
Switch(config)#ip igmp snooping vlan vlan-id static mac-address
    interface interface-id
```

NOTE   The command syntax of some of the commands might be different for different switch platforms. Refer to the product documentation for more information. Also refer to the following document on Cisco.com for more information about Multicast Layer 2 support on Cisco Catalyst switches: "Multicast Catalyst Switches Support Matrix," Document ID: 29480.

To configure IGMP snooping on Catalyst switches running Cisco CatOS, perform the following steps:

Step 1   Configure IGMP snooping on the switch.

```
Console> (enable) set igmp enable
```

Step 2   (Optional.) By default, IGMP flooding is enabled on the switch such that the switch floods multicast traffic for a few seconds after the last multicast host on a VLAN leaves the group. When disabled, this feature only sends multicast traffic to the multicast router port.

```
Console> (enable) set igmp flooding {enable | disable}
```

Step 3   (Optional.) Configure the IGMP mode to detect the multicast ports, if needed. The default is auto.

```
Console> (enable)  set igmp mode {igmp-only | igmp-cgmp | auto}
```

Step 4   (Optional.) Enable IGMP fast leave, if required.

```
Console> (enable) set igmp fastleave enable
```

Step 5   (Optional.) By default, the switch automatically learns multicast router ports once IGMP is enabled. However, if required, configure the multicast router port statically. Again, static configurations are usually only necessary in troubleshooting scenarios.

```
Console> (enable) set multicast router mod-num/port-num
```

NOTE   IGMP snooping is enabled by default in Cisco CatOS software release 5.5(9) and later and software release 6.3(1) and later.

Monitoring and Verifying IP Multicast Traffic

To verify and monitor IP multicast traffic, use a variety of **show** commands to display specific statistics, shown in Table 11-9, such as the contents of IP routing tables.

Table 11-9   *IP Multicast Routing Commands*

Command	Description
ping [*group-name* | *group-address*]	Sends an ICMP echo request to a multicast group address
show ip mroute [*hostname* | *group-number*]	Displays the contents of the IP multicast routing table
show ip pim interface [*type number*] [**count**]	Displays information about interfaces configured for PIM
show ip pim interface	Displays PIM information for all interfaces

Example 11-4 shows the sample output from the **show ip mroute** command for a router operating in PIM sparse mode. For every (S,G) entry, there is a corresponding parent entry. (*,G) entries maintain information about whole groups, such as the group operating mode,

RFP neighbor, IP address, and so on. This information is mainly used to populate the outgoing interface list of any newly created (S,G). In Example 11-4, (*, 224.0.255.3) illustrates that the multicast group 224.0.255.3 is operating in sparse mode with RPF neighbor 198.92.37.2. (10.92.46.1, 224.0.255.3) represents the source of the group with its outgoing multicast list.

Example 11-4 *Using the* **show ip mroute** *Command for PIM Sparse Mode*

```
Switch#show ip mroute

IP Multicast Routing Table
Flags: D - Dense, S - Sparse, C - Connected, L - Local, P - Pruned
R - RP-bit set, F - Register flag, T - SPT-bit set
Timers: Uptime/Expires
Interface state: Interface, Next-Hop, State/Mode

(*, 224.0.255.3), uptime 5:29:15, RP is 198.92.37.2, flags: SC
  Incoming interface: Tunnel0, RPF neighbor 10.3.35.1, Dvmrp
  Outgoing interface list:
    Ethernet0, Forward/Sparse, 5:29:15/0:02:57

(10.92.46.1, 224.0.255.3), uptime 5:29:15, expires 0:02:59, flags: C
  Incoming interface: Tunnel0, RPF neighbor 10.3.35.1
  Outgoing interface list:
    Ethernet0, Forward/Sparse, 5:29:15/0:02:57
```

NOTE   Output interface timers are not updated for hardware-forwarded packets or at specific intervals such as 5 minutes. Entry timers are updated approximately every 5 seconds.

Example 11-5 illustrates sample output from the **show ip mroute** command with the **summary** keyword.

Example 11-5 *Using the* **show ip mroute summary** *Command*

```
Switch#show ip mroute summary

IP Multicast Routing Table
Flags: D - Dense, S - Sparse, C - Connected, L - Local, P - Pruned
       R - RP-bit set, F - Register flag, T - SPT-bit set, J - Join SPT
Timers: Uptime/Expires
Interface state: Interface, Next-Hop, State/Mode

(*, 224.255.255.255), 2d16h/00:02:30, RP 10.69.10.13, flags: SJPC

(*, 224.2.127.253), 00:58:18/00:02:00, RP 10.69.10.13, flags: SJC

(*, 224.1.127.255), 00:58:21/00:02:03, RP 10.69.10.13, flags: SJC

(*, 224.2.127.254), 2d16h/00:00:00, RP 10.69.10.13, flags: SJCL
  (10.9.160.67/32, 224.2.127.254), 00:02:46/00:00:12, flags: CLJT
  (10.48.244.217/32, 224.2.127.254), 00:02:15/00:00:40, flags: CLJT
```

Example 11-5 *Using the* **show ip mroute summary** *Command (Continued)*

```
(10.207.8.33/32, 224.2.127.254), 00:00:25/00:02:32, flags: CLJT
(10.243.2.62/32, 224.2.127.254), 00:00:51/00:02:03, flags: CLJT
(10.173.8.3/32, 224.2.127.254), 00:00:26/00:02:33, flags: CLJT
(10.69.60.189/32, 224.2.127.254), 00:03:47/00:00:46, flags: CLJT
```

Example 11-6 shows sample output from the **show ip mroute** command with the **active** keyword to show the rate of the multicast streams for the active multicast entries.

Example 11-6 *Using the* **show ip mroute active** *Command*

```
Switch#show ip mroute active

Active IP Multicast Sources - sending >= 4 kbps

Group: 224.2.127.254, (sdr.cisco.com)
   Source: 10.137.28.69 (mbone.ipd.anl.gov)
     Rate: 1 pps/4 kbps(1sec), 4 kbps(last 1 secs), 4 kbps(life avg)

Group: 224.2.201.241, ACM 97
   Source: 10.129.52.160 (webcast3-e1.acm97.interop.net)
     Rate: 9 pps/93 kbps(1sec), 145 kbps(last 20 secs), 85 kbps(life avg)

Group: 224.2.207.215, ACM 97
   Source: 10.129.52.160 (webcast3-e1.acm97.interop.net)
     Rate: 3 pps/31 kbps(1sec), 63 kbps(last 19 secs), 65 kbps(life avg)
```

Example 11-7 shows sample output from the **show ip mroute** command with the **count** keyword where it shows additional traffic statistics of the multicast groups.

Example 11-7 *Using the* **show ip mroute count** *Command*

```
Switch#show ip mroute count

IP Multicast Statistics - Group count: 8, Average sources per group: 9.87
Counts: Pkt Count/Pkts per second/Avg Pkt Size/Kilobits per second

Group: 224.255.255.255, Source count: 0, Group pkt count: 0
  RP-tree: 0/0/0/0

Group: 224.2.127.253, Source count: 0, Group pkt count: 0
  RP-tree: 0/0/0/0

Group: 224.1.127.255, Source count: 0, Group pkt count: 0
  RP-tree: 0/0/0/0

Group: 224.2.127.254, Source count: 9, Group pkt count: 14
  RP-tree: 0/0/0/0
  Source: 10.2.6.9/32, 2/0/796/0
  Source: 10.32.131.87/32, 1/0/616/0
  Source: 10.125.51.58/32, 1/0/412/0
  Source: 10.207.8.33/32, 1/0/936/0
  Source: 10.243.2.62/32, 1/0/750/0
```

continues

Example 11-7 *Using the* **show ip mroute count** *Command (Continued)*

```
        Source: 10.173.8.3/32, 1/0/660/0
        Source: 10.137.28.69/32, 1/0/584/0
        Source: 10.69.60.189/32, 4/0/447/0
        Source: 10.162.119.8/32, 2/0/834/0
    Group: 224.0.1.40, Source count: 1, Group pkt count: 3606
      RP-tree: 0/0/0/0
      Source: 10.69.214.50/32, 3606/0/48/0, RPF Failed: 1203

    Group: 224.2.201.241, Source count: 36, Group pkt count: 54152
      RP-tree: 7/0/108/0
      Source: 10.242.36.83/32, 99/0/123/0
      Source: 10.29.1.3/32, 71/0/110/0
      Source: 10.9.160.96/32, 505/1/106/0
      Source: 10.32.163.170/32, 661/1/88/0
      Source: 10.115.31.26/32, 192/0/118/0
      Source: 10.146.111.45/32, 500/0/87/0
      Source: 10.183.33.134/32, 248/0/119/0
      Source: 10.195.7.62/32, 527/0/118/0
      Source: 10.223.32.25/32, 554/0/105/0
      Source: 10.223.32.151/32, 551/1/125/0
      Source: 10.223.156.117/32, 535/1/114/0
      Source: 10.223.225.21/32, 582/0/114/0
      Source: 10.89.142.50/32, 78/0/127/0
      Source: 10.99.50.14/32, 526/0/118/0
      Source: 10.129.0.13/32, 522/0/95/0
      Source: 10.129.52.160/32, 40839/16/920/161
      Source: 10.129.52.161/32, 476/0/97/0
      Source: 10.221.224.10/32, 456/0/113/0
      Source: 10.146.32.108/32, 9/1/112/0
```

Example 11-8 shows sample output from the **show ip pim interface** command.

Example 11-8 *Using the* **show ip pim interface** *Command*

```
Switch#show ip pim interface

Address          Interface        Mode     Neighbor  Query     DR
                                           Count     Interval
10.92.37.6       Ethernet0        Dense    2         30        10.92.37.33
10.92.36.129     Ethernet1        Dense    2         30        10.92.36.131
10.1.37.2        Tunnel0          Dense    1         30        0.0.0.0
```

Example 11-9 shows sample output from the **show ip pim interface** command with the **count** option.

Example 11-9 *Using the* **show ip pim interface count** *Command*

```
Switch#show ip pim interface count

Address          Interface        FS   Mpackets In/Out
10.69.121.35     Ethernet0        *    548305239/13744856
10.69.121.35     Serial0.33       *    8256/67052912
10.92.12.73      Serial0.1719     *    219444/862191
```

Example 11-10 shows another sample output from the **show ip pim interface** command with the **count** option when IP multicast is enabled in hardware. This example lists the PIM interfaces that are fast-switched and process-switched and the packet counts for these. The "H" is added to interfaces where IP multicast forwarding is done in hardware (MMLS or CEF-based MLS), as shown in Example 11-10 for VLANs 10, 11, and 12.

Example 11-10   *Using the* **show ip pim interface count** *Command When IP Multicast Is Enabled*

```
Switch#show ip pim interface count

States: FS - Fast Switched, H - Hardware Switched
Address         Interface         FS  Mpackets In/Out
10.1.10.2       Vlan10            * H 40886/0
10.1.11.2       Vlan11            * H 0/40554
10.1.12.2       Vlan12            * H 0/40554
10.1.23.2       Vlan23            *   0/0
10.1.24.2       Vlan24            *   0/0
```

To monitor the RP mapping information, use the commands shown in Table 11-10.

Table 11-10   *Multicast PIM* **show** *Commands*

Command	Description
show ip pim bsr	Displays information about the currently elected BSR
show ip pim rp-hash *group*	Displays the RP that was selected for the specified group
show ip pim rp [*group-name* | *group-address* | **mapping**]	Displays how the router learns of the RP (via bootstrap or Auto-RP mechanism)
show mls ip multicast summary	Displays rate-limiting information of RPF failure

To display IGMP snooping information, use the commands shown in Table 11-11.

Table 11-11   *IGMP Snooping* **show** *Commands*

Command	Description
show ip igmp snooping mrouter interface	Displays information about IGMP snooping configured interfaces
show mac-address-table multicast *vlan-id* [**count**]	Displays the multicast MAC address for a VLAN
show ip igmp interface *vlan-id*	Displays IGMP snooping information on a VLAN interface

To clear IP multicast caches, tables, and databases, use the commands shown in Table 11-12.

Table 11-12 *Multicast **clear** Commands*

Command	Description
clear ip mroute	Deletes entries from the IP routing table
clear ip cgmp	Deletes all group entries the Catalyst switches have cached
clear ip pim auto-rp *rp-address*	Deletes all the Auto-RP cache entries
clear ip igmp group [*group-name* | *group-address* | *interface*]	Deletes entries from the IGMP cache

Study Tips

The following bullets review important BCMSN exam preparation points of this chapter. The bullets only briefly highlight the important concepts. Consult the text of this chapter for additional information regarding these topics:

- Using multicasting to transmit traffic reduces bandwidth consumption by forwarding one copy of each packet to registered hosts, unlike broadcast traffic, which forwards each packet to all the hosts in the broadcast domain regardless of whether the host is interested in the packet.

- Multicast uses multicast IP addresses to specify a group of hosts that are interested in receiving the multicast traffic.

- Multicast addresses belong to the Class D range (224.0.0.0 to 239.255.255.255). The first four bits of the IP address always begin with 1110, and the rest of the 28 bits represents the multicast group ID.

- Multicast addresses map to multicast MAC addresses, although not always uniquely. A multicast MAC address always starts with 0x01-00-5E-xx-xx-xx with the 25th bit set to 0. The rest of the 23 bits maps into the multicast IP address, which results in a lack of uniqueness for 5 bits in the IP-to-MAC mapping.

- Multicast only forwards packets if the packets passed the Reverse Path Forwarding test, which means a router or switch received the traffic on an interface to which the multicast packet's source IP address is connected or routed.

- Multicast uses distribution trees to forward traffic to all registered hosts from a source. Source-based distribution trees are based around the source and take the shortest path to reach all the receivers. Shared tree distribution uses a common root called the rendezvous point (RP) to forward packets to all the receivers. In shared tree, traffic from the source is forwarded to RP, where it branches out the traffic to all the receivers.

- PIM is a popular multicast routing protocol that is responsible for creating multicast trees and forwarding multicast packets.

- The PIM dense mode is based on a source-tree distribution and is most suitable for networks with a relatively small number of senders compared to receivers.

- The PIM sparse mode uses the shared tree distribution method to forward multicast traffic. Sparse mode is commonly deployed where multicast receivers are sparsely distributed throughout the network and tight control of multicast forwarding paths is needed.

- The PIM sparse-dense configuration is the most commonly recommended configuration for the enterprise networks. When a router or switch runs PIM sparse-dense mode, it uses sparse mode if the RP information is available for the group; otherwise, the router or switch falls back to dense mode for multicast forwarding.

- Auto-RP is the recommended method to automate the distribution of group-to-RP mapping for the networks composed of Cisco routers and switches.

- IGMP is the multicast management protocol that hosts use to register themselves in a multicast group to receive multicast streams.

- IGMP version 2 provides leave group messages and group-specific query messages that optimize multicast packet forwarding that did not exist in IGMP version 1.

- IGMP query messages use the destination IP address 224.0.0.1 with a TTL 1 to address the all-hosts group.

- IGMP version 3 supports source filtering by using the INCLUDE or EXCLUDE modes in the report query messages.

- Current multilayer switches use special ASICs that support multicast forwarding in hardware using the MMLS, MMLS-CEF, or MFIB features to accomplish high performance multicast forwarding in hardware.

- CGMP and IGMP snooping are two Layer 2 multicast protocols that control multicast traffic at Layer 2. However, CGMP is a legacy protocol supported only on legacy Catalyst switches.

- The recommended practice is to run IGMP snooping on all Catalyst switches that have special ASICs to support IGMP snooping to control multicast flooding at Layer 2. IGMP snooping is supported on all currently shipping Catalyst switches including the Catalyst 6500, 4500, 3750, 3560, 3550, 2960, and 2950 families of switches and enabled by default.

Table 11-13 *Commands to Review*

Command	Description
ip igmp snooping	Enables IP IGMP snooping. By default, IGMP snooping is enabled on Cisco Catalyst switches.
ip igmp snooping fast-leave	Enables IP IGMP snooping fast leave on Cisco Catalyst 6500 series switches.
ip igmp snooping immediate-leave	Enables IP IGMP snooping fast leave on Cisco Catalyst 2950/2955/2970 3550/3650/ 3560 and 4500 series switches.
ip multicast-routing	Globally enables multicast routing.
ip pim send-rp-announce *interface_type slot/ port* **scope** *num* **group-list** *num*	Configures RP candidates for RP-to-group mapping.
ip pim send-rp-discovery scope *num*	Configures the RP mapping agent.
ip pim sparse-dense-mode	Enables PIM sparse-dense mode on the interface.
ip pim sparse-mode	Enables PIM sparse-dense on the respective interface.
show ip igmp interface *vlan_ID*	Displays IGMP snooping information on a VLAN interface.
show ip igmp snooping mrouter interface	Displays IGMP snooping multicast router interfaces.
show ip mroute [hostname | *group_number***]**	Displays multicast routing information.
show ip pim interface [{{vlan *vlan_ID***}** | **{***type slot/port***}** | **{port-channel** *number***}}]** **count**	Displays IP multicast Layer 3 switching state information for all MSFC IP PIM Layer 3 interfaces.
show mac-address-table multicast *vlan_ID* **[count]**	Displays multicast MAC address entries for a VLAN.
show mls ip multicast summary	Displays rate-limiting information of RPF failures.

Summary

This chapter discussed the IP multicast routing protocols and their implementation and functionality in detail.

In summary, IP multicast is the transmission of an IP data frame to a host group that is defined by a single multicast IP address. IP multicast–capable routers create distribution trees that control the path that IP multicast traffic takes through the network.

In reference to routing protocols, PIM is an IP multicast routing mechanism that leverages existing unicast IP routing protocols used to populate the unicast routing table. PIM works in dense, sparse, sparse-dense, and bidirectional modes. PIM dense mode is the most commonly deployed IP multicast routing protocol, but PIM sparse-dense mode is the most commonly deployed multicast routing protocol in large enterprise networks to minimize the complexity of the multicast topology. Bidirectional PIM is suited for multicast with larger numbers of sources.

In terms of host registration, IGMP is used to dynamically register individual hosts in a multicast group.

IGMP snooping and CGMP are the Layer 2 multicast protocols to maintain the multicast MAC address forwarding table to identify the location of multicast clients. CGMP is a client/server-based model in which the router receives all the multicast packets and informs the switches which host joins or leaves the multicast group. IGMP snooping is an IP multicast constraining mechanism that examines Layer 3 information to maintain a Layer 2 multicast table. All recent Cisco Catalyst switches support IGMP snooping due to its support in ASICs and its advantages over CGMP.

Configuration Exercise: Configuring and Verifying Multicast in the Multilayer Switched Network to Support Stock Ticker Video Applications

Complete this configuration exercise to familiarize yourself with the initial configuration of multicast on Cisco IOS–based Catalyst switches.

Required Resources

The only resource necessary for this configuration exercise is access to a Cisco IOS–based Layer 3 Catalyst switch via the console or in-band access such as SSH. Host workstations for testing the configuration of IP multicast routing are optional.

Exercise Objective

The purpose of this configuration exercise is to demonstrate the configuration of IP multicast routing in the multilayer switched environment to run a stock ticker video application. After completing this exercise, you will be able to perform the following types of configurations on Catalyst switches running Cisco IOS:

- Multicast routing using sparse-dense mode on VLAN interfaces
- RP and mapping agents for Auto-RP

This exercise uses a Catalyst 6500 switch running Cisco IOS, but this exercise can be done using any Catalyst Layer 3 switches that support IP multicast routing and IGMP snooping. This includes the Cisco Catalyst 3550/3750 and Catalyst 4500 families of switches. The command syntax may be different for different types of switches. Please refer to the command manual of the specific product for more information.

Network Diagram

Figure 11-18 shows the network layout for this configuration exercise.

Command List

In this configuration exercise, you will use the commands listed in Table 11-14, which are in alphabetical order so that you can easily locate the information you need. Refer to this list if you need configuration command assistance during the configuration exercise. The table includes only the specific parameters used in the example and not all the available options for the command.

Figure 11-18 *Network Layout for Lab Exercise*

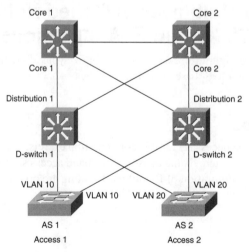

Table 11-14 *Command List for Configuration Exercise*

Command	Description
access-list *num* [**permit** | **deny**] *address mask*	Configures the access list
configure terminal	From privileged EXEC mode, enters global configuration mode
enable password *password*	Sets the password required to enter privileged mode
exit	Exits the current mode
interface FastEthernet | **GigabitEthernet** *slot/ port*	Enters interface configuration mode for a Catalyst switch with a Fast Ethernet or Gigabit Ethernet interface installed
interface loopback *loop-id*	Creates a loopback interface
interface vlan *vlan-id*	Creates the VLAN interface for inter-VLAN routing
IP address *address subnetmask*	Sets the IP address and subnet mask for an interface
ip igmp snooping	Enables IP IGMP snooping
ip igmp snooping fast-leave	Enables IP IGMP snooping fast leave
ip multicast-routing	Globally enables multicast routing
ip pim send-rp-announce *interface-id* **scope** *num* **group-list** *num*	Configures RP candidates for RP-to-group mapping
ip pim send-rp-discovery scope *num*	Configures the RP mapping agent
ip pim sparse-dense-mode	Enables PIM sparse-dense mode on the respective interface
no interface vlan *vlan-id*	Removes the VLAN interface
no switchport	Configures port as Layer 3 routed port
ping *ip-address*	Sends an ICMP echo to the designated IP address, using the default settings of size and response window time
show interface *interface-id* **switchport**	Displays the switchport configuration of the interface
show ip mroute [*hostname* | *group-number*]	Displays the contents of the IP multicast routing table
show ip pim rp [*group-name* | *group-address* | **mapping**]	Displays how the router learns of the RP (via bootstrap or Auto-RP mechanism)
[**no**] **shutdown**	Disables or enables an interface

continues

Table 11-14 *Command List for Configuration Exercise (Continued)*

Command	Description
telnet *ip-address*	Starts a terminal-emulation program from a PC, router, or switch that permits you to access network devices remotely over the network
vlan database	Enters VLAN configuration mode
vlan *vlan-id*	Creates a VLAN in either VLAN database or configuration mode

Task 1: Configure Multicast Routing with Sparse-Dense Mode on Distribution Switches

Step 1 Enter the privileged EXEC mode of the Distribution Layer Switch D-switch1 using the **enable** command, and then enter global configuration mode using the **configure terminal** command.

```
D-switch1>enable
Password:
D-switch1#configure terminal
Enter configuration commands, one per line.  End with CNTL/Z.
```

Step 2 From global configuration mode, enable multicast routing and configure PIM sparse-dense mode on the VLAN interfaces.

```
D-switch1(config)#ip multicast-routing
D-switch1(config)#interface vlan 10
D-switch1(config-if)#ip address 10.10.1.1 255.255.255.0
D-switch1(config-if)#ip pim sparse-dense-mode
D-switch1(config-if)#no shut
D-switch1(config-if)#interface vlan 20
D-switch1(config-if)#ip address 10.20.1.1 255.255.255.0
D-switch1(config-if)#ip pim sparse-dense-mode
D-switch1(config-if)#no shut
D-switch1(config-if)#end
```

Step 3 From global configuration mode, enable the IGMP snooping and IGMP snooping fast leave features.

```
D-switch1(config)# ip igmp snooping
D-switch1(config)#interface vlan 10
D-switch1(config-if)#ip igmp snooping fast-leave
```

```
D-switch1(config)#interface vlan 20
D-switch1(config-if)#ip igmp snooping fast-leave
```

Task 2: Configure the RP/Mapping Agent for Auto-RP on the Core Switches

Step 1   Configure a loopback interface with an IP address to advertise the candidate RP on core 1. Also enable PIM sparse-dense mode on all the interfaces connected to the distribution switches.

```
core1(config)#interface loopback1
core1(config-if)#ip address 10.100.1.254 255.255.255.0
core1(config-if)#ip pim sparse-dense-mode
core1(config-if)#interface gigabitethernet 1/1
core1(config-if)#ip address 10.200.1.1 255.255.255.0
core1(config-if)#ip pim sparse-dense-mode
```

Step 2   Configure a candidate RP and a mapping agent on core 1 for the 239.0.0.0– 239.255.255.255 multicast administrative group using the group list.

```
core1(config)#ip pim send-rp-announce  loopback 1 scope  15 group-list 1
core1(config)#ip pim send-rp-discovery scope 15
core1(config)#access-list 1 permit 239.0.0.0 0.255.255.255
```

Review Questions

For multiple-choice questions, there might be more than one correct answer.

1   True or False: The default value for the maximum response time in an IGMPv2 membership query is 10 seconds.

2   True or False: IGMPv1 supports host membership leave messages.

3   True or False: IP multicast uses destination IP addresses in the 224.0.0.0 to 239.255.255.255 range.

4   True or False: IP multicast addresses map to the ffff.ffff.ffff broadcast MAC address.

Questions 5 through 7 are based on the configuration in Example 11-11.

Example 11-11 *Configuration Example for Questions 5 Through 7*

```
Switch#show ip mroute summary

IP Multicast Routing Table
Flags: D - Dense, S - Sparse, C - Connected, L - Local, P - Pruned
       R - RP-bit set, F - Register flag, T - SPT-bit set, J - Join SPT
Timers: Uptime/Expires
```

continues

Example 11-11 *Configuration Example for Questions 5 Through 7 (Continued)*

```
Interface state: Interface, Next-Hop, State/Mode

(*, 224.255.255.255), 2d16h/00:02:30, RP 10.69.100.13, flags: SJPC

(*, 224.5.127.253), 00:58:18/00:02:00, RP 10.69.100.13, flags: SJC

(*, 224.10.127.253), 00:58:21/00:02:03, RP 10.69.100.13, flags: SJC

(*, 224.2.125.254), 2d16h/00:00:00, RP 10.69.100.13, flags: SJCL
    (10.9.160.67/32, 224.2.125.254), 00:02:46/00:00:12, flags: CLJT
    (10.48.244.217/32, 224.2.125.254), 00:02:15/00:00:40, flags: CLJT
    (10.207.8.33/32, 224.2.125.254), 00:00:25/00:02:32, flags: CLJT
    (10.243.2.62/32, 224.2.125.254), 00:00:51/00:02:03, flags: CLJT
    (10.173.8.3/32, 224.2.125.254), 00:00:26/00:02:33, flags: CLJT
    (10.69.60.189/32, 224.2.125.254), 00:03:47/00:00:46, flags: CLJT
```

5 How does the switch learn about the multicast group 224.2.125.254 based on the configuration in Example 11-11?

   a PIM dense mode

   b PIM sparse mode

   c None of the above

6 Based on the configuration in Example 11-11, what is the RP IP address for multicast group 224.2.125.254?

   a 10.173.8.3

   b 10.69.60.189

   c 224.10.127.253

   d 10.69.100.13

7 How many sources are used in forwarding the multicast traffic for group 224.2.125.254?

   a 1

   b 5

   c 6

   d 3

8 What differentiates IP multicast from other transmission modes?

   a   IP multicast sends packets to a single host.

   b   IP multicast sends packets to groups of hosts where specific hosts process the packet.

   c   IP multicast sends packets to all hosts sequentially.

   d   IP multicast sends packets to all hosts simultaneously.

9 What is one potential drawback to source distribution trees compared to shared distribution trees?

   a   Increased latency

   b   Increased memory overhead

   c   Suboptimal path calculations

   d   Increased bandwidth utilization

10 Under which condition should you choose PIM sparse mode as opposed to PIM dense mode?

   a   Bandwidth is plentiful.

   b   The multicast group has many members.

   c   The hosts in the multicast group are widely dispersed.

   d   Almost all hosts on the network belong to the multicast group.

11 Which version of IGMP added support for source filtering?

   a   IGMPv1

   b   IGMPv2

   c   IGMPv3

   d   IGMPv3 lite

12 Which of the following is a potential drawback of IGMP snooping on a switch without special ASICs?

   a Increased latency

   b Reduced bandwidth

   c Degraded performance

   d Increased administrative complexity

13 Which command correctly enables the preferred mode of PIM for IP multicast?

   a **ip pim dense-mode**

   b **ip pim sparse-mode**

   c **ip pim sparse-dense-mode**

   d **ip pim dense-sparse-mode**

14 What is the purpose of a bootstrap router in PIM version 2?

   a To ensure RP availability

   b To provide redundant RPs

   c To provide RP discovery and distribution

   d To configure a single RP for multiple groups

15 Which command correctly displays the contents of the IP multicast routing table?

   a **show ip mfib**

   b **show ip mroute**

   c **show mroute table**

   d **show ip pim interface**

16 What are the two mechanisms that automate the distribution of RP in sparse mode?

   a Auto-RP

   b RP

   c BSR

   d IGMP snooping

17 In what PIM mode or modes do you have to specify the RP manually? (Choose all that apply.)

   a PIM dense mode

   b PIM sparse-dense mode

   c PIM sparse mode

   d IGMP snooping

18 What does IGMP snooping look for in Layer 3 information?

   a IGMP join/leave messages

   b IGMP membership reports

   c IGMP membership queries

   d IGMP INCLUDE messages

This chapter covers the following topics:

- Using Network-Level and Device-Level (Fault Tolerance) Redundancy to Yield High Availability
- Implementing Redundant Supervisor Engines in Catalyst Switches Running Cisco IOS
- Implementing Redundant Supervisor Engine Uplink Ports in Catalyst Switches
- Understanding Single Router Mode with Hybrid OS on the Catalyst 6500 Family of Switches
- Understanding Cisco IOS Software Modularity and In-Service Software Upgrade (ISSU)
- Implementing Redundant Power Supplies
- Understanding Router Module Redundancy in Catalyst Switches
- Understanding and Configuring the Hot Standby Routing Protocol
- Understanding and Configuring the Virtual Router Redundancy Protocol
- Understanding and Configuring the Gateway Load Balancing Protocol
- Understanding and Configuring the Cisco IOS Server Load Balancing Feature

Design Network Resiliency, Redundancy, and High Availability in Multilayer Switched Networks

The term *high availability* is used to describe a device or network that requires no unscheduled downtime. The term *fault tolerance* describes the ability of a device or network to recover from the failure of a component or device. Achieving high availability requires the elimination of any single points of failure, the deployment of fault-tolerant network devices, and the distribution of intelligence throughout the architecture. Adding redundant components, including redundant network devices and connections to redundant services, increases availability. An example of adding redundancy is to deploy redundant Data Center access layer switches with dual-homed servers. The servers can also have redundancy with a second server acting as a backup server. With a proper multilayer switched network design, no single component (software or hardware) failure affects the availability of any part of the enterprise or service provider network.

This chapter reviews both system component redundancy features and router redundancy features. It concludes with a discussion of a server redundancy feature.

Achieving High Availability in Multilayer Switches

To achieve high network availability, the following network components are required:

- **Reliable, fault-tolerant network devices**—Hardware and software reliability to automatically identify and overcome failures.

- **Device and link redundancy**—Entire devices may be redundant, or modules within devices may be redundant. Links may also be redundant.

- **Resilient network technologies**—Intelligence that ensures fast recovery around any device or link failure.

- **Optimized network design**—Well-defined network topologies and configurations designed to ensure that there is no single point of failure.

- **Best practices**—Documented procedures for deploying and maintaining a robust network infrastructure.

- **Change control**—Better control over changes made to network devices and maintenance of documentation regarding those changes.

One approach to building highly available networks is to use fault-tolerant network devices throughout the network. Fault tolerance provides redundancy within each network device for critical components such as processing engines and power supplies. In brief, fault tolerance offers the following benefits:

- Minimizes times during which the system is nonresponsive to requests (for example, while the system process is being restarted after a software or hardware component failure)

- Eliminates all single points of failure that would cause a system-wide outage

- Provides disaster protection by allowing the major system components to be geographically separated

Although fault tolerance is desirable, trying to achieve high network availability solely through device-level fault tolerance has some drawbacks:

- Massive redundancy within each device adds significantly to its cost, while at the same time reducing physical capacity by consuming slots that could otherwise house network interfaces or provide network services.

- Redundant subsystems within devices are often maintained in a hot standby mode, where they cannot contribute additional performance because they are only fully activated when the primary component fails. However, high-end and future Catalyst switches can overcome this limitation with proper configurations.

Focusing on device-level hardware reliability may result in a number of other failure mechanisms being overlooked. Network elements are not standalone devices but are components of a network system whose internal operations and system-level interactions are governed by software and configuration parameters. Figure 12-1 displays a switched network with a single point of failure—there is only one forwarding path. Failure in devices along the path in Figure 12-1 would be disastrous, because it would isolate parts of the network.

A complementary way to build highly available networks is to provide reliability through redundancy in the network topology rather than primarily within the network devices themselves. A proper balance of fault tolerance and network redundancy is critical to a high-availability network. In the campus network design shown in Figure 12-2, there is a backup for every link and every network device in the path between the client and server.

Using network redundancy (with fault-tolerant network devices) offers the following advantages:

- The network devices that provide redundancy do not need to be co-located in the same physical location. This reduces the probability that problems with the physical environment, such as a power outage or other environmental issue, will interrupt service.

- Problems with software bugs and upgrades, or configuration errors and changes, can be dealt with separately in the primary and secondary forwarding paths without completely interrupting service. Therefore, network-level redundancy can also reduce the impact of nonhardware failure mechanisms.

Figure 12-1 *Switched Network with Fault-Tolerant Devices with Single Point of Failure in Forwarding Path*

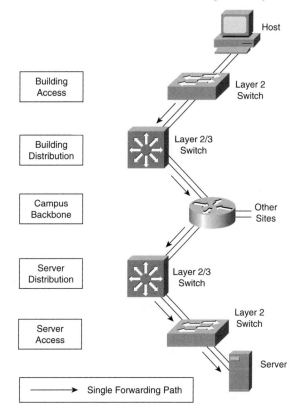

- With the redundancy provided by the network, each network device no longer needs to be configured for optimal standalone fault tolerance. Device-level fault tolerance can be concentrated in the core and distribution layers of the network where a hardware failure would affect the largest number of users. By partially relaxing the requirement for device-level fault tolerance, the cost per network device is reduced, to some degree offsetting the requirement for more devices.

- With appropriate resiliency features combined with careful design and configuration, the traffic load between the respective layers of the network topology (that is, Building Access submodule to Building Distribution submodule) can be shared between the primary and secondary forwarding paths. Therefore, network-level redundancy can also provide increased aggregate performance and capacity.

- Redundant networks can be configured to automatically fail over from primary to secondary facilities without operator intervention. The duration of service interruption is equal to the time it takes for failover to occur. Failover times as low as a few seconds are possible.

Figure 12-2 *Redundant Switched Network with No Single Point of Failure*

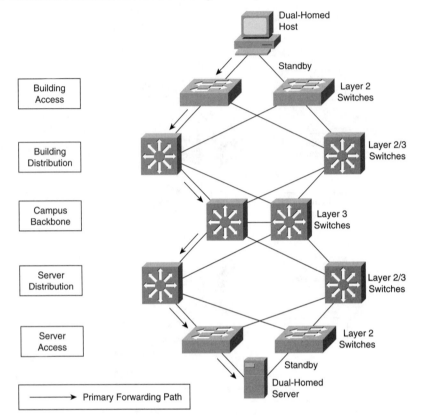

Another way to achieve high availability is link redundancy. An example of network-level redundancy using link redundancy is EtherChannel. Fast EtherChannel and Gigabit EtherChannel are link-aggregation (and access-link) technologies that are based on grouping together multiple full-duplex Fast Ethernet or Gigabit Ethernet ports to provide fault-tolerant high-speed links between switches, routers, and servers. EtherChannel uses a peer-to-peer control protocol that provides auto-configuration and minimal convergence times for parallel links.

The drawbacks of link redundancy include the following:

- Increased cabling costs
- Increased difficulty of management and troubleshooting

Hence, a combination of device-level fault tolerance, network-level redundancy, link redundancy, and redundancy built into the design of network services is essential to achieve true high availability in a multilayer switched network.

The following sections cover redundancy topics in the order in which they appear here:

- Implementing redundant Supervisor Engines in Catalyst switches using high-availability features on Cisco CatOS–based switches and Route Processor Redundancy (RPR) or RPR+ mode in Cisco IOS–based switches (device-level redundancy)

- Implementing Stateful Switchover (SSO)

- Implementing Non-stop Forwarding (NSF) with SSO

- Understanding router module (MSFC) redundancy using Single Router Mode (SRM) on the Catalyst 6500 family of switches in hybrid mode software (device-level redundancy)

- Understanding Cisco IOS Software Modularity and In-Service Software Upgrade (ISSU)

- Implementing redundant Supervisor Engine uplink ports in Catalyst switches (device-level and link redundancy)

- Implementing redundant power supplies (device-level redundancy)

- Implementing default gateway router redundancy in a multilayer switched network

- Implementing Cisco IOS Server Load Balancing (SLB)

Implementing Redundant Supervisor Engines in Catalyst Switches

The Supervisor Engine is the most important component in Catalyst modular switches, which are typically found in the Campus Backbone and Building Distribution submodules. If the Supervisor Engine fails, the switch fails to forward traffic. As a result, providing redundancy for the Supervisor Engine is the most critical form of high availability. Not all Catalyst switches are modular, and not all Catalyst switches provide redundant Supervisor Engine capability. The Catalyst 4500 and 6500 families of switches, however, do provide options for redundant Supervisor Engines.

Configuring dual Supervisor Engines within a Catalyst family of switches, as shown in Figure 12-3, ensures high availability by providing redundancy without requiring the deployment of an entire separate switch. This solution is a cost-effective alternative to deploying multiple switches for redundancy. Even in networks that deploy multiple redundant switches, configuring redundant Supervisor Engines adds an extra level of availability assurance.

The Catalyst 4500 and Catalyst 6500 families of switches support redundant Supervisor Engines. The Catalyst 6500 family supports redundant Supervisor Engines on all chassis models, whereas the Catalyst 4500 supports redundant Supervisor Engines only in 4057R and 4510R chassis.

Figure 12-3 *Redundant Supervisor Engines in Catalyst 6500 Switches*

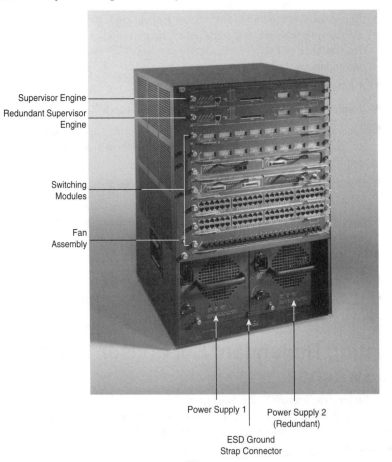

Table 12-1 shows various redundancy features supported on the Catalyst 4500 and Catalyst 6500 families of switches running Cisco IOS.

Table 12-1 *Redundancy Features Supported on the Catalyst 4500 and Catalyst 6500 Families of Switches*

Redundancy Feature	Catalyst 4500	Catalyst 6500
RPR	Supported in Cisco IOS Software Release 12.1(12c)EW and later	Supported in Cisco IOS Software Release 12.1(11b)EX and later
RPR+	Not available	Supported in Cisco IOS Software Release 12.1(11b)EX and later
SSO	Supported in Cisco IOS Software Release 12.2(20)EWA and later	Supported in Cisco IOS Software Release 12.2(17b)SXA and later
NSF with SSO	Supported in Cisco IOS Software Release 12.2 (31) and later	Supported in Cisco IOS Software Release 12.2(18)SXD and later

The "Route Processor Redundancy," "Route Processor Redundancy Plus," "Stateful Switchover (SSO)," and "NSF with SSO" sections of this chapter discuss details of these redundancy features on Cisco IOS–based Catalyst 6500 and 4500 switches. NSF with SSO provides the highest level of high availability in the Catalyst 6500 and Catalyst 4500 families of switches.

In addition, the Catalyst 6500 supports high availability with hybrid systems. Hybrid systems are Catalyst 6500 switches where the Supervisor Engine runs the Cisco CatOS image while the Multilayer Switch Feature Card (MSFC) runs the Cisco IOS image. Catalyst 6500 Supervisor Engines consist of a Network Management Processor (NMP) and a routing daughter card, MSFC. The Cisco CatOS Software provides for NMP high availability, which synchronizes the features such as Spanning Tree Protocol, trunking, Port Aggregation Protocol (PAgP), and so on.

To configure system high availability in Cisco CatOS, use the following command:

```
set system high-availability enable
```

NOTE	For more information about high-availability features on the NMP, refer to the "Configuring Redundancy" section of the Cisco Catalyst 6500 product software configuration guide documentation on Cisco.com.

NOTE	High availability for the MSFC is provided by SRM. More information about SRM is available in the "Router Redundancy Using Single Router Mode on the Catalyst 6500 Series of Switches" section of this chapter.

Table 12-2 shows redundancy options available in Cisco CatOS–based and Cisco IOS–based Catalyst 6500 switches.

Table 12-2   *Redundancy Features for Catalyst 6500 Switches*

Systems	Redundancy Feature(s)
Supervisor Engine (Hybrid)	High Availability
MSFC (Hybrid)	SRM
Supervisor Engine/MSFC (Cisco IOS–based)	RPR, RPR+, SSO, and NSF with SSO

Route Processor Redundancy

Route Processor Redundancy (RPR) was the first form of high availability feature in Cisco IOS Software starting with Cisco IOS Software Release 12.1(13)E. Although RPR is still available in Cisco IOS, it is no longer preferred. NSF with SSO provides better convergence time than RPR or RPR+.

This section briefly reviews the RPR and RPR+ features. The Catalyst 4500 and Catalyst 6500 families of switches support high availability by allowing a redundant Supervisor Engine to take over if the primary Supervisor Engine fails for both Layer 2 and Layer 3 functions. Table 12-3 shows the failover times of RPR and RPR+ on the Catalyst 6500 and 4500 families of switches.

Table 12-3   *RPR and RPR+ Failover Time Intervals*

Redundancy	Catalyst 6500 Failover Time	Catalyst 4500 Failover Time
RPR	2–4 minutes	Less than 60 seconds
RPR+	30–60 seconds	—

The Supervisor Engine involved in forwarding of traffic at both the Layer 2 and Layer 3 levels is called the active Supervisor Engine. The other Supervisor Engine, which is not forwarding traffic but is instead in a standby mode monitoring the active Supervisor Engine, is called the standby Supervisor Engine. The active and standby Supervisor Engines monitor each other through periodic communication for failure.

With RPR, any of the following events triggers a switchover from the active to the standby Supervisor Engine:

- RP or SP crash on the active Supervisor Engine
- A manual switchover from the CLI
- Removal of the active Supervisor Engine
- Clock synchronization failure between Supervisor Engines

In a switchover, the redundant Supervisor Engine becomes fully operational, and the following events occur on the remaining modules during an RPR failover:

- All switching modules are power cycled.
- Remaining subsystems on the MSFC (including Layer 2 and Layer 3 protocols) are initialized on the prior standby, now active, Supervisor Engine.
- ACLs based on the new active Supervisor Engine are reprogrammed into the Supervisor Engine hardware.

NOTE   In an RPR switchover, there is a disruption of traffic because routing states, such as OSPF states, must rebuild along with Layer 2 states, such as the MAC address table. All traffic flows normally after all states are restored to previous conditions.

Route Processor Redundancy Plus

With RPR+, the redundant Supervisor Engine remains fully initialized and configured, which shortens the switchover time if the active Supervisor Engine fails or if the network administrator performs a manual switchover.

NOTE   The active Supervisor Engine checks the image version of the standby Supervisor Engine when the standby Supervisor Engine comes online. If the image on the standby Supervisor Engine does not match the image on the active Supervisor Engine, RPR redundancy mode is used.

RPR+ enhances Supervisor redundancy compared to RPR by providing the following additional benefits:

- **Reduced switchover time**—Depending on the configuration, the switchover time is in the range of 30 to 60 seconds.

- **No reloading of installed modules**—Because both the startup configuration and the running configuration stay continually synchronized from the active to the redundant Supervisor Engine during a switchover, no reloading of line modules occurs.

- **Synchronization of OIR events between the active and standby**—This occurs such that modules in the online state remain online and modules in the down state remain in the down state after a switchover.

Configuring and Verifying RPR+ Redundancy

RPR+ redundancy configurations are straightforward, as illustrated in the following steps:

Step 1   Enter the following command to start configuring redundancy modes:

```
redundancy
```

Step 2   Use the following command under redundancy configuration submode to configure RPR+:

```
mode rpr-plus
```

Example 12-1 illustrates a user configuring RPR+ redundancy on a Catalyst 6500 and verifying the configuration. In Example 12-1, the standby supervisor is currently not present; hence, the peer state is disabled in the display.

Example 12-1 *Configuring and Verifying RPR+ Redundancy*

```
Switch#configure terminal
Enter configuration commands, one per line.  End with CNTL/Z.
Switch(config)#redundancy
Switch(config-red)#mode rpr-plus
Switch(config-red)#^Z
Switch#show redundancy states
```

Example 12-1 *Configuring and Verifying RPR+ Redundancy (Continued)*

```
          my state = 13 –ACTIVE
        peer state = 1  -DISABLED
             Mode = Simplex
             Unit = Primary
          Unit ID = 1

Redundancy Mode (Operational) = Route Processor Redundancy Plus
Redundancy Mode (Configured)  = Route Processor Redundancy Plus
      Split Mode = Disabled
    Manual Swact = Disabled  Reason: Simplex mode
 Communications = Down       Reason: Simplex mode

    client count = 11
 client_notification_TMR = 30000 milliseconds
         keep_alive TMR = 4000 milliseconds
       keep_alive count = 0
   keep_alive threshold = 7
         RF debug mask = 0x0
```

Stateful Switchover (SSO)

RPR and RPR+ recover traffic forwarding of the switch in about a minute after a switchover of the Supervisor Engine; however, RPR and RPR+ disruptions are not transparent to the end user. For example, if the user were using an IP phone, the call would be dropped. Even though a minute-long outage might not be significant to a typical Internet user, it is critical for IP phone users or database applications. Hence, this poses the need for a better redundancy protocol to minimize the disruption of traffic. The Catalyst 4500 and Catalyst 6500 families of switches support SSO to provide minimal Layer 2 traffic disruption during a Supervisor switchover.

In SSO mode, the redundant Supervisor Engine starts up in a fully initialized state and synchronizes with the startup configuration and the running configuration of the active Supervisor Engine. The standby Supervisor in SSO mode also keeps in sync with the active Supervisor Engine for all changes in hardware and software states for features that are supported via SSO. Any supported feature interrupted by failure of the active Supervisor Engine is continued seamlessly on the redundant Supervisor Engine.

The following list details the current protocols and features that SSO modes support for Layer 2 redundancy. For a complete and up-to-date list, refer to Cisco.com:

- 802.3x (Flow Control)
- 802.3ad (LACP) and PAgP
- 802.1X (Authentication) and Port security
- 802.3af (Inline power)
- VTP

- Dynamic ARP Inspection/DHCP snooping/IP source guard
- IGMP snooping (versions 1 and 2)
- DTP (802.1q and ISL)
- MST/PVST+/Rapid-PVST
- PortFast/UplinkFast/BackboneFast /BPDU Guard and filtering
- Voice VLAN
- Unicast MAC filtering
- ACL (VACLs, PACLs, RACLs)
- QOS (DBL)
- Multicast storm control/broadcast storm control

In SSO mode, ports that were active before the switchover remain active because the redundant Supervisor Engine recognizes the hardware link status of every link. The neighboring devices do not see the link-down event during the switchover except the link to the previous active Supervisor. On the Catalyst 4500 switches, the uplink on the previous active Supervisor Engine is also retained even though that Supervisor Engine may be rebooting. In such a case, no spanning-tree topology changes occur because no link states change.

On the Catalyst 6500 family of switches, the time it takes for the Layer 2 traffic to be fully operational following a Supervisor failure is between 0 and 3 seconds.

On the Catalyst 6500 family of switches, you can combine SSO with Single Router Mode (SRM) so that the new active Supervisor Engine continues to use the Layer 3 entries created by the previous active Supervisor Engine until the newly activated Supervisor Engine has time to relearn and re-establish Layer 3 information. As a result, Layer 3 traffic continues to forward during a failover. This Layer 3 information that is maintained during a failover includes hardware-based CEF and adjacency tables. Consequently, when combining SSO with SRM, Layer 2 and Layer 3 disruption is minimal following a Supervisor switchover.

On the Catalyst 4500, sub-second switchover can be achieved for Layer 2 traffic. Layer 3 information, however, needs to be relearned after a Supervisor Engine failover with just the SSO mode of redundancy, but the newly active Supervisor Engine continues to use existing Layer 2 switching information to continue forwarding traffic until Layer 3 information is relearned. This relearning involves rebuilding ARP tables and Layer 3 CEF and adjacency tables. Until the routing converges and CEF and adjacency tables are rebuilt, packets that need to be routed are dropped.

Configuring and Verifying SSO

SSO redundancy configurations are straightforward, as illustrated in the following steps:

Step 1   Enter the following command to start configuring redundancy modes:

> `redundancy`

Step 2   Use the following command under redundancy configuration submode to configure SSO:

> `mode sso`

Example 12-2 illustrates a user configuring SSO redundancy on a Catalyst 4500 and verifying the configuration.

Example 12-2 *Configuring and Verifying SSO Redundancy*

```
Switch#configure terminal
Enter configuration commands, one per line.  End with CNTL/Z.
Switch(config)#redundancy
Switch(config-red)#mode sso
Changing to sso mode will reset the standby. Do you want to continue? [confirm]
Switch(config-red)#^Z
Switch# show redundancy states
        my state = 13 -ACTIVE
      peer state = 8   -STANDBY HOT
            Mode = Duplex
            Unit = Primary
         Unit ID = 2

Redundancy Mode (Operational) = Stateful Switchover
Redundancy Mode (Configured)  = Stateful Switchover
      Split Mode = Disabled
     Manual Swact = Enabled
  Communications = Up

     client count = 21
 client_notification_TMR = 240000 milliseconds
          keep_alive TMR = 9000 milliseconds
        keep_alive count = 0
    keep_alive threshold = 18
            RF debug mask = 0x0
```

NSF with SSO

The Catalyst 4500 and 6500 family of switches supports another form of redundancy called *NSF with SSO*.

NSF with SSO redundancy includes the standard SSO for Layer 2 switching; however, it also minimizes the amount of time that a Layer 3 network is unavailable following a Supervisor Engine switchover by continuing to forward IP packets using CEF entries built from the old active Supervisor. Zero packet loss or near-zero packet loss is achieved with NSF with SSO redundancy mode.

When using the NSF with SSO feature, reconvergence of supported Layer 3 routing protocols (BGP, EIGRP, OSPFv2, and IS-IS) happens automatically in the background while packet forwarding continues. The standby Supervisor Engine maintains the copy of the CEF entries from the active Supervisor Engine, and upon switchover, the new active Supervisor Engine uses the CEF entries while the routing protocol converges without interruption to user traffic. Once the routing protocol has converged and the Routing Information Base (RIB) has been built afresh on the route processor, any stale CEF entries are removed, and packet forwarding is fully restored.

Changes have been made to the routing protocols so that upon switchover, an NSF-enabled router sends special packets that trigger routing updates from the NSF-aware neighbors without resetting the peer relationship. This feature prevents route flapping and routing changes during a Supervisor failover. NSF-aware routers understand that a neighboring NSF router can still forward packets when an RP switchover happens. NSF-aware routers are not required to be NSF routers themselves. For example, the Catalyst 4500 series of switches are currently only NSF-aware.

For information about the NSF operations for each of the routing protocols, refer to the "Configuring NSF with SSO Supervisor Engine Redundancy" configuration section of the Catalyst 6500 configuration guide at Cisco.com.

In summary, Cisco NSF provides the following benefits:

- **Improved network availability**—NSF continues forwarding network traffic and application state information so that user traffic is not interrupted after a Supervisor switchover.

- **Overall network stability**—Network stability is improved by maintaining routing protocol neighbor relationships during Supervisor failover.

Configuring and Verifying NSF with SSO

NSF is an additional configuration option of configuring SSO. For an example of how to configure SSO, refer to Example 12-3. To configure NSF for OSPF, EIGRP, and IS-IS, use the **nsf** router-level command. To configure BGP for NSF support, use the **bgp graceful-restart** router-level command.

Example 12-3 illustrates a user configuring NSF support for BGP and OSPF and verifying the configuration output.

Example 12-3 *Configuring and Verifying NSF Support for BGP and OSPF Routing Protocols*

```
Switch#configure terminal
Enter configuration commands, one per line.  End with CNTL/Z.
Switch(config)#router bgp 100
Switch(config-router)#bgp graceful-restart
Switch(config-router)#exit
```

Example 12-3 *Configuring and Verifying NSF Support for BGP and OSPF Routing Protocols (Continued)*

```
Switch(config)#router ospf 200
Switch(config-router)# nsf
Switch(config-router)#end
Switch#show ip bgp neighbors 192.168.200.1

BGP neighbor is 192.168.200.1, remote AS 200, external link
  BGP version 4, remote router ID 192.168.200.1
  BGP state = Established, up for 00:01:23
  Last read 00:00:17, hold time is 180, keepalive interval is 60 seconds
  Neighbor capabilities:
    Route refresh:advertised and received(new)
    Address family IPv4 Unicast:advertised and received
    Address family IPv4 Multicast:advertised and received
    Graceful Restart Capability:advertised and received
      Remote Restart timer is 120 seconds
      Address families preserved by peer:
        IPv4 Unicast, IPv4 Multicast
  Received 1539 messages, 0 notifications, 0 in queue
  Sent 100 messages, 0 notifications, 0 in queue
  Default minimum time between advertisement runs is 30 seconds

Switch# show ip ospf

Routing Process "ospf 200" with ID 192.168.20.1 and Domain ID 0.0.0.1
Supports only single TOS(TOS0) routes
Supports opaque LSA
SPF schedule delay 5 secs, Hold time between two SPFs 10 secs
Minimum LSA interval 5 secs. Minimum LSA arrival 1 secs
Number of external LSA 0. Checksum Sum 0x0
Number of opaque AS LSA 0. Checksum Sum 0x0
Number of DCbitless external and opaque AS LSA 0
Number of DoNotAge external and opaque AS LSA 0
Number of areas in this router is 1. 1 normal 0 stub 0 nssa
External flood list length 0
Non-Stop Forwarding enabled, last NSF restart 00:02:36 ago (took 34 secs)
Area BACKBONE(0)
Number of interfaces in this area is 1 (0 loopback)
 Area has no authentication
 SPF algorithm executed 3 times
```

Router Redundancy Using Single Router Mode on the Catalyst 6500 Series of Switches

The Catalyst 6500 family of switches running hybrid mode software (Cisco CatOS on the Supervisor Engine and Cisco IOS on the MSFC or MSFC2) also supports dual Supervisor Engines in a chassis for redundancy. Even though the Supervisor Engine is in redundant state and only one Supervisor Engine is active at any time, the MSFC on both Supervisor Engines is active in the default mode.

In a typical network, the design would include redundant paths using two switches for chassis redundancy, making the network difficult to troubleshoot with four active routers. Cisco introduced SRM redundancy as an alternative to internally redundant (dual) MSFC configurations where both MSFCs are active at the same time, reducing the number of active routers to two instead of four.

To use SRM with hybrid mode software, the requirements are as follows:

- Both MSFCs must run the same Cisco IOS image and have identical configurations.
- The high availability feature must be enabled on the Supervisor Engine.

In hybrid mode, only one of the MSFCs programs the active Supervisor Engine's PFC hardware with CEF or MLS flows. MSFC maintains the Cisco IOS routing table and ARP, based on which it builds the CEF FIB table and adjacency table for high-performance packet routing. (For more details on CEF and MLS, refer to Chapter 9, "Understanding and Configuring Multilayer Switching." The MSFC that is programming the hardware is called the designated router; the other MSFC is called the nondesignated router.

With SRM redundancy, only the designated router is visible to the network at any given time. The nondesignated router is booted up completely and participates in configuration synchronization, which is automatically enabled when SRM is configured. The configuration and state of the nondesignated router is the same as that of the designated router, but its interfaces are kept in a line-down state and are not available for network traffic. Processes, such as routing protocols, are created on the nondesignated router and on the designated router, but because all nondesignated router interfaces are in a line-down state, the interfaces on the nondesignated router do not send or receive updates from the network. Therefore, the processes on the nondesignated router have no state.

When the designated router fails, the nondesignated router changes its state from a nondesignated router to a designated router, and its interface state changes to link up. This means that if the designated router fails, there is a delay before the nondesignated router has a complete routing table. To help account for switching of traffic in the interim, the existing Supervisor Engine switch processor entries are used to forward Layer 3 traffic. After the newly designated router builds its routing table, the entries in the switch processor are updated with any new information from the new designated router. (Recall that even when using RPR redundancy, chassis and link redundancy should be used to minimize loss of traffic due to failover.)

NOTE   In the SRM mode, the configuration is allowed only on the designated MSFC.

Table 12-4 illustrates the advantages and disadvantages of SRM in Catalyst 6500 hybrid software systems.

Table 12-4   *Advantages and Disadvantages of SRM*

Advantages	Disadvantages
Conserves IP addresses.	Uses an old FIB built from the old routing table even though the router that created the old routing table is no longer online. There is a risk of routing packets to an invalid destination during the table-update-delay time interval.
Reduces routing protocol peering.	Can be disruptive to the network, because the routing table needs to be calculated from the start on the new DR.
The configuration is much simpler; no risk of running unsupported mismatched configurations.	

SRM Failure Scenario with a Catalyst 6500 Supervisor Engine II and MSFC2

Because the Supervisor Engine II and MSFC2 in a Catalyst 6500 use CEF-based MLS instead of traditional MLS, their failure recovery is slightly different from the failure recovery with a Supervisor Engine IA in a Catalyst 6500. Supervisor Engine 720 uses CEF-based MLS; hence, the behavior is similar to Supervisor Engine II–based systems. When the designated MSFC2 on the Supervisor Engine II crashes or reloads with SRM, the following events occur to failover:

Step 1   The new designated router moves its VLAN interfaces into the up state.

Step 2   The Supervisor Engine maintains the CEF FIB entries in hardware on the active Supervisor Engine, and traffic is switched using this FIB table for 2 minutes after a failure of the designated router (by default). Furthermore, the new designated router does not update the Supervisor Engine for 2 minutes while it is building its routing table. This results in continued traffic flow and reduced disruption for currently flowing traffic.

Step 3   After 2 minutes, the CEF table of the new designated router is downloaded to the Supervisor Engine, whether or not the routing protocol has completed its convergence.

Step 4   As routing protocol neighbors have their adjacencies cleared, there may still be a forwarding outage on other devices after the switchover.

In the more recent software releases, Catalyst 6500 switches allow the tuning of the interval between using the old FIB table and accepting the new one from the new DR using the following Cisco IOS command on the MSFC:

```
single-router-mode failover table-update-delay delay-in-seconds
```

SRM Failure Scenario with Supervisor Engine IA

NOTE	Before converting from dual-router mode to SRM redundancy, Cisco recommends that the non-SRM configuration be saved in case the administrator wants to revert back to the dual-router configuration in the future.

SRM Configuration

This section describes the steps necessary to configure the SRM on the Catalyst 6500 family of switches running hybrid-mode software.

Before configuring SRM, perform the following steps to make sure the SRM requirements are met:

Step 1   Check to ensure that both the Supervisor Engines are running Cisco Catalyst OS version 6.3(1) or later.

Step 2   Check to ensure that both the MSFCs are running Cisco IOS release 12.1(8a)E2 or later.

Step 3   Check to ensure that Supervisor Engine system high availability is enabled using the **show system high-availability** command.

If one or more of the preceding checks is not satisfied, SRM cannot be enabled.

After the requirements have been met, use the following steps to configure SRM. (This procedure assumes that the designated router is the MSFC2 in slot 1, the nondesignated router is the MSFC2 in slot 2, the active Supervisor Engine is in slot 1, and the standby Supervisor Engine is in slot 2.)

Step 1   Enable SRM on the designated router, and then enable SRM on the nondesignated router, as shown in the following configuration:

```
MSFC_1(config)#redundancy
MSFC_1(config-r)#high-availability
MSFC_1(config-r-ha)#single-router-mode
MSFC_2(config)#redundancy
MSFC_2(config-r)#high-availability
MSFC_2(config-r-ha)#single-router-mode
```

Step 2   Enter the **copy running-config startup-config** command on the designated router to save the running configuration to the startup configuration. This step also ensures that the startup configuration of the nondesignated router is synced with SRM configuration commands.

Step 3   Reload the nondesignated router. When prompted whether the configuration should be saved, enter **no**, as shown in the following configuration:

```
MSFC_2#reload

System configuration has been modified. Save? [yes/no]: no
Proceed with reload? [confirm]
Console(enable)
```

Step 4   The nondesignated router comes up in standby mode.

To verify the SRM status, issue the **show redundancy** command, as shown in Example 12-4. The **session 15** and **session 16** commands provide access to the MSFC in slot 1 and slot 2, respectively.

Example 12-4 *Displaying SRM Status*

```
Console (enable)   session 15
Trying Router-15...
Connected to Router-15.
Escape character is '^]'.

MSFC_1>enable
MSFC_1#
MSFC_1#show redundancy
Designated Router: 1 Non-designated Router: 2

Redundancy Status: designated

Config Sync AdminStatus  : disabled

Config Sync RuntimeStatus: disabled

Single Router Mode AdminStatus  : enabled

Single Router Mode RuntimeStatus: enabled

MSFC_1#exit
Console (enable) session 16
Trying Router-16...
Connected to Router-16.
Escape character is '^]'.

MSFC_2>enable
MSFC_2#show redundancy
Designated Router: 1 Non-designated Router: 2

Redundancy Status: non-designated

Config Sync AdminStatus  : disabled

Config Sync RuntimeStatus: disabled
```

Example 12-4 *Displaying SRM Status (Continued)*

```
Single Router Mode AdminStatus  : enabled

Single Router Mode RuntimeStatus: enabled

MSFC_2#exit
Console (enable)
```

Understanding Cisco IOS Software Modularity and In-Service Software Upgrade (ISSU)

The Catalyst 6500 family of switches offers the highest level of high availability on Catalyst switches with the introduction of Cisco IOS Software Modularity. The modular Cisco IOS Software on the Catalyst 6500 switches minimizes unplanned downtime and reduces the length of time necessary to apply corrective patches.

Cisco IOS Software includes multiple processes, and they share the common memory space in the Switch Supervisor Engine. In rare instances, a software anomaly might result in one of these processes crashing or causing memory malfunction (memory leak). When such an event happens, the whole Cisco IOS has to reload to correct itself. If there is a standby Supervisor Engine, the failure time is greatly minimized, as discussed earlier with NSF with SSO. If only one Supervisor Engine exists in the system, however, the whole system needs to reload completely, which may take a few minutes to recover.

The purpose of Cisco IOS Software Modularity on the Catalyst 6500 family of switches is to provide a high-availability infrastructure such that processes run in modular fashion (meaning the processes run in their own protected memory space within the Supervisor Engine's main memory). If a fault happens on one of these processes, the process can restart without affecting the rest of the system. Because the Catalyst 6500 switch offers control and data plane separation, these faults or restarts of processes do not cause packet loss.

The capability to restart processes also enables patching of these processes at run time. The patches can fix any problems in the processes without affecting the rest of the system and, more importantly, the packets being switched and routed through the Catalyst 6500 switch.

The biggest benefit of Cisco IOS Software Modularity is that it provides high availability with just a single Supervisor Engine. Having dual Supervisors further increases the availability of the system.

Another benefit of Cisco IOS Software Modularity is the capability to minimize the time needed to certify new Cisco IOS Software. With traditional Cisco IOS, rebuilds are the way to fix issues. However, Cisco IOS rebuilds might have many bug fixes; hence, to certify the image, complete testing of the system is involved. This complete testing might require a lot of effort on the part of the customer. Fortunately, with Cisco IOS Software Modularity, the patching is specific, and the user knows which features are being fixed and thus can concentrate on testing the fixes on that specific issue. This limited testing saves a lot of effort and, at the same time, increases the stability of the patched version.

Cisco IOS Software Modularity on Catalyst 6500 switches allows multiple patches to be applied simultaneously. Also, Cisco IOS Software allows rollback of the desired patches (in reverse order) if desired. Cisco IOS Software Modularity is similar in functionality to the existing Cisco IOS on Catalyst 6500 (also known as Native IOS), and the CLI is the same.

Cisco IOS Software Modularity can be run in the following two modes:

- **Binary image**—This mode is similar to existing traditional Cisco IOS. This mode enables you to restart processes and protects against memory leaks and other caveats, but it does not allow you to apply patches.

- **Installed image**—This mode provides the protection of the preceding mode and allows patching of affected processes.

For more details on Cisco IOS Software Modularity and how to upgrade patches, refer to the following white paper on Cisco.com:

Cisco IOS Software Modularity on the Cisco Catalyst 6500 Series Switches

Patching of Cisco IOS is called subsystem In-Service Software Upgrade (ISSU) because the Cisco IOS subsystems can be patched while the system is in service. Although this provides a sophisticated way to apply patches, full-system ISSU is still required for a complete image upgrade. A complete image upgrade allows you to apply not only bug fixes but also new software features and support for new hardware, which is not available via patching. ISSU is planned to be released on the Catalyst 4500 and Catalyst 6500 switches in an upcoming release. Full-system ISSU allows a nondisruptive full Cisco IOS Software upgrade.

Implementing Redundant Supervisor Uplink Modules in Catalyst Switches

The uplink ports on a redundant Supervisor Engine are active even when the Supervisor Engine is in standby mode on the Catalyst 6500 series of switches. This allows redundant uplink connections from different cards, removing a single-point-of-failure concern. This section discusses redundant Supervisor Engine uplink modules.

A high-availability network design calls for redundancy throughout the network. When setting up links between Building Distribution and Campus Backbone switches, for example, providing redundancy can reduce the chance of total connectivity failure by providing an alternate hardware path to the Campus Backbone submodule. The uplink ports on a Supervisor Engine are available for this purpose. With both links originating from the same Supervisor Engine, however, the connectivity is completely lost if the Supervisor Engine fails.

By using the uplink ports on the redundant Supervisor Engine, connectivity is maintained if the link from the primary Supervisor Engine should fail, or if the entire primary Supervisor Engine should fail.

Table 12-5 shows the uplink ports supported on various Catalyst 4500 Supervisor Engines.

Table 12-5 *Catalyst 4500 Supervisor Uplink Port Support*

Supervisors	Uplinks in Nonredundant Mode	Uplinks in Redundant Mode
Supervisor Engine II+ and IV	Two GE (Ports 1/1 and 2/1)	Two GE (Ports 1/1 and 2/1)
Supervisor Engine V	Two GE (Ports 1/1 and 2/1)	Four GE (Ports 1/1,1/2, 2/1, and 2/2)
Supervisor Engine V-10GE	Two 10 GE (Ports 1/1 and 1/2) and Four GE (Ports 1/3,1/4,1/5, and 1/6)	Two 10 GE (Port 1/1 and 2/1) and Four GE (Ports 1/3,1/4, 2/3, and 2/4) (except in 4510R chassis use either 10 GE or GE ports)

On Catalyst 6500 switches, all available uplinks on the Supervisor Engines are supported in redundant mode.

Implementing Redundant Power Supplies

The Catalyst 6500 and Catalyst 4500 series of switches support dual power supplies. Depending on the specific power supplies installed and the power consumption of the modules installed in the switch, both supplies may be necessary to provide sufficient power to the switch to enable all line modules. However, if one of the power supplies is sufficient for meeting the power requirements of the entire switch, the second power supply should be used as a redundant backup in case the primary power supply fails. This configuration helps ensure availability of the switch and therefore of the connectivity it provides.

From global configuration mode, enter the **power redundancy-mode combined | redundant** command to disable or enable redundancy. (Redundancy is enabled by default.) Configuration change of the mode of power supplies to redundant or combined is possible at any time, and no downtime will occur.

Specifying the **combined** keyword disables redundancy. In a nonredundant configuration, the power available to the system is the combined power capability of both power supplies on a Catalyst 6500 family of switches. With this configuration, the system powers up as many modules as the combined capacity allows; however, this configuration is not fully redundant.

NOTE   On Catalyst 4500 switches, the available power is less than the sum of both the power supplies. For more information, refer to the environment-monitoring and power-management section of the Cisco software configuration product documentation on Cisco.com.

In a combined power configuration, however, if one supply fails and there is not enough power for all previously powered up modules, the system powers down those modules for which there is not enough power.

Specifying the **redundant** keyword enables redundancy. In a redundant configuration, the total power drawn from both supplies is at no time greater than the capability of one supply. If one supply malfunctions, the other supply can take over the entire system load. With two power supplies installed, each concurrently provides approximately half of the required power to the system. Load sharing and redundancy are enabled automatically; no software configuration is required.

Use the **show power** command to view the current state of modules and the total power available for modules, as illustrated in Example 12-5.

Example 12-5 *Displaying System Power Details on a Cisco IOS–Based Catalyst 6500 Switch*

```
Switch#show power
system power redundancy mode = redundant
system power total =      1153.32 Watts (27.46 Amps @ 42V)
system power used =        456.12 Watts (10.86 Amps @ 42V)
system power available =   697.20 Watts (16.60 Amps @ 42V)
                          Power-Capacity PS-Fan Output Oper
PS   Type                 Watts   A @42V Status Status State
---- ------------------   ------- ------ ------ ------ -----
1    WS-CAC-1300W         1153.32 27.46  OK     OK     on
2    none

                          Pwr-Requested  Pwr-Allocated  Admin Oper
Slot Card-Type            Watts   A @42V Watts   A @42V State State
---- ------------------   ------- ------ ------- ------ ----- -----
1                          -       -     118.86  2.83   -     -
2    WS-X6K-SUP1A-2GE     118.86  2.83   118.86  2.83   on    on
3    WS-X6416-GBIC        118.02  2.81   118.02  2.81   on    on
4    WS-X6148-RJ45V       100.38  2.39   100.38  2.39   on    on
                          Inline         Inline
                          Pwr-Requested  Pwr-Allocated
Slot Card-Type            Watts   A @42V Watts   A @42V
---- ------------------   ------- ------ ------- ------
4    WS-X6148-RJ45V        -       -      -       -
```

It is possible to power down a module from the CLI by entering the **no power enable module** *slot* command on a Catalyst 6500 switch.

NOTE   When the **no power enable module** *slot* command is configured to power down a module, the module's configuration is not saved.

From global configuration mode, enter the **power enable module** *slot* command to turn the power on for a module that was previously powered down. Then, from global configuration mode, enter the **power cycle module** *slot* command to power-cycle (reset) a module; the module powers off for 5 seconds and then powers on.

NOTE   The Catalyst 4500 series of switches currently does not support powering down line modules.

It is important to maintain power budgets, especially when using inline power modules to support IP telephony.

Implementing Default Gateway Router Redundancy in Multilayer Switched Networks

The availability of a default gateway router is a must for hosts in a multilayer switched network. There are several ways a LAN host can determine which router should be the first hop to a particular remote destination. The host can use a dynamic process or static configuration.

Examples of dynamic router discovery are as follows:

- **Proxy ARP**—The host uses Address Resolution Protocol (ARP) to determine the next-hop MAC address for off-network destinations. Local routers respond to the ARP request with their own MAC address.

- **Routing protocol**—The host listens to dynamic routing protocol updates (for example, Routing Information Protocol [RIP]) and forms its own routing table.

- **ICMP Router Discovery Protocol (IRDP) client**—The host runs an Internet Control Message Protocol (ICMP) router discovery client.

The drawback to dynamic discovery protocols is that they incur some configuration and processing overhead on the LAN host. Also, in the event of a router failure, the process of switching to another router can be slow. In addition, dynamic discovery protocols require administrative and management configuration of every end device in the network. As a result, the use of these protocols and methods is rare.

In the next sections, we will review the proxy ARP and IRDP in more detail to understand their mechanism and their drawbacks.

Proxy ARP

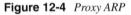A host uses ARP for devices in the same subnet as itself but needs a router to reach other subnets. Cisco IOS Software uses proxy ARP (as defined in RFC 1027) to help hosts with no knowledge of routing determine the MAC addresses of hosts on other networks or subnets. For example, if the router receives an ARP request for a host that is not on the same interface as the ARP request sender, and if the router has all its routes to that host through other interfaces, then it generates a proxy ARP reply packet giving its own local MAC address. The host that sent the ARP request then sends its packets to the router, which forwards them to the intended host. Proxy ARP is enabled by default.

With proxy ARP, the host behaves as if the destination device is connected to the same segment of the network, as shown in Figure 12-4. If the responsible router fails, the source end station continues to send packets for the destination to the MAC address of that router. Those packets subsequently are discarded.

Figure 12-4 *Proxy ARP*

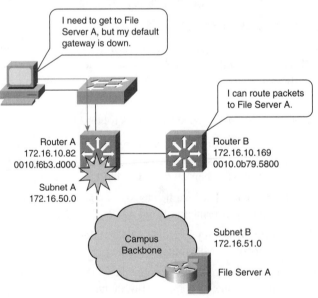

To acquire the MAC address of the failover router, the source end station must either initiate another ARP request or wait for the ARP entry to be flushed dynamically. The ARP flush timer determines the period in which the source end station cannot communicate with the destination even though the routing protocol has converged. Once the ARP flushes the entry due to flush timer expiry, the host recovers the default gateway MAC address. Nevertheless, Cisco does not recommend the use of proxy ARP, because it makes troubleshooting difficult. In addition, proxy ARP does not scale at all in medium-size to large networks.

IRDP

IP hosts may use IRDP to find a new path when an existing primary router becomes unavailable, as shown in Figure 12-5. IRDP is not a routing protocol like RIP or the Interior Gateway Routing Protocol (IGRP). Rather, IRDP is an extension to ICMP that provides a mechanism for routers to advertise useful default routes. IRDP offers several advantages over other methods of discovering addresses of neighboring routers. For example, IRDP does not require hosts to recognize routing protocols, nor does IRDP require manual configuration by an administrator.

Figure 12-5 *IRDP*

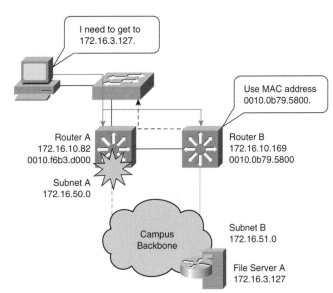

A host that uses IRDP listens for hello multicast messages from the preferred default router. The IRDP-based advertisements are considered valid only for a predefined lifetime value. If a new advertisement is not seen during that lifetime, the router address is considered invalid, and the host removes the corresponding default route. The IRDP protocol allows for varying timing values. A lifetime value is included in the header of every IRDP advertisement and applies to all addresses included in the packet. A host uses the router address only for the specified number of lifetime seconds after the most recent advertisement.

Advertisements are sent every 7 to 10 minutes; the default lifetime is 30 minutes. However, the router has complete control over the interval and lifetime values, and thus can control the period during which the addresses are considered valid.

IRDP has two separate interval times: a minimum and a maximum advertisement interval. All unsolicited advertisements are sent in the window of time defined by these two values. IRDP is covered in greater detail in RFC 1256. As with other host redundancy methods, IRDP is not common and is difficult to troubleshoot in medium-size to large networks.

Most enterprise and service provider networks do not use dynamic discovery protocols, and instead rely on administrators to statically (or through DHCP) configure a default router on end devices.

Static Default Gateway Configuration

The most popular method for hosts to reach subnets outside the local subnet is to configure a default gateway on the host statically or through Dynamic Host Configuration Protocol (DHCP). The default gateway is the IP address of the next-hop router for all destinations beyond the local subnet.

For example, in Figure 12-6, Router A is responsible for routing packets for subnet A, and Router B is responsible for handling packets on subnet B. If Router A becomes unavailable to the end user, fast-converging routing protocols can respond within seconds. After convergence, Router B is prepared to transfer packets that would otherwise have gone through Router A.

Figure 12-6 *Using Default Gateway*

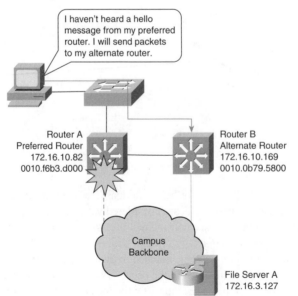

However, it is not the responsibility of the workstations, servers, and printers to exchange dynamic routing information, nor is routing on such devices a recommended practice. These devices typically are configured with a single default gateway IP address. If the router that is the default gateway fails, the device is limited to communicating only on the local IP network segment and is effectively disconnected from the rest of the network. Even if a redundant router exists that could serve as a default gateway, there is no dynamic method by which these devices can switch to a new default gateway IP address in the scenario presented in Figure 12-6.

As you can see, this approach simplifies end-device configuration and processing but creates a single point of failure. If the default gateway fails, the end device is limited to communicating only on the local IP network segment and is cut off from the rest of the network.

Fortunately, Cisco IOS offers several features to provide a redundant default gateway to end devices. With default gateway redundancy, a protocol is used to identify two or more routers as the devices responsible for a single virtual router MAC address and IP address. End devices send traffic to the virtual router. The actual router that handles the forwarding of that traffic is transparent to the end devices. The redundancy protocol provides the mechanism for determining which router should take the active role in forwarding traffic and when that role must be taken over by one of the other routers. The transition from one forwarding router to another is transparent to the end devices.

The following are the default gateway redundancy features supported by Cisco IOS routers and switches:

- Hot Standby Routing Protocol (HSRP)
- Virtual Router Redundancy Protocol (VRRP)
- Gateway Load Balancing Protocol (GLBP)

Hot Standby Routing Protocol

HSRP is a popular default gateway redundancy protocol that is widely used with Cisco multilayer switched networks. HSRP, a Cisco proprietary protocol, supplies a method of providing nonstop path redundancy for IP by sharing protocol and MAC addresses between redundant gateways. The protocol consists of a virtual MAC address and IP address that are shared between two routers, and a process that monitors both LAN and serial interfaces via a multicast protocol. HSRP supports additional routers acting as additional backups for HSRP.

An HSRP standby group consists of the following entities:

- **One active router**—The active router forwards traffic destined to the virtual IP address.
- **One standby router**—The standby router is the backup router in case the active router fails for the subnet. In that case, the standby router becomes the active router and starts forwarding traffic destined to the virtual IP address.

- **One virtual router**—The virtual router is not an actual router. Rather, it is a concept of the entire HSRP group acting as one virtual router as far as hosts on the subnet are concerned, as shown in Figure 12-7. In the figure, the host connected to the switch sends the packet destined for the virtual router, but in reality, the active router does the packet forwarding.

- **Additional HSRP member routers**—The additional routers are neither active nor standby, but they are configured to participate in the same HSRP group. They monitor the current active and standby routers and transition into one of those roles if the current router fails for the subnet.

Figure 12-7 *HSRP Virtual Router*

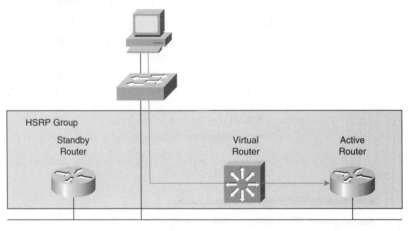

Within each standby group, which is a set of routers participating in HSRP that jointly emulate a virtual router, one router is elected as the active router. The function of the active router is to forward packets sent to the virtual IP address. The active router assumes and maintains its active role through the transmission of hello messages. The hello interval time defines the interval between successive HSRP hello messages sent by active and standby routers. The router with the highest standby priority in the group becomes the active router. The default priority for an HSRP router is 100; however, this option is configurable on a per-standby-group basis.

NOTE   When the preempt option is not configured, the first router to initialize HSRP becomes the active router.

The second router in the HSRP group to initialize is elected as the standby router. The function of the standby router is to monitor the operational status of the HSRP group and to quickly assume packet-forwarding responsibility if the active router becomes inoperable. The standby router also transmits hello messages to inform all other routers in the group of its standby router role and status.

With regard to the redundant gateway functionality, the virtual router presents a consistent available router (default gateway) to the hosts. The virtual router is assigned its own IP address and virtual MAC address; however, the active router acting as the virtual router actually forwards the packets.

An HSRP standby group may contain additional HSRP member routers. These routers in listen state monitor the hello messages but do not respond. These routers do forward any packets addressed to their assigned interface IP addresses but do not forward packets destined for the virtual router because they are not the active router.

When the active router fails, the other HSRP routers stop receiving hello messages, and the standby router assumes the role of the active router. This occurs when the *holdtime* expires. The *holdtime* is defined as the interval between the receipt of a hello message and the presumption that the sending router has failed. Therefore, the length of time it takes to fail over from the active to standby router is dependent on the *holdtime*.

Because the new active router assumes both the IP address and virtual MAC address of the virtual router, the end stations see no disruption in service. The end-user stations continue to send packets to the virtual router's virtual MAC address and IP address where the new active router delivers the packets to the destination.

If both the active and standby routers fail, all routers in the HSRP group contend for the active and standby router roles. When only the active router fails, the standby takes over. If there are other routers participating in the group, those routers then contend to be the new standby router. The following sections discuss HSRP mechanics in more detail.

HSRP States

HSRP defines the following six states in which an HSRP-configured router may exist. When a router is in one of the six states, the router performs the necessary actions required for that state.

- **Initial state**—All routers begin in the initial state. This is the starting state of HSRP and indicates that HSRP is not yet fully operational. This state is entered via a configuration change or when an interface is initiated.

- **Learn state**— In the learn state, the router has not determined the virtual IP address and has not yet seen a hello message from the active router. In this state, the router is still waiting to hear from the active router.

- **Listen state**—In the listen state, the router knows the virtual IP address but is neither the active router nor the standby router. The router listens for hello messages from those routers for its configured *holdtime*. All other routers participating in the HSRP group besides the active or standby routers reside in this state. Routers in the listen state remain in that state until they no longer hear HSRP hello messages from the active or standby HSRP router. At that point, all routers in the listen state participate in an election process for either or both the standby and active router.

- **Speak state**—HSRP routers in the speak state send periodic hello messages and actively participate in the election of the active or standby router.

- **Standby state**—In the standby state, the HSRP router is a candidate to become the next active router and sends periodic hello messages. There must be at least one standby router in the HSRP group.

- **Active state**—In the active state, the router is currently forwarding packets that are sent to the virtual MAC and IP address of the HSRP group. The active router also sends periodic hello messages.

Not all HSRP routers transition through all states. For example, a router that is not the standby or active router does not enter the standby or active states.

HSRP Virtual MAC Address

The active router in the HSRP group responds to traffic for the virtual router. If an end station sends a packet to the virtual router MAC address, the active router receives and processes that packet. If an end station sends an ARP request with the virtual router IP address, the active router replies with the virtual router's MAC address.

In Figure 12-8, Router A has a priority of 200 and Router B has a default priority of 100. Router A assumes the active router role and forwards all frames addressed to the well-known MAC address of 0000.0c07.ac*xx*, where *xx* is the HSRP group identifier.

Figure 12-8 *HSRP Operation*

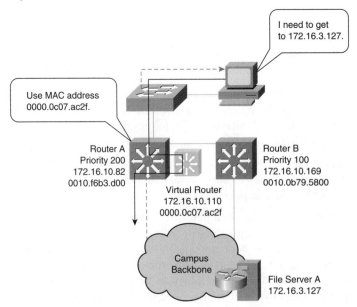

In Figure 12-9, if the HSRP group number of Router A is 47, the MAC address that corresponds to the virtual IP address is 0000.0c07.ac2f. The HSRP group number is the standby group number (47) converted to hexadecimal (2f).

NOTE   The **show ip arp** command for the virtual IP address provides the virtual MAC address, as shown in Figure 12-9. The **show standby** command also provides the information about the HSRP virtual router IP address and virtual MAC address. More information on the **show standby** command is available in the section titled "Verifying HSRP" later in this chapter.

Figure 12-9 *Display HSRP Virtual MAC Address*

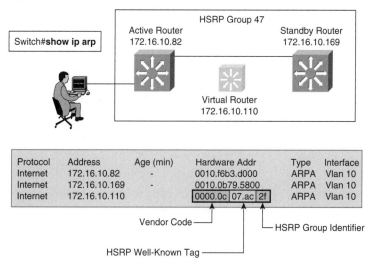

HSRP Load Balancing

To facilitate load sharing, a single router may be a member of multiple HSRP standby groups on a single segment or VLAN. Configuring multiple standby groups further enables redundancy and load sharing within networks and allows redundant routers to be more fully utilized. While a router is actively forwarding traffic for one HSRP group, it can be in the standby or listen state for another group. Each standby group emulates a single virtual router. There can be up to 255 standby groups on any VLAN or interface.

CAUTION   Increasing the number of groups in which a router participates increases the management load on the router and may affect the performance of the router for very large numbers of HSRP groups.

In Figure 12-10, both Router A and Router B are members of groups 1 and 2. However, Router A is the active forwarding router for group 1 and the standby router for group 2. Router B is the active forwarding router for group 2 and the standby router for group 1.

Figure 12-10 *Multiple HSRP Groups*

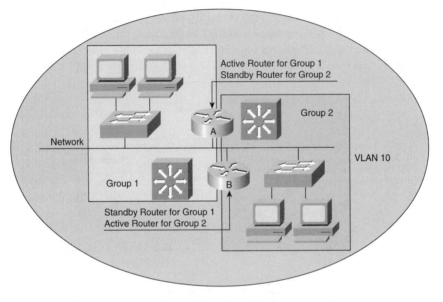

In Figure 12-11, two HSRP-enabled routers participate in two separate VLANs using Inter-Switch Link (ISL) or 802.1Q. Trunking allows users to configure HSRP redundancy between multiple routers to eliminate situations in which a single point of failure causes traffic interruptions.

Figure 12-11 *HSRP Groups Across Trunk Links*

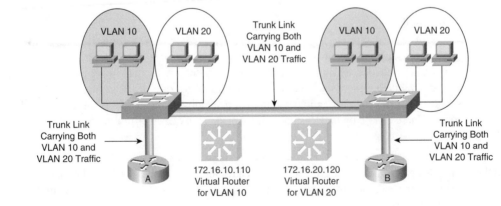

Routers or Layer 3 switches can belong to multiple groups within multiple VLANs, as shown in Figure 12-12. As members of multiple hot standby groups, routers can simultaneously provide redundant backup and perform load sharing across different IP subnets.

Figure 12-12 *Multiple HSRP Groups in Multiple VLANs*

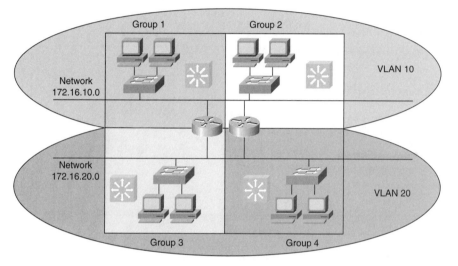

NOTE	One or more HSRP groups need to be configured for each VLAN or subnet. HSRP is not a global configuration.

Configuring HSRP

HSRP has many configuration options; the following sections discuss the common parameters configured for HSRP.

Defining the HSRP Group

To configure a router as a member of an HSRP standby group, enter this command in interface configuration mode:

```
standby group-number ip virtual-ip-address
```

group-number refers to the HSRP standby group number. The group number can range from 0 to 255. *virtual-ip-address* indicates the virtual IP address of the HSRP group.

While running HSRP, it is important that the end-user stations do not discover the actual MAC addresses of the routers in the standby group. Any protocol that informs a host of the router's actual address must be disabled. Enabling HSRP on a Cisco router interface automatically disables ICMP redirects on that interface to ensure that the actual addresses of the participating HSRP routers are not discovered.

Example 12-6 shows interface VLAN 10 configured as a member of the HSRP standby group 47. The virtual router IP address for that group is 172.16.10.110, and ICMP redirects are disabled.

Example 12-6 *Sample Configuration of HSRP Group*

```
Switch#show running-config
Building configuration...

Current configuration:
!
(text deleted)
interface Vlan10
ip address 172.16.10.82 255.255.255.0
no ip redirects
standby 47 ip 172.16.10.110
!
(text deleted)
!
```

NOTE   Using the VLAN ID as the HSRP standby group identifier makes troubleshooting HSRP issues easier. However, it may not always be possible because the group identifier can only be specified in the range of 0 to 255.

Configuring Router HSRP Group Priority

Each standby group has its own active and standby routers. The network administrator can assign a priority value to each router in a standby group, allowing the administrator to control the order in which active routers for that group are selected.

To set the priority value of a router, enter this command in interface configuration mode:

   standby *group-number* **priority** *priority-value*

The *priority-value* indicates the number that prioritizes a potential standby router. The range is 0 to 255; the default is 100. During the election process, the router in an HSRP group with the highest priority becomes the forwarding router. If several routers have the same priority, the physical IP address of the router's interface is used as a tiebreaker. The router with the numerically highest IP address wins.

Example 12-7 shows the configuration of an interface VLAN 10 configured with a priority value of 150 in HSRP standby group 47. The higher the standby group priority value, the greater the chances that this router becomes the active router for the group.

Example 12-7 *Sample Configuration of Router HSRP Priority*

```
Switch#show running-config
Building configuration...

Current configuration:
!
(text deleted)
interface Vlan10
ip address 172.16.10.32 255.255.255.0
no ip redirects
standby 47 priority 150
standby 47 ip 172.16.10.110
!
```

Configuring HSRP Preempt

The standby router automatically assumes the active router role when the active router fails or is removed from service. This new active router remains the forwarding router even when the former active router with the higher priority regains service in the network.

The former active router can be configured to resume the forwarding router role from a router with a lower priority. This feature is useful for consistently having the same routers in the active state on a per–standby group basis after state changes. This consistency facilitates troubleshooting. To enable a router to resume the active state after a state change, enter the following command in interface configuration mode:

standby [*group-number*] **preempt** [{**delay**} [**minimum** *delay*] [**sync** *delay*]]

To remove the interface from preemptive status, enter the following command:

no standby *group-number* **preempt**

Example 12-8 shows the required configuration for interface VLAN 10 to resume its role as the active router in HSRP group 47, assuming interface VLAN 10 on this router has the highest priority in that standby group.

Example 12-8 *Sample Configuration of HSRP Preempt*

```
Switch#show running-config
Building configuration...

Current configuration:
!
(text deleted)
interface Vlan10
ip address 172.16.10.82 255.255.255.0
no ip redirects
!
standby 47 priority 150
standby 47 preempt
standby 47 ip 172.16.10.110
```

Configuring HSRP Group Timers

An HSRP-enabled router sends hello messages to indicate that the router is running and is capable of becoming either the active or standby router. The hello message contains the priority of the router, as well as a *hellotime* and *holdtime* value. The *hellotime* value indicates the interval between the hello messages that the router sends. The *holdtime* value indicates the amount of time that the current hello message is considered valid. The standby timer includes an *msec* parameter for specifying faster failover times.

If an active router sends a hello message, then receiving routers consider that hello message to be valid for one *holdtime*.

NOTE   The *holdtime* should be at least three times the value of the *hellotime*.

Both the *hellotime* and the *holdtime* parameters are configurable. To configure the time between hello messages and the time before other group routers declare the active or standby router to be nonfunctioning, enter this command in interface configuration mode:

```
standby group-number timers hellotime holdtime
```

The value of the *hellotime* parameter is in seconds, 3 seconds being the default value. The *hellotime* parameter value varies from 1 to 255.

The value of the *holdtime* parameter is also in seconds, 10 seconds being the default value. The *holdtime* parameter value varies from 1 to 255.

To reinstate the default standby timer values, enter the following command:

```
no standby group-number timers
```

Configuring HSRP Interface Tracking

In some situations, the status of an interface directly affects which router needs to become the active router. This is particularly true when each of the routers in an HSRP group has a different path to resources within the campus network.

In Figure 12-13, Router A and Router B reside in a branch office. These two routers each support a T1 link to headquarters. Router A has the higher priority and is the active forwarding router for standby group 47. Router B is the standby router for that group. Routers A and B are exchanging hello messages through their E0 interfaces.

The T1 link between the active forwarding router for the standby group and headquarters experiences a failure. Without HSRP enabled, Router A would detect the failed link and send an ICMP redirect to Router B. However, when HSRP is enabled, ICMP redirects are disabled. Therefore, neither Router A nor the virtual router sends an ICMP redirect, and although the S1 interface on Router A is no longer functional, Router A still sends hello messages out interface E0, indicating that Router A is still the active router. Packets sent to the virtual router for forwarding to headquarters cannot be routed.

Figure 12-13 *HSRP Interface Tracking*

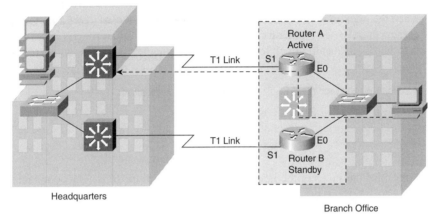

Interface tracking enables the priority of a standby group router to be automatically adjusted based on availability of the other interfaces on that router. When a tracked interface becomes unavailable, the HSRP priority of the router is decreased. The HSRP tracking feature ensures that an HSRP active router with an unavailable key egress interface does not remain the active router.

In Figure 12-14, the E0 interface on Router A tracks the S1 interface. If the link between the S1 interface and headquarters fails, the router automatically decrements its priority on that interface and stops transmitting hello messages out interface E0. Router B assumes the active router role when no hello messages are detected for the specific *holdtime* period.

Figure 12-14 *HSRP Interface Tracking Scenario*

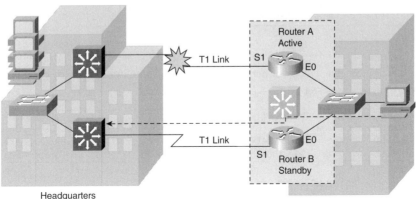

To configure HSRP tracking, use the following command in interface configuration mode:

```
standby [group-number] track interface-type interface-id [interface-priority]
```

The *interface-priority* parameter indicates the amount by which the hot standby priority for the router is decremented when the tracked interface becomes unavailable and incremented when the track interface becomes available. The default value of the *interface-priority* parameter is 10. Careful planning of standby priorities for all routers is needed to ensure that the HSRP standby track lowers priorities enough for standby routers to take active roles.

To disable interface tracking, use the following command:

```
no standby group-number track
```

Verifying HSRP

To display the status of the HSRP router, enter one of the following commands:

```
show standby [interface-type [group]] [active | init | listen | standby][brief]
show standby delay [interface-type number]
```

If the optional interface parameters are not indicated, the **show standby** command displays HSRP information for all interfaces. Example 12-9 shows the output of the **show standby** command.

Example 12-9 *Displaying HSRP Standby Group Information*

```
Switch#show standby Vlan10 47
Vlan10 - Group 47
  Local state is Active, priority 150, may preempt
  Hellotime 3 holdtime 10
  Next hello sent in 00:00:02.944
  Hot standby IP address is 172.16.10.110 configured
  Active router is local
  Standby router is 172.16.10.82 expires in 00:00:08
  Standby virtual mac address is 0000.0c07.ac2f
  Tracking interface states for 1 interface, 1 up:
    Up  Vlan51 Priority decrement: 40
```

Example 12-10 illustrates a user displaying HSRP standby group information with the **brief** parameter. The **brief** parameter displays a summary of standby groups.

Example 12-10 *Displaying Brief HSRP Standby Group Information*

```
Switch#show standby brief
Interface  Grp   Prio P State   Active addr     Standby addr    Group addr
V110       47   150  P Active   local           172.16.10.82    172.16.10.110
V112       12   100    Standby  172.16.102.82   local           172.16.12.10
```

HSRP Debugging

The Cisco IOS implementation of HSRP supports the **debug** command. Enabling the debug facility displays the HSRP state changes and debugging information regarding transmission and receipt of HSRP packets. To enable HSRP debugging, enter this command in privileged EXEC mode:

```
debug standby
```

CAUTION	Because debugging output is assigned high priority in the CPU process, this command can render the system unusable. Use the conditional debug using the **debug condition standby vlan** *vlan-id group-number* command to limit the output of **debug standby** to the specific VLAN interface and specific HSRP group.

Use either the **no debug standby** or the **no debug all** command to disable the debugging feature.

Example 12-11 illustrates the debugs generated using the **debug standby** command when Router A, which is the only HSRP group router on the subnet and not configured with the HSRP preempt option, goes through all the HSRP states before becoming the active router. Notice at timestamp Mar 8 20:34:10.221 that the interface comes up, and Router A enters the listen state. The router stays in the listen state for the *holdtime* of 10 seconds. Router A then goes into the speak state at timestamp Mar 8 20:34:20.221 for 10 seconds. When the router is speaking, it sends its state out every 3 seconds according to its hello interval. After 10 seconds in speak state, the router has determined that there is no standby router at timestamp Mar 8 20:34:30.221 and enters standby state. The router has also determined that there is not an active router and therefore immediately enters the active state at timestamp Mar 8 20:34:30.221. From then on, the active router will send its active state hello every 3 seconds. Because there are no other routers on this broadcast domain, there are no hello messages being received.

Example 12-11 *Sample Debug Output of HSRP Router Initializing with No Other Routers on the Subnet*

```
RouterA(config)#interface vlan 11
RouterAconfig-if)#no shut
*Mar  8 20:34:10.213: %LINK-3-UPDOWN: Interface Vlan11, changed state to up
*Mar  8 20:34:10.221: SB:  Vl11 Interface up
*Mar  8 20:34:10.221: SB11: Vl11 Init: a/HSRP enabled
*Mar  8 20:34:10.221: SB11: Vl11 Init -> Listen
*Mar  8 20:34:11.213: %LINEPROTO-5-UPDOWN: Line protocol on Interface Vlan11,
changed state to up
*Mar  8 20:34:20.221: SB11: Vl11 Listen: c/Active timer expired (unknown)
*Mar  8 20:34:20.221: SB11: Vl11 Listen -> Speak
*Mar  8 20:34:20.221: SB11: Vl11 Hello  out 172.16.11.111 Speak   pri 100 ip
172.16.11.115
```

Example 12-11 *Sample Debug Output of HSRP Router Initializing with No Other Routers on the Subnet (Continued)*

```
*Mar  8 20:34:23.101: SB11: Vl11 Hello  out 172.16.11.111 Speak   pri 100 ip
172.16.11.115
*Mar  8 20:34:25.961: SB11: Vl11 Hello  out 172.16.11.111 Speak   pri 100 ip
172.16.11.115
*Mar  8 20:34:28.905: SB11: Vl11 Hello  out 172.16.11.111 Speak   pri 100 ip
172.16.11.115
*Mar  8 20:34:30.221: SB11: Vl11 Speak: d/Standby timer expired (unknown)
*Mar  8 20:34:30.221: SB11: Vl11 Standby router is local
*Mar  8 20:34:30.221: SB11: Vl11 Speak -> Standby
*Mar  8 20:34:30.221: SB11: Vl11 Hello  out 172.16.11.111 Standby pri 100 ip
172.16.11.115
*Mar  8 20:34:30.221: SB11: Vl11 Standby: c/Active timer expired (unknown)
*Mar  8 20:34:30.221: SB11: Vl11 Active router is local
*Mar  8 20:34:30.221: SB11: Vl11 Standby router is unknown, was local
*Mar  8 20:34:30.221: SB11: Vl11 Standby -> Active
*Mar  8 20:34:30.221: %STANDBY-6-STATECHANGE: Vlan11 Group 11 state Standby ->
Active
*Mar  8 20:34:30.221: SB11: Vl11 Hello  out 172.16.11.111 Active  pri 100 ip
172.16.11.115
*Mar  8 20:34:33.085: SB11: Vl11 Hello  out 172.16.11.111 Active  pri 100 ip
172.16.11.115
```

Example 12-12 illustrates a scenario in which Router A is configured with a priority of 100, which is higher than the current active Router B (172.16.11.112), which has a priority of 50. Router A is not configured with the **preempt** keyword. Only when a router is configured with **preempt** will a router with a higher priority immediately become the active router. After Router A goes through the HSRP initialization states, it establishes itself as the standby router, as illustrated in the debug output in Example 12-11.

Example 12-12 *Sample Debug Output of Higher-Priority Router Coming Online Without Preempt*

```
RouterA(config)#interface vlan 11
RouterA(config-if)#no shut
*Mar  1 00:12:16.871: SB11: Vl11 Hello  in  172.16.11.112 Active  pri 50 ip
172.16.11.115
*Mar  1 00:12:16.871: SB11: Vl11 Active router is 172.16.11.112
*Mar  1 00:12:18.619: %LINK-3-UPDOWN: Interface Vlan11, changed state to up
*Mar  1 00:12:18.623: SB:  Vl11 Interface up
*Mar  1 00:12:18.623: SB11: Vl11 Init: a/HSRP enabled
*Mar  1 00:12:18.623: SB11: Vl11 Init -> Listen
*Mar  1 00:12:19.619: %LINEPROTO-5-UPDOWN: Line protocol on Interface Vlan11,
changed state to up
*Mar  1 00:12:19.819: SB11: Vl11 Hello  in  172.16.11.112 Active  pri 50 ip
172.16.11.115
*Mar  1 00:12:19.819: SB11: Vl11 Listen: h/Hello rcvd from lower pri Active router
(50/172.16.11.112)
*Mar  1 00:12:22.815: SB11: Vl11 Hello  in  172.16.11.112 Active  pri 50 ip
172.16.11.115
*Mar  1 00:12:22.815: SB11: Vl11 Listen: h/Hello rcvd from lower pri Active router
(50/172.16.11.112)
*Mar  1 00:12:25.683: SB11: Vl11 Hello  in  172.16.11.112 Active  pri 50 ip
172.16.11.115
```

Example 12-12 *Sample Debug Output of Higher-Priority Router Coming Online Without Preempt (Continued)*

```
*Mar  1 00:12:25.683: SB11: Vl11 Listen: h/Hello rcvd from lower pri Active router
(50/172.16.11.112)
*Mar  1 00:12:28.623: SB11: Vl11 Listen: d/Standby timer expired (unknown)
*Mar  1 00:12:28.623: SB11: Vl11 Listen -> Speak
*Mar  1 00:12:28.623: SB11: Vl11 Hello  out 172.16.11.111 Speak   pri 100 ip
172.16.11.115
*Mar  1 00:12:28.659: SB11: Vl11 Hello  in  172.16.11.112 Active  pri 50 ip
172.16.11.115
*Mar  1 00:12:28.659: SB11: Vl11 Speak: h/Hello rcvd from lower pri Active router
(50/172.16.11.112)
*Mar  1 00:12:31.539: SB11: Vl11 Hello  in  172.16.11.112 Active  pri 50 ip
172.16.11.115
*Mar  1 00:12:31.539: SB11: Vl11 Speak: h/Hello rcvd from lower pri Active router
(50/172.16.11.112)
*Mar  1 00:12:31.575: SB11: Vl11 Hello  out 172.16.11.111 Speak   pri 100 ip
172.16.11.115
*Mar  1 00:12:34.491: SB11: Vl11 Hello  in  172.16.11.112 Active  pri 50 ip
172.16.11.115
*Mar  1 00:12:34.491: SB11: Vl11 Speak: h/Hello rcvd from lower pri Active router
(50/172.16.11.112)
*Mar  1 00:12:34.547: SB11: Vl11 Hello  out 172.16.11.111 Speak   pri 100 ip
172.16.11.115
*Mar  1 00:12:37.363: SB11: Vl11 Hello  in  172.16.11.112 Active  pri 50 ip
172.16.11.115
*Mar  1 00:12:37.363: SB11: Vl11 Speak: h/Hello rcvd from lower pri Active router
(50/172.16.11.112)
*Mar  1 00:12:37.495: SB11: Vl11 Hello  out 172.16.11.111 Speak   pri 100 ip
172.16.11.115
*Mar  1 00:12:38.623: SB11: Vl11 Speak: d/Standby timer expired (unknown)
*Mar  1 00:12:38.623: SB11: Vl11 Standby router is local
*Mar  1 00:12:38.623: SB11: Vl11 Speak -> Standby
*Mar  1 00:12:38.623: SB11: Vl11 Hello  out 172.16.11.111 Standby pri 100 ip
172.16.11.115
*Mar  1 00:12:40.279: SB11: Vl11 Hello  in  172.16.11.112 Active  pri 50 ip
172.16.11.115
*Mar  1 00:12:40.279: SB11: Vl11 Standby: h/Hello rcvd from lower pri Active router
(50/172.16.11.112)
*Mar  1 00:12:41.551: SB11: Vl11 Hello  out 172.16.11.111 Standby pri 100 ip
172.16.11.115
```

Example 12-13 illustrates the scenario in which Router A is configured with the **preempt** option and has a priority of 100. This priority is higher than the active Router B (172.16.11.112), which has a priority of 50. Only when a router is configured with the HSRP **preempt** option does the router with a higher priority transition into the active state after a state change. Furthermore, at timestamp Mar 1 00:16:43.099, the interface VLAN 11 on Router A comes up and transitions into the listen state. At timestamp Mar 1 00:16:43.295, Router A hears a hello from the active router, Router B. Router A determines that the active router has a lower priority than itself. Router A immediately at timestamp Mar 1 00:16:43.295 sends out a coup message indicating that it is transitioning into the active router. Router B enters the speak state and eventually becomes the standby router.

Example 12-13 *Sample Debug Output of Higher-Priority Router Coming Online with Preempt*

```
RouterA(config)#interface vlan 11
RouterA(config-if)#no shut
*Mar  1 00:16:43.095: %LINK-3-UPDOWN: Interface Vlan11, changed state to up
*Mar  1 00:16:43.099: SB:  Vl11 Interface up
*Mar  1 00:16:43.099: SB11: Vl11 Init: a/HSRP enabled
*Mar  1 00:16:43.099: SB11: Vl11 Init -> Listen
*Mar  1 00:16:43.295: SB11: Vl11 Hello  in  172.16.11.112 Active  pri 50 ip
172.16.11.115
*Mar  1 00:16:43.295: SB11: Vl11 Active router is 172.16.11.112
*Mar  1 00:16:43.295: SB11: Vl11 Listen: h/Hello rcvd from lower pri Active router
(50/172.16.11.112)
*Mar  1 00:16:43.295: SB11: Vl11 Active router is local, was 172.16.11.112
*Mar  1 00:16:43.295: SB11: Vl11 Coup   out 172.16.11.111 Listen  pri 100 ip
172.16.11.115
*Mar  1 00:16:43.299: %STANDBY-6-STATECHANGE: Vlan11 Group 11 state Listen -> Active
*Mar  1 00:16:43.299: SB11: Vl11 Hello  out 172.16.11.111 Active  pri 100 ip
172.16.11.115
*Mar  1 00:16:43.303: SB11: Vl11 Hello  in  172.16.11.112 Speak   pri 50 ip
172.16.11.115
*Mar  1 00:16:44.095: %LINEPROTO-5-UPDOWN: Line protocol on Interface Vlan11,
changed state to up
*Mar  1 00:16:46.187: SB11: Vl11 Hello  in  172.16.11.112 Speak   pri 50 ip
172.16.11.115
*Mar  1 00:16:46.207: SB11: Vl11 Hello  out 172.16.11.111 Active  pri 100 ip
172.16.11.115
*Mar  1 00:16:49.095: SB11: Vl11 Hello  in  172.16.11.112 Speak   pri 50 ip
172.16.11.115
*Mar  1 00:16:49.195: SB11: Vl11 Hello  out 172.16.11.111 Active  pri 100 ip
172.16.11.115
*Mar  1 00:16:52.079: SB11: Vl11 Hello  in  172.16.11.112 Speak   pri 50 ip
172.16.11.115
*Mar  1 00:16:52.147: SB11: Vl11 Hello  out 172.16.11.111 Active  pri 100 ip
172.16.11.115
*Mar  1 00:16:53.303: SB11: Vl11 Hello  in  172.16.11.112 Standby pri 50 ip
172.16.11.115
*Mar  1 00:16:53.303: SB11: Vl11 Standby router is 172.16.11.112
172.16.11.115
```

Virtual Router Redundancy Protocol

Like HSRP, VRRP is a default gateway redundancy method. VRRP enables a group of routers to form a single virtual router. The VRRP standard (RFC 2338) solves the static default gateway configuration problem. VRRP is similar in functionality to HSRP; hence, the LAN hosts can be configured with the virtual router as their default gateway. The virtual router, representing a group of routers, is known as a VRRP group.

Cisco switches and routers support VRRP on Ethernet, Fast Ethernet, and Gigabit Ethernet interfaces and on MPLS VPNs and VLANs.

VRRP Scenarios

Figure 12-15 shows a LAN topology with Router A, Router B, and Router C, which are VRRP-enabled routers that form a virtual router. The IP address of the virtual router is the same as that configured for the Ethernet interface of Router A (10.0.0.1).

Figure 12-15 *VRRP Scenario*

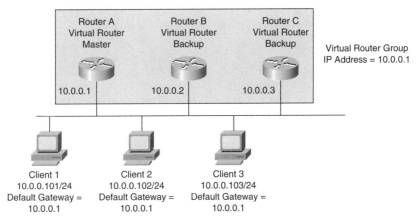

Because the virtual router uses the IP address of the physical Ethernet interface of Router A, Router A assumes the role of the master virtual router and is known as the IP address owner. As the master virtual router, Router A controls the IP address of the virtual router and is responsible for forwarding packets sent to this IP address. Hosts 1 through 3 are configured with the default gateway IP address of 10.0.0.1.

Routers B and C function as backup virtual routers. If the master virtual router fails, the router configured with the higher priority will become the master virtual router and provide uninterrupted service for the LAN hosts. When Router A recovers, it becomes the master virtual router again.

Figure 12-16 shows a LAN topology in which VRRP is configured such that Routers A and B share the traffic to and from hosts 1 through 4 and act as backup virtual routers to each other if either router fails.

In the topology shown in Figure 12-16, two virtual routers exist. For virtual router 1, Router A is the owner of IP address 10.0.0.1 and is the master virtual router, and Router B is the backup virtual router to Router A. Hosts 1 and 2 are configured with the default gateway IP address of 10.0.0.1.

For virtual router 2, Router B is the owner of IP address 10.0.0.2 and is the master virtual router, and Router A is the backup virtual router to Router B. Hosts 3 and 4 are configured with the default gateway IP address of 10.0.0.2.

Figure 12-16 *Multiple Virtual Routers with VRRP*

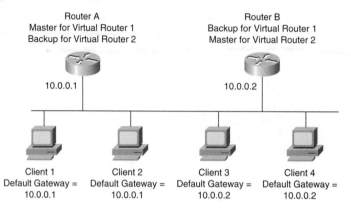

VRRP Operation Details

If an interface IP address is configured with the virtual IP address for the VRRP group, the owning router must be the master in a VRRP group. In addition, the priority associated with that interface must be configured as 255. Otherwise, the highest priority wins the election and is the master. Backup values range from 1 to 254; the default value is 100. If the VRRP group is configured with zero (0) priority, the master or any router releases responsibility for being the virtual router for that VRRP group.

With regard to how VRRP routers communicate with one another, the IP number assigned by the Internet Assigned Numbers Authority (IANA) for VRRP is 112. The router that is acting as the VRRP master sends advertisements using this IP number 112 to the multicast address 224.0.0.18. The default advertisement interval is 1 second but can be modified. The virtual MAC address for the VRRP group is of the form 00-00-5e-00-01-{VRID}, where VRID is the VRRP group number in hexadecimal format.

VRRP also has a coup message that is found in HSRP. However, VRRP calls this message a VRRP flow message. With VRRP, preventing preemption after state changes is achieved through a nondefault configuration.

VRRP supports a resign function similar to HSRP, where the master transitions to a backup router. To trigger this behavior, configure the router acting as the master with a priority of 0.

In terms of failover, the takeover time of a standby router to an active router depends on two timers: the advertisement interval and the master-down interval. The *advertisement interval* is the interval between advertisements (seconds). The default is 1 second. The *master-down interval* is the time interval for backup to declare the master down (seconds). The master-down interval is not configurable and is chosen to be at least three times the value of the advertisement interval. The higher the advertisement interval, the more time the peer router takes to detect the failure of the master, and hence, failover.

Configuring and Verifying VRRP

Like HSRP, VRRP has many parameters to configure. To define a VRRP group, use the following command:

vrrp *group-number* **ip** *virtual-IP-address*

To define the VRRP router priority, use the following command:

vrrp *group-number* **priority** *priority-value*

Example 12-14 illustrates a user configuring and verifying VRRP on Router A and Router B.

Example 12-14 *Configuring and Verifying VRRP*

```
RouterA#configure terminal
Enter configuration commands, one per line.  End with CNTL/Z.
RouterA(config)#interface vlan 1
RouterA(config-if)#ip address 10.0.2.2 255.255.255.0
RouterA(config-if)#vrrp 1 ip 10.0.2.254
RouterA(config-if)#end
```

```
RouterB#configure terminal
Enter configuration commands, one per line.  End with CNTL/Z.
RouterB(config)#interface vlan 1
RouterB(config-if)#ip address 10.0.2.1 255.255.255.0
RouterB(config-if)#vrrp 1 ip 10.0.2.254
RouterB(config-if)#vrrp 1 priority 90
RouterB(config-if)#end
```

```
RouterA#show vrrp interface vlan 1
Vlan1 - Group 1
  State is Master
  Virtual IP address is 10.0.2.254
  Virtual MAC address is 0000.5e00.0101
  Advertisement interval is 1.000 sec
  Preemption is enabled
    min delay is 0.000 sec
 Priority is 100
  Master Router is 10.0.2.2 (local), priority is 100
  Master Advertisement interval is 1.000 sec
  Master Down interval is 3.609 sec
```

```
RouterB#show vrrp interface vlan 1
Vlan1 - Group 1
  State is Backup
  Virtual IP address is 10.0.2.254
  Virtual MAC address is 0000.5e00.0101
  Advertisement interval is 1.000 sec
  Preemption is enabled
    min delay is 0.000 sec
  Priority is 90
  Authentication is enabled
  Master Router is 10.0.2.2, priority is 100
  Master Advertisement interval is 1.000 sec
  Master Down interval is 3.609 sec (expires in 2.745 sec)
```

A main difference between HSRP and VRRP is that in VRRP, the backup router does not send advertisements. Therefore, as seen in Example 12-14, the VRRP master is not aware of the current backup router.

In summary, VRRP is similar to HSRP in functionality, but it is standard compared to the Cisco proprietary HSRP. Nevertheless, in enterprise and service provider networks, HSRP deployments far outnumber VRRP deployments.

Gateway Load Balancing Protocol

While HSRP and VRRP provide gateway resiliency, the standby members of the redundancy group remain underutilized along with their upstream bandwidth. Only the active router for the HSRP group handles traffic for the virtual MAC and IP address. Currently, the Catalyst 6500 series of switches supports GLBP in Cisco IOS Software Release 12.2(17d)SXB or later.

Cisco designed GLBP to allow automatic selection and simultaneous use of multiple available gateways and to provide automatic detection and failover to a redundant path in the event of failure to any active gateway. With GLBP, it is possible to fully use resources without the extra administrative burden of configuring multiple groups and managing multiple default gateway configurations.

A GLBP group can have up to four member routers acting as IP default gateways. These gateways are known as the *active virtual forwarders* (AVF). The GLBP automatically manages the virtual MAC address assignment, determines who handles the forwarding, and ensures that each station has a forwarding path in the event of failures to gateways or tracked interfaces. These functions are accomplished by one of the routers in the group acting as the active virtual gateway (AVG).

If failures occur, the load-balancing ratio is adjusted among the remaining AVFs so that resources are used in the most efficient way.

In the default mode, GLBP attempts to balance traffic on a per-host basis using a round-robin scheme, as shown in Figure 12-17. When a device sends an ARP message for the gateway IP address, the AVG returns a MAC address based on its load-balancing algorithm. When a second device sends an ARP message, the AVG returns the next virtual MAC address from the list of available gateways.

Note that only the AVG, otherwise known as the master gateway, responds to ARP requests. The AVG is responsible for managing the members of the GLBP group, as indicated earlier.

GLBP supports the following operational modes for load balancing:

- **Weighted load-balancing algorithm**—The amount of load directed to an AVF depends on the weighting value advertised by the gateway containing that AVF.

- **Host-dependent load-balancing algorithm**—A host is guaranteed to use the same virtual MAC address as long as that virtual MAC address is participating in the GLBP group.

- **Round-robin load-balancing algorithm**—Each virtual forwarder MAC address takes turns being included in address resolution replies for the virtual IP address. The round-robin load-balancing algorithm is the default.

Figure 12-17 *GLBP Default Scenario*

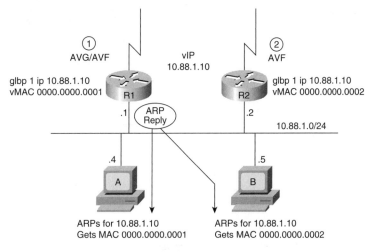

Figure 12-18 illustrates the use of GLBP. Hosts A and B send their off-network traffic to separate next-hop routers because they each have cached a different MAC address for the single virtual gateway IP address—in this case, 10.88.1.10. Each GLBP router is an AVF for the MAC address it has been assigned.

Figure 12-18 *GLBP Load Balancing*

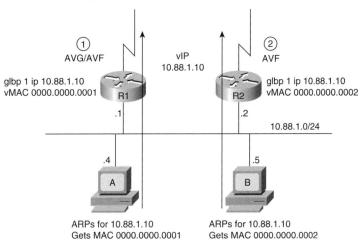

Like HSRP, GLBP can be configured to track interfaces. In Figure 12-19, the link from Router R1 is lost. GLBP detects the failure.

Figure 12-19 *GLBP Load-Balancing Scenario with Link Failure*

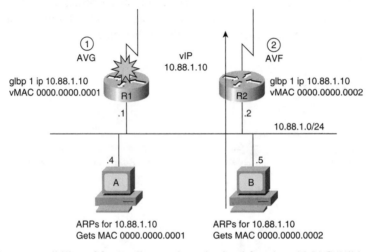

The responsibility of forwarding packets destined for virtual MAC "1" in Figure 12-20 is taken over by the secondary virtual forwarder (Router R2).

Figure 12-20 *GLBP Interface Tracking Mechanism*

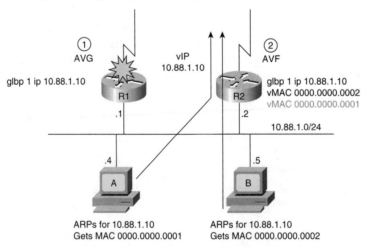

Configuring and Verifying GLBP

Like HSRP and VRRP, GLBP has many parameters to configure. Table 12-6 describes the GLBP commands and the associated parameters.

Table 12-6   *GLBP Commands*

Command	Description
(config-if)#**glbp** *group-number* **ip** *virtual-gateway-address*	Configures the interface of a member of the virtual group with the identified virtual IP address.
(config-if)#**glbp** *group-number* **priority** *priority-value*	Configures the priority of configured router. The highest value wins election as active router. The default is 100. If routers have the same GLBP priority, the gateway with the highest real IP address becomes the AVG.
(config-if)#**glbp** *group-number* **timers** *hello-value holdtime-value*	Configures the hello timer and hold timer values. Place the argument *msec* before the values to specify subsecond values.

Example 12-15 illustrates a user configuring GLBP on interface VLAN 7 on Switch A and Switch B.

Example 12-15   *Configuring GLBP*

```
SwitchA(config)#interface vlan7
SwitchA(config-if)#ip address 10.1.7.5 255.255.255.0
SwitchA(config-if)#glbp 7 ip 10.1.7.1
SwitchA(config-if)#glbp 7 priority 150
SwitchA(config-if)#glbp 7 timers msec 250 msec 750

SwitchB(config)#interface vlan7
SwitchB(config-if)#ip address 10.1.7.6 255.255.255.0
SwitchB(config-if)#glbp 7 ip 10.1.7.1
SwitchB(config-if)#glbp 7 priority 100
SwitchB(config-if)#glbp 7 timers msec 250 msec 750
```

To verify the GLBP operation, issue the following command:

```
show glbp interface interface-id
```

GLBP, although similar to HSRP and VRRP in its ability to provide default gateway redundancy, adds the ability to load-balance between the redundant routers, and thereby efficiently uses the network resources. Nevertheless, in terms of deployment numbers, GLBP is a distant third compared to HSRP and VRRP.

Cisco IOS Server Load Balancing

Cisco IOS Server Load Balancing (SLB) intelligently load-balances TCP/IP traffic across multiple servers, as illustrated in Figure 12-21. Cisco IOS SLB is a Layer 4 or Layer 7 switching feature, depending on configuration. Currently, the only Catalyst switch that supports Cisco IOS SLB is the Catalyst 6500 switch. Cisco IOS SLB is a software-based feature. For high-performance, hardware-based server load balancing, Cisco recommends the Cisco Application Control Engine (ACE) service module for the Catalyst 6500 switches. The ACE service module can help to achieve performance up to 16 Gbps. Also, the ACE service module provides security via SSL encryption/decryption and bidirectional support for content inspection.

Cisco IOS SLB presents a single virtual server IP address to requesting clients. For example, clients make IP requests, such as HTTP Get, to this virtual IP address. The switch then distributes (load-balances) these requests across a series of servers (real servers). The switch load-balancing request is based on numerous factors, such as TCP and UDP protocol, load, and other load-balancing characteristics. Furthermore, the switch forwards requests from clients to the same server when necessary, such as with FTP when a client must communicate with the same server throughout the entire sequence or flow. Generally, client devices resolve the virtual server IP address through DNS.

Figure 12-21 *Server Load Balancing*

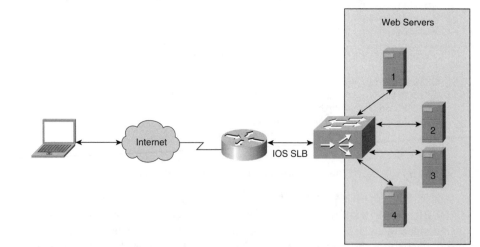

Using Cisco IOS SLB for redundancy, scalability, and performance (load balancing) provides the following benefits:

- High performance is achieved through the distribution of client requests across a cluster of servers.

- Administration of server applications is easier. Clients know only about virtual servers; no administration is required for real server changes, making Cisco IOS SLB highly scalable.

- Security of the real server is provided because its address is never announced to the external network. Users are familiar only with the virtual IP address. Additionally, filtering of unwanted traffic can be based on both IP address and IP port numbers.

- Ease of maintenance with no downtime is achieved by allowing physical (real) servers to be transparently placed in or out of service while other servers handle client requests.

- Switches detect servers that are not responding and do not further requests to those servers until they begin to respond to polls from the switch.

In summary, Cisco IOS SLB allows users to represent a group of network servers (a server farm in a Data Center) as a single server instance, balance the traffic to the servers, and limit traffic to individual servers. The single server instance that represents a server farm is referred to as a *virtual server.* Figure 12-22 illustrates a Cisco IOS SLB applied to a server farm in a Data Center. The virtual web server IP address is 192.168.1.200 on port 80, and the real web servers are 192.168.1.1 and 192.168.1.2. Any request to the virtual web server address is served by the two real servers.

Figure 12-22 *SLB Virtual Server and Server Farm*

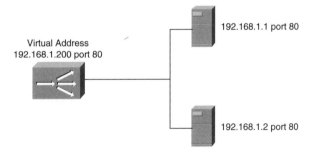

Virtual Address
192.168.1.200 port 80

192.168.1.1 port 80

192.168.1.2 port 80

Cisco IOS SLB Modes of Operation

In an SLB environment, clients connect to the IP address of the virtual server. When a client initiates a connection to the virtual server, the SLB function chooses a real server for the connection based on a configured load-balancing algorithm.

Cisco IOS SLB supports the following redirection modes:

- **Dispatched mode**—In dispatched mode, each of the real servers is configured with the virtual server address as a loopback address or secondary IP address. Cisco IOS SLB redirects packets to the real servers at the MAC layer. Because the virtual server IP address is not modified in dispatched mode, the real servers must be Layer 2–adjacent to Cisco IOS SLB, or intervening routers might not be able to route to the chosen real server.

- **Directed mode**—In directed mode, the virtual server can be assigned an IP address that is not known to any of the real servers in a Data Center. Cisco IOS SLB translates packets exchanged between a client and a real server, translating the virtual server IP address to a real server address via Network Address Translation (NAT). For more information about Cisco IOS SLB support of different NAT types, refer to the Cisco IOS SLB configuration section of the Cisco product documentation for the Catalyst 6500 switches.

Configuring Cisco IOS SLB involves identifying server farms, configuring groups of real servers in Data Centers, and configuring the virtual servers that represent the real servers to the clients. The following sections provide a sample configuration of Cisco IOS SLB.

Configuring the Server Farm in a Data Center with Real Servers

The following steps describe how to configure Cisco IOS SLB in a server farm in a Data Center with real servers:

Step 1 Define the server farm.

```
ip slb serverfarm serverfarm-name
```

Step 2 Associate the real server with the server farm.

```
real ip-address-of-the-real-server
```

Step 3 Enable the real server defined to be used for the Cisco IOS server farm.

```
inservice
```

Example 12-16 shows a user configuring two server farms in a Data Center, PUBLIC and RESTRICTED. The PUBLIC server farm has associated with it three real servers: 10.1.1.1, 10.1.1.2, and 10.1.1.3. The RESTRICTED server farm has two real servers associated with it: 10.1.1.20 and 10.1.1.21. Figure 12-23 visually depicts the configuration.

Figure 12-23 *Configuration Scenario of Cisco IOS SLB for Webserver Farms in a Data Center*

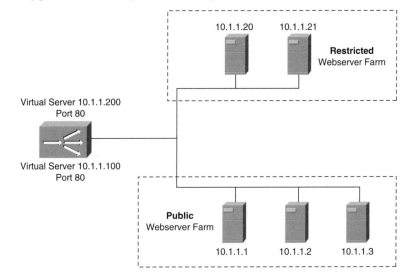

Example 12-16 *Configuring Server Farm with Real Servers*

```
Switch#configure terminal
Enter configuration commands, one per line. End with CNTL/Z.
Switch(config)# ip slb serverfarm PUBLIC
Switch(config-slb-sfarm)#real 10.1.1.1
Switch(config-slb-real)#inservice
Switch(config-slb-real)#exit
Switch(config-slb-sfarm)#real 10.1.1.2
Switch(config-slb-real)#inservice
Switch(config-slb-real)#exit
Switch(config-slb-sfarm)#real 10.1.1.3
Switch(config-slb-real)#inservice
Switch(config-slb-real)#exit
Switch(config-slb-sfarm)#exit
Switch(config)#ip slb serverfarm RESTRICTED
Switch(config-slb-sfarm)#real 10.1.1.20
Switch(config-slb-real)#inservice
Switch(config-slb-real)#exit
Switch(config-slb-sfarm)#real 10.1.1.21
Switch(config-slb-real)#inservice
Switch(config-slb-real)#end
Switch#
```

Example 12-17 shows a user displaying the status of the server farms PUBLIC and RESTRICTED, the associated real servers, and their status, respectively.

Example 12-17 *Displaying SLB Real Servers*

```
Switch#show ip slb real

real                    farm name        weight   state          cons
- - - - - - - - - - - - - - - - - - - - - - - - - - - - - - - - - - - - - - - - - -
10.1.1.1                PUBLIC           8        OPERATIONAL    0
10.1.1.2                PUBLIC           8        OPERATIONAL    0
10.1.1.3                PUBLIC           8        OPERATIONAL    0
10.1.1.20               RESTRICTED       8        OPERATIONAL    0
10.1.1.21               RESTRICTED       8        OPERATIONAL    0
```

Example 12-18 shows a user displaying the configuration and status of server farms PUBLIC and RESTRICTED, respectively.

Example 12-18 *Displaying SLB Server Farm*

```
Switch# show ip slb serverfarm

server farm      predictor    nat    reals   bind id
- - - - - - - - - - - - - - - - - - - - - - - - - - - - - - - -
PUBLIC           ROUNDROBIN   none   3       0
RESTRICTED       ROUNDROBIN   none   2       0
```

Configuring Virtual Servers

The following steps describe how to configure virtual servers in Cisco IOS SLB:

Step 1   Define the virtual server.

> `ip slb vserver` *vserver-name*

Step 2   Configure the IP address of the virtual server.

> `virtual` *ip-address* [*network-mask*] {`tcp` | `udp`} [*port-number* | `wsp` |
> `wsp-wtp` | `wsp-wtls` | `wsp-wtp-wtls`] [`service` *service-name*]

Step 3   Associate the primary and secondary server farm to the virtual server.

> `serverfarm` *primary-serverfarm-name* [`backup` *backup-serverfarm-name*
> [`sticky`]]

Step 4   Enable the virtual server.

> `inservice`

Step 5   Specify the clients allowed to access the virtual server.

> `client` *ip-address network-mask*

Example 12-19 shows a user configuring the virtual servers PUBLIC_HTTP and RESTRICTED_HTTP, respectively, with the latter configuration showing how to restrict access to clients in the network 10.4.4.0.

Example 12-19 *Configuring Virtual Servers*

```
Switch#configure terminal
Enter configuration commands, one per line. End with CNTL/Z.
Switch(config)# ip slb vserver PUBLIC_HTTP
Switch(config-slb-vserver)# virtual 10.1.1.100 tcp www
Switch(config-slb-vserver)# serverfarm PUBLIC
Switch(config-slb-vserver)# inservice
Switch(config-slb-vserver)#exit
Switch(config)#ip slb vserver RESTRICTED_HTTP
Switch(config-slb-vserver)#virtual 10.1.1.200 tcp www
Switch(config-slb-vserver)#client 10.4.4.0 255.255.255.0
Switch(config-slb-vserver)#serverfarm RESTRICTED
Switch(config-slb-vserver)#inservice
Switch(config-slb-vserver)#end
Switch#
```

Example 12-20 shows a user verifying the configuration of the virtual servers PUBLIC_HTTP and RESTRICTED_HTTP, respectively.

Example 12-20 *Displaying SLB Virtual Servers*

```
Switch#show ip slb vserver
slb vserver      prot  virtual              state          cons
---------------------------------------------------------------
PUBLIC_HTTP      TCP   10.1.1.100:80        OPERATIONAL    0
RESTRICTED_HTTP  TCP   10.1.1.200:80        OPERATIONAL    0
```

Example 12-21 shows a user verifying the restricted client access and status, respectively.

Example 12-21 *Displaying the Current SLB Connections*

```
Switch#show ip slb connections
vserver          prot client            real              state     nat
-----------------------------------------------------------------------
RESTRICTED_HTTP TCP  10.4.4.0:80        10.1.1.20         CLOSING   none
```

Example 12-22 shows a user displaying detailed information about the restricted client access status.

Example 12-22 *Displaying Detailed Information for an SLB Client*

```
Switch#show ip slb connections client 10.4.4.0 detail
VSTEST_UDP, client = 10.4.4.0:80
  state = CLOSING, real = 10.1.1.20, nat = none
  v_ip = 10.1.1.200:80, TCP, service = NONE
  client_syns = 0, sticky = FALSE, flows attached = 0
```

Example 12-23 shows a user displaying detailed information about the Cisco IOS SLB network status.

Example 12-23 *Displaying SLB Statistics*

```
Switch#show ip slb stats
Pkts via normal switching:  0
Pkts via special switching: 6
Connections Created:        1
Connections Established:    1
Connections Destroyed:      0
Connections Reassigned:     0
Zombie Count:               0
Connections Reused:         0
```

Study Tips

The following bullets review important BCMSN exam preparation points of this chapter. The bullets only briefly highlight the main points of this chapter related to the BCMSN exam. Consult the text of this chapter for additional information regarding these topics. Table 12-7 lists important commands to review for the BCMSN exam:

- When designing a highly available network (uptime of 99.999%), all single points of failure need to be considered and removed by adding network and component redundancy.

- Network redundancy (multiple devices, multiple paths, redundant links) and device-level redundancy (redundant supervisors, redundant power supplies) are required to guarantee a highly available and reliable multilayered switched network.

- On Cisco IOS based Catalyst switches, RPR, RPR+, SSO, and NSF with SSO are the various modes of Supervisor redundancy available. The preferred mode is the NSF with SSO because it provides both Layer 2 and Layer 3 protocol state syncing between active and standby Supervisors, hence guaranteeing the least amount of network impact due to failover, if any at all.

- SSO on Catalyst 4500 and SSO with SRM on Catalyst 6500 provide almost zero interruption for Layer 2 switched traffic during a Supervisor failover.

- For the Catalyst 6500 family of switches running hybrid mode software, the Supervisor Engine high availability feature with Cisco CatOS and the SRM feature for the MSFC provide the lowest-impact redundancy configuration in hybrid mode.

- Power supply redundancy provides protection against power supply failure. The power can be run in redundant or combined mode. In combined mode, both the power supplies operate to provide system power. This configuration is not considered a redundancy feature.

- Various default gateway redundancy protocols exist including HSRP, VRRP, and GLBP. Currently, HSRP is the most popular choice.

- HSRP operates with one router acting as active and the other backup router as a standby router. The active, standby, and other HSRP routers use a virtual IP address for redundancy to hosts. In case the active router fails, the standby router becomes the active router and takes responsibility of the destination MAC and IP of the virtual IP address. In this manner, HSRP failover is transparent to the host.

- Routers running HSRP can be configured for pre-emption such that if a higher priority HSRP peer comes online, the higher-priority router takes over the active router role. Otherwise, the latest active router remains the active router when new HSRP peers come online.

- VRRP is similar to HSRP except that VRRP is an industry standard, whereas HSRP is a Cisco proprietary protocol.

- GLBP is another industry standard feature in which multiple routers not only act as backup default gateway routers but also share load in forwarding traffic, unlike HSRP and VRRP, where only the active router forwards traffic. Note that HSPR and VRRP may be distributed across VLANs, achieving load balancing using VLANs.

- The Cisco IOS SLB features enable load balancing of connections to a group of real servers and hence provide fault tolerance for the group of real servers. With this feature, hosts connect to a single virtual server, which in turn is supported by many real servers that are transparent to the host. IOS SLB also supports many forms of load balancing and redundancy.

Table 12-7   *Commands to Review*

Command	Description
(config-if)#**glbp** *group-number* **ip** *virtual-gateway-address*	Configures the interface of a member of the virtual group with the identified virtual IP address.
(config-if)#**glbp** *group-number* **priority** *priority-value*	Configures the priority of the configured router. The highest value wins election as active router. The default is 100. If routers have the same GLBP priority, the gateway with the highest real IP address becomes the AVG.
(config-if)#**glbp** *group-number* **timers** *hello-value holdtime-value*	Configures the hello timer and hold timer values. Place the argument *msec* before the values to specify subsecond values.
(config-if)#**standby** *group-number* **ip** *virtual-IP-address*	Configures the HSRP standby group with a specified group number and virtual IP address.

continues

Table 12-7 *Commands to Review (Continued)*

Command	Description
(config-if)#**standby** *group-number* **preempt**	Configures HSRP for pre-emption such that the HSRP router may take over if it has higher priority than the current active router.
(config-if)#**standby** *group-number* **priority** *priority_value*	Configures HSRP standby group priority.
(config-if)#**standby** *group-number* **track interface** *interface-id*	Configures HSRP standby group ###.
(config-if)#**vrrp** *group-number* **ip** *virtual-IP-address*	Configures the VRRP group and virtual IP address.
(config-if)#**vrrp** *group-number* **priority** *priority-value*	Configures the VRRP group priority value.
(config-r)#**high-availability**	Enters the HA configuration submode in MSFC IOS.
(config-red)#**mode {rpr|rprplus|sso}**	Configures the redundancy mode.
(config-r-ha)#**single-router-mode**	Configures SRM redundancy mode for hybrid software-based Catalyst 6500 series of switches.
(config)#**redundancy**	Enters the redundancy configuration submode.
(config)#**ip slb serverfarm** *serverfarm-name*	Configures a Cisco IOS SLB server farm.
(config)#**ip slb vserver** *vserver-name*	Configures a Cisco IOS SLB virtual server.
(config-slb-sfarm)#**real** *ip-address-of-the-real-server*	Configures the association of the real server with the SLB server farm.
(config-slb-vserver)#**client** *ip-address network-mask*	Configures the clients allowed to access the virtual server.
(config-slb-vserver)#**inservice**	Enables the virtual server.
(config-slb-vserver)#**serverfarm primary-***serverfarm-name* [**backup** *backup-serverfarm-name* [**sticky**]]	Configures the association of the primary and secondary server farm to the virtual server.
(config-slb-vserver)#**virtual** *ip-address* [*network-mask*] {**tcp** | **udp**} [**port-number** | **wsp** | **wsp-wtp** | **wsp-wtls** | **wsp-wtp-wtls**] [**service** *service-name*]	Configures parameters of an IOS SLB virtual server.
show glbp	Displays the GLBP configuration and status of the configured interfaces.
show ip slb connections	Displays the information regarding clients currently connected to the virtual servers.

Table 12-7   *Commands to Review (Continued)*

Command	Description
show ip slb vserver	Displays configured virtual servers and operation status.
show redundancy	Displays the redundancy state on MSFC IOS on hybrid software-based system.
show redundancy states	Displays the redundancy state of the active and standby Supervisor Engine.
show spanning-tree summary	Displays spanning-tree summary information for each VLAN configured on a switch.
show standby	Displays the details of HSRP standby groups configured on the Catalyst switch.
show vrrp interface *interface-id*	Displays VRRP configuration and status for an interface.

Summary

Providing redundancy in a multilayer switched network is accomplished through subsystem (device-level) redundancy, link redundancy, and network design redundancy.

Configuration Exercise: Configuring and Verifying RPR+ and HSRP

Complete this configuration exercise to practice working with features discussed in this chapter.

Required Resources

The following resources and equipment are required to complete this exercise:

- Catalyst 6500 switches or equivalent, as shown in Figure 12-24
- A terminal server connected to the console port of each laboratory device
- A PC connected to the terminal server to access the devices

Exercise Objective

The devices in the network should be connected and ready for use. In this configuration exercise, you will configure and verify some of the features reviewed in this chapter. After completing this exercise, you will be able to do the following:

- Configure and verify RPR+
- Configure and verify HSRP

This exercise assumes that the switches are running currently in RPR mode of Supervisor Engine redundancy, and that VLAN 1 and VLAN 2 are configured with the IP addresses shown in Figure 12-24.

Network Diagram

Figure 12-24 shows the network layout for this configuration exercise.

Figure 12-24 *Configuration Topology*

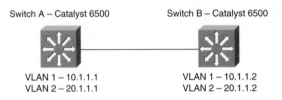

Switch A – Catalyst 6500   Switch B – Catalyst 6500

VLAN 1 – 10.1.1.1   VLAN 1 – 10.1.1.2
VLAN 2 – 20.1.1.1   VLAN 2 – 20.1.1.2

Command List

In this configuration exercise, you will use the commands listed in Table 12-8. The commands are listed in alphabetical order so that you can easily locate the information you need. Refer to this list if you need configuration command assistance during the lab exercise.

Table 12-8 *Command List for Configuration Exercise*

Command	Description
configure terminal	From privileged EXEC mode, enters global configuration mode
end	Exits configuration mode
exit	Exits the current mode
interface VLAN *vlan-id*	Enters interface configuration mode of VLAN interface for a Catalyst switch
mode rpr-plus	Configures RPR+ redundancy mode
redundancy	Enters the redundancy subconfiguration mode
show redundancy states	Displays the redundancy state
show standby	Displays the details of HSRP standby groups configured on the Catalyst switch
standby *group-number* **ip** *virtual_IP_address*	Configures HSRP standby group with the specified group and virtual IP address
standby *group-number* **preempt**	Configures HSRP preempt such that the HSRP router may take over if it has higher priority than the current active router
standby *group-number* **priority** *priority_value*	Configures HSRP standby group priority to change from the default value of 100

Task 1: Configure and Verify RPR+

Step 1 Configure RPR+ using the **mode rpr-plus** command under **redundancy** configuration on switches A and B.

```
SwitchA#configure terminal
Enter configuration commands, one per line.  End with CNTL/Z.
SwitchA(config)#redundancy
SwitchA(config-red)#mode rpr-plus
SwitchA(config-red)#end
SwitchA#

SwitchB#configure terminal
Enter configuration commands, one per line.  End with CNTL/Z.
SwitchB(config)#redundancy
SwitchB(config-red)#mode rpr-plus
SwitchB(config-red)#end
SwitchB#
```

Step 2 Using the **show redundancy states** command, verify that switches A and B are running RPR+ mode.

```
SwitchA#show redundancy states
       my state = 13 -ACTIVE
     peer state = 8  -STANDBY HOT
           Mode = Duplex
           Unit = Secondary
        Unit ID = 2

Redundancy Mode (Operational) = Route Processor Redundancy Plus
Redundancy Mode (Configured)  = Route Processor Redundancy Plus
     Split Mode = Disabled
   Manual Swact = Enabled
 Communications = Up

   client count = 11
 client_notification_TMR = 30000 milliseconds
        keep_alive TMR = 9000 milliseconds
      keep_alive count = 0
  keep_alive threshold = 18
         RF debug mask = 0x0
SwitchB#show redundancy states
       my state = 13 -ACTIVE
     peer state = 8  -STANDBY HOT
           Mode = Duplex
           Unit = Secondary
        Unit ID = 2
```

```
Redundancy Mode (Operational) = Route Processor Redundancy Plus
Redundancy Mode (Configured)  = Route Processor Redundancy Plus
          Split Mode = Disabled
       Manual Swact = Enabled
     Communications = Up

       client count = 11
  client_notification_TMR = 30000 milliseconds
           keep_alive TMR = 9000 milliseconds
         keep_alive count = 0
     keep_alive threshold = 18
             RF debug mask = 0x0
```

Task 2: Configure and Verify HSRP

Step 1   Configure an HSRP standby group on VLAN 1 with a virtual address of 10.1.1.254 on switches A and B. Use the **standby** *group-number* **ip** *virtual_IP_address* command to define the group.

```
SwitchA#configure terminal
Enter configuration commands, one per line.  End with CNTL/Z.
SwitchA(config)#interface vlan 1
SwitchA(config-if)#standby 1 ip 10.1.1.254
SwitchA(config-if)#end
SwitchB#configure terminal
Enter configuration commands, one per line.  End with CNTL/Z.
SwitchB(config)#interface vlan 1
SwitchB(config-if)#standby 1 ip 10.1.1.254
SwitchB(config-if)#end
```

Step 2   Configure an HSRP group priority of 150 for the standby group configured on the VLAN 1 interface on switch A so that it has a higher group priority than switch B. Use the **standby** *group-number* **priority** *priority_value* command to configure the priority.

```
SwitchA#configure terminal
Enter configuration commands, one per line.  End with CNTL/Z.
SwitchA(config)#interface vlan 1
SwitchA(config-if)#standby 1 priority 150
SwitchA(config-if)#end
```

Step 3   Configure the HSRP standby group on VLAN 2 with a virtual address of 20.1.1.254 on switch A and switch B. Use the **standby** *group-number* **ip** *virtual_IP_address* command to define the group.

```
SwitchA#configure terminal
```

```
Enter configuration commands, one per line.  End with CNTL/Z.
SwitchA(config)#interface vlan 2
SwitchA(config-if)#standby 2  ip 20.1.1.254
SwitchA(config-if)#end
SwitchA#
SwitchB#configure terminal
Enter configuration commands, one per line.  End with CNTL/Z.
SwitchB(config)#interface vlan 2
SwitchB(config-if)#standby 2 ip 20.1.1.254
SwitchB(config-if)#end
SwitchB#
```

Step 4   Configure an HSRP group priority of 150 for the standby group
configured on the VLAN 2 interface on switch B to make sure that it has
a higher group priority than switch A. Use the **standby** *group-number*
priority *priority_value* command to configure the priority.

```
SwitchB#configure terminal
Enter configuration commands, one per line.  End with CNTL/Z.
SwitchB(config)#interface vlan 2
SwitchB(config-if)#standby 2 priority 150
SwitchB(config-if)#end
```

Step 5   Using the **show standby** command, verify that switch A is the active
router for standby group 1 and switch B is the active router for standby
group 2. The splitting up of the active router responsibilities ensures load
sharing.

```
SwitchA#show standby
Vlan1 - Group 1
  Local state is Active, priority 150
  Hellotime 3 sec, holdtime 10 sec
  Next hello sent in 2.120
  Virtual IP address is 10.1.1.254 configured
  Active router is local
  Standby router is 10.1.1.2 expires in 7.816
  Virtual mac address is 0000.0c07.ac01
  2 state changes, last state change 00:07:04
  IP redundancy name is "hsrp-Vl1-1" (default)
Vlan2 - Group 2
  Local state is Standby, priority 100
  Hellotime 3 sec, holdtime 10 sec
  Next hello sent in 1.476
  Virtual IP address is 20.1.1.254 configured
  Active router is 20.1.1.2, priority 150 expires in 9.672
  Standby router is local
1 state changes, last state change 00:02:16
  IP redundancy name is "hsrp-Vl2-2" (default)
```

```
SwitchB#show standby
Vlan1 - Group 1
  Local state is Standby, priority 100
  Hellotime 3 sec, holdtime 10 sec
  Next hello sent in 1.476
  Virtual IP address is 10.1.1.254 configured
  Active router is 10.1.1.1, priority 150 expires in 9.400
  Standby router is local
  1 state changes, last state change 00:01:11
  IP redundancy name is "hsrp-Vl1-1" (default)
Vlan2 - Group 2
  Local state is Active, priority 150
  Hellotime 3 sec, holdtime 10 sec
  Next hello sent in 0.360
  Virtual IP address is 20.1.1.254 configured
  Active router is local
  Standby router is 20.1.1.1 expires in 8.748
  Virtual mac address is 0000.0c07.ac02
  2 state changes, last state change 00:04:28
  IP redundancy name is "hsrp-Vl2-2" (default)
```

Step 6 Using the **standby** *group-number* **preempt** command, configure the HSRP preempt option on switches A and B such that switches A and B remain the active routers for groups 1 and 2, respectively, after any failures. This will ensure load sharing.

```
SwitchA#configure terminal
Enter configuration commands, one per line.  End with CNTL/Z.
SwitchA(config)#interface vlan 1
SwitchA(config-if)#standby 1 preempt
SwitchA(config-if)#end
SwitchA#SwitchB#configure terminal
Enter configuration commands, one per line.  End with CNTL/Z.
SwitchB(config)#interface vlan 2
SwitchB(config-if)#standby 2 preempt
SwitchB(config-if)#end
SwitchB#
```

Review Questions

For multiple-choice questions, there may be more than one correct answer.

1 True or False: SRM on a hybrid mode Catalyst 6500 switch allows configuration only on the designated MSFC.

2 True or False: Redundancy within network devices is enough to guarantee no single point of failure.

3 True or False: VRRP allows the use of multiple master routers for a VRRP group.

4 How long does a standby router take to detect the loss of the active router in HSRP with default timer values?

a   15 seconds

b   3 seconds

c   10 seconds

d   9 seconds

e   <1 second

5 What is the default advertisement of the VRRP master router?

a   3 seconds

b   1 second

c   10 seconds

d   2 seconds

e   None of the above

6 Which of the following is one of the SLB redirection modes?

a   Hybrid mode

b   Native mode

c   Indirect mode

d   Directed mode

7 What is the default GLBP load-balancing method?

a   Round-robin

b   Weighted

c   Host-dependent

d   Dispatched

e   Directed

8 How many member routers can be forwarding in a GLBP group?

   a 4

   b 1

   c 2

   d 3

   e No limit

9 What is the expected failover time for NSF with SSO on the Catalyst 6500 family of switches?

   a 2 to 4 minutes

   b 0 to 3 seconds

   c 30 to 60 seconds

   d About 15 minutes

   e None of the above

10 Which of the following routing protocols is not supported as part of NSF?

   a BGP

   b OSPF

   c ISIS

   d EIGRP

   e RIP

11 What is the expected failover time for SSO mode for Layer 2 switching on the Catalyst 4500 family of switches?

   a 2 to 4 minutes

   b 30 to 60 seconds

   c Less than 3 seconds

   d Subsecond

   e None of the above

This chapter covers the following topics:

- Identifying the Network and Device Design Considerations Used to Support Voice Traffic
- Implementing Voice VLANs for Carrying Voice Traffic
- Explaining the Recommendations for Implementing IP Telephony in the Multilayer Switched Network

## CHAPTER 13

Best Practices for Deploying Cisco IP Telephony Using Cisco Catalyst Switches

Deploying IP telephony as part of a converged network has many benefits, including more efficient use of network resources, consolidation of expenses, increased revenue, and innovation that leads to improved productivity.

However, deploying IP telephony as part of a converged network also places strict design requirements (also known as *best practices*) on the network infrastructure. For example, for IP telephony to maintain its required five nines (99.999%) uptime, the multilayer switched network must provide sufficient bandwidth and quick convergence after network failures or changes. Providing sufficient bandwidth to IP telephony requires a well-planned network design with the use of quality of service (QoS). Providing five nines uptime is not difficult, but it also requires a well-planned network design and QoS plus additional redundancy and resiliency features. This chapter introduces and recaps these design considerations that are used to support IP telephony. Most of the features discussed in the book thus far, such as Hot Standby Routing Protocol (HSRP), QoS, and so on, are used in providing five nines uptime to IP telephony. The following list summarizes the layout of this chapter:

- Why Include VoIP When Building a Converged Network?
- Introduction to IP Telephony Components
- Network design Recommendations for IP Telephony
- Best pPractices for Deploying IP Telephony in the Enterprise Composite Network Model

Why Include VoIP When Building a Converged Network?

This section explains in more detail the business value of including VoIP when building a converged network. The justifications include the following:

- **More efficient use of bandwidth and equipment**—For example, traditional telephony networks use a 64-kbps channel for every voice call. Packet telephony shares bandwidth among multiple logical connections and offloads traffic volume from existing voice switches.

- **Lower costs for telephony network transmission**—A substantial amount of equipment is needed to combine 64-kbps channels into high-speed links for transport across the network. Packet telephony statistically multiplexes voice traffic alongside data traffic. This consolidation represents substantial savings on capital equipment and operations costs.

- **Consolidation of voice and data network expenses**—Data networks that function as separate networks from voice networks become major traffic carriers. The underlying voice networks are converted to use the packet-switched architecture to create a single integrated communications network with a common switching and transmission system. The benefit is significant cost savings on network equipment and operations.

- **Increased revenue from new services**—For instance, packet telephony enables new integrated services, such as broadcast-quality audio, unified messaging, and real-time voice and data collaboration. These services increase employee productivity and profit margins well above those of basic voice services. In addition, these services enable companies and service providers to differentiate themselves and improve their market position.

- **Capability to leverage access to new communications devices**—Using packet technology enables companies and service providers to reach devices that are largely inaccessible to the time-division multiplexing (TDM) infrastructures of today. Examples of such devices are computers, wireless devices, household appliances, personal digital assistants, and cable set-top boxes. Intelligent access to such devices enables companies and service providers to increase the volume of communications they deliver, the breadth of services they offer, and the number of subscribers they serve. Packet technology, therefore, enables companies to market new devices, including videophones, multimedia terminals, and advanced IP phones.

- **Flexible pricing structures**—Companies and service providers with packet-switched networks can transform their service and pricing models. Because network bandwidth can be dynamically allocated, network usage no longer needs to be measured in minutes or distance. Dynamic allocation gives service providers the flexibility to meet the needs of their customers in ways that bring them the greatest benefits.

- **Emphasis on greater innovation in services**—Unified communications use the IP infrastructure to consolidate communication methods that were previously independent; for example, fax, voice mail, e-mail, wireline telephones, cellular telephones, call centers, and the web. The IP infrastructure provides users with a common method to access messages and initiate real-time communications—independent of time, location, or device.

This section described the business reasons for a converged network with VoIP. The remaining sections of this chapter focus on the technical details.

Introduction to IP Telephony Components

IP telephony is a term used to describe the technology for transmitting voice communications over a data network using open-standards-based IP. Cisco IP Telephony solutions use multilayer switched networks. As such, multilayer switched networks provide a single network infrastructure for the transmission of data, voice, and video traffic—delivering the business benefits of a converged network. The benefit of using a single network for data, voice, and video is increased productivity, greater business flexibility, productivity, and reduced operational costs.

With Cisco IP Telephony, you have a comprehensive suite of IP-based hardware and software solutions to choose from that scale to individual network needs. For example, Cisco IP Telephony solutions include solutions for as few as 20 phones to more than 10,000. In addition, this suite of solutions can integrate with existing systems to help you migrate to full IP Communications and protect your existing technology investments.

Aside from the standard data network, the Cisco IP Telephony solution has four primary components:

- **Infrastructure**—The network infrastructure includes components used to translate calls from the IP network to the traditional analog voice networks. These components include Public Switched Telephone Network (PSTN) gateways, analog phone support, and digital signal processor (DSP), farms. Cisco IP Telephony infrastructure solutions can support multiple client types such as hardware phones, software phones, and video devices, and they can provide options for integrating traditional PBX, voice mail, and directory systems.

- **IP phones**—Cisco IP Phones combine the functions of a traditional telephone with an Ethernet connection and optional customizations, such as access to stock quotes, employee extension numbers, and web-based content. In addition, Cisco IP Phones support customization via XML for voice applications. The Cisco IP Communicator is a Windows-based application for the PC that offers IP functionality in conjunction with a Cisco IP Phone or as a standalone end station.

- **Cisco CallManager**—This software-based call processing agent extends enterprise telephony features and functions to packet telephony network devices such as IP phones, media processing devices, VoIP gateways, and multimedia applications. In brief, Cisco CallManager is responsible for call processing (that is, call routing).

- **Voice applications**—Voice applications are physically independent from the call processing and voice processing infrastructure, and they may reside anywhere within your network. Voice applications can include a call center application used to record incoming calls.

Figure 13-1 summarizes the VoIP components.

Figure 13-1 *VoIP Components Template*

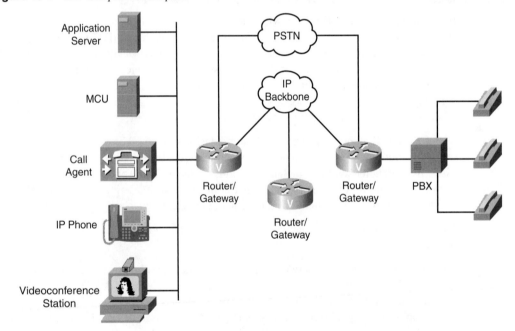

Cisco.com discusses each of these components in more detail. For the purposes of this chapter and for the BCMSN switching exam, the component explanations are sufficient for understanding their role in the multilayer switched network.

Network Design Recommendations for IP Telephony

Most IP telephony installations use an existing network infrastructure. Generally, these network infrastructures require enhancements or additional configurations to correctly manage IP telephony solutions. Foremost, VoIP and voice signaling traffic require strict priority over all other data traffic. Chapter 10, "Understanding and Implementing Quality of Service in Cisco Multilayer Switched Networks," discusses many QoS solutions for providing priority to IP telephony. However, QoS is only one requirement for a network to support IP telephony. The following list summarizes the design recommendations for supporting IP telephony:

- Implement network and Catalyst switch component redundancy as best as possible. Avoiding outages due to simple cable, component, or power supply failures is crucial. Having multiple redundant network paths allows for large network failures to be isolated and prevents VoIP outages. However, keep in mind that VoIP should not use asynchronous paths.

- Implement QoS classification, marking, and congestion management for IP telephony components such as Cisco IP Phones, Cisco CallManagers, Cisco IP Phone clients, IP gateways, and so on. Chapter 10 discusses how to apply QoS and discusses several examples that are applicable to Cisco IP Phones. At minimum, the QoS design should classify VoIP traffic as high priority and schedule the traffic out of transmit queues with high priority. WAN interfaces that carry VoIP traffic in the Enterprise Edge submodules require additional QoS configurations; these configurations are summarized in Chapter 10.

- Place VoIP traffic on a separate VLAN. A simple method of deploying a separate VLAN for Cisco IP Phones is via the use of voice VLANs (auxiliary VLANs). The "Voice (Auxiliary) VLANs" section of this chapter discusses this method of segmentation.

- Consider using inline power to supply power to Cisco IP Phones. Cisco IP Phones require power either via a power supply or via inline power on the cabling plant. Using inline power to provide power to IP phones yields flexibility in phone placement. The following Cisco IOS–based Catalyst switches support inline power: Catalyst 3550, 3560, 3750, 4500, and 6500. Redundant power for network routers and switches is another consideration for high availability.

- Verify whether the physical cable plant is sufficient to support IP telephony. At minimum, IP telephony and VoIP solutions require Category 5 cable plants. Cable plants in this context refer to the physical cable and interconnects in your facility. Improper or deficient cable plants affect the operability of IP telephony.

The following subsections go into more detail about the following recommended features and design criteria for deploying IP telephony in a multilayer switched network:

- QoS
- Voice (auxiliary) VLANs
- Network Bandwidth Provisioning
- Power Considerations
- Network Management
- IP Telephony High Availability
- Security

QoS

VoIP traffic has strict requirements concerning delay and *jitter* (variance in packet delay). To meet the requirements for IP telephony, the Cisco AVVID IP telephony solution uses a range of IP QoS features, such as classification, queuing, congestion detection, traffic shaping, and compression. Figure 13-2 illustrates the differences between VoIP traffic and data traffic.

Figure 13-2 *Differences in IP Flow Behavior Between Data and Voice Traffic*

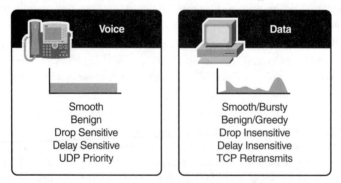

Voice	Data
Smooth	Smooth/Bursty
Benign	Benign/Greedy
Drop Sensitive	Drop Insensitive
Delay Sensitive	Delay Insensitive
UDP Priority	TCP Retransmits

The overall goal of QoS in the network is to minimize packet loss, delay, and jitter. A network that experiences congestion also experiences these problems. QoS configurations give critical applications a higher priority for service such that the critical applications experience less service degradation during times of congestion. In many networks, IP telephony is the most critical application. However, in many large enterprise networks, other applications are equally critical, such as financial transaction processing, stock tickers, and so on.

Applying classification, marking, traffic conditioning, congestion avoidance, and congestion management, as discussed in Chapter 10, allows you to design a network that is capable of supporting IP telephony with other critical applications. The next section discusses another useful tool in deploying IP telephony with Cisco IP Phones: voice VLANs.

Voice (Auxiliary) VLANs

Cisco IP Phones have an additional port for a PC connection; as a result, many Cisco IP Phone installations daisy-chain a PC to the Cisco IP Phone. Because both the Cisco IP Phone and the workstation reside on the same interface, configuring the respective Catalyst switch interface for a specific VLAN results in both the Cisco IP Phone and workstation residing in the same VLAN. Figure 13-3 illustrates the Cisco IP Phone and workstation topology.

Figure 13-3 *Cisco IP Phone Daisy-Chain Topology*

Cisco Catalyst switches support a unique feature, referred to as voice VLANs in Cisco IOS, that places the Cisco IP Phone and workstation in separate VLANs. Voice VLANs allow a single access port to overlay a second VLAN for strictly VoIP traffic.

Besides the Catalyst switch configuration, no additional configuration is necessary on the Cisco IP Phone to use voice VLANs. The following steps detail, at a high level, how voice VLANs, configured with a specific VLAN ID, operate on Catalyst switches:

Step 1 The user attaches a Cisco IP Phone to a Catalyst switch configured for voice VLANs.

Step 2 The Catalyst switch immediately sends Cisco Discovery Protocol (CDP) frames to the Cisco IP Phone on link-up with the typical CDP information, including the voice VLAN-ID.

Step 3 The Cisco IP Phone receives these CDP frames, interprets the voice VLAN-ID, and begins sending VoIP traffic with 802.1Q tags for the respective voice VLAN.

Cisco IP Phones also mark their egress frames with specific differentiated services code point (DSCP) and class of service (CoS) values. With voice VLANs, the Cisco IP Phone still sends ingress frames from the workstation attached to the PC port of the phone without a VLAN tag. As a result, the attached workstation still operates in the access VLAN. Figure 13-4 depicts a logical representation of voice VLANs.

Figure 13-4 *Logical Depiction of Voice VLANs*

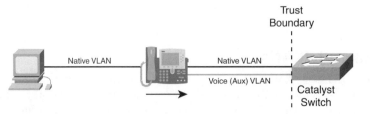

With Cisco IP Phones in their own IP subnets and VLANs, network administrators can easily identify and troubleshoot network problems. In addition, network administrators can create and enforce QoS or security policies on a per-VLAN basis. With the voice VLAN feature, Cisco enables network administrators to gain all the advantages of physical infrastructure convergence while maintaining separate logical topologies for voice and data terminals, creating an effective way to manage a multiservice network.

To configure Catalyst switches running Cisco IOS for voice VLANs, use the following command:

```
switchport voice vlan {vlan-id | dot1p | none | untagged}
```

vlan-id refers to the 802.1Q tagged VLAN that is used for traffic to and from the Cisco IP Phone. The switch informs the Cisco IP Phone of this VLAN by using CDP. This is the recommended configuration for Catalyst switches using Cisco IP Phones. The **dot1p** option configures the switch to inform the Cisco IP Phone to use 802.1P priority tagging for IP phone traffic and to use the default native VLAN (VLAN 0) for all traffic. This configuration is useful in trusting ingress CoS values from IP phones without using a separate voice VLAN. This configuration is common for third-party IP phones that do not support CDP. The **none** option effectively disables the voice VLAN feature, and the Cisco IP Phone uses its own configuration to send untagged frames. The **untagged** option configures the switch to inform the Cisco IP Phone to explicitly use untagged frames.

Example 13-1 illustrates an interface configured for voice VLANs. Note that the voice VLAN feature refers to the native VLAN as the access VLAN.

Example 13-1 *Sample Interface Configuration for Voice VLANs in Cisco IOS*

```
(text deleted)
!
mls qos
!
(text deleted)
!
interface FastEthernet0/24
 switchport access vlan 2
```

Example 13-1 *Sample Interface Configuration for Voice VLANs in Cisco IOS (Continued)*

```
 switchport mode dynamic desirable
 switchport voice vlan 700
 mls qos trust cos
 spanning-tree portfast
 !
(text deleted)
 !
```

In Example 13-1, the Cisco IP Phone transmits all of its frames with an 802.1Q tag for VLAN 700. The workstation that is attached to the Cisco IP Phone resides in VLAN 2, and both the Cisco IP Phone and the Catalyst switch transmit and receive all traffic to and from the workstation without a VLAN tag on the native (access) VLAN. The switch also trusts all ingress CoS values in the configuration shown in Example 13-1; refer to Chapter 10 for more details on the QoS configurations.

Cisco CatOS refers to voice VLANs as auxiliary VLANs. To configure auxiliary VLANs in Cisco CatOS, use the following command:

```
set port auxiliaryvlan  mod/ports  {vlan  |  untagged  |  dot1p  |  none}
```

Network Bandwidth Provisioning

Properly provisioning the network bandwidth is a major component of designing a successful IP telephony network. The sum of the calculated bandwidth of all applications, including those for voice, video, and data, should not exceed approximately 75 percent of the total available bandwidth for any specified link. Seventy-five percent is a recommended threshold in preventing congestion, because traffic flows tend to burst above the required bandwidth. Note that even when the total required bandwidth for all applications is under 75 percent of available bandwidth, a QoS design is still necessary and recommended. Nevertheless, if the applications need more than 75 percent of bandwidth, design the network for additional links or higher-bandwidth links.

From a traffic standpoint, a single IP telephony call consists of two data flows:

- The voice carrier stream, which consists of Real-Time Transport Protocol (RTP) packets that contain the actual voice samples.

- The call control signaling, which consists of packets belonging to one of several protocols, according to the endpoints involved in the call—for example, H.323, SIP, or Media Gateway Control Protocol (MGCP), and so on. Call control functions include steps to set up, maintain, tear down, or redirect a call.

Bandwidth provisioning calculations need to include not only the voice stream traffic, but also the call control traffic.

A VoIP packet consists of the Layer 2 link header, IP header, User Datagram Protocol (UDP) header, RTP header, and voice payload. The link header varies in size according to the Layer 2 media used. Table 13-1 lists the sizes of the other headers.

Table 13-1 *VoIP Packet Overhead for Ethernet Frames*

Header	Size
Ethernet header	14 bytes
IP header	20 bytes
UDP header	8 bytes
RTP header	12 bytes

The VoIP packet overhead is significant because it is a factor in determining the necessary bandwidth requirements in the multilayer switched network. Moreover, the voice sampling rate determines the bit rate. The sampling rate varies based on voice codec. The most popular codecs are G.711 and G.729, which use a total bandwidth (including the IP and Ethernet headers) of 87.2 Kbps and 31.2 Kbps, respectively. When designing a multilayer switched network, determining the amount of bandwidth needed for the maximum concurrent voice calls is a requirement, especially for low-speed WAN interfaces, using the total frame bit rate including all the headers.

For a complete discussion on bandwidth provisioning for IP telephony solutions, refer to the following document on Cisco.com:

"Voice Quality: Voice Over IP – Per Call Bandwidth Consumption"
http://www.cisco.com/en/US/tech/tk652/tk698/
technologies_tech_note09186a0080094ae2.shtml

Cisco.com also includes the TAC Voice Bandwidth Codec Calculator tool for calculating bandwidth requirements for VoIP calls.

Power Considerations

Campus and building power availability potentially affect IP telephony solutions. IP phones can use power from several different sources. These sources include power directly from Catalyst switches with inline power capabilities, an inline power patch panel, or an AC power supply. For more information about provisioning the Catalyst 6500 family of switches for inline power, refer to the following document on Cisco.com:

"Understanding IP Phone In-Line Power Provisioning on the Catalyst 6500/6000 Switch" http://www.cisco.com/en/US/products/hw/switches/ps708/
products_tech_note09186a0080114add.shtml

Moreover, the loss of power does not affect one device at a time, and generally affects an entire building or multiple buildings. As a result, a significant power outage may affect all devices in the IP telephony solution, including the Building Distribution and Campus Backbone submodules, telephony gateways, and call-processing equipment such as Cisco CallManager servers.

To maintain a highly available IP telephony solution during power anomalies, campus networks require a power-protection strategy.

Providing high availability with a power-protection strategy requires the use of uninterruptible power supply (UPS) systems with a minimum battery life of 1 hour and a 4-hour repair time for UPS system failures. In addition, a power generator is an alternate means of providing power during an outage. The recommendation for any IP telephony solution includes a UPS or generator backup. In addition, the power-protection strategy should include UPS systems that have auto-restart capability and a service contract for 4-hour repair for the UPS system or generator.

In summary, recommendations for a power-protection strategy for an IP telephony solution deployed in a multilayer switched network include the following:

- UPS systems that can provide sufficient power at full load for at least 1 hour. For example, if your Catalyst switch uses 20 amps at 208 volts during steady-state, use a UPS that can provide 1 hour of standby time at 20 amps. Undersizing UPS is common; make sure you specify the UPS power requirements based on the power requirements of the switch and the necessary Power-over-Ethernet (PoE) requirements.

- UPS or generator backup sufficient for providing uninterrupted power to all IP telephony devices for at least 1 hour with an ideal run time of 4 hours.

- UPS systems with auto-restart capability after power is restored.

- UPS system-monitoring software and features for preventive maintenance.

- Four-hour service response for UPS system repairs.

For more information about power protection requirements for IP telephony networks, consult the following white paper on Cisco.com:

"IP Telephony: The Five Nines Story"

Network Management

In traditional voice networks, there is a distinct set of voice management concepts and processes. The convergence of voice and data has brought about a similar merge of data network and voice-only management.

In fact, this merging of management tasks and processes is one of the key benefits of using a converged network as opposed to a dedicated voice-only network. However, it is still necessary to understand the traditional voice-only management concepts to relate the features available in that technology to the converged network management techniques.

When deploying IP telephony in a multilayer switched network, evaluate and design a sufficient voice network management system. For more information on network management for IP telephony solutions, refer to the following web page on Cisco.com:

"IP Telephony Management" http://www.cisco.com/en/US/netsol/ns340/ns394/ns107/ns167/networking_solutions_package.html

IP Telephony High Availability

Cisco SONA telephony is based on a distributed model for high availability. Cisco CallManager clusters support redundancy. All IP telephony gateways support the ability to "re-home" to a secondary Cisco CallManager in the event that a primary Cisco CallManager fails, thereby providing redundancy. This differs from call survivability in the event of a Cisco CallManager or network failure, where the call is routed to an alternate gateway, such as an MGCP gateway.

As with any network capability, you need to plan redundancy for critical components such as the CallManager and the associated gateway and infrastructure devices that support the voice network. In terms of the multilayer switched network, additional switch ports and switches may be necessary for deploying high availability within the IP telephony solution. For more information about CallManager redundancy, consult the following document on Cisco.com:

"CallManager: Redundancy"

Security

With the advent of IP telephony, which uses IP data network devices for voice communication, the potential exists for malicious attacks on call-processing components and IP telephony applications. As such, with any data network, IP telephony solutions require security methods.

To help safeguard against attacks on IP telephony components, you should implement the same security features as you would for any other network devices. In regards to the multilayer switched network, consider deploying the following security measures when deploying IP telephony solutions as a first-level security model:

- Data and voice segmentation using features such as voice VLANs
- Access control and packet filtering up to Layer 7 using firewalls and access lists on routers and switches
- 802.1X with voice VLANs to prevent unauthorized access to the network
- Intrusion detection systems (IDS) to detect malicious behavior in the network
- Private VLANs to isolate traffic and prevent direct user-to-user communication

- Port security restricting access to a maximum of two devices
- Network Access Control (NAC)
- Firewalls and VPN integration, where appropriate

As a second level of security in an IP telephony-enabled multilayer switched network, the recommended practice is to deploy the following:

- Use Digital Certificates on all Cisco IP Phones and Cisco CallManager servers.
- Use authenticated and encrypted Transport Layer Security (TLS or SSL version 3.0) signaling to avoid spoofing (man-in-the middle) attacks.
- Use Secure Real-Time Protocol (SRTP) media encryption to prevent eavesdropping of calls.
- Use Integrated Cisco Security Agent in Cisco CallManager servers and Cisco Unity servers to prevent host-based hijacks, worms, viruses, and attacks.
- Use Layer 3 VPNs and route authentication.
- Deploy IP Source Guard, additional firewalls, intrusion detection, and intrusion protection systems to prevent, mitigate, and quickly find malicious entities.
- Deploy AAA for a higher level of security and monitoring.
- Deploy protection against DHCP spoofing.
- Disable GARP and PC access to voice VLAN through IP phone.
- Enable IPsec encryption to gateways.
- Disable and minimize unused services.
- Deploy QoS to mitigate network-based traffic attacks.

Best Practices for Deploying IP Telephony in the Enterprise Composite Network Model

This section discusses deploying IP telephony in the composite network model. Specifically, it discusses the recommended Catalyst switch features for deployment in all the submodules of the Enterprise Composite Network Model. Most of the features listed are standard features for data networks and not necessarily specific to IP telephony deployments.

In the network topology shown in Figure 13-5, the Building Access submodule connects the IP telephony user devices, such as Cisco IP Phones. The Data Center access submodule connects the call-processing devices such as Cisco CallManagers. The Enterprise Edge submodule connects the Internet routers, firewalls, and IP gateways to the network.

In terms of features, consider deploying these features in the Building Access submodule for IP telephony deployments:

- QoS to differentiate service for VoIP and signaling traffic
- Voice VLANs for segmentation of data and voice traffic
- Spanning Tree Protocol (STP) PortFast for immediate forwarding of VoIP traffic on switch interfaces
- STP UplinkFast for higher availability in Layer 2–only access layer switches
- STP Root Guard for protection against anomalous switches becoming root bridge in the spanning-tree topology
- Aggressive mode Unidirectional Link Detection (A-UDLD) to achieve higher availability and redundancy

The current recommendation for most network designs is to apply Layer 3 to the Building Distribution submodules. As a result, typical redundancy features are necessary in this submodule. These features include the following:

- Layer 3 redundancy using Hot Standby Routing Protocol (HSRP) or Virtual Router Redundancy Protocol (VRRP)
- Open Shortest Path First (OSPF) or Enhanced Interior Gateway Routing Protocol (EIGRP) with adequately tuned timers
- A-UDLD
- QoS to differentiate service to VoIP and signaling traffic

In the Campus Backbone submodule, deploy the following features for IP telephony solutions. This submodule generally has sufficient redundancy as deployed with data-only networks:

- A-UDLD
- QoS to differentiate service to VoIP and signaling traffic

Figure 13-5 *Example Network Topology Deploying Cisco VoIP*

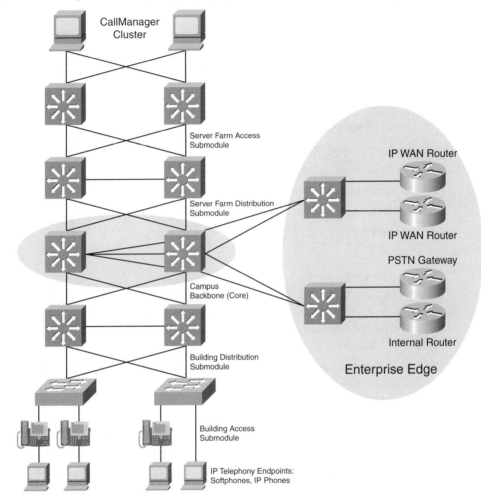

Study Tips

The following bullets review important BCMSN certification exam preparation points of this chapter. The bullets briefly highlight the main points of this chapter related to the BCMSN exam and should be used only as supplemental study material. Consult the text of this chapter for additional information regarding these topics. Table 13-2 lists important commands to review for the BCMSN certification exam:

- *IP telephony* is the term used to describe the technology for transmitting voice communications over a data network using open-standards-based IP.

- IP telephony reduces infrastructure and support costs, increases flexibility, and adds numerous features to telephony.

- With a Cisco multilayer switched network, data, voice, video, and storage can be transmitted simultaneously over the same network infrastructure.

- The four main components of IP telephony in reference to building Cisco multilayer switched networks are as follows:

    — Infrastructure

    — IP phones

    — Cisco CallManager servers

    — Voice applications

- The infrastructure component of IP telephony includes the following devices:

    — PSTN gateways

    — DSP farms

    — PBXs

    — Directory systems

- The IP phones of the IP telephony design are used to place IP calls over an Ethernet network. An IP phone might be a standalone device such as the Cisco IP Phone 7970 or a Cisco IP Communicator, which runs under Microsoft Windows 2000, XP, 2003, or Vista (future).

- The Cisco CallManager component of IP telephony is responsible for "routing" calls (call processing). The Cisco CallManager server directs calls to other IP phones, PSTN gateways, multimedia applications, and so on.

- The Voice Application component of IP telephony includes applications that use both the data and voice capabilities of the Cisco multilayer switched network. Voice applications include call center applications and call ordering applications.

- QoS is an important feature of IP telephony. Prioritizing IP telephony over all other traffic in the network is important. Even if there is ample bandwidth and no congestion in a multilayer switched network, QoS can shield IP telephony from broadcast storms, Layer 2 loops, and malicious traffic.

- In terms of configuring QoS for IP telephony, classify the traffic accordingly and prioritize QoS over all other traffic using congestion management (scheduling). IP telephony does not require large output queue (buffer) sizes because "late" packets should be dropped rather than delivered.

- Voice (auxiliary) VLANs provide an easily configurable and automatic method of separating data and voice traffic onto separate VLANs.

- In terms of provisioning network bandwidth for voice traffic over low-speed or congestion links, always reserve enough bandwidth for the maximum number of calls crossing a link, consider a different codec if bandwidth is limited, always enable QoS regardless of bandwidth, and never design the interface to use more than 75 percent of its bandwidth.

- When building a multilayer switched network, consider the infrastructure power consideration carefully such that backup systems can provide up to one hour of standby power. In addition, inline power for IP phones requires additional power; therefore, design the infrastructure appropriately.

- To maintain the five nines uptime requirement for VoIP, utilize network management software to aid in maintaining your multilayer switched network.

- High availability is a key design requirement for IP telephony.

Table 13-2   *Commands to Review*

Command	Description
(config)#**mls qos**	Globally enables QoS on the Catalyst 2950, 3550, 3750, and 6500 families of switches.
(config-if)#**mls qos trust cos**	Configures an interface to trust the ingress CoS values of frames.
(config-if)#**mls qos trust device cisco-phone**	Configures an interface to trust the ingress CoS values or ingress DSCP of frames based on whether a Cisco IP Phone is learned through CDP. The command works in conjunction with the **mls qos trust dscp** or **mls qos trust cos** commands.
(config-if)#**mls qos trust dscp**	Configures an interface to trust the ingress DSCP values of packets.
(config-if)#**priority-queue out**	Configures an interface on a Catalyst 3550 for an expedite queue; this queue is serviced before all other queues. By default, CoS values of 5 and DSCP values of 46 do not use this queue on the Catalyst 3550, and CoS/DSCP mapping to queue mapping is necessary to properly place voice packets into the expedite queue.
(config-if)#**switchport voice vlan** *vlan-id*	An interface-level configuration command for designating the voice (aux) VLAN.
show interfaces *interface-id* **switchport**	Displays the important configuration options and current operational status of an interface.
show mls qos interface *interface-id*	Displays the QoS configuration of an interface.

Summary

This chapter briefly introduced some design topics for deploying IP telephony in multilayer switched networks. Note that this chapter only introduced the topics and does not provide the full details of each topic necessary for deploying IP telephony in the multilayer switched network. As such, consult the following resource on Cisco.com for additional information on deploying IP telephony in a multilayer switched network:

"Cisco IP Telephony Solutions"

Configuration Exercise: Configuring Voice VLANs on a Catalyst Switch

Complete this configuration exercise to familiarize yourself with voice VLAN configurations on Cisco IOS–based Catalyst switches.

Required Resources

The following resources and equipment are required to complete this exercise:

- A Catalyst 3550 switch. (You can also use a Catalyst 3560, 3750, 4500, or 6500 switch for this exercise.)

- Terminal server or workstation connected directly to the console port of the Catalyst 3550 or in-band access to the Catalyst 3550.

- Cisco IP Phones with the infrastructure to support voice calls. (This resource verifies the configuration and is not mandatory.)

Exercise Objective

The purpose of this exercise is to configure interfaces of a Catalyst IOS–based switch for voice VLANs using the following parameters:

- Configure the workstations attached to the Cisco IP Phones in VLAN 2.

- Configure the Cisco IP Phones to reside in VLAN 5.

- Configure the VLAN 2 and VLAN 5 interfaces for 10.1.1.1/24 and 10.2.1.1/24, respectively.

- Apply a standard QoS configuration for differentiating service to VoIP traffic.

Network Diagram

Figure 13-3, earlier in this chapter, illustrates the network layout for this configuration exercise.

Command List

In this configuration exercise, you use the commands listed in Table 13-3, which are in alphabetical order so that you can easily locate the information you need. Refer to this list if you need assistance during the configuration exercise. The table includes only the specific parameters used in the example and not all the available options for the command.

Table 13-3   *Command List for Configuration Exercise*

Command	Description
configure terminal	Enters the configuration mode.
copy running-config startup-config	Copies the running configuration to NVRAM.
enable	Enters the privileged mode.
end	Ends the configuration mode.
exit	Ends the current configuration mode leaf.
interface fastethernet | gigabitethernet *interface*	Enters an interface configuration mode.
interface vlan *vlan-id*	Enters the VLAN configuration interface mode.
ip address *ip_addr subnet_mask*	Configures the IP address and subnet mask of an interface.
mls qos trust cos	Trusts CoS values for ingress frames.
mls qos	Globally enables QoS.
mls qos trust device cisco-phone	Trusts when a Cisco Phone is learned via CDP on the respective interface. This command works in conjunction with the **mls qos trust dscp** and **mls qos trust cos** commands.
no shutdown	Configures an interface in the Administrative UP state.
priority-queue out	Configures queue 4 on the Catalyst 3550 family of switches as a priority queue.
spanning-tree portfast	Configures an interface for the spanning-tree PortFast feature.

continues

Table 13-3 *Command List for Configuration Exercise (Continued)*

Command	Description
switchport	Configures an interface for Layer 2 operation.
switchport access vlan *vlan-id*	Configures an interface for a specific VLAN-ID.
switchport voice vlan *vlan-id*	Configures the voice VLAN-ID.
vlan *vlan-id*	Adds or removes a VLAN-ID in the VLAN database.
wrr-queue bandwidth *weight1 weight2 weight3 weight4*	For *weight1 weight2 weight3 weight4*, enter the ratio, which determines the ratio of the frequency in which the WRR scheduler dequeues packets. Separate each value with a space. The range is 1 to 65536.
wrr-queue cos-map *queue-id cos1 ... cos8*	Configures CoS value to egress queue mapping.

Task 1: Configure Access and Voice VLAN

Step 1   Connect the Catalyst switch to a terminal server or directly to a workstation's serial port for in-band connectivity.

Step 2   Configure the native (access) and voice VLANs.

```
Switch#configure terminal
Switch(config)#vlan 2
Switch(config-vlan)#name Workstation_VLAN
Switch(config-vlan)#exit
Switch(config-if)#vlan 5
Switch(config-vlan)#name Voice_VLAN
Switch(config-vlan)#exit
```

Step 3   Configure the native (access) and voice VLAN interfaces for Layer 3 routing.

```
Switch(config)#interface vlan 2
Switch(config-if)#ip address 10.1.1.1 255.255.255.0
Switch(config-if)#no shut
Switch(config-if)#exit
Switch(config)#interface vlan 5
Switch(config-if)#ip address 10.2.1.1 255.255.255.0
Switch(config-if)#no shut
Switch(config-if)#exit
```

Task 2: Configure Interfaces for Access and Voice VLANs

Step 1   Enter the **range** command to configure multiple interfaces simultaneously.

```
Switch(config)#interface range FastEthernet 0/1 -10
```

Step 2   Configure the interface range for the access VLAN.

```
Switch(config-if-range)#switchport access vlan 2
```

Step 3   Configure the interface range for the voice VLAN.

```
Switch(config-if-range)#switchport voice vlan 5
```

Step 4   Configure the interfaces for spanning-tree PortFast.

```
Switch(config-if-range)#spanning-tree portfast
%Warning: portfast should only be enabled on ports connected to a single
host. Connecting hubs, concentrators, switches, bridges, etc... to this
interface when portfast is enabled, can cause temporary bridging loops.
Use with CAUTION
%Portfast will be configured in 10 interfaces due to the range command
but will only have effect when the interfaces are in a non-trunking mode.
Switch(config-if-range)#exit
```

Task 3: Configure Interface FastEthernet 0/1 Through 0/10 for a Recommended QoS Configuration for Congestion Management

---

NOTE   Refer to Chapter 10 for details about QoS configurations.

Step 1   Globally enable QoS features on the switch.

```
Switch(config)#mls qos
```

Step 2   Configure interfaces for mapping CoS values associated with voice frames to egress queue 4.

```
Switch(config)#interface range FastEthernet 0/1 -10
Switch(config-if-range)#wrr-queue cos-map 4 5
Switch(config-if-range)#wrr-queue cos-map 3 4 6 7
```

Step 3   Configure queue 4 as a strict priority queue.

```
Switch(config-if-range)#priority-queue out
```

Task 4: Configure Interface FastEthernet 0/1 for a Classification Based on Trusting CoS

Step 1 Configure Interface FastEthernet 0/1 for trusting CoS.

```
Switch(config)#interface FastEthernet 0/1
Switch(config-if)#mls qos trust cos
```

Task 5: Configure Interface FastEthernet 0/2 for Classification Based on Trusting DSCP

Step 1 Configure Interface FastEthernet 0/2 for trusting DSCP.

```
Switch(config)#interface FastEthernet 0/2
Switch(config-if)#mls qos trust dscp
```

Task 6: Configure Interfaces FastEthernet 0/3 Through 0/10 for Trusting CoS Based on Whether an IP Phone Is Attached to the Interface

Step 1 Configure Interface FastEthernet 0/3 through 0/10 for trusting CoS if an IP phone is attached.

```
Switch(config)#interface range FastEthernet 0/3 -10
Switch(config-if)#mls qos trust cos
Switch(config-if)#mls qos trust device cisco-phone
```

Task 7: Verify the Voice VLAN Configuration of the FastEthernet Interfaces

Step 1 Verify the configuration; interface FastEthernet 0/1 is shown as an example.

```
Switch#show interfaces FastEthernet 0/1 switchport
Name: Fa0/1
Switchport: Enabled
Administrative Mode: dynamic desirable
Operational Mode: static access
Administrative Trunking Encapsulation: negotiate
Operational Trunking Encapsulation: native
Negotiation of Trunking: On
Access Mode VLAN: 2 (Workstation_VLAN)
Trunking Native Mode VLAN: 1 (default)
Voice VLAN: 5 (Voice_VLAN)
Administrative private-vlan host-association: none
Administrative private-vlan mapping: none
```

```
Administrative private-vlan trunk native VLAN: none
Administrative private-vlan trunk encapsulation: dot1q
Administrative private-vlan trunk normal VLANs: none
Administrative private-vlan trunk private VLANs: none
Operational private-vlan: none
Trunking VLANs Enabled: ALL Pruning VLANs Enabled: 2-1001
Capture Mode Disabled Capture VLANs Allowed: ALL Protected: false
Unknown unicast blocked: disabled
Unknown multicast blocked: disabled
Appliance trust: none
```

Review Questions

For multiple-choice questions, there might be more than one correct answer.

1 True or False: When designing a multilayer switched network for IP telephony applications, QoS is not necessary if all interfaces carry traffic 75 percent or lower than the interface bandwidth.

2 What are two benefits of the voice (auxiliary) VLAN feature of Catalyst switches? (Choose two.)

   a Reduced bandwidth utilization

   b Easier troubleshooting

   c Data and voice segmentation

   d Redundancy

Example 13-2 *Catalyst Switch Configuration for Question 3*

```
(text deleted)
!
mls qos
!
(text deleted)
!
interface FastEthernet0/24
 switchport access vlan 2
 switchport mode dynamic desirable
 switchport voice vlan 10
 mls qos trust cos
 spanning-tree portfast
!
(text deleted)
!
```

3 For the interface configuration in Example 13-2, which statement is true?

  a The switch associates frames received from the workstation as from VLAN 10 and transmits frames to the workstation without an 802.1Q VLAN tag.

  b The switch associates frames received from the workstation with VLAN 2 and transmits frames to the workstation without an 802.1Q VLAN tag.

  c The switch associates frames received from the workstation in VLAN 2 and transmits frames to the workstation with an 802.1Q VLAN tag of 2.

4 For the interface configuration in Example 13-2, if no Cisco IP Phone is attached to the interface and a workstation is attached to the interface, what VLAN would be used to send traffic to and from the workstation?

  a VLAN 1

  b VLAN 2

  c VLAN 10

5 What transport protocol does VoIP use and why?

  a TCP/IP

  b UDP

  c ICMP

6 Which of the following statements is true regarding the interface QoS configuration shown in Example 13-2?

  a The switch will trust the CoS value on all incoming frames.

  b The switch will trust the CoS value on frames only from Cisco IP Phones.

  c The switch will treat the interface as untrusted and mark all CoS values to 1.

7 Which of the following features is used to distinguish voice VLAN traffic from access (data) traffic in a packet?

  a ISL encapsulation

  b DHCP

  c HSRP

  d 802.1Q tagging

  e marking

8 By default, Cisco IP Phones mark traffic at the IP layer as well as at Layer 2. Which of the following fields is marked in the IP header by Cisco IP Phones to indicate priority at Layer 3?

a CoS

b TTL

c DSCP

d Checksum

e Identifier

9 Which of the following features increases the time that a Cisco IP Phone is available for placing calls after a reboot when connected to a Cisco Catalyst switch?

a Voice VLANs

b QoS classification, marking, and trusting

c STP PortFast

d STP Root Guard

e CEF-based MLS

10 Which of the following features is necessary for all submodules of the Enterprise Composite Network Model for IP telephony deployments?

a Aggressive mode Unidirectional Link Detection (A-UDLD)

b HSRP or VRRP

c QoS

d Spanning-tree Root Guard

This chapter covers the following topics:

- Introduction to Layer 2 Security and Types of Layer 2 Attacks
- Explaining the Management Security Configurations for the Multilayer Switched Network
- Understanding and Configuring AAA on Catalyst Switches
- Understanding and Configuring Port Security
- Understanding and Configuring Port-Based Authentication with 802.1X
- Understanding Cisco Network Admission Control (NAC) on Catalyst Switches
- Applying Security Using Access Lists
- Securing Networks Using Firewalls
- Security Using Network Address Translation (NAT)
- Understanding and Configuring DHCP Snooping
- Understanding and Configuring IP Source Guard (IPSG)
- Understanding and Configuring Dynamic ARP Inspection (DAI)
- Understanding the Role of Private VLANs as a Security Feature
- Understanding the Role of QoS as a Security Feature
- STP Security Mechanisms Review
- Case Study: Understanding and Protecting Against VLAN Hopping

Securing Your Multilayer Switched Network to Minimize Service Loss and Data Theft

Network-security vulnerabilities, as discussed in this chapter, include loss of privacy, data theft, impersonation, and loss of integrity. This chapter begins with an introduction of various types of Layer 2 attacks and covers several important features that aid in the prevention of network-security vulnerabilities. This chapter discusses many features covered in earlier chapters but presents those features from a security perspective. In addition, this chapter focuses on port security, DHCP snooping, IP Source Guard (IPSG), Dynamic ARP Inspection (DAI), 802.1X, Network Admission Control (NAC), and access list applications (data plane security features). This chapter also includes brief discussions on management security features such as authentication, authorization, and accounting (AAA), intended only as an introduction. Refer to the references at the end of the "Configuring AAA" section for a complete review of AAA.

Introduction to Layer 2 Security and Types of Layer 2 Attacks

Much industry attention centers on security attacks from outside the walls of an organization that are directed at the upper Open System Interconnection (OSI) layers. Network security often focuses on edge-routing devices and the filtering of packets based upon Layer 3 and 4 headers, ports, stateful packet inspection, and so forth. Network security includes all issues surrounding Layer 3 and above, as traffic makes its way into the campus network from the Internet. Campus access devices and Layer 2 communication are left largely unconsidered in most security discussions.

The default state of networking equipment highlights this focus on external protection and internal open communication. Firewalls, placed at the organizational borders, arrive in a secure operational mode and allow no communication until configured to do so. Routers and switches placed internally in an organization and designed to accommodate communication, delivering needful campus traffic, have a default operational mode that forwards all traffic unless configured otherwise. Their function as devices to facilitate communication often results in minimal security configuration and renders them targets for malicious attacks. If an attack is launched at Layer 2 on an internal campus device, the rest of the network can be quickly compromised, often without detection.

A new security focus centers on attacks launched by maliciously leveraging normal Layer 2 switch operations. Security features exist to protect switches and Layer 2 operations, but a policy must be established and appropriate features configured to protect against potential malicious acts while maintaining daily network operations.

Understand How a Rogue Device Gains Unauthorized Access

Rogue access comes in several forms, as shown in Figure 14-1. For example, because unauthorized rogue access points are inexpensive and readily available, employees sometimes plug them into existing LANs and build ad hoc wireless networks without IT department knowledge or consent. These rogue access points can be a serious breach of network security because they can be plugged into a network port behind the corporate firewall. Because employees generally do not enable security settings on the rogue access points, it is easy for unauthorized users to use the access points to intercept network traffic and hijack client sessions.

Figure 14-1 *Rogue Network Devices*

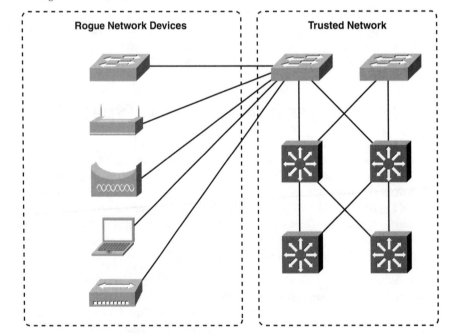

Malicious rogue access points, while much less common than employee-installed rogue access points, are also a security concern. These rogue access points create an unsecured wireless LAN connection that puts the entire wired network at risk. Malicious rogue access points present an even greater risk and challenge because they are intentionally hidden from physical and network view.

Other types of rogue devices include the following:

- **An unauthorized switch connected by an employee to extend the network**—This might result in the newly introduced switch becoming root of the STP.

- **A hub device connected by an employee**—This might potentially cause a network loop.

- **Unauthorized laptops or workstations connected to the network**—The newly introduced laptops or workstations might not have proper virus or OS patches installed. Such a device might infect other employee devices with a worm or virus, thus causing loss of productivity.

Categories of Layer 2 Attacks

Layer 2 malicious attacks are typically launched by a device connected to the campus network. This can be a physical rogue device placed on the network for malicious purposes or an external intrusion that takes control of and launches attacks from a trusted device. In either case, the network sees all traffic as originating from a legitimate connected device.

Attacks launched against switches and at Layer 2 can be grouped as follows:

- Attacks on switch configuration/management
- MAC layer attacks
- Spoof attacks
- VLAN attacks
- STP attacks
- VTP attacks

Subsequent sections of this chapter cover the significant attacks in these categories that are prevalent at the time of this writing. Each attack method is accompanied by a standard measure for mitigating the security compromise.

Table 14-1 briefly describes the types of attacks and indicates the mitigation steps available.

Table 14-1 *Layer 2 Attacks*

Attack Method	Description	Mitigation
Switch Device Attacks		
CDP manipulation	Information sent through CDP is transmitted in clear text and unauthenticated, allowing it to be captured, thus divulging network topology information.	Disable CDP on all ports except on links between networking devices.
SSH and Telnet attacks	Telnet packets can be read in clear text.	SSH is an option but has security issues in version 1, so use SSH version 2 instead. Telnet with vty ACLs.
MAC Layer Attack		
MAC address flooding	Frames with unique, invalid source MAC addresses flood the switch, exhausting MAC address table space, thus disabling the ability to add new entries from valid hosts. Traffic to valid hosts is subsequently flooded out to all ports.	Port security. MAC address VLAN access maps.
Spoofing Attacks		
DHCP address exhaustion and DCHP server spoofing	An attacking device can exhaust the address space available to the DHCP servers or establish itself as a DHCP server to cause denial of service.	DHCP snooping.
MAC spoofing	An attacking device spoofs the MAC address of a valid host currently in the MAC address table. The switch then forwards frames destined for that valid host to the attacking device.	Port security.
ARP spoofing	An attacking device crafts ARP replies intended for valid hosts. This enables the attacking device to man-in-the-middle attack without either the source or destination device knowing that it is communicating through the attacking device.	Dynamic ARP Inspection.

Table 14-1   *Layer 2 Attacks (Continued)*

Attack Method	Description	Mitigation
IP address spoofing	The attacking device spoofs the IP address of a valid host either to bypass Layer 3 security measures or to bypass the DHCP mechanism and self-assign an IP address for unauthorized access.	IP Source Guard.
VLAN Attacks		
VLAN hopping	By altering VLAN IDs on packets encapsulated for trunking, an attacking device can send or receive packets on various VLANs, bypassing Layer 3 security measures.	Tighten up trunk configurations and the negotiation state of unused ports.
Attacks between devices on a common VLAN	Devices may need protection from one another, even though they are on a common VLAN. This is especially true on service provider segments supporting devices from multiple customers.	Implement private VLANs (pVLANs).
STP Attacks		
An unauthorized device taking over root of the STP	An unauthorized switch can lower its bridge priority below the current root to take over as the root of the STP.	Implement Root Guard on access ports.
Unauthorized hubs or switches attached to the access layer to extend the network	Unauthorized hub or switch devices can be connected to the access layer network to provide connectivity to an unauthorized number of devices on a user port.	Implement BPDU Guard and port security.
Looping of network traffic on to an access port	Attack includes looping one access port back to another access port, creating a loop in the VLAN.	Implement BPDU Guard along with BPDU PortFast.
VTP Attack		
Unauthorized devices sending bogus VLAN database	An unauthorized device sends a bogus VLAN database to overwrite the production switches' VLAN database, resulting in network disruption.	Configure VTP password for the VTP domain.

Besides the types of attacks and mitigation steps mentioned in Table 14-1, this chapter covers other types of attacks and useful techniques for mitigating them, including the use of firewall devices, NAT, ACLs, and STP security mechanisms to prevent network outages.

Catalyst Switch Configurations for Security in Multilayer Switched Networks

Implementation of a basic security configuration on every installed Cisco device is a requirement for preventing network vulnerabilities. Cisco recommends the following security measures on every Cisco device in your network to aid in network-security protection:

- Configure strong system passwords
- Restrict management access using access control lists (ACL)
- Secure physical access to the console
- Secure access to vty lines
- Configure system warning banners
- Disable unneeded or unused services
- Trim and minimize the use of CDP
- Disable the integrated HTTP daemon (where appropriate)
- Configure basic system logging (syslog)
- Secure SNMP
- Limit trunking connections and propagated VLANs
- Secure the Spanning-Tree topology

The techniques listed here are simple and easy to understand for those interested in implementing a minimum level of security on Cisco IOS and Cisco CatOS switches. This list is not a complete list, and you should review additional product security configurations per platform. Furthermore, these security principles are applicable to other Cisco products, including routers, SAN switches, and network appliances. The following sections discuss each item in the previous list in more detail.

NOTE   In addition to recommendations from Cisco Systems, Inc., the National Security Agency (NSA) publishes a recommended list of security features for Cisco IOS and the Microsoft Windows operating systems on its website (http://www.nsa.gov). Although the recommended security feature lists of the NSA do not include the most recent security features available in Cisco IOS, the lists are still a valuable, supplemental guideline for implementing security features in Cisco IOS.

Configuring Strong System Passwords

Use the **enable secret** command to set a password that grants enabled access to the Cisco IOS system, instead of using the **enable** command. Because the **enable secret** command simply implements an MD5 hash on the configured password, that password remains vulnerable to dictionary attacks. Therefore, standard practices in selecting a feasible password apply. Try to pick passwords that contain letters, numbers, and special characters. An example of a feasible password is "$pecia1$"—that is, the word "specials", where each "s" has been replaced by "$" and the letter "l" has been replaced with the numeral "1." (Chapter 3, "Initial Configuration and Troubleshooting of Cisco Multilayer Switches," discusses configuring system passwords in more detail and includes examples.)

Restricting Management Access Using Access Control Lists

Creating ACLs to limit management and remote access traffic aids in prevention of unauthorized access and denial of service (DoS) attacks against management interfaces. For example, consider a multilayer switched topology that uses the subnet 10.1.2.0/24 for accessing all network devices for management purposes. This subnet does not pass user data traffic. Limiting access to this subnet for system administrators in another specific subnet, for example 10.1.3.0/24, prevents typical enterprise users from accessing the management subnet. As a result, ACLs that limit management traffic reduce vulnerability of the network devices and limit unauthorized access to the management subnet.

Example 14-1 illustrates a sample ACL configuration that limits traffic to the management VLAN (in this case, VLAN 601) to only system administrators in the 10.1.3.0/24 subnet.

Example 14-1 *Sample ACL for Restricting Access to Management Subnet*

```
(text deleted)
!
interface Vlan600
 description User LAN
 ip address 10.1.1.1 255.255.255.0
!
interface Vlan601
 description Management VLAN
 ip address 10.1.2.1 255.255.255.0
 ip access-group 100 out
!
interface Vlan602
 description IT LAN
 ip address 10.1.3.1 255.255.255.0
!
(text delete)
!
!
access-list 100 permit ip 10.1.3.0 0.0.0.255 10.1.2.0 0.0.0.255
access-list 100 deny   ip any any log
!
```

For more details on configuring ACLs, consult Cisco.com.

Securing Physical Access to the Console

Physical security of switches or routers is often overlooked but is a valuable security precaution. Console access requires a minimum level of security both physically and logically. An individual who gains console access to a system gains the ability to recover or reset the passwords or to reload the system, thereby enabling that individual to bypass all other security measures implemented on that system. Consequently, it is imperative to physically secure access to the console by using security personnel, closed circuit television, card-key entry systems, locking cabinets, access logging, or other means to control physical access as standard practice.

Securing Access to vty Lines

The minimum recommended security practices for securing access to vty lines are as follows:

- Apply ACLs on all vty lines to limit in-band access only to management stations from specific subnets.

- Configure strong passwords for all configured vty lines.

- Use Secure Shell Protocol (SSH) instead of Telnet to access the device remotely. Refer to Chapter 3 for examples of configuring SSH.

Configuring System Warning Banners

For both legal and administrative purposes, configuring a system warning banner to display prior to login is a convenient and effective way of reinforcing security and general usage policies. Clearly stating the ownership, usage, access, and protection policies prior to a login aids in stronger prosecution in the event of unauthorized access.

Disabling Unneeded or Unused Services

By default, in Cisco IOS versions 11.2 and earlier, Cisco routers implement multiple TCP and UDP servers to facilitate management and integration into existing environments. However, in Cisco IOS versions 11.3 and later, most TCP and UDP servers are disabled by default. In addition, most installations do not require these services, and disabling them reduces overall security exposure. Multilayer switched networks typically do not use the following services:

- TCP Small Servers (Echo, Chargen, Discard, Daytime)

- UDP Small Servers (Echo, Discard, Chargen)

- Finger
- Auto config
- Packet Assembler and Disassembler (PAD)
- BOOTP server
- Identification service
- NTP without authentication
- Source routing
- IP Proxy-ARP
- ICMP unreachables
- ICMP redirects
- Directed broadcast forwarding
- Maintenance Operation Protocol (MOP)

For a description and the associated commands to disable these services, consult Cisco.com.

For a secure network, you should carefully evaluate every device configuration before applying it. For example, only appropriate VLANs should be allowed on the trunk to other devices, instead of allowing all VLANs. Another example is disabling Dynamic Trunk Protocol (DTP) and Port Aggregation Protocol (PAgP) protocols on end user ports where those features are not needed. Some of these features are enabled by default on Catalyst switches, so you need to make careful considerations for the default configuration as well as for additional configuration by the user. Avoiding unneeded services and making the configuration deterministic makes the network less susceptible to attack. The premise of "plug-n-play" might bode well for ease of installation, but it tremendously increases vulnerability of your network. Cisco Systems customers generally want plug-n-play for ease of use, and as the products evolve, more and more security features become plug-n-play. Nevertheless, using a default security configuration on any device, Cisco or not, is a security risk.

Keep in mind that this chapter focuses on the discussion of Cisco devices. Securing your network includes securing not only your Cisco devices but also your hosts, servers, and any other network device.

Trimming and Minimizing Use of CDP

Security with CDP remains fairly controversial. Although CDP propagates detailed information about respective network devices, correct planning and configuration of CDP enables it to be a fairly safe protocol. This is a great advantage because auxiliary VLANs and specific solutions in many multilayer switched networks require CDP. For a practical and secure deployment of CDP, adhere to the following CDP configuration guidelines:

- Disable CDP on a per-interface basis. Run CDP only for administrative purposes, such as on inter-switch connections and interfaces where IP Phones reside.

- Confine CDP deployment to run between devices under your control. Because CDP is a link-level (Layer 2) protocol, it does not propagate end-to-end over a MAN or WAN unless a Layer 2 tunneling mechanism is in place. As a result, for MAN and WAN connections, CDP tables may include the service provider's next-hop router or switch and not the far-end router under your control.

- Do not run CDP to any unsecured connection such as Internet connections.

For a detailed discussion of how CDP operates and how to configure CDP as discussed in this section, refer to the "CDP" section of Chapter 7, "Enhancing Network Stability, Functionality, Reliability, and Performance Using Advanced Features."

Disabling the Integrated HTTP Daemon

Although Cisco IOS provides an integrated HTTP server for ease of management, the recommendation is to disable this feature, especially in multilayer switched networks that do not use this method for management. Otherwise, any unauthorized user might be able to gain access via the web interface and make configuration changes. A user might also send numerous HTTP requests to the switch or router, which might cause high CPU utilization, resulting in a DoS-type attack on the system. In Cisco IOS, the integrated HTTP server is disabled by default. If HTTP access is necessary, use a different HTTP port and use ACLs to isolate access from only trusted subnets or workstations. Use the following command in Cisco IOS to disable HTTP server access on a switch:

```
no ip http server
```

Use the following command in Cisco CatOS to disable HTTP server access on a switch:

```
set ip http server disable
```

Examples 14-2 and 14-3 illustrate disabling HTTP server access in Cisco IOS and Cisco CatOS, respectively.

Example 14-2 *Disabling IP HTTP Server Access in Cisco IOS*

```
svs-san-msfc#configure terminal
Enter configuration commands, one per line.  End with CNTL/Z.
svs-san-msfc(config)#no ip http server
svs-san-msfc(config)#end
```

Example 14-3 *Disabling IP HTTP Server Access in Cisco CatOS*

```
Console> (enable)  set ip http server disable
```

Configuring Basic System Logging

To assist and simplify both problem troubleshooting and security investigations, monitor switch subsystem information received from the logging facility. To render the on-system logging useful, increase the default buffer size; generally, the default buffer size is not adequate for logging most events. For more information about system logging, refer to the "System Logging" section of Chapter 3.

Securing SNMP

Whenever possible, avoid using SNMP read-write features. SNMPv2c authentication consists of simple text strings that are communicated between devices in clear, unencrypted text. In most cases, a read-only community string is sufficient. To use SNMP in secure method, use SNMPv3 with an encrypted password and use ACL to limit SNMP from only trusted workstations and subnets. For more information on how to secure SNMP, refer to the following document on Cisco.com:

"Securing Simple Network Management Protocol," Document ID: 20370
http://www.cisco.com/en/US/tech/tk648/tk362/
technologies_tech_note09186a0080094489.shtml

Limiting Trunking Connections and Propagated VLANs

By default, specific models of Catalyst switches that are running Cisco IOS and Cisco CatOS automatically negotiate trunking capabilities. This poses a security risk because the negotiation allows the introduction of an unauthorized trunk port into the network. If an unauthorized trunk port is used for traffic interception and to generate DoS attacks, the consequences can be far more serious than if only an access port is used. (A DoS attack on a trunk port may affect multiple VLANs, whereas a DoS attack on an access port affects only a single VLAN.) To prevent unauthorized trunks, disable automatic negotiation of trunking on host and access ports. In addition, remove unused VLANs from trunks manually or by using VTP. Refer to Chapter 4, "Implementing and Configuring VLANs," for more information on how to disable automatic negotiation of trunking and other VLAN configurations such as VTP.

Securing the Spanning-Tree Topology

It is important to protect the Spanning Tree Protocol (STP) process of the switches that compose the infrastructure. Inadvertent or malicious introduction of STP BPDUs potentially overwhelms a device or creates a DoS. The first step in stabilizing a Spanning-Tree installation is to positively identify the intended root and designated bridge in the design and to hard-set that bridge's STP bridge priority to an acceptable root value.

Configuring specific bridge priorities aids in prevention of inadvertent shifts in the STP root due to an uncontrolled introduction of a new switch.

In addition, use the STP BPDU Guard feature to prevent host devices from maliciously sending BPDUs to a port. This feature, when enabled, works in conjunction with the STP PortFast feature to protect the network from unwanted BPDU traffic injection. Upon receipt of an unauthorized STP BPDU, the feature automatically disables the port until user intervention occurs or a time-out value is reached. For more information on configuring the STP parameters and the BPDU Guard feature, refer to Chapter 5, "Understanding and Configuring the 802.1D, 802.1s, and 802.1w Spanning Tree Protocols," and Chapter 6, "Adding Resiliency to Spanning Tree Using Advanced Features and Troubleshooting STP Issues," respectively.

Configuring AAA

The AAA network-security services provide the primary framework through which you set up access control on a Cisco IOS or Cisco CatOS switch. AAA is an architectural framework for configuring a set of three independent security functions in a consistent manner. AAA provides a modular way of performing the following services:

- Authentication
- Authorization
- Accounting

NOTE   Be extremely careful when configuring AAA because you might accidentally lock yourself out of the router or switch, in which case you might have to initiate password recovery to return to the original state.

Authentication

Authentication provides a method for handling the following:

- User identification
- Login and password dialog
- Challenge and response
- Messaging
- Encryption

Authentication identifies users prior to accessing the network and network services. AAA configures authentication by defining a named list of authentication methods and then applying that list to various interfaces. The method list defines the types of authentication performed and their sequence. These methods are applicable on a per-interface basis. However, all interfaces on Cisco routers and switches adhere to a default method list named "Default" when no other authentication methods are defined. A defined method list always overrides the default method list.

All authentication methods, except for local, line password, and enable authentication, require the use of AAA.

Authorization

Authorization provides the method for remote access control. This remote access control includes one-time authorization or authorization for each service on a per-user account list or a user group basis. Authorization on Cisco switches and routers is multi protocol and supports IP, Internetwork Packet Exchange (IPX), AppleTalk Remote Access (ARA), Telnet, and SSH.

The AAA authorization process on switches or routers works by contacting a common, centralized database of a set of attributes that describe the network user's authorized services, such as access to different parts of the network. The centralized server returns a result of allowed services to the switch or router in question to execute the user's actual capabilities and restrictions. This database is generally a centrally located server, such as a RADIUS or TACACS+ security server. However, using a local database is possible. The remote security servers, such as RADIUS and TACACS+, authorize users for specific rights by associating their attribute-value pairs (AVP). TACACS+ and RADIUS use these AVPs for configurations that are applied to users or a group of users. Each AVP consists of a type identifier associated with one or more assignable values. AVPs specified in user and group profiles define the authentication and authorization characteristics for their respective users and groups.

For example, with TACACS+ authorization, an AVP of Outacl=10 applies the out ACL 10 to a user; the AVP of Idletime=30 sets an idle timeout value for a user to 30 minutes.

AVPs are usually in the form a=b or a*b, in which a is the attribute and b is the value. The = separator indicates that the AVP is mandatory. The * separator indicates that the AV pair is optional. Tables 14-2 and 14-3 illustrate examples of RADIUS AVPs and TACACS+ AVPs, respectively.

Table 14-2   *Examples of RADIUS AVPs*

Attribute	Type of Value
User-Name	String
Password	String
CHAP-Password	String
Client-Id	IP address

continues

Table 14-2 *Examples of RADIUS AVPs (Continued)*

Attribute	Type of Value
Login-Host	IP address
Login-Service	Integer
Login-TCP-Port	Integer

Table 14-3 *Examples of TACACS+ AVPs*

Attribute	Type of Value
Inacl	Integer
Addr-pool	String
Addr	IP address
Idletime	Integer
Protocol	Keyword
Timeout	Integer
Outacl	Integer

All authorization methods require the use of AAA. As with authentication, AAA authorization is applicable on a per-interface basis.

Accounting

Accounting provides the method for collecting and sending security server information used for billing, auditing, and reporting. This type of information includes user identities, network access start and stop times, executed commands (such as PPP), number of packets, and number of bytes. This information is useful for auditing and improving security as each switch or router monitors each user.

In many circumstances, AAA uses protocols such as RADIUS, TACACS+, or 802.1X to administer its security functions. If your switch is acting as a network access server, AAA is the means through which a switch establishes communication between your network access server and your RADIUS, TACACS+, or 802.1X security server.

AAA is dynamic in that it allows configuration of authentication and authorization on a per-line (per-user) or per-service (for example, IP, IPX, or virtual private dial-up network [VPDN]) basis. Creating method lists and then applying those method lists to specific services or interfaces achieves the per-line or per-user application.

Configuring AAA Authentication

The AAA security services facilitate a variety of login authentication methods. Before configuring any AAA security, use the **aaa new-model** command to initialize a AAA access control model on Cisco IOS switches or routers. Furthermore, use the **aaa authentication login** command to enable AAA login authentication in Cisco IOS. In conjunction with the **aaa authentication login** command, configure one or more lists of authentication methods that each switch or router tries per user during login. These lists are configurable using the following Cisco IOS configuration commands:

```
login authentication line {default | list-name} method1 [method2...]
```

list-name defines the list name, whereas *method1 [method2...]* defines the authentication methods in order, such as TACACS+ or RADIUS. *list-name* is case-sensitive, as with any other Cisco named lists.

To apply the authentication list to an input line, use of the following line command:

```
login authentication {default | list-name}
```

Example 14-4 illustrates configuring of the VTY terminals in Cisco IOS for TACACS+ authentication as the first method. The second method, local login, occurs when the TACACS+ server is unreachable.

Example 14-4 *Example of Configuring AAA Authentication in Cisco IOS*

```
Switch(config)#aaa new-model
Switch(config)#aaa authentication login TEST tacacs+
Switch(config)#tacacs-server host 192.168.100.100
Switch(config)#line vty 0 4
Switch(config-line)#login authentication TEST
```

The equivalent commands in Cisco CatOS for configuring AAA authentication are **set authentication login local enable** and **set authentication login tacacs enable**. Example 14-5 shows a user configuring AAA authentication in Cisco CatOS.

Example 14-5 *Example of Configuring AAA Authentication in Cisco CatOS*

```
Console> (enable)set authentication login local enable
local login authentication set to enable for console, telnet and http session.
Console> (enable)set authentication login tacacs enable
tacacs login authentication set to enable for console, telnet and http session.
Console> (enable)set tacacs server 192.168.100.100
```

Configuring AAA Authorization

Switches and routers use AAA authorization to limit the services that are available to specific users. AAA authorization uses information retrieved from the user's profile, which is located either in the local user database on the switch or on the security server, to configure the user's session. Afterward, the switch or router grants access to services requested by the user only if the information in the user profile allows for it. These services include the ability to execute commands, use network access such as PPP, or enter configuration options.

In addition, you should create method lists, which are similar to the AAA authentication configuration, to define authorizations. Method lists are specific to the authorization type requested. The following options are available for AAA authorization:

- **Auth-proxy**—Auth-proxy applies security policies on a per-user basis. With the use of auth-proxy, each user brings up a web browser to authenticate to a TACACS+ or RADIUS server before accessing the network. Upon successful authentication, the authentication server passes additional ACL entries and profile information to the router or switch to allow the users into the network.

- **Commands**—Command authorization applies authorization to all EXEC commands, including configuration commands associated with a specific privilege level. An example is limiting network operation users to only **show** commands when accessing switches and routers in the enterprise network for normal operations.

- **EXEC**—EXEC refers to the attributes associated with a user EXEC terminal session.

- **Network**—Network authorization applies to the types of network connections. An example of using network authorization is authorization granting remote users access to network protocols such as PPP, SLIP, or ARAP during login for remote access.

- **Reverse access**—Reverse access refers to reverse Telnet sessions commonly used on console servers for access to different lines.

Similar to the configuration of AAA authentication, AAA authorization uses named method lists in its configuration. AAA supports the following five different methods of authorization:

- **TACACS+**—TACACS+ is a client/server method that stores specific rights for users by associating AVPs for each user. The AAA authorization daemon on the Cisco switch or router communicates with the TACACS+ server to determine correct authorization for different options, such as EXEC and network access.

- **RADIUS**—RADIUS is similar to TACACS+ in that RADIUS is also a server/client model for a Cisco router or switch to request authorization about a specific user. RADIUS servers store specific rights about users by associating specific attributes.

- **If-authenticated**—The if-authenticated method allows a user to access any requested function as long as the AAA daemon previously and successfully authenticated the user.

- **None**—The none option effectively disables authorization for the respective interface.

- **Local**—The local method of authorization uses a database of usernames and passwords configured on the respective switch or router. Local databases on Cisco IOS routers and switches configure using the **username** command and allow only a subset of feature-controlled functions.

To configure AAA authorization using named method lists, use the following commands in the global and interface configuration modes, respectively:

```
aaa authorization {auth-proxy | network | exec | commands level | reverse-access |
configuration | ipmobile} {default | list-name} [method1 [method2...]]
authorization {arap | commands level | exec | reverse-access} {default | list-
name}
```

To have the multilayer switch request authorization information via a TACACS+ security server, use the **aaa authorization** command with the **group tacacs+** method keyword. The **group tacacs+** method instructs the switch to use a list of all TACACS+ servers for authentication; refer to the Cisco IOS command reference for AAA on the Cisco.com website for additional methods. To allow users to have access to the functions they request as long as they have been authenticated, use the **aaa authorization** command with the **if-authenticated** method keyword. If you select this method, all requested functions are automatically granted to authenticated users.

To select local authorization, which means that the router or access server consults its local user database to determine which functions a user is permitted to use, use the **aaa authorization** command with the **local** method keyword. The functions associated with local authorization are defined by using the **username** global configuration command. To have the network access server request authorization via a list of RADIUS security servers, use the **aaa authorization** command with the **group radius** method keyword. Example 14-6 illustrates configuring AAA authorization for users via VTY access for shell commands.

Example 14-6 *Configuring AAA Authorization in Cisco IOS*

```
Switch(config)#aaa new-model
Switch(config)#aaa authorization commands 0 default if-authenticated group tacacs+
Switch(config)#line vty 0 4
Switch(config-line)#authorization commands 0 default
```

Cisco CatOS supports AAA authorization for the following three types of access options:

- Commands
- EXEC mode (user login)
- Enable mode (privilege login)

The commands to configure these access options are as follows, respectively:

```
set authorization commands enable {config | all} {option}{fallbackoption}
[console | telnet | both]
set authorization exec enable {option}{fallbackoption} [console | telnet |
both]
set authorization enable enable {option} {fallbackoption} [console | telnet |
both]
```

Configuring AAA Accounting

AAA supports the following six different accounting types:

- **Network accounting**—Provides information for all PPP, SLIP, or ARAP sessions, including packet and byte counts.

- **Connection accounting**—Provides information about all outbound connections made from the network, such as Telnet and rlogin.

- **EXEC accounting**—Provides information about user EXEC terminal sessions (user shells) on the network access server, including username, date, start and stop times, the access server IP address, and (for dial-in users) the telephone number from which the call originated.

- **System accounting**—Provides information about all system-level events (for example, when the system reboots and when accounting is turned on or off).

- **Command accounting**—Provides information about the EXEC shell commands for a specified privilege level that are being executed on a network access server.

- **Resource accounting**—Provides start and stop record support for calls that have passed user authentication.

To configure AAA accounting in Cisco IOS, first configure the global accounting method list and enable accounting using the following command:

```
aaa accounting {system | network | exec | connection | commands level} {default
| list-name} {start-stop | stop-only | none} [method1    [method2...]]
```

Second, apply the accounting method to an interface or line using the following command:

```
accounting {arap | commands level | connection | exec} {default | list-name}
```

Example 14-7 illustrates configuring accounting on the vty lines.

Example 14-7 *Configuring EXEC Accounting on vty Lines*

```
Switch(config)#aaa new-model
Switch(config)#aaa accounting exec default start-stop group tacacs+
Switch(config)#line vty 0 4
Switch(config-line)#accounting exec default
```

Table 14-4 illustrates the tasks and commands in Cisco CatOS to configure AAA accounting.

Table 14-4 *AAA Accounting Commands for Cisco CatOS*

Task	Command
Enable accounting for connection events	**set accounting connect enable {start-stop| stop-only} {tacacs+ | radius}**
Enable accounting for EXEC mode	**set accounting exec enable {start-stop | stop-only} {tacacs+ | radius}**
Task	**Command**

Table 14-4   *AAA Accounting Commands for Cisco CatOS (Continued)*

Enable accounting for system events	**set accounting system enable {start-stop | stop-only} {tacacs+ | radius}**
Enable accounting of configuration commands	**set accounting commands enable {config | all} {stop-only} tacacs+**
Enable suppression of information for unknown users	**set accounting suppress null-username enable**
Configure accounting to be updated as new information is available	**set accounting update {new-info | {periodic [*interval*]}}**

A Step-by-Step Example of Configuring Cisco AAA on a Cisco IOS-Based Catalyst Switch

First-time users of AAA might find the configuration daunting. With some practice, though, configuring AAA becomes fairly simple. When configuring AAA, always use a console connection to avoid locking yourself out of the router or switch through misconfiguration. To illustrate the simplicity of configuring AAA, the following example presents a step approach to configuring AAA for authentication using TACACS+ on a Catalyst 3750 running Cisco IOS:

Step 1   Configure the TACACS+ server for a test user.

When using Cisco ACS for Microsoft Windows, create a new test user without a specific options.

Step 2   Configure new network device on the TACACS+ server.

When using Cisco ACS for Microsoft Windows, create a new network device by specifying the DNS name and IP address, and specify a key to be used for TACACS+.

Step 3   Access the switch using the Console (out-of-band) connection.

Step 4   Enable AAA globally:

```
svs-san-3550-1(config)#aaa new-model
```

Step 5   Configure the TACACS+ server and key:

```
svs-san-3550-1(config)#tacacs-server host 172.18.114.33
svs-san-3550-1(config)#tacacs-server key bcmsn
```

Step 6   Configure the default login access:

```
svs-san-3550-1(config)#aaa authentication login default group tacacs+
enable
```

Step 7   Test the login using a separate connection.

This allows you to troubleshoot and make changes in real-time while testing the configuration.

Additional Resources for Understanding and Configuring AAA

The previous sections introduced AAA in Cisco IOS and Cisco CatOS. For a thorough understanding of AAA, consult the following resources:

- *Cisco IOS Security Configuration Guide, Release 12.2*, "AAA Overview" http://www.cisco.com/en/US/products/sw/iosswrel/ps1835/products_configuration_guide_chapter09186a00800ca7a7.html

- *Cisco IOS Security Configuration Guide, Release 12.3*, "Part 1: Authentication, Authorization, and Accounting (AAA)" http://www.cisco.com/en/US/products/sw/iosswrel/ps5187/prod_configuration_guide09186a008017d583.html#wp1000714

- *Managing Cisco Network Security,* by Mike Wenstrom (Cisco Press, 2001; ISBN: 1578701031)

Port Security

In today's enterprise networks, security is the top concern. Because most desktops have Fast Ethernet or Gigabit Ethernet connections, traffic from users, maliciously or inadvertently, can cause congestion or result in a denial of service (DoS) attack and a subsequent network outage. Hence, it is imperative that the network administrators allow only legitimate users on the enterprise network and deny unauthorized users. Port security is a Layer 2 feature that provides the following five protective features:

- Allows traffic based on host MAC addresses
- Restricts traffic based on host MAC addresses
- Blocks unicast flood packets on configured ports
- Prevents MAC flooding attacks
- Prevents MAC spoofing attacks

The Cisco port security feature has some similarity to IEEE 802.1X, which is a client/server–based access control and authentication protocol that restricts unauthorized devices from connecting to switch ports. 802.1X is described later in this chapter.

Allowing Traffic Based on Host MAC Addresses

Port security allows traffic based on host MAC addresses. The individual port can allow more than one MAC address, up to a specific number of MAC addresses. The maximum number of MAC addresses varies on each Catalyst switch. The port security feature is useful in dictating the number of hosts per port. For example, restricting user ports to one learned MAC address and restricting conference rooms to ten MAC addresses assist in avoiding unauthorized access to the network.

For example, the Catalyst 6500 family of switches supports 1024 MAC addresses plus one default MAC address, for a total of 1025 MAC addresses on a global basis. These 1025 MAC addresses are allocated in different ways on a per-port basis. The following combinations are valid allocations:

- 1025 (1 + 1024) MAC addresses on one port and 1 MAC address on the remaining ports.

- 201 (1 + 200) on one port, 701 (1 + 700) on another port, 125 (1 + 124) on the third port, and 1 address each on the rest of the ports.

NOTE   The Catalyst 6500 family of switches supports a maximum of 4097 MAC addresses since Cisco CatOS version 8.1(1) and later.

Use the following command in Cisco CatOS–based switches to configure the maximum number of MAC addresses allowed per port:

```
set port security {mod/port} { maximum-number-of-mac-addresses }
```

In Cisco IOS–based switches, use the following interface-level command:

```
switchport port-security maximum {maximum-number-of-mac-addresses}
```

Catalyst switches support securing MAC addresses by manual configuration or by learning an initial MAC address dynamically.

To configure the MAC address manually on Cisco CatOS–based Catalyst switches, use the following command:

```
set port security {mod/port} {mac-address}
```

In Cisco IOS–based Catalyst switches, use the following interface-level command:

```
switchport port-security mac-address {mac-address}
```

To configure the duration before dynamically learned MAC addresses age, use the following command in Cisco CatOS–based Catalyst switches:

```
set port security {mod/port} age {time}
```

The *time* parameter represents the time, in seconds, after dynamically learned MAC addresses age.

In Cisco IOS–based Catalyst switches, use the following interface-level command:

```
switchport security aging time {time}
```

Violations in port-security terminology refer to an unauthorized use of the network resources as defined by the port-security configuration.

Violations occur for two possible reasons:

- A frame with an unauthorized source MAC address is received on a secure port.
- A port receives a new frame when it has already learned the maximum number of MAC addresses allowed on that port.

Upon security violation detection, the switch can perform one of the following:

- **Shutdown**—Err-disable the port permanently or for a specified period of time.
- **Restrict**—Continue to operate but drop frames from unauthorized hosts.
- **Protect (on Cisco IOS–based switches only)**—Continue to operate, but drop frames from newer hosts when the maximum number of learned addresses has been exceeded.

The security violation action chosen depends on the nature of the port. If it is a critical server farm switch, then the network administrator can choose to use the restrictive option such that operation of the servers is not affected upon any violation. Consequently, if the switch in question is an access layer switch, the network administrator can configure the shutdown option with a specified timer such that accidental unauthorized movements of user devices do not require manual intervention by the network administrator to re-establish connectivity. To summarize, the action chosen depends on the individual network scenario, the switch location, and the degree of security desired.

To configure the err-disable timer of shutdown mode in Cisco CatOS–based switches, use the following commands:

```
set err-disable-timeout enable  reason_for_err-disable
set err-disable-timeout interval  time-interval
```

The *time-interval* parameter represents the time, in seconds, after which the switch re-enables the interface after being disabled due to error condition.

In Cisco IOS–based switches, use the following global configuration commands:

```
err-disable recovery cause secure-violation
err-disable recovery interval {time-interval}
```

To summarize, enable port security to allow traffic based on host MAC addresses by using the following steps:

Step 1 Enable port security for the port in question.

Step 2 Specify the maximum number of MAC addresses for dynamic learning or host MAC addresses that need to be secured.

Step 3 Specify the security violation action. (The default is to shut down the port permanently.)

Step 4   Configure the err-disable timer if the security-violation action is to shut down the port. The err-disable timer is a global value for all features that puts the port in err-disable state on certain conditions.

Figure 14-2 depicts an access layer Catalyst 6500 switch scenario. A real-time media server plugs into switch port 3/47. The switch port needs port security to prevent any unauthorized devices from plugging into the same port. The administrator has configured preferential QoS policies based on all traffic received on the port as well as other security ACLs. The network administrator requirement is not to shut down the port of the server but rather to restrict the port to only the authorized MAC address. In addition, the network administrator configures the switch to shut down port 2/2 in the guest lobby if any unauthorized workstation plugs into that port.

Figure 14-2   *Scenario of Port Security in Cisco Catalyst Switches*

Access Layer Catalyst

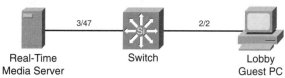

Real-Time   Switch   Lobby
Media Server   Guest PC

Example 14-8 shows the configuration and verification of the scenario depicted in Figure 14-1.

Example 14-8   *Configuration of Port Security on Cisco CatOS–Based Switch*

```
6500> (enable)  set port security 3/47 enable
Port 3/47 security enabled.
Trunking disabled for Port 3/47 due to Security Mode.
6500> (enable)  set port security  3/47 00-00-00-00-00-08
Mac address 00-00-00-00-00-08 set for port 3/47.
6500> (enable)  set port security 3/47 maximum 1
Port 3/47 security maximum address 1.
6500> (enable)  set port security 3/47 age 0
Port 3/47 security age time 0.
6500> (enable)  set port security 3/47 violation restrict
Port 3/47 security violation mode restrict.
6500> (enable)  set port security 2/2 enable
Port 2/2 security enabled.
Trunking disabled for Port 2/2 due to Security Mode.
6500> (enable)  set port security 2/2 00-00-00-00-11-18
Mac address 00-00-00-00-11-18 set for port 2/2.
6500> (enable)  set port security 2/2 maximum 1
Port 2/2 security maximum address 1.
6500> (enable)  set port security 2/2 age 0
Port 2/2 security age time 0.
6500> (enable)  set port security 2/2 shutdown 300 violation shutdown
Port 2/2 security shutdown time 300, violation mode shutdown.
```

The error message that you would see when a violation occurs on the secure port 2/2 is as follows:

```
2003 May 20 17:56:15 %SECURITY-1-PORTSHUTDOWN:Port 2/2 shutdown due to security
violation
2003 May 20 17:56:15 %ETHC-5-PORTFROMSTP:Port 2/2 left bridge port
```

Use the following command in Cisco CatOS–based switches to find out which MAC address caused the security violation:

show port security {*mod/port*}

Example 14-9 shows a user determining which MAC address caused a security violation on port 2/2. The output shows the configured MAC address as 00-00-00-00-11-18 and the violating MAC address as 00-00-00-00-00-05.

Example 14-9 *Determining the Violating MAC Address on a Cisco CatOS–Based Catalyst Switch*

```
6500> (enable)  show port security 2/2
* = Configured MAC Address
Port  Security Violation Shutdown-Time Age-Time Max-Addr Trap     IfIndex
----- -------- --------- ------------- -------- -------- -------- -------
 2/2   enabled  shutdown        300        0         1 disabled      57
Port  Num-Addr Secure-Src-Addr    Age-Left Last-Src-Addr     Shutdown/Time-Left
----- -------- ----------------   -------- ----------------- ------------------
 2/2        1 00-00-00-00-11-18 *    - 00-00-00-00-00-05       yes          289
Port  Flooding on Address Limit
----- -----------------------
 2/2                     Enabled
```

To configure the switch to automatically re-enable the port after a certain time, configure the err-disable timeout value.

Example 14-10 illustrates the configuration required for the scenario as shown in Figure 14-1 if a Cisco IOS–based access layer Catalyst 4500 switch were to be used.

Example 14-10 *Configuration of Port Security on Cisco IOS–Based Catalyst Switches*

```
4503(config)#interface  FastEthernet 3/47
4503(config-if)#switchport
4503(config-if)#switchport mode access
4503(config-if)#switchport port-security
4503(config-if)#switchport port-security mac-address 0000.0000.0008
4503(config-if)#switchport port-security maximum 1
4503(config-if)#switchport port-security aging static
4503(config-if)#switchport port-security violation restrict
4503(config)#interface FastEthernet 2/2
4503(config-if)#switchport
4503(config-if)#switchport mode access
4503(config-if)#switchport port-security
4503(config-if)#switchport port-security mac-address 0000.0000.1118
4503(config-if)#switchport port-security maximum 1
4503(config-if)#switchport port-security aging static
4503(config-if)#switchport port-security violation shutdown
```

Although port security restricts the access to a single MAC address, it does not restrict to a specific MAC address unless manually configured to do so. In a large enterprise network, it is time consuming to manually configure all the user ports in this fashion, so the general practice is to allow the switch to dynamically secure the MAC address. However, such a configuration allows for a malicious user to get access to the network as long as he can find an unconnected LAN port. The port security will learn the new address when this user connects to the network.

To prevent this scenario from happening, Cisco Catalyst switches support the port security sticky feature, which restricts the port access to a specific MAC address but doesn't require manual configuration of that MAC address.

When the port security sticky feature is used, the switch port converts dynamically learned MAC addresses to sticky MAC addresses and subsequently adds them to the running configuration as if they were static entries for a single MAC address to be allowed by port security. Sticky secure MAC addresses will be added to the running configuration but will not become part of the startup configuration file unless the running configuration is copied to the startup configuration after addresses have been learned. If they are saved in the startup configuration, they will not have to be relearned upon switch reboot. This provides a higher level of network security and a faster configuration option for the network administrators.

The following command will convert all dynamic port security–learned MAC addresses to sticky secure MAC addresses:

```
switchport port-security mac-address sticky
```

Restricting Traffic Based on Host MAC Addresses

The MAC filtering feature restricts traffic based on host MAC addresses. With this feature, the switch drops the traffic sourced from a configured MAC address. Network administrators use this feature to prevent a particular unauthorized host from sending traffic into the network. This feature is different from the port security feature, where the traffic from the specified MAC addresses is allowed. In the MAC filtering feature, traffic from the unauthorized MAC address is restricted.

NOTE   Catalyst switches allow the filtering of only unicast source MAC address traffic, not multicast source MAC address traffic. It is nonetheless against specification to originate packets with multicast source MAC addresses. The switch should not be receiving such packets.

Example 14-11 shows a user configuring the MAC filtering feature on an access layer Catalyst 6500 switch to prevent users with the host MAC addresses of 00-00-00-00-00-08 and 00-00-00-00-00-11 from accessing the network in VLAN 99. Figure 14-3 represents the network topology for Example 14-11.

Figure 14-3   *MAC Filtering Feature on Cisco Catalyst Switch*

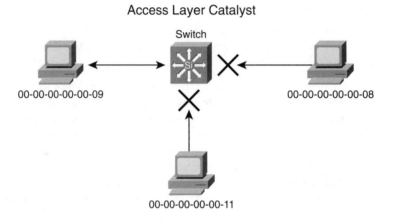

Access Layer Catalyst
Switch

00-00-00-00-00-09   00-00-00-00-00-08

00-00-00-00-00-11

Example 14-11   *Configuration and Verification of the MAC Filtering Feature on Cisco CatOS–Based Catalyst Switches*

```
6500> (enable)  set cam static filter 00-00-00-00-00-08 99
Filter entry added to CAM table.
6500> (enable)  set cam permanent filter 00-00-00-00-00-11 99
Filter entry added to CAM table.
6500> (enable)  show cam static
* = Static Entry. + = Permanent Entry. # = System Entry. R = Router Entry.
X = Port Security Entry $ = Dot1x Security Entry
VLAN  Dest MAC/Route Des    [CoS]  Destination Ports or VCs / [Protocol Type]
----  -----------------     -----  ------------------------------------------
99    00-00-00-00-00-08   *   FILTER Total Matching CAM Entries Displayed  =1
6500> (enable)
6500> (enable)  show cam permanent
* = Static Entry. + = Permanent Entry. # = System Entry. R = Router Entry.
X = Port Security Entry $ = Dot1x Security Entry
VLAN  Dest MAC/Route Des    [CoS]  Destination Ports or VCs / [Protocol Type]
----  -----------------     -----  ------------------------------------------
99    00-00-00-00-00-11   +   FILTER Total Matching CAM Entries Displayed  =1
```

The difference between static and permanent filters lies in whether the filter remains configured when the switch is reset. Catalyst switches retain permanent filters until the administrator manually clears the configuration, unlike the static filters, which are cleared after a reset. Typically static filters are used as a temporary policy, whereas permanent filters are used as a long-term policy because the permanent filters remain after resets.

In Cisco IOS–based switches, the unicast filtering feature is equivalent to the MAC filtering feature. Catalyst switches allow for the configuration of unicast filtering on a VLAN basis or on an individual interface basis. Cisco IOS–based switches support only unicast filtering that persists on reload. To configure this feature on Cisco IOS–based Catalyst switches, use the following command:

```
mac-address-table static  mac-address  vlan  vlan-id  drop
```

<table>
<tr><td>NOTE</td><td>The Cisco IOS unicast filtering (**mac-address-table**) command uses the **static** keyword, but the filter remains after the switch resets. Do not confuse this behavior with Cisco CatOS static filters, which are cleared after a reset. Cisco IOS unicast filtering behaves like the permanent filters present in Cisco CatOS switches. Cisco IOS does not have an equivalent to the static filters present in Cisco CatOS.

Refer again to the topology in Figure 14-2 for the configuration of the MAC filtering feature with a Cisco IOS–based Catalyst 4500 switch demonstrated in Example 14-12. Example 14-12 shows a user configuring unicast filtering to filter the 0000.0000.0008 and 0000.0000.0011 MAC addresses in VLAN 1.</td></tr>
</table>

Example 14-12 *Configuring and Verifying Unicast Filtering on a Cisco IOS–Based Catalyst Switch*

```
4503(config)#mac-address-table static 0000.0000.0008 vlan 1 drop
4503(config)#mac-address-table static 0000.0000.0011 vlan 1 drop
4503#show mac-address-table static vlan 1
Unicast Entries
 vlan   mac address      type      protocols          port
-------+---------------+--------+--------------------+------------------
    1   0000.0000.0008    static ip,ipx,assigned,other  Drop
    1   0000.0000.0009    static ip,ipx,assigned,other  FastEthernet3/2
    1   0000.0000.0011    static ip,ipx,assigned,other  Drop
    1   0009.e845.64bf    static ip,ipx,assigned,other  Switch
Multicast Entries
 vlan   mac address      type    ports
-------+---------------+--------+-----------------------------------------
    1   ffff.ffff.ffff   system Switch,Fa3/14,Fa3/38
```

Blocking Unicast Flooding on Desired Ports

By default, switches flood packets with unknown destination MAC addresses to all ports in the same VLAN as the received port's VLAN. Some ports do not require flooding. For example, a port that has only manually assigned MAC addresses and that does not have a network device connected to that port other than the configured MAC address does not need to receive flooded packets. In addition, a port security–enabled port with a configured secure MAC address or port does not need to receive unknown unicast flooding if the port has already learned the maximum number of MAC addresses. If the network exhibits asymmetrical routing, excessive unicast flooding can occur and might cause all the devices in that VLAN to suffer as they receive the unneeded traffic. With asymmetrical routing, transmit and receive packets follow different paths between a host and the destination device. For more information about asymmetrical routing, see the following technical document at Cisco.com:

"Unicast Flooding in Switched Campus Networks," Document ID: 23563
http://www.cisco.com/en/US/products/hw/switches/ps700/products_tech_note
09186a00801d0808.shtml

The unicast flood-blocking feature prevents the forwarding of unicast flood traffic on unnecessary ports. Restricting the amount of traffic on a per-port basis adds a level of security to the network and prevents network devices from unnecessarily processing non-directed packets.

Use the following command on Cisco CatOS–based switches to enable or disable the unicast flood feature:

set port unicast-flood {*mod/port*} {**enable** | **disable**}

Cisco IOS–based switches can restrict flooding of unknown multicast MAC-addressed traffic on a per-port basis, in addition to restricting flooding of unknown unicast destination MAC addresses. Use the following interface-level command:

switchport block {**unicast** | **multicast**}

Example 14-13 shows a user configuring unicast and multicast flood blocking on an access layer Cisco IOS–based Catalyst 4500 switch.

Example 14-13 *Configuration of Unicast and Multicast Flood Filtering on a Cisco IOS–Based Catalyst Switch*

```
4503#configure terminal
Enter configuration commands, one per line.  End with CNTL/Z.
4503(config)#interface FastEthernet 3/22
4503(config-if)#switchport block unicast
4503(config-if)#switchport block multicast
```

Port Security Summary

In summary, the port security features enable network administrators to restrict access to network by devices. Port security not only prevents unauthorized access but also prevents several types of malicious network DoS attacks, such as MAC flooding and spoofing. Unicast and multicast flooding prevents unnecessary traffic from being sent to all ports in the VLAN and acts as a security mechanism by preventing unauthorized devices from analyzing the type of traffic and devices in the network. 802.1X is emerging rapidly as the popular standard for network access control in the industry. 802.1X is discussed in the next section.

Network Access Security Using IEEE 802.1X

This chapter discusses several network access security features such as MAC address filtering, port security, and protocol filtering. However, these features are not available across all Cisco platforms and do not offer a centralized method of administration. The IEEE 802.1X access control feature is an industry-standard method of Layer 2 access control that offers centralized management. The IEEE 802.1X access control feature is also commonly found in wireless networks. The IEEE 802.1X feature is available on currently shipping Catalyst switches. Figure 14-4 illustrates the basic topology for 802.1X.

Figure 14-4 *IEEE 802.1X Topology*

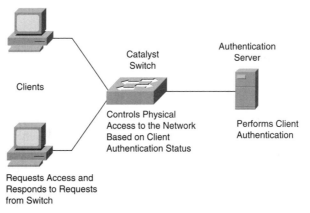

With 802.1X, an authentication server authenticates each workstation connected to a switch port before accepting any packets from the workstation. Until the authentication server authenticates the workstation, 802.1X access control allows only Extensible Authentication Protocol over LAN (EAPOL) traffic through the port to which the workstation connects. After authentication is successful, normal traffic may pass through the port.

With 802.1X port-based authentication, three defined devices exist:

- **Client**—The client is essentially the workstation that is requesting authentication to the network using 802.1X. Currently, only Microsoft Windows XP and Windows 2003 natively support 802.1X.

- **Authentication server**—The authentication server is responsible for validating requests from clients forwarded by the switch. Currently, the authentication servers are RADIUS servers with the Extensible Authentication Protocol (EAP) extension loaded.

- **Switch**—The switch is responsible for forwarding the 802.1X request from the clients to the authentication server and granting access to the network based on successful authentication. The switch is essentially a proxy in the 802.1X process.

The switch port state determines whether the client is granted access to the network. The port starts in the unauthorized state. While in this state, the port disallows all ingress and egress traffic except for 802.1X protocol packets. When a client is successfully authenticated, the port transitions to the authorized state, allowing all traffic for the client to flow normally. If the switch requests the client's identity (authenticator initiation) and the client does not support 802.1X, the port remains in the unauthorized state and the client is not granted access to the network.

In contrast, when an 802.1X-enabled client connects to a port and the client initiates the authentication process (supplicant initiation) by sending the EAPOL-start frame to a switch not running the 802.1X protocol and no response is received, the client begins sending frames as if the port were in the authorized state.

Configuring IEEE 802.1X

Catalyst switches support control of the port authorization state of 802.1X. The following three options are available:

- **Force-authorized**—Disables 802.1X port-based authentication and causes the port to transition to the authorized state without requiring an authentication exchange. The port transmits and receives normal traffic without 802.1X-based authentication of the client. This is the default setting.

- **Force-unauthorized**—Causes the port to remain in the unauthorized state, ignoring all attempts by the client to authenticate. The switch cannot provide authentication services to the client through this port.

- **Auto**—Enables 802.1X port-based authentication and causes the port to begin in the unauthorized state, allowing only EAPOL frames to be sent and received through the port. The authentication process begins when the link state of the port transitions from down to up (authenticator initiation) or when an EAPOL-start frame is received (supplicant initiation). The switch requests the identity of the client and begins relaying authentication messages between the client and the authentication server. The switch uniquely identifies each client that is attempting to access the network by using the client's MAC address.

If the client is successfully authenticated (receives an Accept frame from the authentication server), the port state changes to authorized, and all frames from the authenticated client are allowed through the port. If the authentication fails, the port remains in the unauthorized state. In this state, the port only allows authentication retries and does not pass a other user traffic. If the authentication server is not reachable, the switch may retransmit the request. If the switch does not receive a response from the server after a specified number of attempts, the authentication fails and the switch does not grant network access. Moreover, when a client logs off, the client sends an EAPOL-logoff message, causing the switch port to transition to the unauthorized state.

IEEE 802.1X must be enabled globally before it can be applied to specific ports. Use the following command sequence to configure 802.1X globally:

```
aaa new-model
aaa authentication dot1x  {default}   method1   [method2...]
dot1x system-auth-control
```

To configure an interface for 802.1X port-based authentication after globally configuring 802.1X, use the following interface command:

```
dot1x port-control auto
```

Example 14-14 illustrates enabling of AAA and configuring 802.1X on FastEthernet port 5/1 of a Catalyst IOS switch.

Example 14-14   *Enabling 802.1X Access Control in Cisco IOS*

```
Switch#configure terminal
Switch(config)#aaa new-model
Switch(config)#aaa authentication dot1x default group radius
Switch(config)#dot1x system-auth-control
Switch(config)#interface fastethernet 5/1
Switch(config-if)#dot1x port-control auto
Switch(config-if)#end
```

To enable 802.1X globally in Cisco CatOS, use the **set dot1x system-auth-control enable** command. To enable an interface for 802.1X access control after enabling 802.1X globally, use the **set port dot1x** *mod/port* **port-control auto** command. Example 14-15 illustrates configuring of 802.1X in Cisco CatOS.

Example 14-15   *Enabling 802.1X Globally and Per Interface in Cisco CatOS*

```
Console> (enable)set dot1x system-auth-control enable
dot1x system-auth-control enabled.
Console> (enable)set port dot1x 4/1 port-control auto
Port 4/1 dot1x port-control is set to auto.
Trunking disabled for port 4/1 due to Dot1x feature.
Spantree port fast start option enabled for port 4/1.
```

NOTE   IEEE 802.1X requires the use of a RADIUS server for access control. These configurations do not include the steps necessary to configure the RADIUS server.

IEEE 802.1X access control on Catalyst switches supports a multitude of additional features, such as 802.1X with voice VLANs, guest VLANs, and port security. IEEE 802.1X on Catalyst switches supports many additional configuration options; consult the configuration guides on Cisco.com for each platform for documentation on these additional features and options.

Understanding Cisco Network Admission Control on Catalyst Switches

Cisco Network Admission Control (NAC) is a solution that uses the network infrastructure to enforce security policies on all devices seeking to access network computing resources.

NAC helps ensure that all hosts comply with the latest corporate security policies, such as antivirus, security software, and operating system patches, prior to obtaining normal network access. Vulnerable and noncompliant hosts will be isolated (quarantined) or given limited access until they reach compliance. In addition, Cisco NAC has the capability to perform user authentication at the network level so that only devices with proper user credentials are permitted network access.

Switches are the first line of defense in a multilayer switched network, as Figure 14-5 illustrates. All the Catalyst switches are enabled for providing the NAC solution. NAC identifies not only who the user is but also whether the devices the users are using are healthy enough to access the network.

Figure 14-5 *NAC and Catalyst Switches*

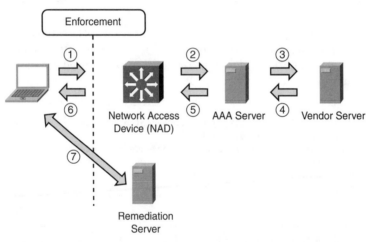

The steps involved in a Catalyst switch–based NAC solution (as depicted in Figure 14-5) are as follows:

1 Clients send credentials to the switch, also known as a Network Access Device (NAD).

2 The switch relays the credentials to the AAA server for user identification and policy check.

3 The AAA server authenticates the user and sends credentials of the host to appropriate vender servers to ascertain the health of the host based on the corporate policy defined by the system administrators.

4 The vendor servers respond with the result on the status check of the host based on the credentials sent.

5 The AAA server sends the response back to the switch. The response could indicate that the host is healthy enough to be allowed to access the network or that the host needs to be quarantined or denied access due to its unhealthy status.

6 The switch, based on the decision provided by the AAA server, configures the appropriate VLAN (normal VLAN or remediation VLAN) and any ACL and QoS features and sends the notification back to the device.

7 If the host is unhealthy and the switch assigns the host to the remediation VLAN, the host accesses the remediation server for the latest virus or OS patch to become healthy. Once the host becomes healthy, it goes back to Step 1 and sends the updated credentials to the NAD again to gain network access.

For more information about the Cisco NAC solution, refer to the following document on Cisco.com:

"Network Admission Control Framework"
http://www.cisco.com/en/US/partner/netsol/ns617/
networking_solutions_sub_solution_home.html

Applying Security Using Access Control Lists

Access control lists are essential for maintaining a secure network. Cisco Catalyst switches use specialized hardware components to switch traffic at line-rate speeds. These specialized hardware components support a limited number of ACL entries and features compared to software-switching methods typically found in Cisco routers. Furthermore, most Catalyst switches support only four ACL lookups per packet: an input and output security ACL, and an input and output QoS ACL. Furthermore, Cisco Layer 3 multilayer switches recognize four types of ACLs:

- **Router access control lists (RACL)**—RACLs are standard Cisco IOS–configured ACLs applied to routed interfaces.

- **VLAN access control lists (VACL)**—VACLs, also known as VLAN access-maps, apply to all traffic in a VLAN. VACLs support filtering based on Ethertype and MAC addresses. VACLs are order-sensitive, similar to Cisco IOS–based route maps. VACLs are capable of controlling traffic flowing within the VLAN or controlling switched traffic, whereas RACLs control only routed traffic.

- **QoS access control lists**—QoS ACLs define packets that are to be applied to QoS classification, marking, policing, and scheduling. Refer to Chapter 10, "Understanding and Implementing Quality of Service in Cisco Multilayer Switched Networks," for more details about QoS ACLs.

- **Port access control lists (PACL)**—ACLs applied on a Layer 2 port to control traffic entering or leaving the port.

To conserve the use of ternary content addressable memory (TCAM) space for ACLs, Catalyst switches merge ACLs entries for optimal use of memory space in TCAM. Generally, switches can combine several ACL entries into a single ACL entry. For example, 128 ACL entries for denying all class C subnets between 192.168.0.0 and 192.168.127.0 can be combined into a single ACL of denying traffic for 192.168.0.0 255.255.248.0 (192.168.0.0/25). Refer to Chapter 9, "Understanding and Configuring Multilayer Switching," for more information about TCAM.

Catalyst switches use two methods of performing an ACL merge:

- **Order independent**—With an order-independent merge, switches transform ACLs from a series of order-dependent actions to a set of order-independent masks and patterns. The resulting ACL entry is generally large. In addition, the merge is processor- and memory-intensive.

- **Order dependent**—The order-dependent merge is a recent improvement on newer Catalyst switches where ACLs in TCAM retain their order-dependent aspect. The computation is much faster and is less processor-intensive.

For more information regarding ACL merge algorithms, refer to the following white paper on Cisco.com:

"Understanding ACL Merge Algorithms and ACL Hardware Resources on Cisco Catalyst 6500 Switches"

RACLs

RACLs define security policies on routed interfaces for control plane and data plane traffic. Catalyst switches support RACLs in hardware with permit and deny actions. All Catalyst switches perform ACL (RACL and VACL) lookups regardless of whether ACLs exist; as a result, ACLs (RACLs and VACLs) have no effect on the switching performance. With RACLs, limitations exist in statistic and logging information per platform. RACLs are configured in the same way as normal Cisco IOS ACLs.

In Catalyst switches, you can apply RACLs to any routed interface such as the following:

- SVI (VLAN interfaces)
- L3 port or routed port
- L3 port-channel
- Other L3 interfaces

Figure 14-6 shows a network in which administrative policy restricts clients in VLAN 1 from accessing Server B.

Figure 14-6   *Example of Using RACL on a Catalyst Switch*

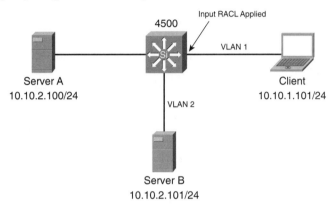

Example 14-16 illustrates an administrator configuring an ACL to prevent clients in VLAN 1 from talking to Server B due to a certain administrative policy. The ACL 101 would prevent traffic received on VLAN 1 interface from being delivered to Server B.

Example 14-16   *Configuring RACL on Catalyst IOS-Based Switch*

```
Switch#configure terminal
Enter configuration commands, one per line.  End with CNTL/Z.
Switch(config)#access-list 101 deny ip 10.10.1.0 0.0.0.255 host 10.10.2.101
Switch(config)#access-list 101 permit ip any any
Switch(config)#interface vlan 1
Switch(config-if)#ip access-group 101 in
Switch(config-if)#end
Switch#
```

VACLs

Currently, the Catalyst 6500 family of switches supports several types of VACL actions:

- **Forward (Permit)**—The forward (permit) VACL action forwards the frame as normal. Furthermore, the permit action with the capture option is essentially a switch port analyzer (SPAN) option, a troubleshooting feature used to copy frames to a monitor port. This type of VACL is useful for configuring multiple SPAN ports and attaching network-monitoring equipment such as third-party IDS equipment.

- **Drop (Deny)**—When a flow matches a drop (deny) ACL entry, it will be checked against the next ACL in the same sequence or the next sequence. If a flow does not match an ACL entry, the packet is denied.

- **Redirect**—The VACL redirect action is useful for redirecting specific traffic for monitoring, security, or switching purposes.

Other Catalyst switches currently support a subset of these actions but intend to support all actions in later software releases or hardware revisions.

NOTE   Check the respective Catalyst family release notes on Cisco.com for information about support of VACL and RACL features.

As mentioned previously, RACLs are configured in the same way as normal Cisco IOS ACLs. VACL configuration is similar. When configuring VACLs, use the following steps to configure a VLAN access map, **match** clause, **action** clause, and VLAN application respectively:

Step 1   Name and sequence the VLAN access map:

         vlan access-map *map-name* [*seq#*]

Step 2   Configure the match class:

         match {**ip address** {*1-199* | *1300-2699* | *acl-name*} | **ipx-address** {*800-999* | *acl-name*} | {**mac address** *acl-name*}

Step 3   Configure the ACL action:

         action {**drop** [**log**]} | {**forward** [**capture**]} | {**redirect** {{**fastethernet** | **gigabitethernet** | **tengigabitethernet**} *slot/port*} | {**port-channel** *channel-id*}}

Step 4   Attach the VLAN access map to respective VLANs:

         vlan filter *map-name* **vlan-list** *list*

Example 14-17 illustrates an example of configuring a VACL in Cisco IOS. In this example, the switch drops all ingress traffic on TCP port 10000. A practical example of the use of this VACL is in this case of stopping an Internet worm from transmitting traffic on TCP port 10000.

Example 14-17   *Configuring a VACL in Cisco IOS*

```
Switch#configure terminal
Switch(config)#access-list 100 permit tcp any any eq 10000
Switch(config)#vlan access-map BCMSN 100
Switch(config-access-map)#match ip address 100
Switch(config-access-map)#action drop
Switch(config-access-map)#exit S
witch(config)#vlan filter BCMSN vlan-list 1
Switch(config)#end
```

In Cisco CatOS, many permutations of commands for configuring VACLs exist. Consult the configuration and command references on Cisco CatOS for configuration details of VACLs in Cisco CatOS. Example 14-18 illustrates a sample configuration of a VACL in Cisco CatOS for restricting DHCP requests to a specific DHCP server in VLAN 10.

Example 14-18   *Sample VACL Configuration in Cisco CatOS*

```
Console(enable)#set security acl ip SERVER permit udp host 10.2.1.4 any eq 68
Console(enable)#set security acl ip SERVER deny udp any any eq 68
Console(enable)#set security acl ip SERVER permit any
Console(enable)#commit security acl SERVER
Console(enable)#set security acl map SERVER 10
```

Port ACLs

A port ACL (PACL) provides another level of granularity by controlling traffic at the port level. PACLs are applied to a Layer 2 switch port, trunk port, or EtherChannel port. The PACL feature is available only on Cisco IOS-based Catalyst switches.

The following ACLs are supported on Layer 2 interfaces using PACLs:

- Standard IP access lists using source addresses
- Extended IP access lists using source and destination addresses and optional Layer 4 protocol type information
- MAC extended access lists using source and destination MAC addresses and optional Layer 3 protocol type information

When you apply a PACL to a trunk port, the ACL filters traffic on all VLANs present on the trunk port. When you apply a PACL to a port with a voice VLAN, the ACL filters traffic on both the data and voice VLANs.

With PACLs, you can filter IP traffic by using IP access lists or non-IP traffic by using MAC ACLs. In addition, you can filter both IP and non-IP traffic on the same Layer 2 interface by applying both an IP access list and a MAC access list to the interface.

PACL features form the underlying mechanism of IPSG and DAI, which will be discussed later in this chapter.

Example 14-19 shows a user configuring IP access-list 101 and MAC access-list BCMSN

and applying them on interface FastEthernet 2/5, which is a Layer 2 switchport.

Example 14-19   *Configure PACL on a Catalyst Switch*

```
Switch#configure terminal
Enter configuration commands, one per line.  End with CNTL/Z.
Switch(config)#mac access-list extended BCMSN
Switch(config-ext-macl)#permit host 0011.abcd.abcd  host 0011.1111.1111
Switch(config-ext-macl)#exit
Switch(config)#access-list 101 deny ip 10.10.1.0 0.0.0.255 host 10.10.2.101
Switch(config)#access-list 101 permit ip any any
```

continues

Example 14-19 *Configure PACL on a Catalyst Switch (Continued)*

```
Switch(config-if)#interface fastEthernet 2/5
Switch(config-if)#switchport
Switch(config-if)#ip access-group 101 in
Switch(config-if)#mac access-group BCMSN in
Switch(config-if)#end
Switch#
```

Securing Networks Using Firewalls

Firewalls are used to prevent unauthorized access from external networks to the internal network. Firewalls can also be used within an organization to prevent one part of the network from accessing another part of the network. For example, a firewall could add protection for a firm's financial department network or human resources department network from standard users. Another practical example of firewalls deployed in the LAN is with company mergers and network integrations.

Resources such as web or FTP servers, which are generally accessed by external networks or through the Internet, are generally in a separate, secure network called the demilitarized zone (DMZ). Access to this network is also controlled by a firewall. If these publicly accessible devices are attacked, the use of the DMZ aids in protecting the internal network from such attacks. Figure 14-7 shows a typical firewall scenario, protecting an internal network and DMZ from the Internet.

Figure 14-7 *Typical Firewall Scenarios in a Network*

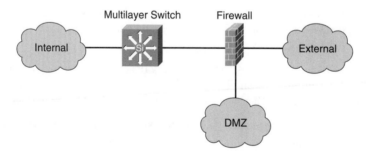

Cisco Systems does offer standalone firewalls such as the PIX 501. However, the Catalyst 6500 offers the integrated Firewall Services Module (FWSM), which is available as a line card with high performance and stateful inspection, which are crucial to internal LAN performance and availability.

The FWSM features include bidirectional NAT, policy NAT, URL filtering, and ACL filtering. The FWSM protection features include ARP inspection, DNS guard, flood guard, fragment guard, ICMP filtering, mail guard, TCP intercept, and Unicast Reverse Path Forward (uRPF) check. For more details about these features, refer to Cisco.com.

The stateful inspection feature enables the FWSM to inspect all traffic passing through the firewall using the adaptive security algorithm (ASA) to determine whether each packet needs to be allowed or dropped.

FWSM checks for new or established connections. If the connection is new, the FWSM creates a NAT translation and performs an ACL check, route lookup, IP checksum verification, session lookup, and TCP sequence check before establishing a "fast path." Subsequent packets from the established connection go through the "fast path," and thus FWSM is able to provide high performance without compromising security or CPU resources.

The FWSM does not include any external physical interfaces. Instead, it uses internal VLAN interfaces. For example, you assign VLAN 101 to the FWSM inside interface and VLAN 100 to the outside interface. You assign these VLANs to physical switch ports, and hosts connect to those ports. When communication occurs between VLANs 101 and 100, the FWSM is the only available path between the VLANs, forcing traffic to be statefully inspected.

Figure 14-8 shows a typical FWSM implementation on a Catalyst 6500 with four interfaces:

- One outside interface (VLAN 100)
- One DMZ interface (VLAN 102)
- Two inside interfaces (VLAN 101 and 103)

FWSM protects traffic between the HR department and inside network VLAN. FWSM also acts as a firewall to the Internet and protects the DMZ VLAN.

Figure 14-8 *Typical FWSM Implementation on a Catalyst 6500 Switch*

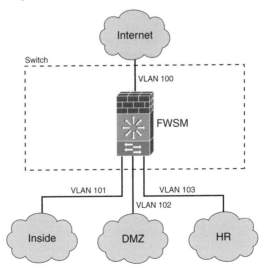

The Catalyst 6500 switches also support the traditional IOS firewall feature set without the need for the FWSM; however, the FWSM is recommended for higher performance because it provides 5.5 Gbps of throughput, up to 100 connections per second, and 1 million concurrent connections using Cisco PIX technology. You can install up to four FWSMs in a chassis to provide up to 20 Gbps throughput. For more information about the IOS firewall feature, refer to Cisco.com.

Security Through Network Address Translation (NAT)

NAT is typically used to convert private IP addresses from internal networks to public IP addresses for accessing the Internet. NAT is typically used in following forms:

- **Static NAT**—Statically configured one-to-one mapping between the internal and external IP address. Used in scenarios where the internal device needs to be accessed from external networks without dynamic port mapping.

- **Dynamic NAT**—Cisco IOS dynamically allocates NAT translations from a pool of available IP addresses. Probably the most popular method of NAT because it conserves public address space.

- **Port Address Translation (Overloading)**—A variation of dynamic NAT in which all the internal devices' communications are mapped to various ports of a single external IP address. Used in scenarios where the availability of multiple IP addresses is an issue.

There are multiple reasons to use NAT, such as saving the need for a unique public IP address for each internal device. Dynamic NAT is also a very useful security feature. With dynamic NAT, connections that originate from within the internal network are hidden. In other words, external networks cannot initiate connections to the internal network, thereby providing an effective mechanism against attacks from outside networks.

The Catalyst 6500 family of switches supports NAT. With the Supervisor Engine 720, NAT is supported in the hardware forwarding path. NAT will be supported on other Catalyst switches in future hardware or software revisions. NAT is used in the Enterprise Edge at distribution layer.

For a thorough understanding of NAT, consult the following resources on Cisco.com:

- "How NAT Works" http://www.cisco.com/en/US/tech/tk648/tk361/technologies_tech_note09186a0080094831.shtml

- "Cisco IOS Network Address Translation Overview" http://www.cisco.com/en/US/tech/tk648/tk361/technologies_white_paper09186a0080091cb9.shtml

DHCP Snooping

DHCP snooping is a DHCP feature that provides security by filtering untrusted DHCP messages from hosts or other devices in the network. DHCP snooping accomplishes this level of security by building and maintaining a DHCP snooping binding table.

An untrusted DHCP message is a DHCP message that the switch receives from outside the network or firewall or from an unauthorized DHCP server that can cause security attacks within a network. DHCP snooping is used along with the interface tracking feature, which inserts option 82 in the DHCP messages by the switch. Option 82 is the Relay Agent Information Option as described in RFC 3046.

The use of DHCP snooping extends existing security capabilities, including the capability to trust a port as a DHCP server and preventing unauthorized DHCP server responses from untrusted access ports. Another DCHP snooping supported feature is per-port DHCP message rate limiting, which is configurable in packets per second (pps) and is used to prevent DoS attacks. The DCHP snooping feature is useful in ISP networks, university campuses, and Long Range Ethernet (LRE) network scenarios to prevent misconfigured or malicious DHCP servers from causing user-connectivity problems (such as giving out bogus DHCP addresses).

DHCP snooping builds a DHCP binding table that contains client IP addresses, MAC addresses, ports, VLAN numbers, leases, and binding types. Switches support the enabling of the DHCP snooping feature on a per-VLAN basis. With this feature, the switch intercepts all DHCP messages within the Layer 2 VLAN domain. With option 82 enabled, the Supervisor Engine adds the ingress module, port, VLAN, and switch MAC address to the packet before forwarding the DHCP request to the DHCP server. The DHCP server can track the IP address that it assigns from the DHCP pool.

With this feature, the switch restricts end-user ports (untrusted ports) to sending only DHCP requests, while all other types of DHCP traffic, such as DHCP offer responses, are dropped by the switch. DHCP snooping trusted ports are the ones connected to the known DHCP servers or uplink ports to the distribution switch that provides the path to the DHCP server. Trusted ports can send and receive any DHCP message. In this manner, the switch allows only trusted DHCP servers to give out DHCP addresses via DHCP responses. Therefore, this feature prevents users from setting up their own DHCP servers and providing unauthorized addresses.

Figure 14-9 illustrates a typical use of DHCP untrusted and trusted ports. The recommendation is to enable trusting on the legitimate DHCP server port and interconnection ports between the access layer switches and the distribution layer switches, as shown in Figure 14-9. In addition, the recommendation is to leave the end-user workstation ports on the access layer switches at the default port state of untrusted for DCHP snooping.

Example 14-20 shows the configuration of DHCP snooping with option 82 on VLAN 10 on an access layer or distribution layer Cisco IOS–based Catalyst 4500 switch. In this scenario, the DHCP server connects to interface FastEthernet 4/10 while the clients connect on all the ports of module 3. In addition, the configuration rate limits DHCP requests in an effort to prevent DHCP DoS attacks.

Figure 14-9   *DHCP Snooping in Multilayer Switched Networks*

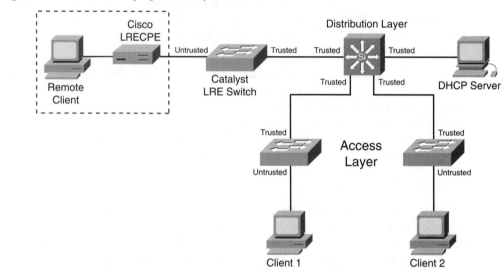

Example 14-20   *Configuration and Verification of DHCP Snooping on Cisco IOS–Based Switches*

```
4503(config)#ip dhcp snooping
4503(config)#ip dhcp snooping vlan 10
4503(config)#ip dhcp snooping information option
4503(config)#interface FastEthernet 4/10
4503(config-if)#ip dhcp snooping trust
4503(config)#interface range FastEthernet 3/1 - 48
4503(config-if-range)#ip dhcp snooping limit rate ?
  <1-4294967294>  DHCP snooping rate limit
4503(config-if-range)#ip dhcp snooping limit rate 100
4503#show ip dhcp snooping
Switch DHCP snooping is enabled
DHCP snooping is configured on following VLANs:
1,10
Insertion of option 82 is enabled
Interface              Trusted      Rate limit (pps)
-------------------    -------      ----------------
FastEthernet3/1        no           100
FastEthernet3/2        no           100
FastEthernet3/3        no           100
FastEthernet3/4        no           100
Output truncated
FastEthernet4/10       yes          unlimited
```

To summarize, DHCP snooping with option 82 provides an excellent mechanism to prevent DHCP DoS attacks or misconfigured clients from causing anomalous behavior in the network.

IP Source Guard

The IP Source Guard (IPSG) feature is a Layer 2 interface feature that is similar to the Unicast Reverse Path Forwarding (uRPF) check for Layer 3 or routed interfaces. In other words, IPSG provides a check to ensure that the packet received on an interface is supposed to be received on the respective interface. If the check succeeds, the packet is allowed; otherwise, a violation occurs. IPSG makes sure that in a Layer 2 network, the IP addresses of end devices are not hijacked, or that an unauthorized device does not self-assign IP addresses in an effort to access the network or cause a network disruption or outage.

For more information about uRPF for routed interfaces, refer to the "Configuring Unicast Reverse Forwarding Path section of the Cisco IOS Release 12.2" software configuration guide on Cisco.com.

IPSG derives the valid source port information with the help of the DHCP snooping binding table or static IP source binding. DHCP snooping provides dynamic binding and hence is more scalable in an enterprise network with many end-users. Static IP source binding needs to be used on ports where the end device has a static IP address. Usually, servers that are assigned a static IP address are candidates for IPSG and need static IP source binding. With IPSG configured, on link up, the only packets allowed are the DHCP packets. Once the DHCP server assigns the IP address, the DHCP snooping binding is updated. IPSG then automatically installs a per-port VLAN ACL (PVACL) for the interface. This process restricts the client IP traffic to those source IP addresses configured in the binding. Any IP traffic from the host port with a source IP address other than that in the IP source binding will be filtered out. This filtering limits a host's capability to attack the network by claiming a neighbor host's IP address.

IP Source Guard supports Layer 2 interfaces only, including both access and trunk interfaces. For each untrusted Layer 2 interface, there are two levels of IP traffic security filtering:

- **Source IP address filter**—IP traffic is filtered based on its source IP address. Only IP traffic with a source IP address that matches the IP source binding entry is permitted. An IP source address filter is changed when a new IP source entry binding is created or deleted on the port. The port PVACL will be recalculated and reapplied in the hardware to reflect the IP source binding change. By default, if the IP filter is enabled without any IP source binding on the port, a default PVACL that denies all IP traffic is installed on the port. Similarly, when the IP filter is disabled, any IP source filter PVACL will be removed from the interface.

- **Source IP and MAC address filter**—IP traffic is filtered based on its source IP address as well as its MAC address; only IP traffic with source IP and MAC addresses matching the IP source binding entry are permitted.

When IPSG is enabled in IP and MAC filtering mode, the DHCP snooping option 82 must be enabled to ensure that the DHCP protocol works properly. Without option 82 data, the switch cannot locate the client host port to forward the DHCP server reply. Instead, the DHCP server reply is dropped, and the client cannot obtain an IP address.

Configuring IPSG

IPSG requires that DHCP snooping be enabled on the required VLAN to enable automated IP source bindings. Refer to the DHCP snooping section for more information about configuring DHCP snooping.

To enable IPSG with source MAC and IP filtering, use the following interface-level command on desired interface:

```
ip verify source vlan dhcp-snooping port-security
```

To configure a static IP source binding, use the following global configuration command:

ip source binding *mac-address* **vlan** *vlan-id* *ip-address* **interface** *interface-id*

For more information on how to configure IPSG on CatOS-based Catalyst 6500 switches, refer to the "Configuring DHCP snooping and IP Source Guard" section of the software configuration guide on Cisco.com.

Figure 14-10 shows a scenario in which a workstation using DHCP for acquiring IP addresses and a server that uses a static IP address connect to a Catalyst switch. Example 14-21 shows configuration and verification of IPSG for the scenario in Figure 14-10.

Figure 14-10 *IP Source Guard on Catalyst IOS-Based Switches*

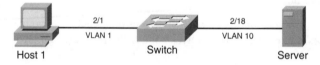

Host 1   2/1   VLAN 1   Switch   2/18   VLAN 10   Server

Example 14-21 *Configuration and Verification of IPSG on Catalyst Switch*

```
Switch#configure terminal
Enter configuration commands, one per line.  End with CNTL/Z.
Switch(config)#ip dhcp snooping
Switch(config)#ip dhcp snooping vlan 1,10
Switch(config)#ip dhcp snooping verify mac-address
Switch(config)#ip source binding 0000.000a.000b vlan 10 10.1.10.11 interface Fa2/18
Switch(config)#interface fastethernet 2/1
Switch(config-if)#switchport
Switch(config-if)#switchport mode access
```

Example 14-21 *Configuration and Verification of IPSG on Catalyst Switch (Continued)*

```
Switch(config-if)#switchport port-security
Switch(config-if)#ip verify source vlan dhcp-snooping port-security
Switch(config)#interface fastethernet 2/18
Switch(config-if)#switchport
Switch(config-if)#switchport mode access
Switch(config-if)#switchport port-security
Switch(config-if)#ip verify source vlan dhcp-snooping port-security
Switch(config-if)#end
Switch#show ip source binding
MacAddress          IpAddress       Lease(sec)  Type            VLAN  Interface
-----------------   --------------- ----------  ------------    ----  -------------
00:02:B3:3F:3B:99   10.1.1.11       6522        dhcp-snooping   1     FastEthernet2/1
00:00:00:0A:00:0B   10.1.10.11      infinite    static          10    FastEthernet2/18
Switch#show ip verify source
Interface Filter-type  Filter-mode  IP-address      Mac-address         Vlan
--------- -----------  -----------  --------------- -----------------   ----------
Fa2/1     ip-mac       active       10.1.1.11       00:02:B3:3F:3B:99   1
Fa2/18    ip-mac       active       10.1.10.11      00:00:00:0a:00:0b   10
```

Figure 14-11 shows that an attacker is connected to interface 2/10 and is trying to spoof the IP address of the server. The Catalyst switch detects and drops the packets in the hardware path. Currently, the Catalyst 4500 does not provide any error message upon violation if only the IP address is spoofed, but the switch is protected against IP spoofing attack. Port security takes the necessary action in the case of MAC address spoofing by the attacker in this scenario. The Catalyst 6500 does provide an error message to indicate the violation in the case of IP spoofing.

Figure 14-11 *IPSG Protecting Against an Attacker on Catalyst Switch*

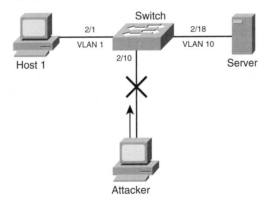

IPSG is an essential security feature to prevent IP address spoof attacks at the Layer 2 level. Recommended practice is to enable IPSG on access layer switches in a multilayer switched network.

Dynamic ARP Inspection

Dynamic ARP Inspection (DAI) is a security feature that validates Address Resolution Protocol (ARP) packets in a network. DAI enables a network administrator to intercept, log, and discard ARP packets with invalid MAC address-to-IP address bindings. This capability protects the network from certain "man-in-the-middle" attacks.

Figure 14-12 shows three hosts connected to a Catalyst switch in the same VLAN. Host A needs to communicate with Host B and sends an ARP request for the Host B MAC address. The ARP request is sent as broadcast in the subnet. Host B receives the ARP request and creates or updates its ARP cache with Host A's MAC address and IP address, and Host B sends an ARP response. The ARP response is sent as a unicast packet. Host A, upon receiving the ARP response, updates the ARP entry for Host B.

Figure 14-12 *Man-in-the-Middle Attack*

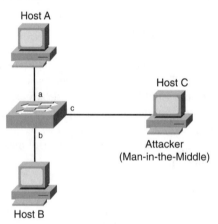

In this scenario, Host C can act as a man-in-the-middle by sending a forged broadcast ARP response as Host B but with the MAC address of itself. Host A, upon receiving the ARP response, would incorrectly have an ARP entry for Host B's IP address with Host C's MAC address. Host C can also forge the ARP response with Host A's IP address and its own MAC address, whereas Host B now thinks Host C's MAC address maps to Host A's IP address.

Any communication between Host A and B is now sent to Host C, who can then redirect the traffic after reading the content. This scenario is called a man-in-the-middle attack and can be easily achieved.

To prevent such attacks in the Layer 2 network, Catalyst switches have introduced DAI. The switch makes sure that ARP packets are originated from the correct ports and are not spoofed by an attacker. The switch is able to determine the correct port by manual configuration or dynamically using the DHCP snooping binding table. If the switch determines that packets are coming from the wrong port, it drops the packets and also logs the violation. Logging the violation helps the administrator to identify the attacker or unauthorized devices in the switched network. In addition, the violator port is err-disabled, and hence the attacker will not be able to cause further disruption to the network.

To illustrate DAI operation in a multilayer switched network, consider the network shown in Figure 14-13 with two switches, switches A and B. Host 1 is connected to switch A, and Host 2 is connected to switch B. The DHCP server is connected to switch A. DHCP snooping is enabled on both switch A and switch B as a prerequisite for DAI. The inter-switch links are configured as DAI trusted ports, and the user ports are left in the default untrusted state.

Figure 14-13   *DAI Enabled Catalyst Switches*

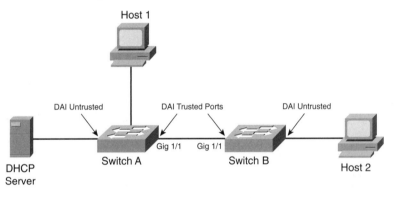

Example 14-22 shows the configuration and verification of the switches for DAI for the scenario in Figure 14-13. Assume that all the devices are in VLAN 10 in this scenario. (The switches are connected to each other via uplink ports GigabitEthernet 1/1.)

Example 14-22   *Configuration and Verification of DAI on Catalyst Switch*

```
SwitchA#configure terminal
Enter configuration commands, one per line.  End with CNTL/Z.
SwitchA(config)#ip arp inspection vlan 10
SwitchA(config)#interface gigabitEthernet 1/1
SwitchA(config-if)#ip arp inspection trust
SwitchA(config-if)#end
SwitchA#
SwitchB#configure terminal
Enter configuration commands, one per line.  End with CNTL/Z.
 SwitchB(config)#ip arp inspection vlan 10
SwitchB(config)#interface gigabitEthernet 1/1
SwitchB(config-if)#ip arp inspection trust
SwitchB(config-if)#end
SwitchB#
Switch#show ip arp inspection interfaces
Interface        Trust State    Rate (pps)    Burst Interval
---------------  -----------    ----------    --------------
```

continues

Example 14-22 *Configuration and Verification of DAI on Catalyst Switch (Continued)*

```
Gi1/1                Trusted               None               N/A
Gi1/2                Untrusted             15                 1
Fa2/1                Untrusted             15                 1
Fa2/2                Untrusted             15                 1
Fa2/3                Untrusted             15                 1
Fa2/4                Untrusted             15                 1
<output skipped>
SwitchA#show ip arp inspection vlan 10
Source Mac Validation      : Disabled
Destination Mac Validation : Disabled
IP Address Validation      : Disabled
Vlan      Configuration    Operation   ACL Match          Static ACL
 ----     -------------    ---------   ---------          ----------
   10     Enabled          Active
Vlan      ACL Logging      DHCP Logging
 ----     -----------      ------------
   10     Deny             Deny
SwitchA#
SwitchA#show ip dhcp snooping binding
MacAddress          IpAddress        Lease(sec)  Type            VLAN   Interface
------------------  ---------------  ----------  -------------   ----   --------------
00:01:00:01:00:01   10.10.10.1       4995        dhcp-snooping   10     FastEthernet2/1
SwitchB#show ip arp inspection interfaces
Interface           Trust State      Rate (pps)  Burst Interval
---------------     -----------      ----------  --------------
 Gi1/1              Trusted          None               N/A
 Gi1/2              Untrusted        15                 1
 Fa2/1              Untrusted        15                 1
 Fa2/2              Untrusted        15                 1
 Fa2/3              Untrusted        15                 1
 Fa2/4              Untrusted        15                 1
<output skipped>
SwitchB#show ip arp inspection vlan 10
Source Mac Validation      : Disabled
Destination Mac Validation : Disabled
IP Address Validation      : Disabled
Vlan      Configuration    Operation   ACL Match          Static ACL
 ----     -------------    ---------   ---------          ----------
   10     Enabled          Active
Vlan      ACL Logging      DHCP Logging
 ----     -----------      ------------
   10     Deny             Deny
SwitchB#
SwitchB#show ip dhcp snooping binding
MacAddress          IpAddress        Lease(sec)  Type            VLAN   Interface
------------------  ---------------  ----------  -------------   ----   --------------
00:02:00:02:00:02   10.10.10.2       4995        dhcp-snooping   10     FastEthernet2/2
```

Now if an attacker is connected to switch B, as shown in Figure 14-14, and tries to send a bogus ARP request, switch B will detect it and drop the ARP request packet. The switch can also err-disable or shut down the port and send a log message to alert the administrator. DAI will discard any ARP packets with invalid MAC address-to-IP address bindings.

Figure 14-14   *DAI Prevents Attacker's Bogus ARP Request*

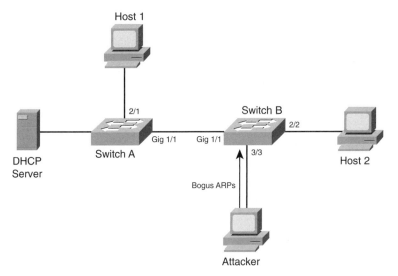

The error message displayed on the switch when such a security violation occurs is as follows:

```
02:46:49: %SW_DAI-4-DHCP_SNOOPING_DENY: 1 Invalid ARPs (Req) on Fa3/3, vlan
10.([0001.0001.0001/10.10.10.1/0000.0000.0000/0.0.0.0/09:23:24 UTC Thu Nov 27
2003])
```

DAI is also used to rate-limit the incoming ARP packets (ARP throttling) and then err-disable the interface if the rate is exceeded. Use the following Cisco IOS command at interface-level to implement this action:

```
ip arp inspection limit  rate  0-2048
```

DAI is a powerful security feature along with DHCP snooping and IPSG and offers the protection needed in the multilayer switched network access layer against ARP spoofing or ARP flood attacks.

Understanding the Role of Private VLANs as a Security Feature

Service provider customers usually connect multiple servers to the Internet, isolating their own traffic from other customers' traffic while maintaining communication between their own servers. The traditional solution to this requirement is for the ISP to provide one VLAN per customer, with each VLAN having its own IP subnet. A Layer 3 device aggregates the subnets to provide interconnectivity between VLANs and to route traffic to the Internet. Problems with the traditional end-to-end VLAN solutions include the following:

- Supporting a separate VLAN per customer requires a high number of interfaces on the service provider's network devices.

- The solution does not scale well because spanning tree becomes more complicated with the addition of multiple VLANs.

- Maintaining multiple VLANs means maintaining multiple ACLs, increasing network-management complexity.

Private VLANs provide Layer 2 isolation between ports within the same private VLAN. This eliminates the need for a separate VLAN per customer, as well as the requirement of a separate IP subnet per customer. A range of addresses from a single IP network can be assigned to each customer. This functionality of private VLANs yields a secure environment in which multiple devices, hosts, or customer networks reside on the same Layer 2 network, purely isolated from each other.

Figure 14-15 illustrates private VLAN behavior in an enterprise network. Chapter 4 discusses private VLAN configuration and terminology in detail.

Figure 14-15   *Pictorial View of Private VLANs*

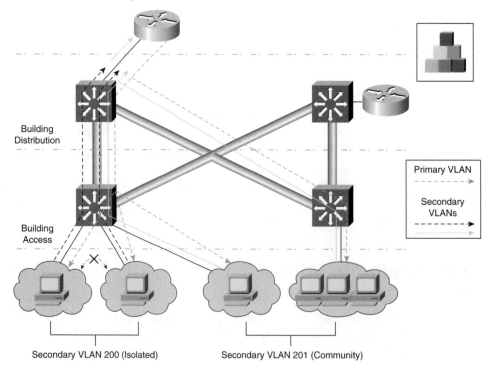

Understanding the Role of QoS as a Security Feature

Because QoS applies classification, marking, policing, queuing, and scheduling to frames passing in the network, QoS is also a security feature. With QoS, it is possible to minimize DoS attacks and limit traffic with classification and policing. For example, limiting specific Internet gaming traffic to a low rate, such as 1 to 2 Mbps, prevents a DoS attack using gaming traffic profiles from consuming the network with large amounts of traffic. In addition, reducing traffic flows of specific types based on UDP and TCP port numbers also minimizes the effects of DoS attacks. Moreover, features such as marking and scheduling prevent DoS attacks from taking priority over high-priority traffic such as voice traffic or iSCSI traffic. Scheduling achieves this security level by transmitting packets with specific priorities before other packets. Switches use QoS classification and marking to ensure that only the correct frames, such as voice frames, are designated as high priority. For a complete discussion of QoS, refer to Chapter 10.

STP Security Mechanisms Review

STP is essential in a Layer 2 topology to prevent loops in a redundantly configured network. However, STP is a protocol that can be taken advantage of either intentionally or unintentionally in the network.

Some of the preventable common network attacks involving STP are the following:

- **Connecting an unauthorized hub**—Users may plug in a unauthorized hub in their workspace to extend the network. But by connecting two switch ports into the hub, the user may create an STP loop. To prevent this type of network issue, use the BPDU Guard feature. BPDU Guard detects the loop and effectively err-disables the user port. For more information about BPDU Guard, refer to Chapter 6.

- **Connecting an unauthorized access switch**—Users may plug in an unauthorized access switch in their workspace to extend the network. Unlike the previous scenario with a hub, connecting an access switch will not cause a network loop but it may result in a topology change in the network. If the access switch has a better BPDU, then it may become the root of the network, resulting in network performance degradation due to an undesirable network topology. To prevent this type of scenario from happening, use the Root Guard feature. This feature will detect the BPDU sent by this newly added access switch and will disable the user port. For more information about the Root Guard feature, refer to Chapter 6.

- **Unidirectional link due to faulty cabling or device**—One of the rarer but definite possibilities in a network is that a cable fault or device will cause switch links to become unidirectional. Such a condition will result in an STP loop (as described in the Chapter 6 section "Preventing Forwarding Loops and Black Holes"). Unidirectional links result in a blocking port going into the forwarding state, because the downstream switch is not receiving BPDUs. With no blocking port in the Layer 2 topology, a loop results, causing network downtime. To prevent this failure, use the UDLD feature, which detects and err-disables the offending link. Although the UDLD feature is not part of the STP features, it is mentioned in this section because it is closely related. For more information about the UDLD feature, refer to Chapter 6.

- **Blocking port erroneously moving to forwarding state**—You just read that a unidirectional link can cause a blocking port to move to the forwarding state due to hardware problems. A software inconsistency or BPDU loss can also cause this to occur. The switch erroneously puts a port in the forwarding state even though it should be blocking, causing a loop in the network. To prevent this type of rare issue, use the Loop Guard feature, which will detect such a condition and put the blocking switch port into an inconsistent state, thus preventing the loop. For more information about the Loop Guard feature, refer to Chapter 6.

Case Study: Understanding and Preventing VLAN Hopping Attacks

VLAN hopping attacks refer to a malicious device attempting to access VLANs for which it is not configured. There are two forms of VLAN hopping attacks.

The first form is due to the default configuration of the Catalyst switchport. Cisco Catalyst switches enable trunking in auto mode by default. As a result, the interface becomes a trunk upon receiving a DTP frame. An attacker can use this default behavior to access VLANs configured on the switch through one of the following methods:

- An attacker can send a malicious DTP frame. Upon receiving the frame, the switch would form a trunk port, which would then give the attacker access to all the VLANs on the trunk. In Figure 14-16, the attacker port becomes a trunk port, and the attacker is able to attack a victim in any VLAN carried on the trunk.

- An attacker can connect via an unauthorized Cisco switch, which can send DTP frames and form a trunk. The attacker again has access to all the VLANs through the trunk. In Figure 14-17, an unauthorized switch is able to form a trunk with the Cisco switch. The attacker device connects to the unauthorized switch and is able to attack a victim in another VLAN.

Figure 14-16 *Single-Tagged 802.1Q VLAN Hopping Attack with Default Trunk Configuration*

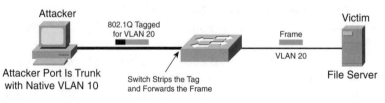
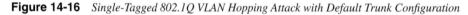

Figure 14-17   *Single-Tagged 802.1Q VLAN Hopping Using an Unauthorized Switch*

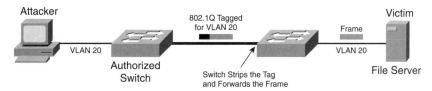

Protecting against the first type of VLAN hopping is simple. Configure all user ports with the trunking feature turned off. On Cisco IOS-based Catalyst switches, use the **switchport mode access** interface-level command to disable trunking. Another way to configure interface connecting to the host is to use the **switchport mode host** interface-level command, which turns off PAgP and DTP negotiation and enables STP PortFast configuration.

The second form of VLAN hopping attack is possible even if the trunking feature is turned off on the switchport. The attack involves sending frames with a double 802.1Q tag. This attack requires the client to be on a switch other than the attacking switch. Another requirement is that these two switches must be connected in the same VLAN as the attacking switchport or native VLAN of the trunk between the switch and the attacked VLAN.

The outer tag is tagged with the attacker VLAN or VLAN configured on the switchport, and the inner tag is tagged with the VLAN of the intended victim. The switch, upon receiving the frame, removes the first 802.1Q tag but does not remove the second tag. This packet is flooded to all the ports in that VLAN as the switch does not have the MAC address in the table because the switch does not recognize that there is a second tag. This packet would be flooded to the victim's switch on the native VLAN with the inner tag sent by the attack, which is removed by that switch to forward the frame to the victim in a VLAN other than the attacker.

Figure 14-18 shows the second type of VLAN hopping attack. The attacker is in VLAN 10, and the intended victim is in VLAN 20. The attacker sends double-tagged 802.1Q frames with the outer tag marked with VLAN 10 and the inner tag marked with VLAN 20. Switch A removes the first tag and floods the packet to switch B on the native VLAN. Switch B receives the frame with 802.1Q and does not differentiate between this packet and a normal packet tagged received for VLAN 20 and hence forwards the frame to the victim device on VLAN 20.

Figure 14-18 *Example of Double-Tagged 802.1Q VLAN Hopping Attack*

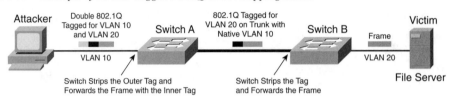

To protect against a double-tagged 802.1Q VLAN hopping attack, make sure that the native VLAN of the trunk between switches is not an end-user VLAN. Typically, the recommended practice is to configure a VLAN that will never be assigned to users.

In the scenario described in Figure 14-18, a native VLAN configuration of, say, VLAN 999 would result in the traffic from the attacker VLAN remaining within the same VLAN.

Study Tips

The following bullets review important BCMSN exam preparation points of this chapter. The bullets only briefly highlight the main points of this chapter related to the BCMSN exam. Consult the text of this chapter for additional information regarding these topics. Table 14-5 lists important commands to review for the BCMSN exam. Table 14-5 repeats commands found in earlier chapters because these commands are applicable to content in this chapter:

- Switch security is a critical element of overall network security.

- Different types of attacks happens at Layer 2, including MAC flooding, IP address spoofing, DHCP spoofing, ARP spoofing, VLAN hopping, intra-VLAN attacks, and SSH/Telnet attacks. Catalyst switches provide a variety of security features to deal with these types of attacks.

- Port security prevents unauthorized access to the network by limiting the number of MAC addresses that are able to access a network port as well as by specifying the exact MAC address that can access the network through the respective port. Violation options include shutting down the port or logging violation messages.

- DHCP snooping prevents unauthorized DHCP servers from disrupting the network by providing invalid or unauthorized IP addresses. It also prevents DoS attacks on the legitimate DHCP server.

- IP Source Guard (IPSG) provides IP address verification on a Layer 2 interface. IPSG derives the needed information from DHCP snooping and drops spoofed IP packets.

- The Dynamic ARP Inspection (DAI) feature prevents ARP spoofing or man-in-the-middle attacks. DAI also uses DHCP snooping information for validating ARP packets.

- The Firewall Services Module (FWSM) module provides integrated high performance and firewall support for the Catalyst 6500 switches. The Cisco IOS firewall feature can also be used on the Catalyst 6500 to provide firewall functionality.

- Network Address Translation (NAT) in dynamic form is a powerful security tool because it doesn't allow external network traffic to initiate sessions.

- 802.1X port-based authentication is defined as a client/server access control and authentication protocol that restricts unauthorized clients from connecting to a LAN through publicly accessible ports.

- NAC is a Cisco solution to prevent unhealthy hosts from accessing the network even though these hosts belong to legitimate employees.

- Cisco Catalyst switches provide security through different types of ACLs: Router ACLs, Port ACLs, VLAN ACLs, and QoS ACLs.

- The private VLAN feature provides the capability to limit Layer 2 connectivity between devices while providing Layer 3 connectivity through promiscuous interfaces.

- STP security mechanisms such as BPDU Guard and Root Guard help to prevent unauthorized devices being connected at the access layer, while features like Loop Guard help to prevent unidirectional links from causing network loop.

- AAA is used for robust authentication, authorization, and accounting services for network devices through TACACS+ and RADIUS.

- You should use secure passwords for console/vty lines and use SSH instead of Telnet for remote access for a higher level of security.

- General security protections include disabling unneeded services, configuring warning banners, disabling integrated HTTP daemon, securing access to the console and enable logging. See Chapter 3 for additional recommendations.

Table 14-5 *Commands to Review*

Command	Description
aaa authentication dot1x	Specifies one or more AAA methods for use on interfaces running IEEE 802.1X
aaa new-model	Enables AAA globally
aaa authentication login {**default**	*list-name*} **method1** [*method2...*]	Configures switch AAA authentication list
crypto key generate rsa	Initiates configuration of RSA keys for SSH access
dot1x port-control {**auto**	**force-authorized**	**force-unauthorized**}	Configures interface for authorization state of 802.1X
dot1x system-auth-control	Enables 802.1X globally

continues

Table 14-5   *Commands to Review (Continued)*

Command	Description
hostname *hostname*	Configures switch with a descriptive name
login authentication {**default** | *list-name*}	Applies the AAA authentication list to a line or set of lines
(config-if)#**ip arp inspection trust**	Enables DAI trust for the interface
ip arp inspection vlan vlan-id	Enables DAI for the specified VLAN
ip dhcp snooping	Enables DHCP snooping
(config-if)#**[no]ip dhcp snooping trust**	Enables or disables DHCP snooping trust for the interface
ip dhcp snooping vlan *vlan-id*	Enables DHCP snooping for the specified VLAN
ip domain-name *domain-name*	Configures the Internet domain suffix for the switch name
ip source binding *mac-address* **vlan** *vlan-id ip-address* **interface** *interface-id*	Configures a static IP source binding
(config-if)#**ip verify source vlan dhcp-snooping**	Enables IPSG for the specified interface and uses DHCP snooping information
mac-address-table static *mac- address vlan* **vlan-id drop**	Configures MAC address filtering for the specified MAC address in the specified VLAN
no ip dhcp snooping information option	Disables DHCP option 82 tagging by the switch
ping *ip-address*	Pings the specified IP address
show ip arp inspection	Displays configuration and statistics for DAI
show ip dhcp snooping	Displays DHCP snooping configuration and status
show ip dhcp snooping binding	Displays DHCP snooping bindings
Show ip source binding	Displays IP Source Guard bindings
show ip verify source	Displays the IPSG status for the configured interfaces
show mac-address-table static vlan *vlan-id*	Displays static entries in the MAC address table for the specified VLAN
switchport access vlan *vlan-id*	Configures an interface for a specific VLAN-ID
switchport block unicast | **multicast**	Configures unicast or multicast flooding blocking feature
switchport port-security	Enables port security feature for the interface

Table 14-5   *Commands to Review (Continued)*

Command	Description
switchport port-security aging {static | time | type}	Specifies port security aging options
switchport port-security mac-address *mac-address*	Specifies secure MAC address for the interface
switchport port-security maximum *<number>*	Specifies maximum number of allowed MAC addresses for the interface
switchport port-security violation {restrict | shutdown}	Specifies the violation action for the interface for port security
transport input	Configures the virtual terminal for allowable protocols
username *username* **password** *password*	Configures local username and password database
vlan access-map *name* [*number*]	Configures or modifies a VLAN map entry for VLAN packet filtering
vlan filter *mapname* **vlan-list** *list*	Assigns a VLAN access-map to a VLAN or a range of VLANs

Summary

Security is a primary concern in maintaining a secure, stable, and uninterrupted network. Network security goes far beyond the information in this chapter, and includes topics such as intrusion detection, firewalls, virus protection, and operating system patching. Unless you recognize and understand the importance of network security, your network is at risk. The following list summarizes the aspects and recommended practices for avoiding, limiting, and minimizing network vulnerabilities strictly related to Catalyst switches as a single network entity:

- Layer 2 attacks vary in nature and include spoofing attacks, VLAN attacks, MAC flood attacks, and switch device attacks, among others.

- Use strong passwords with SSH access instead of Telnet exclusively to Cisco network devices.

- Disable unused services such as TCP and UDP small services where appropriate.

- Use AAA for centralized authentication, authorization, and accounting of network devices and remote access.

- Use an access control feature such as 802.1X or port security to restrict workstation access to Catalyst switches.

- NAC helps to prevent hosts infected with viruses or worms or otherwise unhealthy hosts from accessing the network.

- Use DHCP snooping to prevent rogue DHCP servers on the network.

- Use IPSG and DAI with DHCP snooping to prevent IP address and ARP spoofing attacks.

- Apply management ACLs to limit remote access to Cisco network devices.

- Apply data plane security ACLs to filter unwarranted traffic in the network.

- Use private VLANs where appropriate to limit communication in specific VLANs.

- Apply QoS to limit and medicate anomalous traffic.

- Configure QoS to maintain network stability for high-priority traffic such as voice traffic during possible DoS or other anomalous security threats.

- STP security mechanisms such as BPDU Guard, Root Guard, Loop Guard, and UDLD prevent more types of network attacks and guard against certain failure scenarios.

Configuration Exercise 1: AAA, 802.1X, and VACLs

Complete this configuration exercise to familiarize yourself with the basic configuration of AAA, 802.1X, and VACLs.

Required Resources

The resources and equipment required to complete this exercise are as follows:

- A Cisco IOS–based Catalyst switch such as a Catalyst 2950, 3550, 4500, or 6500

- A terminal server or workstation connected directly to the console port of the Catalyst switch or remote access to the switch

- A Microsoft Windows XP workstation preconfigured with 802.1X

- Optionally, a traffic generator to verify VACLs

Exercise Objective

The purpose of this exercise is to demonstrate, on a small scale, AAA authentication, 802.1X configuration, and a VACL configuration. This exercise represents only a small-scale configuration; larger-scale implementations of these features are more realistic. Nevertheless, this exercise presents the necessary CLI commands to configure equivalent large-scale networks with the AAA, 802.1X, and VACL features.

Network Diagram

The network layout for this exercise is simplistic because it involves only a single standalone switch with an attached workstation capable of 802.1X. The switch also needs to be able to communicate with a RADIUS server via IP for testing AAA configurations.

Command List

In this configuration exercise, you will use the commands listed in Table 14-6, which are listed in alphabetical order so that you can easily locate the information you need. Refer to this list if you need configuration command assistance during the exercise. The table includes only the specific parameters used in the example and not all the available options for the command.

Table 14-6   *Command List for Lab Exercise*

Command	Description
aaa authentication dot1x	Specifies one or more AAA methods for use on interfaces running IEEE 802.1X
aaa new-model	Enables AAA globally
aaa authentication login {default | *list-name*} *method1* [*method2...*]	Configures switch AAA authentication list
configure terminal	EXEC command to enter the configuration mode
crypto key generate rsa	Initiates configuration of RSA keys for SSH access
dot1x port-control {auto | force-authorized | force-unauthorized}	Configures interface for authorization state of 802.1X
dot1x system-auth-control	Enables 802.1X globally
end	Configuration EXEC command to end the configuration mode
exit	Configuration EXEC command to end the current configuration mode leaf
hostname *hostname*	Configures switch with a descriptive name
interface FastEthernet *interface*	Configuration command to enter an interface configuration mode
interface range *range*	Groups interfaces together for applying configurations simultaneously
ip domain-name *domain-name*	Configures the Internet domain suffix for the switch name
login authentication {default | *list-name*}	Applies the AAA authentication list to a line or set of lines

continues

Table 14-6 *Command List for Lab Exercise (Continued)*

Command	Description
switchport access vlan *vlan-id*	Configures an interface for a specific VLAN-ID
transport input	Configures the virtual terminal for allowable protocols
username *username* **password** *password*	Configures local username and password database
vlan access-map *name* [*number*]	Configures or modifies a VLAN map entry for VLAN packet filtering
vlan filter *mapname* vlan-list *list*	Assigns a VLAN access-map to a VLAN or a range of VLANs

Task 1: Enable AAA, Disable Telnet, and Enable SSH

Step 1 Enable AAA authentication for SSH connectivity.

```
Switch#configure terminal
Enter configuration commands, one per line.  End with CNTL/Z.
Switch(config)#aaa new-model
```

Step 2 Configure the host name for the switch.

```
Switch(config)#hostname AL1
```

Step 3 Configure local usernames and passwords for switch access when out-of-band servers are not available.

```
AL1(config)#username cisco password cisco
```

Step 4 Configure the switch for SSH.

```
AL1(config)#ip domain-name cisco.com
AL1(config)#crypto key generate rsa
The name for the keys will be: AL1.cisco.com
Choose the size of the key modulus in the range of 360 to 2048 for your
General Purpose Keys. Choosing a key modulus greater than 512 may take
  a few minutes.
How many bits in the modulus [512]: 2048
Generating RSA keys ...
[OK]
```

Step 5 Configure the switch for in-band connectivity via SSH exclusively.

```
AL1(config)#line vty 0 15
AL1(config-line)#transport input ssh

AL1(config-line)#exit

AL1(config)#exit
```

Task 2: Configure AAA Authentication for VTY Access Using RADIUS and the Local Username and Password Database if the Radius Server Is Unavailable

Step 1   Enable AAA authentication to use RADIUS and the local username database, respectively.

```
AL1(config)#aaa authentication login TEST group radius line
```

Step 2   Configure VTY lines for the appropriate AAA authentication group.

```
AL1(config)#line vty 0 15
AL1(config-line)#login authentication TEST
AL1(config-line)#exit
```

Task 3: Configure 802.1X on a Per-Interface Basis

Step 1   Enable 802.1X for RADIUS authentication.

```
AL1(config)#aaa authentication dot1x default group radius
```

Step 2   Enable 802.1X globally.

```
AL1(config)#dot1x system-auth-control
```

Step 3   Configure the interface for 802.1X.

```
AL1(config)#interface range FastEthernet0/2 -10
AL1(config-if-range)#switchport access vlan 10
AL1(config-if-range)#dot1x port-control auto
```

Task 4: Configure VACL to Drop All Ingress Frames on TCP Port 8889

Step 1   Configure an ACL to match packets against TCP port 8889.

```
AL1(config)#access-list 100 permit tcp any any eq 8889
```

Step 2   Configure the VLAN access-map.

```
AL1(config)#vlan access-map DROP_WORM 100
AL1(config-access-map)#match ip address 100
AL1(config-access-map)#action drop
AL1(config-access-map)#exit
```

Step 3   Attach the VLAN access-map to the appropriate VLANs.

```
AL1(config)#vlan filter DROP_WORM vlan 10-20
```

Configuration Exercise 2: Securing a Cisco Multilayer Switched Network Using DHCP Snooping, IPSG, and DAI

Complete this configuration exercise to familiarize yourself with the basic configuration of securing a Cisco multilayer switched network using DHCP snooping, IPSG, and DAI.

Required Resources

The resources and equipment required to complete this exercise are as follows:

- Two Cisco IOS–based Catalyst switches such as a Catalyst 3550, 4500, or 6500
- A terminal server or workstation connected directly to the console port of the Catalyst switch or remote access to the switch
- DHCP Server (or Cisco IOS router) and 2 workstations (for example, PC running Windows OS)
- Optionally, a traffic generator to verify VACLs

Exercise Objective

The purpose of this exercise is to demonstrate, on a small scale, configuration of security features such as DHCP snooping, IPSG, and DAI. This exercise represents only a small-scale configuration; larger-scale implementations of these features are more realistic. Nevertheless, this exercise presents the necessary CLI commands to configure features in an equivalent large-scale network with servers at distribution layer and workstations on access layer switches.

Network Diagram

Figure 14-19 shows the network layout for this configuration exercise. Switch A acts as the distribution layer switch, and switch B acts as the access layer switch. PC A, PC B, and the DHCP Server might not necessarily be used for the configuration but are needed to test the configuration.

Figure 14-19 *Network Diagram for Configuration Exercise*

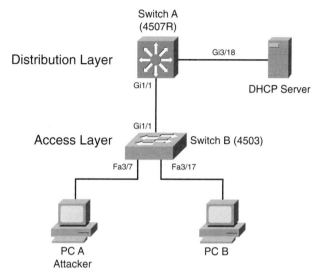

Note: All ports are in VLAN 10.

Command List

In this configuration exercise, you will use the commands listed in Table 14-7, which are listed in alphabetical order so that you can easily locate the information you need. Refer to this list if you need configuration command assistance during the exercise. The table includes only the specific parameters used in the example, not all the available options for the commands.

Table 14-7 *Command List for Lab Exercise*

Command	Description
configure terminal	EXEC command to enter the configuration mode
end	Configuration EXEC command to end the configuration mode
exit	Configuration EXEC command to end the current configuration mode leaf
**interface FastEthernet	GigabitEthernet** *interface*	Configuration command to enter an interface configuration mode
(config-if)#**ip arp inspection trust**	Enables DAI trust for the interface
ip arp inspection vlan *vlan-id*	Enables DAI for the specified VLAN

continues

Table 14-7   *Command List for Lab Exercise (Continued)*

Command	Description
ip dhcp snooping	Enables DHCP snooping
(config-if)#[**no**]**ip dhcp snooping trust**	Enables or disables DHCP snooping trust for the interface
ip dhcp snooping vlan *vlan-id*	Enables DHCP snooping for the specified VLAN
ip source binding *mac-address* **vlan** *vlan-id ip-address* **interface** *interface-id*	Configures a static IP source binding
(config-if)#**ip verify source vlan dhcp-snooping**	Enables IPSG for the specified interface and uses DHCP snooping information
no ip dhcp snooping information option	Disables DHCP option 82 tagging by the switch
ping *ip-address*	Pings the specified IP address
show ip arp inspection	Displays configuration and statistics for DAI
show ip dhcp snooping	Displays DHCP snooping configuration and status
show ip dhcp snooping binding	Displays DHCP snooping bindings
show ip source binding	Displays IP Source Guard bindings
show ip verify source	Display IPSG status for the configured interfaces

Task 1: Enable DHCP Snooping

Step 1   Enable DHCP snooping on switches A and B for VLAN 10. Because a Cisco IOS DHCP server that doesn't support option 82 is used here, option 82 tagging has been disabled on switches A and B.

```
SwitchA#configure terminal
Enter configuration commands, one per line.  End with CNTL/Z.
SwitchA(config)#ip dhcp snooping
SwitchA(config)#ip dhcp snooping vlan 10
SwitchA(config)#no ip dhcp snooping information option
SwitchB#configure terminal
Enter configuration commands, one per line.  End with CNTL/Z.
SwitchB(config)#ip dhcp snooping
SwitchB(config)#ip dhcp snooping vlan 10
SwitchB(config)#no ip dhcp snooping information option
```

Step 2 Configure the DHCP trust for the interface connecting to the DHCP server on switch A and configure interface connection to PC A and PC B as untrusted on switch B. Also the uplink's interfaces needs to configured for DHCP snooping trust.

```
SwitchA(config)#interface gigabitEthernet 3/18
SwitchA(config-if)#ip dhcp snooping trust
SwitchA(config-if)#interface gigabitEthernet 1/1
SwitchA(config-if)#ip dhcp snooping trust
SwitchB(config)#interface fastEthernet 3/7
SwitchB(config-if)#no ip dhcp snooping trust
SwitchB(config-if)#interface fastEthernet 3/17
SwitchB(config-if)#no ip dhcp snooping trust
SwitchB(config-if)#interface gigabitEthernet 1/1
SwitchB(config-if)#ip dhcp snooping trust
```

Step 3 Configure IP Source Guard for the end-user ports PC A and PC B to verify the IP address.

```
SwitchB(config-if)#interface fastEthernet 3/7
SwitchB(config-if)#ip verify source vlan dhcp-snooping
SwitchB(config-if)#interface fastEthernet 3/17
SwitchB(config-if)#ip verify source vlan dhcp-snooping
```

Step 4 Configure a static IP Source binding for the DHCP server whose IP address is 10.10.1.101 on switch A.

```
SwitchA(config)#ip source binding 000A.4172.DF7F vlan 10 10.10.1.101
interface Gi3/18
```

Step 5 Configure DAI for VLAN 10 on switches A and B.

```
SwitchA(config)#ip arp inspection vlan 10
SwitchB(config)#ip arp inspection vlan 10
```

Step 6 Configure the uplink interfaces as DAI trusted interfaces on switches A and B.

```
SwitchA(config)#interface gigabitEthernet 1/1
SwitchA(config-if)#ip arp inspection trust
SwitchA(config-if)#end
SwitchA#
SwitchB(config)#interface gigabitEthernet 1/1
SwitchB(config-if)#ip arp inspection trust
SwitchB(config-if)#end
SwitchB#
```

Task 2: Verify DHCP Snooping, IPSG, and DAI Status

Step 1   Verify DHCP snooping status and binding table on switches A and B.

```
SwitchA#show ip dhcp snooping
Switch DHCP snooping is enabled
DHCP snooping is configured on following VLANs:
10
Insertion of option 82 is disabled
Verification of hwaddr field is enabled
Interface                 Trusted      Rate limit (pps)
------------------------   -------      ----------------
GigabitEthernet1/1        yes          unlimited
GigabitEthernet3/18       yes          unlimited
SwitchB#show  ip dhcp snooping
Switch DHCP snooping is enabled
DHCP snooping is configured on following VLANs:
10
Insertion of option 82 is disabled
Verification of hwaddr field is enabled
Interface                 Trusted      Rate limit (pps)
------------------------   -------      ----------------
GigabitEthernet1/1        yes          unlimited
SwitchB#show ip dhcp snooping binding
MacAddress        IpAddress      Lease(sec) Type         VLAN   Interface
-----------       -----------    ---------- ------------ ----   -------
00:04:9A:80:A7:FF  10.10.1.102   85682      dhcp-snooping 10
FastEthernet3/17
Total number of bindings: 1
```

Step 2   Verify IP Source Guard binding and status on switches A and B.

```
SwitchA#show ip source binding
MacAddress         IpAddress      Lease(sec) Type    VLAN   Interface
----------------   -----------    ---------- -----   ------  ----------
00:0A:41:72:DF:7F  10.10.1.101    infinite   static  10
GigabitEthernet3/18
SwitchB#show ip source binding
MacAddress         IpAddress      Lease(sec) Type      VLAN   Interface
----------------   -----------    ---------- --------- ----   -------
00:04:9A:80:A7:FF  10.10.1.102    85609      dhcp-snooping 10
FastEthernet3/17
Total number of bindings: 1
SwitchB#show ip verify source
Interface Filter-type Filter-mode IP-address      Mac-address
Vlan
--------- ----------- ----------- --------------- ----------------
Fa3/7     ip          active      deny-all                          10
Fa3/17    ip          active      10.10.1.102                       10
```

Step 3 Verify DAI status and statistics on switches A and B.

```
SwitchA#show ip arp inspection
Source Mac Validation      : Disabled
Destination Mac Validation : Disabled
IP Address Validation      : Disabled
Vlan      Configuration      Operation    ACL Match          Static ACL
----      -------------      ---------    ---------          ----------
   1      Disabled           Inactive
  10      Enabled            Active
Vlan      ACL Logging        DHCP Logging
----      -----------        ------------
   1      Deny               Deny
  10      Deny               Deny
Vlan      Forwarded          Dropped      DHCP Drops      ACL Drops
----      ---------          -------      ----------      ----------
   1             0                 0               0               0
  10             3                 0               0               0
Vlan   DHCP Permits    ACL Permits    Source MAC Failures
----   ------------    -----------    -------------------
   1             0              0                  0
Vlan   DHCP Permits    ACL Permits    Source MAC Failures
----   ------------    -----------    -------------------
  10             1              0                  0
Vlan   Dest MAC Failures   IP Validation Failures
----   -----------------   ----------------------
   1             0                   0
  10             0                   0
SwitchB#show ip arp inspection
Source Mac Validation      : Disabled
Destination Mac Validation : Disabled
IP Address Validation      : Disabled
Vlan      Configuration      Operation    ACL Match          Static ACL
----      -------------      ---------    ---------          ----------
   1      Disabled           Inactive
  10      Enabled            Active
Vlan      ACL Logging        DHCP Logging
----      -----------        ------------
   1      Deny               Deny
  10      Deny               Deny
Vlan      Forwarded          Dropped      DHCP Drops      ACL Drops
----      ---------          -------      ----------      ----------
   1             0                 0               0               0
  10             4               361             361               0
Vlan   DHCP Permits    ACL Permits    Source MAC Failures
----   ------------    -----------    -------------------
```

```
       1              0                0                        0
Vlan  DHCP Permits   ACL Permits   Source MAC Failures
....  ............   ...........   ...................
      10              2                0                        0
Vlan  Dest MAC Failures   IP Validation Failures
....  .................   ......................
       1                    0                        0
      10                    0                        0
```

Task 3: Simulate an IP Source Guard and DAI Violation

Step 1 Configure PC A for the same IP address as PC B and ping from switch B to PC B IP address. Because PC B is configured for same IP address to spoof ARP, it responds as well, but it is dropped by switch B. Currently, there is no log message for violation for IPSG on Catalyst 4500, but all the packets sourced by PC B with the same IP address as PC A are dropped in the hardware path, and thus the IP and ARP spoofing attack is prevented.

```
SwitchB#ping 10.10.1.102
Type escape sequence to abort.
Sending 5, 100-byte ICMP Echos to 10.10.1.102, timeout is 2 seconds:
.!!!!
Success rate is 80 percent (4/5), round-trip min/avg/max = 8/10/16 ms
SwitchB#
03:46:18: %SW_DAI-4-DHCP_SNOOPING_DENY: 1 Invalid ARPs (Res) on Fa3/7,
vlan 10.([000a.4172.df7f/10.10.1.102/0009.e845.4fff/10.10.1.2/22:55:08
UTC Mon Nov 24 2003])
```

Review Questions

For multiple-choice questions, there may be more than one correct answer.

1 True or False: When configuring SNMP on Cisco routers and switches, use SNMPv2c because SNMP version 2c supports the use of encrypted passwords for authentication rather than the use of simple text or unencrypted passwords, as in version 1.

2 True or False: Using the 802.1X access control feature is preferable to using port security because the 802.1X protocol is a standards-based feature that supports centralized management.

3 True or False: The DHCP snooping trust interface is enabled only on ports with DHCP clients.

4 Which of the following is not a recommended management security configuration on Catalyst switches?

   a Using SSH and disabling Telnet service

   b Disabling unnecessary or unused services such as MOP or Proxy-ARP

   c Configuring ACLs to restrict specific users to manage the network devices

   d Policing to limit specific types of traffic to specific bandwidth parameters

   e Disabling remote access to switches

   f Physically preventing access to console ports

5 Which command correctly enables Catalyst switches to enact AAA security configurations?

   a ppp authentication chap

   b aaa new-model

   c aaa authentication login default group radius

   d **username** *name* **password** *password*

6 What is the purpose of the if-authenticated configuration option for a specific function, such as granting access to the EXEC shell?

   a Always allowing access to the function

   b Allowing access to the function based on the local user database

   c Allowing access to the function if the user was authenticated by AAA

   d Allowing access to the function based on RADIUS authentication

7 Which of the following is not a supported 802.1X port authorization state?

   a Force-authorized

   b Force-unauthorized

   c Auto

   d Desirable

8 Which of the following features is a requirement for configuring DAI?

  a IPSG

  b DHCP snooping

  c IGMP snooping

  d Proxy ARP

9 Which of the following methods can prevent a single 802.1Q tag VLAN hopping attack?

  a Turn off auto-negotiation of speed/duplex

  b Turn off trunk negotiation

  c Turn off PAgP

  d Turn on PAgP

10 Which of the following will prevent MAC address spoofing?

  a Port security

  b DHCP snooping

  c IGMP snooping

  d MAC notification

11 Which of the following features is similar to IPSG but for a Layer 3 interface?

  a RFP

  b RPF

  c uRPF

  d SFP

12 Which of the following types of ACLs can be applied to a Layer 2 port? (choose all that apply)

   a RACL

   b QACL

   c PACL

   d VACL

   e All of the above

13 Which of the following features can be used to prevent an ARP spoofing attack?

   a IP Source Guard

   b DHCP snooping

   c DAI

   d Port security

   e All of the above

14 Sticky port security allows for easier configuration of MAC addresses that need to be secured. True or False?

15 Which of the following solutions can be used to prevent a host infected with a virus from accessing the network?

   a IP Source Guard

   b DHCP snooping

   c NAC

   d Port security

   e All of the above

This chapter covers the following topics:

- Catalyst 6500
- Catalyst 4500
- Catalyst 3750
- Catalyst 3560
- Catalyst 2960

## CHAPTER 15

Introduction to the Catalyst Switching Architectures

Understanding the features and limitations of any Cisco Catalyst switch is critical in effectively deploying the switch in a multilayer switched network. Cisco Systems, Inc., has introduced many families of switches through the past years, from the Catalyst 5500 to the more recent Catalyst 4500 and 6500 families of switches. Each of these switches is designed for different functions in the multilayer switched network. For example, Catalyst 2960 switches are primarily designed for the Building Access submodule, whereas Catalyst 6500 switches are designed more for the Campus Backbone submodule. Designing the network with appropriate Catalyst switches for each of the core, distribution, and access layers is a critical success factor. Troubleshooting is another advantage of understanding the architecture; for troubleshooting complex problems, knowing the architecture is paramount.

This chapter goes beyond the description of Catalyst switches found in Chapter 1, "Introduction to Building Cisco Multilayer Switched Networks." Chapter 1 focused on all performance, scalability, and availability options. This chapter focuses on performance and switching architectures. Upon completion of this chapter, you will understand the basics of the switching architecture on the Catalyst switches discussed, how to effectively place them in your network, and how to troubleshoot the switches.

NOTE   Most of this chapter is outside the spectrum of the CCNP certification exam. However, the concepts presented in this chapter are essential for a complete understanding of the Catalyst switches.

Catalyst 6500

The Catalyst 6500 is the premier intelligent multilayer switch among the Cisco Catalyst family of products. The Catalyst 6500, used in Campus Backbone submodules, Building Distribution submodules, and the Enterprise Edge module, offers high-performance, scalability, and high-availability features such as Non-Stop Forwarding (NSF) with stateful switchover (SSO). The Catalyst 6500 family of switches also supports the Cisco modular IOS, which allows unprecedented availability and run-time patching capabilities. The Catalyst 6500 family of switches is also commonly deployed in every submodule, end-to-end, in large enterprise networks. Moreover, the Catalyst 6500 is a modular switch with different chassis options, as shown in Table 15-1.

Table 15-1 *Catalyst 6500 Chassis Models*

Chassis	Description
WS-C6503-E	3-slot chassis
WS-C6504-E	4-slot chassis
WS-C6506-E	6-slot chassis
WS-C6509-E	9-slot chassis
WS-C6509-NEB-A	9-slot chassis, Network Equipment Business System (NEBS) compliant
WS-C6513	13-slot chassis

Figure 15-1 shows a Catalyst 6509-NEB-A switch.

Figure 15-1 *A Catalyst 6509-NEB-A Switch*

The Catalyst 6500 supports the following types of interfaces:

- Fast Ethernet
- Gigabit Ethernet
- 10-Gigabit Ethernet (10GE)
- WAN interface through Enhanced FlexWAN modules and Shared Port Adapter Interface Processor (SIP) modules

In addition, the Catalyst 6500 provides many service modules, such as the following:

- Content Services Gateway (CSG)
- Application Control Engine (ACE)
- Firewall Services Module (FWSM)
- IPsec Shared Port Adapter (SPA) VPN Module (IVSM)
- Intrusion Detection System Module (IDSM)
- Network Analysis Module (NAM)
- Anomaly Detection Module (ADM)
- Anomaly Guard Module (AGM)
- Communication Media Module (CMM)
- Wireless Service Module (WiSM)

Catalyst 6500 Supervisor Engines are available in many different hardware configurations, as shown in Table 15-2.

Table 15-2   *Catalyst 6500 Supervisor Engines*

Supervisor Engine	Description
WS-X6K-S2-PFC2	Supervisor Engine II with Layer 3 engine (Note: End of Sale as of March 1, 2007)
WS-X6K-S2-MSFC2	Supervisor Engine II with MSFC2. (Note: End of Sale as of March 1, 2007)
WS-SUP32-GE-3B	Supervisor Engine 32 with eight Gigabit Ethernet (GE) uplinks and PFC3B (includes MSFC2A)
WS-SUP32-10GE-3B	Supervisor Engine 32 with two 10GE uplinks and PFC3B (includes MSFC2A)
WS-SUP720-3B	Supervisor Engine 720 (includes MSFC3)

In brief, Catalyst 6500 architecture supports the following data paths in the system:

- **Data bus (D-bus)**—The 32-Gbps full-duplex data bus (also known as classic bus) is available with all Supervisor Engines and chassis.

- **256-Gbps fabric**—The 256-Gbps full-duplex fabric requires the Supervisor Engine II, Switch Fabric Module, and specific model of line modules.

- **720-Gbps fabric**—The 720-Gbps full-duplex fabric is provided in addition to D-bus on Supervisor Engine 720–based systems only.

Catalyst 6500 line cards are also available in different hardware and performance configurations. Fabric line cards interface with the fabric module and might or might not have a connection to the D-bus, whereas the non-fabric module only interfaces with the D-bus. Table 15-3 illustrates the different types of line cards.

Table 15-3   *Types of Line Cards on Catalyst 6500*

Line Cards	Description	Example
Non-fabric	Connects only to the backplane D-bus	WS-X6148A-RJ45
256-Gbps fabric enabled (single) with or without distributed forwarding option	Connects to D-bus and has one fabric connection (16-Gbps full duplex)	WS-6516-GBIC
256-Gbps fabric only (dual) with Distributed Forwarding Card	Connects only to fabric through two connectors (16-Gbps full duplex each)	WS-X6816-GBIC
720-Gbps fabric enabled with or without Distributed Forwarding Card	Connects to the D-bus and has two fabric connections (40-Gbps full duplex each)	WS-X6704-10GE

Catalyst 6500 Supervisor Engine 32

The Supervisor Engine 32 features are similar to the Supervisor Engine 720 features but at a lower performance level, targeted for the access layer or WAN edge deployments. Supervisor Engine 32 uses a CEF forwarding mechanism. The performance of the Catalyst 6500 with Supervisor Engine 32 is limited to 15 million packets per second (Mpps).

Supervisor Engine 32 comes with the MSFC2A routing engine by default and consists of the following three components. The ingress module sends the received packet to the D-bus, which is seen and stored by other modules in their module ASIC buffers.

- **Network Management Processor (NMP)**—Maintains and controls the Layer 2 protocols, such as Spanning Tree Protocol, and line-card and system management communications.

- **Policy Feature Card 3B (PFC 3B)**—A Layer 3 forwarding ASIC controlled by the NMP and performs Layer 3 hardware switching, Quality of Service (QoS), and security ACL lookups.

- **Multilayer Switch Feature Card 2A (MSFC 2A)**—The router module performs routing with the assistance of NMP and PFC. The MSFC runs the router IOS and supports all the features of a normal router.

All modules in the chassis connect to the backplane D-bus through connectors. The Supervisor NMP module receives copies of every packet on the D-bus that it stores in a buffer while making forwarding decisions. NMP makes the forwarding decision on the packet based on the source and destination MAC, IP address, source and destination VLAN, security features, QoS, and other features configured on the system. After the decision has been made to either forward the frame or drop it; that decision is communicated to all the modules. Only the correct egress interfaces forward the traffic; the rest of the modules flush the packet from buffers. In other words, with a Supervisor Engine 32 in a Catalyst 6500, the switch copies ingress packets to every other module buffers, and the NMP signals exactly which ports forward the packet. The performance of this behavior is limited by the speed of the BUS and the NMP.

Catalyst 6500 with Supervisor Engine II

The Supervisor Engine II is the second-generation Supervisor Engine for the Catalyst 6500 platform. The Supervisor Engine II introduced CEF-based MLS on the Catalyst 6500 switch series. The details of CEF-based MLS are described in Chapter 9, "Understanding and Configuring Multilayer Switching."

NOTE   Supervisor Engine II will go End of Sale (EoS) March 1, 2007. Newer deployments should use Supervisor Engine 720, which offers higher performance and throughput.

The Supervisor Engine II introduced support for the following features and components:

- **Switch Fabric Module (SFM)**—256-Gbps full-duplex cross-bar fabric

- **Distributed Forwarding Card**—Provides distributed CEF-based MLS

With SFM and fabric-enabled line cards, the Supervisor Engine II can achieve forwarding rate increases up to 30 Mpps. With SFM and distributed fabric-enabled line cards, forwarding rates increase to 210 Mpps. Catalyst 6500 provides SFM redundancy in the case of active SFM failure with support for a standby SFM.

The SFM module plugs into specific dedicated slots on the chassis. Table 15-4 shows the location on various chassis models.

Table 15-4 *SFM Chassis Slot Dependency*

Chassis	SFM (Active and Standby) Slot Number
WS-C6506-E, WS-C6509-E	5, 6
WS-C6513	7, 8 (needs WS-C6500-SFM2)

With non-fabric-enabled line cards, the operations are similar to the behavior described for the Supervisor Engine I–based systems.

With SFM, the packets are sent over the SFM if possible, because it is faster than the D-bus. SFM operates in one of the following modes:

- **Compact mode**—The most efficient mode of operation without DFC-equipped cards present in the chassis. Compact mode is achieved when all line cards in the chassis are fabric enabled, and packets traveling between modules flow through the fabric. Only a compact header with enough information is sent on the D-bus so that the Supervisor Engine can make the forwarding decision. The actual data frame is sent over the SFM yielding the improved performance.

- **Truncated mode**—Less efficient than Compact mode because one or more non-fabric-enabled line cards are present in the chassis. The non-fabric-enabled line card forces the fabric-enabled line cards to use the D-bus to communicate to these non-fabric-enabled cards. In this mode, the traffic between the fabric-enabled module and the non-fabric-enabled modules goes through the switch fabric channel to the Supervisor Engine, which then forwards the frame via D-bus to the destination module. In case of traffic between fabric-enabled modules, only the truncated data (the first 64 bytes of the frame) is sent over the switch fabric channel, and actual data goes through the fabric.

- **BUS mode**—Uses the D-bus for all traffic communication except when fabric-only line cards are present. Traffic between fabric-only line cards is switched through the Supervisor Engine to the D-bus to the destination module. BUS mode is the least efficient because its maximum forwarding rate is limited to 15 Mpps.

- **Distributed CEF 256 (dCEF256) mode**—Used when DFC-equipped line cards are present. If all the line cards are equipped with DFC, the combination with an SFM achieves the highest forward rate. DFC downloads the CEF-forwarding information from the Supervisor Engine (CEF-based MLS), and hence forwarding decisions are made locally on the line cards. If the source and destination of the traffic are local to the line card, then the DFC switches the packet locally without needing the full packet to go over the fabric or BUS. Only the truncated header is sent over the fabric to the Supervisor Engine for statistics purposes.

For more information about the SFM, refer to the following Cisco.com document:

"Understanding the Catalyst 6500 Switch Fabric Module with Supervisor Engine 2," Document ID: 23221

http://www.cisco.com/en/US/products/hw/switches/ps700/ products_tech_note09186a00801c6652.shtml

Catalyst 6500 with Supervisor Engine 720

Supervisor Engine 720 is the third-generation Catalyst 6500 Supervisor Engine; the Supervisor Engine 720 includes an integrated fabric module and MSFC module where previous Supervisors used a separate line module for the fabric module. The highlight of this Supervisor Engine is the high forwarding capabilities—up to 400 Mpps over a 720-Gbps fabric.

Supervisor Engine 720 adds hardware-switching support for the following features in addition to features of Supervisor Engine II:

- IPv6
- IPv4 NAT
- MPLS
- GRE and IP in IP tunneling

NOTE   Supervisor Engine 720 uses the slot dedicated for SFM modules. Previous Supervisor Engines used slots 1 and 2.

The fabric connections of the line cards (6700 series) for Supervisor Engine 720 operate at 40-Gbps full duplex and hence provide the ability to support a high data rate through the module and the switch.

Catalyst 6500 Modules

The Catalyst 6500 offers a variety of line modules suited for all environments. Table 15-5 lists and describes the most popular modules at press time. For a complete current list of all module types, refer to Cisco.com.

Table 15-5　*List of Select Catalyst 6500 Modules*

Module	Description
WS-X6704-10GE	4-port 10-Gigabit Ethernet Module with 40-Gigabit Fabric connectivity
WS-X6708-10GE-3C/3C-XL	8-port 10-Gigabit Ethernet Module with 40-Gigabit Fabric connectivity (2:1 oversubscribed)
WS-X6724-SFP/WS-X6748-SFP	24-port and 48-port SFP Gigabit Ethernet interface module with 40-Gigabit Fabric connectivity
WS-X6748-GE-TX	48-port 10/100/1000 Ethernet Module with 40-Gigabit Fabric connectivity
WS-X6148A-GE-45AF	48-port 10/100/1000 Ethernet Module with IEEE 802.3af support
WS-X6148A-45AF	48-port 10/100 Ethernet Module with IEEE 802.3af support

Catalyst 6500 Service Modules

The Catalyst 6500 also supports various types of service modules. Table 15-6 provides a brief description of each of these modules. For a complete current list of service modules and more information, refer to Cisco.com.

Table 15-6　*Catalyst 6500 Services Modules*

Service Module	Description
Wireless Service Module (WS-SVC-WISM-1-K9)	Enables secure wireless LAN deployment with support for up to 10,000 wireless LAN users and 300 lightweight access points
Persistent Storage Device (WS-SVC-PSD-1)	Provides an extension to the Cisco CSG storage to prevent loss of billing information due to failures to reach billing collections from CSG
Multiprocessor WAN Application Module (WS-SVC-MWAM-1)	Enables service providers to deploy, provision, and manage value-added services at the network edge
Content Services Gateway (WS-SVC-CSG-1)	Provides dynamic content examination, subscriber service access control, and subscriber account balance enforcement and provides the capability for billing, traffic analysis, and data mining in a highly scalable, fault-tolerant package in a service provider environment
Communication Media Module (WS-SVC-CMM)	Provides high-performance and high-density Voice over IP (VoIP) gateways and Media Services

Table 15-6   *Catalyst 6500 Services Modules (Continued)*

Service Module	Description
Application Control Engine (ACE10-6500-K9)	Delivers the highest level of application infrastructure control, application performance, application security, and infrastructure simplification. ACE scales up to 16 Gbps throughput, 6.5 Mpps, and 4 million concurrent connections.
Firewall Services Module (WS-SVC-FWM-1-K9)	Provides integrated 5.5 Gbps throughput, 100 connections per second, and 1 million concurrent connections using Cisco PIX technology. Up to 4 can be installed in a chassis to provide up to 20 Gbps throughput.
Intrusion Detection System Module (WS-SVC-IDSM2-K9)	Enable organizations to protect their connected business assets from threats and increase the operating efficiency of intrusion protection
Network Analysis Module (WS-SVC-NAM-2)	Provides integrated monitoring up to application layer level for both LAN and WAN environments

Catalyst 6500 Summary

Switches in the Catalyst 6500 family are widely deployed in multilayer switched networks and provide the highest forwarding performance rate among the Catalyst family of switches. They provide critical features such as security, high availability, and services that are necessary in enterprise and service provider environments.

Table 15-7 lists the recommended Catalyst 6500 deployment scenarios.

Table 15-7   *Catalyst 6500 Deployment Scenarios*

Supervisor Engine	Deployment Scenarios
WS-SUP720-3B	Enterprise Campus Backbone and Building Distribution submodules, Data Center modules, and service provider networks
WS-SUP32-10GE-3B and WS-SUP32-GE-3B	Enterprise Building Access submodules and Enterprise Edge

Catalyst 4500

The Catalyst 4500 family of switches is the second generation of the previous-generation Catalyst 4000 family of switches. Catalyst 4500 provides many of the features provided by Catalyst 6500, but with lower performance metrics and lower cost. The Catalyst 4500 architecture is based on low latency, centralized shared memory switching fabric, and centralized switching.

The Catalyst 4500 family of switches offers the following key features:

- Supervisor Engine redundancy via NSF/SSO
- Power supply redundancy
- IEEE 802.3af PoE
- 102-Mpps performance capability
- Full suite of QoS features
- Superior Catalyst security features

The Catalyst 4500 is a modular switch with different chassis options, as shown in Table 15-8.

Table 15-8 *Catalyst 4500 Chassis Models*

Chassis	Description
WS-C4503	3-slot chassis
WS-C4506	6-slot chassis
WS-C4507R	7-slot chassis
WS-C4510R	10-slot chassis

NOTE The first generation Catalyst 4000 family of switches included the WS-C4003 (3-slot chassis) and WS-C4006 (6-slot chassis). The Catalyst 4500 family of switches listed in Table 15-8 replaces the first generation of the Catalyst 4000 family of switches.

Catalyst 4500 switches also offer fixed configuration models, as shown in Table 15-9, for high-end Data Center environments offering line-rate performance on all ports.

Table 15-9 *Catalyst 4500 Fixed Configuration Models*

Model	Description
WS-C4948	48 10/100/1000T including 4 ports alternatively wired for 1000 SPF 96-Gbps switching capacity 72-Mpps throughput
WS-C4948-10GE	48 10/100/1000T with two 10GE uplink ports 136-Gbps switching capacity 102-Mpps throughput

Similar to the Catalyst 6500, the Catalyst 4500 family of switches supports a range of Supervisor Engines, as shown in Table 15-10, offering different feature options.

Table 15-10 *Catalyst 4500 Family of Switches Supervisor Engines*

Supervisor Engine	Description
WS-X4013+	Supervisor Engine II+ provides Layer 2 and basic Layer 3 functionality (RIP and static routes along with QoS and security ACL support). Redundancy option available in 4507R and supported in 4006, 4503, and 4506 chassis. 64-Gbps switching capacity. 48-Mpps throughput.
WS-X4013+ TS	Supervisor Engine II plus provides Layer 2 and basic Layer 3 functionality. Supported only on the Catalyst 4503 chassis. Provides 20 Gigabit Ethernet ports on the Supervisor Engine module. 64-Gbps switching capacity. 48-Mpps throughput.
WS-X4013+10GE	Supervisor Engine II+ with two 10GE uplink ports provides Layer 2 and basic Layer 3 functionality (RIP and static routes along with QoS and security ACL support). Redundancy option available in 4507R and supported in 4006, 4503, and 4506 chassis. Up to 108-Gbps switching capacity. Up to 81-Mpps throughput.

continues

Table 15-10 *Catalyst 4500 Family of Switches Supervisor Engines (Continued)*

Supervisor Engine	Description
WS-X4515	Supervisor Engine IV provides Layer 2 and Layer 3 functionality.
	NetFlow service card optionally available for NetFlow data collection.
	Redundancy option available in 4507R and supported in 4006, 4503, and 4506 chassis.
	64-Gbps switching capacity.
	48-Mpps throughput.
WS-X4516	Supervisor Engine V provides Layer 2 and Layer 3 functionality.
	NetFlow service card optionally available for NetFlow data collection.
	Redundancy option available in 4507R and 4510R and supported in 4503 and 4506.
	96-Gbps switching capacity.
	72-Mpps throughput.
WS-X4516-10GE	Supervisor Engine V provides Layer 2 and Layer 3 functionality. Supports two 10GE uplinks or four 1-Gigabit Ethernet uplinks on the Supervisor.
	NetFlow service card integrated into the supervisor for NetFlow data collection.
	Redundancy option available in 4507R and 4510R and also supported in 4503 and 4506.
	136-Gbps switching capacity.
	102-Mpps throughput.

All Catalyst 4500 Supervisor Engines run Cisco IOS. Each module on Catalyst 4500 is connected to the Supervisor Engine central ASIC through 6 individual full-duplex Gigabit Ethernet connections. All Cisco IOS–based Supervisor Engines use the CEF-based MLS forwarding architecture.

The following are the series of steps performed upon packet reception on an interface by members of the Catalyst 4500 family of switches:

1 The receiving interface forwards the frame to the Supervisor Engine through the module backplane connector.

2 The packet is received by the packet-processing engine, which stores the packet in packet memory and forwards the packet descriptor to the forwarding engine.

3 The forwarding engine uses the packet descriptor to perform Layer 2 lookup, Layer 3 lookup, ACL processing, and QoS processing.

4 If the packet needs to be discarded or forwarded, the decision is sent to the packet-processing engine with the necessary rewrite information.

5 The packet-processing engine does the necessary rewrite and sends the packet to the destination module.

6 The egress module receives the packet to forward it out the necessary egress interface.

NOTE   If the Layer 2 or Layer 3 lookup does not yield information, the packet may be forwarded to the CPU for software-switching or dropped in hardware, depending on software configuration or switch design.

In the case of multicast packets, the forwarding engine generates a copy of the packet for each egress port, which is then forwarded to the appropriate egress modules by the packet-processing engine.

Catalyst 4500 series of switches are typically used in Building Distribution submodules, the Enterprise Edge, and Data Center modules in enterprise networks. As with any switch, however, the Catalyst 4500 can be found throughout the network.

Catalyst 3750

The Cisco Catalyst 3750 family of switches is the newest generation of standalone switches. Catalyst 3750 switches can be stacked using the Cisco StackWise technology, which provides a high level of resiliency, automation, and performance. It is possible to create a single 32-Gbps switching unit with up to nine individual Catalyst 3750 switches. Table 15-11 shows the various models available in the Catalyst 3750 family of switches. Note that all models of the Catalyst 3750 have a 32-Gbps switching capacity.

Table 15-11 *Catalyst 3750 Family of Switches*

Model	Description
WS-C3750G-24PS	24 Ethernet 10/100/1000 ports and 2 SFP-based Gigabit Ethernet uplinks 38.7-Mpps throughput IEEE 802.3af and Cisco pre-standard PoE
WS-C3750G-48PS	48 Ethernet 10/100/1000 ports and 4 SFP-based Gigabit Ethernet uplinks 38.7-Mpps throughput IEEE 802.3af and Cisco pre-standard PoE

continues

Table 15-11 *Catalyst 3750 Family of Switches (Continued)*

Model	Description
WS-C3750-24TS	24 Ethernet 10/100 ports and 2 SFP-based Gigabit Ethernet uplinks 6.5-Mpps throughput
WS-C3750-48TS	48 Ethernet 10/100 ports and 4 SFP-based Gigabit Ethernet uplinks 13.1-Mpps throughput
WS-C3750G-24T	24 autosensing 10/100/1000 Ethernet ports 35.7-Mpps throughput
WS-C3750G-24TS	24 autosensing 10/100/1000 Ethernet ports and 4 SFP-based Gigabit Ethernet uplinks 38.7-Mpps throughput
WS-C3750G-48T	48 10/100/1000 Ethernet ports 35.7-Mpps throughput
WS-C3750G-48TS	48 Ethernet 10/100/1000 ports and 4 SFP-based Gigabit Ethernet uplinks 38.7-Mpps throughput
WS-C3750G-16TD	16 Ethernet 10/100/1000 ports and 1 10-Gigabit Ethernet uplink 35.7-Mpps throughput
WS-C3750G-12S	12 SFP-based Gigabit Ethernet ports 17.8-Mpps throughput

Catalyst 3750 brings the following to the standalone switches typically available on modular switches:

- High availability and fault tolerance
- Seamlessly integrated CLI for configuration of member switches
- Port density and a variety of ports in a single switch

Catalyst 3750 also provides additional critical features, such as the following:

- IEEE 802.3af and Cisco pre-standard PoE
- 10/100/1000 speed and SFP connections
- Full suite of QoS
- Jumbo frames
- IPv6 in hardware capable
- Security features
- Border Gateway Protocol (BGP), Open Shortest Path First (OSPF), and Enhanced Interior Gateway Routing Protocol (EIGRP)

The Catalyst 3750 is designed to be used in a stack. The Cisco StackWise technology provides a new method for collectively using the capabilities of a stack of switches. Individual switches intelligently join to create a single switching unit with a 32-Gbps switching stack interconnect. Configuration and routing information is shared by every switch in the stack, creating a single switching unit. Catalyst 3750 switches can be added and deleted from a working stack without affecting performance.

The switches are united into a single logical unit via special stack interconnect cables that create a bidirectional closed-loop path. This bidirectional path acts as a switch fabric for all the connected switches. Network topology and routing information is updated continuously through the stack interconnect. All stack members have full access to the stack interconnect bandwidth.

The stack is managed as a single unit by a master switch. Each switch in the stack has the capability to behave as a master or subordinate in the hierarchy. The master switch is elected from one of the stack member switches. The subordinates act as forwarding processors. As many as nine separate switches can be joined.

Each stack of Cisco Catalyst 3750 series switches has a single IP address and is managed as a single object. This single IP management applies to activities such as fault detection, VLAN creation and modification, security, and QoS controls. Each stack has only one configuration file, which is distributed to each member in the stack. This allows each switch in the stack to share the same network topology, MAC address, and routing information. For more information on Cisco StackWise technology, refer to the following white paper at Cisco.com:

"Cisco StackWise Technology" http://www.cisco.com/en/US/products/hw/switches/ps5023/products_white_paper09186a00801b096a.shtml

Within each Catalyst 3750, the front panel connects to a port ASIC, which in turn connects to an internal stack ring, which is the actual 32-Gbps switching fabric. The CPU controls all the port ASICs. The following events happen when a port receives a frame:

1 The ingress port ASIC makes the forwarding decision using CEF-based MLS (Layer 2, Layer 3), considering ingress policing and ingress marking as well.

2 The ingress port ASIC determines the destination port and sends the header and frame data to the stack ring.

3 The egress port ASIC receives the frame and does egress processing, including processing against any egress ACLs.

4 The egress port ASIC performs any rewrites and transmits the frame out the egress port. The Catalyst 3750 family of switches is typically used in Building Distribution and Building Access submodules.

Catalyst 3560

The Cisco Catalyst 3560 family of switches is one of the latest additions to the range of standalone switches. The Catalyst 3560 is based on the Catalyst 3750; however, unlike the Catalyst 3750 family of switches, the Catalyst 3560 family of switches cannot be stacked using Cisco StackWise technology.

Table 15-12 shows the various models available in the Catalyst 3560 family of switches.

Table 15-12 *Catalyst 3560 Family of Switches*

Model	Description
WS-C3560-24TS	24 Ethernet 10/100/1000 ports and 2 SFP-based Gigabit Ethernet uplinks 8.8-Gbps switching capability 6.6-Mpps throughput
WS-C3560-48TS	48 Ethernet 10/100/1000 ports and 4 SFP-based Gigabit Ethernet uplinks 17.6-Gbps switching capability 13.1-Mpps throughput
WS-C3560-24PS	24 10/100/1000 Ethernet ports and 2 SFP-based Gigabit Ethernet uplinks IEEE 802.3af and Cisco pre-standard PoE 8.8-Gbps switching capability 6.6-Mpps throughput
WS-C3560G-48PS	48 10/100/1000 Ethernet ports and 4 SFP-based Gigabit Ethernet uplinks IEEE 802.3af and Cisco pre-standard PoE 17.6-Gbps switching capability 13.1-Mpps throughput

The Catalyst 3560 provides additional critical features, such as the following:

- IEEE 802.3af and Cisco pre-standard PoE
- Full suite of QoS
- Jumbo frame support
- IPv6 in hardware capable
- Security features
- BGP, OSPF, and EIGRP support

Within each Catalyst 3560, the front panel ports connect to a port ASIC. The CPU controls all the port ASICs. The following events happen when a port receives a frame:

1 The ingress port ASIC makes the forwarding decision using CEF-based MLS (Layer 2, Layer 3), considering ingress policing and ingress marking as well.

2 The ingress port ASIC determines the destination port and sends the header and frame data to the internal ring connecting other port ASICs.

3 The egress port ASIC receives the frame and does egress processing, including processing against any egress ACLs.

4 The egress port performs any layer rewrites and transmits the frame out the egress port. The Catalyst 3560 family of switches is typically used in Building Access submodules.

Catalyst 2960

The Catalyst 2960 family of switches offers intelligent wire-rate Layer 2 switching with high-end features such as QoS policing and security filtering. Catalyst 2960 switches have up to 32-Gbps switching fabric and support up to a 39-Mpps throughput. The Catalyst 2960 family of switches includes fixed configuration switches offering Fast Ethernet and Gigabit Ethernet ports. Catalyst 2960 can be managed as a standalone switch, or a group of them can be managed via a single IP address using stack configuration.

The Catalyst 2960 family of switches supports only the LAN BASE feature set software image. The Catalyst 2960 family of switches is supported in the Cisco Network Assistant (CNA) software tool for graphical user management. CNA is a freely available software tool for small-sized networks.

The Catalyst 2960 family of switches is available in different hardware and software configurations, which include support for the following types of interfaces:

* 10/100BASE-T

* 100BASE-FX

* 10/100/1000BASE-T

* GBIC-based 1000BASE-SX and 1000BASE-LX

* Small Form Pluggable (SFP)-based 1000BASE-SX and 1000BASE-LX

The Catalyst 2960 family of switches supports port densities of 24 to 48 ports per standalone unit. In addition, Catalyst 2960 is based on a shared memory architecture with centralized switching. All front panel ports connect to the switching fabric through forwarding engines. A central CPU controls the system and protocol table management. The following events occur for packet forwarding:

1 The packet is received by the ingress forwarding engine connected to the ingress port.

2 The ingress forwarding engine makes a forwarding decision (Layer 2, ingress policing, ingress marking).

3 The ingress forwarding engine sends the frame to the switching fabric.

4 The switching fabric schedules the frame for the egress frame based on QoS egress CoS parameters.

5 The egress forwarding engine receives the frame and forwards the frame out the egress port.

The Catalyst 2960 family of switches is intended for Building Access submodules only, because these switches do not support Layer 3 routing.

Study Tips

The following bullets review important BCMSN exam preparation points of this chapter. The bullets only briefly highlight the main points of this chapter related to the BCMSN exam. Consult the text of this chapter for additional information regarding these topics:

- The Catalyst 6500 series of switches support a variety of special-purpose service modules, including the NAM, IDSM, and WiSM.

- The Catalyst 4500 and Catalyst 6500 support redundant Supervisors as well as high, availability features, such as SSO and NSF with SSO.

- The IEEE 802.3af PoE is supported on the Catalyst 6500, Catalyst 4500, Catalyst 3560, and Catalyst 3750.

- All Layer 3 Cisco Catalyst switches perform CEF–based MLS forwarding.

Summary

Cisco offers a wide range of Catalyst switches with varied performance and feature capabilities.

Cisco Systems continues to evolve its Catalyst switch product line with the introduction of 10-Gigabit Ethernet technology and SFP connections. Deploying the correct Catalyst switches necessary for your network requirements will enhance the applications and services run on your network and increase the overall productivity of your network.

Review Questions

For multiple-choice questions, there might be more than one correct answer.

1 True or False: Catalyst 3560 switches offer Layer 3 functionality.

2 True or False: Catalyst 2960 offers no QoS features.

3 True or False: The Catalyst 4500 family of switches supports WAN interfaces.

4 Name one feature that is not supported in the Cisco IOS IP base feature set in the Catalyst 3560 family of switches.

   a PAgP

   b STP

   c BGP

   d RIP

   e All of the above

5 What is the forwarding capacity of Catalyst 4500 Supervisor Engine V-10GE?

   a 18 Mpps

   b 64 Mpps

   c 72 Mpps

   d 108 Mpps

6 Catalyst 4500 supports redundancy on which of the following chassis?

   a 4006

   b 4503

   c 4506

   d 4507R

   e All of the above

7 On which slot can the Supervisor Engine 720 reside in the Catalyst 6513 chassis?

   a 1

   b 2

   c 5

   d 6

   e 7

8 What is the maximum forwarding rate on a Catalyst 6500 with Supervisor Engine 720?

   a 72 Mpps

   b 210 Mpps

   c 400 Mpps

   d 720 Mpps

   e None of the above

9 If all modules in the Catalyst 6500 switch are fabric enabled, in what mode does the fabric operate?

   a BUS mode

   b Compact mode

   c Truncated mode

   d dCEF mode

10 How many Catalyst 3750s can exist in a stack?

   a 3

   b 6

   c 12

   d 9

   e Catalyst 3750 can only operate as a standalone switch.

11 Which of the following Cisco Catalyst switches supports the Cisco StackWise technology?

   a Catalyst 3560

   b Catalyst 3750

   c Catalyst 3550

   d Catalyst 3500 XL

   e Catalyst 4500

12 Which of the following service modules for the Catalyst 6500 provides packet monitoring up to the application layer level?

   a WS-SVC-CMM

   b WS-SVC-SSL-1

   c WS-SVC-MWAM

   d WS-SVC-NAM-2

   e None of the above

This chapter covers the following topics:

- Cisco Metro Networking Solutions
- Criteria Used to Evaluate Metro Ethernet Connectivity Options
- Benefits and Disadvantages of Transparent LAN Service
- Benefits and Disadvantages of Directed VLAN Service
- Benefits and Disadvantages of DWDM as a Layer 1 Implementation of Metro Ethernet
- Benefits and Disadvantages of SONET as a Layer 1 Implementation of Metro Ethernet
- Benefits and Disadvantages of CWDM as a Layer 1 Implementation of Metro Ethernet

Designing, Building, and Connecting Cisco Multilayer Switched Networks Using Metro Solutions

Metro Ethernet is no longer part of the BCMSN switching course or examination. As such, a significant amount of content regarding Metro Ethernet has been removed from the previous edition for this updated edition. However, retaining the content about deploying Ethernet over long-range networks for synchronous data solutions seemed warranted for practical reasons. This chapter is important to customers deploying multilayer switched networks for remote data centers and disaster recovery sites.

Applying metro solutions is necessary when building multilayer switched networks that connect multiple sites over long-distance metropolitan area networks (MANs) or WANs. A single main enterprise campus does not satisfy the redundancy and disaster-recovery requirements necessary for large enterprise networks. Large enterprise networks require co-locations, redundant Data Centers, and disaster-recovery sites in the event of a network, environmental, or other critical business interruption. As a result, many enterprise customers architect a disaster-recovery site for the purposes of data recovery and enterprise operation continuance during different types of anomalous situations and disasters.

In addition, several draft standards and best practice documents in the proposal process highly recommend or require financial institutions to adhere to strict disaster-recovery guidelines. These draft guidelines propose maintaining a backup site at least 200 km away from the main operations site that has the ability to achieve full network and data operation within two hours of a major disaster at the main operations facility. These types of redundancy requirements require high bandwidth at low latency between the main and backup operation facilities, which is achievable only through metro solutions.

Consequently, enterprise networks are now locating new disaster-recovery sites and data centers in a MAN within 200 km to 600 km from the main campus or in more distant locations using WAN technologies. For proper data backups to occur between the main operations facility and its disaster-recovery sites, a fair amount of bandwidth at low latency is necessary for synchronous data transfers between sites. Synchronous data transfers are necessary to avoid data loss. They avoid data loss by maintaining multiple simultaneous copies of data between the main operations facility and its disaster-recovery sites. Figure 16-1 illustrates a sample method of synchronous data.

Figure 16-1 *Synchronous Data Example*

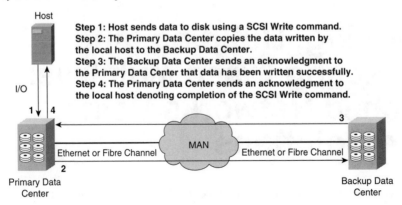

Cisco metro solutions provide enterprise customers with the following design characteristics:

- High bandwidth in terms of 1 to 10 Gbps
- High availability in terms of 10-ms failovers
- Low latency, where latency is a factor of distance, exclusively
- Scalability
- Modularity

MANs also fit well into WAN environments to connect multiple remote sites at high bandwidth.

This chapter introduces, in brief, the Cisco metro solutions as applied to building Cisco multilayer switched networks at high speeds over long distances. This chapter does not discuss, as with the previous edition, tunneling options, EoMPLS, or MPLS. For a complete discussion of all Cisco metro solutions, options, and products, consult Cisco.com.

Introduction to Cisco Metro Solutions

The Cisco metro solutions deliver a comprehensive multilayer service portfolio for service providers and enterprises who manage their own MAN and WAN solutions. This portfolio of metro solutions, which includes metro IP, metro Ethernet switching, metro storage transports, and metro optical transport platforms and technologies, ensures a flexible and efficient foundation for profitable metro services for service providers and high availability and scalability to the enterprise.

Moreover, the Cisco metro solutions enable service providers to grow quickly and profitably with a comprehensive multilayer service portfolio for those customers who choose to use a service provider to manage their metro solution. The metro service portfolio, achieved through a modular system, offers to service providers deployment flexibility with operational consistency across all metro environments. The Cisco modular system supports metro solutions with up to 10 Gigabit Ethernet, 2, 4, or 10 Gigabit Fibre Channel, and 10-Gbps Synchronous Optical Network/Synchronous Digital Hierarchy (SONET/SDH) OC-192. These high data rates coincide with the high-availability transport, scalability, and data integrity of the metro solution.

Figure 16-2 illustrates a sample Cisco metro solution. In this figure, multiple protocols, including Ethernet, Enterprise Systems Connection (ESCON), Fibre Connection (FICON), and Fibre Channel, transfer the metro solution. The metro solution in this example uses a metro optical solution for transporting data at high bandwidth and low latency. The metro optical solution uses the Cisco ONS 15540s as the optical platform and dense wavelength division multiplexing (DWDM) as the optical transport medium. Catalyst Ethernet switches connect to the Cisco ONS 15540s as a metro Ethernet (access) platform.

Figure 16-2 *Cisco Metro Solution Example*

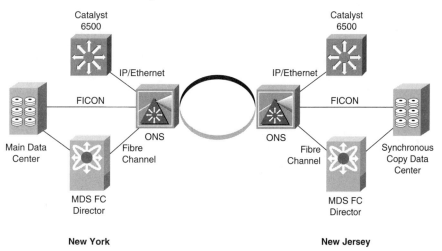

Figure 16-3 illustrates the generic metro solution hierarchy. The definitions for the acronyms and abbreviations used in the figure are as follows:

- Ethernet in the first mile (EFM)
- Dynamic Packet Transport (DPT)
- Layer 2 Ethernet Virtual Private Networks (L2 Ethernet VPNs)
- Synchronous Optical Network/Synchronous Digital Hierarchy (SONET/SDH)
- Wavelength division multiplexing (WDM)

Figure 16-3 *Generic Cisco Metro Solution Hierarchy*

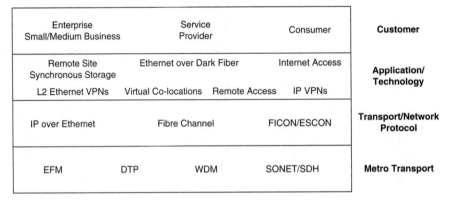

Metro Ethernet

Service providers often build networks that integrate with legacy infrastructures and are flexible to respond to changing market conditions such as reduction in bandwidth costs and diverse customer requirements varying from DWDM to SONET. This is especially important when service providers provide MANs with connectivity to enterprises. As a result, Ethernet emerged as a leading access medium for enterprise MANs for the following reasons:

- Enables most cost-effective services

- Provides ample bandwidth between the enterprise and the metro

- Eliminates access bottlenecks

- Allows service providers to deliver multiple data, voice, and video services to enterprise and consumer customers over a high-speed access connection

- Supports QoS

- Inherits low latency of the protocol

The Cisco metro Ethernet platforms move Ethernet data from the enterprise or local network to the metro optical platform. The metro optical platforms transport the Ethernet frames to remote sites using one of the available optical transport mechanisms, such as DWDM or SONET. The following section introduces this concept of metro Ethernet. Later subsections discuss metro Ethernet over the different transports. In brief, this section discusses the following topics:

- Metro Ethernet connectivity and transport

- Metro Ethernet over SONET

- Metro Ethernet over DWDM

- Metro Ethernet over CWDM

Metro Ethernet Connectivity and Transport

Transmitting Ethernet packets across the MAN is applicable using a variety of methods. These methods depend on factors such as cost effectiveness, service levels, transparency, and scalability. Several options are available for sending Ethernet frames across the WAN, ranging from using point-to-point Layer 1 connections such as DWDM to more complex Layer 2 and 3 encapsulation protocols that allow Ethernet services to be emulated over packet networks such as 802.1Q-in-Q tunneling and VPN tunneling. Each option has different advantages and disadvantages. In brief, this chapter discusses the following leading enterprise methods of Layer 1 metro Ethernet connectivity:

- SONET

- DWDM

- CWDM

This section discusses the criteria for choosing a metro Ethernet solution in general. Later sections discuss the properties of the SONET, DWDM, and CWDM metro Ethernet solutions, specifically, and their characteristics applicable to this section.

Figure 16-4 illustrates the optical and IP hierarchy for this chapter. IP runs over SONET, ATM, or Ethernet, which uses the optical transport. Fibre Channel runs directly on an optical network. Although not depicted in the figure, Fibre Channel can run on top of IP.

Figure 16-4 *Optical and IP Hierarchy*

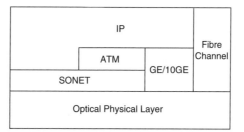

In brief, use the following criteria for determining the best available option for metro Ethernet connectivity in any campus design:

- **Cost-effectiveness**—For metro Ethernet access services to be cost-effective, the metro Ethernet access solutions must deliver network architectures of an initial low-capital expenditure with a relatively low sustaining and operation cost. For example, metro Ethernet connectivity using DWDM may have a high initial capital cost; however, the use of DWDM results in lower sustaining costs because it scales easily to accommodate growth.

- **Service level**—Service providers offer different levels of service for network availability, class of services, latency, and committed transfer rates. These service levels dictate the metro Ethernet connectivity solution. For instance, DWDM offers very high bandwidth connectivity with low latency compared to packet switched networks that offer low bandwidth and inherently higher latency.

- **Point-to-point versus multipoint**—With metro Ethernet access services, the concept of multipoint connectivity is slightly different from typical Frame Relay–like multipoint connections. Instead of the CPE supporting multiple virtual circuits (VC) over a single physical interface, there is only a single logical interface from the CPE to the provider edge (PE). At the PE, this single logical interface maps into multiple point-to-point circuits to establish a single Layer 2 broadcast domain. With this model of multipoint connectivity, it is possible, but not necessarily desirable, to eliminate the Layer 3 function on the CPE. For larger multipoint topologies, enterprises need to consider a Layer 3 method of transport, such as MPLS VPN, for security and ease-of-management purposes.

- **Transparency**—Because Ethernet is the predominant technology used in enterprise networks, metro Ethernet can accommodate a transparent interface to the enterprise. Because the medium is transparent, the metro solution can pass standard Ethernet frames and 802.1Q tagged frames without any modification to the frame. As a result, a Layer 2 network may span across the metro solution. This capability did not exist with traditional data-communication services such as ATM, Frame Relay, or leased lines. Layer 2 transport protocols were different from the Ethernet Layer 2 protocol used in the enterprise's LAN. The different transport protocol forced Layer 3 interfaces between the enterprise and service provider.

- **Scalability**—As the name suggests, metro Ethernet access services originated to provide high-speed connectivity within a metro service area. However, as metro Ethernet access services evolved, enterprises desired an Ethernet service interface that connects the enterprise to the service provider for general-purpose WAN connectivity to either private or public networks. Some service providers choose to offer metro Ethernet services to a specific metropolitan area, such as the New York City area. Other service providers choose to scale metro Ethernet services to inter-metro distances, such as the New York City metro area to include New Jersey. In either case, the control plane must allow new metro access and aggregation network elements to connect into the core metro network without major disruption or reconfiguration.

Two types of metro Ethernet connectivity options, transparent LAN services and directed VLAN services, determine frame handling as the frame passes through the center of the metro network. With a transparent LAN service, the metro solution forwards traffic as a multipoint-to-multipoint connection, whereas all connected sites in the metro solution see all traffic. With directed VLAN service, the metro solution forwards the traffic according to the campus VLAN topology. The next two sections discuss transparent and directed LAN services in more detail.

Transparent LAN Services

Transparent LAN service (TLS) refers to adjoining multiple sites over a metro solution using a single subnet or VLAN. TLS is easy to implement but presents scalability issues and a single failure domain for all customers using the metro solution. TLS supports point-to-point and point-to-multipoint operation.

In a transparent LAN service, data transmitted across the metro solution acts in a manner similar to an Ethernet hub using a single broadcast domain. This type of behavior presents a single failure domain to all customers of the metro solution. One traffic flow from a single customer within the core network of the metro solution may affect traffic from another customer. Figure 16-5 illustrates a TLS metro solution where the metro solution acts as a single broadcast domain.

Figure 16-5 *Sample TLS Topology*

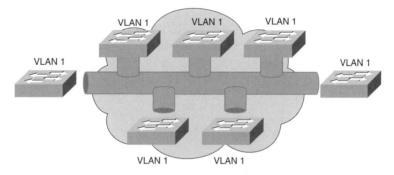

For the enterprise using a TLS metro solution, all of its routers and multilayer switches reside on the same subnet on the edge. The service provider easily provides a TLS solution for the enterprise by maintaining the same VLAN across its entire infrastructure. However, a TLS metro solution has two potentially serious performance implications for the enterprise:

- Broadcasts are sent to all sites that connect to the TLS metro solution.

- All routers must peer with each other across the MAN, which may cause a scalability problem for routers that maintain large routing tables. Multipoint solutions where remote site routers only peer with a central site tend to scale better than fully meshed networks where all remote site routers peer with each other.

The key benefit of TLS is that its shared backbone provides simplicity of implementation. All remote locations appear on a single subnet and in a single VLAN. Service providers and enterprise customers use VLANs to segment and differentiate traffic across a TLS metro solution. However, from a service provider standpoint, only 4096 individual VLANs are available for customer use. Generally, 4096 VLANs are insufficient for service providers who provide multiple VLANs on metro Ethernet solutions to multiple customers. In addition, supporting multicast and implementing QoS on TLS metro solutions is difficult because no discrete method of traffic separation exists.

In summary, only enterprises that purchase their own dark fiber and implement their own metro solution platforms use the TLS design, with or without the use of VLANs. Generally, service providers use directed VLAN services, as discussed in the next section, to take advantage of the cable plant while maintaining differentiated and autonomous metro Ethernet solutions to enterprise customers.

Directed VLAN Service

In a directed VLAN service (DVS), the metro solution uses VLAN IDs to forward traffic to select destinations. DVS supports both point-to-point and point-to-multipoint operations. Typically, DVS isolates VLANs of the enterprise from the VLANs of the network by using additional header information. As such, enterprise VLANs are separate from the metro VLANs. One such example is to add a second 802.1Q header to a frame to achieve a Q-in-Q transport.

Figure 16-6 *Metro Solution Deploying DVS*

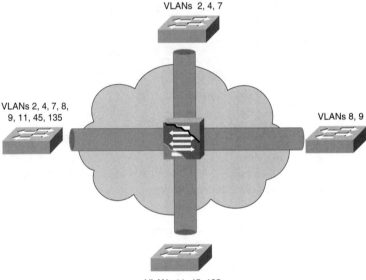

VLANs 2, 4, 7

VLANs 2, 4, 7, 8,
9, 11, 45, 135

VLANs 8, 9

VLANs 11, 45, 135

The switch in the core sees the VLANs defined at the edge of the network and provides VLAN switching. Note that these VLANs are not the VLANs configured in the multilayer switched network, but rather VLANs locally significant only to the metro solution. In DVS, the core switch must know the enterprise VLAN assignments. This implementation requires Per VLAN Spanning Tree Plus (PVST+).

DVS allows enterprises to support VLANs that appear in multiple locations across the core. In Figure 16-7, VLAN 10 appears in Remote Offices 1 and 3, whereas VLAN 20 appears in remote offices 2 and 3. The core switch in the cloud, generally physically located in Enterprise Edge of the Campus network, provides VLAN switching capability. As a result, the core switch knows about VLAN assignments on the remote location switches.

Figure 16-7 *Sample DVS Metro Solution*

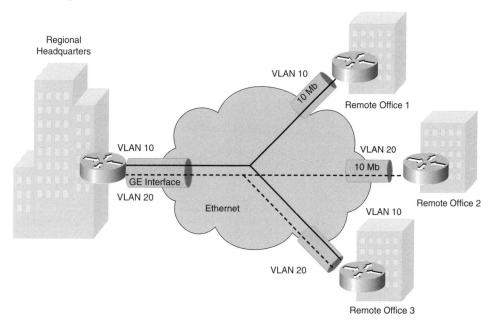

Metro Ethernet over SONET

Irrespective of the connectivity method, TLS or DVS, the metro solutions move Ethernet frames across a metro optical platform using several transports. One such transport is SONET.

SONET standards specified in ANSI T1.105, ANSI T1.106, and ANSI T1.117 define optical signals and a synchronous frame structure for multiplexed digital traffic. SONET carries numerous signals of different capacities through a synchronous, flexible, optical hierarchy. From the perspective of metro Ethernet over SONET, the SONET network is completely transparent. Figure 16-8 illustrates a sample network topology using SONET on OC-48 as a metro Ethernet solution.

NOTE   SDH, founded in Europe by the International Telecommunication Union Telecommunication Standardization Sector (ITU-T), is a similar synchronous framing standard and is regarded as equivalent to SONET. North American service providers generally use SONET while the rest of the world uses SDH.

Figure 16-8 *Metro Solution Using SONET*

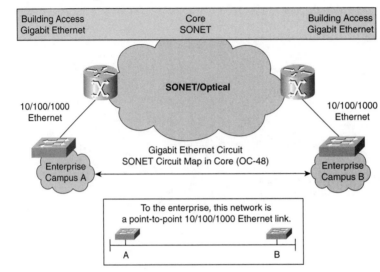

Because of its history in legacy telephony networks, service providers leverage well-established and entrenched SONET infrastructures for MAN deployments. Metro Ethernet over SONET takes advantage of the management and fault-tolerance mechanisms of this widely deployed SONET technology. Specifically, SONET supports up to a 50-millisecond internal failover. In addition, SONET uses a byte-interleaved multiplexing scheme for increasing bandwidth. Byte-interleaving simplifies multiplexing and presents end-to-end network management capability.

The base signal of SONET is the synchronous transport signal–level 1 (STS-1); this signal operates at 51.84 Mbps. SONET supports a hierarchy of signaling speeds by interleaving multiple STS-1 signals. Table 16-1 illustrates the hierarchical signaling speeds for SONET. In Table 16-1, the term *OC* refers to the optical carrier. Typically, service providers refer to the SONET signaling speeds in terms of the OC speeds, such as OC-48.

Table 16-1 *SONET Signaling Hierarchy*

SONET, Signal	SDH	Bit Rates (Mbps)
STS-1, OC-1		51.840
STS-3, OC-3	STM-1	155.520
STS-12, OC-12	STM-4	622.080
STS-48, OC-48	STM-16	2488.320
STS-192, OC-192	STM-48	9953.280

As illustrated in Table 16-1, SONET multiplexes several lower-speed signals together to achieve higher-level signals. For example, 12 STS-1 signals multiplex together to form an STS-12 (OC-12) signal. In addition, note that 10 Gigabit Ethernet operates at a rate that maps directly into OC-192.

Figure 16-8 also illustrates the transparency of using SONET as a metro solution. In this figure, the SONET metro Ethernet network appears to the end user as a point-to-point Gigabit Ethernet link. The metro Ethernet system essentially creates a long extension cord for the Gigabit Ethernet transmission between enterprise campus A and enterprise campus B. In this figure, the metro solution connects in the Building Access submodule of the Enterprise Edge submodule. Connecting submodules to the SONET network requires the use of Catalyst switches or Cisco IOS routers with specific port adapters and interfaces in the service provider network.

Figure 16-9 illustrates a sample network topology using SONET. The figure demonstrates how to configure a metro Ethernet solution using a SONET ring infrastructure. The Cisco ONS 15454 provides support for both Ethernet and SONET/SDH interfaces, allowing enterprises to build metro-to-metro or city-to-city metro Gigabit Ethernet networks.

Figure 16-9 *Sample Metro Network Using SONET*

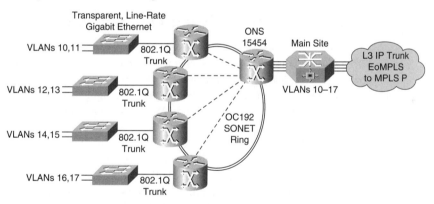

In addition, the ONS 15454 supports port-based VLANs that group ports into virtual workgroups. These port-based VLANs ensure that Ethernet ports see only traffic from ports within the same VLAN. The different VLANs communicate with each other through a router that spans multiple VLANs by using router ports in each VLAN, or through a router that understands IEEE 802.1Q. In Figure 16-9, the main site uses a router capable of IEEE 802.1Q routing.

SONET encompasses far more technical detail than the information provided in this chapter. For additional information on SONET, refer to the following document on Cisco.com:

"A Brief Overview of SONET Technology," Document ID: 13567
http://www.cisco.com/en/us/tech/tk482/tk607/technologiestechnote
09186a0080094313.shtml

In brief, SONET offers several advantages to a metro Ethernet solution. These advantages are as follows:

- Internal 50-ms failover mechanism through protection switching
- Support for management and alarms natively
- Generally available in metro areas for reasonable cost

Conversely, SONET has its disadvantages. A summary of its disadvantages is as follows:

- Available only in bandwidth increments of 51.84 Mbps
- Core equipment is costly where existing equipment is not available
- Redundant circuits are generally idle and do not take advantage of additional resources
- Not able to statistically multiplex traffic across its backbone to increase available bandwidth of circuit

Choosing SONET as part of a metro solution requires careful consideration, planning, and availability of SONET through service providers.

Metro Ethernet over Wavelength Division Multiplexing Optical Solutions

Metro Ethernet over WDM solutions are metro implementation options that provide 1-, 2-, and 10-Gbps rates with ease of configuration, high scalability, transparency, and optical protection. WDM technology over long distances for ultra-high-bandwidth transports is becoming increasing popular. The scalability of WDM solutions for long-distance, high-bandwidth requirements versus the laying of additional fibers is tremendous and results in significant cost savings. WDM achieves the same effects of multiple strands of fiber by offering multiple channels for discrete isolation of network traffic. At a high-level overview, WDM maps multiple optical signals to individual wavelengths and multiplexes the wavelengths over a single fiber. This multiplexing achieves multiple distinct optical paths across a single pair of fiber. This section discusses the two variations of WDM solutions available on Cisco platforms:

- Metro Ethernet over DWDM
- Metro Ethernet over coarse wavelength division multiplexing (CWDM)

Metro Ethernet over DWDM

At a high-level overview, DWDM provides a transparent medium for Ethernet connectivity similar to SONET. In Figure 16-10, the DWDM metro Ethernet network appears to the end user as a point-to-point Gigabit Ethernet link. As with SONET, the metro Ethernet system essentially creates a long extension cord for the Gigabit Ethernet transmission between enterprise campus A and enterprise campus B.

Figure 16-10 *Metro Solution Using DWDM*

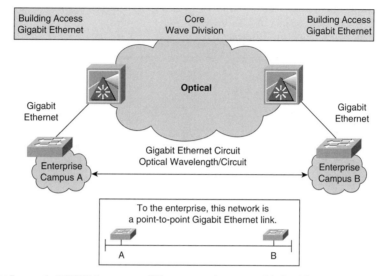

At Layer 1, DWDM converts Ethernet packets on a bit-by-bit basis into an optical stream at 1, 2, or 10 Gbps. DWDM does not perform framing conversion and simply performs optical conversion. As a result, Ethernet over DWDM does not require specific encapsulation. The core network moves data bits transparently from campus to campus. Because DWDM simply converts data bits to an optical stream, DWDM suffices as a transport media for not only Ethernet, but also storage protocols such as Fibre Channel, FICON, and ESCON.

Figure 16-11 illustrates a sample deployment of DWDM for multiple protocols and autonomous networks.

Figure 16-11 *Sample Metro Solution Using DWDM*

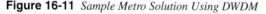
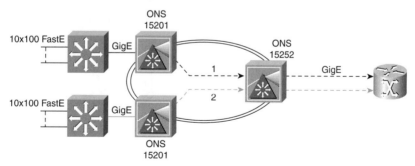

The two most commonly used wavelength regions for optical transmission over long distances are 1310 nanometers (nm) and 1550 nm. Short distance requirements commonly use the 850-nm window. These 1310-nm (S band) and 1550-nm (C band) windows, along with a fourth window at 1625 nm (L band) for upcoming technologies, have significantly lower optical loss compared to other windows near the same wavelength range. Figure 16-12 illustrates the optical loss characteristics at different wavelengths.

Figure 16-12 *Optical Loss at Different Wavelengths*

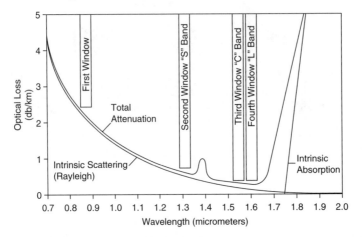

Transmissions using the 1310-nm wavelength (band) are popular for metropolitan or short-range applications because of their relatively low cost. The 1310-nm single-mode GBICs are readily available for Catalyst switches. Because transmissions in the 1550-nm band can travel greater distances because of that band's intrinsic properties, the 1550-nm range is preferable for very long-distance transmissions (between 100 km and 600 km). The increased cost in CPE equipment to process wavelengths in the 1550-nm range is still cheaper than the aggregate cost associated with continuous retransmission of a 1310-nm range optical signal. Figure 16-13 illustrates these windows relative to the electromagnetic spectrum.

Figure 16-13 *Wavelength Bands in the Electromagnetic Spectrum*

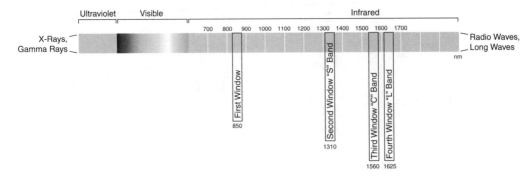

DWDM technology assigns incoming optical signals to specific frequencies of light (wavelengths, or lambdas) within the 1550-nm frequency band. Figure 16-14 illustrates the principle of multiplexing different wavelengths across a single medium.

Figure 16-14 *Illustrative DWDM Functional Schematic*

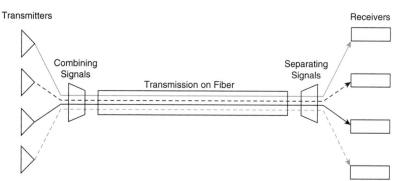

This multiplexing closely resembles the way radio stations broadcast on different wavelengths without interfering with each other. Because each channel transmits at a different frequency, a tuner is necessary to select the desired channel.

NOTE   This chapter uses the term *wavelength* instead of the term *frequency* to avoid confusion with other uses of frequency. The term *lambda* and *wavelength* are interchangeable and relate to Layer 1 optical functionality. *Channel* describes a Layer 2 (Ethernet, Fibre Channel) link mapping onto a wavelength. A single wavelength can carry multiple channels in the form of an Ethernet trunk channel, or an EtherChannel.

Current models of the Cisco optical platforms support up to 32 usable lambdas plus a 33rd lambda for management. DWDM optical platforms use different frequencies and wavelengths of the ITU draft standard G.692 for systems based on 100-GHz wavelength spacing with a center wavelength at 1553.52 nm. Table 16-2 illustrates the ITU grid for these types of DWDM systems.

Table 16-2   *ITU Grid*

ITU Grid Frequency (THz)	Wavelength (nm)	Frequency (THz)	Wavelength (nm)	Frequency (THz)	Wavelength (nm)
196.1	1528.77	194.6	1540.56	193.1	1552.52
196.0	1529.55	194.5	1541.35	193.0	1553.33
195.9	1530.33	194.4	1542.14	192.9	1554.13
195.8	1531.12	194.3	1542.94	195.8	1554.94
195.7	1531.9	194.2	1543.73	192.7	1555.75
195.6	1532.68	194.1	1544.53	192.6	1556.56
195.5	1533.47	194.0	1545.32	195.5	1557.36

continues

Table 16-2   *ITU Grid (Continued)*

ITU Grid Frequency (THz)	Wavelength (nm)	Frequency (THz)	Wavelength (nm)	Frequency (THz)	Wavelength (nm)
195.4	1534.25	193.9	1546.12	192.4	1558.17
195.3	1535.04	193.8	1546.92	192.3	1558.98
195.2	1535.82	193.7	1547.72	192.2	1559.79
195.1	1536.61	193.6	1548.51	192.1	1560.61
195.0	1537.40	193.5	1549.32	192.0	1561.42
194.9	1538.19	192.4	1550.12	191.9	1562.23
194.8	1538.98	193.3	1550.92	191.8	1563.05
194.7	1539.77	193.2	1551.72	191.7	1563.86

As mentioned previously, most LAN-based Cisco IOS routers and Catalyst switches use either the 850-nm band or the 1310-nm band for optical transmission. For a DWDM system to transmit a signal in the 1550-nm range, it converts the ingress 850- or 1310-nm signal into a 1550-nm signal using a device called a *transponder*. Transponders accomplish the wavelength altering by doing an optical-to-electric-to-optical (OEO) conversion. In addition, transponders support regeneration, reshaping, and retiming functionality.

DWDM systems use optical multiplexers and de-multiplexers to combine and separate the multiple wavelengths for transmission and upon reception of optical signals, respectively. Optical amplifiers increase optical signals as they transmit across the optical fiber. Optical amplifiers differ from traditional amplifiers in that the optical signals are not converted to electrical signals for amplification. Erbium doped fiber amplifiers (EDFA) are the most commonly used optical amplifier in today's DWDM system.

Furthermore, DWDM systems use optical add/drop multiplexers (OADM) to drop or add a single lambda at a specific location. OADMs are useful in aggregating remote sites where each remote site uses only a subset of lambdas. For instance, Figure 16-15 illustrates the use of an OADM. In this DWDM system, the New York metro site only uses one lambda. As a result, the DWDM topology uses an OADM to add and drop a single lambda at this location.

This section is meant to be only a brief overview of DWDM; for a complete understanding of DWDM, consult Cisco.com.

Metro Ethernet over CDWM

CWDM technology harnesses the same WDM technologies as DWDM systems. DWDM and CDWM primarily differ in distance ranges, spacing of lambdas, number of channels, and the ability to amplify optical signals. In brief, CDWM uses 8 lambdas using a 20-nm wavelength grid, whereas DWDM technology has 32 or more lambdas using a 1-nm wavelength grid. CWDM technology does allow for optical signal amplification using any external amplifier, which limits its capability to transmit under 100 Km. CWDM basically provides for the same topology as DWDM except the Cisco IOS routers or Catalyst switches originate the signal and OADMs add or drop lambdas at a specific location. As such, CWDM is far less complex than DWDM, requires less hardware, and is easier to install. Figure 16-16 illustrates a sample metro Ethernet over CDWM topology.

Figure 16-15 *Sample OADM Use in DWDM Topology*

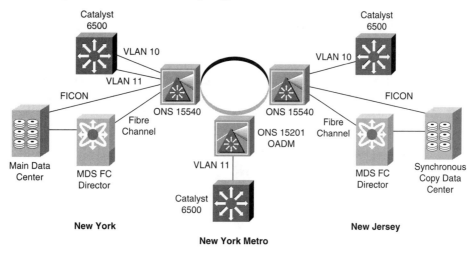

Figure 16-16 *Sample Metro Ethernet Deployment over CDWM Topology*

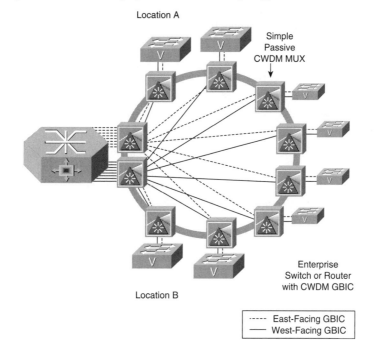

The CDWM solution uses two main components:

- **CWDM GBIC modules**—The Cisco CWDM GBICs convert Gigabit Ethernet electrical signals into optical signals at a specified wavelength (color). As a result, these GBICs are available in a variety of colors, including the 1470, 1490, 1510, 1530, 1550, 1570, 1590, and 1610 nm wavelengths.

- **CWDM OADM modules**—The Cisco CWDM OADMs are passive devices that provide the ability to multiplex/de-multiplex or add/drop wavelengths from multiple fibers onto one fiber. The OADM connects directly to the color-matching Cisco CWDM GBICs.

CWDM does support EtherChannel using multiple CWDM GBICs and OADM modules between sites. An alternative to EtherChannel is using multiple Layer 3 equal-cost paths over multiple CWDM connections. In summary, CWDM has the following benefits as a metro Ethernet solution:

- Metro distance range of approximately 100 km

- Inexpensive compared to DWDM

- Viable alternative to 10 Gigabit Ethernet over DWDM using EtherChannel over CWDM

- The Catalyst 6500, 4500, 4000, 3550, and 2950 families of switches support CWDM GBICs

- Cisco MDS Fibre Channel switches support CWDM GBICs

The only main downside to deploying CWDM as a metro solution is distance; CWDM does not support amplification, which limits distances to 100 km for 30-dB optical budgets.

Optical Distance Challenges

Several factors limit distances of unamplified optical fiber transmission. The root cause of these challenges is the transmission of light in optical fiber. These challenges can be summarized into one of the following three categories:

- **Attenuation**—*Attenuation* is the loss of light pulses as the pulses travel down the fiber. Attenuation is a factor of internal and external properties such as scattering, absorption, physical bending, and other environmental properties. If there is too much attenuation in an optical cable between a transmitter and receiver, the receiver may not be able to decode the optical pattern, rendering the fiber plant useless or problematic depending on the level of attenuation.

- **Dispersion**—*Dispersion* is the spreading of light pulses as the pulses travel down the optical fiber. Figure 16-17 illustrates dispersion. Two main types of dispersion affect optical systems: chromatic dispersion, which is linear, and polarization mode dispersion (PMD), which is nonlinear. Chromatic dispersion is related only to the wavelength of the optical signal. For a given fiber type and wavelength, the spectral line width of the transmitter and the bit rate of the laser determine the chromatic dispersion tolerance of a system. PMD has essentially the same effect on the system performance as chromatic dispersion, which causes errors in the optical signal. However, PMD has a different origin from chromatic dispersion; PMD occurs when different polarization states propagate through the fiber at slightly different velocities. PMD is a major concern for 10 Gbps and greater transmission speeds. Dispersion in optical fibers may make optical signals unreadable at receivers, rendering fiber plants useless or problematic. Dispersion is a factor of wavelength and distance, as illustrated in Figure 16-17. Cisco optical products adhere to specific dispersion characteristics and design guides.

Figure 16-17 *Dispersion Example*

Original Wave Pulse   Transmitted over   Received Wave Pulse
                                Distance

Note	In reference to optical fibers, multimode fiber generally suffers from chromatic dispersion that can be compensated with dispersion-shifted fiber that uses a graduated index of reflection between the core and cladding. Multimode fiber also suffers from multimodal dispersion where many paths at varying lengths exist in the fiber, resulting in light photons spreading out over time where some light photons take faster paths while the others take slower paths. Conversely, single-mode fiber mainly suffers from PMD and is affected by chromatic dispersion when using physically dirty lasers.

- **Nonlinearities**—Nonlinear properties of the optical fiber lead to transmission effects that further degrade the optical signal over long distances. For more information on nonlinear properties, refer to Cisco.com and other texts regarding fiber optics.

All these issues are critical criteria for designing optical networks, especially those exceeding 100 km. This section discusses these optical characteristics only in brief; consult Cisco.com for additional design guides, fiber budget documentation, and Cisco optical product limitations.

NOTE	This chapter does not include a Study Tips section because this chapter contains material outside the scope of the BCMSN examination, although still possibly relevant to CCNP certification holders.

Summary

This chapter introduced several metro Ethernet solutions, covering specifically deploying metro Ethernet over optical solutions such as CDWM, DWDM, and SONET.

The information in this chapter can be summarized as follows:

- Cisco metro Ethernet solutions provide high bandwidth and low latency Ethernet and Fibre Channel connectivity options.

- Current design requirements and recommendations for disaster-recovery planning require high bandwidth with low latency connectivity between enterprise sites and campuses.

- Enterprises choose whether to implement their own metro solution by purchasing dark fiber or purchasing Ethernet ports from service providers.

- The Cisco wide range of optical and Catalyst switching products fits into various metro Ethernet solutions depending on specific application.

- Metro Ethernet and Fibre Channel solutions using SONET, DWDM, and CDWM are high-bandwidth options available with Cisco optical platforms.

- TLS solutions forward traffic to all interfaces in the topology, whereas DVS solutions switch traffic, transparently to the enterprise, to specific interfaces.

- Metro solutions using SONET are widely available from service providers and support high availability.

- Metro solutions using DWDM are highly scalable and offer extremely high performance compared to metro solutions using SONET.

- Metro solutions using CDWM offer similar benefits to metro solutions using DWDM at a lower cost, but they do not support the long-range distances (in excess of 100 km) of DWDM.

Review Questions

For multiple-choice questions, there might be more than one correct answer.

1 True or False: To increase the distance of optical fibers using CDWM, use an amplifier.

2 Which of the following are advantages to using SONET as part of a metro solution?

   a Internal 50-ms failover mechanisms

   b General availability through service providers

   c Native support of load balancing through service provider

   d New core network equipment implements at very low costs

3 SONET interleaves a base signal to achieve higher levels of throughput. At which of the following bandwidth rates does the base signal for SONET operate?

a   1.54 Mbps

b   3.08 Mbps

c   10 Mbps

d   45 Mbps

e   51.84 Mbps

4 Which of the following devices converts optical signals of 850-nm and 1310-nm frequencies commonly found in enterprise networks to lambdas in the 1550-nm band used in DWDM systems?

a   EDFA

b   Amplifier

c   Transponder

d   Multiplexer

e   De-multiplexer

5 Which drawback does metro Ethernet over SONET share with metro Ethernet over DWDM?

a   Not designed for LAN traffic

b   Lack of bandwidth granularity

c   No backbone statistical multiplexing

d   Inefficient fault-tolerance mechanism

6 What is one drawback of metro Ethernet over CWDM compared to metro Ethernet over DWDM?

a   Increased cost

b   Distance limitations

c   Complexity

d   Service availability

This chapter covers the following topics:

- Using Techniques to Enhance Performance
- Monitoring Performance with SPAN and VLAN SPAN
- Monitoring Performance with Remote SPAN
- Monitoring Performance with Enhanced Remote SPAN
- Monitoring Performance Using VLAN ACL with the Capture Option
- Troubleshooting Using L2 Traceroute
- Enhancing Troubleshooting and Recovery Using Cisco IOS Embedded Event Manager
- Employing the Network Analysis Module for the Catalyst 6500 Family of Switches

## CHAPTER 17

Performance and Connectivity Troubleshooting Tools for Multilayer Switches

Previous chapters described troubleshooting methodology applied to Cisco multilayer switched networks. For you to be able to perform these complex troubleshooting and performance analyses, Cisco provides software and hardware tools to help you monitor and analyze the traffic on your network, which is the first step to optimizing performance. Traffic monitoring allows you to identify bottlenecks, underused resources, and places where you may implement improvements such as port aggregation (increasing link bandwidth by combining several physical ports into a single virtual link). Optimizing the performance of your Cisco multilayer switched network helps to maximize use of existing resources and reduces unnecessary duplication of network components. This ensures that the network runs efficiently and supports multiple solutions. This chapter explains some of the most commonly used features to monitor and understand performance and aid in troubleshooting Cisco multilayer switched networks.

This chapter covers these multilayer switch performance and troubleshooting tools and features with a brief description of each feature's functionality and its support on various switches. Each section also includes a small case study on how to use these tools in real network troubleshooting scenarios using Cisco CatOS– and Cisco IOS–based switches. Upon completion of this chapter, you will understand how to use these tools to effectively monitor performance and troubleshoot network issues in a Cisco multilayer switched network.

Techniques to Enhance Performance

Performance management includes maintaining internetwork performance at acceptable levels by measuring and managing various network performance variables. This section covers some of the techniques used to enhance network performance.

Critical performance-management issues are as follows:

- **User/application performance**—For most users, response time is the critical performance success factor. This variable may shape the perception of network success by both your users and application administrators.

- **Capacity planning**—Capacity planning is the process of determining future network resource requirements to prevent a performance or availability impact on business-critical applications.

- **Proactive fault management**—Fault management involves both responding to faults as they occur and implementing solutions that prevent faults from affecting performance.

The critical success tasks that need to be performed for performance management are as follows:

1 **Gather a baseline for both network and application data**.

   This step aids in troubleshooting performance issues during network operations. A typical router or switch baseline report would include capacity issues related to CPU, memory, buffer management, link utilization, and throughput. In addition, there are other types of baseline data that need to be included depending on your defined objectives. For instance, an availability baseline would demonstrate increased stability and availability of the network environment. Perform a baseline comparison between old and new environments to verify solution requirements. Develop a good network topology diagram as part of this step.

2 **Perform a what-if analysis on your network and applications**.

   A what-if analysis involves modeling and verifying solutions. Before adding a new solution to the network, document some of the alternatives. The documentation for this analysis includes major questions, methodology, data sets, and configuration files. The essential what-if analysis should contain enough information for someone other than the author to re-create the solution.

3 **Perform exception reporting for capacity issues**.

   If capacity requirements outstrip available resources, there should be in place a mechanism to notify network administrators of that fact. This could include setting up periodical SNMP polling on some key parameters of the network devices, such as CPU and memory, and having the network management station alert the administrator in the event of anomalous behavior.

4 **Determine the network management overhead for all proposed or potential network management services**.

   Network management services affect network and application performance. Make sure that the network measurement planning takes into account the additional resources required to perform measurement and management. For instance, SNMP polling of devices needs CPU cycles from the switch or router. If the device is already running at an above-average CPU utilization, the management services may further strain the device. In addition, the bandwidth required for these management functions should be considered if the links are heavily utilized to avoid oversubscription.

5 **Analyze the capacity information**.

Examine all the data you have gathered to determine capacity and management requirements. This is the most important task, forming the basis for the next step.

6 **Periodically review capacity information, baseline, and exceptions for the network and applications**.

Periodically repeat your analysis to identify changes in network use and growth patterns. The time interval chosen for measurement depends on the nature of the network being measured, and it may vary over weekdays versus weekends and also on a monthly or yearly basis. Reviewing the capacity periodically is critical to avoid unexpected network or application downtime and to plan for future growth.

7 **Maintain upgrade or tuning procedures that are set up to handle capacity issues on both a reactive and longer-term basis**.

Set up procedures to handle future capacity requirements. For instance, if you think that your network may need another link addition to a port channel based on certain thresholds, make sure that you plan for this change. Having the cabling and configuration procedure in place in advance minimizes the time required to make the change and ensures that the network runs smoothly without major downtime.

This section outlined some best-practice tasks essential for good performance management. The remainder of this chapter focuses on the various Cisco Catalyst switches and modules that assist in performance management and troubleshooting network exceptions.

Monitoring Performance with SPAN and VSPAN

The Switched Port Analyzer (SPAN) feature is an important aid in performance management and troubleshooting. SPAN copies network traffic from a VLAN or group of ports to a selected port. This port is usually connected to a network analyzer, such as a SwitchProbe device, a workstation running a packet-capturing application, or a remote monitoring (RMON) probe. SPAN does not affect the switching of network traffic on source ports or VLANs.

Local SPAN involves configuring source ports, source VLANs, and destination ports on the same Catalyst switch. Local SPAN, which involves configuring one or more VLANs as the source of the SPAN session, is also called VSPAN. All ports in the source VLANs become source ports in a VSPAN. Local SPAN copies traffic from one or more source ports in any VLAN or from one or more VLANs to a destination port for analysis. For example, as shown in Figure 17-1, the switch copies all traffic transmitted to and from port 3/1 (the source port) to port 3/5 (the destination port). A workstation running a packet-capturing application on port 3/5 thus receives all network traffic received and transmitted on port 3/1.

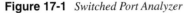

Figure 17-1 *Switched Port Analyzer*

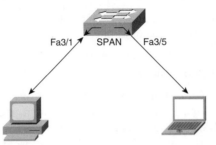

SPAN sessions support the monitoring of only ingress network traffic (ingress SPAN), only egress network traffic (egress SPAN), or traffic flowing in both directions. Ingress SPAN copies network traffic received by the source ports and VLANs for analysis to the destination port. Egress SPAN copies network traffic transmitted from the source ports and VLANs to the destination port. When the **both** keyword is used, SPAN copies the network traffic received and transmitted by the source ports and VLANs to the destination port.

By default, local SPAN monitors all network traffic, including multicast and bridge protocol data unit (BPDU) frames.

NOTE On a Cisco CatOS–based Catalyst switch, it is possible to disable multicast traffic monitoring from the source ports or VLAN. On Cisco IOS–based switches, this feature is currently not available, but Catalyst 4500 switches provide destination port filters using ACLs to remove any unneeded traffic for monitoring.

SPAN supports the configuration of both switched and routed ports as SPAN source ports. SPAN can monitor one or more source ports in a single SPAN session. Configuring source ports in any VLAN is allowed. Trunk ports are valid source ports mixed with nontrunk source ports. However, trunk encapsulation (dot1q or ISL) configuration of the destination port determines the encapsulation of the packets forwarded to the destination port. If the destination port is not configured for trunk encapsulation, the ISL or dot1q is removed from the frame before egress transmission. Refer to Chapter 4, "Implementing and Configuring VLANs," for more details on trunk encapsulations.

NOTE	In Cisco IOS–based Catalyst switches, you must dedicate the destination port for SPAN use because the port does not learn MAC addresses. For the Catalyst 2950, 3550, 4000, and Catalyst 4500 families of switches, it is possible for the device connected on the destination port to send traffic to the switch. The switch forwards these incoming frames out to the other ports based on the destination MAC address and IP address. An intrusion prevention system (IPS) typically uses the ingress feature on the destination port to thwart attacks in the network by sending TCP resets to the attacker TCP session or sending alarms to network management stations. In later Cisco IOS versions, Catalyst switches can be configured to dynamically learn MAC addresses on the destination SPAN port using the **learning** keyword.

The following additional guidelines or restrictions apply to local SPAN:

- Both Layer 2 switched ports (LAN ports configured with the **switchport** command) and Layer 3 ports (LAN ports configured with the **no switchport** command) can be configured as source or destination ports in Cisco IOS–based switches.

- A port can act as the destination port for only one SPAN session.

- A port cannot be configured as a destination port if it is a source port of a span session.

- Port channel interfaces (EtherChannel) can be configured as source ports:

  — A member port of an EtherChannel configured as a SPAN source port transitions into the suspended state and carries no traffic on Cisco IOS–based Catalyst 6500 with releases earlier than Cisco IOS 12.1(13)E.

  — Active member ports of an EtherChannel cannot be configured as source ports on Cisco IOS–based Catalyst 6500 with Cisco IOS 12.1(13)E and later releases. Inactive member ports of the EtherChannel go into suspended state if they are configured as source ports and carry no traffic.

- A port channel interface (EtherChannel) cannot be a destination port:

  — A member port of an EtherChannel configured as a SPAN destination port goes into suspended state and carries no traffic with releases earlier than Cisco IOS 12.1(13)E.

  — Active member ports of an EtherChannel cannot be configured as destination ports on Cisco IOS–based Catalyst 6500 with Cisco IOS 12.1(13)E and later releases. Inactive member ports of the EtherChannel go into suspended state if they are configured as destination ports and carry no traffic.

- SPAN supports configuration of source ports belonging to different VLANs.

- Local SPAN uses any previous configuration when enabled in Cisco CatOS. Always check for a previous configuration before enabling SPAN in Cisco CatOS to avoid unwarranted situations. For instance, the prior configuration SPAN destination port may now be connected to another switch. By enabling SPAN, the SPAN session results in loss of connectivity to the new switch or possible Spanning Tree Protocol (STP) issues.

- Traffic direction is "both" by default for SPAN sources.

- Destination ports never participate in a spanning-tree instance. Local SPAN includes BPDUs in the monitored traffic, so any BPDUs seen on the destination port are from the source port. As a result, SPAN destination ports should not be connected to another switch, because this may cause a network loop.

- Destination ports get a copy of all packets switched through the switch regardless of whether or not the packets actually leave the switch due to STP blocking state on an egress port.

The following additional guidelines or restrictions apply to VSPAN:

- VSPAN sessions, with both ingress and egress options configured, forward duplicate packets from the source port only if the packets get switched in the same VLAN. One copy of the packet is from the ingress traffic on the ingress port, and the other copy of the packet is from the egress traffic on the egress port.

- VSPAN only monitors traffic that leaves or enters Layer 2 ports in the VLAN:
  - Routed traffic that enters a monitored VLAN is not captured if the SPAN session is configured with that VLAN as an ingress source, because traffic never appears as ingress traffic entering a Layer 2 port in the VLAN.
  - Traffic that is routed out of a monitored VLAN, which is configured as an egress source in a SPAN session, is not captured because the traffic never appears as egress traffic leaving a Layer 2 port in that VLAN.

The destination port of SPAN can be configured with the **inpkts** keyword option in Cisco CatOS–based switches, which allows the destination port to receive packets from the network analyzer device and forward the packets to other ports in the switch. In Cisco IOS–based switches, the **ingress vlan** keyword is used instead of the **inpkts** keyword. The **inpkts** or **ingress vlan** features are useful when the monitoring station, such as an intrusion detection system, needs to send TCP resets upon TCP attack detection in the network. Table 17-1 shows the support of this feature in various Catalyst switches. The **inpkts** option is also useful for remotely accessing network analyzers.

Table 17-1 *Support of the inpkts/ingress vlan Feature on Catalyst Switches*

Catalyst Switch	inpkts/ingress vlan Feature (Minimum Software Version)
Catalyst 2950/Catalyst 2955	12.1(13)EA1
Catalyst 3550	12.1(12c)EA1
Catalyst 3750/Catalyst 3560	All versions

Table 17-1 *Support of the inpkts/ingress vlan Feature on Catalyst Switches (Continued)*

Catalyst Switch	inpkts/ingress vlan Feature (Minimum Software Version)
Catalyst 4500 Cisco IOS family	12.1(19)EW
Catalyst 6500 Cisco CatOS family	5.1
Catalyst 6500 Cisco IOS family	12.2(33)SXH

Example 17-1 shows the configuration and verification of a local SPAN session on a Cisco CatOS–based switch. The source port is 3/1, and the destination port is 3/21. The SPAN session is configured to only capture traffic in the receive direction on the source port. In addition, destination port 3/21 is configured for the **inpkts** and **learning** optional features.

Example 17-1 *Local SPAN Configuration and Verification on Cisco CatOS–Based Switches*

```
6500> (enable)  set span 3/1 3/21 rx inpkts enable learning enable
2003 May 04 20:46:02 %SYS-5-SPAN_CFGSTATECHG:local span session active for
destination port 3/21
Destination      : Port 3/21
Admin Source     : Port 3/1
Oper Source      : None
Direction        : receive
Incoming Packets: enabled
Learning         : enabled
Multicast        : enabled
Filter           : -
Status           : active
Warning: The destination port will not participate in the spanning tree protocol and
may cause spanning tree loops.
6500> (enable)  show span
Destination      : Port 3/21
Admin Source     : Port 3/1
Oper Source      : None
Direction        : receive
Incoming Packets: enabled
Learning         : enabled
Multicast        : enabled
Filter           : -
Status           : active
Total local span sessions:  1
```

On Cisco IOS–based switches, use the following commands in configuration mode to configure local SPAN.

```
monitor session session source {interface interface-id | vlan vlan-id [,][-] {rx |
tx | both}
monitor session session destination interface interface-id [encapsulation {dot1q |
isl}] [ingress vlan  vlan-id]
```

Example 17-2 shows the configuration and verification of a local SPAN session on a Cisco IOS–based switch. The source interface is FastEthernet 3/1, and the destination interface is FastEthernet 3/21.

Example 17-2 *Local SPAN Configuration and Verification on Cisco IOS–Based Catalyst Switches*

```
4506(config)#monitor session 1 source interface FastEthernet 3/1
4506(config)#monitor session 1 destination interface FastEthernet 3/21
4506(config)#end
1d01h: %SYS-5-CONFIG_I: Configured from console by bsivasub on console
4506#show monitor session 1
Session 1
----------
Type              : Local Session
Source Ports      :
    Both          : Fa3/1
Destination Ports : Fa3/21
    Encapsulation : Native
          Ingress : Disable
```

Example 17-3 shows the configuration and verification of a VSPAN session for capturing traffic on a Cisco CatOS–based Catalyst switch. This VSPAN only captures traffic in the receive (rx) direction for VLAN 10 and VLAN 20. The destination port for this VSPAN session is 3/21.

Example 17-3 *VSPAN Configuration and Verification on Cisco CatOS–Based Catalyst Switches*

```
6500> (enable)  set span 10,20 3/21 rx
2003 May 04 21:08:32 %SYS-5-SPAN_CFGSTATECHG:local span session active for
destination port 3/21
Destination      : Port 3/21
Admin Source     : VLAN 10,20
Oper Source      : None
Direction        : receive
Incoming Packets: disabled
Learning         : enabled
Multicast        : enabled
Filter           : -
Status           : active
6500> (enable)  show span
Destination      : Port 3/21
Admin Source     : VLAN 10,20
Oper Source      : None
Direction        : receive
Incoming Packets: disabled
Learning         : enabled
Multicast        : enabled
Filter           : -
Status           : active
Total local span sessions:  1
```

NOTE	Cisco CatOS–based Catalyst switches do not allow source ports to have different characteristics with regard to direction of traffic in SPAN sessions. In Cisco IOS–based switches, it is possible for different source ports to have different directions of traffic in SPAN sessions.

Example 17-4 shows the configuration of a VSPAN session on a Cisco IOS–based Catalyst switch with rx-only traffic for VLAN 10, and tx-only traffic for VLAN 20 and destination port interface FastEthernet 3/4.

Example 17-4 *VSPAN Configuration and Verification on Cisco IOS–Based Catalyst Switches*

```
cat4k(config)#monitor session 1 source vlan 10 rx
cat4k(config)#monitor session 1 source vlan 20 tx
cat4k(config)#monitor session 1 destination interface FastEthernet 3 /4
cat4k#show monitor session 1
Session 1
---------
Type               : Local Session
Source VLANs       :
    RX Only        : 10
    TX Only        : 20
Destination Ports  : Fa3/4
    Encapsulation  : Native
          Ingress  : Disabled
```

Using SPAN to Monitor the CPU Interface of Switches

The sc0 interface represents the management interface of the Supervisor Engine on switches running CatOS. The ability to span the sc0 interface is available on all Cisco CatOS switches with the exception of the Catalyst 4000 and 4500 families of switches.

NOTE	Currently, only Catalyst 4500 Cisco IOS–based switches support an equivalent CPU monitoring feature among the Cisco IOS–based switches. The Catalyst 6500 family of switches plans to support CPU monitoring in Cisco IOS Release 12.2(33)SXH.

The ability to span the CPU comes in handy when you are trying to troubleshoot traffic destined to the CPU of the Supervisor Engine. Traffic destined to the Supervisor Engine includes the control traffic, such as BPDUs, SNMP traffic, and so on. Normal switch traffic is not forwarded to the CPU and is handled via hardware switching. Captured traffic also includes Telnet traffic and broadcast traffic seen in the same subnet as the Supervisor Engine.

To configure SPAN to monitor the sc0 interface, enter the following command:

```
set span sc0 {mod/dest_port} [rx | tx | both] [inpkts {enable | disable}] [learning
{enable | disable}] [multicast {enable | disable}] [filter vlans] [create]
```

Example 17-5 illustrates a user configuring a SPAN session to monitor the sc0 interface with the SPAN destination port as 3/27.

Example 17-5   *Configuration and Verification of SPAN Session to Switch CPU Port (sc0)*

```
cat6k> (enable)  set span sc0 3/27
2003 Apr 28 17:54:08 %SYS-5-SPAN_CFGSTATECHG:local span session active for
destination port 3/27
Destination       : Port 3/27
Admin Source      : Inband Port (sc0)
Oper Source       : Inband Port (sc0)
Direction         : transmit/receive
Incoming Packets: disabled
Learning          : enabled
Multicast         : enabled
Filter            : -
Status            : active
```

To configure a SPAN to monitor the CPU traffic on the Catalyst 4000 and 4500 Cisco IOS–based switches, use the keyword **cpu** in the monitor session source configuration, as shown in Example 17-6.

Example 17-6   *Configuration and Verification of SPAN to Monitor the CPU Port on Catalyst 4000 and 4500 Cisco IOS–Based Switches*

```
4506(config)#monitor session 1 source cpu ?
  both    Monitor received and transmitted traffic
  queue   SPAN source CPU queue
  rx      Monitor received traffic only
  tx      Monitor transmitted traffic only
  <cr>
4506(config)#monitor session 1 source cpu queue ?
  <1-32>        SPAN source CPU queue numbers
  acl           Input and output ACL [13-20]
  adj-same-if   Packets routed to the incoming interface [7]
  all           All queues [1-32]
  bridged       L2/bridged packets [29-32]
  control-packet Layer 2 Control Packets [5]
  mtu-exceeded  Output interface MTU exceeded [9]
  nfl           Packets sent to CPU by netflow (unused) [8]
  routed        L3/routed packets [21-28]
  rpf-failure   Multicast RPF Failures [6]
  span          SPAN to CPU (unused) [11]
  unknown-sa    Packets with missing source address [10]
4506(config)#monitor session 1 source cpu
4506(config)#monitor session 1 destination interface fastEthernet 3/21
4506(config)#end
1d00h: %SYS-5-CONFIG_I: Configured from console by bsivasub on consmonitor session 1
4506#show monitor session 1
```

Example 17-6   *Configuration and Verification of SPAN to Monitor the CPU Port on Catalyst 4000 and 4500 Cisco IOS–Based Switches (Continued)*

```
Session 1
----------
Type               : - Source Ports      :
    Both           : CPU Destination Ports : Fa3/21
    Encapsulation : Native
            Ingress : Disabled
```

Case Study: Troubleshooting a Catalyst 6500 Using a SPAN Session to Monitor the sc0 Interface

This case study provides a practical scenario to illustrate the use of the SPAN session sourcing the sc0 interface in troubleshooting network issues. The switch in this case study is displaying the following error messages in the console and syslog:

```
%IP-3-UDP_SOCKOVFL:UDP socket 161 overflow
%IP-3-UDP_SOCKOVFL:UDP socket 161 overflow
```

The switch generates this syslog message when the buffer allocated for incoming packets on the specified socket (UDP destination port) is full because the rate of traffic destined for that socket is too high for the switch to process. If the switch generates an excessive number of these messages, use a network analyzer to identify the source of the traffic and reduce the rate of traffic.

NOTE   UDP port 161 represents the well-known port number for SNMP protocol polling.

Because this is a well-known port for SNMP polling, it is most likely that the polling frequency needs to be reduced. To confirm this theory, the administrator connects the network analyzer to the switch and configures a SPAN session with the sc0 interface as the source. After analyzing the captured output, the administrator determines that a device in his network is sending an excessive amount of unauthorized SNMP polling queries to the switch. When the device is disabled, the switch stops reporting the error messages.

TIP   It is recommended to configure the capture filter in the network analyzer to narrow the capture only to traffic destined to a particular source or destination or a type of traffic. This greatly reduces the time required to analyze the captured data for interesting traffic and reduces the amount of buffer space required to capture the frames. In addition, using display filters in the analyzer helps to better analyze the captured frames.

Monitoring Performance with RSPAN

Remote SPAN (RSPAN) is similar to SPAN, but it supports source ports, source VLANs, and destination ports on different switches, which provide remote monitoring of multiple switches across a switched network. Each RSPAN session carries the SPAN traffic over a user-specified RSPAN VLAN. This VLAN is dedicated for that RSPAN session in all participating switches.

The RSPAN source ports can be trunks carrying the RSPAN VLAN. Local SPAN and RSPAN do not monitor the RSPAN traffic in the RSPAN VLAN seen on a source trunk. For example, if the source port carries VLAN 1 through 10, with 10 being the RSPAN VLAN, the local span of that port does not mirror the RSPAN traffic to the destination port. However, the local SPAN correctly monitors traffic for the other VLANs 1 through 9. To receive the RSPAN traffic on a destination port, the port must be configured as the RSPAN destination port for that RSPAN VLAN.

The destination ports in the RSPAN VLAN receive RSPAN traffic from the source ports or source VLANs. The source ports or VLANs in an RSPAN session may be different on different source switches, but they must be the same for all sources on each RSPAN source switch. Each RSPAN source switch must have either ports or VLANs as RSPAN sources.

Figure 17-2 shows an RSPAN configuration across multiple switches. Access switches A and B act as the RSPAN source, distribution switch C acts as the intermediate switch, and data center switch D acts as the RSPAN destination switch where the probe is connected. Without RSPAN, the user has to go to each of the closet switches and manually configure local SPAN to monitor the traffic. For example, the administrator charged with monitoring ports A1 and A2 has to configure a local SPAN session on switch A and then configure a separate local SPAN session to monitor ports B1, B2, and B3. This type of configuration is obviously not scalable for geographically separated switch closets; RSPAN enables the administrator to monitor these remote ports from the data center switch. In this case, the trunks between the switches carry RSPAN VLAN traffic for the RSPAN to work correctly.

RSPAN consists of an RSPAN source session, an RSPAN VLAN, and an RSPAN destination session. It is advisable to configure separate RSPAN source sessions and destination sessions on different network devices. To configure an RSPAN source session on one network device, associate a set of source ports and VLANs with an RSPAN VLAN. To configure an RSPAN destination session on another device, associate the destination port with the RSPAN VLAN.

In addition to the guidelines and restrictions that apply to SPAN, these guidelines apply to RSPAN:

- Configure the RSPAN VLANs in all source, intermediate, and destination network devices. If enabled, the VLAN Trunking Protocol (VTP) can propagate configurations of VLANs numbered 1 through 1024 as RSPAN VLANs. Manually configure VLANs numbered higher than 1024 as RSPAN VLANs on all source, intermediate, and destination network devices.

- Network devices that support RSPAN VLANs can act as an RSPAN intermediate device.

Figure 17-2 *Remote RSPAN Example*

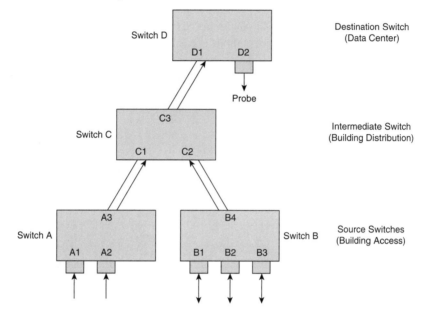

- Switches impose no limit on the number of RSPAN VLANs configured.
- Intermediate switches might impose limits on the number of RSPAN VLANs that they can support, depending on their capacity. For instance, some low-end switches like Catalyst 2950 support only 250 VLANs with the Enhanced Image software image.
- RSPAN VLANs carry only RSPAN traffic.
- Do not configure a VLAN used to carry management traffic as an RSPAN VLAN.
- Do not assign access ports to RSPAN VLANs.
- Do not configure ports in an RSPAN VLAN except those selected to carry RSPAN traffic.
- RSPAN VLAN has MAC address learning disabled.
- RSPAN source ports and destination ports must reside on different network devices.
- RSPAN does not support BPDU monitoring.
- Do not configure RSPAN VLANs as sources in VSPAN sessions.
- Configure any VLAN as an RSPAN VLAN as long as all participating network devices support configuration of RSPAN VLANs and use the same RSPAN VLAN for each RSPAN session.

- Entering SPAN configuration commands does not clear previously configured SPAN parameters. Enter the **no monitor session** command to clear previously configured SPAN parameters.

RSPAN configuration involves the following two steps:

1 Configure the RSPAN VLAN in the VTP server. This VLAN is then dedicated for RSPAN. If VTP transparent mode is used, configure RSPAN in all the devices in the domain consistently.

2 Configure the RSPAN session in the source and destination switches and ensure that the intermediate switches carry the RSPAN VLAN across respective VLAN trunks. Table 17-2 shows software support of the RSPAN feature on different Catalyst families of switches.

Table 17-2 *Support of RSPAN Feature on Catalyst Switches*

Catalyst Switch	RSPAN (Minimum Software Version)
Catalyst 2950/Catalyst 3550	12.1(11)EA1
Catalyst 2955	All versions
Catalyst 3750/Catalyst 3560	All versions
Catalyst 4500 Cisco IOS family	12.1(20)EW
Catalyst 6500 Cisco CatOS family	5.3
Catalyst 6500 Cisco IOS family	12.1(13)E

On Cisco IOS–based Catalyst switches, use the following commands in configuration mode to configure RSPAN.

On the source switch:

```
monitor session session source {interface interface-id | vlan vlan-id} [,][-] {rx |
tx | both}
monitor session session destination remote vlan vlan-id
```

On the destination switch:

```
monitor session  session  source remote vlan  vlan-id
monitor session  session  destination interface  interface-id [encapsulation {dot1q
|
isl}] [ingress vlan  vlan-id]
```

Example 17-7 shows the configuration and verification of an RSPAN session between two Catalyst 2950 switches. Switch 2950-1 is the source switch for the RSPAN session, and 2950-2 is the destination switch with the network analyzer. Only the Catalyst 2950 and Catalyst 2955 series switches require an additional port to be designated as the reflector port. The reflector should be left unconnected and is used internally by the Catalyst 2950 for implementing RSPAN. In Example 17-7, the reflector port is interface FastEthernet 0/24. The reflector port is used on the Catalyst 2950 switches as a way to overcome the limitation of that switch architecture in regards to SPAN. Figure 17-3 depicts the network scenario for this example.

Figure 17-3 *RSPAN Using Cisco IOS–Based Catalyst 2950 Switches*

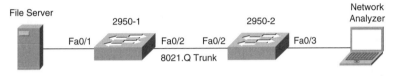

Example 17-7 *RSPAN Configuration and Verification on Cisco IOS–Based Catalyst Switches*

```
2950-1(config)#vlan 100
2950-1(config-vlan)#remote-span
2950-1(config-vlan)#exit
2950-1(config)#monitor session 1 source interface FastEthernet 0/1
2950-1(config)#monitor session 1 destination remote vlan 100 reflector-port
FastEthernet 0/24
2950-1(config)#in FastEthernet 0/2
2950-1(config-if)#switchport mode trunk
2950-1(config-vlan)#end
2950-1#
```
```
2950-2(config)#monitor session 2 source remote vlan 100
2950-2(config)#monitor session 2 destination interface FastEthernet 0/3
2950-2(config)#in FastEthernet 0/2
2950-2(config-if)#switchport mode trunk
2950-2(config-vlan)#end
2950-2#
```
```
2950-1#show monitor
Session 1
---------
Type               : Remote Source Session
Source Ports       :
    Both           : Fa0/1
Reflector Port     : fa0/24
Dest RSPAN VLAN    : 100
2950-1#show interfaces trunk
Port       Mode         Encapsulation  Status         Native vlan
Fa0/2      on           802.1q         trunking       1
Port       Vlans allowed on trunk
Fa0/2      1-4094
Port       Vlans allowed and active in management domain
Fa0/2      1-30,100
Port       Vlans in spanning tree forwarding state and not pruned
Fa0/2      1-30,100
```
```
2950-2#show interfaces trunk
Port       Mode         Encapsulation  Status         Native vlan
Fa0/2      on           802.1q         trunking       1
```

continues

Example 17-7 *RSPAN Configuration and Verification on Cisco IOS–Based Catalyst Switches (Continued)*

```
Port        Vlans allowed on trunk
Fa0/2       1-4094
Port        Vlans allowed and active in management domain
Fa0/2       1-30,100
Port        Vlans in spanning tree forwarding state and not pruned
Fa0/2       1-30,100
2950-2#show monitor session 2
Session 2
---------
Type             : Remote Destination Session
Source RSPAN VLAN : 100
Destination Ports : Fa0/3
    Encapsulation: Native
            Ingress: Disabled
```

Example 17-8 shows the configuration and verification of an RSPAN session between two Catalyst 6500 switches running Cisco CatOS. Switch 6509-1 is the source switch for the RSPAN session and 6509-2 is the destination switch with the network analyzer. Figure 7-4 depicts the network scenario for this example.

Figure 17-4 *RSPAN Using Cisco CatOS–Based Catalyst 6500 Switches*

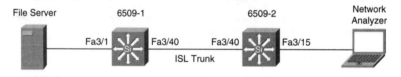

Example 17-8 *RSPAN Configuration and Verification on Cisco CatOS–Based Catalyst Switches*

```
6509-1> (enable)  set vlan 100  rspan
VTP advertisements transmitting temporarily stopped,
and will resume after the command finishes.
Vlan 100 configuration successful
6509-1> (enable)  set rspan source 3/1 100
Rspan Type      : Source
Destination     : - Rspan Vlan    : 100
Admin Source    : Port 3/1
Oper Source     : None
Direction       : transmit/receive
Incoming Packets: - Learning       : -
Multicast       : enabled
Filter          : -
Status          : active
6509-1> (enable) 2003 May 06 21:18:47 %SYS-5-SPAN_CFGSTATECHG:remote span source
session active for remote span vlan 100
6509-1> (enable)  set trunk 3/40 isl desirable
Port(s)  3/40 trunk mode set to desirable.
```

Example 17-8   *RSPAN Configuration and Verification on Cisco CatOS–Based Catalyst Switches (Continued)*

```
6509-2> (enable) set trunk 3/40 isl desirable
Port(s)  3/40 trunk mode set to desirable.
6509-2> (enable) set rspan destination 3/15 100
2003 May 06 21:20:07 %SYS-5-SPAN_CFGSTATECHG:remote span destination session active
for destination port 3/15
Rspan Type       : Destination
Destination      : Port 3/15
Rspan Vlan       : 100
Admin Source     : - Oper Source    : - Direction      : -
Incoming Packets: disabled Learning      : enabled Multicast      : -
Filter           : - Status          : active
```
```
6509-1> (enable) show rspan
Rspan Type       : Source Destination    : -
Rspan Vlan       : 100
Admin Source     : Port 3/1
Oper Source      : None
Direction        : transmit/receive
Incoming Packets: - Learning       : - Multicast       : enabled Filter       : -
Status           : active
Total remote span sessions:  1
```
```
6509-2> (enable) show rspan
Rspan Type       : Destination
Destination      : Port 3/15
Rspan Vlan       : 100
Admin Source     : - Oper Source    : - Direction      : -
Incoming Packets: disabled Learning      : enabled Multicast      : -
Filter           : - Status          : active
Total remote span sessions:  1
```
```
6509-1> (enable)  show trunk 3/40
* - indicates vtp domain mismatch
# - indicates dot1q-all-tagged enabled on the port
Port      Mode          Encapsulation Status        Native vlan
--------  -----------   ------------- ------------  -----------
 3/40     desirable     isl           trunking      1
Port      Vlans allowed on trunk
--------  ----------------------------------------------------------------
 3/40     1-1005,1025-4094
Port      Vlans allowed and active in management domain
--------  ----------------------------------------------------------------
 3/40     1,10,20,100
Port      Vlans in spanning tree forwarding state and not pruned
--------  ----------------------------------------------------------------
 3/40     1,10,20,100
```
```
6509-2> (enable)  show trunk 3/40
* - indicates vtp domain mismatch
# - indicates dot1q-all-tagged enabled on the port
Port      Mode          Encapsulation Status        Native vlan
--------  -----------   ------------- ------------  -----------
```

continues

Example 17-8 *RSPAN Configuration and Verification on Cisco CatOS–Based Catalyst Switches (Continued)*

```
  3/40     desirable    isl              trunking     1
  Port     Vlans allowed on trunk
 --------  ------------------------------------------------------------------
  3/40     1-1005,1025-4094
  Port     Vlans allowed and active in management domain
 --------  ------------------------------------------------------------------
  3/40     1,10,20,100
  Port     Vlans in spanning tree forwarding state and not pruned
 --------  ------------------------------------------------------------------
  3/40     1,10,20,100
```

Monitoring Performance with ERSPAN

Enhanced Remote SPAN (ERSPAN) is similar to RSPAN, but it supports source ports, source VLANs, and destination ports on different switches, even across the Layer 3 boundary, which provides remote monitoring of multiple switches across a switched or routed network. Each ERSPAN session carries the SPAN traffic over a GRE tunnel. The source and destination switches must support GRE in hardware. Currently, the ERSPAN feature is supported only on the Catalyst 6500 family of switches.

To configure an ERSPAN source session on one switch, you associate a set of source ports or VLANs with a destination IP address, ERSPAN ID number, and, optionally, a VRF name. To configure an ERSPAN destination session on another switch, you associate the destination ports with the source IP address, ERSPAN ID number, and, optionally, a VRF name.

ERSPAN source sessions do not copy locally sourced RSPAN VLAN traffic from source trunk ports that carry RSPAN VLANs. ERSPAN source sessions do not copy locally sourced ERSPAN GRE-encapsulated traffic from source ports.

Each ERSPAN source session can have either ports or VLANs as sources, but not both.

The ERSPAN source session copies traffic from the source ports or source VLANs and forwards the traffic using routable GRE-encapsulated packets to the ERSPAN destination session. The ERSPAN destination session switches the traffic to the destination ports, as shown in Figure 17-5.

Figure 17-5 *ERSPAN Using Cisco Catalyst 6500 Switches*

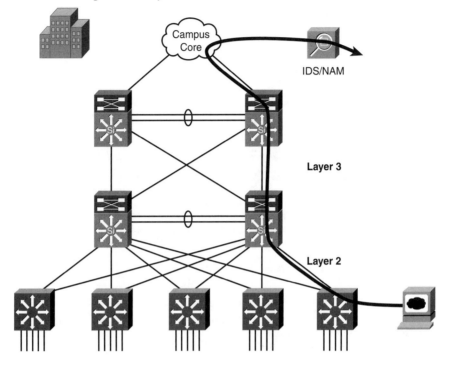

The following guidelines and restrictions apply to ERSPAN:

- The payload of a Layer 3 ERSPAN packet is a copied Layer 2 Ethernet frame, excluding any ISL or 802.1Q tags.

- ERSPAN adds a 50-byte header to each copied Layer 2 Ethernet frame and replaces the 4-byte cyclic redundancy check (CRC) trailer.

- ERSPAN supports jumbo frames that contain Layer 3 packets of up to 9202 bytes. If the length of the copied Layer 2 Ethernet frame is greater than 9170 bytes (9152-byte Layer 3 packet), ERSPAN truncates the copied Layer 2 Ethernet frame to create a 9202-byte ERSPAN Layer 3 packet.

- Regardless of any configured MTU size, ERSPAN creates Layer 3 packets that can be as long as 9202 bytes. ERSPAN traffic might be dropped by any interface in the network that enforces an MTU size smaller than 9202 bytes.

- With the default MTU size (1500 bytes), if the length of the copied Layer 2 Ethernet frame is greater than 1468 bytes (1450-byte Layer 3 packet), the ERSPAN traffic is dropped by any interface in the network that enforces the 1500-byte MTU size.

- All ERSPAN source sessions on a switch must use the same origin IP address, configured with the **origin ip address** command.

- All ERSPAN destination sessions on a switch must use the same IP address on the same destination interface. You enter the destination interface IP address with the **ip address** command.

ERSPAN configuration involves the following two steps:

Step 1 Configure the source ERSPAN session.

Step 2 Configure the destination ERSPAN session on a different switch.

Example 17-9 shows the configuration and verification of ERSPAN on the source and destination switches.

Example 17-9 *ERSPAN Configuration and Verification on a Catalyst 6500 Switch*

```
Switch1(config)#monitor session 66 type erspan-source
Switch1(config-mon-erspan-src)#source interface gigabitethernet 6/1
Switch1(config-mon-erspan-src)#destination
Switch1(config-mon-erspan-src-dst)#ip address 10.10.10.10
Switch1(config-mon-erspan-src-dst)#origin ip address 20.20.20.200
Switch1(config-mon-erspan-src-dst)#erspan-id 111


Switch1#show monitor session 66
Session 66
----------
Type                   : ERSPAN Source Session
Status                 : Admin Enabled
Source Ports           :
    Both               : Gi6/1
Destination IP Address : 10.10.10.10
Destination ERSPAN ID  : 111
Origin IP Address      : 20.20.20.200
Switch2(config)#monitor session 60 type erspan-destination
Switch2(config-erspan-dst)#destination interface gigabitethernet 6/1
Switch2(config-erspan-dst)#source
Switch2(config-erspan-dst-src)#ip address 10.10.10.10
Switch2(config-erspan-dst-src)#erspan-id 111
Switch2#show monitor session 60
Session 60
----------
Type                   : ERSPAN Destination Session
Status                 : Admin Enabled
Destination Ports      : Gi6/1
Source IP Address      : 10.10.10.10
Source ERSPAN ID       : 111
```

The number of supported local SPAN, RSPAN, and ERSPAN sessions varies on different Catalyst switches. Table 17-3 provides a summary of the number of local and remote SPAN sessions supported on Cisco CatOS–based Catalyst families of switches, and Table 17-4 provides the summary for Cisco IOS–based Catalyst switches.

Table 17-3   *Summary of SPAN and RSPAN Session Support on Cisco CatOS–Based Catalyst Switches*

Feature	Catalyst 4000/4500 (Cisco CatOS)	Catalyst 6000/6500 (Cisco CatOS)
rx or both SPAN sessions	5	2
tx SPAN sessions	5	4
rx, tx, or both RSPAN source sessions	5	1
RSPAN destination	5	24
ERSPAN	—	—
Total sessions	5	30

Table 17-4   *Summary of SPAN/RSPAN Session Support on Cisco IOS–Based Catalyst Switches*

Feature	Catalyst 3750	Catalyst 4500	Catalyst 6500 (Cisco IOS)
rx or both SPAN sessions	2	2	2
tx SPAN sessions	2	4	2 (16 with 12.2 [33] SXH)
rx, tx, or both RSPAN source sessions	6 (2 rx, 4 tx or 2 both, 2 tx)	1 (with 1 rx SPAN session)	1 (with 1 rx SPAN session)
RSPAN destination	2	2	64
ERSPAN destination	—	—	23
Total sessions	2	6	89

Monitoring Performance Using VACLs with the Capture Option

The Catalyst 6500 family of switches offers an additional feature to monitor traffic flows through the switch. SPAN, VSPAN, and RSPAN configuration applies to all traffic on the source port or source VLAN in one or both directions. Using VACLs with the capture option, the network analyzer only receives a copy of traffic matching the configured ACL. Because the ACL may match Layer 2, 3, or 4 information, the VACL with the capture option offers a useful and powerful complementary value to the SPAN and RSPAN features.

The VACL with the capture option on the Catalyst 6500 family of switches also overcomes the session number limit, as listed in Table 17-3 and Table 17-4, thus increasing the monitoring capability. The VACL with capture option works by a user setting up a VACL to match the interesting traffic and then configuring the capture port, which receives the copy of the matched traffic.

The following configuration guidelines apply to using the capture option in VACL:

- The capture port cannot be an ATM port.
- The capture port needs to be in the spanning-tree forwarding state for the VLAN.
- The switch has no restriction on the number of capture ports.
- The capture port captures only packets permitted by the configured ACL.
- Capture ports only transmit traffic belonging to the capture port VLAN. To capture traffic going to many VLANs, configure the capture port as a trunk carrying the required VLANs.

In Figure 17-6, a user is troubleshooting a session timeout between a server and client. Example 17-10 shows the user configuring VACL with the capture option to monitor communication between a client and a server on Cisco CatOS–based Catalyst switches.

Figure 17-6 *Capturing Using a VACL*

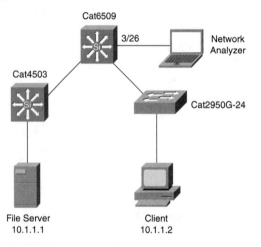

Cat6509

3/26 — Network Analyzer

Cat4503

Cat2950G-24

File Server
10.1.1.1

Client
10.1.1.2

Example 17-10 *Configuration and Verification of VACL with the Capture Option on Cisco CatOS–Based Catalyst 650*

```
cat6k> (enable)  set security acl ip bcmsn_VACL permit ip host 10.1.1.1 host
  10.1.1.2 capture
bcmsn_VACL editbuffer modified. Use 'commit' command to apply changes.
cat6k> (enable)  set security acl ip bcmsn_VACL permit ip host 10.1.1.2 host
10.1.1.1 capture
bcmsn_VACL editbuffer modified. Use 'commit' command to apply changes.
cat6k> (enable)  commit security acl bcmsn_VACL
ACL commit in progress.
ACL 'bcmsn_VACL' successfully committed.
cat6k> (enable)  set security acl map bcmsn_VACL 1
Mapping in progress.
ACL bcmsn_VACL successfully mapped to VLAN 1.
```

Example 17-10 *Configuration and Verification of VACL with the Capture Option on Cisco CatOS–Based Catalyst 650 (Continued)*

```
cat6k> (enable)  set security acl capture-ports 3/26
Successfully set 3/26 to capture ACL traffic.
cat6k> (enable)  show security acl info all
set security acl ip bcmsn_VACL
------------------------------------------------------
arp permit
1. permit ip host 10.1.1.1 host 10.1.1.2 capture
2. permit ip host 10.1.1.2 host 10.1.1.1
capture cat6k> (enable)  show security acl capture-ports
ACL Capture Ports: 3/26
```

Example 17-11 shows the VACL with the capture option configuration and verification for the troubleshooting scenario presented in Figure 17-5 on the Cisco IOS–based Catalyst 6500 family of switches.

Refer to the VACL section in Chapter 14, "Securing Your Multilayer Switched Network to Minimize Service Loss and Data Theft," for additional information about various VACL configuration options.

Example 17-11 *Configuration and Verification of VACL with the Capture Option on Cisco IOS–Based Catalyst 6500*

```
cat6k(config)#access-list 101 permit ip host 10.1.1.1 host 10.1.1.2
cat6k(config)#access-list 101 permit ip host 10.1.1.2 host 10.1.1.1
cat6k(config)#vlan access-map bcmsnvacl
cat6k(config-access-map)#match ip address 101
cat6k(config-access-map)#action forward capture
cat6k(config-access-map)#exit
cat6k(config)#vlan filter bcmsnvacl vlan-list 1
cat6k(config)#in GigabitEthernet 3/26
cat6k(config-if)#switchport
cat6k(config-if)#switchport capture allowed vlan 1
cat6k(config-if)#switchport capture
cat6k(config-if)#end
cat6k#show vlan access-map
Vlan access-map "bcmsnvacl"  10
        match: ip address 101
        action: forward capture
cat6k#show vlan filter
VLAN Map bcmsnvacl:
        Configured on VLANs:  1
            Active on VLANs:  1
```

Troubleshooting Using L2 Traceroute

Layer 2 (L2) traceroute is equivalent to the IP **traceroute** command except that this trace is for Layer 2 connectivity troubleshooting based on MAC addresses. L2 traceroute is a powerful tool for determining the path of a frame through the Layer 2 topology. The administrator needs to know only the source and destination MAC addresses of the devices in question. L2 traceroute also identifies the physical connection of any device in the network, freeing the administrator from having to manually check each switch.

To illustrate a typical troubleshooting scenario, consider a situation in which the connection between a server and client is slow. To troubleshoot this problem, identify the source and destination IP addresses of this session. Once the IP addresses are determined, you can easily find the MAC address of these devices by consulting the ARP tables of the workstation, client, and adjacent routers. Next, you need to locate the ports where the actual client and server are connected in the Layer 2 infrastructure. If, however, the L2 topology is large, it may be difficult to find out where these two devices are connected with just their IP addresses and MAC addresses unless the ports are clearly labeled and the network is clearly organized.

L2 traceroute is useful in these situations to trace the device connection into the network using just the MAC addresses. The L2 **traceroute** command also works with IP addresses being specified as part of the command for directly connected subnet devices. In the case of Cisco CatOS switches, the devices that you are troubleshooting must reside in the same subnet as the sc0 or sl0 interface. In the case of Cisco IOS switches, the devices being traced must be in the same subnet as any of the switched virtual interfaces (SVI) configured on those switches.

Many Catalyst families of switches support L2 traceroute. Table 17-5 shows the availability on various Catalyst switches.

Table 17-5   *L2 Traceroute Availability on Catalyst Switches*

Catalyst Switch	L2 Traceroute (Minimum Software Version)
Catalyst 2950	12.1(12c)EA1
Catalyst 2955	All versions
Catalyst 3550	12.1(12c)EA1
Catalyst 3560/3750	All versions
Catalyst 4500	12.1(13)EW
Catalyst 6500 Cisco CatOS family	6.1
Catalyst 6500 Cisco IOS family	12.2(18)SXE

L2 traceroute requires the following conditions to function properly:

- All the switches and interfaces in the network require CDP to be running and functioning properly.
- All intermediate switches between the source and device in question must support the L2 traceroute feature. Refer to Table 17-5 for a list of switches and software supporting this feature.

In Figure 17-7, a user needs to identify the performance and path on a hop-by-hop basis for a specific server and client exhibiting slow file-transfer performance. Example 17-12 shows a user using the L2 traceroute feature with the source MAC address of the server, 0000.0000.0007, to the destination MAC address of the client, 0000.0000.0011. To perform L2 tracerouting, the user may choose any switch in the network as long as that switch has both the source and destination MAC addresses in the MAC address table. In this example, the user performed the L2 **traceroute** command on the Catalyst 2950 of Figure 17-7.

Example 17-12   *L2 traceroute Output from Cisco IOS–Based Switches*

```
2950G#traceroute mac 0000.0000.0007 0000.0000.0011
Source 0000.0000.0007 found on 4503
4503 (14.18.2.132) : Fa3/48 => Fa3/2
6500 (14.18.2.145) :  3/40 =>  3/24
2950G (14.18.2.176) : Fa0/24 => Fa0/23
2948G (14.18.2.91) :  2/2 =>  2/24
Destination 0000.0000.0011 found on 2948G Layer 2 trace completed
```

Example 17-13 shows the same user using the L2 traceroute feature from the same source and destination as in the previous example; this time, however, the commands were executed from the Catalyst 2948G switch running Cisco CatOS software. Figure 17-7 shows the network topology for this example's output.

Figure 17-7   *L2 Traceroute Example*

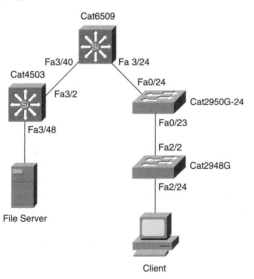

Example 17-13   *L2 Traceroute Output from Cisco CatOS–Based Switches*

```
2948G> (enable)l2trace 00-00-00-00-00-11 00-00-00-00-00-07
Starting L2 Trace
 2/24 : 14.18.2.91 :  2/2
 Fa0/23 : 14.18.2.176 : Fa0/24
 3/24 : 14.18.2.145 :  3/40
Fa3/2 : 14.18.2.132 : Fa3/48
```

The output from the L2 traceroute helps the user focus on troubleshooting the links between the source and destination devices without the user having to worry about building a network diagram or the spanning-tree topology.

To summarize, L2 traceroute is useful and applicable to any switch in the network in determining the path from any source to any destination. This feature offers flexibility and reduces time in troubleshooting individual host issues in large networks.

Enhancing Troubleshooting and Recovery Using Cisco IOS Embedded Event Manager

The Embedded Event Manager (EEM) feature has the capability to monitor events happening in the switch using embedded event collectors. The events tracked could be a generation of a syslog message, incrementing of a certain counter, or the result of a Generic Online Diagnostic (GOLD) test. Based on the detection of these events, custom actions could be performed, including configuration changes, e-mail notification, or paging the system administrator. The EEM feature is currently available only on the Catalyst 6500 switches running Modular IOS Software. Cisco plans to introduce this feature in future releases of other Catalyst switches. EEM is available in Cisco routers starting in Cisco IOS Software Release 12.2(18)SXF4.

EEM greatly improves troubleshooting and recovery of network failures by providing the capability not only to detect a great variety of events in the switch but also to take immediate actions without user invention.

Table 17-6 shows a sample set of events and typical actions that can be automated with EEM. It is important to remember that actions based on an event are fully user configurable.

Table 17-6   *Sample EEM Scenarios*

Event (User Configurable)	Action (User Defined)
A specific interface error crosses a user-defined threshold.	Disable the interface and bring up a backup interface.
Configuration changes are made during production hours.	Deny the configuration changes and send an e-mail alert.

Table 17-6   *Sample EEM Scenarios (Continued)*

Event (User Configurable)	Action (User Defined)
A GOLD diagnostic test fails.	Generate a custom syslog message indicating the action to take for Level 1 network operators.
A user logs into the system.	Generate a custom login message based on the user ID.
Unauthorized hardware is removed or added from the switch.	Send a page to the administrator.
It is necessary to collect data for capacity planning.	Run a user-defined set of commands to collect the capacity information at regular intervals.

The EEM feature on Catalyst 6500 is configurable in the following two ways:

- **EEM using applet CLI**—Cisco IOS CLI–based configuration that provides a limited set of actions and detection
- **EEM using Tool Command Language (TCL) script**—Provides full flexibility in defining the events and the subsequent actions

EEM allows customers to define their own custom TCL script that can be executed on the Catalyst switch. For more information about EEM, refer to the following documentation on Cisco.com (requires a Cisco.com username and password):

"Embedded Event Manager 2.0" http://www.cisco.com/en/US/partner/products/sw/iosswrel/ps1838/products_feature_guide09186a008025951e.html

Performance Monitoring Using the Network Analysis Module in the Catalyst 6500 Family of Switches

The Network Analysis Module (NAM) for the Cisco Catalyst 6500 family of switches is part of the end-to-end network management and monitoring solution. Network administrators need to collect statistics about voice, video, and data applications. The NAM gathers multilayer information about voice, video, and data flows up through the application layer, helping to simplify the task of managing multiservice switched LANs that support a variety of data, voice, and video applications.

The NAM monitors and analyzes network traffic using RMON, RMON extensions for switched networks, and other Management Information Bases (MIB).

Cisco has three NAM versions:

- **WS-X6380-NAM**—The first-generation NAM. It has a connection only to the data bus with no fabric connections.

- **WS-SVC-NAM-1**—A second-generation NAM with higher performance and a dual-processor architecture. It is scalable to support large switching environments running up to gigabit speeds. NAM-1 consists of 512-MB RAM with a 96-MB capture buffer.

- **WS-SVC-NAM-2**—Another second-generation NAM. In addition to NAM-1, NAM-2 has another accelerator card that provides extra-high packet-processing performance for full-scale gigabit monitoring. NAM-2 consists of 1-GB RAM with a 128-MB capture buffer.

The embedded NAM Traffic Analyzer software in the NAM gives any web browser access to the RMON1 (RFC 1757), RMON2 (RFC 2021), SMON (RFC 2613), DSMON (RFC 3287), and voice-monitoring features of the NAM. Furthermore, the NAM software provides the ability to troubleshoot and monitor network availability and health.

In addition to extensive MIB support, the NAM can also monitor individual Ethernet VLANs, which allows the NAM to serve as an extension to the basic RMON support provided by the Catalyst Supervisor Engine.

The TrafficDirector application, or any other IETF-compliant RMON application, can access link, host, protocol, and response-time statistics for capacity planning and real-time application protocol monitoring. Filters and capture buffers are also available for troubleshooting the network.

The NAM requires the following basic configuration via root access before use:

- IP address
- Subnet mask
- IP broadcast address
- IP host name
- Default gateway
- Domain name
- DNS name server, if a domain name service is used

If you are using an external SNMP manager to communicate with the NAM, configure the following:

- SNMP MIB variables
- Access control for the SNMP agent
- System group settings on the NAM
- The web server (using the **ip http server enable** command)

Example 17-14 shows the configuration and verification of the basic parameters on the WS-X6380-NAM. Use the root account to configure these parameters. The default login for the root account is **root**, and the password is **root**. Change the default password for this root account before beginning configuration.

Example 17-14 *Configuration and Verification of Basic Parameters on the NAM*

```
root@localhost#password
Changing password for user root
New UNIX password:
Retype new UNIX password:
passwd: all authentication tokens updated successfully
root@localhost#ip address 14.18.2.190 255.255.255.0
root@localhost#ip broadcast 14.18.2.255
root@localhost#ip host cat6knam
root@cat6knam#ip gateway 14.18.2.21
root@cat6knam#ip domain cisco.com
root@cat6knam.cisco.com#ip nameserver 14.18.2.200
root@cat6knam.cisco.com#show ip
IP address:        14.18.2.190
Subnet mask:       255.255.255.0
IP Broadcast:      14.18.2.255
DNS Name:          cat6knam.cisco.com
Default Gateway:   14.18.2.21
Nameserver(s):     14.18.2.200
HTTP server:       Disabled
HTTP secure server: Disabled
HTTP port:         80
HTTP secure port:  443
TACACS+ configured: No
Exsession:         Off
root@cat6knam.cisco.com#snmp location 1stFloor
root@cat6knam.cisco.com#snmp contact JohnDoe
root@cat6knam.cisco.com#snmp name cat6k
root@cat6knam.cisco.com#snmp community cisco rw
root@cat6knam.cisco.com#snmp community cisco123 ro
root@cat6knam.cisco.com#show snmp
SNMP Agent:   cat6knam.cisco.com   14.18.2.190
SNMPv1:  Enabled SNMPv2C: Enabled SNMPv3:  Disabled
community   cisco    write community   cisco123 read community    private  write
community   public   write community   ww       write
sysDescr        Catalyst 6000 Network Analysis Module (WS-X6380-NAM)
sysObjectID     enterprises.9.5.1.3.1.1.2.223
sysContact      JohnDoe sysName          cat6k sysLocation       1stFloor
```

The NAM supports having multiple data sources simultaneously. The NAM can use the following data sources for traffic analyses:

- Ethernet, Fast Ethernet, Gigabit Ethernet, trunk port, or Fast EtherChannel; SPAN or RSPAN source port; VSPAN and VACL with the capture option.

- Locally generated NetFlow Data Export (NDE) records. The NDE feature collects individual flow statistics of the traffic switched through the switch. NDE can also export the collected information to external flow collectors such as the NetFlow FlowCollector application. The NAM is another example of such a flow collector.

NOTE   With NDE records as source, the NAM only monitors the protocol (RMON2 protocol distribution table), the host (RMON2 nlHost and alHost tables), and the conversation (RMON2 nlMatrix and alMatrix tables) collection types. NDE records have insufficient information to implement other collection types.

To configure SPAN as a traffic source, use the CLI or NAM Traffic Analyzer application. Example 17-15 shows a user configuring a VSPAN source for the NAM in slot 4 of a Cisco IOS–based Catalyst 6500 switch.

Example 17-15   *User Configuration and Verification of VSPAN with NAM Port as Destination on Cisco IOS–Based Catalyst 6500 Switch*

```
Cat6kIOS(config)#monitor session 1 source vlan 10
Cat6kIOS(config)#monitor session 1 destination interface GigabitEthernet 4/1
Cat6kIOS(config)#end
Cat6kIOS#show monitor
Session 1
- - - - - - - - - -
Source Ports:
RX Only: None
TX Only: None
Both: None
Source VLANs:
RX Only: None
TX Only: None
Both: 10
Destination Ports:Gi4/1
Filter VLANs: None
```

NOTE   The SPAN destination for the NAM must always be port 1.

Example 17-16 shows the user configuring and verifying a SPAN configuration for the NAM in slot 4 of a Cisco CatOS–based Catalyst 6500 switch.

Example 17-16 *Configuration and Verification of SPAN to NAM Port in Cisco CatOS–Based Catalyst 6500 Switch*

```
6500> (enable)  set span 2/1 4/1 both create
Destination      : Port 4/1
Admin Source     : Port 2/1
Oper Source      : None
Direction        : transmit/receive
Incoming Packets: disabled
Learning         : enabled
Multicast        : enabled
Filter           : -
Status           : active
6500> (enable) 2003 May 10 18:50:15 %SYS-5-SPAN_CFGSTATECHG:local span session
active for destination port 4/1
6500> (enable)  show span
Destination      : Port 4/1
Admin Source     : Port 2/1
Oper Source      : None
Direction        : transmit/receive
Incoming Packets: disabled
Learning         : enabled
Multicast        : enabled
Filter           : -
Status           : active
Total local span sessions:  1
```

To use NDE as a traffic source for the NAM, enable the NetFlow Monitor option to allow the NAM to receive the NDE stream. The NAM receives NDE statistics automatically.

NDE makes traffic statistics available for analysis by an external data collector. Use NDE to optionally monitor all Layer 3 switched traffic and all routed IP unicast traffic.

When configuring the NAM as an NDE collector, use only the IP address of the NAM on the Cisco IOS–based Catalyst 6500 family of switches.

Example 17-17 shows a user configuring the NAM IP address as the NDE destination on a Catalyst 6500 switch running Cisco IOS. The **mls nde sender** command enables the NDE export feature on the PFC for exporting statistics for Layer 3 switched traffic. The **ip route-cache flow** interface-level command enables NetFlow switching so that statistics are collected for NDE export.

Example 17-17 *Enabling NDE as Source for NAM on Cisco IOS–Based Catalyst 6500 Switches*

```
Cat6kIOS(config)#mls nde sender
Cat6kIOS(config)#mls rp nde-address 14.18.2.190
Cat6kIOS(config)#mls flow ip full
Cat6kIOS(config)#mls nde flow include protocol udp
Cat6kIOS(config)#ip flow-export destination 14.18.2.190 3000
Cat6kIOS(config)#ip flow-export source vlan 1
Cat6kIOS(config)#interface vlan 10
Cat6kIOS(config-if)#ip route-cache flow
```

Example 17-18 shows a user configuring NDE as a source for the NAM in Cisco CatOS–based Catalyst switches.

Example 17-18 *Enabling NDE as Source for NAM on Cisco CatOS–Based Catalyst 6500 Switches*

```
6500> (enable)  set snmp extendedrmon netflow enable 4
Snmp extended RMON netflow enabled to module 4
6500> (enable)  show snmp
SNMP:                        Enabled
RMON:                        Disabled
Extended RMON Netflow Enabled : Module 4
Memory usage limit for new RMON entries: 85 percent
EngineId: 00:00:00:09:00:30:7b:4e:34:00:00:00
Chassis Alias: Traps Enabled: None
Port Traps Enabled: None
Community-Access     Community-String
----------------     --------------------
read-only            public
read-write           private
read-write-all       secret
Additional-                             Access-
Community-String     Access-Type     Number  View
------------------   --------------  ------- ------------------------------------
Trap-Rec-Address Trap-Rec-Community Trap-Rec-Port Trap-Rec-Owner Trap-Rec-Index
---------------- ------------------ ------------- -------------- --------------
6500> (enable)  set mls nde enable
Netflow export to Network Analysis Module
6500> (enable) 2003 May 10 19:01:12 %MLS-5-NDEENABLED:Netflow Data Export enabled
```

The **autostart** command is used on NAM initialization to configure several RMON collections on every available data source (including all known VLANs). Alternatively, RMON collections may be explicitly configured through SNMP by a management station on only some data sources. Collections that are explicitly configured through SNMP take precedence over autostart collections, so if both are configured, only the explicitly configured collections are started on each data source when the NAM initializes.

The NAM allows the automatic starting of the following collection types:

- **addressMap**—addressMapTable from RMON2-MIB (RFC 2021)
- **art**—artControlTable from draft-warth-rmon2-artmib-01.txt
- **etherStat**—etherStatsTable from RMON-MIB (RFC 1757)
- **prioStats**—smonPrioStatsControlTable from SMON-MIB (RFC 2613)
- **vlanStats**—smonVlanStatsControlTable from SMON-MIB (RFC 2613)

NOTE   For data sources that are already configured through SNMP, the autostart collection type configuration does not apply.

To enable or disable autostart collection, use the **autostart** *collection* {**enable** ı **disable**} command.

To enable etherStat and vlanStat autostart collections, respectively, issue the following command:

```
root@cat6knam.cisco.com#autostart etherstats enable
root@cat6knam.cisco.com#autostart vlanstats enable
```

To disable etherStat and vlanStat autostart collections, respectively, issue the following command:

```
root@cat6knam.cisco.com#autostart etherstats disable
root@cat6knam.cisco.com#autostart vlanstats disable
```

NOTE   If the autostart collection configuration is enabled or disabled, the NAM requires rebooting for the new configuration to take effect.

The application response time (ART) MIB measures the response time on the network at the transport layer. ART MIB can be enabled and disabled globally using the **rmon artmib** {**enable** ı **disable**} privileged command. To enable ART MIB, use the following:

```
root@cat6knam.cisco.com#rmon artmib enable
```

NOTE   An ART MIB license from Cisco Systems must be purchased before enabling and using the ART MIB feature.

Verification of the NAM Configuration

To verify the NAM configuration, use the **show** commands from the NAM console. The commonly used **show** commands are as follows:

- **show ip**—Displays the IP configuration of the NAM and HTTP server status.
- **show snmp**—Displays the community strings and SNMP MIB variables.
- **show options**—Specifies whether ART MIB and voice monitoring are enabled.
- **show autostart**—Displays the autostart collection configuration status.
- **show tech-support**—Displays system information that the Cisco TAC might need for troubleshooting. This command is available with the root account only.

To verify whether the switch Supervisor Engine recognizes the NAM and whether the NAM is online, use the **show module** command. Example 17-19 illustrates the **show**

module command output in Cisco IOS–based switches, and Example 17-20 illustrates the **show module** command output in Cisco CatOS–based switches.

Example 17-19 *Verifying the Status of NAM in Cisco IOS–Based Switches*

```
cat6k#show module
Mod Ports Card Type                             Model               Serial No.
--- ----- -------------------------------       ------------------  ----------
  1    2  Catalyst 6000 supervisor 2 (Active)   WS-X6K-S2U-MSFC2    SAD0628035C
  3   16  Pure SFM-mode 16 port 1000mb GBIC     WS-X6816-GBIC       SAL061218K3
  4    2  Network Analysis Module               WS-X6380-NAM        SAL061218K8
  5    0  Switching Fabric Module-136 (Active)  WS-X6500-SFM2       SAD061701YC

Mod MAC addresses                       Hw     Fw            Sw            Status
--- --------------------------------    ------ ------------  ------------  -------
  1 0001.6416.0342 to 0001.6416.0343    3.9    6.1(3)        7.5(0.6)HUB9  Ok
  3 0005.7485.9518 to 0005.7485.9527    1.3    12.1(5r)E1    12.1(13)E4,   Ok
  4 0003.32bb.dacb to 0003.32bb.dacc    1.4    4B4LZ0XA      2.1(2),       Ok
  5 0001.0002.0003 to 0001.0002.0003    1.2    6.1(3)        7.5(0.6)HUB9  Ok
<output skipped>
```

Example 17-20 *Verifying the Status of NAM in Cisco CatOS–Based Switches*

```
6500> (enable)  show module
Mod Slot Ports Module-Type            Model                 Sub Status
--- ---- ----- ---------------------- --------------------  --- -------
 2   2    2    1000BaseX Supervisor   WS-X6K-SUP1A-2GE      yes ok
16   2    1    Multilayer Switch Feature WS-F6K-MSFC2       no  ok
 3   3   48    10/100BaseTX Ethernet  WS-X6148-RJ45V        yes ok
 4   4    2    Network Analysis Module WS-X6380-NAM         no  ok

Mod Module-Name          Serial-Num
--- -------------------- -----------
 2                       SAD0507003F
16                       SAL063453F6
 3                       SAL0710A226
 4                       SAD062302PK

Mod MAC address(es)                     Hw     Fw          Sw
--- ----------------------------------  ------ ----------  ----------------
 2  00-01-97-2d-c1-94 to 00-01-97-2d-c1-95 7.3  5.3(1)     7.6(1)
    00-01-97-2d-c1-92 to 00-01-97-2d-c1-93
    00-30-7b-4e-34-00 to 00-30-7b-4e-37-ff
16  00-09-11-ed-3e-40 to 00-09-11-ed-3e-7f 2.5  12.1(8a)E3 12.1(8a)E3
 3  00-0b-fd-f1-54-f0 to 00-0b-fd-f1-55-1f 1.2  5.4(2)     7.6(1)
 4  00-03-fe-a9-ce-f4 to 00-03-fe-a9-ce-f5 1.4  4B4LZ0XA   2.1(2)

Mod Sub-Type             Sub-Model       Sub-Serial   Sub-Hw Sub-Sw
--- -------------------- --------------- -----------  ------ ------
 2  L3 Switching Engine  WS-F6K-PFC      SAD043405Z9  1.1
 3  Inline Power Module  WS-F6K-VPWR                  2.0    1.0
```

Troubleshooting Common Problems with the NAM

Table 17-7 describes several common potential problems encountered in the NAM and offers possible solutions.

Table 17-7   *Common Problems and Solutions in the NAM*

Symptom	Possible Cause	Recommended Action
The user cannot enable the HTTP server.	The NAM could not determine the server's fully qualified domain name.	Reboot the NAM.
The user cannot connect to the server.	The initial configuration is incorrect or the NAM is not configured.	Configure or reconfigure the NAM with the correct IP address and the NAM switch port in the correct VLAN.
The user cannot connect to the NAM Traffic Analyzer application.	The configuration for the HTTP server is incorrect.	Check whether the HTTP server and HTTP port are configured correctly using the **show ip** command.

Study Tips

The following bullets review important BCMSN exam preparation points of this chapter. The bullets only briefly highlight the main points of this chapter related to the BCMSN exam. Consult the text of this chapter for additional information regarding these topics. Table 17-8 lists important commands to review for the BCMSN exam:

- The following functions are essential for effective performance management:
  — Gather a baseline for both network and application data.
  — Perform a what-if analysis on your network and applications.
  — Perform exception reporting for capacity issues.
  — Determine the network management overhead for all proposed or potential network management services.
  — Analyze the capacity information.
  — Periodically review capacity information, baseline, and any exceptions for the network and applications.
  — Maintain upgrade or tuning procedures that are set up to handle capacity issues on both a reactive and longer-term basis.
- Two variations of SPAN exist: local SPAN and remote SPAN.
- SPAN monitors either individual or group interfaces, single or multiple VLANs, or a combination.

- Local SPAN is a SPAN session in which the source interface and the destination interface belong to the same switch.

- Remote SPAN is a SPAN session in which the source interface or VLAN is on a different switch than the destination interface.

- The NAM services module allows integrated monitoring on the Catalyst 6500 series of switches.

- The NAM supports multiple data sources, including local and remote SPANs, VACL with capture option, and NDE.

Table 17-8   *Commands to Review*

Command	Description
(config)#**monitor session** *session* **source** {**interface** *interface-id*}|{**vlan** *vlan-id* [**rx**	**tx**	**both**]	**remote vlan** *rspan vlan-id*	Configures the data source of the SPAN session
(config)#**monitor session** *session* **destination** {**interface** *interface-id*}{**vlan** *vlan-id* {**remote vlan** *vlan-id*}	Configures the destination parameters of the SPAN session
(config-vlan)#**remote-vlan**	Configures a VLAN as a remote VLAN
show autostart	Displays the autostart collection configuration status on NAM services module
show ip	Displays the IP configuration of the NAM service module and HTTP server status
show module	Displays the module type and status information
show monitor session *session*	Displays SPAN session configuration
show snmp	Displays the community strings and SNMP MIB variables on NAM services module

Summary

Keep internetwork performance at acceptable levels by measuring and managing various network performance variables. This chapter reviewed and demonstrated the following tools:

- Local SPAN/VSPAN
- RSPAN
- VACL with the capture option
- L2 traceroute
- NAM

The first three features in the preceding list are primarily ways to capture traffic for performance monitoring and troubleshooting purposes. Local SPAN is used when the source port and the network analyzer are connected to the same switch. VSPAN is similar to local SPAN but is used when the entire VLAN needs monitoring. The RSPAN feature allows the monitoring of source ports or VLAN on a different switch than the network analyzer, even through multiple intermediate switches. L2 traceroute is purely a troubleshooting tool, providing critical information about the path of the frame and identifying port connections of the devices for easier troubleshooting. The NAM, on the other hand, which is used to monitor performance and for troubleshooting, can capture and decode packets. The NAM is available on the Catalyst 6500 family of switches.

Review Questions

For multiple-choice questions, there might be more than one correct answer.

1 What is the default direction of traffic capture in a SPAN session?

   a rx

   b tx

   c Both

   d None

2 How many SPAN destination ports are allowed for local SPAN?

   a 2

   b 1

   c No limit

   d 6

3 If you want to capture multiple VLAN packets and be able to distinguish between them, how does the SPAN destination port need to be configured?

   a Routed port

   b Access port

   c Trunk port

   d Isolated PVLAN port

4 What type of devices connect to the SPAN destination port with the **inpkts** option in CatOS–based switches or the **ingress vlan** option in Cisco IOS–based switches?

    a Routers

    b Servers

    c Hubs

    d IPS

    e Switches

5 True or False: User ports may be configured on the RSPAN VLAN.

6 Which of the following commands can be used to verify the status of the HTTP server on the Catalyst 6500 NAM?

    a **show ip**

    b **show server**

    c **show http**

    d **show http status**

    e None of the above

7 Select the best tool from the following list for capturing the intended traffic, if the sniffer device is not in the same location as the switch being monitored.

    a Local SPAN

    b VSPAN on the client switch

    c L2 traceroute

    d Remote SPAN

    e None of the above

8 A network administrator does not know the port in which a server connects into the switch. The administrator does know the IP address of the server. Which tool can the administrator use to determine which port the server is connected to?

    a VACL with capture option

    b NAM

    c   L2 traceroute

    d   Local SPAN

    e   None of the above

9 A network administrator needs to quickly analyze the traffic belonging to a certain VLAN for information such as the top talker, conversation statistics, and protocol distribution. Select the best tool that the administrator can use to obtain this information from the following list.

    a   SPAN

    b   RSPAN

    c   Catalyst 6500 NAM

    d   VACL with capture option

    e   None of the above

10 Which of the following commands is needed to configure a VSPAN with source of VLAN 10 in the receive direction only?

    a   **monitor session 1 source 10 rx**

    b   **monitor session 1 destination 10 rx**

    c   **monitor session 1 source-vlan 10**

    d   **monitor session 1 source vlan 10**

    e   **monitor session 1 source vlan 10 rx**

11 Which of the following commands is needed to configure an RSPAN with the source being the RSPAN VLAN 10?

    a   **monitor session 1 source 10 rx**

    b   **monitor session 1 destination remote 10**

    c   **monitor session 1 source vlan 10 rx**

    d   **monitor session 1 source remote vlan 10**

    e   **monitor session 1 source vlan remote 10 rx**

12 Which of the following commands is needed to configure an RSPAN with a destination of RSPAN VLAN 10?

   a   monitor session 1 destination 10

   b   monitor session 1 destination vlan 10 tx

   c   monitor session 1 destination remote 10 tx

   d   monitor session 1 destination remote vlan 10 tx

   e   monitor session 1 destination remote vlan 10

13 Which of the following encapsulation types is used in the ERSPAN feature?

   a   IPIP

   b   PPP

   c   GRE

   d   DES

   e   None of the above

14 Which of the following scripting languages is supported in the EEM feature?

   a   PERL.

   b   TCL.

   c   EXPECT.

   d   JAVA.

   e   Any script language is acceptable.

This chapter covers the following topics:

- WLAN and Ethernet Similarities
- WLAN and Ethernet Differences
- WLAN Components
- Wireless Network Implementations
- Building Blocks of AP WLAN Topologies
- Building Blocks of a Bridging WLAN
- Topology Implementation
- Wireless Theory and Standards
- 802.11 Operational Standards
- Implementing WLANs
- Cisco WLANs
- Cisco Wireless Clients
- Configuring a Basic WLAN

## CHAPTER 18

Introducing Wireless into the Campus Network

The wireless LAN (WLAN) evolution started in the 1980s using 900-MHz Direct Sequence Spread Spectrum (DSSS) technology. The 900-MHz systems were fairly easy to deploy because one access point (AP) could cover large areas and no licenses were required in the approved countries. One problem for 900-MHz technology was that only a few countries allowed it.

As time progressed, the need for faster speeds, open standards, and global acceptance forced the manufacturers of WLAN products to engineer newer products using the 2.4-GHz band. The 2.4-GHz technology was well received because the throughput grew from 860 kbps to 54 Mbps using the 802.11g modulation scheme called Orthogonal Frequency-Division Multiplexing (OFDM).

Today, WLANs are pervasive, and implementations have grown significantly in many industries such as education, health care, retail, and others. Wireless Internet service providers (WISPs) are providing hot spots at airports, coffee shops, malls, and so on, so people can surf the web or connect back to work. The WLAN can extend wired LANs in classrooms, hospitals, or historical buildings where cabling is difficult or structural changes are forbidden.

WLANs Explained

Wireless networks solve the data exchange problem without wires. There are many different types of wireless data communication methods, each of which has its advantages and drawbacks:

- **Infrared (III)**—Very high data rates, lower cost, and very short distance
- **Narrowband**—Low data rates, medium cost, license required, limited distance
- **Spread spectrum**—Limited to campus coverage, medium cost, high data rates
- **Personal Communications Service (PCS)**—Low data rates, medium cost, citywide coverage
- **Cellular**—Low to medium cost, national and worldwide coverage (typical cell phone carrier)

The spread spectrum wireless focus is on the three unlicensed bands: 900 MHz, 2.4 GHz, and 5 GHz. The 900-MHz and 2.4-GHz bands are referred to as the Industrial, Scientific, and Medical (ISM) bands, and the 5-GHz band is commonly referred to as the Unlicensed National Information Infrastructure (UNII) band.

Figure 18-1 refers to the frequencies for these bands. They are as follows:

- **900-MHz band**—902 to 928 MHz
- **2.4-GHz band**—2.4 to 2.483 GHz (in Japan extends to 2.495 GHz)
- **5-GHz band**—5.150 to 5.350 MHz, 5.725 to 5.825 MHz, with some countries supporting middle bands between 5.350 and 5.825 MHz

Figure 18-1 *Unlicensed Frequency Bands*

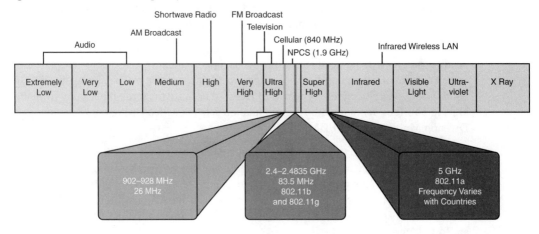

A wireless communications system uses radio frequency (RF) energy to transmit data from one point to another through the air. Many people use the term *signal* to refer to the RF energy over the air. The transmitted data is first modulated onto a carrier so that it can be sent out to the receivers. The modulated signal is then received and demodulated so the data can be processed.

There are many different types of networks offered. Each unique network provides some defined coverage area. Figure 18-2 lists each wireless technology and illustrates the corresponding coverage areas. The following is a brief discussion of the wireless networks, starting with the smallest area:

- **Personal-area network (PAN)**—Typically designed to cover your personal workspace. Radios are typically very low powered, do not offer options in antenna selection, and limit the size of the coverage area to approximately 15 to 20 feet radially. One such PAN network is Bluetooth. Good examples of this technology are communications between PCs and peripherals or between wireless phones and headsets. In the PAN wireless network, the customer owns 100 percent of the network; therefore, no airtime charges are incurred.

- **LAN**—Designed to be an enterprise-based network that allows for complete suites of enterprise applications to be used without wires. A LAN typically delivers Ethernet-capable speeds (up to 54 Mbps). In the LAN wireless network, the customer owns 100 percent of the network; therefore, no airtime charges are incurred.

- **Metropolitan-area network (MAN)**—Deployed inside a metropolitan area, allowing wireless connectivity throughout an urban area. A MAN typically delivers up to broadband speeds (similar to digital subscriber line [DSL]) but is not capable of Ethernet speeds. In the wireless MAN, the wireless network may be from a licensed carrier, requiring the customer to purchase airtime, or it may be built out and supported by one entity, such as a police department.

- **WAN**—Typically slower in speed but offers more coverage, sometimes including rural areas. Because of their vast deployment, all wireless WANs require that a customer purchase airtime for data transmission.

Figure 18-2 *Wireless Technologies*

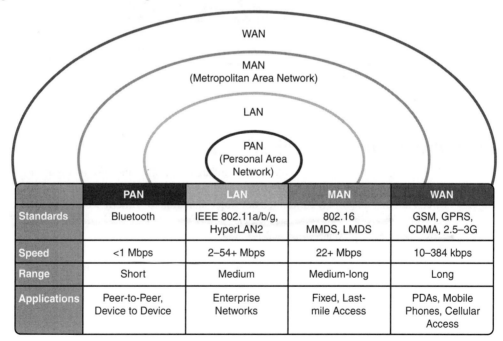

	PAN	LAN	MAN	WAN
Standards	Bluetooth	IEEE 802.11a/b/g, HyperLAN2	802.16 MMDS, LMDS	GSM, GPRS, CDMA, 2.5–3G
Speed	<1 Mbps	2–54+ Mbps	22+ Mbps	10–384 kbps
Range	Short	Medium	Medium-long	Long
Applications	Peer-to-Peer, Device to Device	Enterprise Networks	Fixed, Last-mile Access	PDAs, Mobile Phones, Cellular Access

The Cisco Aironet wireless products are considered to be LAN, not WAN, wireless products. They are intended for in-building wireless networks or line-of-sight outdoor bridging applications. No license is required for the spread spectrum and OFDM devices in most countries. They are not designed for a mesh or citywide wireless network. They are not WAN or MAN devices; cellular phones, pagers, or Mobitex; or PCS devices. There are no rental, ongoing, or licensing fees for the use of Cisco Aironet wireless devices. To help clear up any confusion, Figure 18-3 illustrates the coverage areas and data rates of various wireless data networks in use today.

Figure 18-3 *Wireless Data Networks*

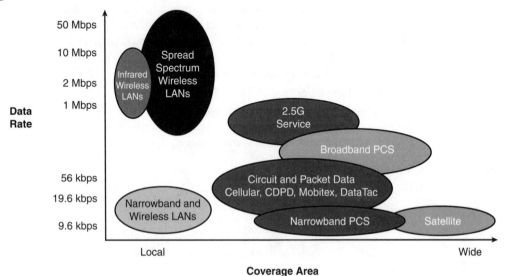

WLAN and Ethernet Similarities

The IEEE 802 committee develops open standards for LANs and WANs. Figure 18-4 provides a layout of the 802 framework. For example, the 802.3 (the standard defining wired Ethernet networks) committee develops standards for Ethernet-based wired networks. The 802.11 (a group of wireless networking standards, also known as Wi-Fi) committee develops standards for WLANs.

Figure 18-4 *IEEE 802 Framework*

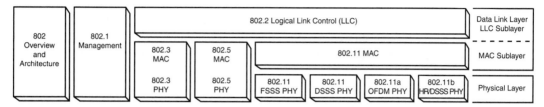

In July 1997, the IEEE ratified the 2.4-GHz standard that included DSSS technology, Frequency Hopping Spread Spectrum (FHSS) technology, and infrared light, commonly referred to as IR, at the physical layer. The standard specified 1 Mbps as the standard speed and 2 Mbps as a "turbo" mode. In September 1999, the IEEE 802.11a standard (5 GHz at 54 Mbps) and the IEEE 802.1lb standard (2.4 GHz at 11 Mbps) were ratified by the IEEE. In June 2003, the IEEE ratified the 802.11g standard (2.4 GHz at 54 Mbps). This standard is backward compatible with 802.11b systems because both use the same 2.4-GHz bandwidth.

802.11 is based on the IEEE 802.3 standard. Moreover, 802.3 and 802.11 standards evolved based on bandwidth demands by both applications and the number of users. Ethernet scaled from 10 Mbps (Ethernet or 10BASE-T), 100 Mbps (Fast Ethernet), and 1 Gbps (Gigabit Ethernet) to 10 Gbps. Wireless scaled from 1 and 2 Mbps (802.11), 5.5, and 11 Mbps (802.11b, including 1- and 2-Mbps rates for backward compatibility) to 54 Mbps (802.11a and 802.11g). Both wireless and Ethernet use carrier sense multiple access (CSMA). Ethernet adds collision detection (CD), and wireless uses a modified form of collision avoidance (CA).

Ethernet CSMA/CD is designed to easily detect or sense a collision based on the wire voltage. The wired LAN uses unshielded twisted-pair (UTP) copper cables that have electrical pulses to transmit data back and forth. When two stations transmit simultaneously, the wire voltage is raised, signifying a collision. WLANs are not afforded the same luxury due to the inability to control air waves. Each client or station (an end-user device such as a laptop or PC) must wait for the active station to be done. Once the active station is done, another station wanting to speak announces itself and how long it wants to speak. The station knows its transmission was successful only if it receives an acknowledgement. If two stations transmit data simultaneously, the absence of the positive acknowledgement implies a collision. Both stations then use a backoff algorithm to wait prior to transmitting data again.

All the upper-level services work the same. Without additional tools, the upper-level services such as DHCP and SNMP can take advantage of wireless. The user experience is like being connected to the wired network. Telecommuters can connect to their workplace through a Virtual Private Network (VPN) IPsec tunnel created over a wired or wireless connection. Home users can access the Internet while roaming around.

Remote and wireless users should be authenticated prior to access to an enterprise network. Cisco Secure Access Control Server (ACS) provides a centralized identity networking solution and simplified user management experience across all Cisco devices and security-management applications. Cisco Secure ACS ensures enforcement of assigned policies by allowing network administrators to control authentication, authorization, and accounting (AAA).

WLAN and Ethernet Differences

A view of the physical (Layer 1) and data link (Layer 2) layers of the OSI model will help you to understand how the 802.11 Physical (PHY) components relate. The PHY components are MAC, Physical Layer Convergence Procedure (PLCP), and the Physical Medium Dependent (PMD). Figure 18-5 breaks down the PHY components.

Figure 18-5   *PHY Components*

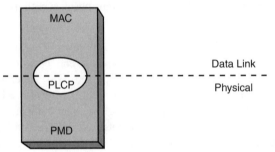

Consider how the data link layer can be broken into the MAC and LLC sublayers. The PHY continues to use the MAC portion while replacing the LLC with the PLCP. The PLCP provides a common interface to the MAC sublayer and is more unique in that it transcends into the physical layer, too. The PLCP creates frames from the MAC layer PDUs (MPDUs) by adding the correct header based on the PMD's selected modulation. When receiving frames from the PMD, the PLCP header is stripped off and sent to the MPDU of the MAC sublayer. The PMD component is responsible for modulating and transmitting the frames received from the PLCP. It also processes received signals from other transmitters, demodulates them, and sends those frames to the PLCP component.

802.11 uses the same frequency for both transmitting and receiving (half duplex, sometimes called simplex). The bandwidth is shared by all the computers on the wireless network. A WLAN can handle several client stations but can become unusable with too many clients.

Physically, the main difference between wireless and wired networks is, of course, the presence or absence of cables for the communications medium. Wired networks transfer through cables electrical signals that represent information, whereas wireless networks transfer data through the air. WLAN users are able to roam around without getting disconnected from the network while in RF range.

Privacy Concerns

Roaming comes at a cost. A hacker with the right wireless components could wreak havoc on a WLAN. Unlike the physical security with wired LANs, WLANs are open and should always be secured as if they were a publicly accessible network. Preventing hackers from listening to a WLAN is not realistic. The real solution is making your WLAN data indiscernible through power and encryption security services. Too much power creates an easy target due to the signal-to-noise ratio. Too little power causes reachability problems due to the signal-to-noise ratio as well.

Privacy is addressed by 802.11 by an optional service called Wired Equivalent Privacy (WEP). WEP is based on the RC4 algorithm, which the encryption keys must match on both the client and the AP for frame exchanges to succeed. Any diligent hacker can break WEP because it is not a strong encryption method. WEP is analogous to speaking privately in a foreign language. After someone understands that language, the conversation is no longer private. So, simple abuses, such as neighbors leeching onto your Internet access, can be stopped by using WEP, but not much more than that.

Environmental Concerns

Other problems may arise in the WLAN. Knowing the common issues prior to design will help mitigate them. Just as light and sound bounce off objects, so do RF signals. This means that there can be many RF paths from the transmit (Tx) to receive (Rx) antennas. These multiple signals combine to cause distortion of the signal. The higher the number of radios in a cell, the higher the noise level in the cell. Because of multipath reception, the signal strength might be strong, but it might also be distorted. Proximity does not guarantee better performance.

Coverage holes are the voids where the RF signal is not discernable. A perfect survey can get coverage holes if environmental changes are made. Such RF examples would be the addition of plants, office furniture getting moved, or walls getting changed from structural modifications. RF gets absorbed or reflected so that the signal becomes too weak for the station to pick out the signal from the noise. The closer the antennas are to each other, the stronger all paths are, including reflected paths, which increases the possibility of interference from reflected paths. The farther the antennas are from each other, the greater the difference between reflected and direct (primary) signal. So farther distance makes for decreased signal strength but also reduces the strength of any reflected signal.

Environmental factors such as reflections, refractions, and diffractions (all of which can cause multipath interference) can degrade a signal between the transmitter and receiver.

Multipath interference can cause high signal strength yet low signal quality, so that the data would be unreadable. One indication that you are experiencing multipath interference is that signal strength and signal quality fluctuate drastically, even when you are moving the client only a little (inches). You can relate this to a common occurrence in your car. As you pull up to a stop sign, you might notice static on the radio. But as you move forward a few inches or feet, the station starts to come in more clearly. By rolling forward, you move the antenna slightly, away from the point where the multipath signals converge.

Interference occurs when another RF source produces a signal on the same channel. If there is severe signal interference in one area, it is possible to change to another channel and totally avoid the interference. Normally, changing channels does not happen automatically in DSSS and must be done with reconfiguration to the AP. Cisco firmware will allow an AP to search for the least-congested channel.

Compression Concerns

As the data is further compressed, it requires a stronger signal as compared to the noise level. More noise means slower speed for the data to be received correctly. The same is true in radio. As a receiver moves farther from a transmitter, the signal gets weaker, and the difference between the signal and noise decreases. At some point, the signal cannot be distinguished from the noise, and loss of communication occurs. The amount of compression (or modulation type) at which the signal is transmitted determines the amount of signal necessary to be clearly received through the noise. As transmission or modulation schemes (compression) become more complex and the data rate goes up, immunity to noise decreases and coverage goes down. Or, stated simply, when frequency and speeds are increased, the cell coverage distances are decreased.

Mobility Concerns

Mobility is the freedom from constraints such as physical connections (power cords, network cables, and so on). Mobile devices contain client software to manage the WLAN client cards. WLAN client cards can have a significant impact on the battery life of a mobile device. One or two surveys will burn that into your brain. Moreover, using 802.11a drains the battery life faster than 802.11b or 802.11g.

To help reduce the battery drain problem, Cisco client cards use power save mode to preserve battery life while maintaining association. The AP buffers data during power save mode, which reduces the overall throughput.

Regulatory Concerns

Different countries have different regulatory bodies and may have as many as 14 channels available. Table 18-1 gives the channel set breakdown on several regulatory domains. In some countries, this might mean that the number of nonoverlapping channels is reduced to one, and an aggregate data rate of 33 Mbps might not be possible.

Table 18-1 *2.4-GHz Regulated Channels Table*

Channel Identifier	Center Frequency	Regulatory Domain			
		Americas	Europe, Middle East, and Asia	Japan	Israel
1	2412 MHz	✓	✓	✓	
2	2417 MHz	✓	✓	✓	✓
3	2422 MHz	✓	✓	✓	✓
4	2427 MHz	✓	✓	✓	✓
5	2432 MHz	✓	✓	✓	✓
6	2437 MHz	✓	✓	✓	✓
7	2442 MHz	✓	✓	✓	✓
8	2447 MHz	✓	✓	✓	✓
9	2452 MHz	✓	✓	✓	✓
10	2457 MHz	✓	✓	✓	
11	2462 MHz	✓	✓	✓	
12	2467 MHz		✓	✓	
13	2472 MHz		✓	✓	
14	2484 MHz			✓	

There are 11 channels available in the United States; however, only three of these channels (1, 6, and 11) are nonoverlapping. In the European Telecommunications Standards Institute (ETSI) domains, there are 13 available channels, but again there are only three nonoverlapping channels. In Japan, there is an additional channel located at the top end of the band. It is possible to use this along with three other channels for a total of four nonoverlapping channels.

WLAN Components

The wireless connection can be as simple as two wireless laptops or two PCs equipped with wireless adapter cards. A wireless connection requires little to no setup for the WLAN to work. This connection type is used when transferring information directly between stations as long as they remain within radio range. Cisco does not consider this to be a WLAN.

Clients refers to end-user hardware such as PCs, laptops, and personal digital assistants (PDAs). WLAN client adapter cards can enable stations to have network and Internet access anywhere within a building that is equipped with a wireless network infrastructure. Client adapters can connect to a wireless network in either *ad hoc* (peer-to-peer) mode or *infrastructure* mode using APs. The following list describes the two WLAN client adapters:

- **Cisco Aironet 802.11a/b/g CardBus Wireless LAN Client Adapter**—This 802.11a/b/g-compliant CardBus client adapter is ideal for laptops and tablet PCs and complements the 1100 and 1200 Series APs.

- **Cisco Aironet 802.11a/b/g PCI Wireless LAN Client Adapter**—This 802.11a/b/g-compliant low-profile PCI client adapter is ideal for slim desktop and point-of-sale devices and complements the 1100 and 1200 Series APs.

The APs themselves can be put in either one of Cisco's two WLAN architectures: Autonomous and Lightweight. Autonomous APs were once called thick, fat, or decentralized, and lightweight APs were called thin or centralized.

Both autonomous and lightweight APs use the network infrastructure, which may require additional design considerations to support the WLAN. Various switches, routers, and VPN concentrators may be needed. Network services such as AAA, certificate authority (CA), DHCP, and DNS can be valuable for security reasons.

Autonomous APs

An autonomous AP has local configurations requiring local management (for example, Telnet to each device to add an infrastructure SSID), which might make consistent configurations difficult and add to the cost of network management. The following APs are autonomous:

- **1100 Series**—An affordable, easy-to-install, single-band AP.

- **1130 Series**—An all-in-one dual-band 802.11a/b/g AP that has all the radios and antennas included.

- **1200 Series**—A dual-band 802.11a/b/g AP; was the first versatile enterprise-class AP.

- **1230AG Series**—A dual-band 802.11a/b/g AP designed for harsh WLAN environments or installations that require specialized antennas. It includes hardware encryption.

- **1240AG Series**—IEEE 802.11a/b/g access, second-generation, versatile AP.

Lightweight APs

A lightweight AP receives control and configuration from a WLAN controller to which it is associated. This reduces the security concern of a stolen AP and provides a single point of management. The Cisco Aironet 1000 Series Lightweight AP is an 802.11a/b/g dual-band device. The following autonomous APs are lightweight capable:

- **1130 Series Lightweight**—An all-in-one dual-band 802.11a/b/g AP
- **1200 Series Lightweight**—A single-band lightweight AP
- **1240AG Series Lightweight**—A dual-band 802.11a/b/g AP

The lightweight Wireless LAN Controllers communicate with Cisco 1000 Series or lightweight-capable APs over any Layer 2 (Ethernet) or Layer 3 (IP) infrastructure using the Lightweight Access Point Protocol (LWAPP). These devices support automation of numerous WLAN configuration and management functions. Wireless LAN Controllers are responsible for centralized system-wide WLAN management functions, such as security policies, intrusion prevention, RF management, quality of service (QoS), and mobility. Stated simply, this is where the instructions are processed. They work in conjunction with Cisco 1000 Series Lightweight APs and the Cisco Wireless Control System (WCS) to support business-critical wireless applications. Cisco wireless LAN controllers provide the control, scalability, security, and reliability that network managers need to build secure, enterprise-scale wireless networks—from branch offices to main campuses.

Cisco Systems currently offers the following controllers:

- **2000 Series**—Can handle up to six lightweight APs. Ideal for smaller enterprises.
- **4400 Series**—Can handle up to 100 lightweight APs. Ideal for large enterprises.
- **4100 Series**—Can handle up to 36 lightweight APs. An Enhanced Security Module (ESM) is available to offload processor-intensive security options. Ideal for medium enterprises.
- **Catalyst 6500 Series Wireless Services Module (WiSM)**—Ideal for medium to large enterprises with clustering capabilities.
- **Wireless LAN Controller Module (WLCM) for Cisco Integrated Services Routers (ISR)**—Ideal for small to medium businesses and enterprise branch offices.

Wireless Network Implementations

Wireless networks have two main categories: WLANs (in-building or mesh), and wireless bridges (building-to-building). Figure 18-6 illustrates two WLAN users connecting locally with a wireless bridge connection to the remote building.

Figure 18-6 *Wireless LAN and Bridge*

WLANs replace the Layer 1 transmission medium of a traditional wired network (usually Category 5 cable) with radio transmission over the air. WLANs can plug into a wired network and function as an overlay to traditional or wired LANs, or they can be deployed as a standalone LAN where wired networking is not feasible. WLANs permit the use of desktop or portable computers or specialty devices in a system where connection to the network is essential. A computer with a wireless network interface card (NIC) can connect to the wired LAN through the AP. WLANs are typically located within a building and are used for distances up to 1000 feet. Properly deployed WLANs can provide instant access to the network from anywhere in a facility. Users can roam without losing network connection.

Mesh networks are scalable outdoor networks that continuously communicate with each other to determine link paths. If a link is degraded, the AP will determine whether a better path exists and will route traffic through a more optimal node.

Intelligent wireless routing is provided by the patent-pending Adaptive Wireless Path (AWP) protocol. This enables each AP to identify its neighbors and intelligently choose the optimal path to the wired network by calculating the cost of each path in terms of signal strength and the number of hops required to get to a controller.

The Cisco Aironet 1500 Series Lightweight Outdoor Mesh AP operates with Cisco wireless LAN controllers and Cisco WCS software. The AP dedicates the 5-GHz radio frequency for backhaul operations to reach a wired network and uses the 2.4-GHz radio frequency for wireless clients.

Wireless bridges allow two or more networks that are physically separated to be connected on one LAN, without the time or expense of dedicated cable or T1 lines.

Building Blocks of AP WLAN Topologies

WLAN designs build upon the components of wireless. *Basic Service Sets* (BSSs) are the building block modes used to design wireless network solutions. The BSS is where mobile clients use a single AP for connectivity to each other or wired network resources. The *Extended Services Set* (ESS) is two or more BSSs connected by the distribution system. Independent (ad hoc) mode and infrastructure mode are the two BSS modes.

NOTE   Many clients default to ad hoc mode, which has a negative impact on infrastructure WLAN in regard to both bandwidth usage and network security.

Independent mode, also known as *ad hoc mode*, is a peer-to-peer network where mobile clients connect directly without an intermediate AP, sharing files between two or more mobile clients directly. This mode is called an *Independent Basic Service Set* (IBSS).

Infrastructure mode adds greater diversity and control for larger environments. Infrastructure mode incorporates APs, which are used to provide stations with communication.

Figure 18-7 illustrates both BSS modes. The left side is a simple peer-to-peer connection, and the right side is a typical infrastructure WLAN.

Figure 18-7   *BSS Modes—Independent and Infrastructure*

IBSS (Ad Hoc) Mode   Infrastructure Mode

In BSS infrastructure mode, the AP attaches to the Ethernet backbone and communicates with all the wireless devices in the cell area. The AP is the master for the cell and controls traffic flow to and from the network. The remote devices do not communicate directly with each other; they communicate with the AP.

An aspect of the BSS is the basic service area (BSA), which is the cell area of RF coverage provided by an AP, also referred to as a *microcell*.

To extend the BSA, or to simply add wireless devices and extend the range of an existing wired system, an AP can be added. (As the name *access point* indicates, this unit is the point at which wireless clients can access the network.)

If a single cell does not provide enough coverage, any number of cells can be added to extend the range. This is known as an *extended service area* (ESA). It is recommended that the ESA cells have 10 to 15 percent overlap to allow remote users to roam without losing RF connections. Bordering cells should be set to different nonoverlapping channels for best performance.

In an environment where extended coverage is needed but access to the backbone is not practical or available, a wireless repeater can be used (see Figure 18-8). A *wireless repeater* is simply an AP that is not connected to the wired backbone. This requires a 50 percent overlap of the AP on the backbone and the wireless repeater. Receive and retransmit times involved will decrease because of data rates. The repeater must be on the same channel as the root (the AP connected to Ethernet).

Figure 18-8   *Wireless Repeater*

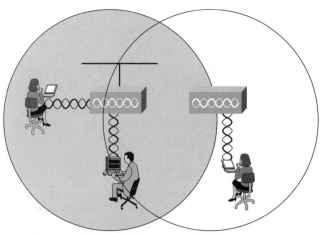

A wireless bridge can act as an AP in some applications by communicating with clients at the remote sites. This is accomplished with a Cisco Work Group Bridge (WGB), such as shown in Figure 18-9. The WGB allows up to eight wired machines to be attached to the same radio device. The WGB is ideal for connecting remote workgroups to a wired LAN and provides a single MAC address connection into an AP and onto the LAN backbone. The WGB cannot be used in a peer-to-peer mode connection and must communicate to an AP or a bridge in AP mode. The WGB has an 802.11b radio that communicates with Cisco Aironet APs and bridges with 802.11b or 802.11g radios.

Figure 18-9   *Wireless Work Group Bridge*

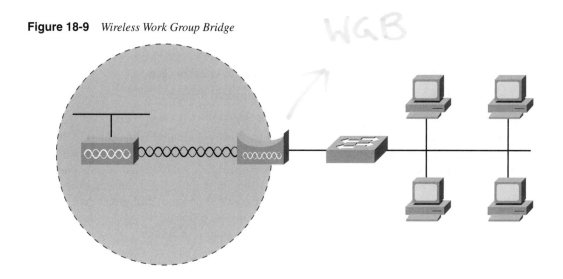

Building Blocks of a Bridging WLAN

Bridges such as the Cisco 1300 and 1400 Series are used to connect two or more wired LANs, usually located within separate buildings, to create one large LAN. Cisco Aironet bridges operate at the MAC address layer (data link layer), which means they have no routing capabilities. A router must be put in place if IP subnetting is needed within the network.

The Cisco 1300 and 1400 Series Wireless Bridges are designed to be mounted outdoors, typically on a tower or a tall building. Choosing a good mounting location for the bridge is important because it affects the reliability of the wireless link and the maximum data rates that it can support. The most important considerations are distance between bridges and clearance from obstacles. The mounting location can be the top or side of a building, in a window, on a tower or mast providing a clear unobstructed line of sight to the remote bridges, or any suitable flat surface.

Bridging has quickly become one of the most popular uses of wireless networks. This development is in part due to the ease of installation and setup. But it is also due to the variety of emerging markets where WLAN bridging can be applied.

The Root setting is normally used for the "main" side of the bridge. This bridge provides connectivity to the main LAN for other wireless clients or wired clients that are being connected wirelessly. Only one bridge in a WLAN can be set as the root bridge. This is the default setting for Cisco bridges.

In root mode, the bridge supports the following by default:

- **Non-root bridges**—Typically considered the remote side of the bridge connection
- **Wireless client cards**—PC card, PCI card end-user connections
- **WGB**—A bridge that can directly connect wired devices
- **Repeater**—An AP that helps extend the reachability

Bridges offer many advantages over other, more costly alternative connections such as T1 lines, cabling, and microwave connections. A bridge can be used in point-to-point or point-to-multipoint connections. Regardless of the connection type, there can be only one root bridge, as shown in Figure 18-10. Figure 18-10 has the point-to-point connection on the left with the root bridge on top of the black building and the non-root bridge on top of the gray building. Moreover, it has the point-to-multipoint connection on the right with a black building (root bridge) and multiple gray buildings (non-root bridges).

Figure 18-10 *Wireless Bridge Connections*

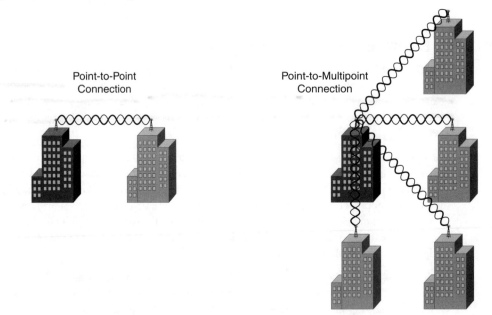

A T1 line typically costs from $200 to more than $1000 per month. For a site with four buildings, the cost could be anywhere from $10,000 to $36,000 per year. If such sites were connected via local bridges, the payback for the hardware costs incurred could actually be realized in less than a single year. The hardware cost for wireless bridging can range from $1000 to $10,000, depending on the design configuration.

Another popular option for smaller businesses might be a cable or DSL modem. This solution sometimes offers faster download speeds but slower upload speeds. Reliability is often an issue. Cable users are often forced to "share" connections with other nearby businesses, sometimes causing a sacrifice in speed.

Microwave is a solution for some sites where distance is short, reliability is not critical, and money is not an issue. With licensed microwave, a U.S. Federal Communications Commission (FCC) license is required. The cost of the equipment is typically more than $10,000 per site, not including installation items. In heavy fog, rain, or snow, performance is questionable. Multipoint connections are usually not possible.

Topology Implementation

An enterprise WLAN consists of tens or hundreds of APs covering floors, buildings, and whole campuses too. Each AP microcell is carefully designed. Figure 18-11 illustrates microcells with laptop computers and pen-based computers. The WLAN can include printers and any other devices that are found on typical wired networks.

Figure 18-11   *Microcellular Architecture*

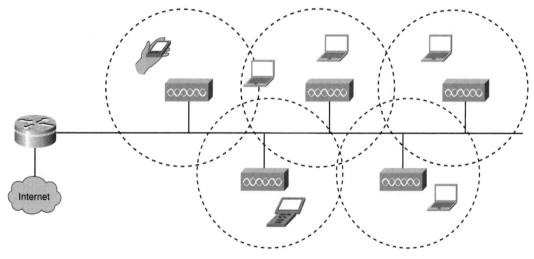

The user has the ability to move freely anywhere the microcells permit.

The following are the benefits of a microcell architecture:

- **Seamless roaming**—Roaming across APs allows users to maintain connection while moving around a facility or campus environment.

- **Power management**—Managing the radio results in better battery life for portable devices.

- **Dynamic load balancing**—Users can be dynamically distributed among APs to increase the throughput of each user.

- **Fault tolerance**—WLAN backbones can be provided with the use of APs with overlapping coverage cells.

Wireless Theory and Standards

Radio frequencies are high-frequency, alternating current (AC) signals that are radiated into the air via an antenna, creating radio waves. Radio waves propagate away from the antenna in a straight line in all directions at once just like "light" from a light bulb. Just as spreading more light bulbs around the room provides better overall lighting, spreading more antennas around a service area provides a stronger average signal for mobile clients.

RF Basics

When radio waves hit a wall, door, or any obstruction, there is attenuation of the signal, which weakens the signal and may reduce throughput.

Several natural causes impact radio waves/RF:

- **Reflection**—Occurs when RF bounces off objects (such as metal or glass surfaces).

- **Refraction**—Occurs when RF passes through objects and changes direction (such as glass surfaces).

- **Absorption**—Occurs when RF is absorbed by an object (such as a wall or furniture).

- **Scattering**—Occurs when an RF wave strikes an uneven surface and is reflected in many directions. Also occurs when an RF wave travels through a medium that consists of objects that are much smaller than the wavelength of the signal (such as heavy dust).

- **Diffraction**—Occurs when an RF wave strikes sharp edges (such as external corners of buildings), which bends the signal.

RF wave propagation naturally encounters the attenuation factors in the preceding list, all of which need to be considered when designing, implementing, and troubleshooting WLANs. Figure 18-12 represents each RF impact.

Figure 18-12 *RF Impacts*

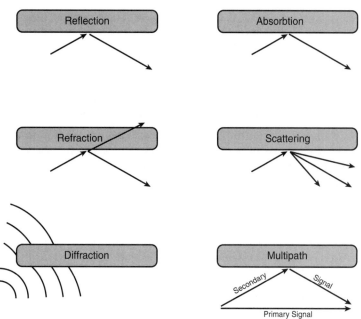

NOTE   Reflection may cause signal gain, and if increased power is not required, an AP's power can be reduced.

Some form of absorption occurs with almost all materials, which reduces the overall signal strength.

Multipath interference is less of an issue when using an OFDM technology because multipath is frequency selective. DSSS comprises a single signal, whereas OFDM comprises multiple signals. While multipath interference affects an entire DSSS signal, it affects only a subset of the OFDM signals.

Cisco 1000 series APs address multipath interference issues by providing multiple antennas that support diversity for the 802.11b band. Even with multiple antennas, multipath interference can occur.

WLAN: RF Math

WLANs transmit power just like radio stations do to reach listeners. The power levels for wireless are in milliwatts, whereas the power levels for radio stations are in megawatts.

Here are some units of measure to help you better understand the RF math:

- **dB (decibel)**—The difference or ratio between two signal levels. Used to measure relative gains or losses in an RF system. Named after Alexander Graham Bell and used to describe the effect of system devices on signal strength.

- **dBm (decibels per milliwatt)**—A signal strength or power level. Zero dBm is defined as 1 mW of power into a terminating load such as an antenna or power meter. Small signals are negative numbers (such as –83 dBm).

- **dBW (decibels per watt)**—A signal strength or power level compared to 1 watt (0 dBw = 1W). One ampere (1A) of current at one volt (1V).

- **dBi (isotropic)**—The gain a given antenna has over a theoretical isotropic (point source) antenna. Unfortunately, an isotropic antenna cannot be made in the real world, but it is useful for calculating theoretical fade and system operating margins.

The math formula used in WLANs is too complex for most people to solve without a calculator. The formula requires adding gains or losses, described in decibels, and then converting those results into an absolute power, described in milliwatts or watts.

The formula is

Transmit Power (dBm) = 10 * log[Transmit Power (mW)]

You can easily see, using Table 18-2, how the gains and losses relate to power levels. Refer to this table to help out whenever needed.

Table 18-2   *Decibel to Milliwatt Conversion Table*

dBm	mW		dBm	mW
0	1		10	10
3	2		20	100
6	4		30	1000 or 1W
9	8		40	10,000 or 10W
12	16		50	100,000 or 100W

RF math can be made easier by understanding a few key points:

- Every 3 dB will double when gaining (gain) or decrease by half when losing (loss).

- Every 10 dB will increase by a factor of 10 when gaining (gain) or decrease by a factor of 10 when losing (loss).

- Add all the gains and losses to come up with the end result and convert.

A 9-dB loss can be broken down into –3 dB + –3 dB + –3 dB. A signal level of 200 mW will be decreased to 25 mW. It can be broken down as follows:

- 200 mW + –3 dB = 100 mW
- 100 mW + –3 dB = 50 mW
- 50 mW + –3 dB = 25 mW
- 25 mW is the end result

Gain increases the RF signal amplitude. Two common sources for gain are amplifiers and antennas.

Loss is a decrease in the RF signal strength. Losses impact the WLAN design and are part of our everyday world. All the cables and connections between the AP and the antenna cause loss. Losses are the real concern, and the common causes of loss are distance, resistance of cables and connectors, mismatched impedance in cables and connectors, and objects such as the following in the path of a signal that absorb or reflect RF signals:

- Fixed walls: 3.0 dB
- Movable walls: 1.4 dB
- Doors: 2.0 dB
- Metal partitions: 5.0 dB
- Windows: 2.0 dB
- Exterior walls: 10.0 dB
- Basement walls: 20.0 dB

Antennas

Antennas used in WLANs come in many shapes and sizes based on the differing RF characteristics desired. The physical dimension of an antenna is directly related to the frequency at which the antenna transmits or receives radio waves. As the gain increases, the coverage area becomes more focused. High-gain antennas offer longer coverage areas than low-gain antennas at the same input power level. As frequency increases, the wavelength and the antennas become smaller.

Antennas can be categorized into one of three types:

- **Omnidirectional**—The most widely used today but not always the best solution. The shape of the radiant energy is a doughnut-shaped pattern.
- **Semidirectional**—Offer the ability to direct and apply gain to the signal. The shape of the radiant energy is a cowbell-shaped pattern.
- **Highly directional**—Intended for highly directed signals that must travel a long distance. The shape of the radiant energy is a telescope pattern.

NOTE Reducing power or applying different antennas is not a security option. Even if you direct the signal away from vulnerable spots, a high-gain receiver may still be able to pick up the signal.

NOTE The Cisco 1000 Series AP can be configured to provide semidirectional capability by disabling one internal antenna or connecting an external antenna. An external antenna can be used to solve the problem of providing outside coverage areas, because the Cisco 1000 Series AP is designed only for indoor use.

Designing the right WLAN solution requires using the right antenna. Table 18-3 provides a helpful generic guide to antenna selection. Each antenna type is included with its ranges for both gain and EIRP. Reviewing the manufacturers' antenna specifications provides the specific details.

Table 18-3 *Antenna Selection Guide*

Antenna Type	Application	Gain	EIRP Ranges	
			Azimuth	Elevation
Omnidirectional	Indoor/outdoor: open spaces and office cubicles	2–5 dBi	360°	25–75°
Semidirectional	Indoor/outdoor: longer hallways with offices and warehouse isles	6–13 dBi	60–80°	50–70°
Highly directional	Outdoor: between buildings	14–21 dBi	30–55°	50–70°

Omnidirectional antennas have the following characteristics:

- Radiate equally in all directions around their axis.
- Most common antenna used in WLANs, APs, and Personal Computer Memory Card International Association (PCMCIA) cards. This antenna is frequently used in open space or larger cubicle areas.
- The shape of the radiant energy is that of a doughnut or bagel.
- The higher the gain of the antenna, the more the doughnut gets squeezed flat.

NOTE The transmit signal is weak or lost directly under the AP due to the shape of the signal.

Semidirectional antennas have the following characteristics:

- Direct the energy more in one particular direction.
- In WLANs, Yagi antennas are frequently used semidirectional antennas.
- Very effective in directing signal into hard-to-reach locations such as long hallways or distant corners.

Highly directional antennas have the following characteristics:

- Radiate equally in all directions around their axis.
- Emit a very narrow beam and long distance.
- Typically concave, dish-shaped devices.
- Ideal for long-distance, point-to-point applications such as communications between buildings.
- Achieve distance with a very narrow signal.

Antenna diversity refers to the condition under which multiple antennas are receiving signals from a single source and the AP's ability to respond using the best antenna. Antenna diversity reduces multipath issues.

NOTE   A Cisco Airespace AP will not support an external antenna and an internal antenna simultaneously. When the external antenna is enabled, the software will disable the internal antenna.

CAUTION   You should not enable an external antenna without having an external antenna physically attached to the AP, because doing so may damage the radio.

The most commonly used antenna connectors are male connectors with reverse-polarity TNC jacks (RP-TNC connectors). It is the same connector type that Cisco uses on its APs.

Cisco Airespace APs are certified for any external 2.4-GHz or 5-GHz patch antenna with 6-dBi gain or less.

Regulatory Agencies and Standards

Wireless is the result of organizational standards and regulatory guidelines. With hundreds of countries around the world, it is a welcome relief to have organizations and consortiums providing standards and guidelines.

Some of the wireless regulatory agencies and standards are as follows:

- **IEEE**—Institute of Electrical and Electronic Engineers (http://www.ieee.org) creates and maintains operational standards.

- **ETSI**—European Telecommunications Standards Institute (http://www.etsi.org) is chartered to produce common standards in Europe.

- **Wi-Fi Alliance**—Wi-Fi Alliance (http://www.wi-fi.com) promotes and tests for WLAN interoperability.

- **WLANA**—Wireless LAN Association (http://www.wlana.org) educates and raises consumer awareness regarding WLANs.

In the United States, the Federal Communications Commission (FCC) does the following:

- Regulates the use of wireless devices in the United States. The FCC established the rules limiting the frequencies that wireless bands can use and the output power for the bands.

- Specifies that WLANs can use the license-free ISM bands. The ISM bands start at 902 MHz, 2.4 GHz, and 5.8 GHz. ISM bands vary in width from 26 MHz to 150 MHz.

- Specifies that WLANs can use three UNII bands. UNII bands are at 5 GHz and are 100-MHz wide. Moreover, they are intended for indoor (lower band), indoor/outdoor (middle band), and outdoor (upper band) uses. All are currently being used for indoor use today.

NOTE   Regulations may differ from country to country.

802.11 Operational Standards

The IEEE has made an extensive effort to create open standards. The following IEEE 802.11 standards exist today:

- **802.11a**—5 GHz, ratified in 1999

- **802.11b**—11 Mbps, 2.4 GHz, ratified in 1999

- **802.11d**—World mode, ratified in 2001

- **802.11e**—Quality of service, ratified in 2005

- **802.11F**—Inter-Access Point Protocol (IAPP), withdrawn in 2006

- **802.11g**—Higher data rate (>20 Mbps) 2.4 Mbps, ratified in 2003

- **802.11h**—Dynamic Frequency Selection and Transmit Power Control mechanisms, ratified in 2003

- **802.11i**—Authentication and security, ratified in 2005
- **802.11j**—Additional Japanese frequencies, ratified in 2005
- **802.11k**—Radio resource management draft, planned to be ratified in 2007
- **802.11n**—High throughput draft, planned to be ratified in 2007

The 802.11a, b, and g specifications all relate to WLAN physical layer standards.

Cisco APs currently support the 802.11d standard for world mode. World mode enables the AP to inform an 802.11d client device which radio setting the device should use to conform to local regulations.

The IEEE 802.11e standard is being developed to enhance the current 802.11 MAC to expand support for applications with QoS requirements and improve the capabilities and efficiency of the protocol. This standard will assist with voice, video, and other time-sensitive applications.

The IEEE 802.11F standard was a recommended practice guideline, defining a protocol for intercommunication between APs, to assist in roaming and handoff of traffic. The IEEE administratively withdrew 802.11F in February 2006. Most vendors have implemented their own proprietary IAPP for use with their own APs.

The IEEE 802.11h standard is supplementary to the MAC layer to comply with European regulations for 5-GHz WLANs. Most European radio regulations for the 5-GHz band require products to have Transmission Power Control (TPC) and Dynamic Frequency Selection (DFS). TPC limits the transmitted power to the minimum needed to reach the farthest user. DFS selects the radio channel at the AP to minimize interference with other systems, particularly radar.

The IEEE 802.11i standard is intended to enhance the current 802.11 MAC to provide improvements in security.

The IEEE 802.11j standard is intended to enhance the 802.11 standard and amendments, to add channel selection for 4.9 GHz and 5 GHz in Japan to conform to Japanese rules on operational mode, operational rate, radiated power, spurious emissions, and channel sense.

The IEEE 802.11k task group was developed to define and expose radio and network information as well as facilitate the management and maintenance of a wireless and mobile LAN. It is also expected to enable new applications based on this radio information—for example, location-enabled services.

The IEEE 802.11n task group was created to improve the WLAN user experience by providing significantly higher throughput of at least 200+ Mbps over the air, 100 Mbps measured at the MAC data service AP. Changes to the PHY/MAC functionality helped to increase the bandwidth. More issues need to be resolved, such as the use of Multiple Input, Multiple Output (MIMO) antennas and getting 40-MHz channels approved. Designing WLAN solutions based on draft standards is not a best practice.

IEEE 802.11 Standards in the 2.4-GHz Band

2.4-GHz 802.11b/g has three nonoverlapping channels. This means that three APs could operate in the same cell area without sharing the media. An AP on channel 1 does not share time with an AP on channel 6, because they do not have common frequencies. There is no degradation in throughput when three APs are in the same cell area if the APs are each on a nonoverlapping channel. Three APs in the same cell using three non-overlapping channels provide an aggregated data rate of 33 Mbps with an aggregated throughput of 18.6 Mbps. If the same three APs shared the same channel, the aggregate data rate would still be 33 Mbps with the aggregated throughput of 7 Mbps.

All channels are known by their center frequency, and they are as follows: 1 (2412); 2 (2417); 3 (2422); 4 (2427); 5 (2432); 6 (2437); 7 (2442); 8 (2447); 9 (2452); 10 (2457); 11 (2462); 12 (2467); and 13 (2472). The top part of Figure 18-13 illustrates this information along with the starting frequency on the bottom.

Figure 18-13   *2.4-GHz Channels*

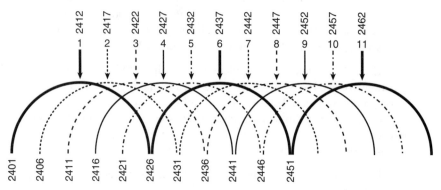

The 802.11g standard was ratified in June 2003. It operates in the same 2.4-GHz band as 802.11b and uses the same three nonoverlapping channels. Moreover, there is full backward compatibility with 802.11b.

The 802.11g specification uses Orthogonal Frequency Division Multiplexing (OFDM) modulation for 802.11g data rates and Complementary Code Keying (CCK) modulation for 802.11b data rates.

The 802.11g data rates are 54, 48, 36, 24, 18, 12, 9, and 6 Mbps. The 802.11b data rates are 11, 5.5, 2, and 1 Mbps. The 2.4-GHz channels are 22-MHz wide. Figure 18-14 provides a comparison of the 2.4-GHz common data rates and ranges.

Figure 18-14 *2.4-GHz Common Data Rate Comparison*

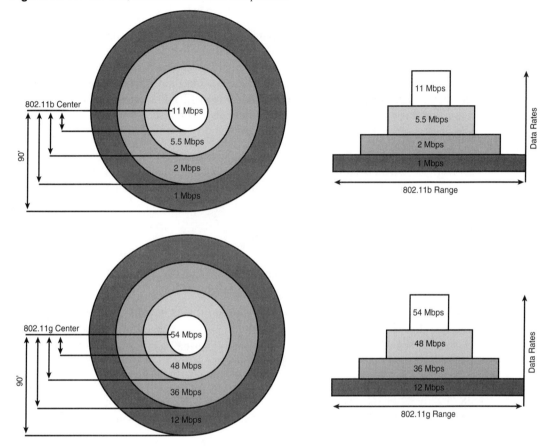

The relationships between data rates and distance for 802.11g are similar to 802.11b, but the data rates themselves are higher. The difference between 802.11b and 802.11g is how the data is transmitted over the airwaves, not in the antennas or radios themselves. One radio handles both protocols but not simultaneously.

NOTE It requires greater signal-to-noise ratio to receive a signal with more complex modulation. Higher data rates require more complex modulation than lower dates rates. Therefore, higher data rates can only be received at shorter distances because signal strength decreases with distance while the noise floor stays constant. At greater distances, the signal-to-noise ratio is lower than at shorter distances.

Different countries allow different channels and allow different amounts of transmit power.

Part of the 802.11g protocol design ensures 802.11b backward compatibility by detecting and supporting those clients who end up reducing the 802.11g throughput.

Protection mode or mixed mode is enabled when an 802.11b client associates to an 802.11g AP. Additionally, it can be enabled by another 802.11g that can hear the beacons from another 802.11g AP having an 802.11b client associated. The Non-ERP Present bit is set by an 802.11g AP when it has an 802.11b client associated to it. The Use Protection bit is set when an 802.11g AP hears a beacon with the Non-ERP Present bit set on the same channel as it is operating or it has an 802.11b client associated.

With protection, broadcasts must support 802.11b clients as well as the fact that an 802.11b client will transmit at slower data rates than an 802.11g client. Mixed environments will generally have a maximum of 18 Mbps independent of frame transmission rate for the 802.11g devices. 802.11g-only environments can obtain rates over 20 Mbps.

802.11a Standards in the 5-GHz Band

802.11a-compliant devices operate in the 5-GHz UNII band. 802.11a and 802.11b are not compatible due to differences in frequencies. 802.11a requires a different radio and antenna.

The 5-GHz UNII band is made up of three separate 100-MHz-wide bands known as the lower, middle, and upper bands. Within each of these three bands are four nonoverlapping channels. The FCC specifies that the lower bands be used indoors, the middle bands indoors/outdoors, and the upper bands outdoors.

The channels and center frequencies are as follows: 36 (5.180); 40 (5.200); 44 (5.220); 48 (5.240); 52 (5.260); 56 (5.280); 60 (5.300); 64 (5.320); 149 (5.745); 153 (5.765); 157 (5.785); and 161 (5.805). Figure 18-15 illustrates the channels in the UNII bands.

Figure 18-15 *5-GHz Channels*

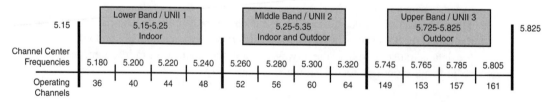

The capability to use 4, 8, or 12 nonoverlapping channels is an improvement. However, this improvement depends on the vendor's implementation and the country-specific regulations. Having additional nonoverlapping channels is an advantage when implementing an enterprise WLAN solution. The additional channels are an advantage when dense, high-bandwidth requirements are needed.

Pico cells solve the high-density and bandwidth-requirement issues and are used in places such as stock exchanges and trading floors. Smaller than microcells and solution specific, the use of pico cells needs to be discussed first with the manufacturer's sales team due to solution-specific configuration/supplicant.

OFDM modulation technology is less susceptible to noise and multipath issues when compared to DSSS. OFDM is a more efficient modulation technique that enables the high data rates of 6, 9, 12, 18, 24, 36, 48, and 54 Mbps. Figure 8-16 shows the 802.11a common data rates.

Figure 18-16   *5-GHz Common Data Rates*

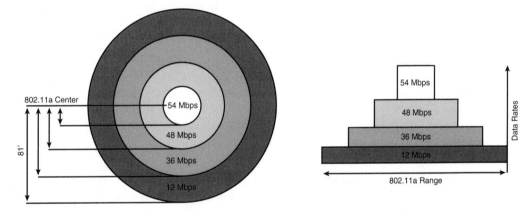

Comparing the 802.11 Standards

Understanding the advantages and disadvantages of each standard helps in knowing which one to choose.

802.11a provides the better throughput because it does not deal with any backward-compatibility issues. 802.11a has more channels, which provides less overall interference. Fewer APs will be operating on the same channel.

802.11g gives most organizations an easy migration plan and backward compatibility with 802.11b. The roaming distance is greater than 802.11b, resulting in fewer APs being deployed.

Antenna selection is much greater with 802.11g than with 802.11a. Moreover, most countries support 802.11g, allowing world mode functionality. The regulatory issues with 802.11a are more complicated outside the United States.

NOTE	There are benefits and drawbacks of operating with unlicensed frequency. Unlicensed bands are flexible and can be used without significant regulatory overhead. However, other unlicensed devices might use the same frequency, such as 2.4-GHz cordless phones, baby monitors, Bluetooth devices, and microwave ovens, to name a few.

Implementing WLANs

Learning the fundamental concepts and the physical and technological components is required prior to implementing WLANs. How can anything be accomplished without first understanding it?

The implementation of WLANs will draw on all the prior concepts, such as what components are used in a given indoor or outdoor situation. The basics teach us how to ask greater solution-oriented questions about the implementation. Implementing WLANs generically addresses the channel limitation, users versus bandwidth, signaling, and power issues.

802.11b/g Channel Reuse

802.11b/g networks require a well-thought-out plan. A channel reuse plan is required because only three nonoverlapping channels exist. Those channels are 1 (2412 MHz), 6 (2437 MHz), and 11 (2462 MHz).

Channel reuse eliminates microcell overlapping. You can correlate this concept to the placement of FM radio stations throughout the country. You will never find two radio stations in the same geographic area on the same channel. The same concept holds true for channels and cells. Figure 18-17 helps to depict this concept.

802.11a Channel Reuse

802.11a cells are easier to deploy because there are 12 different channels. These 12 nonoverlapping channels can provide a simpler channel reuse schema, as illustrated in Figure 18-18. Due to the size of the microcell, there are more cells on a per-area basis as compared to 802.11b/g.

Figure 18-17   *2.4-GHz Channel Reuse*

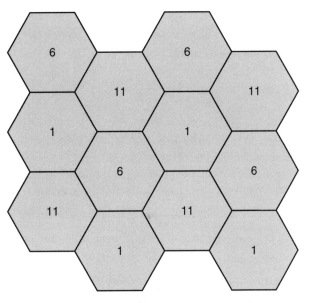

No two adjacent cells use the same channel.

Figure 18-18   *5-GHz Channel Reuse*

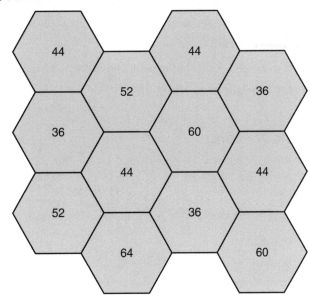

No two adjacent cells use the same channel.

It is recommended that neighboring cells not be placed on neighboring frequencies. Two other key points to keep in mind are as follows:

- Seven users per AP with no conference rooms provides 4.5 Mbps per user.
- Seven users plus one conference room (10 users), which equals 17 total users, provides 1.8 Mbps per user.

Best Practices

The best practices for bandwidth in an 802.11a/b/g WLAN are based on the number of users. The bandwidth requirements are different for 802.11a, 802.11b, and 802.11g because applications require more bandwidth at higher frequencies. The wireless best practices for cell bandwidth are broken down into the three IEEE standards.

The following are the 2.4-GHz 802.11b bandwidth calculations:

- **25 users per cell**—General office maximum users limited by bandwidth.
- **Peak true throughput 6.8 Mbps**—6.8 Mbps × 1024/25 = 278.5 kbps per user.
- **Cell density**—Maximum number of users per cell. Cell size and maximum data rates.

The following are the 2.4-GHz 802.11g bandwidth calculations:

- **20 users per cell**—General office maximum users limited by bandwidth.
- **Peak true throughput 32 Mbps**—32 Mbps × 1024/20 = 1683 kbps per user.
- **Cell density**—Maximum number of users per cell. Cell size and maximum data rates.

The 5-GHz 802.11a bandwidth calculations follow:

- **15 users per cell**—General office users limited by coverage, not bandwidth.
- **Peak true throughput 32 Mbps**—32 Mbps × 1024/15 = 2188 kbps per user.

Bridge Path Considerations

Root bridge is the setting that is normally used for the "main" bridge that is connected to the main network. This bridge provides connectivity to the main LAN for other wireless clients or wired clients that are being connected wirelessly.

In this mode, the bridge supports the following types by default:

- Non-root bridges
- Wireless client cards (PC card, PCI card)
- Work Group Bridges (WGBs)
- Access points configured as repeaters

Only one bridge in a WLAN can be set as the root bridge. This is the default setting for Cisco Aironet bridges.

For two or more Cisco wireless bridges to communicate, you must configure one bridge to root bridge mode and the rest of the bridges to non-root mode. The function of a non-root bridge is to actively seek out a radio connection to the root bridge. This must occur before data can be transferred or bridged across a link. Recalling Figure 18-10, the black buildings were the root bridge, whereas the gray buildings were non-root bridges.

The characteristics of a root bridge (parent) are as follows:

- Accepts associations and communicates with non-root bridge (child) devices
- Will not communicate with other root bridge devices
- Communicates with multiple non-root bridges

The characteristics of a non-root bridge (child) are as follows:

- Can associate and communicate with root devices or clients
- Will not communicate with other root bridge devices
- Will communicate with other non-root devices, provided the other non-root devices are communicating with a root

A single parent bridge can support numerous child bridges. The number of child bridges that should be attached to a parent bridge is determined by usage and throughput needs. There is only one exception—a non-root bridge communicates with another non-root bridge as long as one of the non-root bridges has a root bridge in its uplink.

This setting is normally used for a bridge that is used to connect a remote wired LAN and will only communicate with another root bridge. In this mode, the bridge will refuse associations from wireless clients.

One of the most important concepts in installing bridges is line of sight. Wireless bridges are unlicensed devices and are not designed to penetrate objects such as mountains, trees, or buildings. The signal will be either absorbed or reflected, and the end result will be that the bridges will be unable to connect. If there are trees between the bridges, much of the signal will be absorbed.

For a typical 6-foot (183-cm) person, the horizon appears at about 6 miles (9.7 km). Its disappearance is determined by the height of the observer. If you have two 10-foot (305-cm) structures, the top of one will have a line of sight to the other at about 16 miles (26 km), but it will have minimum clearance at the horizon point.

The Fresnel zone is an elliptical area immediately surrounding the visual path. It varies depending on the length of the signal path and the frequency of the signal. Figure 18-19 illustrates a simple Fresnel zone between two buildings. The Fresnel zone can be calculated, and it must be taken into account when designing a wireless link. If the Fresnel zone is obstructed, then the line of sight is not clear and the link might be unreliable.

Figure 18-19 *Fresnel Zone*

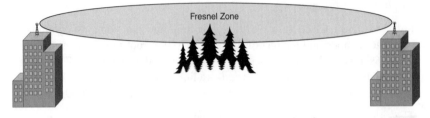
Fresnel Zone

Power Implementation

Inline power, or Power-over-Ethernet (PoE), provides source operating current from the Ethernet port, over the Category 5 cable. It is line power configuration compliant with all Cisco line power–enabled devices. Switches and line power patch panels can reach distances up to 100 meters.

To decrease the cost and complexity of the installation, the Cisco APs can be powered over an Ethernet cable, eliminating the need to run expensive AC power to remote AP installation locations.

For 802.11b-only configurations, line power–enabled devices such as switches and patch panels may be used instead of power injectors. Remember that the standard Cat 5 cable requirements still apply (maximum 328 feet or 100 meters).

Inline power further reduces installation costs, because an electrician is not required. Anyone qualified to run Cat 5 cable can install the cabling required to power Cisco Aironet APs.

NOTE   Cisco Aironet Power Injector products are designed for use with Aironet 350, 1100, and 1200 Series APs and bridges only.

Cisco Aironet Power Injector products increase the deployment flexibility of Cisco Aironet wireless APs and bridges by providing an alternative powering option to local power, inline power–capable multiport switches, and multiport power patch panels.

An end-span device is a unit that has PoE integrated and thus does not require a midspan device. A midspan device is a standalone unit that adds the PoE capability to existing networking equipment. The unit is inserted into the LAN between the Ethernet switch and the peripherals.

NOTE   Some midspan devices (such as power injectors), although 802.3af compliant, provide only Class 1 or 2 power and will not adequately power the Cisco Airespace AP. See Table 18-4 for a summary of class power.

The power injector for Cisco Aironet 1100 and 1200 Series APs works with the power supply provided with the AP.

The Power Injector Media Converter converts fiber media to Category 5 media and combines the resulting data signal with power for delivery to the AP or bridge. The power injector media converter accepts 48-VDC power from either the barrel connector of the local power supply or an alternative 48-VDC power source. When powered by an alternate 48-VDC power source connected using the provided power supply pigtail, the Power Injector Media Converter is UL2043 certified and suitable for installation in environmental air spaces. The local power supply is provided with the Cisco Aironet 1100 and 1200 Series APs.

The IEEE 802.3af power specification created a standard for powering devices over copper wire. Table 18-4 provides the classes defined along with the default setting.

Table 18-4 *802.3af Power Specification*

Class	Usage	Range of Maximum Power
0	Default	0.44 to 12.95 watts
1	Optional	0.44 to 3.84 watts
2	Optional	3.84 to 6.49 watts
3	Optional	6.49 to 12.95 watts
4	Not allowed	Reserved for future use

The Cisco Airespace AP is a Class 3 device with an average draw of approximately 8W and a maximum of 10W.

Table 18-5 defines an EIA/TIA 568A and 568B standard straight-through cable.

Table 18-5 *EIA/TIA 568A and 568B Cabling Standard*

Pin	Usage	Pin	Usage
1	RD+	1	TD+
2	RD-	2	TD-
3	TD+	3	RD+
4	PoE+	4	PoE+
5	PoE+	5	PoE+
6	TD-	6	TD-
7	PoE-	7	PoE-
8	PoE-	8	PoE-

Cisco WLANs

The pervasive nature of wireless has caused enterprise customers to address common issues prior to WLAN implementation. Cisco Unified Wireless Network products address the integration, control, scalability, security, and reliability issues of the wired and wireless networks.

The unified network services are provided across a variety of platforms including WLAN controllers and integrated switches and routers, allowing network managers to build secure, enterprise-class wireless networks.

Enterprise WLAN Issues

It is easy to plug in an access point, but it is difficult to build a business-critical enterprise WLAN.

The new paradigm for IT managers will enable them to deal with limited bandwidth by making the most efficient use of it, while contending with the adverse effects of coverage holes, environmental coverage area changes, inherent security issues, and other interfering issues that crop up over time.

NOTE   Cisco Airespace asked Fortune 500 companies for their input into the requirements for an effective enterprise WLAN solution for business-critical applications. Their general response was that current WLAN solutions are complex and burdened by multiple devices or software programs for a complete solution. They also responded that current WLAN solutions lack the capability to control RF effectively, do not have the security options required for many applications, and are not built for rigorous real-time applications such as voice over IP (VoIP).

Here are the top ten enterprise WLAN issues at the time of this writing:

1 Can you prevent wireless deployment until you are ready?

2 Is every element of your system secure?

3 Are your access points a security risk?

4 Can your security framework support heterogeneous users?

5 Can you apply wired security policies to your WLAN?

6 Can you extend identity or VPN technology to a mobile environment?

7 Can your WLAN address security threats in real time?

8 How does your system address dictionary attacks?

9 Can you accurately locate the source of a security risk?

10 Will your WLAN support future innovations?

The Cisco Airespace solution attempts to address all of these issues.

NOTE   Cisco Airespace was founded on the principal that security is the primary concern.

Overview of Cisco WLAN

As WLANs become increasingly mission-critical and evolve in terms of scale and capabilities, the way the wireless deployment is managed must evolve as well. Because each customer and each deployment is unique, Cisco provides differing feature sets and differing management paradigms to address these customer-specific requirements.

The Cisco Unified Wireless Network is a unified wired and wireless solution to address the WLAN security, deployment, management, and control issues facing enterprises. This integrated end-to-end solution addresses all layers of the WLAN, from client devices and APs, to the network infrastructure, to network management, to the delivery of mobility services. The Cisco Unified Wireless Network addresses the deployment, management, and RF challenges associated with building business-critical WLANs.

The Cisco Unified Wireless Network is deployable in corporate offices, hospitals, retail stores, manufacturing floors, warehouse environments, educational institutions, financial institutions, local and national government organizations, and other locations worldwide. It supports Wi-Fi-enabled business applications for a variety of uses, including mobile healthcare, inventory management, retail point-of-sale, video surveillance, real-time data access, asset tracking, and network visibility.

The Cisco Unified Wireless Network enables on-the-road access from venues such as public hotspots, hotels, convention centers, and airports for mobile users and traveling executives. It delivers real-time access to a variety of business environments, providing secure mobility and guest access for campus and branch offices. Customers can confidently deploy the Cisco Unified Wireless Network knowing that their investment is protected.

The five interconnecting elements of the Cisco Unified Wireless Network and their characteristics are as follows:

- **Client devices**—90 percent of Wi-Fi silicon is Cisco Compatible certified. Proven Aironet platform. "Out-of-the-box" wireless security.

- **Mobility platform**—Ubiquitous network access in the indoor and outdoor environments. Enhanced productivity. Proven platform with large install base and 61 percent market share. Plug and play.
- **Network unification**—Secure WLAN controllers. Integration into selected switching and routing platforms.
- **World-class network management**—Same level of security, scalability, reliability, ease of deployment, and management for WLANs as wired LANs.
- **Unified advanced services**—Unified Wi-Fi VoIP, advanced threat detection, identity networking, location-based security, asset tracking, and guest access.

Cisco provides a core feature set that includes autonomous APs and the CiscoWorks Wireless LAN Solution Engine (WLSE) management appliance. The core feature set provides a base set of capabilities that are required for enterprise deployments. Core features include secure connectivity through support for 802.11i/Wi-Fi Protected Access 2 (WPA2), fast and secure Layer 2 roaming, and interfaces to a variety of third-party applications and products. Most Cisco APs are available in versions designed for autonomous operation. These devices may be upgraded in the field to lightweight mode, thereby providing customers with a smooth path from core to advanced features.

The Cisco advanced WLAN feature set is delivered by lightweight APs, wireless LAN controllers, and the WCS management application. The advanced feature set represents the most comprehensive set of capabilities in the industry, including guest access, wireless intrusion detection, scalable Layer 3 mobility, and available location services. Most Cisco Aironet APs are available in versions designed for lightweight operation.

Cisco WLAN controllers are part of the Cisco advanced WLAN feature set and are responsible for handling system-wide WLAN functions across an entire wireless network. Cisco WLAN controllers are designed to smoothly integrate into existing enterprise networks. They communicate with Cisco Aironet 1000 Series Lightweight APs over any Layer 2 (Ethernet) or Layer 3 (IP) infrastructure using LWAPP.

Comparing Autonomous and Lightweight APs

Enterprise wireless networks must meet requirements in five fundamental areas:

- **Client devices**—Because more than 95 percent of today's notebooks are Wi-Fi enabled and many specialized client devices are now available for industry-specific applications, WLAN solutions must ensure that client devices interoperate securely with the WLAN infrastructure. WLANs must also consistently provide the features required to support an array of client devices.
- **Mobility platform**—WLAN solutions must provide 802.11a/b/g connectivity for WLAN clients via APs that facilitate specialized RF deployment, management, and performance features.

- **Network unification**—WLAN solutions must integrate the wired and wireless network. Network unification is critical for network control, scalability, security, and reliability. System-wide WLAN functions, such as security policies, intrusion prevention, RF management, QoS, and mobility, must be available to support enterprise applications.

- **Network management**—WLAN solutions must allow IT managers to design, control, and monitor their enterprise wireless networks from a centralized location. Centralized network management is critical for simplifying operations and reducing total cost of ownership.

- **Unified advanced services**—A robust WLAN must support new mobility applications, emerging Wi-Fi technologies, and advanced threat detection and prevention capabilities. This support must be cost-effective and easy to deploy and implement.

Table 18-6 reflects the Cisco AP Series operational modes. The Lightweight solution combines the best elements of wireless and wired networking to deliver scalable, manageable, and secure WLANs. It includes innovative RF capabilities that enable real-time access to core business applications and provides proven enterprise-class secure connectivity. The Cisco Unified Wireless Network delivers the same level of security, scalability, reliability, ease of deployment, and management for WLANs that organizations expect from their wired LANs.

Table 18-6   *Access Point Operational Modes*

Cisco Series	Autonomous Operation	Lightweight Operation
1000 Series	No	Yes
1100 Series	Yes	No
1130AG Series	Yes	Yes
1200 Series	Yes	Yes
1230AG Series	Yes	Yes
1240AG Series	Yes	Yes
1300 Series	Yes	No
1400 Series	Yes	No
1500 Series	No	Yes

Wireless LAN Management

Network managers need reliable, cost-effective tools for WLAN planning, configuration, and management. These tools must be centrally available and must support simplified operations and easy-to-use graphical interfaces. Cisco Wireless LAN Management options are determined based on the type of APs deployed and the features required.

Lightweight APs may be managed with Cisco WLAN controllers and the Cisco Wireless Control System (WCS). A Cisco Wireless Location Appliance may be added for advanced features such as wireless VoIP and location services, as well as advanced wireless security features such as Network Admission Control (NAC), the Cisco Self-Defending Network, and guest access.

Autonomous APs may be configured with the CiscoWorks WLSE or the CiscoWorks WLSE Express.

Cisco provides several unified wireless products to meet the various enterprise WLAN management solutions. The sections that follow cover the Cisco Wireless Control System, Cisco Catalyst 6500 Series Wireless Services Module, Cisco wireless LAN controller Module for ISRs, CiscoWorks Wireless LAN Solution Engine, and the Cisco Wireless Location Appliance.

Cisco Wireless Control System

Cisco WCS is a Windows or Linux server-based platform for WLAN planning, configuration, and management. It provides a powerful foundation on which IT managers can design, control, and monitor enterprise wireless networks from a centralized location, simplifying operations and reducing total cost of ownership.

Cisco Catalyst 6500 Series Wireless Services Module (WiSM)

The Cisco WiSM is a member of the Cisco wireless LAN controller family. It works in conjunction with Cisco Aironet lightweight APs, Cisco WCS, and the Cisco Wireless Location Appliance to support mission-critical wireless data, voice, and video applications. The Cisco WiSM provides real-time communication between lightweight APs and other WLAN controllers to deliver a secure and unified wireless solution. The Supervisor Engine that is compatible with the WiSM is any one of the Supervisor Engine 720 modules with native Cisco IOS Software.

Cisco Wireless LAN Controller Module (WLCM) for Integrated Services Routers (ISR)

The Cisco WLCM allows small and medium-sized businesses (SMB) and enterprise branch offices to cost-effectively deploy and manage secure WLANs. The module provides unparalleled security, mobility, and ease of use for business-critical WLANs, delivering the most secure enterprise-class wireless system available. As a Cisco ISR module, it delivers centralized security policies, wireless intrusion prevention system (IPS) capabilities, award-winning RF management, QoS, and Layer 3 fast secure roaming for WLANs. The Cisco WLCM manages up to six Cisco Aironet lightweight APs and is supported on Cisco 2800/3800 Series ISRs and Cisco 3700 Series routers.

CiscoWorks Wireless LAN Solution Engine (WLSE)

The CiscoWorks WLSE is available as a management tool for Cisco Aironet autonomous APs and wireless bridges. The CiscoWorks WLSE is a turnkey and scalable management platform for managing hundreds to thousands of Cisco Aironet autonomous APs and wireless bridges.

CiscoWorks WLSE Express

The WLSE Express is a complete WLAN management solution with an integrated AAA server for small to medium-sized enterprise facilities or branch offices using Cisco Aironet autonomous APs and wireless bridges.

Cisco Wireless Location Appliance

The Cisco Wireless Location Appliance is the industry's first location solution that simultaneously tracks thousands of devices from directly within the WLAN infrastructure—bringing the power of a cost-effective, high-resolution location solution to critical applications such as high-value asset tracking, IT management, and location-based security. This easy-to-deploy solution smoothly integrates with Cisco WLAN controllers and Cisco Aironet lightweight APs to track the physical location of wireless devices, including Wi-Fi-enabled laptops, voice handsets, Wi-Fi tags, and rogue devices, to within a few meters.

By centralizing intelligence within these devices, security, mobility, QoS, and other functions essential to WLAN operations can be efficiently managed across an entire wireless enterprise.

Comparing Core and Advanced Feature Roaming

One way to determine a design solution is to review the requirements and compare them to the various WLAN features. While comparing features with requirements may be a design methodology, it requires extensive product knowledge. Such is the case with the Cisco Auto RF and mobility group features.

The Auto RF feature enables the Cisco Airespace controllers to "self-heal" by continually monitoring and adjusting the network. The end result is a dynamically managed network with seamless roaming capabilities throughout the WLAN. Auto RF works hand in hand with other features, which can significantly affect the network design.

One such feature is group mode, which provides dynamic grouping and has two modes: on and off. When the grouping feature is off, there is no dynamic grouping. Each controller optimizes its own Cisco Airespace AP's parameters. When grouping is on, the controller forms groups and elects leaders to perform better dynamic parameter optimization.

Another complex feature is the mobility group. A set of controllers can be configured as a mobility group to allow seamless client roaming within a group of shared controllers. By creating a mobility group, multiple controllers can dynamically share information and forward data traffic when inter-controller or inter-subnet roaming occurs. Controllers can share the context and state of client devices and controller loading information. With this information, the network can support inter-controller WLAN roaming and controller redundancy.

NOTE   A maximum of 24 controllers can be part of a mobility group. Cisco recommends that no more than 12 controllers be contained within a mobility group.

NOTE   All controllers in a mobility group must be configured on all other members of the mobility group in a consistent manner. This can be done via either the Edit All feature or WCS templates.

In the current Cisco Airespace mobility paradigm, the client obtains its IP *point of presence* (IP address, subnetwork, and so on) from the controller with which it first associates (anchor) to the mobility group. If the client associates to an AP associated to another controller in the mobility group that is on a different subnetwork, a "foreign" session is established with the original "anchor" switch. Packets from the client are forwarded from the controller to the wired network normally, but packets to the client are received by the anchor controller and forwarded to the foreign controller via Ethernet over IP (EoIP) encapsulation. The foreign controller de-encapsulates the packet and forwards it to the client.

When a client attempts to associate to a Cisco Airespace controller that is part of a mobility group, the Cisco Airespace controller will confirm if the client has an active session in the mobility group based on the MAC address of the client. If it does, the session will be moved from the anchor Cisco Airespace controller to the foreign Cisco Airespace controller. The client will retain its IP address (static or DHCP) and presence on the wired network at the anchor Cisco Airespace controller.

Cisco Airespace Roaming

Roaming refers to movement of clients across Cisco Airespace APs, Cisco Airespace Remote Edge Access Points (REAP), and third-party APs. Roaming will not occur across different mobility groups. The Airespace controller can reside in only a single mobility group. A maximum of 24 Cisco Airespace controllers may reside in any single mobility group.

Cisco Airespace mobility groups require consistent group membership, code across all member controllers and ACLs, and the same Layer 2 or 3 LWAPP mode across all member controllers. The LWAPP roaming types are Layer 2 (intra-subnetwork) and Layer 3 (inter-subnetwork) roaming.

NOTE   Same-controller intra-subnetwork roaming requires less than 10 ms, whereas multiple-controller intra-subnetwork roaming requires less than 20 ms. Inter-subnetwork roaming requires less than 30 ms to complete. These estimates do not account for congestion across the enterprise infrastructure.

Cisco Airespace Layer 2 Roaming

Layer 2 (intra-subnetwork) roaming can be used with a single controller or with multiple controllers in the same subnetwork. Regardless, it is transparent to the client. The client's session is sustained during connection to the new AP. The client continues using the same DHCP-assigned or static IP address. Figure 18-20 illustrates Layer 2 roaming (intra-subnetwork).

Figure 18-20   *Layer 2 Roaming (Intra-Subnetwork)*

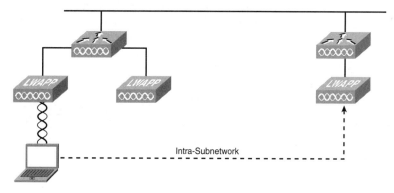

Reauthentication is required if the client sends a DHCP Discover packet with a 0.0.0.0 client IP address or a 169.254.*.* client auto-IP address or when the operator-set session timeout is exceeded.

Cisco Airespace Layer 3 Roaming

Layer 3 (inter-subnetwork) roaming can be used with multiple Cisco Airespace controllers in different subnetworks. It is still transparent to the client. The session connection to the new AP is sustained as well. Figure 18-21 illustrates Layer 3 roaming (inter-subnetwork).

Figure 18-21 *Layer 3 Roaming (Inter-Subnetwork)*

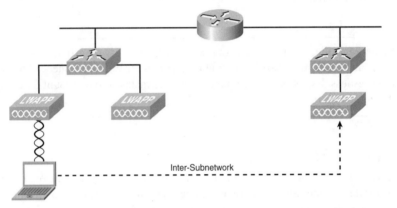
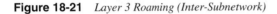
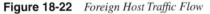

Tunneling requires special handling of the client traffic between the anchor and foreign controllers. Tunneling the traffic allows the client to continue using the same DHCP-assigned or client-assigned IP address while keeping an active session.

Figure 18-22 illustrates the path traffic takes when on a foreign host subnetwork. First, the client requests information from another host computer and is properly routed to that device. The return path goes back to the anchor controller and is redirected to the foreign controller for final delivery back to the client.

Figure 18-22 *Foreign Host Traffic Flow*

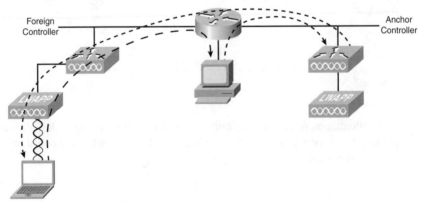

Reauthentication is required if the client sends a DHCP Discover packet with a 0.0.0.0 client IP address or a 169.254.*.* client auto-IP address or when the operator-set session timeout is exceeded.

Split MAC

Features such as the "split MAC" architecture allow the splitting of 802.11 protocols between the AP and the WLAN controller. The Cisco Airespace AP handling the real-time portions of the 802.11 protocols is split from the WLAN controller that handles those items that are not time sensitive.

This patent-pending architecture has revolutionized enterprise wireless networking by splitting the processing of the 802.11 data and management protocols between two devices: the AP and a centralized Cisco Airespace controller. By innovating the way that WLAN controllers handle 802.11 packets, Cisco Airespace has created a robust platform upon which enterprises can deliver business-critical wireless services.

The AP handles the portions of the protocol that have real-time requirements, which include the following:

- The frame exchange handshake between a client and AP when transferring a frame over the air
- The transmission of beacon frames
- The buffering and transmission of frames for clients in power save mode
- The response to Probe Request frames from clients
- Forwarding notification of received Probe Requests to the controller
- Providing real-time signal-quality information to the controller with every received frame
- Monitoring each of the radio channels for noise, interference, and other WLANs
- Monitoring for the presence of other APs
- Encryption and decryption, except in the case of VPN/IPsec clients

All remaining functionality is handled in the Cisco Airespace controller, whereby time-sensitivity is not a concern and controller-wide visibility is required. Some of the MAC layer functions provided in the WLAN controller include the following:

- 802.11 authentication
- 802.11 association and reassociation (mobility)
- 802.11 frame translation and bridging

LWAPP AP Association

LWAPP is an open protocol for AP management. In this mode of operation, a WLAN controller system is used to create and enforce policies across multiple different lightweight APs. All functions essential to WLAN operations are centrally controlled by WLAN controllers. In this mode of operation, Cisco APs run a simplified version of Cisco IOS. It is not possible to enter into configuration mode and configure APs individually in this mode.

LWAPP is used for low-overhead communication between the AP and Cisco Airespace controller and is used to encrypt and secure control traffic between the AP and controller.

The UDP control messages are encrypted with an X.509 PKI using Advanced Encryption Standard-Counter Mode with Cipher Block Chaining Message Authentication Code Protocol (AES-CCMP). Data traffic is not encrypted in LWAPP and is switched at the WLAN controller. LWAPP will require 1–4 kbps overhead with associated clients.

Both data traffic and control traffic between the AP and controller are encapsulated. UDP source port 1024 is used for both control and data. Destination port 12222 is used for the data port, and 12223 is used for the control port.

An unknown AP will not be able to "spoof" a Cisco Airespace AP because an X.509 certificate is used. It is used to set up the connection, and encryption keys are dynamically set and rotated.

NOTE   Time and date are critical in any network using Public Key Infrastructure. Each certificate has validity dates. If the time and date on the Cisco Airespace controller are outside the validity dates on the certificate on the AP, the control channel will not be able to be negotiated.

NOTE   Although LWAPP is a proprietary protocol, it is being widely adopted because it features very low overhead while allowing such advantages as central control of APs from a WLAN controller.

APs are using LWAPP to connect to the controller, so the following topics deserve a brief discussion:

- Layer 2 LWAPP
- Layer 3 LWAPP
- Access point association

- Access point association order
- Access point association Layer 2 controller response
- Access point association Layer 3 controller response

Layer 2 Lightweight AP Protocol

Layer 2 LWAPP is encapsulated in an Ethernet frame. The controller and AP must be either directly connected or connected to the same VLAN/subnetwork, as illustrated in Figure 18-23.

Figure 18-23   *Layer 2 LWAPP*

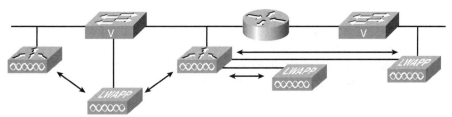

Layer 3 Lightweight AP Protocol

Layer 3 LWAPP is encapsulated in UDP and then an IP packet. The controller and AP can be directly connected, connected to the same VLAN/subnetwork, or connected to a different VLAN/subnetwork, as illustrated in Figure 18-24.

Figure 18-24   *Layer 3 LWAPP*

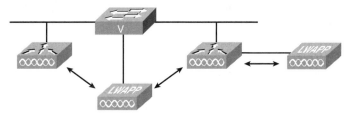

Layer 3 LWAPP requires Cisco Airespace APs to obtain an IP address using DHCP.

NOTE   An AP always attempts discovery with Layer 2 mode first and then Layer 3 mode. The AP continues to alternate between Layer 2 mode and Layer 3 mode until it discovers a controller.

Access Point Association

The AP attempts to associate using Layer 2 first. Upon failing Layer 2 association, the AP makes a DHCP request and attempts to establish a Layer 3 association. If the Layer 3 association attempt fails, the AP reboots and attempts a Layer 2 association again.

Access Point Association Order

Responses to an AP association request proceed in an orderly fashion. Tthe request is sent, in order until a response is received, to the primary configured controller, the secondary configured controller, and the tertiary configured controller. If no configured controller responds, the response will be from a master controller. Finally, if no master controller responds, the response from the least-loaded controller will then be used.

Access Point Association Layer 2 Controller Response

The Layer 2 communications between the AP and controller use MAC addresses to create the Layer 2 association. The steps applying to all Layer 2 controllers are as follows:

1 The AP sends an LWAPP Discovery Request to the switch management MAC address via a broadcast.

2 The switch responds with a Discovery Response from the MAC that includes the current number of APs associated to the controller.

3 The AP chooses the MAC address with the least number of APs and sends the Join Request.

Access Point Association Layer 3 Controller Response

Enabling Layer 3 communications provides additional features and requires additional steps during the AP and controller association process. Moreover, the Layer 3 communications steps are different depending upon the controller platform used.

The steps applying to the 2006 and 4102 Layer 3 controllers are as follows:

1 The AP sends an LWAPP Discovery Request to the switch management IP address via a directed broadcast.

2 The switch responds with a Discovery Response from the AP manager IP address that includes the number of APs currently associated to that AP-manager interface.

3 The AP chooses the AP-manager IP address with the least number of APs and sends the Join Request.

4 All subsequent communication is to the switch's AP-manager IP address.

The steps applying to the 4400 Series Layer 3 controllers are as follows:

1 The AP sends an LWAPP Discovery Request to the switch management IP address via a directed broadcast.

2 The switch responds with a Discovery Response from the switch management IP address.

3 The Discovery Response is modified to contain a list of <AP Manager IP Addresses, Number APs Associated to each Interface> tuples.

4 The AP chooses the AP-manager IP address with the least number of APs and sends the Join Request.

5 All subsequent communication is to the switch's AP-manager IP address.

Mixing LWAPP with Autonomous APs

Although autonomous APs have a significant deployment base, companies may want to start migrating to a more centralized design. WLANs already running in autonomous mode can have a migration path to a centralized lightweight solution. Some APs may already be lightweight capable, such as the Cisco 1200, 1230AG, and 1240AG Series APs.

These APs only need to use the Cisco Autonomous to Lightweight upgrade tool. The APs are upgraded through this tool and have limited capabilities, which include disabled radios until the controller sends the full LWAPP image. The converted AP or lightweight AP is then able to participate in the WLAN via the controller.

During the configuration of the AP, the mode—either local or monitor can be selected. Local mode is the default and is used for most WLANs. Monitor mode is a listen mode for monitoring services.

The lightweight APs offer the same 802.11a/b/g solution as do the autonomous APs. The Cisco 1000 Series Lightweight AP contains a pair of high-gain internal antennas for unidirectional (180-degree) or omnidirectional (360-degree) coverage. The Cisco 1030 Series Lightweight APs are designed for remote edge deployment, and Radio Resource Management (RRM) control via a WAN link includes connectors for external antennas.

NOTE   The primary difference between the Cisco Airespace APs and Cisco Airespace 1030 APs is that the 1030 APs do not use the data component of LWAPP. The 1030 APs perform local bridging of client traffic, acting much like traditional APs. However, the 1030 APs do have the benefit of being managed by a Cisco Airespace controller via LWAPP, providing the same level of WLAN management available from the Cisco Airespace APs.

The Cisco Remote Edge Access Point (REAP) allows a remote AP to be controlled across a WAN link while keeping client bridged data local. REAPs are implemented in Layer 3 AP mode.

REAPs are designed to support remote offices by extending LWAPP control timers. Control traffic is still LWAPP encapsulated and sent to the controller. Client data is not LWAPP encapsulated but is locally bridged. All management control and RF management is available when the WAN link is up and connectivity is available to the controller. A REAP will continue to provide local connectivity even if the WAN is down.

The controller will support the same number of REAPs as local APs. REAPs can support up to 16 WLANs if controller connectivity is enabled. If controller connectivity is disabled, REAPs goes into standalone mode. REAPs associated to the same controller can provide aggressive load balancing for the wireless clients.

Cisco Wireless Clients

All load balancing for the wireless clients goes unnoticed, as it should. The wireless clients roam around, having liberties that are not afforded to the wired world such as a continuous connection while moving from room to room. Users are able to reach into the enterprise network with advanced security features that meet or exceed security guidelines and policies.

Client devices need only to make an association to the new AP either by actively looking for the specific AP or by surveying it passively with wireless discovery tools.

Wireless Client Association

Wireless clients first send probe requests prior to any associations. The two methods employed to discover APs are passive and active scanning.

The passive scanning steps are as follows:

1 APs send out beacons announcing the name of the WLAN (SSID), supported rates, and other information.

2 The client passively scans radio channels for beacons and probe responses, which allows the client to catalog information.

3 The client chooses an AP sending a beacon with the "right" SSID name and attempts association.

4 When multiple APs use the same basic service set identifier (BSSID), the client attempts to connect to the AP with the strongest signal and the lowest bit error rate.

5 The client continues to scan even after connecting to an AP, to efficiently roam from one AP to another or to reduce the reconnection time if it is disconnected from an AP.

NOTE	The Cisco Airespace controller supports 16 BSSIDs plus one third-party BSSID for a total of 17. With the Cisco Airespace solution, it is possible to turn off broadcast for an SSID on a per-AP basis.

The active scanning steps are as follows:

1 The client sends out a probe request announcing the name of the WLAN (SSID), supported rates, other information.

2 The client sends a probe request, actively seeking to join a WLAN. The probe request contains either the SSID of the WLAN the client wants to join or a broadcast indicator.

3 If the probe request contains an SSID, only the APs that know that SSID will respond.

4 If the probe request contains a broadcast indicator, then all APs will respond.

Clients can probe for a specific SSID.

Open Authentication

The open authentication method allows authorization and associations with or without a WEP key. If the client does not use a WEP key, the client undergoes the normal association process with the AP. The user is then granted access to the network.

If a WEP key is used, both the client and the AP must have matching WEP keys. If the client uses a WEP key that is different from the WEP key of the AP, data traffic cannot be passed because the data is encrypted. Keep in mind that the header is not encrypted; only the payload (or data) is encrypted.

Using open authentication, the client goes through the normal association process, whether or not the client is using a WEP key. Once the client is associated and data transmission begins, a client using a WEP key encrypts the data. If the WEP key on the AP does not match, then the AP is unable to decrypt the data, so it is impossible to send the data via the WLAN.

The initial connection to an AP consists of the following steps:

1 The client sends a probe request.

2 Access points A and B each send a probe response. The client evaluates the AP responses and selects the best AP, A in this example.

3 The client sends an authentication request to access point A.

4 Access point A confirms authentication and registers the client.

5 The client sends an association request to access point A.

6 Access point A confirms association and registers the client.

Pre-shared Key Authentication (WEP)

A wireless client using pre-shared key authentication attempts to associate with an AP. Steps 1 through 3 are the same as those for open authentication:

1 The client sends an authentication request to access point A.

2 Access point A sends an authentication response. The authentication response from the access point to the client is sent containing challenge text. This packet is unencrypted.

3 The client then uses the text from the authentication response to form another authentication packet, which will be encrypted using one of the client WEP keys, and sends this as a response to the access point.

4 Access point A compares the encrypted challenge text to the access point copy of the encrypted challenge text. If the encrypted text is the same, then the access point allows the client on the WLAN.

Pre-shared key authentication is considered less secure than open authentication because of the challenge text packet. Because this packet is sent unencrypted and then returned as an encrypted packet, it may be possible to capture both packets and determine the stream cipher.

Introducing WLAN Security

WLAN security is one of the most important things to consider when designing a WLAN. The importance is one of the reasons so many people discuss and research it.

Enhanced 802.11 security incorporates two elements to improve upon standard or "basic" 802.11 security. Authentication and encryption are used with enhanced security both to check user credentials before granting access and to increase the security integrity of the user's session after association to the network.

Authentication in 802.11 leverages the IEEE 802.1X standard to authenticate users and to permit policy assignment to those users as a result of the authentication transaction. Basing the authentication transaction on user rather than machine credentials reduces the risk of security compromise from lost or stolen equipment. 802.1X authentication also permits flexible credentials to be used for client authentication; password, one-time tokens, PKI certificate, or device ID may be used for authentication. Using 802.1X for wireless client authentication also has the advantage that dynamic encryption keys may be distributed to users each time that they authenticate to the network.

Encryption for 802.11 is enhanced with multiple mechanisms, to aid in protecting the system from malicious exploits against the WEP key and in protecting investment in the system by facilitating encryption improvements in existing hardware.

Temporal Key Integrity Protocol (TKIP) protects the WEP key from exploits that seek to derive the key using packet comparison. Message Integrity Check (MIC) is a mechanism for protecting the wireless system from "inductive attacks," which seek to induce the system to send either key data or a predictable response that can be analyzed (compared) to known data to derive the WEP key.

Both TKIP and MIC are elements of the Wi-Fi Protected Access (WPA) standard, which is intended to secure a system against all known WEP key vulnerabilities. Note that Cisco implemented a pre-standard version of TKIP and MIC in late 2001 and also supports the Wi-Fi industry-standard TKIP or MIC version.

802.11i encompasses a number of security improvements, including those implemented in WPA. Additionally, 802.11i standardized on a new form of encryption for 802.11, which is wireless Advanced Encryption Standard (AES). AES is recognized as a stronger security algorithm than the RC4 stream cipher used with WEP, although AES is undeniably more processor intensive. Hardware updates will be required to move to AES encryption while maintaining comparable throughput. Table 18-7 summarizes the security evolution overview.

Table 18-7   *The Evolution of Wireless LAN Security*

Past	First-generation encryption (WEP)
	No strong authentication, static (breakable keys), not scalable
Interim	WPA standardized: improved encryption
	Strong, user-based authentication (e.g., LEAP, PEAP, EAPFAST)
Present	Wireless IDs: identify and protect against attacks
	IEEE 802.11i: AES encryption, 802.1X authentication, dynamic key management
	WPA 2 (WPA2): provides stronger encryption through AES
Future	Improvements to hashing algorithms and key management in conjunction with AES—192-bit and 256-bit keys

Cisco Client Cards

The Cisco Aironet 802.11a/b/g Wireless LAN Client Adapters (CB21AG and PI21AG) support 802.11a, 802.11b, and 802.11g (2.4 GHz and 5 GHz). Theses cards connect mobile computing devices to the WLAN.

The Cisco Aironet Configuration Administration Tool (ACAT) enables an administrator to install the Aironet Client Utility (ACU) across a network, eliminating the need to install and configure ACU on each wireless client. The auto-installer runs in a silent batch mode and installs and configures ACU (thus configuring the Cisco Aironet client adapter) on a computer running the Windows operating system.

The Cisco Aironet Client Administration Utility (ACAU) enables an administrator to install the Aironet Desktop Utility (ADU) across a network, eliminating the need to install and configure ADU on each wireless client. The auto-installer runs in a silent batch mode and installs and configures ADU (thereby configuring the Cisco Aironet client adapter) on a computer running the Windows operating system.

ACAU and ACAT have virtually identical abilities, just slightly different user interfaces.

On Windows XP, configuration can be done by the Cisco Aironet Wireless LAN Client Adapter through ADU or a third-party tool, such as the Microsoft Wireless Configuration Manager. Because third-party tools may not provide all of the functionality available in ADU, Cisco recommends using ADU. (Please note that a patch from Microsoft might be required to use the Microsoft tool with WPA security.)

NOTE   If you are selecting a third-party tool, some of the ADU features will not be available. To activate those features, you must install the ADU.

ADU works only with the PC-CardBus card (AIR-CB21AG) and PCI card (AIR-PI21AG). The abilities of ADU are similar to those of ACU; ADU simply has a different look and feel.

ACU is a Windows GUI diagnostic and configuration utility. It allows you to upgrade firmware, edit configuration, and perform RF link testing. ACU allows the wireless client to use different profiles to connect to different WLANs. Each profile allows the user to selectively configure all parameters on the client card. The profile manager can then be used to change profiles. When the user selects a different profile, the settings for the client card are changed without requiring a reboot. ACU can accommodate a maximum of 16 profiles.

Cisco Compatible Extensions

The Cisco Compatible Extensions (CCX) program for WLAN devices provides tested compatibility with licensed Cisco infrastructure innovations. Compatibility is assured through extensive, independent testing of third-party devices. The CCX program enables the widespread availability of wireless client devices that take advantage of the Cisco Aironet wireless network, accelerating the availability of innovative features while maintaining interoperability.

With the CCX program, WLAN client suppliers (the program's participants) license, at no charge, Cisco WLAN technology innovations in a specification. Participants implement all elements of the specification and undergo extensive testing at an independent third-party test lab. The testing helps to ensure support for innovative features pioneered by Cisco Systems, as well as interoperability with Cisco WLAN infrastructure products.

The CCX program helps to ensure that client devices from a variety of suppliers can leverage Cisco-based WLANs. To make it easy to find these devices, Cisco has licensed the Cisco Compatible logo for use by participants whose products pass all tests at the independent third-party test lab. Locating approved wireless devices is as easy as looking for the logo.

The CCX program for WLAN devices provides tested compatibility with licensed Cisco infrastructure innovations.

Configuring a Basic WLAN

Lightweight APs are centrally managed via the controller, providing greater scalability than autonomous APs. The centrally managed controller provides various interfaces for connecting and configuring the WLAN. An all-in-one-stop device is available for configuration and verification now.

Available Interfaces for WLAN Configuration

The WLAN controller provides multiple interface options for configuration. Interfaces are logical entities on the controller. An interface has multiple parameters associated with it, including an IP address, default gateway (for the IP subnet), primary physical port, secondary physical port, VLAN identifier, and DHCP server.

These five types of interfaces are available on the controller:

- **Management**—Static and configured at setup time; mandatory
- **AP-manager**—When using Layer 3 LWAPP, static and configured at setup time; mandatory
- **Virtual**—Static and configured at setup time; mandatory
- **Service-port**—Static and configured at setup time; optional
- **Dynamic**—User defined, such as VLANs

NOTE   Four of these interfaces are static and are configured at setup time.

Each interface is mapped to at least one primary port, and some interfaces (management and dynamic) can be mapped to an optional secondary (or backup) port. If the primary port for an interface fails, the interface automatically moves to the backup port. In addition, multiple interfaces can be mapped to a single controller port.

Management Interface

The management interface is the default interface for in-band management of the controller and connectivity to enterprise services such as AAA servers. The management interface has the only consistently "pingable" in-band interface IP address on the controller. You can access the controller's GUI by entering the controller's management interface IP address in Internet Explorer's Address field.

The management interface is also used for Layer 2 communications between the controller and Cisco 1000 Series Lightweight APs. It must be assigned to distribution system port 1, but it can also be mapped to a backup port and can be assigned to WLANs if desired. It may be on the same VLAN or IP subnet as the AP-manager interface. However, the management interface can also communicate through the other distribution system ports.

When LWAPP communications are set to Layer 2 (same subnet) mode, the controller requires one management interface to control all inter-controller and controller-to-AP communications, regardless of the number of ports. When LWAPP communications are set to Layer 3 (different subnet) mode, the controller requires one management interface to control all inter-controller communications and one AP-manager interface to control all controller-to-AP communications, regardless of the number of ports.

AP-Manager Interface

A controller has one or more AP-manager interfaces, which are used for all Layer 3 communications between the controller and lightweight APs after the APs have joined the controller. The AP-manager IP address is used as the tunnel source for LWAPP packets from the controller to the AP and as the destination for LWAPP packets from the AP to the controller.

The static (or permanent) AP-manager interface must be assigned to distribution system port 1 and must have a unique IP address. It cannot be mapped to a backup port. It is usually configured on the same VLAN or IP subnet as the management interface, but this is not a requirement. The AP-manager interface can communicate through any distribution system port.

Virtual Interface

The virtual interface is used to support mobility management, Dynamic Host Configuration Protocol (DHCP) relay, and embedded Layer 3 security such as guest web authentication and VPN termination. It also maintains the DNS gateway host name used by Layer 3 security and mobility managers to verify the source of certificates when Layer 3 web authorization is enabled.

Specifically, the virtual interface plays these three primary roles:

- It acts as the DHCP server placeholder for wireless clients that obtain their IP address from a DHCP server.
- It serves as the redirect address for the Web Authentication Login window.
- It acts as part of the IPsec configuration when the controller is used to terminate IPsec tunnels between wireless clients and the controller.

The virtual interface IP address is used only in communications between the controller and wireless clients. It never appears as the source or destination address of a packet that goes out a distribution system port and onto the switched network. For the system to operate correctly, the virtual interface IP address must be set (it cannot be 0.0.0.0), and no other device on the network can have the same address as the virtual interface. Therefore, the virtual interface must be configured with an unassigned and unused gateway IP address, such as 1.1.1.1. The virtual interface IP address is not pingable and should not exist in any routing table in your network. In addition, the virtual interface cannot be mapped to a backup port.

Service-Port Interface

The service-port interface controls communications through and is statically mapped by the system to the service port. It must have an IP address on a different subnet from the management, AP-manager, and any dynamic interfaces, and it cannot be mapped to a backup port. This configuration enables you to manage the controller directly or through a dedicated operating system network, such as 10.1.2.x, which can ensure service access during network downtime.

The service port can obtain an IP address using DHCP, or it can be assigned a static IP address, but a default gateway cannot be assigned to the service-port interface. Static routes can be defined through the controller for remote network access to the service port.

Dynamic Interface

Dynamic interfaces, also known as VLAN interfaces, are created by users and designed to be analogous to VLANs for WLAN clients. A controller can support up to 512 dynamic interfaces (VLANs). Each dynamic interface is individually configured and allows separate communication streams to exist on any or all of a controller's distribution system ports. Each dynamic interface controls VLAN and other communications between controllers and all other network devices, and each acts as a DHCP relay for wireless clients associated to WLANs mapped to the interface. You can assign dynamic interfaces to distribution system ports, WLANs, the Layer 2 management interface, and the Layer 3 AP-manager interface, and you can map the dynamic interface to a backup port.

You can configure zero, one, or multiple dynamic interfaces on a distribution system port. However, all dynamic interfaces must be on a different VLAN or IP subnet from all other interfaces configured on the port. If the port is untagged, all dynamic interfaces must be on a different IP subnet from any other interface configured on the port.

Connecting to the Controller

Connecting to the controller is similar to the standard switch connection. Configure the terminal emulator (HyperTerminal, ProComm, and so on) with the following parameters: 9600 baud, 8 data bits, 1 stop bit, no parity, and no hardware flow control.

Next, use a null-modem serial cable to connect the CLI console to the controller console port.

NOTE   The controller end of the cable is female DB-9. The other end should be any kind of connector that plugs into your VT-100 terminal emulator (usually a laptop or palmtop computer).

The initial setup for all controllers can be done through the serial port. Moreover, the Service Interface port is another setup option available only on the 4400 Series controllers.

Using the serial port requires a male DB-9 pin connector that supports pins 2, 3, and 5. This is the default port configuration.

The serial port of all WLAN controllers is dedicated to the management of the AireOS operating system. It ensures access to AireOS in the event of a network failure and can be used for initial installation too. The serial port access will only be available from the CLI—not the GUI.

On the 4400 WLAN controller, the Service Interface port is dedicated to AireOS management in addition to the Serial port. The Service Interface port ensures access to AireOS in the event of a network failure and can be used for initial configuration or out-of-band (OOB) management from the management network.

The Service Interface port is an auto-sensing 10/100BASE-TX Ethernet port. The WLAN controller is a DTE type device that requires a crossover cable for other DTE devices such as a router or end station. Standard Category 5 Ethernet cables are used when connecting to a DCE device such as a switch or modem. By default, the port IP address assigned is 192.168.1.1/24.

NOTE   The controller supports five Telnet/SSH sessions plus one serial port connection simultaneously by default. The serial port can support up to a 115-kbps baud rate.

After the connection is made and power is applied to the WLAN controller, the boot sequence will provide additional options. The boot options available, because this is set in PROM to ensure controller recovery, are as follows:

1   Run primary image

2   Run backup image

3   Manually upgrade primary image

4   Change active boot image

5   Clear configuration

NOTE   The clear configuration option allows you to remove the current configuration and return to factory defaults. This is a two-step process. You must first choose option 5 and then choose an image.

Connection to the controller can be made from a web browser after bootup. Cisco Switch Web Configuration Wizard Login is a GUI tool with an easy-to-use interface. The initial system configuration supports only HTTP access, so if you attempt to use HTTPS, you will receive an error.

The default IP address for Cisco WLAN controllers is 192.168.1.1/24. The default username/password combination is admin/admin.

Configuring the Controller

When selecting the primary or backup image at the Boot Options menu, the system automatically starts if the Esc key is not pressed. After the boot image loads, the Airespace AireOS starts up.

NOTE   The message "Checking for new bootloader: Not found" will be observed only after initial controller boot or controller upgrade.

Watching the bootup messages enables you to follow the overall process, such as:

- APs will not light up until the PoE services are okay as displayed by the message 'Starting Power Over Ethernet Services: ok'.

- Web Authentication Certificate not found (error) is only after the initial controller boot or controller upgrade.

- The Cisco Airespace Wizard Configuration Tool begins automatically if there are no saved binary configuration files. The bootup script will run either the CLI or Switch Web Interface Configuration Wizard.

NOTE   Power-on self test (POST) and controller boot will normally take about 3 minutes. If an Enhanced Security Module (ESM) is installed, it might take an additional 60 seconds for the boot process to complete.

If there is a configuration saved on the controller, the bootup script will prompt for the administrator username and password. Once logged in to the controller AireOS, the **show running configuration** command provides a general summary of the configuration. It is not in a command syntax format and contains no MAC address information, which allows it to be ported to multiple controllers. Be aware of duplicate IP addresses.

As the switches have both a running-configuration and a saved-configuration, so does the controller. So the running-configuration is any command executed and not saved, whereas saved changes create the saved-configuration in NVRAM. Otherwise, a power cycle will drop all running-configuration changes.

When the controller boots at factory defaults, the bootup script runs the configuration wizard, which prompts the installer for initial configuration settings. Follow these steps to enter settings using the wizard on the CLI:

Step 1   Connect your computer to the controller using a DB-9 null-modem serial cable.

Step 2   Open a terminal emulator session and connect to the WLAN controller.

Step 3   At the prompt, log into the CLI. The default username is **admin**, and the default password is **admin**.

Step 4   If necessary, enter **reset system** to reboot the unit and start the wizard.

Step 5   The first wizard prompt is for the system name. Enter up to 32 printable ASCII characters.

Step 6   Enter an administrator username and password, each up to 24 printable ASCII characters.

Step 7   Enter the service-port interface IP configuration protocol: none or DHCP. If you do not want to use the service port or if you want to assign a static IP address to the service port, enter **none**.

Step 8   If you entered **none** in Step 7 and need to enter a static IP address for the service port, enter the service-port interface IP address and netmask for the next two prompts. If you do not want to use the service port, enter **0.0.0.0** for the IP address and netmask.

Step 9   Enter the management interface IP address, netmask, default router IP address, and optional VLAN identifier (a valid VLAN identifier, or **0** for untagged).

Step 10   Enter the Network Interface (Distribution System) Physical Port number. For the controller, the possible ports are 1 through 4 for a front-panel GigE port.

Step 11   Enter the IP address of the default DHCP server that will supply IP addresses to clients, the management interface, and the service-port interface if you use one.

Step 12   Enter the LWAPP Transport Mode: LAYER2 or LAYER3.

Step 13   Enter the Virtual Gateway IP Address. This address can be any fictitious, unassigned IP address (such as 1.1.1.1) to be used by Layer 3 security and mobility managers.

Step 14   Enter the Cisco WLAN Solution Mobility Group (RF group) name.

Step 15   Enter the WLAN 1 SSID, or network name. This is the default SSID that lightweight APs use to associate to a controller.

Step 16   Allow or disallow static IP addresses for clients. Enter **yes** to allow clients to supply their own IP addresses. Enter **no** to require clients to request an IP address from a DHCP server.

Step 17   If you need to configure a RADIUS server, enter **yes**, and enter the RADIUS server IP address, the communication port, and the shared secret. If you do not need to configure a RADIUS server or you want to configure the server later, enter **no**.

Step 18   Enter a country code for the unit. Enter **help** to list the supported countries.

Step 19   Enable or disable support for 802.11b, 802.11a, and 802.11g.

Step 20   Enable or disable Radio Resource Management (RRM) (Auto RF).

The CLI allows operators to use a VT-100 emulator to locally or remotely configure, monitor, and control a WLAN controller and its associated lightweight APs. The CLI is a simple text-based, tree-structured interface that allows up to five users with Telnet-capable terminal emulators to access the controller. The CLI basic command set is as follows:

- **linktest**—If the client is a Cisco client, the Cisco Airespace controller will run the Cisco linktest program to test connectivity. If the client is not a Cisco client, 20 pings are sent to the destination MAC address, which will return a Relative Signal Strength Indicator (RSSI) value. You cannot use variables for the MAC address.

- **logout**—Exit the current CLI session.

- **ping**—Packet internet groper sends three Internet Control Message Protocol (ICMP) requests to a specified IP address.

- **reset**—Allows soft reboot of the Cisco Airespace controller.

- **save configuration**—Data is saved to NVRAM and is preserved in the event of a power cycle.

The GUI allows up to five users to simultaneously browse into the controller http or https (http + SSL) management pages to configure, control, and monitor the operational status for the controller and its associated lightweight APs. The GUI menu bar is as follows:

- **MONITOR**—Provides a view of this controller, its APs, and wireless clients

- **WLANs**—Provides WLAN configurations such as SSIDs and security policies for all user groups

- **SWITCH**—Provides controller-wide configurations, such as Layer 2/3 mode, multicast, and mobility settings

- **WIRELESS**—Provides AP configurations, client management, and various RF settings

- **SECURITY**—Provides integration into the security structure, such as RADIUS connectivity

- **MANAGEMENT**—Provides integration into the network, such as IP addressing and SNMP

- **COMMANDS**—Provides administrative options, such as upgrades and backups

- **Logout**—Exits the current switch web interface session

- **PING**—Sends three ICMP requests to a specified IP address

- **Save configuration**—Saves data to NVRAM and preserves it in the event of a power cycle

NOTE   The switch web interface will refresh every 5 minutes, but when looking at statistics, it is recommended to observe the latest information, which can be provided by clicking Refresh. The switch web interface has a default inactivity timeout of 10 minutes.

After Switch Web Configuration Wizard saves the configuration and reboots the controller, HTTPS access will be enabled whereas HTTP access will be disabled by default.

NOTE	You can connect using either HTTP://*controller-IP-Address* or HTTPS://*controller-IP-address* but HTTP is disabled by default. You can disable either HTTP or HTTPS access. If you receive a "The page cannot be displayed" error message, check to see if the corresponding access method has been disabled.

Verifying Controller Configuration

Knowledge and awareness are gained via the **show** commands. They are a set of robust commands that display what the current WLAN configuration is running.

show 802.11 Commands

Use the **show 802.11** commands to display configuration parameters.

To display basic 802.11a options and settings, use the following command:

```
show 802.11a
```

Table 18-8   *Syntax Description*

show	Display Configurations
802.11a	802.11a configurations

Defaults: None

Related commands: **show 802.11b**

show advanced 802.11 Commands

Use the **show advanced** commands to display advanced configuration parameters.

To display the 802.11a advanced options and settings, use the following command:

```
show advanced 802.11a summary
```

Table 18-9   *Syntax Description*

show	Display Configurations
advanced	Advanced parameters
802.11a	802.11a configurations
summary	Cisco 1000 Series Lightweight AP name, channel, and transmit level summary

Defaults: None

Related commands: **show advanced 802.11b summary**

show ap Commands

Use the **show ap** commands to display AP parameters.

To display the detailed configuration for an 802.11b/g Cisco 1000 Series Lightweight AP, use the following command:

```
show ap config {802.11a | 802.11b | general} Cisco_AP
```

Table 18-10 *Syntax Description*

show	Display Configurations
ap config	**Cisco radio**
802.11a	802.11a settings
802.11b	802.11b/g settings
general	General settings
Cisco_AP	Cisco 1000 Series Lightweight AP name

Defaults: None

Related commands: **show ap auto-rf, show ap bmode, show ap bhrate, show ap core-dump, show ap crash-file, show ap stats, show ap summary, show ap wlan, show arp switch, show auth-list, show boot**

show stats Commands

Use the **show stats** commands to display controller statistics.

To show physical port receive and transmit statistics, use the following command:

```
show stats port {detailed port | summary port}
```

Table 18-11 *Syntax Description*

show	Display Configurations
stats	Statistics
port	Port
detailed	Display detailed port statistics
summary	Display port summary statistics

Table 18-11 *Syntax Description (Continued)*

show	Display Configurations
port	Physical port number:
	•1 through 4 on Cisco 2000 Series WLAN controllers
	•1 or 2 on Cisco 4100 Series WLAN controllers
	•1 or 2 on Cisco 4402 Series WLAN controllers
	•1 through 4 on Cisco 4404 Series WLAN controllers
	•1 on Cisco WLCM Series WLAN controllers

Defaults: None

Related commands: **show stats switch**, **show switchconfig**, **show sysinfo**, **show syslog**, **show tech-support**, **show time**, **show trapflags**, **show traplog**, **show watchlist**, **show wlan**, **show wps**

show client Commands

Use the **show client** commands to display client settings.

To display the clients on a Cisco 1000 Series Lightweight AP, use the following command:

```
show client ap {802.11a | 802.11b} Cisco_AP
```

NOTE The **show client ap** command may list the status of automatically disabled clients. Use the **show exclusionlist** command to view clients on the exclusion list (blacklisted).

Table 18-12 *Syntax Description*

show	Display Configurations
client ap	Cisco radio
802.11a	802.11a settings
802.11b	802.11b/g settings
Cisco_AP	Cisco 1000 Series Lightweight AP name

Defaults: None

Related commands: **show client ap**, **show client detail**, **show client summary**, **show client username**, **show country**, **show cpu**, **show custom-web**, **show database summary**,

show debug, **show dhcp**, **show eventlog**, **show exclusionlist**, **show ike**, **show interface**, **show inventory**, **show ipsec**, **show known ap**, **show l2tp**, **show load-balancing**, **show location summary**, **show loginsession**, **show macfilter**

show radius Commands

To display the RADIUS accounting server statistics for the Cisco WLAN controller, use the following command:

```
show radius acct statistics
```

Table 18-13 *Syntax Description*

show	Display Configurations
radius acct	RADIUS accounting server
statistics	Display RADIUS accounting server statistics

Defaults: None

Related commands: **show radius auth statistics**, **show radius rfc3576 statistics**, **show radius summary**

show rogue ap Commands

Use the **show rogue ap** commands to display rogue AP settings.

To show details of rogue AP clients detected by the Cisco WLAN controller, use the following command:

```
show rogue ap clients MAC
```

Table 18-14 *Syntax Description*

show	Display Configurations
rogue ap	Rogue access point
detailed	Display detailed information
MAC	Rogue access point MAC address

Defaults: None

Related commands: **show rogue ap clients**, **show rogue ap summary**

show rogue client Commands

Use the **show rogue client** commands to display the rogue client settings.

To show details of a rogue client detected by a Cisco WLAN controller, use the following command:

```
show rogue client detailed MAC
```

Table 18-15 *Syntax Description*

show	Display Configurations
rogue client	Rogue client
detailed	Provide detailed information for a rogue client
MAC	Rogue client MAC address

Defaults: None

Related commands: **show rogue client summary**

Additional **show** commands exist covering configuration designs such as mobility, X.509 certificates, RFIDs, and mesh networking. All require further exploration into the world of wireless networking.

Summary

The move to 2.4 GHz put WLAN products into a "cleaner" radio frequency (RF) environment, making it possible to deploy data collection systems without the worries of 900-MHz interference. WLAN products are designed using the IEEE 802 family of LAN specifications, which 802.11 falls under. Understanding the similarities between Ethernet and wireless makes it easier to understand 802.11. However, the security, connectivity, regulatory, and power-related issues associated with WLANs make the differences start to stand out.

Wireless components such as the client cards, APs, and controllers are obvious differences from Ethernet that are required to make WLANs work. WLAN components are the building blocks of AP topologies such as infrastructure, bridging, or mesh designs. Those building blocks and RF knowledge create the foundation to any wireless design. The results are always better when considering RF propagation issues such as reflection, refraction, diffraction, and absorption. Losses and gains, also, come into play for RF absorption, antenna types, and distances. All those losses and gains require RF math skills to know the end results.

Adding antenna gains and losses requires an understanding of gain and how each type of antenna is used. Moreover, the RF coverage area provided by the antenna defines a microcell layout. Microcells designed for 802.11a do not have the same effective RF coverage area as 802.11b/g microcells.

Omnidirectional antennas are the most widely used, followed by semidirectional antennas for both indoors and outdoors. Highly directional antennas are mostly used for bridging between distant buildings. Keep in mind that all RF links between buildings or indoors are subject to regulatory agency compliance, which may impact the WLAN design. The outdoor antennas need to keep Fresnel zone interferences to less than 40 percent and ideally to less than 25 percent.

The wireless frequency standards provide effective transmissions and reliability of data. Currently, wireless transmission and reliability are so effective that most customers are focusing on other issues such as bandwidth and backward compatibility. 802.11g is meeting the needs of most customers regardless of the channel reuse issues. A well-designed WLAN considers the three separated channels on the ISM band, which are 1, 6, and 11. Moreover, the design may include 802.11a, UNII band, which provides greater ease on channel reuse because 12 channels exist. Using best practices during the design phase reduces a number of issues and eases the implementation phase.

Getting power to the APs cannot be overlooked, and easing that burden is why power injectors and 802.3af-compliant devices exist. The power issue is one of the common concerns enterprises have regarding wireless. That is one of the reasons why Cisco came out with the Unified Wireless Network solution, which has three goals: maintaining network security, managing the network, and unifying the network.

The requested features most enterprises wanted form the core AireOS feature set. Layer 2 roaming is a core feature and is included in the advanced features set. The advanced features provide Layer 3 roaming and advanced security. Most features are carried out on the controller and not on the lightweight AP. The split MAC architecture allows the lightweight AP to split the 802.11 function between the AP and controller. Authentication, reassociation, and frame translation are all handled in the controller. The controller also maintains association to the APs using the Lightweight Access Point Protocol (LWAPP), the low-overhead management protocol. Some autonomous APs can be converted to use LWAPP, such as in an enterprise migration plan.

Cisco wireless clients can create an association either actively or passively. The clients actively send AP authentication requests after the AP probe request. After both responses come back, the AP association request is sent. Passively, the client does not send probes; it is a listen-only mode until the reassociation occurs. The reassociation or association process may include open or pre-shared (WEP) key information for authentication. It is recommended to use a stronger mechanism for security purposes, such as WPA2. Client cards are available from Cisco, and other vendors now support the Cisco Compatibility Extensions (CCX) program.

WLAN controllers that have multiple interfaces support up to five interfaces:

- **Management**—Static and configured at setup time; mandatory
- **AP-manager**—When using Layer 3 LWAPP, static and configured at setup time; mandatory
- **Virtual**—Static and configured at setup time; mandatory

- **Service-port**—Static and configured at setup time; optional
- **Dynamic**—User defined, such as VLANs

The connection to the controller can be accomplished using the CLI or service port for web access. Gathering all the pertinent information prior to the configuration is a best practice and may eliminate potential conflicts. Once the configuration setup is complete, use the **show** commands to verify the configuration.

Planning, designing, implementing, operating, and troubleshooting an enterprise wireless network requires a greater understanding than this brief chapter can provide. Many materials are offered to enable you to learn about and better understand wireless networks, including books, software, websites, and instructor-led courses.

Review Questions

1 What does DSSS stand for?

2 What two frequency bands does wireless mostly use?

3 What technology group does Bluetooth fall under?

4 What medium standard is used in wireless to avoid collisions?

5 What environmental factors can cause multipath interference?

6 How does 802.11 address privacy?

7 What country permits all 14 channels within the 2.4-GHz spectrum?

8 What does a lightweight AP get from the controller once it associates?

9 What does the Cisco Unified Wireless Network address?

10 What two implementation categories does wireless have?

11 What are the two BSS modes?

12 Is dBi or dBw used when calculating antenna gain?

13 A 3-dB loss will reduce 100 mW to what new power?

14 What are the three antenna types?

15 Why is a channel reuse plan required in the 2.4-GHz spectrum?

16 In a bridging WLAN, how many root bridges can exist?

17 How many users do best practices suggest for 2.4-GHz 802.11g?

18 What is PoE?

19 True or False: Cisco lightweight APs can be managed by a wireless LAN controller and WCS.

20 What are the two methods employed to discover APs?

21 WPA uses what two elements to secure WEP from vulnerabilities?

22 What is the Cisco Compatible Extensions program designed to help?

23 Which WLAN controller interface is known as a VLAN?

24 What command is used to display basic 802.11a options and settings?

Answers to Review Questions

Chapter 1

1 True. Applying security in the multilayer switched network is crucial to provide a secured environment.

2 True. Security is the most important aspect of building multilayer switched networks today.

3 True. Hardware-switching of frames scales the number of wire-speed ports by implementing features such as distributed CEF.

4 True. The Enterprise Composite Network Model adds modularity to the hierarchical network design.

5 True. The Data Center is evolving as its own functional area of the enterprise network.

6 Answers:

a. Layer 3. Switching per IP destination occurs at the network layer (Layer 3).

b. Layer 3. IP precedence is denoted by bits in the IP header to signify priority. Applying QoS based on these IP precedence bits is a Layer 3 switching feature.

c. Layer 3. Restricting IP broadcast traffic requires a switch to inspect the destination IP address of a packet; therefore, restricting IP broadcast traffic is a Layer 3 switching feature.

d. Layer 2. Applying 802.1x authentication is purely a Layer 2 switching feature because 802.1x authentication only requires the switch to read the Layer 2 MAC addresses of a frame.

e. Layer 4. Distributing TCP sessions requires Layer 4 inspection of the frame by a switch.

f. Layer 7. Blocking web cookies requires content-intelligence, a Layer 7 feature.

g. Layer 4. Network Address Translation requires Layer 3 and Layer 4 inspection of IP frames.

h. Layer 2. CoS bits are bits in the Layer 2 802.1Q tag that signify priority.

7 e. DSCP values are contained within the IP header.

8 Answers:

1-b. The Enterprise Edge functional area interconnects the Enterprise Campus to the Service Provider Edge and contains the Remote Access and VPN module.

2-a. The Enterprise Campus functional area contains the Building Access, Building Distribution, and Campus Backbone submodules that are used to build a campus infrastructure that offers high performance, scalability, and availability.

3-c. The Service Provider Edge functional area integrates ISP services into the enterprise network.

9 Answers:

1-a. The Edge Distribution module connects the Enterprise Campus module with Enterprise Edge services and modules.

2-d. The Network Management module monitors the network for performance, system alerts, and anomalous events, all of which are useful in troubleshooting.

3-c. The Campus Infrastructure module provides many services and functions, including connecting the Server Farm and Edge Distribution modules.

4-b. The Data Center module contains many types of Internet servers, including e-mail and DNS servers.

10 Answers:

1-c. The E-Commerce module integrates the applications and services for Internet-based commerce and information.

2-d. The Internet Connectivity module consists of servers, including e-mail servers for exchanging e-mail globally.

3-b. The Remote Access and VPN module terminates VPN and remote-access traffic from remote users or remote sites.

4-a. The WAN module consists of routers and switches that connect remote sites with central sites over point-to-point connections.

11 Answers:

1-c. The PSTN module uses legacy phone technologies such as POTS and ISDN to provide for remote access to the enterprise network.

2-b. The Frame Relay/ATM/PPP module includes WAN technologies for connecting remote sites or users using permanent, point-to-point connections.

3-a. The ISP module connects the enterprise network to the Internet and includes components for security.

12 a, b, and c. The Catalyst 2950 family of switches is the only Cisco Catalyst switch listed that does not support IP routing.

13 b. The Catalyst 4500 family of switches offers specialized line modules of high port density for high-speed metro Ethernet deployment over long distances. The Catalyst 2950 LRE switch also provides for metro Ethernet functionality but is limited in port density and speed.

14 a, b, c, and d. All Catalyst families of switches in the list support power redundancy either via dual internal power supplies or via external RPSs.

15 a and b. The Catalyst 3550 and 3760 are families of switches are the only switches in the list that are not modular and that are of fixed port density.

16 a. The Catalyst 6500 family of switches is the only switch in the list that supports ATM interfaces through special modules.

17 a. The Catalyst 6500 family of switches supports any role within the Enterprise Composite Network Model because of its versatility, its available interface types, and its performance, scalability, and availability features.

18 a, b, and c. Using modular switches rather than fixed port density switches provides for additional performance, scalability, and availability. Modular switches generally use higher-performance ASICs, including ASICs at specific line modules for increased performance. Modular switches achieve scalability because of their ability to swap line modules for different interface types and increased port density. With regard to availability, modular switches generally support redundant supervisors.

19 b. Stacking applies a few modular switch benefits to the fixed port density switches, such as link redundancy and scalability.

20 The destination MAC address of the frame at Location A is 0000.0cbb.000a because Workstation A sends frames to its default gateway to be routed to other subnets.

21 The source MAC address, the destination MAC address, and the destination IP address of the frame at Location B are 0000.0cbb.001a, 0000.0cbb.001b, and 10.1.2.2, respectively. Routers rewrite the MAC address in the path from source to destination at each Layer 3 boundary. The IP address does not change from source to destination in this topology.

22 The source MAC address, the destination MAC address, and the destination IP address of the frame at Location C are 0000.0cbb.000b, 0000.0c00.0012, and 10.1.1.2, respectively. Routers rewrite the MAC address in the path from source to destination at each Layer 3 boundary. The IP address does not change from source to destination in this topology.

Chapter 2

1 False. If both link partners are operating at full duplex, collisions cannot occur.

2 False. Per the IEEE 802.3ab specification, auto-negotiation with Gigabit Ethernet over copper is required.

3 c. A duplex mismatch will occur if the manually configured link partner is set to 100 Mbps, full duplex. This is because the auto-negotiation link partner does not see auto-negotiation parameters from its peer and defaults to 100-Mbps, half-duplex operation.

4 b, c, and f. Layer 3 switches and routers differ only in physical aspects such as design, implementation, and port density.

5 b, e, and f. 10-Gigabit Ethernet is an emerging technology currently limited to connecting clusters of servers, high-speed switches, and multiple campuses.

6 c. The Data Center module connects to the Campus Backbone submodule with more than one connection for high-availability purposes.

7 b. Servers connect to switches via two autonomous NICs to protect against failure of internal components of the NIC, which is not the case with a single NIC with dual ports.

8 a and b. Servers in the Data Center module may reach storage devices with the iSCSI protocol over TCP/IP or via Fibre Channel using HBAs. It is not common for intranet servers to communicate with storage devices via web access.

9 d and e. Switches in the E-Commerce module are deployed to interconnect servers and storage devices and to switch traffic between edge routers and the rest of the module.

10 a. The best Cisco solution for this small company involves a small-scale network design consisting of Catalyst 3560s because these switches support inline power and work as well as access layer and distribution layer switches.

11 b. Because of the large size of the corporate network and the growth projections, a large-scale network design with Catalyst 6500 in every module is the best choice for the listed requirements.

12 c. The best Cisco solution for this network is a medium-scale network. The company has only 1000 employees but requires a vast storage infrastructure with moderate bandwidth requirements. For such large storage requirements, a SAN works best for this network.

13 Layer 3 routing in the distribution layer is needed in all medium-sized and large networks. Layer 3 routing in the distribution layer is quickly becoming an important design criterion for all networks.

14 SANs integrate in the Campus Infrastructure module when using FCIP to connect remote SANs with Fibre Channel running over TCP/IP or using iSCSI to allow for storage hosts to directly attach to Fibre Channel storage devices.

Chapter 3

1 True. Telnet sends passwords in clear-text. Use SSH instead of Telnet for in-band access.

2 False. Layer 3 switches configured for routing may use a gateway of last resort and routing protocols to reach remote subnets.

3 True. Despite major attempts by hardware and software manufacturers and standards organizations, hackers always seem to find new vulnerabilities in protocols and features.

4 False. Default gateways are necessary only for Layer 2–only switches or Layer 3 switches with IP routing disabled. Layer 3 switches with routing enabled use the IP routing table to reach non-local subnets.

5 True. TFTP is neither a reliable nor a secure protocol for transferring images to and from Catalyst switches.

6 b. The **no shutdown** command administratively enables an interface.

7 c and d. The **show ip interface brief** and **show interface status** commands display a port's link state.

8 e. The only listed file system not supported in any Catalyst switch is the NFS file system.

9 d. The Catalyst 6500 with a Supervisor Engine 720 with MSFC3 and PFC3 uses a unique prefix for the Cisco IOS Software image of s72033.

10 a and c. Both the **undebug all** and **no debug all** commands immediately disable all running debugs.

11 b and c. The rollover cable and the straight-through cable are the only cable types used on Catalyst switch console ports depending on platform and console port settings. Legacy Catalyst switches such as the Catalyst 1900 used a null modem cable for console port connectivity.

12 The strings **public** and **private** are used commonly as default read-only and read-write community strings. For security purposes, recommended practice is to use different strings if SNMPv3 is not a possible option.

13 The default console baud rate is 9600, and it can be changed. If 9600 baud does not work when connecting to a Cisco router, switch, or device, attempt to use a baud rate of 38400 instead. Occasionally, the baud rate is used for special debugging purposes.

14 The **show module** command shows the hardware modules installed in a Cisco Catalyst switch.

15 The **show tech** command is generally required for all Cisco TAC cases.

16 Both the **dir** *device* and the **show flash** commands illustrate the contents of the IFS and the remaining space available.

17 The **show version** command displays the current software version and the uptime of a switch.

18 The **copy running-config startup-config** command saves the running configuration to NVRAM.

19 The **copy ftp disk0:** command copies an image from an FTP server to the disk0:. Note that Cisco IOS requires global configuration of the FTP username and password prior to executing this form of the command.

20 The **copy tftp: running-config** command copies a configuration file from TFTP and merges it with the running configuration.

Chapter 4

1 False. ISL trunking doesn't require the same Native VLAN because it encapsulates all the VLANs, including the Native VLAN.

2 False. The Catalyst 6500 family of switches supports up to 4094 VLANs in recent Cisco IOS Software versions.

3 False. If you remove the VLAN 1 from the trunk, it still carries CDP, PAgP, and DTP on VLAN 1, and it only removes the data traffic from VLAN 1.

4 False. All members of same community pVLANs can communicate with all other members of the same community pVLAN.

5 False. Switches can add or delete VLANs only in the VTP server or transparent mode.

6 False. Token Ring support is available starting in VTP version 2.

7 a. Native VLAN is always 1 by default in Cisco IOS.

8 d. The interface is manually configured for 801.1Q trunking.

9 c. The interface is a member of access VLAN and may negotiate to a trunk port.

10 b. VLAN 2 is the trunk native VLAN based on the configuration shown in Example 4-32.

11 c. The interface can negotiate to become a trunk port if the peer interface is configured for dynamic, desirable, or trunk.

12 a. VLAN 1 is the access mode VLAN as indicated by the access mode VLAN output in configuration Example 4-32.

13 b. One of the benefits of implementing VLANs is that doing so constrains broadcast traffic.

14 a and c. Local VLANs, typically used in the Building Access submodule, are easier to manage and conceptualize than VLANs that span different areas of the network.

15 b. Switch(vlan)# indicates that the switch is in the VLAN database configuration mode of Cisco IOS.

16 a. Access ports do not listen to or send DTP packets.

17 a. ISL-encapsulated frames have a 4-byte FCS field. This field contains a 32-bit CRC value, based on header information in the ISL frame.

18 b. 802.1Q trunking adds a tag in the standard Layer 2 Ethernet header after the SA (source MAC address) field and before the Type (ethertype) field.

19 c. The **switchport trunk encapsulation isl** command is used to configure trunks for ISL encapsulation.

20 d. The command **switchport trunk native vlan** *vlan-id* is used to configure the native VLAN when an interface is operating as a trunk.

21 a and e. Trunks are only established between link partners operating in auto trunk or dynamic desirable modes.

22 c. All Cisco Catalyst products operate in VTP server mode by default.

23 d. In VTP version 2, the switch performs consistency checks on new information entered through CLI or SNMP.

24 d. The **vtp version 1** or **no vtp version 2** command can be used to configure VTP version 1 in Cisco IOS.

25 b, c, and d. VTP versions 1 and 2 support server, client, and transparent mode.

26 a. The **show vtp status** command is the command to verify the VTP configuration in Cisco IOS.

27 d. The **vtp password** *password-string* command is used to configure or change VTP passwords.

28 VTP pruning uses VLAN advertisements to determine when a trunk connection is flooding traffic needlessly.

29 pVLANs provide security and reduce the use of IP subnets by isolating traffic between the end stations even though they are in the same VLAN.

30 If workstations A and B are members of the same community pVLAN, they can communicate with each other, but they cannot communicate if each workstation is a member of a different community pVLAN or a member of the same isolated pVLAN. In any case, all ports that are members of either isolated or community pVLANs can communicate with promiscuous ports.

Chapter 5

1 False. If redundant paths exist, a Layer 2 loop will occur if STP is disabled. STP prevents loops in such scenarios by blocking redundant paths, providing a single, loop-free topology.

2 False. If you have only a few VLANs, the amount of CPU resource usage saved with MST is not significant enough to warrant changes from default STP mode.

3 False. Secondary root bridges typically have a higher bridge priority than the primary root bridge.

4 a. The lowest bridge priority possible is zero and hence is the best possible bridge priority for a root switch.

5 e. The **show spanning-tree root** Cisco IOS command shows the root bridge information for all VLANs configured on a switch.

6 b. The **spanning-tree vlan** *vlan-id* **root primary** command configures a distribution switch to be the primary root switch.

7 c. Refer to Figure 5-22. RSTP has three operational states: discarding, learning, and forwarding.

8 b. STP operates on Layer 2 of the OSI model and operates independent of the upper-level protocols.

9 e. The time it takes for the proposal and agreement to be exchanged between the two switches on a link is less than 1 second.

10 d. The default message interval for BPDUs in RSTP remains at 2 seconds, identical to the 802.1D hello interval. The hello interval can be modified by a CLI command.

11 Bridge A is elected root because it has a lower MAC address compared to the other switches with equal priority values.

12 The port on root bridge A would be the designated port. The designated port is the port sending the best BPDU on a segment. Because root bridge A has the best BPDU, its port would act as the designated port.

13 The primary root switch needs to be centrally located in the network with enough switching capacity to accommodate all the packets that need to pass through the root switch between different building distribution and access layer switches. In addition, the CPU power of the primary root switch needs to be sufficiently high to handle all functions needed.

Chapter 6

1 False. You should enable the PortFast feature only on host ports. Enabling PortFast on ports connected to switching devices can cause bridging loops.

2 False. Loop Guard and UDLD aggressive-mode are complementary features and could both be enabled on the same interface.

3 True. STP actually tries to prevent bridging loops. If STP is disabled, you would always see a bridging loop if there are redundant paths or there is a physical loop in the network. If there is no redundancy in the network, then a bridging loop will not occur.

4 d. Without BackboneFast enabled, switches take 50 seconds to change to the forwarding state. This is in part because during the first 20 seconds (equal to max age), the switch ignores the inferior BPDU from the connected switch.

5 c. UplinkFast is the feature used to detect and recover from direct link failures.

6 a. PortFast must be enabled for BPDU Guard to work.

7 e. With UplinkFast enabled, the switch will start forwarding traffic over the backup link typically in less than 1 second.

8 a. The port unblocks and moves through the STP transition after it stops receiving superior BPDUs.

9 a. BPDU filtering causes the switch not to send BPDUs out the PortFast-enabled port; hence, it is recommended that the feature be enabled, if needed, only on host ports to prevent STP loops or undesired behavior.

10 c. Rebooting the root switch or secondary root switch is not a recommended activity when troubleshooting STP issues or Layer 2 issues. Rebooting a switch results in the loss of statistics or syslog data stored on that switch. Identifying the root cause of any issue after a reboot is difficult.

11 e. The correct command to enable STP events debugging is the **debug spanning-tree events** command.

Chapter 7

1 False. Aggressive mode UDLD has additional benefits to detect UDLD conditions when one side of the link is up and the other side is down. Also, aggressive mode UDLD detects situations where a link remains up but the port is not communicating due to a software or hardware anomaly.

2 False. LACP is the implementation of the IEEE 803.2ad link aggregation protocol; hence, LACP can be used to form an EtherChannel between Catalyst switches and non-Cisco devices. PAgP, on the other hand, can only be used between Cisco switches. Cisco has licensed PAgP to some NIC vendors.

3 c. The IEEE version of the port channeling protocol, 803.2ad, is referred to in Cisco Catalyst switches as LACP.

4 b. UDLD operates at Layer 2 of the OSI model because it sends frames. UDLD does use Layer 1 mechanisms.

5 d. The maximum default size of Ethernet frames, including the Ethernet header and CRC (FCS), is 1518 bytes.

6 b. The 802.1Q tag is 4 bytes in length; along with the standard Ethernet frame size of 1518 bytes, the total frame size of an 802.1Q tagged frame is 1522 bytes.

7 e. The size of CRC (FCS) in 802.3 Ethernet is 4 bytes. The total header plus CRC overhead is 18 bytes. The maximum payload or data portion of an Ethernet frame is 1500 bytes.

8 d. The default message interval setting of UDLD is 15 seconds, and detection of an UDLD condition is three times the message interval.

9 d. The desirable mode of operation belongs exclusively to Cisco EtherChannel using PAgP.

10 Aggressive mode UDLD offers additional benefits over UDLD, as described in Table 7-6.

11 c. The default recovery time is 300 seconds.

12 d. Route flap is not an error condition that the error-disable feature would act upon.

13 d. IEEE 802.3 defines the standard for the flow control protocol, which is followed between two devices when the downstream switch receiver buffer is congested.

14 CDP sends various information about the sending device as described in the "CDP" section of this chapter, such as the IP addresses of the sending interface, routing or switching platform type, software version, and so on. This information, when exchanged on a public interface, could divulge enough information for an attacker to attack this device with traffic destined to management addresses or exploit any known software vulnerabilities existing in the Cisco IOS version. Hence, it is strongly recommended to turn off CDP on public interfaces.

Chapter 8

1 False. A routed port is a Layer 3 interface similar to interfaces on Cisco IOS routers, whereas an SVI is a virtual VLAN (Layer 3) interface.

2 True. Multilayer switches use hardware switching to route and switch frames. Hardware switching achieves line-rate performance.

3 True. Routers can forward DHCP requests across Layer 3 boundaries using the DHCP relay agent feature.

4 a. Hosts on VLAN 20 can communicate with the hosts on VLAN 10 if both have the proper default gateway defined.

5 b. If a host that resides in VLAN 20 doesn't have a default gateway set to 200.1.1.1, the response packets from the host on VLAN 20 will be dropped because the host does not know where to send the packets.

6 c. The command **switchport** enables an interface for Layer 2 switching. To change an interface from a Layer 2 interface to a Layer 3 interface, use the command **no switchport**.

7 a. Use the **ip routing** command to enable routing on Cisco Catalyst switches.

8 With BVIs, routable traffic is routed across Layer 3 interfaces and bridge-groups, whereas local and nonroutable traffic is bridged among multiple routed domains or VLANs within the same bridge-group. This configuration creates a large, single spanning-tree domain across multiple VLANs. This type of practice complicates spanning-tree troubleshooting and may adversely affect the performance, scalability, and availability of the network.

9 DHCP is a client-server application, in which the DHCP client contacts a DHCP server for configuration parameters using a broadcast request. If a client is in a different subnet than a server, the broadcast is forwarded using the DHCP relay agent feature by the local router or multilayer switch.

10 b and c. The **ip helper-address** feature forwards DNS, NetBIOS, Time, TCP/IP over NetBIOS, TFTP, and BOOTP UDP broadcasts, in addition to DHCP.

Chapter 9

1 False. CEF-based MLS Catalyst switches prepopulate IP CEF FIB and adjacency tables in hardware.

2 True. Distributed switching uses multiple forwarding engines, where the sum of all forwarding engines is the total available bandwidth of the switch.

3 b. Punt adjacencies are used to send frames requiring special handling to the Layer 3 engine.

4 c. The TCAM mask associated with the access list is 16 bits of the source address because the remaining 16 bits are wildcard bits.

5 d. Because the IP routing table and the ARP table build the CEF FIB and adjacency tables, respectively, those tables should be verified as a first step in troubleshooting issues with CEF-based MLS.

6 a. CEF-based MLS Catalyst switches use the IP CEF FIB and adjacency tables to build FIB and adjacency tables in TCAM for hardware switching. CEF-based MLS does not use the IP routing or ARP tables directly to build the FIB and adjacency tables in hardware, nor is CEF-based MLS an on-demand technology.

7 See the section entitled "Sample CEF-Based MLS Operation" earlier in Chapter 9.

Chapter 10

1 True. Always apply QoS as close to the network device as possible, preferably in the access layer.

2 False. RED, WRED, and tail drop are congestion-avoidance QoS features.

3 d. The **mls qos cos 1** command configures an interface to classify and mark the CoS value of ingress frames to 1.

4 d. It is an administrative configuration where Layer 2 or Layer 3 priority designations of frames are either accepted or not.

5 b. Marking only the video-related frames from the server using an ACL would be the best method to prioritize only video traffic from the server.

6 b. IntServ works by deploying QoS mechanisms end-to-end by allocating bandwidth specifically from network resources.

7 a. Shaping is a better choice for TCP traffic.

8 b. It is pointless to buffer VoIP because it is extremely delay sensitive; policing is the obvious choice for conditioning VoIP traffic.

9 b. Because the switch is configured for trusting DSCP and the switch is using the default mapping tables, the internal DSCP is 46.

10 c. Because the switch is configured for trusting CoS, the switch maps the ingress CoS value to an internal DSCP using the CoS-to-DSCP mapping table. By default, an ingress CoS value of 5 maps to an internal DSCP value of 40.

11 d. Because the switch interface is untrusted, the switch associates all incoming frames with an ingress CoS and DSCP value of 0. As a result, the internal DSCP is 0.

12 b. The **police 1536000 20000 exceed-action drop** command defines the action to be taken by the switch for the respective class of traffic.

13 a. For packets that conform to the policing rate, the switch transmits the packets. For packets that do not conform to the policing rate, the switch drops the packets.

Chapter 11

1 True. For the IGMPv2 membership query, the default value is 10 seconds.

2 False. IGMPv1 does not support host membership leave messages.

3 True. Multicast IP addresses are in the range of 224.0.0.0 to 239.255.255.255.

4 False. Multicast IP addresses are always mapped to MAC addresses starting with 0x01-00-5E.

5 b. The group 224.2.125.254 is learned via PIM sparse mode, as indicated by the presence of an RP and the flag S.

6 d. The IP address of the RP for group 224.2.125.254 is 10.69.100.13.

7 c. There are six sources for multicast group 224.2.125.254, as shown under the group (*.224.10.125.254).

8 b. IP multicast sends packets from the source to specific groups of hosts that registered through IGMP.

9 b. Source trees have the advantage of creating the optimal path between the source and the receivers but maintain large databases of source and group mappings.

10 c. PIM sparse mode is not based on flooding, and it is optimal for multilayer switched networks when trying to conserve bandwidth where hosts are widely spread across the network.

11 c. IGMPv3 is the only IGMP version to support source filtering.

12   c. A switch running IGMP snooping must examine every multicast data packet to determine whether it contains any pertinent IGMP control information. If IGMP snooping were implemented on a low-end switch with a slow CPU, this could have a severe performance impact when data is transmitted at high rates due to increase in latency.

13   c. PIM sparse-dense mode is the preferred method, because it works in dense mode if there is no RP present for a specific group.

14   c. BSR is used to automate the RP distribution in a multicast network with the fault-tolerant automated discovery method.

15   b. Use **show ip mroute** to see the multicast routing table.

16   a and c. Auto-RP and BSR are the two mechanisms used to automate the distribution of RP in sparse mode.

17   c. Only in PIM sparse mode do you have to manually specify the RP on each router in the network.

18   a. IGMP snooping looks for IGMP leave and join messages sent between hosts and the first-hop multicast router.

Chapter 12

1   True. SRM on hybrid mode Catalyst 6500 switches allows configuration only on the designated MSFC. Configuration is possible in both designated and nondesignated MSFCs in dual-router mode.

2   False. The use of redundancy within network devices, only, does not guarantee that there will be a single point of failure. Using a combination of device redundancy, link redundancy, and design redundancy is necessary for a highly available network.

3   False. VRRP allows only one master router in a VRRP group. Only GLBP allows the simultaneous use of multiple available gateways.

4   c. The standby router takes 10 seconds to detect active router failure in HSRP. This value is equal to the holdtime value.

5   b. The default advertisement time for the VRRP master router is 1 second.

6   d. Valid SLB redirection modes are directed mode and dispatched mode.

7   a. The GLBP default load-balancing method is round-robin. Weighted and host-dependent are two other methods available for load balancing. Dispatched and directed are two SLB redirecting modes and do not relate to GLBP.

8   a. Four routers can act as forwarding gateways in a GLBP group.

9 b. Expected failover time on the Catalyst 6500 family of switches with the NSF with SSO feature is about 0 to 3 seconds.

10 e. RIP is not a supported routing protocol of NSF.

11 d. Catalyst 4500 in SSO mode provides for subsecond switchover.

Chapter 13

1 False. Deploying QoS is highly recommended in multilayer switched networks, regardless of interface bandwidth.

2 b and c. Voice VLANs separate workstation (data) traffic and IP phone (voice) traffic into separate VLANs. This separation of data and voice traffic also aids in troubleshooting.

3 b. In Example 13-2, the switch is configured for an access VLAN of 2. Therefore, the switch associates the received frames with VLAN 2 and transmits frames to the workstation without an 802.1Q VLAN tag, because VLAN 2 is the access VLAN.

4 b. VLAN 2 is configured as the access VLAN.

5 b. VoIP uses UDP because a retransmission of a VoIP packet is not necessary, as the voice frame is no longer important by the time of retransmission, and UDP has slightly less overhead.

6 a. Although answer b appears to be the correct answer, there is no specific mechanism in the configuration to strictly trust CoS of attached IP phones.

7 d. 802.1Q packet tagging is used to distinguish voice VLAN traffic from the native VLAN.

8 c. Voice traffic is marked at Layer 3 using DSCP values.

9 c. The STP PortFast feature, enabled on a per-port basis, speeds availability of a Cisco IP Phone after reboot because the Catalyst switch ports move immediately into the forwarding state, allowing frames to pass faster than if the feature were not enabled. See Chapters 5 and 6 for more details on the STP PortFast feature.

10 a and c. A-UDLD and QoS are required in every submodule of the Enterprise Composite Network Model for IP telephony deployments. HSRP and VRRP are specific to Layer 3 routing, and spanning-tree features are specific to Layer 2 regions.

Chapter 14

1 False. SNMP version 3 is the SNMP version that supports encrypted passwords.

2 True. The 802.1X access control feature is a standards-based feature that supports centralized management via RADIUS.

3 False. DCHP snooping trust is enabled only on ports connected to an authentic DHCP server or uplink port connecting to a distribution server (providing path to the DHCP server).

4 e. Remote access to switches is necessary for troubleshooting and management purposes regardless of security concerns.

5 b. The **aaa new-model** command configures Catalyst switches to enact AAA configurations.

6 c. The **if-authenticated** option allows access to specific functions based on whether the user was authenticated by AAA.

7 d. The desirable state is not a valid 802.1X port authorization state.

8 b. DHCP snooping is required for DAI to function.

9 b. Turning off trunk negotiation can prevent a single tag VLAN hopping attack.

10 a. Port security will prevent MAC address spoofing, assuming that the proper configuration has been made.

11 c. IPSG is similar to uRPF, but for Layer 2 interfaces, IPSG requires DHCP snooping or manual bindings to work.

12 b, c. QACLs (through service policy) and PACLs can be applied to Layer 2 interfaces. RACLs are applied to Layer 3 interfaces only, and VACLs are applied to entire VLANs.

13 c. DAI (Dynamic ARP Inspection) is used to prevent ARP spoofing attacks.

14 True. Sticky port security features allow the switch to dynamically secure a MAC address and simultaneously store the MAC address as part of the running configuration. The administrator can just save the configuration to permanently secure that address on the learned ports. Without this feature, the administrator has to manually enter the MAC address as part of the port security configuration, a laborious task in a large network.

15 c. NAC (Network Admission Control) is used to prevent infected hosts from joining the network. The infected host is put in a remediation VLAN, where the host can secure the necessary virus patches to clean itself.

Chapter 15

1 True. The Catalyst 3560 family of switches does offer Layer 3 functionality using the EMI software releases.

2 False. The Catalyst 2960 family of switches does offer QoS features, such as ingress classification, policing, marking, and egress scheduling and queuing.

3 False. The Catalyst 4500 family of switches does not support WAN interfaces.

4 c. BGP is not supported in the Cisco IOS IP base feature set on the Catalyst 3560 family of switches.

5 d. Catalyst 4500 Supervisor Engine V-10GE supports up to 108 Mpps of forwarding rate with a 136-Gbps switching fabric.

6 d. Catalyst 4500 supports redundancy on the 4507R and 4510R chassis.

7 e. Supervisor Engine 720 can reside in slot 7 or 8 on the Catalyst 6513 chassis.

8 c. The maximum forwarding rate of Catalyst 6500 with Supervisor Engine 720 with all distributed 720-Gbps fabric-enabled cards is about 400 Mpps.

9 b. If all modules in the Catalyst 6500 switch are fabric enabled, the fabric operates in compact mode. If all the fabric-enabled modules are equipped with DFC-enabled line cards, then the system would operate in dCEF mode.

10 d. As many as nine Catalyst 3750 switches can exist in a stack. A Catalyst 3750 can also operate as a standalone switch.

11 b. The Catalyst 3750 utilizes the Cisco StackWise technology to stack up to 9 switches together.

12 d. The WS-SVC-NAM-2 (Network Analysis Module) provides integrated packet monitoring up to the application layer level.

Chapter 16

1 False. CDWM solutions do not support amplification.

2 a, b. Internal 50-ms failover mechanisms and general availability through service providers are advantages to using SONET, which is very expensive in implementing new core equipment and does not natively support load balancing.

3 e. SONET base signal, STS-1, operates at 51.84 Mbps.

4 c. Transponders for current DWDM systems convert optical signals from the 850-nm or 1310-nm bands into the 1550-nm band.

5 c. Ethernet over SONET and Ethernet over DWDM do not support statistical multiplexing.

6 b. CDWM does not support amplification and thus is limited to 100 km with a 30-dB fiber budget.

Chapter 17

1 c. The default direction of traffic capture in a SPAN session is both ingress and egress.

2 b. Only one destination port is allowed for local SPAN.

3 c. The destination port needs to be configured as a trunk port to be able to receive multiple VLAN packets and to distinguish the various VLAN packets.

4 d. The IPS is typically connected to the destination port. Upon detection of an intrusion, the IPS may take actions to stop the attack and send alarms. For the IPS to perform the function, the **inpkts** option for Cisco CatOS–based switches or the **ingress vlan** option for Cisco IOS–based switches needs to be enabled.

5 False. The RSPAN VLAN carries only RSPAN traffic; hence, user ports can be configured for that VLAN.

6 a. The **show ip** command can be used to verify the status of the HTTP server.

7 d. If the sniffer device is not in the same location as the switch being monitored, RSPAN could be used so that monitored traffic is switched to the location where the sniffer device is available.

8 c. L2 traceroute can use the IP address as an argument to identify the port of the server if the server is connected to the same VLAN as the sc0 interface in Cisco CatOS–based switches or in the same subnet as SVIs defined on the Cisco IOS–based switches. Otherwise, the administrator needs to know the MAC address of the server to be used with L2 traceroute. The MAC address is typically obtained from the ARP table of the default gateway.

9 c. Catalyst 6500 NAM is an in-build module on the switch that can be configured easily to gather information such as top talker, conversation statistics, and so on as desired by the network administrator.

10 e. The Cisco IOS command to configure VSPAN with the source as VLAN 10 in the receive direction only is **monitor session 1 source vlan 10 rx**.

11 d. The Cisco IOS command to configure RSPAN with the source as RSPAN VLAN 10 is **monitor session 1 source remote vlan 10**.

12 e. The Cisco IOS command to configure RSPAN with the destination as RSPAN VLAN 10 is **monitor session 1 destination remote vlan 10**.

13 c. GRE is the encapsulation method used in the ERSPAN feature.

14 b. TCL scripting language is supported with the EEM feature.

Chapter 18

1 DSSS stands for Direct Sequence Spread Spectrum.

2 Wireless mostly uses 2.4 GHz for 802.11b and 802.11g and 5 GHz for 802.11a.

3 Bluetooth falls under the personal-area network (PAN) technology group.

4 Carrier sense multiple access with collision avoidance (CSMA/CA) is used in wireless to avoid collisions.

5 Environmental factors such as reflections, refractions, and diffractions can degrade a signal between the transmitter and receiver and cause multipath interference.

6 Privacy is addressed by 802.11 by an optional service called Wired Equivalent Privacy (WEP).

7 Japan permits all 14 channels within the 2.4-GHZ spectrum.

8 A lightweight AP receives control and configuration from a WLAN controller to which it is associated.

9 The Cisco Unified Wireless Network addresses the deployment, management, and RF challenges associated with building business-critical WLANs.

10 Wireless networks have two main implementation categories: WLANs (in-building or mesh) and wireless bridges (building-to-building).

11 Independent (ad hoc) and infrastructure are the two BSS modes.

12 dBi is the gain that a given antenna has over a theoretical isotropic (point source) antenna.

13 A 3-dB loss will reduce 100 mW by half for a new result of 50 mW.

14 The three antenna types are omnidirectional, semidirectional, and highly directional.

15 A channel reuse plan is required in the 2.4-GHz spectrum because only three nonoverlapping channels exist: 1 (2412 MHz), 6 (2437 MHz), and 11 (2462 MHz).

16 Only one bridge in a WLAN can be set as the root bridge.

17 Twenty users for 2.4-GHz 802.11g is the best practice based on general office users limited by bandwidth.

18 Inline power, or Power over Ethernet (PoE), provides source operating current from the Ethernet port, over the Category 5 cable.

19 True: Lightweight APs can be managed with Cisco WLAN controllers and the Cisco Wireless Control System (WCS).

20 The two methods employed to discover APs are passive and active scanning.

21   Temporal Key Integrity Protocol (TKIP) and Message Integrity Check (MIC) are both elements of the Wi-Fi Protected Access (WPA) standard, which is intended to secure a system against all known WEP key vulnerabilities.

22   The Cisco Compatible Extensions (CCX) program helps to ensure that client devices from a variety of suppliers can leverage Cisco-based WLANs.

23   Dynamic interfaces, also known as VLAN interfaces, are created by users and are designed to be analogous to VLANs for WLAN clients.

24   To display basic 802.11a options and settings, use the **show 802.11a** command.

INDEX

Symbols

! (exclamation point) character, 124
(pound sign) character, 124

Numerics

10GBASE-xyz, naming conventions, 69
10GE, 68
    distance limitations, 70–71
10-Mbps Ethernet, 62
802.1D, compatibility with RSTP, 250
802.1Q, 176
    misconfiguring, 178
802.11 operational standards, 830–831
802.11a standard, 834–835
    calculating bandwidth, 838
    channel reuse, 836–838
802.11b standard, calculating bandwidth, 838
802.11b/g standard, channel reuse, 836
802.11g standard, 832–834
    calculating bandwidth, 838

A

AAA
    accounting, configuring, 660–665
    authentication, configuring, 658–661
    authorization, configuring, 659–663
    on Cisco IOS-based Catalyst switches,
        configuring, 658, 665–666
aaa new-model command, 106
absorption, 824
access layer, 25
access networks, 44
access
    to vty lines, securing, 654
    unauthorized, 95
access-layer switches, 64
accounting, 660
    configuring, 663–665
ACLs (access control lists), 5
    applying, 679–680
    configuring on Cisco Catalyst switches, 653
    PACLs, applying, 683–684
    RACLs, applying, 680–681
    VACLs, applying, 681–683
active keyword, 537
active scanning, 857
ad hoc mode, 815, 819
adding switches, 206
Address Resolution Protocol. *See* ARP
addresses
    globally scoped, 506
    GLOP, 506–507
    IP multicast, 502
    limited-scope, 506
    MAC address notification, 337–338
    reserved link local, 505–506
    source-specific multicast, 506
    virtual MAC, VRRP, 596
adjacencies, 428
adjacency tables, 413–414
ADSL (asymmetric digital subscriber line), 71
ADU (Aironet Desktop Utility), 860
AES (Advanced Encryption Standard), 859
**AES-CCMP (Advanced Encryption Standard-
    Counter Mode with Cipher Block Chaining
    Message Authentication Code Protocol), 852**
agents, DHCP relay, 399
aggregate policers, 468
aggressive mode UDLD, 356–358
    case study, 360–364
    configuration exercises, 374
    versus Loop Guard, 292
answers to review questions
    chapter 1, 881–883
    chapter 10, 892–893
    chapter 11, 893–894
    chapter 12, 894–895
    chapter 13, 895
    chapter 14, 896
    chapter 15, 897
    chapter 16, 897
    chapter 17, 898
    chapter 18, 899–900
    chapter 2, 884–885
    chapter 3, 885–886

B

E

J-K

L

M

X-Y-Z

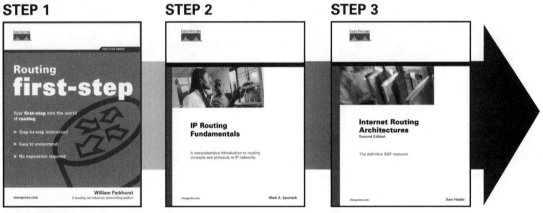

802.11 (WIFI)

802.11a (OFDM) 54 Mb/s